A Companion to Poetic Genre

Blackwell Companions to Literature and Culture

This series offers comprehensive, newly written surveys of key periods and movements and certain major authors, in English literary culture and history. Extensive volumes provide new perspectives and positions on contexts and on canonical and post-canonical texts, orientating the beginning student in new fields of study and providing the experienced undergraduate and new graduate with current and new directions, as pioneered and developed by leading scholars in the field.

Published Recently

A COMPANION TO

POETIC GENRE

EDITED BY
ERIK MARTINY

A John Wiley & Sons, Ltd., Publication

Registered Office
John Wiley & Sons Ltd, The Atrium, Southern Gate, Chichester, West Sussex, PO19 8SQ, United
Kingdom

Editorial Offices
350 Main Street, Malden, MA 02148-5020, USA
9600 Garsington Road, Oxford, OX4 2DQ, UK
The Atrium, Southern Gate, Chichester, West Sussex, PO19 8SQ, UK

For details of our global editorial offices, for customer services, and for information about how to
apply for permission to reuse the copyright material in this book please see our website at www.wiley.
com/wiley-blackwell.

Library of Congress Cataloging-in-Publication Data

A companion to poetic genre / edited by Erik Martiny. – 1st ed.
　　p. cm.
　　Includes bibliographical references and index.
　ISBN 978-1-4443-3673-3 (hardback)
　1. Poetry–History and criticism.　2. Poetics–History.　I. Martiny, Erik.
　PN1300.C66 2011
　809.1–dc23

　　　　　　　　　　　　　　　　　　　　　　2011026045

A catalogue record for this book is available from the British Library.

This book is published in the following electronic formats: ePDFs 9781444344288; Wiley Online
Library 9781444344318; ePub 9781444344295; Mobi 9781444344301

Set in 11 on 13 pt Garamond Three by Toppan Best-set Premedia Limited
Printed and bound in Singapore by Markono Print Media Pte Ltd

1　2012

Contents

Part II

Notes on Contributors

Hélène Aji is Professor of American poetry at the Université du Maine (France). In addition to a number of articles on modernist and contemporary American poetry, she is the author of *Ezra Pound et William Carlos Williams: pour une poétique américaine* (L'Harmattan, 2001), *William Carlos Williams: un plan d'action* (Belin, 2004) and a book-length essay on Ford Madox Ford's *The Good Soldier* (Armand Colin, 2005). Recently she edited *L'Impersonnel en littérature* (Presses universitaires de Rennes, 2008) and, with Helen M. Dennis, an issue of the *European Journal of English Studies* on "Reading the Modernist Past."

Andy Brown is a lyric poet, editor, and a critic. He is Director of Creative Writing at the University of Exeter. His poetry books include *Goose Music* (Salt, 2008, co-written with John Burnside); *The Storm Berm* (Tall Lighthouse, 2008); *Fall of the Rebel Angels: Poems 1996-2006* (Salt, 2006); and five previous volumes of poetry. His forthcoming book of poems is *On the Threshold*. He has also edited two collections of correspondences with contemporary writers, *Binary Myths 1&2* (Stride, 2004). His criticism has most recently appeared in *The Salt Companion to Lee Harwood*.

Stephen Burt is Professor of English at Harvard. His most recent books include *The Art of the Sonnet*, with David Mikics (Harvard University Press, 2010), *Close Calls with Nonsense* (Graywolf, 2009), and *Parallel Play*, a collection of poems (Graywolf, 2006): he is a regular contributor to the *London Review of Books*, the *Boston Review*, and other journals in the US and UK.

David Caplan is Associate Professor of English at Ohio Wesleyan University and the author of *Questions of Possibility: Contemporary Poetry and Poetic Form* (Oxford University Press, 2004), *Poetic Form: An Introduction* (Longman, 2006), and *In the World He Created According to His Will* (poems) (University of Georgia Press, 2010). He serves as a contributing editor to the *Virginia Quarterly Review* and *Pleiades: A Journal of New Writing*, and is an affiliated researcher at the Centre Interdisciplinaire de Poétique Appliquée at the University of Liège. His essays on poetry and poetics have appeared widely in

America and Europe. His current project is *Rhyme's Challenge* (Oxford University Press).

Jennifer Clarvoe is Professor of English at Kenyon College, in Gambier, Ohio. Her first book of poems, *Invisible Tender*, won the Poets Out Loud Prize and the Kate Tufts Discovery Award. In 2002–2003, she held the Rome Prize in Literature at the American Academy in Rome. Her second book of poems, *Counter-Amores*, is forthcoming from the University of Chicago Press in 2011.

Philip Coleman is a Lecturer in the School of English, Trinity College Dublin, where he is Director of the MPhil in Literatures of the Americas and Head of Sophisters. With Maria Johnston he is editing *Reading Pearse Hutchinson*, a collection of essays and reflections on the poet, for the Irish Academic Press. He has edited collections of essays on literature and science and on the poetry of John Berryman. His book *John Berryman and the Public Sphere: Reception and Redress* will be published by University College Dublin Press in 2010.

Bonnie Costello is Professor of English at Boston University. She is the author of many articles on modern poetry and five books, including most recently *Shifting Ground: Reinventing Landscape in Modern American Poetry* (Harvard University Press, 2003) and *Planets on Tables: Poetry, Still Life and the Turning World* (Cornell University Press, 2008). She was the general editor for *The Selected Letters of Marianne Moore* (Penguin, 1997). She focuses on relations between the arts and has written essays on visual artists, including Giorgio Morandi, Joseph Cornell, and Abelardo Morell. Costello has been a recipient of fellowships from the Rockefeller, Guggenheim, and Bogliasco Foundations, and she is a member of the American Academy of Arts and Sciences.

Jonathan Ellis is Lecturer in American Literature at the University of Sheffield. He is the author of *Art and Memory in the Work of Elizabeth Bishop* (2006), as well as articles and essays on Paul Muldoon, Sylvia Plath, and Anne Stevenson. His next book is on twentieth-century letter-writing. He has been the recipient of a Leverhulme Early Career Fellowship, and more recently, a British Academy Research Development Award.

Rainer Emig is Chair of English Literature and Culture at Leibniz University in Hanover, Germany. He is especially interested in the link between literature and the media and in Literary, Critical, and Cultural Theory, especially theories of identity, power, gender, and sexuality. His publications include the monographs *Modernism in Poetry* (1995), *W.H. Auden* (1999), and *Krieg als Metapher im zwanzigsten Jahrhundert* (2001), as well as edited collections on *Stereotypes in Contemporary Anglo-German Relations* (2000), *Ulysses* (2004), and *Gender ↔ Religion* (2008). He has recently completed a monograph entitled *Eccentricity: Culture from the Margins* and co-edited collections on *Hybrid Humour* and *Performing Masculinity* (2009). He is one of the three editors of the *Journal for the Study of British Cultures*.

Rachel Falconer is Professor of Modern and Contemporary Literature in the School of English at the University of Sheffield. She also has research interests in classical and early modern Anglo-European Literatures. Amongst her publications are: *Orpheus Dis-remembered: Milton and the Myth of the Poet-Hero* (Continuum, 1996); co-edited with C. Adlam, V. Makhlin, and A. Renfrew, *Face to Face: Bakhtin Studies in Russian and the West* (Continuum, 1997), including her chapter, "Bakhtin, Milton and the Epic Chronotope"; *Hell in Contemporary Literature: Western Descent Narratives since 1945* (Edinburgh, 2005); *The Crossover Novel: Contemporary Children's Fiction and Its Adult Readership* (Routledge, 2009); "Epic," in *A Companion to English Renaissance Literature and Culture* (Blackwell, 2009); and "Hell in Our Time: Reading 9/11 and Its Aftermath as a Dantean Descent into Hell," in *Hell and Its Afterlife: Historical and Contemporary Perspectives* (Ashgate, 2009).

Karen Jackson Ford is a Professor of English and the Director of the Creative Writing Program at the University of Oregon. She has published two books, *Gender and the Poetics of Excess: Moments of Brocade* and *Split-Gut Song: Jean Toomer and the Poetics of Modernity*. Her scholarship investigates the politics of poetic form, and she is currently at work on a book about race and form in American poetry. Recent essays include "Marking Time in Native America: Haiku, Elegy, Survival," "The Sonnets of Satin-Leg Brooks," "The Lives of Haiku Poetry: Self, Selflessness, and Solidarity in Concentration Camp Haiku," and "The Last Quatrain: Gwendolyn Brooks and the End of Ballads."

Debra Fried teaches English and American poetry and poetics at Cornell University, has published articles on rhymes and puns, twentieth-century sonnets, Dickinson's variants and personification, repetition in epitaphic verse, Spenser's caesura, and on classic American film. Current projects include a study of particularity in nineteenth- and twentieth-century lyric genres.

Kit Fryatt is Lecturer in English, Mater Dei Institute of Education (Dublin City University). Most of her research has been in the field of Irish poetry, with subsidiary interests in British and American poetry. Her book *Austin Clarke: Holy Rage of Argument* will be published by the Research Institute for Irish and Scottish Studies at Aberdeen University. She has published articles on a wide range of Irish and American poetry and also writes non-academic literary criticism and reviews. With her colleague Michael Hinds she edits *POST*, the web-journal of the Irish Centre for Poetry Studies at Mater Dei. Her poetry has appeared in a number of British and Irish magazines.

Jo Gill is Lecturer in twentieth-century literature at the University of Exeter, UK. She is the author of *Anne Sexton's Confessional Poetics* (University Press of Florida, 2007), *Women's Poetry* (Edinburgh University Press, 2007), and *The Cambridge Introduction to Sylvia Plath* (Cambridge University Press, 2008); and the editor of *The Cambridge Companion to Sylvia Plath* (Cambridge University Press, 2007), *Modern Confessional Writing: New Critical Essays* (Routledge, 2006), and, with Simon Barker, *Literature as*

History: Essays in Honour of Peter Widdowson (Continuum, 2009). She is currently working on a new book on *The Poetics of the American Suburbs*.

Peter L. Groves was educated in the United Kingdom at the universities of Exeter and Cambridge, where he wrote his PhD on Shakespeare's metrics. He now teaches Renaissance English literature in the School of English, Communications and Performance Studies at Monash University, Melbourne. His publications on meter include a theoretical monograph, *Strange Music: The Metre of the English Heroic Line* (University of Victoria, 1998), and a series of articles on poets from Chaucer to Philip Larkin. He is currently working on the theory of verse-movement.

Peter Harris teaches American literature and poetry-writing at Colby College in Maine, where he is the Zacamy Professor in English. He has published numerous articles on contemporary American poetry and a chapbook, *Blue Hallelujahs*. His poetry has appeared in many magazines including, *The Atlantic Monthly*, *Epoch*, *Prairie Schooner*, *Ploughshares*, *Rattle*, *Seattle Review*, and *Sewanee Review*. A former Dibner Fellow, he has been awarded residencies at Macdowell, the Guthrie Center, Red Cinder House, and the Virginia Center for the Creative Arts. Harris has also taught at Marie Curie University in Lublin, Poland, and at University College Cork. He is a Zen Buddhist priest.

Michael Hinds is currently Head of English and Humanities at the Mater Dei Institute (Dublin City University), Dublin, and is coordinator of the Irish Centre for Poetry Studies there. Prior to taking up his post at Mater Dei in 2000, he taught at Trinity College Dublin, University College Dublin, Queens University Belfast, International Christian University (Tokyo), and the University of Tokyo, where he was a visiting lecturer from 1996–1999. Amongst others, he has written and published extensively on the poetry of Randall Jarrell and Ciaran Carson, and, in 2005 (with Stephen Matterson), he edited *Rebound: The American Poetry Book*. In 2007, he edited *The Irish Reader: Essays for John Devitt*. He is co-editor of *POST: A Poetry Studies Review* and has reviewed for *METRE* and *The Irish Times*. He is currently researching the Sapphic genes of modern poetry and song.

Romana Huk is an Associate Professor of English at the University of Notre Dame. Her books include *Contemporary British Poetry: Essays in Theory and Criticism* (edited with James Acheson; State University of New York Press, 1996), *Assembling Alternatives: Reading Postmodern Poetries Transnationally* (Wesleyan University Press, 2003), *Stevie Smith: Between the Lines* (Palgrave, 2005), and a forthcoming study of avant-garde poetries, postwar theologies, and postmodern philosophy/sociolinguistic theory. Her many articles on contemporary poetics have appeared in journals as various as *Contemporary Literature*, *The Yale Journal of Criticism*, *Christianity and Literature*, and *Performance Research*, as well as in edited collections from presses such as Cornell University Press, Edinburgh University Press, Ohio University Press, London Macmillan, Blackwell Publishing, and Le Cri Editions.

Patrick Jackson is an Assistant Professor of English at Columbus State University in Columbus, Georgia. He is currently working on *This Side of Despair: Forms of Hopelessness in Modern Poetry*, a book which examines the ways nihilism shapes British and American poetry in the twentieth century. His essays include "The Sublimity of Wilfred Owen's Despair" and "Ned Rorem's Reversal and Resurrection of Sylvia Plath's *Ariel*."

Maria Johnston holds a PhD in English from Trinity College Dublin. She currently lectures in American poetry at Trinity College and also lectures part-time at Mater Dei Institute (Dublin City University) on a variety of courses at both undergraduate and postgraduate level. She is a regular reviewer of contemporary Irish, British, and American poetry and she has contributed essays to a number of books and academic journals. *High Pop: The Irish Times Column of Stewart Parker*, which she edited with Gerald Dawe, was published by Lagan Press in 2008. She is in the process of preparing a monograph on Sylvia Plath and contemporary Irish and British poetry for publication and is also editing a collection of essays by poets from Britain and Ireland on the subject of poetry and politics.

Ann Keniston is an Associate Professor of English at the University of Nevada, Reno, with a specialty in contemporary American poetry. She is the author of two books, a critical study, *Overheard Voices: Address and Subjectivity in Postmodern American Poetry* (Routledge, 2006), and a volume of poems, *The Caution of Human Gestures* (David Robert, 2005). With Jeanne Follansbee Quinn, she edited *Literature after 9/11* (Routledge, 2008). She is at work on a new monograph, "Ghostly Figures: Memory and Belatedness in Postwar American Poetry"; an edited anthology of twenty-first-century American poetry, with Jeffrey Gray; and a collection of poems provisionally titled "Lament/Praise."

Marie-Christine Lemardeley is Full Professor of American literature at the Sorbonne Nouvelle—Paris 3 university, of which she was elected President in 2008. She is the author of a book on Adrienne Rich's poetry, *Cartographies du Silence* (1990), several essays on John Steinbeck, and articles on contemporary American poetry and fiction (Lorine Niedecker, Robert Lowell, Lyn Hejinian, Amy Hempel, Lorrie Moore).

Erik Martiny teaches Anglophone literature in Aix-en-Provence. He has published numerous articles on poets such as Peter Redgrove (*The Wallace Stevens Journal*), Frank O'Hara (*The Cambridge Quarterly*), Sylvia Plath, Paul Durcan, Thomas Kinsella and Paul Muldoon (*Etudes Anglaises*), Ted Hughes and Derek Walcott (*English Studies*). He has also written on the connections between film and fiction, having recently edited a volume of essays for the Sorbonne publisher Sedes (*Lolita: From Nabokov to Kubrick and Lyne*), as well as a personal book on the poetics of filiation: *Intertextualité et filiation paternelle dans la poésie anglophone* (L'Harmattan, 2009).

Fiona McMahon is Senior Lecturer in American Literature at the Université de Bourgogne, Dijon, France. She is the author of articles on poetry in the Objectivist tradition and has published essays on the relationship between the documentary and the lyric in modernist and contemporary poetry. Her book *Charles Reznikoff: une poétique du témoignage* is forthcoming from Editions L'Harmattan (2010).

Bernard O'Donoghue was born in Cullen, Co. Cork in 1945, and he still spends part of the year there. Since 1962 he has lived in the United Kingdom, and he now teaches medieval English at Wadham College, Oxford. He has published books on medieval poetry, including an anthology of medieval European love poetry entitled *The Courtly Love Tradition* (1984), and he published a verse translation of *Sir Gawain and the Green Knight* (Penguin Classics 2006). He has published five volumes of poetry, including *Gunpowder* which won the Whitbread Poetry Prize in 1995. His *Selected Poems* was published by Faber in 2008. He has also published books on modern Irish poetry, including *Seamus Heaney and the Language of Poetry* (1994), and the *Cambridge Companion to Seamus Heaney* (2009).

Nicole Ollier is Professor of American Literature and Translation at the Université Michel de Montaigne, Bordeaux, France. She earned a first Doctorate at the Université Paul Valéry in Montpellier on the work of Mark Twain, and a Comparative Literature "Doctorat d'Etat" on Greek-American Literature at the Université de la Sorbonne Nouvelle. For many years she has translated poetry from English (most publications concerned English and Irish poetry) and Modern Greek. She directs a Translation research group called "Passages" which translates poetry and drama into French—currently Caribbean and Afro-American poets and playwrights—and interprets for the stage and screen, using such mixed media as dance, music, slam. She also teaches gender studies and ethnic literature (Irish, Greek, Chinese diasporas) and directs research on those, on poetry and on such subjects as the translation of aspectual forms, or prosody.

Jahan Ramazani is Edgar F. Shannon Professor of English at the University of Virginia. He is the author of *A Transnational Poetics* (Chicago, 2009), which won the 2011 Harry Levin Prize of the ACLA for the best book of comparative literary history published between 2008 and 2010; *The Hybrid Muse: Postcolonial Poetry in English* (Chicago, 2001); *Poetry of Mourning: The Modern Elegy from Hardy to Heaney* (Chicago, 1994), a finalist for the National Book Critics Circle Award; and *Yeats and the Poetry of Death* (Yale, 1990). He edited the most recent edition of *The Norton Anthology of Modern and Contemporary Poetry* (2003) and, with Jon Stallworthy, *The Twentieth Century and After,* in *The Norton Anthology of English Literature* (2006). He is a recipient of a Guggenheim Fellowship, a National Endowment for the Humanities Fellowship, a Rhodes Scholarship, the William Riley Parker Prize of the Modern Language Association, the National Endowment for the Humanities/Mayo Distinguished Teaching Professorship, and the Jefferson Scholars Faculty Prize at the University of Virginia.

Neil Roberts is Emeritus Professor of English Literature at the University of Sheffield. His publications include *Ted Hughes: A Critical Study* (with Terry Gifford), *The Lover,* *the Dreamer and the World: The Poetry of Peter Redgrove, Narrative and Voice in Postwar Poetry*, and *Ted Hughes: A Literary Life*. He edited the Blackwell *Companion to Twentieth-Century Poetry* and is currently working on a biography of Peter Redgrove.

Lacy Rumsey has lectured in British and American poetry at the Ecole Normale Supérieure Lettres et Sciences Humaines (shortly to be renamed Ecole Normale Supérieure de Lyon) since 2002, having previously taught at King's College London. He is the author of a doctoral thesis (University of London, 2000) on the role of rhythm and intonation in free verse, and of numerous articles on British and American poetry of the nineteenth and twentieth centuries, focusing in particular on questions of poetic form. His current activities include the organization of a conference on rhythm in twentieth-century British poetry (Lyons, November 2009), and the writing of two monographs; one on the theory of free verse, the other on the role of intonation in American poetry since Pound.

Alex Runchman is writing his PhD at Trinity College Dublin on the American writer Delmore Schwartz. His thesis re-evaluates Schwartz's oeuvre, addressing his achievements as a poet, short-story-writer, and essayist, and engaging particularly closely with his interest in the American Dream. He studied for an MA in English Language and Literature at the University of Oxford and an MPhil in American Literature at the University of Cambridge. He has also worked as a teacher of English as a foreign language and as a secondary-school English teacher.

Lisa Sewell is the author of *The Way Out* (Alice James Books), *Name Withheld* (Four Way Books) and *Long Corridor* (Seven Kitchens Press), which won the 2008 Keystone Chapbook Award. She is also co-editor with Claudia Rankine of *American Poets in the 21st Century: The New Poetics* (Wesleyan University Press, 2007) and *American Women Poets in the 21st Century: Between Lyric and Language*, vol. 2, forthcoming from Wesleyan University Press. She has published essays on Louise Gluck, Brenda Hillman, Frank Bidart, and other contemporary poets. Recent poetry is appearing in *Colorado Review*, *Tampa Review*, *American Letters and Commentary*, *Denver Quarterly*, *New Letters*, and *The Journal*. She lives in Philadelphia and teaches at Villanova University.

Eve C. Sorum is an Assistant Professor of English at the University of Massachusetts—Boston, where she teaches courses on British modernism, modern poetry, and the literature of World War I. She has published articles on Virginia Woolf, T.S. Eliot, and Ford Madox Ford in the *Journal of Modern Literature*, *Woolf Studies Annual*, and in the collection *Modernism and Mourning*. Her most recent publication is an essay in *Modernism/Modernity* that examines Thomas Hardy's elegiac sequence, the *Poems of 1912–13*. She is currently working on a book manuscript, *The Terrain of Loss: Geography and Elegiac Modernism*, in which she argues that the creation of a regionally based "New Geography" significantly shaped the elegiac strain of British modernism.

Mark Scroggins is Professor of English at Florida Atlantic University in Boca Raton. He is the author of *Louis Zukofsky and the Poetry of Knowledge* (University of Alabama

Press, 1998), *The Poem of a Life: A Biography of Louis Zukofsky* (Shoemaker & Hoard, 2007), and a book of poems, *Anarchy* (Spuyten Duyvil, 2003). He has edited the collection *Upper Limit Music: The Writing of Louis Zukofsky* (University of Alabama Press, 1997) and a selection of uncollected prose for the latest edition of *Prepositions: The Collected Critical Essays of Louis Zukofsky* (Wesleyan University Press, 2001). He has published widely on modernist and contemporary British and American poetry, and his essays and reviews have appeared in *Parnassus: Poetry in Review*, *Chicago Review*, *Twentieth Century Literature*, *Talisman*, *West Coast Line*, and *The Cambridge Companion to Modernist Poetry*, among other places.

George Szirtes was born in Budapest in 1948 and came to England as a refugee with his family, following the Hungarian Uprising of 1956. Trained in fine art, his first book, *The Slant Door* was joint winner of the Faber Prize in 1980. He has published several books since then that have brought him the Cholmondeley Award and, most recently, the T.S. Eliot Prize for *Reel* (2004). His *New and Collected Poems* were published in 2008 and a new book, *The Burning of the Books and Other Poems* is, at the time of writing, shortlisted for the latest T.S. Eliot Prize. He was elected a Fellow of the Royal Society in 1982 and of the English Association in 2004 and is Reader in Creative Writing at the University of East Anglia.

John Thieme teaches at the University of East Anglia. He has held Chairs at the University of Hull and London South Bank University and has also taught at the Universities of Guyana and North London. His books include *The Web of Tradition: Uses of Allusion in V.S. Naipaul's Fiction* (1987), *The Arnold Anthology of Post-Colonial Literatures in English* (1996), *Derek Walcott* (1999), *Post-Colonial Con-Texts: Writing Back to the Canon* (2001), *Post-Colonial Studies: The Essential Glossary* (2003), and *R.K. Narayan* (2007). He is editor of *The Journal of Commonwealth Literature* and general editor of the Manchester University Press Contemporary World Writers Series.

Yann Tholoniat is Associate Professor at the University of Strasbourg. He has written a number of articles on Robert Burns, William Blake, Thomas De Quincey, Robert Browning, and Joseph Conrad, and also on Pío Baroja, Vicente Huidobro, and Juan Carlos Onetti. He edited *Culture savante, culture populaire dans les pays anglophones* (RANAM 39, 2006), and co-edited *Culture savante, culture populaire en Ecosse* (RANAM 40, 2007). His latest book is *"Tongue's Imperial Fiat": les polyphonies dans l'œuvre poétique de Robert Browning* (Presses universitaires de Strasbourg, 2009). His current project is a study of Robert Burns.

Todd Nathan Thompson is an Assistant Professor of English at Indiana University of Pennsylvania. Thompson has published scholarly articles in the *M/MLA Journal* and the *Journal of American Culture*; he has also written several encyclopedia articles and a review essay. He has performed funded archival research on early American political satire at the Lilly Library at Indiana University, the Abraham Lincoln Presidential Library, and the Library Company of Philadelphia. Thompson earned a PhD in American literature from the University of Illinois at Chicago in

2008 and an MFA in writing from the School of the Art Institute of Chicago in 2000. Thompson's scholarly interests include satire and humor, aesthetics and politics, media history, poetry and poetics, early American culture, and the Harlem Renaissance.

Meg Tyler is Assistant Professor of Humanities at Boston University, where she directs the poetry-reading series. Her book, *A Singing Contest: Conventions of Sound in the Poetry of Seamus Heaney*, was published by Routledge in 2005 in their series, Studies in Major Literary Authors. She writes poetry reviews regularly for *Harvard Review* and has published poems in *Kenyon Review* and *AGNI* literary journal, among others. A recipient of a BU Humanities Foundation fellowship, she is now working on a book project entitled *Broken Sonnets*, which is a study of sonnets by contemporary American, British, and Irish poets.

Geoff Ward is Vice Principal at Royal Holloway, University of London, and Professor of English. He has also worked at the University of Dundee, where he was Head of English and subsequently Deputy Principal, and at the University of Liverpool, having studied at Cambridge. His many academic publications include *Statutes of Liberty: The New York School of Poets* (1993, new edition Palgrave, 2000) and *The Writing of America: Literature and Cultural Identity from the Puritans to the Present* (Polity, 2002). He has lectured widely across Europe, the United States, and Japan, where he worked from 1994 to 1995, and held a Leverhulme Fellowship from 1999 to 2001, researching at the Library of Congress in Washington, DC. He is also an editor of *The Cambridge Quarterly*, and has written and presented programs for BBC Radio 3 on American writers. He has just completed his first novel.

Jeff Westover is an Assistant Professor of English at Howard University, where he teaches American literature. His research focuses on twentieth-century American poetry. His recent publications include a book, *The Colonial Moment: Discoveries and Settlements in Modern American Poetry* (Northern Illinois University Press, 2004), and an article about value in Marianne Moore's poetry (*Paideuma*, 2004). He has also published articles on James Merrill, Henry James, and Herman Melville.

David Wheatley is a Senior Lecturer at the University of Hull. He is the author of four collections of poetry with the Gallery Press: *Thirst* (1997), *Misery Hill* (2000), *Mocker* (2006), and *A Nest on the Waves* (2010). He edited the poetry journal *Metre* for many years with Justin Quinn, and has edited the work of James Clarence Mangan for Gallery Press and Samuel Beckett's *Selected Poems* for Faber and Faber.

Karina Williamson holds degrees from Oxford (MA, BLitt, DLitt), and Stirling (MLitt), and has taught at the universities of Uppsala, Oxford, Edinburgh, and New Mexico. She is editor of *The Poetical Works of Christopher Smart* (6 vols., 1980–1996), *Marly; or, A Planter's Life in Jamaica* (2005), and *Contrary Voices: Representations of West Indian Slavery, 1657–1834* (2008), and has published numerous essays and articles on English, Scottish, and Caribbean literary subjects. Now retired, she remains active in research as Honorary Fellow at the Edinburgh Institute for Advanced Studies in the Humanities, and Supernumerary Fellow of St Hilda's College, Oxford.

Stephen Wilson has a doctorate from Trinity College Dublin and is a professor of American literature, and director of a Masters program entitled Poetry and Poetics, at the University of Coimbra, Portugal. He is also a fellow of the Irish Centre for Poetry Studies. His areas of specialization are American literature and Anglo-American modernism and particularly the work of Ezra Pound (on whom he has published widely). He is currently working on a book *On Pound's American History Cantos*.

Preface

Erik Martiny

Since this book is entirely given over to proclaiming the vigor of traditional genres in modern poetry, let us begin by considering the anti-formalist trend that still often interacts with the notion of genre, if only to reject it. A recent poem by the American poet Sapphire serves to illustrate this particular tendency. The text, entitled "Villanelle," does initially take the late Renaissance genre into perfunctory consideration before it is dismissed:

> At school the workshop focuses on villanelle
> & sestina—the light at the end for counting
> knowing, rhyming, European, white
> I'm interested in the black howl,
> light candles to invoke it.
>
> (ll.1–5)

The speaker later asks:

> Can a French form do anything for me?
> Can the light dying behind my eyes be
> recorded in rhymes schemes?
>
> (ll.20–22)

Admittedly, the poem never dwells on the formula of the fixed form it evokes in the title and develops regardless of the ordered iteration of the villanelle. In the same collection of poems, "Sestina" proceeds along the same disdainful lines, using no more than the word "sestina" to head its entirely organic growth:

> Last night after school I finally got around
> to looking at the formula for a sestina
> & thought of Crazy Horse dancing in the desert

& I asked, Is god gonna appear here?
I want god
   a blue light so dark
it stains everything for centuries
radiative hallucinatory rood smelling
like urine & frankincense.

            (ll.1–9)

Poets like Sapphire are clearly far from considering non-organic forms as conducive to intensity or personal expression and yet even the poems quoted above do betray a certain residual interest in poetry's ancient ancestry. Although Sapphire empties the sestina and the villanelle of their formal characteristics, and ultimately sets them aside, the titles chosen for her poems still nominally offer them as contemporary versions of these ancient genres, betraying at least a modicum of interest in the mysteriousness of archaic form. There is a certain ambivalence about the second poem's discourse after the word "sestina": the vision of absolute freedom embodied by "Crazy Horse dancing in the desert" can be interpreted as being entirely antithetical to the sestina, and yet the fantasy is also triggered by the reading of the fixed form's magic formula, the sestina being a genre which did in fact leave its mark on poetry "for centuries" in a "radiative" manner. The question which the speaker asks herself is perhaps not all that ironic.

Other poems such as Peter Cooley's "Aubade with Dachshund" indicate that even for poets who reject ancient forms or their traditional motifs, there is a longing to connect with notions of genre, no matter how gestural, facetious, or parodic this engagement may be. Many neo-formalist poets are also interested in reconciling the "black howl" with ancient form, making things old and new at the same time, technically demanding yet lyrical; formal and yet charged with emotion, hallucinatory phantasmagoria, or comedy: Robert Creeley's "Ballad of the Despairing Husband" is another delightful case in point.

As the title chosen for this *Companion* suggests, genre is intended here in the broad sense in which it is often spoken of today. Some might object that comic or satirical poetry is closer to being a mode than a genre, serving primarily to inflect genres, yet modes can also be considered in their own right as genres, especially when the main purpose of a poem seems to be humorous or parodic. Likewise, some of the chapters included here might seem to belong more properly under the rubric of themes: war poetry, for instance, could be considered a theme, yet what are genres, in the end, but themes or technical exercises which have recurred over time and accrued into a tradition with its intertextual links, its expectations, its stock characters, images, rhetorical effects, formal trends, and deviations from those trends?

The reach of this *Companion* has been made as large as possible within the constraints of available space. It covers a wide range of cultural traditions from Britain, Ireland, North America, Japan, the Arabic world, and the Caribbean, providing critical overviews of genres that are still in widespread current use today in English-language poetry. While the focus of these essays is primarily contemporary, each chapter charts genres from their initial stages to their most recent renderings so that the reader can perceive in what ways genres from past centuries have evolved over time.

Some readers will perhaps bemoan the jettisoning of such genres as the virelai or the palinode for reasons of space: let me just say that it was hard to let them go, even though there was some comfort in dropping them overboard, knowing that they would not sink but float away to other hands. I thus send out an invitation to harbor them, if enough survivors can be found within the many seas of modern poetry; I wish to make the appeal to poets too for it is they who are the greater conservationists of ancient genres.

Although it is no longer referred to under that appellation, the palinode is arguably just as much alive as it was in times of yore, especially in our politically conscious, postmodernly self-surveying era: in Ancient Greece, the palinode was a poem which withdrew the claims, or redressed the balance, of a previous poem by the same writer. Since Stesichorus poetically retracted his attack on Helen for having caused the Trojan War, many poets have either rewritten their texts in subsequent reprints or addressed their previous poems with self-critical panache. A couple of fine examples spring to mind for those who might be interested in undertaking critical work on the contemporary palinode: Sharon Olds's intratextual poem "The Window" (*The Unswept Room*) and Edward Kamau Brathwaite's response to the reception history of his *Mother Poem* in his later *Ancestors* are well worth delving into.

The *Companion* has been divided into two parts, the first dealing with genres determined primarily by form; the second dealing with genres essentially defined by subject matter. It opens with considerations of ancient genres such as the elegy, the ode, and the ballad, and moves on to Medieval and Renaissance genres originally invented or codified by the Troubadours or poets who followed in their wake. It then approaches genres driven essentially by theme, with few or no formal parameters, also broaching recently emergent genres such as the calypso and found poetry.

A number of these genres were brought into existence possessing formal as well as thematic constraints, sometimes losing the structural element over time: the elegy, for instance, began essentially as a formal genre bound by the distich only to become a theme-based, occasional genre. Likewise, the alba is a genre that did initially have formal constraints such as the repetition of the word "alba" at the end of verses, a rhetorical dialogic structure, as well as stock characters including the pair of doomed lovers, the nightwatchman, and the jealous husband: these were generally lost over time as they blended with the more celebratory and less formally constrained aubade.

The metamorphic nature of most genres has caused some theorists to go so far as to claim that "genres have no essence: they have historically changing use values" (Frow 134). This is a seductive view of genre, even if it is tempting to protest that genres such as the sonnet will always retain its fourteen-line mold, even if its initial amatory theme is only occasionally drawn on today: the valiant, steadfast, inviolate sonnet has resisted attempts to stretch its steel in Meredithian style or trim its edges into curtal brevity. Before Meredith, there were attempts by Coleridge, Thomas Dermody, Charlotte Smith, and others to write extended sonnets during the almost compulsive nineteenth-century era of "sonnetizing"; even Byron, who vowed never to write another sonnet, claiming that it was "the most puling, petrifying, stupidly platonic" of compositions, could not resist its pull in his subsequent work (Duff 16).

The sonnet has resisted periodic overuse, hybridizing fusion, omission of its rhyme, tampering with its pentameter, typographical reshuffling of its outline on the page. No matter how far contemporary experimentation with the sonnet goes, we never seem to lose sight of its initial formulation. It is tempting to see the sonnet as giving birth to mutating offspring but remaining indestructible in its original form. It is as resistant as those small reptiles that survived cataclysmic conditions when the largest saurians did not.

And yet, permanent mutation or even extinction remains a possibility. One might ask: whence the *partimen*, the *plazer* and the *pastorela*? It is, however, ultimately a mistake to conclude that some genres are defunct and gone forever. Poets can at any time resurrect them in their original form, a modernized version, or in a deeply intra-generic or intertextual manner: even extinct volcanoes are really only very dormant.

Genres nowadays have not so much modified, or evolved from, their original for-mulations; modern poems exist together in varying degrees of generic concentration, ranging from strict adherence, to transgression, to parody, to token nominal gesturing in the title, to texts written in complete rejection or disregard for form.

Begun in 2009, the anniversary year of both Darwin and his groundbreaking theo-ries, this volume of essays could be discussed in semi-facetious biomorphic terms: the word "evolution" has often been used to describe how genres develop. Indeed there is a striking resemblance between the prescriptive, normative approach of Neoclassical theorists and artificial selection; natural selection being closer to what happens in contemporary practice. It is hard to imagine sexual selection operating between genres, even if one tries to picture the villanelle leaping backward and forward flash-ing its colors like a bird of paradise trying to attract the sestina's attention, and yet similar things do happen in the metageneric poems of Billy Collins: his "Plight of the Troubadour" or "American Sonnet," not to mention his comically generic hoax poem "Paradelle for Susan," are poems which the reader interested in genre studies would do well to consider. The fact that Collins's tongue-in-cheek creation of the "paradelle" fooled so many critics into believing it was an ancient genre goes to show how relevant and necessary this volume is.

REFERENCES AND FURTHER READING

Boland, Eavan and Mark Strand. *The Making of a Poem: A Norton Anthology of Poetic Forms.* New York: Norton. 2000.

Brathwaite, Edward Kamau. *Ancestors: A Reinvention of Mother Poem, Sun Poem, and X/Self.* New York: New Directions. 2001.

Caplan, David. *Questions of Possibility: Contemporary Poetry and Poetic Form*. Oxford: Oxford University Press. 2006.

Cohen, Ralph (ed.). *The Future of Literary Theory*. New York: Routledge. 1989.

Collins, Billy. *Taking off Emily Dickinson's Clothes*. London: Picador. 2000.

Cooley, Peter. *The Astonished Hours*. New York: Carnegie Mellon University Press. 1992.

Creeley, Robert. *The Collected Poems: 1975–2005*. Berkeley: University of California Press. 2006.

Dubrow, Heather. *Genre*. London: Methuen. 1982.

Duff, David (ed.). *Modern Genre Theory*. Harlow: Longman. 2000.

Duff, David. *Romanticism and the Uses of Genre*. Oxford: Oxford University Press. 2009.

Fowles, Alastair. *Kinds of Literature: An Introduction to the Theory of Genres and Modes*. Cambridge, MA: Harvard University Press. 1982.

Frow, John. *Genre*. London: Routledge. 2006.

Genette, Gérard and Tzvetan Todorov (eds.). *Théorie des genres*. Paris: Seuil. 1986.

Olds, Sharon. *The Unswept Room*. New York: Knopf. 2002.

Sapphire. *Black Wings and Blind Angels*. New York: Vintage. 1999.

Acknowledgments

Erik Martiny

I am particularly grateful to all contributors for the quality of their essays and their faultless cooperation, in spite of the sometimes Herculean teaching and administrative assignments which they have to face. I wish to extend my thanks to Isobel Bainton, Emma Bennett, and Ben Thatcher, the fine editorial team at Wiley-Blackwell for their ever-ready support and enthusiasm. Thanks is also due to Wiley's art department for promoting Polish culture by agreeing to use, and elegantly enhance, Jacek Malczewski's "Hamlet Polski" in the cover illustration.

The authors and publisher gratefully acknowledge the permission granted to reproduce the copyright material in this book:

Chapter 2: H.L. Hix, "July 2003," from *First Fire, Then Birds: Obsessionals 1885–2010*. Copyright © 2010 by H.L. Hix. Reprinted with the permission of Etruscan Press, www.etruscanpress.org.

Chapter 8: Agha Shahid Ali, *Call Me Ishmael Tonight*. New York: W. W. Norton and Co., 2003. Adrienne Rich. From *Ghazals of Ghalib*, edited by Aijaz Ahmed. Copyright © 2010 Colombia University Press. Reprinted with permission of the publisher. Galway Kinnell "Driving West," from *Imperfect Thirst*. Boston, New York: Houghton Mifflin, 1994. Phyllis Webb, *Sunday Water: Thirteen Anti-Ghazals*, from *The Vision Tree: Selected Poems*, Vancouver, BC: Talon Books, 1982.

Chapter 9: Charles Bernstein, "Wherever Angels Go" and "The Ballad of the Girly Man," from *Girly Man*. Chicago and London: University of Chicago Press, 2006.

Chapter 12: Elizabeth Bishop, "One Art," from *The Complete Poems 1927–1979*. Copyright © 1979, 1983 by Alice Helen Methfessel. Reprinted by permission of Farrar, Straus and Giroux, LLC*. Wendy Cope, "Lonely Hearts," from *Making Cocoa for Kingsley Amis* by Wendy Cope. Copyright © 1986, Faber and Faber Ltd. Used by

Every effort has been made to trace copyright holders and to obtain their permission for the use of copyright material. The publisher apologizes for any errors or omissions in the above list and would be grateful if notified of any corrections that should be incorporated in future reprints or editions of this book.

Part I

1
"To Get the News from Poems"
Poetry as Genre

Jahan Ramazani

The difficulty of crafting a precise definition of poetry that could include high-art formalism and Creole performance poetry, sonnets and collage poems, W.B. Yeats and Gertrude Stein, should not be underestimated. Like epics, comedies, novels, and works in other genres and modes, poems are threaded together by family resemblances, but their variousness is hard to fit under one conceptual roof, built out of identifiable formal and thematic characteristics. In the *OED*, poetry is defined as:

> Composition in verse or some comparable patterned arrangement of language in which the expression of feelings and ideas is given intensity by the use of distinctive style and rhythm; the art of such a composition.
>
> Traditionally associated with explicit formal departure from the patterns of ordinary speech or prose, e.g. in the use of elevated diction, figurative language, and syntactical reordering.

In an introduction to a poetry anthology, *The Poet's Tongue*, W.H. Auden famously defined poetry as "memorable speech," explaining that poetry heightens "audible spoken word and cadence," "power of suggestion and incantation," "alternating periods of effort and rest," and "tension between" personal and inherited rhythms, while emphasizing "[s]imiles, metaphors of image or idea, and auditory metaphors such as rhyme, assonance, and alliteration" and "the aura of suggestion round every word" (*English Auden* 327). Though profoundly useful, these and other genre distillations are vexed by what they exclude: poems that avoid patterning or intensity, free-verse poems without mnemonic structures, poems written not in "elevated diction" but in a vernacular or dialect, and so forth. They are also vexed by what they inadvertently include, such as sermons and political speeches, hard-to-forget jingles

A Companion to Poetic Genre, First Edition. Edited by Erik Martiny.
© 2012 John Wiley & Sons, Ltd. Published 2012 by John Wiley & Sons, Ltd.

and James Joyce's novels. Auden was well aware that the qualities he ascribed to poetry—rhythm, figuration, sound patterning, and polysemy—aren't exclusive to it, and so he cited alongside Housman and Shakespeare a popular song and a schoolroom mnemonic for remembering a Latin gender, as well as the "good joke" made by the poetry-phobe who unwittingly "creates poetry" (*English Auden* 329). But this laudable theoretical elasticity doesn't resolve all the issues: if it did, and if Auden thought jokes and schoolroom mnemonics were indeed poems, why didn't he include them alongside the sonnets, ballads, and epigrams indexed in *The Poet's Tongue*?

One way of trying to get around the difficulties of defining poetry is the adoption of a more circumscribed vocabulary of genre, such as "twentieth-century British sonnets" and "modern American elegies." It limits the scope of the problem and avoids flattening historical and cultural differences. Even so, intractable boundary questions remain. What, for example, gets included and shut out by "British," "American," or "modern"? Does "sonnet" mean any fourteen-line poem, or are specific meters and stanzas and themes also prerequisites, and what about near-sonnets? Does "elegy" include only poems of mourning for individuals or also blues poems and group laments and works of self-mourning (Ramazani)? What is the relation between historically and culturally disparate instances of each subgenre? Whether framed broadly as "poetry," or limited to the sonnets and elegies, villanelles and aubades of a particular era and culture, definitions of genre are inherently unsettled by their porous, shifting, and uncertain boundaries.

But to discard genre as an interpretive framework because of its untidiness would be to make unrecognizable the specific ways in which individual works invoke and resist genre conventions. The "transgression requires a law," writes Tzvetan Todorov (14), and Jacques Derrida adds that a text "cannot be without or less a genre. Every text participates in one or several genres, there is no genreless text" (65). Genre descriptors like "poem of mourning for the dead" and "fourteen-line poem"; or "patterned arrangement," "intensity," "distinctive style and rhythm," and "elevated diction, figurative language, and syntactical reordering"; or "speech" made "memorable" by rhythm, figuration, sound patterning, and polysemy, should be seen not as strictly defining elegies, sonnets, and poems but as pragmatically delineating what cognitive psychologists call "schemas" and what Hans Robert Jauss terms "horizons of expectation," which "can then be varied, extended, corrected, but also transformed, crossed out, or simply reproduced" (88). Because genres are historically and culturally differentiated, and because individual works both activate and press against the genre assumptions brought to bear on them, critical use of the term "poetry," as well as "elegy," "sonnet," "ballad," "sestina," "ghazal," "pantoum," and the like, requires a pragmatic awareness both of the power of genre terms and of their unavoidable overreach and imprecision.

A major reason for poetry's ineluctable messiness as a concept is that genres are not sealed off from one another, transmitted in isolation through the centuries, but responsive, in A. K. Ramanujan's words, "to previous and surrounding traditions; they invert, subvert, and convert their neighbours" (8); "a whole tradition may invert,

negate, rework, and revalue another" (9). Genres constantly absorb materials from
other genres, even those against which they define themselves. Hence, all genres are
ineluctably intergeneric, and all genres are *genera mixta*. In a dialogic understanding
of genre, poetry is infiltrated by and infiltrates its generic others. Writers are constantly enlarging (Marianne Moore's poeticization of "business documents and //
school-books" {"Poetry"}) and narrowing (Stéphane Mallarmé's restrictive "Donner un
sens plus pur aux mots de la tribu" ["Le Tombeau d'Edgar Poe"}) the intergeneric
scope of what is understood to be "poetry," "lyric," "sonnet," "elegy," "ballad," and so
forth. Narrow it too much, and a genre risks choking in self-parody. Enlarge it too
much, and it risks vanishing into unrecognizability, unable to activate the genre-based
assumptions that propel the hermeneutic circle of literary engagement.

In "Asphodel, That Greeny Flower," William Carlos Williams implicitly identifies
poetry's specificity by placing the genre in an intergeneric context:

> It is difficult
> to get the news from poems
> yet men die miserably every day
> for lack
> of what is found there.
>
> (ll.317–21)

Although the news is usually seen as essential for modern citizenship, poetry as a
leisure option, Williams's famous declaration of poetry as the soul-sustaining opposite
of the news inverts center and periphery. The implications of his claim may be worth
pursuing for the genre-based study of modern and contemporary poetry, since among
the many genres that constitute the discursive field out of which poems are carved,
the news has a particular power and pervasiveness under modernity. The news is an
especially insistent discursive other in relation to which poetry's distinctiveness can
be understood.

"Every morning brings us the news of the globe," laments Walter Benjamin, "and
yet we are poor in noteworthy stories" ("Storyteller" 89). Benjamin famously theorized
the newspaper as the generic opposite of storytelling. Although his insights have more
often been brought to bear on the novel, much of Benjamin's argument in "The
Storyteller" applies more forcefully to poetry. In his analysis, the news is shallow and
ephemeral, whereas the traditional story is, like a poem in Auden's distillation,
strongly oral, mnemonic, and grounded in a long tradition:

> The value of information does not survive the moment in which it was new. It lives only
> at that moment; it has to surrender to it completely and explain itself to it without
> losing any time. A story is different. It does not expend itself. It preserves and concen-
> trates its strength and is capable of releasing it even after a long time . . . [A] story
> from ancient Egypt is still capable after thousands of years of arousing astonishment
> and thoughtfulness. It resembles the seeds of grain which have lain for centuries in the

chambers of the pyramids shut up air-tight and have retained their germinative power to this day.

There is nothing that commends a story to memory more effectively than that chaste compactness which precludes psychological analysis.

("Storyteller" 90–91)

Concentrated, compact, durable, memorable—these are qualities also invoked by Auden and others to characterize our expectations of poetry, a discourse with "an amplitude that information lacks" ("Storyteller" 89). Whereas the storyteller, like the poet, seeks to instill thoughtfulness and reflection, Benjamin writes in "The Newspaper" that "impatience is the state of mind of the newspaper reader," an "all-consuming impatience," a "longing for daily nourishment" by fragmentary and disconnected facts ("Newspaper" 741). The newspaper, in Benjamin's analysis, commodifies information, "the scene of the limitless debasement of the word" ("Newspaper" 742). If transience, impatience, fragmentation, and linguistic debasement seemed to afflict the newspapers in Benjamin's 1920s and 1930s, the rise of electronic and digital news media since that time has only exacerbated these features of the news. The main requirement for information is the appearance of "prompt verifiability," that it seem "'understandable in itself'" ("Storyteller" 89). In contrast, poetry and storytelling depend on long traditions to legitimize their far-fetched imaginings, their stretch, their amplitude.

If we take our cues from Williams, Auden, and Benjamin, one approach to the impossibly general question, "what is poetry?," is the almost equally general answer: under modernity, poetry is what it is by virtue of not being the news. Compared with the news, poetry seems compressed and memorable, phonetically patterned and figuratively rich, if also slow and often counterfactual; compared with poetry, the news seems instantaneous and transparent and dense with information, if also ephemeral, denotative, and flat. But these contrasts obviously oversimplify, less because the news sometimes aspires to poetry in, for example, punning headlines, than because poetry is itself sometimes shot through with the news. If we turn to a handful of modern and contemporary poems, we see that, in accordance with Mikhail Bakhtin's dialogic model of genre, poetry both incorporates and resists the news. After all, pace Williams, if we tried to get the news of the last century or so from poems, we wouldn't come up empty handed. In English-language poems, we'd learn a great deal about the world wars, especially the first; the Great Depression; the decolonization of European empires since Ireland's Easter Rising; changes in gender relations; the rise of new technologies; the wars in Vietnam and Iraq; and so forth. More recently, the news event that outstripped all others was the September 11 destruction of the World Trade Center, my starting point in analyzing individual poems in relation to the news. By exploring the news as one of modern and contemporary poetry's generic others and simultaneously as one of its generic cousins, I consider both poetry's specificity as genre and its infiltration by, and engagement with, other discourses—that is, how poetry echoes and inverts, plays on, and absorbs the news, among other genres.

Helping examine poetry in its generic particularity and relationality, Seamus Heaney's "Anything Can Happen" might seem an odd example of the newsy poem, since among the many poems about the September 11 attacks, it reworks a 2,000-year-old Latin ode by Horace (*"after Horace, Odes I, 34"*) (11). But this very fact tells us something important about poetry and its distinctive approach to the news:

> Anything can happen. You know how Jupiter
> Will mostly wait for clouds to gather head
> Before he hurls the lightning? Well, just now
> He galloped his thunder-cart and his horses
>
> Across a clear blue sky. It shook the earth
> And clogged underearth, the River Styx,
> The winding streams, the Atlantic shore itself.
>
> (ll.1–7)

The "just now" of Horace's poem (*"nunc"*) is renewed, doubling as the now of the ancient past and the now of the immediate present, unlike the singular "now" of the news. To reiterate and adapt Benjamin, poetry "does not expend itself. It preserves and concentrates its strength and is capable of releasing it even after a long time." Heaney's poem evidences poetry's delayed-release capacity by reawakening an ancient poem, highlighting its surprisingly strong resonances with the contemporary (the cloudless sky, the shaking earth, the rivers and shore, the inversions of fortune). It represents itself as an overlay on an earlier poem, showing poetry to be, in words quoted earlier from Benjamin and perhaps especially appropriate for an ode, "still capable after thousands of years of arousing astonishment and thoughtfulness." One part of our experience of Heaney's poem is the power of its compact and eerie evocation of the 9/11 attacks, another is our wonder at poetry's transhistorical durability and transnational adaptability: "It resembles the seeds of grain which have lain for centuries in the chambers of the pyramids shut up air-tight and have retained their germinative power to this day." Poet and reader encounter the "news event" through a cross-historical and cross-cultural detour into literary antiquity, responding simultaneously to an ancient text and to current reality.

By first publishing the poem then titled "Horace and the Thunder" in *The Irish Times* on November 17, 2001, Heaney emphasized the poem's intersections with the news, but in so doing, he also accentuated the difference between poetry's slow, layered, and indirect way of telling the news and much of what's found in the newspaper. To repeat Benjamin on the news media: "The value of information does not survive the moment in which it was new. It lives only at that moment; it has to surrender to it completely and explain itself to it without losing any time." This is what Benedict Anderson calls the "obsolescence of the newspaper on the morrow of its printing" (35). After the 9/11 attacks, many of us remember feeling that "all-consuming impatience" for news about who, what, when, where, and how, as we scoured newspapers and radio, TV, and the Internet. Heaney's poem adds nothing to this store of information. And yet it has "an amplitude that information lacks."

> Anything can happen, the tallest things
>
> Be overturned, those in high places daunted,
> Those overlooked regarded. Stropped-beak Fortune
> Swoops, making the air gasp, tearing the crest off one,
> Setting it down bleeding on the next.
>
> (ll.8–12)

By intertwining with an ancient poem in another language, Heaney's poem openly declares the transhistorical and transnational dependency of poems on other poems and, more generally, of thoughtful and reflective understanding on long time horizons and vast contexts often absent from the news. Instead of aspiring like the news to what Benjamin calls "prompt verifiability," Heaney's poem isn't "understandable in itself": you have to know something not only about the Twin Tower attacks but also about Horace, Jupiter, the River Styx, and classical Fortune; you have to have some context for the poem's literariness and difficulty, its classical mythology and elevated diction ("Stropped-beak" meaning a beak strop-sharpened like a razor). The poem acknowledges its deep embeddedness within literary tradition, instead of presenting itself as a history-free report of current reality. Like Yeats's "Leda and the Swan," it sees current upheaval as a bird-like assault on the human by the divine. It has, as Heaney says of poetry and Benjamin suggests of storytelling, "a touch of the irrational," "a soothsaying force" (13). With its news orientation and yet also its unpredictable deities, swooping fortune, and hurling lightning, the poem is true to our divided experience of such horrific events, in Heaney's words, "partly as assimilable facts of day-to-day life, partly as some kind of terrible foreboding, as if we were walking in step with ourselves in an immense theatre of dreams" (14).

As memorable speech that remembers prior memorable speech, and yet that also evokes contemporary reality, the poem freely translates Horace to point up references to 9/11, dropping Horace's first stanza and adding a new final stanza:

> Ground gives. The heavens' weight
> Lifts up off Atlas like a kettle lid.
> Capstones shift, nothing resettles right.
> Smoke furl and boiling ashes darken day.
>
> (ll.13–16)

The last line's syntactic complexity ("furl" used not as a verb but as a noun) and its echo of Auden's "In Memory of W.B. Yeats" ("The day of his death was as dark cold day" [*Selected Poems*, ll.6, 31]) complete a poem that has built up intensity by deploying a variety of poetic resources, including apostrophe ("You know . . . "); enjambment (emphasizing "just now" at the end of one line and "Across a clear blue sky" after a stanza break); mixed formal and colloquial registers ("Well . . . "); tension between iambic pentameter and Latinate caesurae; metaphor ("the air gasp") and simile ("like a kettle lid"); and alliteration ("Ground gives"). Poetry isn't the news. But when it tells the news, it tells it slant. It mediates contemporary history through a transnational thicket of long-memoried aesthetic structures that, in Pound's words, help make poetry "the news that STAYS news" (l.29).

Heaney's poetry was often quoted in the days after 9/11, but the most widely circulated poem was Auden's "September 1, 1939," for reasons made obvious by the opening stanza, in which the speaker sitting in one of 52nd Street's "dives" observes:

> Waves of anger and fear
> Circulate over the bright
> And darkened lands of the earth,
> Obsessing our private lives;
> The unmentionable odour of death
> Offends the September night.
>
> (*Selected Poems*, ll.6–11)

That Auden's poem was set in New York City, that it was dated September, that it evoked the onset of violent catastrophe, all seemed, like the Horatian thunderbolt in a cloudless sky, an uncanny anticipation of the Twin Tower attacks—another Benjaminian seed that germinated long after composition. Confirming that even an occasional poem with a date for its name could bear news that stayed news, many news consumers turned to Auden for a more reflective and humanly vulnerable ("Uncertain and afraid"), public yet personal expression of historical trauma (*Selected Poems* 86, l.3).

Toward the end of the poem, which recalls the trimeters and public–private fusing voice of Yeats's "Easter, 1916," Auden sets his poetry in opposition to newspapers:

> All I have is a voice
> To undo the folded lie,
> The romantic lie in the brain
> Of the sensual man-in-the-street
> And the lie of Authority
> Whose buildings grope the sky.
>
> (ll.79–83)

The "folded lie" of the newspaper, as of various ideologies, contrasts with the openness of the poet's demystifying voice. The newspaper, associated here with the deceptions and dishonesties of romantic love, commerce, and the state, may seem plainer than poetry, but its unsuspected convolutions, like the folds of the human "brain," can conceal and distort more than they reveal. This poem joins other "Ironic points of light" that flash affirmatively, despite the overwhelming "Negation and despair" (ll.92, 98). Brightly lit with irony and orality, poetry is seen as affording liberating affiliations among poets, and between poets and readers, in contrast to newspaper-supported political power, with its blindly lustful and coercive "grope." An Englishman in New York, addressing the German invasion of Poland and drawing on Irish, Greek, Russian, and other cultural sources, poetically embodies a complexly enmeshed world that, like that of Heaney's "Anything Can Happen," can't be neatly divided between "national" and "international."

Figured obliquely in the kenning of the "folded lie" (Fuller 292), the newspaper is thematized overtly in other poems. Two years earlier, another of Auden's topical public poems, "Spain," encompasses its frontline report on the urgent present within a panoramic, global vision that extends back to ancient China and prehistoric Northern Europe and looks ahead to a utopian future, including "Poets exploding like bombs" (l.89). This vast timescale is one of the many differences between the poem and a standard news account, glanced at in the depiction of "the poor in their fireless lodgings, dropping the sheets / Of the evening paper" (ll.33–34). They find in the newspaper no delivery from their constraining circumstances. Like "September 1, 1939," "Spain" incorporates news discourse but is anxious to assert its difference from it—broader temporal and cultural horizons, utopian longings and admissions of guilt. A few years earlier, Auden's *The Orators* (1932) included a scathing attack on newspapers, addressed to "Beethameer, Beethameer, bully of Britain," a conflation of the press barons Lord Beaverbrook and Lord Rothermere, the latter of whom subsequently supported Hitler, Mussolini, and the British Blackshirts in his *Daily Mail*:

> In kitchen, in cupboard, in club-room, in mews,
> In palace, in privy, your paper we meet
> Nagging at our nostrils with its nasty news,
> Suckling the silly from a septic teat,
> Leading the lost with lies to defeat.
>
> (ll.8–12)

Newspapers permeate every corner of modern experience, like a false and deceitful god that appears in both private and public spaces, both inside and outside the body. With the recent explosive growth of digital media, the ubiquity of the news has, if anything, been still more fully realized since Auden's riposte. A pretend "prophet," a deceiving "Savior," the newspaper is—as in "September 1, 1939" and in Benjamin's skeptical account—a tool of power, commerce, and the nation-state. "I advertise idiocy, uplift, and fear, / I succour the State, I shoot from the hip . . ." (ll.31–32). Like "September 1, 1939," which links poetry with both love and irony, this poem associates a poetic "awareness of difference" with "love" (75), but sees newspapers as a crushingly homogenizing force: "Newspapers against the awareness of difference" (86). "The newspaper is an instrument of power," writes Benjamin. "It can derive its value only from the character of the power it serves; not only in what it represents, but also in what it does, it is the expression of this power" ("Karl Kraus" 440). Despite its revolutionary potential, the newspaper, in Benjamin's view as in Auden's, "belongs to capital" ("The Author as Producer" 772). This poem's postscript satirically declares the poet's competition with the ephemera reproduced by the mass press: "10,000 Cyclostyle copies of this for aerial distribution" (*English Auden* 87). Poetry can't compete with the mass appeal of the news, nor does it have the coercive power of the press's commercial and political allies, but Auden attributes to it the power to ironize and demystify.

Despite Auden's defiance of the hegemonic news media, he, like Heaney, is much more of a public writer than many modern and contemporary poets. He even remarked: "in literature I expect plenty of news" and recommends the writer take an "interest in objects in the outside world." An artist has to be "a bit of a reporting journalist"— that is, someone for whom "the first thing of importance is subject"—although Auden also warns that too much journalism "can and frequently does kill" the "sensibility" (*English Auden* 357). If even Auden's poetry, including news-inflected public poems such as "Spain" and "September 1, 1939," nevertheless pits itself against the discursive norms of the newspaper, purchased daily at that time by 69 percent of the British public (K. Williams 23), then the large bulk of modern and contemporary poems, most of which have no such direct bearing on public events, should also be seen as carving out discursive alternatives to the news media, though often less overtly so. To write poems, whether about love or nature or grief ("mainstream" lyric), or about contemporary language's infestation by commodity discourse (Language poetry), or about the death of a jazz singer, as reported by *The New York Post* (Frank O'Hara's "The Day Lady Died"), is at some level to propose a different way of telling the news of our outer and inner lives.

Another poet can help explore further the poetry of poetry, as measured in relation to journalism, since her poetry, like Auden's, constantly rubs up against the news, yet might otherwise seem to share little with Auden's and Heaney's high literary verse. A news announcement of sorts, "Wat a joyful news, Miss Mattie," begins Jamaican Creole poet Louise Bennett's best-known poem, "Colonisation in Reverse" (l.1). Bennett's career was entwined with the news media and with newspapers in particular, perhaps more so than that of any significant modern or contemporary poet. Initially, she published many of her poems on a weekly basis in the Jamaican newspaper *The Sunday Gleaner*, and their popularity, despite the editor's initial reluctance, was a boon to the paper's fortunes. Whether published in newspapers, magazines, books, or aired on the radio, many of Bennett's topical poems vernacularize the headline news, such as the 1958 West Indies Federation and Jamaica's 1962 independence, wartime scarcities and victories, public water problems and overcrowded trams, emigration and race relations, and the women's movement, even visits by politicians such as Adlai Stevenson and Creech Jones, and singers such as Marian Anderson and Paul Robeson. It isn't difficult to get the local and global news from Bennett's poems of the 1940s, 1950s, and 1960s.

But does this mean that her poems, initially bound up with the production and circulation system of a national newspaper, approximate Benjamin's characterization of the news—short-lived, lacking amplitude, exhausted in the moment of its telling? After all, they are more topical than most modern and contemporary poems, have little of the high literary allusiveness of Heaney's and Auden's poems, and don't ground themselves in a slow-germinating writerly tradition that goes back to antiquity. But because of their strongly marked oral and narrative texture, Bennett's poems are perhaps even more like Benjaminian storytelling than are Heaney's and Auden's poems. Written and performed in a robust Jamaican Creole that contrasts with the Jamaican newspapers' dryly standardized English, her poetic narratives are propelled by the tetrameter rhythms and alternating rhymes of the ballad quatrain. They recontextualize decontextualized news fragments, situating them within balladic narratives about women's lives and gossip. Many of these orally coded stories, which are as much about the local human impact and circulation of the news as about the news itself, begin in the reading or overhearing of journalism, such as "bans o' big headline" in "Invasion" about the Allied successes toward the end of World War II (line 2). Elated by the news of Nazi and Japanese defeat, the speaker of "Peace" seizes on it to warn two gossips about the danger of deceit and lies:

> Two-face Muriel teck me warnin
> Check yuh wutless 'ceitful way,
> Faas-mout Edna clip yuh long tongue
> Lie an back-bitin noh pay.

> (ll.25–28)

Hybridizing Jamaican oral tale telling, global news reporting, and the British ballad, Bennett shows her characters turning impersonal and faraway news into moral and social meaning, despite the comically disjunctive fit between global and local, public and private. In these transnationally stretched poems, Bennett's speakers don't hesitate to transgress the news's compartmentalizations by making local use of foreign news, rhyming their private lives with global events.

Bennett's news poems are meta-news poems, telling stories in which the material reception and human appropriation of the news is itself the news. Although the news media often present events as if apprehended transparently and objectively, speakers of poems such as "Big Tings" (1947) struggle to get the news, in this case pressing her ears to a hole in the wall ("Mi kotch me aise a one li-hole") to hear the news of a local election ("Miss Mum son dah-read newspapa") (ll.3, 1). The verbal physicality of poetry, as emphasized by Bennett's "auditory metaphors" (Auden) of insistent rhymes, jaunty rhythms, and tight ballad stanzas, accentuates the bodily circumstances of news retrieval. Another speaker has access to the news only through a hole, in a poem about the V-Day Parade in London, written while Bennett was there at the end of World War II. The speaker of "Victory" is trying to witness the unfolding of this momentous news event, including a marching contingent of "coloured bwoys" but a woman's hairdo (a "high upsweep") comically blocks her view (ll.33, 23).

> Me teck time teck me finga bore
> One hole eena de hair,
> An t'rough the gal upsweep me spy
> De whole parade affair!
>
>   (ll.25–28)

As sonically underscored by rhyme, the news "affair" is, for this speaker, inextricable from a woman's upswept "hair." The little hole she has to bore through the woman's hairdo represents her vision as partial, limited, physically located, a parodic and poetic inversion of the reporter's god's eyed omniscience. In Bennett's epistemology, even triumphant news is inseparable from the bodily perception of it, as meaning is from poetic sound.

Bennett's readers and hearers are not passive consumers of the news; they physically re-embody it. In " 'Sir,' " the speaker ridicules by phonetic repetition the newspapers' usual "bus-fuss / An de cuss-cuss an abuse" and "foo-fool / Letta to de edita" (ll.23–24, 27–28), but she is elated to read that a black man, a pre-independence finance minister, has been knighted: "Nayga man tun eena 'Sir'!" she exclaims, adding, "Lawd me pride an head a-swell up" (ll.4, 5). In other poems, when Bennett's speakers try to conjure for themselves the newspaper's huge and impersonal events, they re-imagine them embodied on a human scale. In "Italy Fall," we learn that "Po' Italy kick puppa-lick, / Newspapa say she fall!" (ll.3–4). That is, Italy has somersaulted and fallen, showing an upturned buttock that seems ready for a father's ("puppa") spank ("lick") (*Dictionary of Jamaican English* 367). The poetry physically metaphorizes and sonically indigenizes large events to make them comprehensible in terms of the known world. Regarding Mussolini's disappearance, the speaker remarks: "Soh maybe him dah-hide wey eena / Italy boots toe" (ll.11–12). The clichéd image of Italy as boot-like, ominous under Fascist rule, is imaginatively revitalized in the speaker's cartographic fantasy of Mussolini hiding in Italy's toe. Lamenting Italy's degradation by its alliance with Hitler, the speaker concludes with a proverb about the dangers of consorting with turkey buzzards or carrion crow: "ef yuh fly wid John Crow, yuh / Wi haffe nyam dead meat!" [if you fly with John Crow, you will have to eat dead meat] (ll.31–32). Whereas Auden's and Heaney's lyrics are grounded in a Western literary tradition that self-consciously traces itself back to antiquity, Bennett's poems also have a deeper time than the news: they reanimate the compressed repositories of "folk" wisdom and wit not only in the British ballad but also in Jamaican proverbs, by which she creolizes foreign news. As Benjamin puts it, a proverb "proclaims its ability to transform experience into tradition" ("On Proverbs" 582).

Although the language of poetry is often thought of as being elevated, Bennett's distinguishes itself, paradoxically, by its lowly register, the supposedly subliterary register of West Indian Creole—the use of which delayed her recognition as a poet for decades. The vividly imagistic physicality and phonetic vibrancy of Bennett's poetry set it apart from the disembodiment of the newspaper English she parodies.

The speaker of "Big Wuds" is baffled by a woman's lumbering abstractions, "dem big wud" like "'New Nation', 'Federation', 'Delegation,'" until she realizes she is parroting news reports about plans for the West Indies Federation: "Oh, is newspapa yuh readin / Meck yuh speaky-spoky so!" (ll.2, 3, 9–10). But in the story woven around this tension between discourses, soon the speaker, too, is seduced by big words from the newspaper, such as "development" and "improvement," "delegation" and "population," taking to them with zeal (ll.31, 34). They make her feel learned. But there is one potential problem. To speak in abstractions of political unity is ironically to risk breaking ("bus") her own body:

> Me like sey de big wuds dem, gwan like
> Me learnin is fus rate;
> But me hope dat me jawbone noh bus
> Before we federate.
>
> (ll.37–40)

The newspaper diction is made to seem lifeless and clichéd by comparison with richly poetic Creole descriptions of jawbones in danger of rupture, just as the federation will itself come apart in a few short years. Another poem that quotes "bans o' big wud" from the news (l.9), "Invasion" punningly turns on its head empty news rhetoric by way of explaining the impossibility of anyone with self-respect siding with the nasty Nazis:

> For ef yuh cuss nayga "naasy"
> Dem get bex an feel shame,
> But German bawl out tell de whole worl'
> "Naasy" is dem name!
>
> (ll.25–28)

Bennett's bilingual pun on Nazi ("Naasy") and nasty ("naasy"), comically compressing and bridging transnational distances, exemplifies the sonic association and semantic friction that poetry so readily elicits from words, in contrast with the transparent one dimensionality and ephemerality of most news reports. Her physical re-embodying, narrative re-embedding, and transnational creolizing of the news show up poetry's difference from the news, even when poetry comes closest to it. After Bennett's initial newspaper contributions, she went on to create popular radio and TV shows, continuing to play with and against the media's norms, and since then, poetry's engagement and rivalry with media forms such as TV and the Internet has only intensified, as the news media have ever more thoroughly saturated our lives (Perloff).

Exploring what poetry is not, with the news as our central exhibit, may seem an oddly roundabout way of getting at what it is. But whether overtly or not, all genre definitions depend on contrast, if always complicated by exceptions: a tragedy is a non-comedy, except of course in tragicomedy; epic is neither lyric nor dramatic, though epics can incorporate lyrics and plays can tell epic stories; and so forth. A genre's others are often multiple. Poetry is not prose, except in prose poetry; poetry is not fiction, except in narrative poetry and in poetic novels. Once we look outside literary systems for areas of overlap and differentiation, these generic others multiply. Poems often draw on song, though they also differ in many ways, most obviously by fastening themselves to the page. Poems sometimes approximate prayer, addressing or petitioning or berating a deity, though their self-conscious artifice and idiosyncrasy also often make them hard to reduce to prayer. Poems can emphasize the verbal precision that brings them close to the law, though poems that directly borrow from legal language and norms also often unmake legal hierarchies and procedures. Poems are rich in philosophical and theoretical reflection, though a tradition going back to antiquity also highlights the contention between poetry and philosophy. The extra-literary discourses and speech genres that poetry draws on and yet distinguishes itself from are many, ranging from post it notes and text messages to public oratory and ritual incantations. The news is but one of these other genres, if an especially pressing other under modernity, when the media's assumptions about time, information, language, nation, and representation are everywhere—assumptions that, as we have seen, poets often contest. Not that poetry is pristinely uncontaminated by the news. As we have also seen, poems often adapt news-like consciousness of the historical now, even as, in Heaney, they embed themselves within a slow-germinating aesthetic with wider time horizons than those of the news, or, as in Auden, they wield an ironic and disenchanting discourse meant to undo state and capitalist ideologies, or, as in Bennett, they deploy a vernacular, physically rich, proverb-laden language to re-narrate and creolize public circumstance within lived social experience. Poetry's vigorously transnational energies, forms, and affiliations, observed in all three examples, often confound the nationalist imperatives and geographic compartmentalizations of the news. Poetry will never be satisfactorily defined, but under modernity the news is one of the most prominent discursive others against which it defines itself.

REFERENCES AND FURTHER READING

Anderson, B. *Imagined Communities*. Rev. edn. London: Verso. 1991.

Auden, W.H. *The English Auden*. Ed. Edward Mendelson. London: Faber. 1977.

Auden, W.H. *Selected Poems*. New edn. Ed. Edward Mendelson. New York: Vintage-Random House. 1979.

Bakhtin, M.M. *The Dialogic Imagination: Four Essays*. Ed. M. Holquist. Trans. C. Emerson and M. Holquist. Austin: University of Texas Press. 1981.

Benjamin, W. "The Author as Producer." *Selected Writings*. Vol. 2. Ed. M.W. Jennings, H. Eiland, and G. Smith. Cambridge, MA: Belknap Press; Harvard University Press. 1996. 768–82.

Benjamin, W. "Karl Kraus." Trans. E. Jephcott. *Selected Writings*. Vol. 2. Ed. M.W. Jennings, H. Eiland, and G. Smith. Cambridge, MA: Belknap Press; Harvard University Press. 1996. 433–58.

Benjamin, W. "The Newspaper." Trans. R. Livingstone. *Selected Writings*. Vol. 2. Ed. M.W. Jennings, H. Eiland, and G. Smith. Cambridge, MA: Belknap Press; Harvard University Press. 1996. 741–42.

Benjamin, W. "On Proverbs." Trans. R. Livingstone. *Selected Writings*. Vol. 2. Ed. M.W.

Jennings, H. Eiland, and G. Smith. Cambridge, MA: Belknap Press; Harvard University Press. 1996. 582.

Benjamin, W. "The Storyteller." *Illuminations*. Trans. Harry Zohn. New York: Schocken Books. 1969. 83–109.

Bennett, L. *Jamaica Labrish*. Kingston, Jamaica: Sangster's Book Stores. 1966.

Derrida, J. "The Law of Genre." Trans. A. Ronell. *Critical Inquiry* 7 (1980): 55–81.

The Dictionary of Jamaican English, q.v. "pupa-lick." Ed. F.G. Cassidy and R.B. Le Page. 2nd edn. Kingston, Jamaica: University of West Indies Press. 2002.

Fuller, J. *W.H. Auden: A Commentary*. Princeton: Princeton University Press. 1988.

Heaney, S. *Anything Can Happen: A Poem and Essay*. Dublin: TownHouse. 2004.

Jauss, H.R. *Toward an Aesthetic of Reception*. Trans. Timothy Bahti. Minneapolis: University of Minnesota Press. 1982.

Oxford English Dictionary Online, s.v. "poetry," http://dictionary.oed.com.

Perloff, M. *Radical Artifice: Writing Poetry in the Age of Media*. Chicago: University of Chicago Press. 1991.

Pound, E. *ABC of Reading*. New York: New Directions. 1960.

Ramanujan, A.K. "Where Mirrors Are Windows." *The Collected Essays of A.K. Ramanujan*. Ed. V. Dharwadker. New Delhi: Oxford University Press. 1999. 6–33.

Ramazani, J. *Poetry of Mourning: The Modern Elegy from Hardy to Heaney*. Chicago: University of Chicago Press. 1994.

Todorov, T. *Genres in Discourse*. Trans. C. Porter. Cambridge: Cambridge University Press. 1990.

Williams, K. *British Writers and the Media, 1930–45*. New York: St. Martin's Press. 1996.

Williams, W.C. *The Collected Poems of William Carlos Williams*. Vol. 2. Ed. C. MacGowan. New York: New Directions. 1986.

2
What Was New Formalism?

David Caplan

Two recent movements in American letters awkwardly share an unattractive name. Emerging in the 1980s, a largely American movement promoted the use of metrical verse technique and rhyme. The group published anthologies, poetry collections, and literary criticism, most consciously, *Rebel Angels: 25 Poets of the New Formalism* (1996), Dana Gioia's *Can Poetry Matter?: Essays on Poetry and Poetic Culture* (1992), and Timothy Steele's *Missing Measures: Modern Poetry and the Revolt against Meter* (1990). In the early 1990s Gioia and Michael Peich, publisher of Aralia Press, cofounded an annual conference at West Chester University, "Exploring Form and Narrative." The conference brings together many poets associated with new formalism, who serve as faculty, keynote speakers, and panel participants. Following a pattern in American poetry, the manifestoes that the movement produced drew more attention than the poems they defended. A second "new formalism" emerged during the last decade as literary scholarship displayed an increased interest in form. In a special issue of *Modern Language Quarterly* titled "Reading for Form," Heather Dubrow wrote of the embarrassment the field inspires, "Many scholars are far more comfortable detailing their sexual histories in print than confessing to an interest in literary form" (Dubrow 59). If so, the date of the issue's publication, 2000, marked the year that form came out of the closet. In a 2007 review essay in *PMLA*, Marjorie Levinson observed that the works under consideration, all published since 2000, "aim to recover for teaching and scholarship in English some version of their traditional address to aesthetic form" (Levinson 55). Levinson surveyed a movement too vast for the pages of *PMLA*; she posted online a longer version of the essay, along with a more extensive bibliography divided into three sub-groups, "Alternative Solutions to Problems Raised by New Formalism," "Works Focused on Metrical Study," and "Works Focused on Beauty and Disinterest." As intended Levinson's essay encouraged more discussion. Following

A Companion to Poetic Genre, First Edition. Edited by Erik Martiny.
© 2012 John Wiley & Sons, Ltd. Published 2012 by John Wiley & Sons, Ltd.

decades in which studies of poetic form typically lamented the subject's neglect, scholar after scholar declared its rebirth. Each new work created greater momentum. In the early 1980s, Derek Attridge described a sleepy discipline, lacking vigor and readership, as its books justifiably languished unread. "[B]y and large," he observed of prosody studies, "their undisturbed repose on the library shelves is not unwarranted" (quoted in Holder 241). A year after Levinson's review essay, Attridge appraised a rapidly expanding and energized field, describing the "signs of a revitalization of formal study" (565).

Conjoining this history, my title, then, echoes two earlier works that share the title, "What Is New Formalism?", one devoted to poetic "new formalism" and the other devoted to the subsequent movement in scholarship.[1] My slight revision of the phrase, the use of the past tense instead of the present, signals my belief that the critical task has moved from definition to evaluation.[2] My aim is not to assert a direct connection between the groups, although I will suggest that the poets' interest in form did encourage the scholars'. Instead, I wish to re-examine the earlier poetic movement in order to urge a fuller, more accurate, and generous discussion of form. My hope is that such analysis might prove useful to the scholarly movement as it defines—and refines—its ambitions.

First, let me note one shared tendency—or at the very least a shared point of contention. Levinson decries what she calls "backlash formalism" (559), a threat that also alarms Attridge. He explains:

> One danger is that a return to form would be indeed a return, a turning back of the clock, what Levinson calls 'backlash formalism'. While there are no doubt those who favour the methods of close reading that dominated the mid-twentieth century, the demonstration of the complicity between those methods and unacceptable ethico-political assumptions has surely been too persuasive to allow a simple revival. Although there is more to learn from the best of the early formalist critics than has generally been allowed in recent decades, they also provide a clear lesson in the many hazards of a formalism that fails to take account of the situatedness of writers and readers, that treats works of literature as self-sufficient, organic wholes, and that allies evaluation with questionable human and social values.
>
> (567)

Attridge assumes that an essential connection exists between "methods of close reading" and "unacceptable ethico-political assumptions." He notes that "there are no doubt those who favour the methods of close reading that dominated the mid-twentieth century," before brushing such readers aside as ethically and politically defective. "[T]he demonstration of the complicity," he writes with suave confidence, "has surely been too persuasive." Such close-reading techniques, though, enjoy a greater flexibility than this statement admits. They enable stances far less sinister than complicity. Hardly an apologist for the "unacceptable ethico-political assumptions" that Attridge decries, Edward Said, for instance, celebrated "the enlightening and yes, emancipatory purposes of close reading" (67). However, it is not necessary to accept Attridge's premise to share his belief that "a simple revival" is not possible. As if demonstrating this difficulty, his essay's central metaphor puzzles over the question of how the present scholarly moment relates to those it follows. A question mark punctuates Attridge's title, "A Return to Form?" and the essay's opening sentence adds another reservation, "To speak of returns is to speak of departures" (563). Later in the essay, Attridge drops the question mark, using the phrase "return to form" without this questioning tone. Despite this shift in tone, Attridge consistently fears an unqualified return: "a return to form [that] would be indeed a return," a reactionary setting aside of the last few decades in order to reclaim an earlier age. Paradoxically, he seeks a "return" that also offers a "departure."

Attridge's title repeats a phrase often used to describe poetic new formalism, whether in praise or derision. This coincidence suggests how an overlapping set of underlying concerns guide discussions of both groups. Debates about the relation of literary technique and politics dominated much of the initial reception of poetic new formalism, with the strong assumption that metrical technique marked a deplorable "complicity." During the so-called "poetry wars," some poets and critics attacked contemporary metrical verse as politically and aesthetically reactionary.[3] Dominated more by polemics than careful analysis, such debates obscured many of the underlying issues, but helped to give the field a certain prominence. It suggested the centrality of poetic technique to the art, albeit crudely; in a telling gesture, such debates sought to define certain poets according to the techniques they favored. Complicating matters, a broader poetic new formalism emerged in the movement's wake, as more poets wrote metrical verse yet resisted any group affiliation. Such poetry offers the most visible signs that many writers found the various condemnations of these forms to be unpersuasive. I do not want to linger too long over the heated (and over-heated) discussions of the relation between poetic form and politics that raged in the 1980s and 1990s.[4] It is helpful, though, to note a broad parallel: that these debates anticipate some of the questions raised about the scholarly new formalism and the techniques it employs: in particular, whether it represents a return or a departure—or both.

In the case of the poetic new formalism, for several reasons the widely used metaphor of "return" remains inaccurate. To use a poetic form after a period of neglect is to contend with new linguistic, aesthetic, and formal challenges. To adopt a form from another language necessitates even more transformations. In Attridge's terms, no "revival" is ever "simple," even when it purports to be. As if to demonstrate this point, new formalism helped to popularize many verse forms that remain unusual within the larger sweep of English-language literary history, such as villanelles, pantoums, ghazals, and sestinas. Exploiting both the term's malleability and the literary culture's gullibility, the movement made the "untraditional" seem "traditional." Yet poetic forms resist the claims of timelessness putatively made on their behalf. As Frank Bidart observes, the forms serve as agents of change, not stasis. They compel change from the author and themselves. "We fill pre-existing forms," Bidart notes, "and when we fill them we change them and are changed" (16).

Finally, the phrase, "a return to form," obscures how form offers the opportunity for contestation and disagreement and how it encourages competing and contrary motivations. As I noted in my brief opening summary, the poets and critics associated with new formalism promoted metrical verse and rhyme. This broad similarity, though, scarcely disguised a more telling dispute. While those associated with new formalism agreed that poets should write metrical verse, many disagreed over the reasons why. In his widely anthologized essay, "Notes on the New Formalism," Dana Gioia argued (29–41) that poets should not limit themselves to the range of free-verse prosody. He writes with an air of even-handed neutrality, reminding the reader that he composes both metrical and free-verse poetry. (Indeed, many other poets associated with new formalism have published both kinds of poems.) Gioia's reasons remain pragmatic; he advocates that poets "explore the full resources that the English language offers" (*CPM* 41). "I find it puzzling therefore," he observes, "that so many poets see these modes ['fixed and open forms'] as opposing aesthetics rather than as complementary techniques" (*CPM* 41). As Gioia clearly states, he sees such techniques as socially, politically, and aesthetically neutral:

> Formal verse, like free verse, is neither intrinsically bad nor good. The terms are strictly descriptive not evaluative. They define distinct sets of metrical technique rather than rank the quality or nature of poetic performance. Nor do these techniques automatically carry with them social, political, or even, in most cases, aesthetic values.
>
> (*CPM* 30)

In contrast Timothy Steele ends *Missing Measures: Modern Poetry and the Revolt against Meter* concludes with a call-to-arms that links metrical verse—or as Steele calls it, the "art of measured speech"—with "values," both extensive and specific:

> What is most essential to human life and to its continuance remains a love of nature, an enthusiasm for justice, a readiness of good humor, a spontaneous susceptibility to beauty and joy, an interest in our past, a hope for our future and above all, a desire that others should have the opportunity and encouragement to share in those qualities. An art of measured speech nourishes these qualities in a way no other pursuit can.
>
> (*MM* 294)

Discussions of new formalism frequently quote Steele's statement because it confirms many observers' suspicions that a clear link exists between metrical form and a broader agenda. Eager to link metrical technique with "unacceptable ethico-political assumptions" (to shift Attridge's phrase into this context), some disregard the particulars of Gioia's position, or, even more oddly, ascribe to Gioia the views that Steele holds as if unable to accept that Gioia believes what he writes.

Of course some writers of metrical verse contest the claims I have just made; they present their forms as unchanging, stable, and timeless. Relying on these associations, a certain kind of poetry uses verse technique to strike a defiantly minority gesture. A

subgenre of contemporary metrical verse employs verse technique to criticize its putative "opposite" and the poets who use them, as well as to signal a group allegiance.
The tones range from wry to bitter to outraged. Cody Walker's "Limerick" (56) offers
a short example:

> A new class of antidepressants
> Is targeted at adolescents:
> They lose track of time,
> Of meter, of rhyme,
> It's really sad.
>
> (ll.1–5)

Curmudgeonly the poem enjoys a perceived generational divide. It seeks to distinguish itself from those who "lost track of time, / Of meter, of rhyme." As a demonstration of its argument, these verse techniques proclaim a certain pride in what the
poem is not; it has not forgotten the lost entertainments and virtues of metrical verse
technique. The poem, though, lacks the form's bawdy bad taste. The concluding line
also departs from the typical limerick form, as the final line usually repeats (sometimes
with a variation) the first line. Instead of following this pattern by concluding with
"A new class of antidepressants," the poem more quietly ends, "It's really sad." Blandly
the poem rejects a certain blandness.

Like other in-jokes, the poem relies upon shared commitments. It constructs two
communities—those who share the joke and those who serve as its butt—and uses
verse form straightforwardly: as the means to reinforce this distinction. The verse form
neatly supports the argument. Even with its contemporary reference to "A new class
of antidepressants," though, this recently published poem sounds dated. It returns to
out-worn arguments as if they were still vibrant. Just as such poetry presents a special
case, Steele's position represents only one, highly personal motivation for writing
metrical verse. Whether in prose or in verse, such polemics tempt the reader with
their clarity and self-assurance; they urge him or her to view their eccentric stances
as exemplary. Overlooked remains the fact that verse technique bears a complicated
relationship with ethical and moral values, one that resists the easy elision of, say,
rhyme and meter with specific literary, civic, and political beliefs.

Like other poetic movements, the new formalism favors certain meters and forms
(though individual poets differ in their preference). The contemporary poetic culture
hungers for new yet preexisting forms: it cycles through such structures, seeking both
precedent and novelty. "We have seen," observes the poet-critic William Logan, "the
sestina become the poor man's sonnet, the villanelle the poor man's sestina, and the
pantoum (just in the past decade) the poor man's villanelle" (Logan, unpaginated).
Another reviewer wearily mentions "an obligatory villanelle, sestina, pantoum, and
sonnet" that many collections include (Mlinko, unpaginated). This nearly frantic
cycling through different forms gives the impression that the poets seek to demonstrate a certain skill then quickly weary of it. They add even more outlandish demands

to forms once viewed as forebodingly difficult. Denise Duhamel, for instance, writes a sestina whose end words vary the last name of the actor Sean Penn (21–22).

Duhamel's endwords also mark the distinctive way that some contemporary poets handle metrical forms. As if eager to disprove the claim that pre-existing forms are outmoded, some poets cram theirs with counter-evidence. They aim to sound the moment, as they knowingly detail peculiarly contemporary mores and situations. Their forms do not represent anything as weighty as timelessness, immortality, or endurance; they demonstrate responsiveness to stimuli as they freely accept nearly whatever the contemporary moment allows. In the course of her sestina, Duhamel's endwords mention a "Pentium / Processor," a "ballpoint pen," the talk show host Larry King's iconic "suspenders," the cartoon character "Pig Pen," and "penne / pasta" (ll.4–5, 2, 10, 28, 33–34). With a similar attention to the details of contemporary scene, sonnets by Rafael Campo, Marilyn Hacker, Kate Light, and Rachel Wetzsteon depict the vicissitudes of modern dating, gay and straight, mixing techniques from, among other sources, screwball comedy, feminist theory, queer studies, light verse, and pop culture. In Donald Justice's "Street Musician," "Punk teens, in pink hair-spikes and torn T-shirts / Drift past" (ll.8–9) introduce a touch of local color as a background to the poem's true subject, a jazz saxophonist, a figure of noble dignity. In the next generation of metrical verse, "punk teens" do not "drift past"; they claim center stage. One of Light's "Five Urban Love Songs," a sonnet, devotes fourteen lines to analyzing a sexually ambiguous server's jewelry, noting his (or her) "Pierced tongue. Do-it-yourself-list" (23, l.1) and the effect it has on the speaker and her date.

In this kind of contemporary poetry, a general rule applies; the more staid the form might appear, the more enthusiastically poets inject it with a conspicuous contempo-raneity. Discussing Tennyson's handling of stanzaic form in "In Memoriam," in 1850 Charles Kingsley praised "their metre, so exquisitely chosen, that while the major rhyme in the second and third lines of each stanza gives the solidity and self-restraint required by such deep themes, the mournful minor rhyme of each first and fourth line always leads the ear to expect something beyond" (62). Following Kingsley's "most perceptive comment," subsequent generations of scholars emphasize how the stanza "rises" "and then fades" "into dimness and regret" (Ricks 216). Describing Tennyson's versification, the scholars precisely name the very qualities that contemporary poets who use this form typically avoid. Little "dimness and regret" remains in "In Memoriam" stanzas recast as:

> Darryl Dawkins wrote a book,
> And I might too. He liked the rhymes'
> (*If you ain't groovin'*) paradigms
> (*You best get movin'*). Hook
>
> A chorus and we've got
> A song . . .

(ll.9–14)

In an interview, Erica Dawson names Anthony Hecht, James Merrill, and her teacher Greg Williamson as formative influences. As if rewarding this taste, her collection *Big-Eyed Afraid* won the 2006 Anthony Hecht Poetry Prize, judged by Mary Jo Salter. Yet Dawson's self-dramatizing "Chocolate Thunder" claims a hipper lineage; it not only mentions but quotes the similarly flamboyant Darryl Dawkins, a basketball and sometime poet, famous for his backboard-shattering dunks and the nicknames he coined for them. Dawson adds rhyme to rhyme; the internal quoted lines rhyme with each other, leaving less than two metrical feet to meet the next rhyme. The poem gets as much as possible into its rhymes: to chart only a partial catalogue, it couples English and French, basketball nicknames and literary-critical terms, visual opposites ("Frankenstein" and "fine" [ll.18–19]), and multisyllabic and one-syllable words. To account for this variety, the poem proposes metaphor after metaphor for its handling of form: at times athletic, at times musical, at times linguistic ("logogriph," 23). The poem joyfully flees the form's associations with "solidity and self-restraint." At its most successful such poetry achieves a thrilling movement, daring and excited. In its exuberant commitment to whatever it can rhyme, though, it also risks producing a verse equivalent of what James Woods decries as the contemporary novel's "hysterical realism," "characterised by a fear of silence . . . a perpetual motion machine that appears to have been embarrassed into velocity."

This poetry also employs meter distinctively. In one respect, it is accurate to say that contemporary metrical verse favors iambic rhythm. As the prosodist Thomas Cable observes of new formalist poetry, "As in English poetry, historically the iamb reigns" (333). Cable's formulation suggests one of the two main justifications for the meter: that is, it forms the language's canonical meter. In his poem, "Approaching a Significant Birthday, He Pursues *The Norton Anthology of Literature*," Gwynn wittily makes this point. The twenty-eight-line poem consists wholly of iambic pentameter lines culled from *The Norton Anthology of Literature*, arranged into quatrains:

> All human things are subject to decay.
> Beauty is momentary in the mind.
> The curfew tolls the knell of parting day.
> If Winter comes, can Spring be far away?
>
> (ll.1–4)

If mortality forms English-language poetry's great subject, iambic pentameter serves as its great meter. Some new formalists explain this status on the basis of the meter's "naturalness," with occasionally outlandish theories that range from the biological to the linguistic. In response, Annie Finch has proposed non-iambic meters as an "aesthetic, emotional, and ideological alternative to iambic pentameter" (117). This position, though, exerts little visible influence. Less explored, though, remains the question of how contemporary poets define "the iamb." A carefree attitude toward form inspires contemporary metrical verse. "I count on my fingers," observes Derek Walcott. "Everything else is by accident" (82). As in Walcott's or Seamus Heaney's verse, a careful scansion of much contemporary metrical verse shows an abundance of variations, as accentual-syllabic verse switches into accentual meter and drops or adds syllables, metrical feet, and rhyme schemes. Such poetry values more the sound of the line than its metrical count. In Dawson's passage quoted above, the five complete lines consist of two lines of iambic tetrameter, two lines of iambic trimeter, and a line of tailless trochaic tetrameter.

Informed by such debates, H.L. Hix's recently published *Selected Poems, First Fire, Then Birds: Obsessionals 1985–2010* broods over the question of what, if any, values verse structures embody. Hix has enjoyed a peculiar writing career. "The philosopher who pursues ideas with ardor learns to distrust the idea of ideas," he observes as if speaking of himself impersonally, "and becomes a poet, one pursued by ideas."(Hix, *Fire*, 194) Trained as a philosopher, Hix published two scholarly books about postmodernism before his first poetry collection, which Dana Gioia selected for publication. Hix regularly serves as a faculty member at the West Chester Exploring Form and Narrative Conference and his work often appears in venues familiar to new formalism. Consistently, though, his poetry's admirers struggle to explain their enthusiasm and his work inspires some perplexing claims. *Contemporary American Poetry: A Pocket Anthology* lists Hix, along with Michael Palmer, Susan Howe, and Harryette Mullen, as writers of "Language Poetry": news, I'm sure, to all involved (Gwynn and Lidner 492).

As the subtitle of *Selected Poems, First Fire, Then Birds: Obsessionals 1985–2010* suggests, Hix's obsessions drive his poetry. "I am a person of obsessions," he admits, "and my poems have always come from following those obsessions whether I could justify them or not" (*God Bless*, 72). Two remain particularly prominent. His work features a great number of poems in easily recognizable forms such as sonnets, villanelles, ghazals, couplets, syllabic verse, and nonce forms that include prose. The formal range aims less for a tour de force display of virtuosity than a pained and painful consideration of their limitations. Hix would never say, as Kevin McFadden does in his riotously punning collection *Hardscrabble*, "Horseplay behooves me" (McFadden 34). Hix does not employ intricate forms to project a jaunty cosmopolitanism, whether self-protectively (as in Rachel Wetzsteon's work) or not. Instead, his explorations remain far graver. Added to this effect, certain distinctive thematic concerns compel Hix poetry, or, in the author's own terms, particular "ideas" he is "pursued by." His poems detail scenes of horrific violence, anguishing over what sense should—or should not—be made of them.

At his poetry readings, Hix often explains that nihilism serves as a starting place for his work. Curiously for a poet inspired by such stark premises, he favors a metaphysical vocabulary. His *Selected Poems* refers to "god" 117 times and "love" 129 times (by comparison "devil" appears only 12 times and "divorce" never). His lushly observed, lushly detailed sonnet sequence, "The God of Window Screens and Honeysuckle," suggests why. More than a dozen times throughout the sequence it repeats the phrase, "God: nothing," before a second colon introduces a new phrase to follow this nearly mathematical formula. For Hix, an atheist attentive to the patterns of human existence, "God" introduces a host of shifting meanings. Most commonly in Hix's work, "God" signifies absence. Sometimes, though, it represents the uncontrollable, senseless violence that erratically haunts our lives. In a fearsome rewriting of *The Book of Job*, Hix anthropomorphizes God cruelly, "God's powerful jaws / dwarf his primitive brain" (ll.2–3). More rarely the term serves as shorthand for a redemptive quality absent in the world. "Virtue is a gift of the gods," Hix affirms before characteristically turning against the hopeful thought. "Unfortunately there are no gods" (*Spirits*, 184). If so, we face a necessary question that lacks a definite answer: what virtues should we claim in the gods' absence.

Consider, for instance, a group of poems that appear about two-thirds of the way into his *Selected Poems*, innocuously titled "First Term." An author's note explains Hix's method of composition: "In 'First Term,' the poems designated by a month are constructed entirely of passages from speeches, executive orders, and other public statements of George W. Bush; the 'interleaves' reformulate arguments from the communications of Osama bin Laden" (*Fire*, unnumbered acknowledgments page). The poems switch between the perspectives of George W. Bush and Bin Laden, setting their words into recognizable verse forms. In its most obvious, this strategy complicates any formulation of the relationship between poetic form and politics as the two adversaries, each eager to kill the other, shared several verse structures. Titled "July 2003," one poem recasts Bush's words into a villanelle, a form the sequence also uses for a poem spoken in Bin Laden's voice:

> Our country made the right decision.
> We're realists in this administration.
> I believe God has called us into action.
>
> First of all, the war on terror goes on.
> The first value is, we're all God's children.
> Our country made the right decision.
> I am confident that Saddam Hussein
> had a weapons of mass destruction
> program. God has called us into action.
>
> Nobody likes to have the whistle blown.
> I think the intelligence I get is darn
> good. Our country made the right decision.
>
> I did the right thing. A free Iraq will mean
> a peaceful world. My answer is, bring them on.
> I believe God has called us into action.
>
> The al Qaeda terrorists still threaten
> our country, but they're on the run.

Our country made the right decision.
I believe God has called us into action.

(ll.1–19)

"July 2003" follows several other recent villanelles that revise their most famous precursor: Dylan Thomas's "Do Not Go Gentle into That Good Night." An exchange in May Sarton's novel, *A Reckoning*, attests to the poem's odd status, highly popular yet unfashionable. After a character discloses she has cancer, her aunt tries to encourage her by reciting the refrain of Thomas's poem, "flushed with emotion, and her voice cracked a little as she repeated the famous line." The niece, though, quickly derides the quotation as inappropriate and in bad taste, "It's too big—too important for romantic bluster" (Sarton, *A Reckoning*, 19). For a number of poets, Thomas's "words, so hackneyed by now," as a character in another Sarton novel derides them, (Sarton, *As We are Now*, 121), present a negative model, a model of how not to write in the form.

In contemporary reworkings of "Do Not Go Gentle into That Good Night," its grand, hortatory style turns jokey, sly, or childish. While Thomas rousingly addresses a dying father, they quote questionable advice dispensed as wisdom. The most spectacular example remains Rodney Dangerfield's mock-heroic recitation in the movie *Back to School*, a scene whose barbed vulgarity includes the sight of another character risibly moved to tears and the Dangerfield character's pithy analysis of the villanelle, "It means I don't take shit from no one." The choice of the poem proves telling. Supported by Dangerfield's delivery, its grand style comes off as exaggerated and funny. In short, the very forcefulness of Thomas's poem makes it an easy comic target.

Several recent villanelles employ a similar insight, though with more understatement. Marilyn Nelson Waniek's "Daughters, 1900" features bickering sisters eager to show their maturity. "The eldest has come home," the poem observes, "with new truths she can hardly wait to teach" (ll.2–3). The phrase, "new truths," introduces another irony: the ideas strike only her and her younger sisters as new, not her parents or the reader. Enthusiastically the sisters dispense banalities. The final stanza lists them, even while the girls' behavior hardly follows these genteel ideals:

The eldest sniffs, "A lady doesn't scratch."
The third snorts back, "Knock, knock: nobody home."
The fourth concedes, "Well, maybe not in *church*. . ."
Five daughters in the slant light on the porch.

(ll.16–19)

Denise Duhamel's villanelle extends this strategy; the poem consists almost wholly of misguided advice. It isolates the unfashionable element of Thomas's poem—the heartening refrain, easily quotable to those who face similar circumstances—and turns against it. The setting introduces the work's skeptical tone. Instead of a father's deathbed, the poem finds inspiration in a bathroom stall. "Please Don't Sit Like a Frog, Sit

Like a Queen" takes its title, setting, and repeated line from the same source, graffiti meant to reinforce proper bathroom behavior, and plays changes on this found line:

> Remember to pamper, remember to preen.
> The world doesn't reward a pimply girl.
> Don't sit like a frog, sit like a queen.
>
> (ll.1–3)

The villanelle reproduces the syntax and grammar of counsel but without Thomas's conviction. Sly but not overly subtle, this strategy confused at least one reader. Selecting "Please Don't Sit Like a Frog, Sit Like a Queen" for *The Best American Poetry, 2006*, Billy Collins praised the poem's "motherly advice" (xxii), a misreading that underscores how differently Duhamel uses the villanelle form: for depreciation, not incantation, and thematic counterpoint, not reinforcement. Finally, while Duhamel and Waniek present a specifically female reworking of "Do Not Go Gentle," turning from a son to daughters, Hayden Carruth writes from the perspective of one of the "old men" whom Thomas's villanelle praises as "wise," "good," "wild," or "grave" (ll.4, 7, 10, 13). Carruth recast his speaker, though, with none of these venerable qualities. "[F]eeling old and tired," he resents that he must speak as a poetic sage. His language remains pointedly flat and the verse form adds little solace. "One wonders if a villanelle," the speaker crabbily opines, "Can do the job" (ll.2, 12–13).

Hix similarly drains the villanelle of romantic bluster, but replaces it with a nightmare version of civic discourse. The villanelle works particularly well for Hix's purposes, since Bush's unwillingness to change fascinates Hix. In Hix's handling of the form, the villanelle emphasizes the speaker's unbreakable commitments. Instead of urging steadfastness, though, the poem questions its need. The lines repeat confident assertions of faith such as "I believe God has called us to action." Such statements insist on their unswerving rightness; even their slight revisions over the course of the poem express no hesitancy and admit little qualification of meaning or emphasis. Even when the repeated lines vary their phrases, they convey a stolid determination not to change. A conventional test for a villanelle is whether an example displays a specific artfulness: the ability to make the same lines convey different meanings. "[T]he repeated line," William Empson maintains, "ought to mean something different each time" (quoted in Woods 134). According to this view, the form's repetitions demand such revisions of thought or emphasis. A different imperative drives Hix's villanelle. The lines convey a heavy irony as they repeat Bush's belief in discredited arguments; "I am confident that Saddam Hussein / had a weapons of mass destruction / program" and "I think the intelligence I get is darn / good." "We're realists in this administration," maintains Bush, but the poem presents him as guided more by messianic Christianity than *Realpolitik*. He appears truly dangerous since his commitment to military action remains untested by facts or, according to the poem's perspective, counterfactual. As the poem presents him, only Bush's fellow evangelical Christians view him as a realist. From the poem's perspective, Bush's language conveys his delusions. Expressing the author's distaste for this theology, the villanelle's repetitions make the President sound more than a little deranged.

The fact that Bush shares the villanelle form with his bitter enemy introduces a certain irony. The form suggests that the two adversaries share a certain worldview, a religious framework that shapes and subsumes all disparate experience, regardless of the details of their particular faith traditions. In this respect the poems agree with Bin Laden's taunt, "To attentive observers it may seem / that *we and the White House are on the same team*" (18). In Bush's villanelle, nearly every stanza mentions "God"; the one exception includes a word both orthographically close and semantically distant as if asserting the absence of "God" is in fact "good." In a departure from Hix's characteristic language, Bin Laden's villanelle mentions "god" only once, a striking scarcity given how frequently both poet and speaker use the word:

> It is our meeting with God for which *jihad* prepares.

> Life in this world is an illusory pleasure.

> *The Crusader world has agreed to devour us.*

(ll.10–12)

Adding to this omission, apocalyptic imagery overwhelms the one reference. It falls in the middle of the line, a bland object of a preposition buried within a passive sentence. As if to rectify this near-absence, another poem in Bin Laden's voice consists of couplets whose last word unwaveringly remains "God." "We do not fear death. We do not fear war." Bin Laden proclaims, "We do not fear you. We fear only God" (ll.11–12). Such arguments, such assertions of identity, present God as both their justification and their goal. The elegant verse structure admits no other ending, no other formal possibility. Inevitably every stanza ends with "God"; as in the lives it depicts, every stanza meets this resolution.

Such formal gestures, then, emphasize the dangers of a god-driven politics, regardless of its roots in evangelical Christianity or radical Islam. Yet the Bush villanelle is, in its own way, counterfactual. When George W. Bush declared to a cheering crowd, "I believe God has called us to action," he was not justifying his decision to invade Iraq; rather, he promoted dramatically increased HIV-AIDS funding for Africa. On July 11, 2003, in Entebbe, Uganda, George W. Bush repeated his pledge to "spend $15 billion on the fight to fight AIDS around the world, with special focus here on the continent of Africa." Continuing to applaud, Bush described his and his country's motivation:

> I believe God has called us into action. I believe we have a responsibility—my country has got a responsibility. We are a great nation, we're a wealthy nation. We have a responsibility to help a neighbor in need, a brother and sister in crisis. And that's what I'm here to talk about. And I want to thank you for giving me the chance.

As many commentators noted, Bush's Christian beliefs clearly inspired his commitment to fight HIV-AIDS in Africa, a commitment greater than that of his predecessors and successor. "Almost certainly," one supporter sympathetically noted, "George W. was responding to a call of his conscience as a professed Christian" (Aikman 170). Hix, then, takes a commitment that he likely admires and shifts it to a commitment he clearly despises. In blunt terms, he recasts Bush as a pure villain.

What should a reader make of this strategy? "July 2003" originally appeared in the collection *God Bless: A Political/Poetic Discourse.* The subtitle introduces two competing imperatives, two different modes of language. As a political document, the poem follows a strategy that might strike readers as misleading, perhaps even deplorable: it skews facts to level a harsher attack. In one of the prefaces that Hix wrote for the sequence then abandoned, he deplored Bush for "using false evidence to lead the country into a futile, draining occupation of Iraq" (*GB* 71). In a sense, Hix provides his own "false evidence" against Bush. As a "poetic discourse," though, the poem bears different responsibilities. In his entry on "Poetics" for the *Encyclopedia of Aesthetics,* Hix differentiates poetry from other forms of discourse on the basis of its relation to "empirical fact": "Poetry resembles less an assertion of empirical fact than a performance utterance. It does something, and the doing subjects it to coherence rather than correspondence as the criterion for truth" (*Easy* 71). Continuing, Hix explains, "A poem is no more subject to empirical validation or invalidation than is a symphony," before quoting Wittgenstein's famous injunction, "Do not forget that a poem, even though it is composed in the language of information, is not used in the language game of giving information" (*Easy,* 71). Like the other poems in the sequence, "July 2003" plays a particular language game. Its primary material remains language that the poet chooses but does not create. In this context, the details of when and where Bush said, "I believe God has called us into action," and which policy this statement defended matter less than the action it enacts, its performance utterance.

It is tempting to wonder how satisfactorily the poem reconciles the two elements, the "political" and "poetic" elements of the "discourse," and to judge it accordingly. The slash mark that separates the subtitle's two adjectives records the opposite ambition: that the poem aims neither to choose between them nor to reconcile them. Instead, the villanelle form holds them together as a jagged whole, containing truth and falsity, "empirical fact" and "performance utterance." Bush's vocabulary fascinates Hix in part because of its sheer ugliness: the "bad poetry" of Bush's speeches, the way he truncates "God Bless America" into "God bless," a two-syllable blessing without object, a devout grunt. "Formal versification," observed Allen Tate in a classic New Critical formulation, "is the primary structure of poetic order, the assurance to the reader and to the poet himself that the poet is in control of the disorder both outside him and within his own mind" (256). Hix's poetry eschews this kind of "control"; the form assures neither reader nor poet. Instead, it achieves nearly the opposite effect: propelled by its obsessions, the poem gives little such self-possession, little enforcement of its limits. At times the poem enacts revenge on the President; it rearranges his words to diminish his accomplishments and highlight his failures. To research the sequence, Hix read every public statement that Bush made: in total, more than 9,000 pages of White House manuscripts. The poet immersed himself in the President's speeches, press conferences, and other statements. Sometimes revenge works both ways. If the limits of Bush's language mean the limits of his world, Hix's forms silently bear the limits of that language-world.

Hix's poetry might be labeled "new formalist" since it exhibits the most conspicuous markers; the specific verse forms associated with the movement. New formalism introduced some forms to the literary culture and helped to popularize them. It emphasized the study of versification, both in creative-writing and literature classes. In addition to its other virtues, the subject erodes the unhelpful institutional divisions between creative-writing and other forms of literary study. Indeed, a new generation of poet-critics, poet-scholars, and poet-theorists has written primers on poetic form, anthologies, and writing guides, as well as scholarly monographs. At their best, these books introduce students to a rich and demanding discipline, one essential to both the critical analysis and composition of poetry. At their worst, whether intentionally or not, they give the impression that formal expertise constitutes more a specialist's skill than a mode of discovery and, by doing so, reinforce some oddly persistent prejudices about metrical verse.

"Whatever our position on the New Formalism," Marjorie Perloff observes, "close readings of its exemplars suggests that, like the clothing or the furniture of earlier centuries, the verse form of, say, the Romantic period cannot in fact be replicated except as museum curiosities." After a "close reading" that apparently proves the point, namely, a two-sentence analysis of a five-line passage of contemporary blank verse, Perloff concludes: "[T]he recycling of a verse form that had a raison d'être at a particular moment in history at a particular place cannot be accomplished . . . Specific sound patterns change in response to their time and culture, but the principle that sound structure controls meaning remains the same" (214). In this formulation, Perloff sets aside at least two obvious questions, as well as a great stretch of literary history. If a particular verse structure cannot transcend its "raison d'être at a particular moment in history at a particular place," how did the Romantic poets employ a meter that already enjoyed a long history in the language (much more time separated the Romantics from blank verse's introduction in English than distinguishes the contemporary moment from the Romantics)? If one "period" should not use its predecessor's forms, how does this theory explain major modernist works such as "Sunday Morning," "The Waste Land," and "The Second Coming" that employ the apparently Romantic "form" of blank verse? Perloff's putatively historical informed, formalist analysis rests on several assumptions that more historically rigorous scholars easily rebut. In a throat-clearing aside before he addresses his main subject of "Formalism and History," J. Paul Hunter, for example, decries the "insidious" "habitual assumption that formal strategies do have implications but that what they mean is always rigid, cumbersome, and bad—that form determines content and deters, discourages, or even prevents thinking beyond its repressive governing limits" (Hunter 109). Guided by this assumption, Perloff, a master reader of self-professed "experimental" verse, rarely attends to contemporary metrical verse with similar care because she knows that to write in a form is to "replicate" or "recycle" it. Like "the clothing or the furniture of earlier centuries," its examples inevitably suffer a freakish fate: they languish as "museum curiosities."

As such language suggests, the charges that one "new formalism" faces mimic the charges leveled against the other. More than once, scholarly formalism has been called passé. In the case of poetic new formalism, the accusation sounds almost quaint, given the number of poems that show metrical verse's flexibility, its openness to the contemporary moment and its challenges. But what might be a better approach? A recent anthology proposes that "the hybrid poem" shows contemporary poetry's impatience with such familiar divisions between, for example, Language Poetry and New Formalism; other observers offer different terms to describe similar developments.[5] The best poets remain the most opportunistic and observant, alert to the artistic resources available to them, impatient with limiting notions of what poetry should and should not do. Literary criticism needs a corresponding nimbleness. Wholesale attacks on or defenses of new formalism accomplish as little as similar considerations of language poetry or the assertion that all poems in one form remain essentially the same.[6] To understand contemporary poetry, scholars need to resist committing the representative fallacy, where one poem "represents" a movement. A closer attention shows that the most interesting poems strain against group principles, not demonstrate them. In this respect, poetic new formalism's greatest contribution remains its provocations; it inspired poets and critics to reassess what form can do. The forms that poems share mark their differences and disagreements, their idiosyncrasies and obsessions.

NOTES

1   The two works also differ (slightly) by using or omitting the definite article. See Robert McPhillips, "What is the New Formalism?" in *The New Formalism: A Critical Introduction* (Cincinnati: Textos Books, 2003), 7–12, and Levinson, "What Is New Formalism?"

2   As early as 1999, an edited essay collection referred the situation "after new formalism." See Finch.

3   For two iconic attacks, see Sadoff, and Wakoski.

4   I should note, however, that some of these accusations have achieved the status of received knowledge. In 2007 Michael Collier terms new formalism "a reactionary movement," explaining: "Lamenting the loss of American cultural coherence and purpose last felt in the fifties, New Formalist paralleled the conservative turn that had taken place in America during the seventies and eighties" (122–23).

5   See, for example, St. John and Swensen, and Burt.

6   I take the term, "wholesale attacks," from Perloff. Asked by an interviewer, "What poets do you think are particularly neglected or vilified but deserve our attention," Perloff responds, "I wish the mainstream press would drop its wholesale attack on 'language poetry' and realize that there are, in the end, only individual poets, some much better than others." See "Marjorie Perloff Interview," Argotist Online, undated, available at www. argotistonline.co.uk/Perloff%20interview. htm.

REFERENCES AND FURTHER READING

Aikman, David. *A Man of Faith: The Spiritual Journey of George W. Bush*. Nashville: W Publishing Group. 2004.

Attridge, Derek. "A Return to Form?" *Textual Practice* 22(3). 563–74. 2008.

Bidart, Frank. "Borges and I," *Great American Prose Poems: From Poe to the Present*, ed. David Lehman. New York: Scribner. 2003. 132–34.

Burt, Stephen. "The Elliptical Poets," *A Poetry Criticism Reader*, ed. Jerry Harp and Jan Weissmiller. Iowa City: University of Iowa Press. 2006. 40–51.

Cable, Thomas. "The Prosody of New Formalism," *New Formalist Poets, Dictionary of Literary Biography*, Vol. 282, ed. Jonathan N. Barron and Bruce Meyer. New York: Thomson Gale. 2003. 333–37.

Carruth, Hayden. *Scrambled Eggs & Whiskey: Poems, 1991–1995*. Port Townsend: Copper Canyon Press. 1996.

Collier, Michael. *Make Us Wave Back: Essays on Poetry and Influence*. Ann Arbor University of Michigan Press. 2007.

Collins, Billy. "Introduction," *The Best American Poetry, 2006*. Billy Collins, editor, David Lehman, series editor. New York: Scribner. 2006. xv–xxiii.

Dawson, Erica. *Big-Eyed Afraid*. Surrey: Waywiser Press. 2007.

Dubrow, Heather. "Guess Who's Coming to Dinner?: Reinterpreting Formalism and the Country House Poem," *Modern Language Quarterly*, 61:1 (March 2000): 59–77.

Duhamel, Denise. *Ka-Ching*. Pittsburgh: University of Pittsburgh Press. 2009.

Finch, Annie (ed.). *After New Formalism: Poets on Form, Narrative, and Tradition*. Ashland: Story Line Press. 1999.

Gioia, Dana. *Can Poetry Matter?: Essays on Poetry and Poetic Culture*. St. Paul, MN: Graywolf Press. 1992.

Gwynn, R.S. *No Word of Farewell: Selected Poems 1970–2000*. Ashland: Story Line Press. 2001.

Gwynn, R.S. and April Lidner (eds.). *Contemporary American Poetry: A Pocket Anthology*. New York: Penguin Academics. 2005.

Hilbert, Ernest. "Erica Dawson Interview, *Contemporary Poetry Review*," available at www.cprw.com/Hilbert/dawson.htm.

Hix, H.L. *Easy as Lying: Essays on Poetry*. Silver Spring: Etruscan Press. 2002.

Hix, H.L. *First Fire, Then Birds: Obsessionals 1985–2010*. Silver Spring: Etruscan Press. 2010.

Hix, H.L. *God Bless*. Silver Spring: Etruscan Press. 2007.

Hix, H.L. *Spirits Hovering over the Ashes: Legacies of Postmodern Theory*. Albany: State University of New York Press. 1995.

Holder, Alan. *Rethinking Meter: A New Approach to the Verse Line*. Cranbury: Associated University Presses. 1995.

Hunter, J. Paul. "Formalism and History: Binarism and the Anglophone Couplet," *Modern Language Quarterly* 61:1 (March 2000): 109–27.

Jarman, Mark and David Mason (eds.). *Rebel Angels: 25 Poets of the New Formalism*. Ashland: Story Line Press. 1996.

Justice, Donald. *Collected Poems*. New York: Alfred A. Knopf. 2004.

Kingsley, Charles. "Tennyson" (1850), in *Alfred, Lord Tennyson: Bloom's Classic Critical Views*, ed. Harold Bloom. New York: Infobase Publishing. 2010. 50–63.

Levinson, Marjorie. "What Is New Formalism?" *PMLA* 122:2 (March 2007): 557–69; "What is New Formalism? (Long Version)," available at http://sitemaker.umich.edu/pmla_article/home.

Light, Kate. *The Laws of Falling Body*. Ashland: Story Lines Press. 1997.

Logan, William. "All over the Map," The New Criterion (December 2001), available at www.newcriterion.com/articles.cfm/All-over-the-map–2081.

McFadden, Kevin. *Hardscrabble*. Athens, GA: University of Georgia Press. 2008.

Metter, Alan (dir.). Back to School, MGM Studios. 1986.

Mlinko, Ange. "More than Meets the Eye," *Poetry* (October 2007), available at www.poetryfoundation.org/journal/article.html?id=180081.

Perloff, Marjorie. "The Oulip Factor: The Procedural Poetics of Christian Bök and Caroline Bergvall," *Jacket* 23. "Marjorie Perloff Interview," Argotist Online, n.d., available at www.argotistonline.co.uk/Perloff%20interview.htm.

Ricks, Christopher. *Tennyson*, 2nd edn. Berkeley: University of California Press. 1989.

Sadoff, Ira. "Neo-Formalism: A Dangerous Nostalgia," *American Poetry Review* 19:1 (January–February 1990): 7–13.

Said, Edward. *Humanism and Democratic Criticism.* New York: Columbia University Press. 2004.

St. John, David and Cole Swensen. *American Hybrid: A Norton Anthology of New Poetry.* New York: W.W. Norton. 2009.

Sarton, May. *As We Are Now.* New York: W.W. Norton. 1992.

Sarton, May. *A Reckoning.* New York: W.W. Norton. 1997.

Steele, Timothy. *Missing Measures: Modern Poetry and the Revolt against Meter.* Fayetteville: University of Arkansas Press. 1990.

Tate, Allen. *Essays of Four Decades.* Chicago: The Swallow Press. 1968.

Wakoski, Diane. "Picketing the Zeitgeist: The New Conservatism in American Poetry," American Book Review (May–June 1986): 3.

Walcott, Derek. *Conversations with Derek Walcott,* ed. William Baer. Jackson, MS: University Press of Mississippi. 1996.

Walker, Cody. *Shuffle and Breakdown.* Surrey: Waywiser Press. 2008.

Waniek, Marilyn Nelson. *The Homeplace.* Baton Rouge: Louisiana State University Press. 1990.

White House Office of the Press Secretary. "President Bush Discussed Emergency Plan for AIDS Relief in Uganda" (July 11, 2003), available at http://georgewbush-whitehouse.archives.gov/news/releases/2003/07/20030711-1.html.

Wood, Michael. *Literature and the Taste of Knowledge.* Cambridge, UK: Cambridge University Press. 2005.

Woods, James. "Tell Me How Does it Feel?" The Guardian (October 6, 2001).

3
Meter

Peter L. Groves

Poetry is "memorable speech," as W.H. Auden once remarked: "the stimulus is the audible spoken word and cadence" with "all its power of suggestion and incantation" (Auden v). By "cadence" he meant "rhythmical form," and for most of human history rhythmical form in poetry has been synonymous with meter: meter is to speech what dance is to movement, a way of revealing the potential order and beauty that underlie the chance-prone ungainliness of ordinary human activity. All poetry, including free verse, is rhythmically organized to some degree; we call it meter when one or two aspects of speech-rhythm are pervasively and systematically patterned throughout the poem. Because poems may be indeterminate in length, the constitutive rules of metrical patterning apply not to the poem as a whole but cyclically to successive segments of the poem, called "lines."

The Mechanisms of English Meter

As an organization of speech-rhythm, meter must engage the same mechanisms as speech-rhythm itself. Accounts of English meter usually ascribe speech-rhythm to the functioning of a single feature of prominence, commonly referred to as either "stress" or "accent," but this is a misleading simplification: we need to distinguish between the two. Stress, to begin with, is a built-in feature of lexical or "dictionary" words—nouns, main verbs, adjectives, and so on—in which one syllable is perceived as most prominent (*fénce, defénce, defénsive, defénsible*); some words also have a secondary stress (*ùnknówn; phótogràph, phòtográphic*). By contrast "grammar" words like prepositions, conjunctions, and pronouns have no stress in monosyllables and much weaker stress

---

A Companion to Poetic Genre, First Edition. Edited by Erik Martiny.
© 2012 John Wiley & Sons, Ltd. Published 2012 by John Wiley & Sons, Ltd.

in polysyllables. Stress also has a role in distinguishing grammatical structures: we discriminate between the phrase *{a} blàck bírd* and the compound noun *{a} bláckbìrd* (in the phrase, subordinate stress falls on the first syllable, and in the compound noun on the second).

Stress is part of our knowledge of the language, and so will tend to be perceived whether or not it gets any phonetic prominence in an utterance. In any given utterance, however, we may actively highlight a particular word or syllable, whether stressed or not, by sudden pitch-change, called focal or contrastive accent: *i said IN the fridge, not ON it*; *man proposes, god DISposes.*

In English, however, the main rhythmic mechanism is not stress or accent but the system of "beating." Beats are the means by which we shape utterances in time; they usually represent peaks of muscular effort in articulation (people who tend to gesture will gesture on the beats) and occur at (very roughly) equal intervals, a principle called isochrony (Greek: "equal timing"). Isochrony is normally a rather weak tendency, easily disrupted by interruptions, pauses, hesitations, and so on, and is strongly present only in procedures such as counting (*/One, /two, /three, /four, /five*) and listing (*/Plums, /apples, /figs, /pears*). Most commonly beats fall upon primary stressed syllables (*/drink a /pint of /milk a /day*), though not normally on successive stressed syllables in a phrase (*/old brown /dog, BBC* [*/bee-bee-/see*]); they may also fall upon accented syllables even if those syllables are not stressed: */man pro/póses, /god /DISpóses*. Beats may also fall upon unstressed syllables in order to break up a long run of them: instead of saying *there's a /néw a/méricanist in the de/pártment*, for example, with a scarcely tolerable gabble of six offbeats (underlined), we will tend to say *there's a /néw a/méricanist /in the de/pártment*, with a beat on unstressed *in*. It is important to note that this technique of "Beat Addition" is unobtrusive: it doesn't involve assigning stress or accent, but rather a deceleration in approaching the beated syllable, and in the case of an unstressed syllable like *in*, a slightly greater degree of clarity in enunciating the (normally reduced) vowel. Most oddly, beats—being events rather than kinds of sound—can occur in silence, like a rest in music (indicated in what follows by "<!>"): if I say *I / spoke to the /waiter who /brought my /ORder*, it means something different from *I /spoke to the /WAIter /<!>, who /brought my /ORder*. In verse we distinguish between a sounded beat (an "ictus"—the plural is "ictus," last syllable rhyming with "obtuse") and a silent beat (a rest).

We may think of beats, or syllables of different kinds (depending on the language), as "events"; meter works by regulating the number (and sometimes the arrangement) of events in successive lines ("numbers" is, indeed, an old-fashioned term for meter). We don't consciously count these events, which is why their number must be limited to six or so, roughly the upper limit of items we can "subitize," or intuitively grasp the number of without counting. "Chunking" or subgrouping increases the limits of subitization: we can subitize five dots flashed onto a screen in any arrangement, but we can only subitize eight dots if they are patterned in (say) two squares. Thus the classical French alexandrine is not perceived directly as twelve syllables but as two cola of six each.

Simple Meters

Simple English meter (also called accentual, demotic, or isoictic) is no more than a counting—or rather subitizing—of beats, so many to a line. In simple meter, beats come in pairs, most commonly two pairs to a line to make a four-beat line (in what follows I shall indicate a sounded beat, or ictus, with a capital "I," and an offbeat (a syllable not carrying a beat) with an "o"; I shall indicate a stressed offbeat with a capital "O" and an unstressed beat with a superscript "^{I}"):

```
(1)   /Tom, /Tom, the /piper's /son,
        I     I    o    I o     I

      /Stole a /pig and a/way he /run.
        I    o  I   o   o I  o   I
```
(Trad.)

The first thing we notice about this is its insistent rhythmicality: simple meter co-opts the strong isochrony we find in counting and listing (see above) and tends to distort the performance of the verse away from naturalistic speech, towards chanting. It thus represents a communal verse-form, easily chanted in groups (e.g. of children, Shakespearean witches, protestors, and so on).

The measure—that is, number of syllables between any two ictus within the line—varies from zero to three, though the following well-known couplet has one rare—and uncomfortable—measure with four:

```
(2)   There /was an òld /wóman who /lived in a /shoe;
        o      I  o  O    I o  o    I  o  o    I

      She had /SO many /children, she /didn't know what to /do.
        o  o   I  Oo    I   o     o   I o   O   O    o   I
```
(Trad.)

There are a number of other ways of finding four ictus in the second line, as the complexity of the notation suggests, so that the reader experiences something like the old woman's confusion in the face of a multiplicity of choices.

As these examples suggest, simple four-beat lines do not exist by themselves: they come in couplets of eight beats (examples (1) and (2), with eight ictus, are called octometers). Eight-beat structures themselves tend to be linked into quatrains of sixteen beats, in which the units may be linked by rhyme or by some other device. Where all sixteen beats are sounded (a pair of octometers) we may usefully adapt the hymnodists' name of "long meter": examples below include (3) and (11).

Another linking device is the use of a rest (silent beat) at the end of the octometer, as a sort of terminal punctuation, as in the case of this protest chant:

```
(3)  /What  do  we  /want?   /Ten per/cent!
      I    o   o    I         I   o   I

     /When  do  we  /want it?  /Now!     /<!>
      I    o   o    I    o      I         R
```
(Trad.)

This second form of eight-beat structure (tetrameter (IIII) + trimeter (IIIR)) is very common throughout English poetry, and is called the septenary (Latin *septem*, "seven," for the seven ictus). A stanza made from two septenaries is known as "common meter" by hymnodists, and is the standard form of the ballad, and of anonymous folk-poetry like the following (see also (16) and (18)):

```
(4)  /Hinx,  /minx,  the  /old witch  /stinks,
      I       I      o     I    O      I

     The  /fat be/gins to  /fry      /<!>
      O    I   o  I    o    I         R

     There's  /nobody  /home but  /Jumping  /Joan
       o       I  o     I    o     I    o    I

     /Father,  /mother and  /I.      /<!>
      I   o     I     o  o    I       R
```
(Trad.)

A third kind of eight-beat structure is the senary (IIIR + IIIR), here doubled to form a stanza ("truncated meter"):

```
(5)  /Break,  /break,  /break,      /<!>
      I        I        I            R

     On thy  /cold grey  /stones, O  /Sea:   /<!>
      o   o   I    O       I    O     I       R

     And I  /would that my  /tongue could  /utter    /<!>
      o   o  I     o    o    I     o         I    o    R

     The  /thoughts that a/rise in  /me.     /<!>
      o    I      o    o  I   o      I        R
```
(Tennyson, "Break, Break, Break" ll.1–4)

A persistent rest on the last beat of each line, with its resultant sense of incompleteness, can be a way of supporting a mood of loss, absence or thwartedness.

The last two stanzas of Tennyson's poem exemplify a fourth, widely used kind of
sixteen-beat structure, the senary-plus-septenary or "short meter" (see also (14) and
(19)); in this poem the "complete" line recalls the perfect but unattainable past:

```
(6)   /Break, /break, /break,        /<!>
       I      I       I                  R

      On thy /cold grey /stones, O /Sea:      /<!>
       o   o    I    O     I    O  I              R

      But the /tender /grace of a /day that is /dead
       o    o   I   o    I    o  o  I    o   o   I

      Will /never come /back to /me.      /<!>
       o    I    o   O    I    o   ᴵ          R
```

This last example from Tennyson shows that while simple meter is in generic terms
the primary medium of anonymous, demotic or folk-verse—nursery-rhyme, protest
chants, weather saws, graffiti, advertising jingles, and so on—it has also (since the
Romantics) been a medium of "art-verse." The difference between the two is that in
art-verse, while the length of the measure remains unpredictable, it no longer seems
random or merely adventitious. Throughout John Masefield's "Cargoes," for example,
the differing length of the measure carefully regulate the tempo for mimetic purposes,
suggesting the gaits of the different vessels, and the placement of beats highlights
the "vowel-music" of the poem throughout: in the first line, for example, it underscores the insistent patterning of two close vowels, the long vowel of "beat" (/i:/) and
the short vowel of "b*i*t" (/I/): "qu*I*nqu*I*ri:me of n*I*n*I*vi: from d*I*stant Ophi:r"). The
beats of the second line pick up the open long vowel of "Ophir" and develop a new
vowel-theme ("r*O*wing h*O*me to h*A*ven"):

```
(7)   Quinquireme of Nineveh from distant Ophir,
        I    o O   o   I o o    o  I o  I o

      Rowing home to haven in sunny Palestine,
       I o   O    o  I o  o  I  o  O o  I

      With a cargo of ivory, And apes and peacocks,
        o     o I o o I o o  o   I    o   I  O

      Sandalwood, cedarwood, and sweet white wine.
       I  o  O   I o  O    o   I      O    I
```

(Masefield, "Cargoes")

It should be emphasized that in simple-meter art verse, which flourished in the second half of the nineteenth century and the first of the twentieth, it can be difficult to find the poet's metrical intention, because the prosody may offer a number of competing possibilities: we could, for example, read the second line of "Cargoes" as a senary, but while it would make good metrical sense in its own right it would not fit the equivalent lines in subsequent stanzas:

```
(8)  Rowing home to haven in sunny Palestine,
     I   o   I    o  IoRo I o  I o I   R
```

Similarly, when you first read Hardy's "Afterwards" your initial instinct may be to read the first line as a senary:

```
(9)
When the Present has latched its postern behind my tremulous stay,
 O     o I o    o   I     o   I o Ro I  o  I o o    I R
```

The problem with this reading is not in this line but in the fact that the other odd-numbered lines in the poem are clumsy and awkward as senaries, forcing rests in the middle of phrases like "new-spun <!> silk," "like <!> an eyelid's," "nocturnal <!> blackness," and so on. The reading that fits all equivalent lines is a septenary:

```
(10)
When the Present has latched its postern behind my tremulous stay,
 I     o I o    o   I     o   I o  o I  o  I o o    I R
```

"Afterwards" is an example of "dolnik" (see Tarlinskaja), a partially regulated form, transitional between simple and compound meter, in which the measure varies only between one and two (rather than between zero and three). Dolnik was very popular in the late nineteenth and twentieth centuries:

```
(11)  When the hounds of spring are on winter's traces,
       o    o   I   o   I    o   o  I o      I o

      The mother of months in meadow or plain
       o  I o  o   I      o  I o o   o   I

      Fills the shadows and windy places
       I    o  I o  o   I o I o

      With lisp of leaves and ripple of rain
       o   I   o  I      o   I o  o   I
```
                              (Swinburne, *Atalanta in Calydon* ll.65–68)

To recapitulate: simple (and compound) meter exhibits the following kinds of common line-structures:

Table 3.1 Standard four-beat structures

IIII	tetrameter
IIIR	trimeter
IRIR	extended dimeter

Table 3.2 Standard eight-beat structures

IIII + IIII (tetrameter + tetrameter):	octometer
IIII + IIIR (tetrameter + trimeter):	septenary
IIIR + IIIR (trimeter + trimeter):	senary

Table 3.3 Standard sixteen-beat structures

Octometer + octometer:	long meter
Septenary + septenary:	common meter (e.g. ballads)
Senary + septenary:	short meter (e.g. limerick, Poulter's)
Senary + senary:	truncated meter (mainly art-verse)

Compound Meters

The example of dolnik shows that the regularity of the measure represents a kind of sliding scale: as the number of offbeats grows more and more predictable in a poem, the verse approaches the condition of compound or ictosyllabic meter, where there is both a primary regulation (of beats) and a secondary one (of the measure). It should be noted that a measure lies *between* ictus *within* the line; what precedes the first ictus (the head) or follows the last (the tail) doesn't count as part of the body. In (11), for example, the second line has a head but no tail, the third a tail but no head, and the first line has both. The fact that in (14) below the first two lines have only one offbeat in the head does not, therefore, affect our perception of the regularity of the measure.

Regulated measure is usually either duple (one offbeat) or triple (two offbeats); quadruple measure (three offbeats) is rare (see (16)), and single measure (no offbeats), though found in occasional lines of simple meter ("/Ding /dong /bell /<!>," "/Nine / days/ old /<!>") is almost impossible to sustain as a compound meter for obvious linguistic reasons.

It might be thought that the double regulation of compound meter would render it more sophisticated and mentally engaging than simple meter, but in fact the reverse tends to be the case: it rapidly becomes tedious. It is not only that the metrical pattern itself is unvarying, but also that the inflexibility of that pattern seems to crush all resistance (and thus lifelikeness and interest) out of the language-material:

(12) And the sheen on their spears was like stars on the sea
    o   o I o   o   I   o   o I   o   o I

    When the blue wave rolls nightly on deep Galilee
    O   o I O   O   I   o o I   Oo^I

            (Byron, "The Destruction of Sennacherib" ll.3–4)

In the first of these two lines, the complete co-incidence of meter and prosody represents a kind of tour de force that might be initially striking, but rapidly becomes monotonous; in the second, the disjunctures between the two represent not a struggle (since the meter always wins) but a reduction of the rich prosodic complexity of English speech towards the mechanical binary opposition of the meter itself. One of the first kinds of compound meter used in Modern English was the dreary Poulters' measure of the sixteenth century, short meter in duple measure:

(13)
  The dazzled eyes with pride, which great ambition blinds,
  o   I o I   o   I R o   I o I o   I   R

  Shall be unsealed by worthy wights whose foresight falsehood finds.
  o   I O I   o I o I   o   I o   I   o I R

         (Queen Elizabeth I, "The Doubt of Future Foes" ll.5–6)

The wooden regularity comes at a price, reflected here in the clumsy dislocations of syntax. It is possible that the popularity of the form among courtly Tudor poets—even the great Sir Thomas Wyatt used it—was precisely due to its inflexibility, and the decisive triumph that it seemed to represent of aristocratic order over the slovenly simple-meter doggerel of late medieval culture, as exemplified in the work of a poet such as Barclay or Skelton.

Generically, compound meter could be described as a "middle-brow" form, a favorite with those who feel culturally obliged to admire poetry but don't really enjoy it at any very sophisticated level, like that sizable proportion of the Victorian and Edwardian middle classes for whom contemporary poetry meant Longfellow, Kipling, Robert Service, *Punch* magazine, and (in Australia) "Banjo" Patterson and Henry Lawson. Compound meter is also the form that light verse invariably takes, since such verse requires technical skill and compound meter exhibits a kind of skillfulness that most people can appreciate. One of its most famous forms is the limerick, a stanza of short meter in triple measure:

(14) There was a young man who said "God
      o   ^I o O   I o   o   I R

    Must find it exceedingly odd
    o   I o o I o o I   R

```
That the sycamore tree Still continues to be
 o    o I o o    I   O    o I o   o I

When there's no-one about in the quad."
 o    o    I  o o I o   o I    R
```
(attributed to Ronald Knox)

Triple measure tends generically towards light verse: not necessarily humorous, that is, but certainly uncomplicated, as in the case of (9). Tennyson famously used it mimetically, to suggest the galloping of horses (superscript indicates elision, the quick and light pronunciation of a weak syllable that doesn't count in the metrical tally; in texts from the sixteenth to the eighteenth centuries elisions are often indicated by an apostrophe):

```
(15)  Half a league, half a league, half a league onwards,
       I  o  O      I  o  o     I  o  O    I o

      Into the vall^ey of death rode the six hundred
      I o   o I     o  o  O   I  o  o I  o
```
("The Charge of the Light Brigade" ll.1–4)

Tennyson conveys the idea of a gallop that is at the same time weighty and forceful by making many of the measures *oO* rather than the expected *oo*. But if triple measure is light, quadruple is positively vacuous, only suitable for comic verse or simple narrative, as in the case of this common-meter stanza in quadruple measure:

```
(16)
There was movement at the station, for the word had passed around
 o    o  I o  o   o   o  I o   o   o I   o  O   o I

    That the colt from old Regret had got away
     o    o I   o  o  O  o I   o  O o I  R

And Ohad joined the wild bush-horses; he was worth a thousand pound,
 o   o  I    o o O   O  I o    o  o I   o  Oo   I

    So all the cracks had gathered to the fray.
     o I   o  O    o I  o   o  o I  R
```
(A.B. Paterson, "The Man from Snowy River" ll.1–4)

Quadruple measure can also be seen in the patter-songs of W.S. Gilbert: "I /am <u>the</u> <u>very</u> /model of a /mod<u>ern</u> <u>major</u>-/general." Quadruple meter is not only highly artificial but also unstable, since the middle of the three offbeats is always a candidate to become a beat, and that candidacy is strengthened when the offbeat falls on a stressed syllable surrounded by unstressed ones (I have underlined such *oOo* measures in example (16)). For this reason some writers see quadruple measure as dipodic, which refers to an alternation of unstressed and stressed beats producing a kind of higher-order patterning ("dipod" means "double foot"). Dipody is hard to sustain, though the following line could just about pass as dipodic on the grounds that "passed" is syntactically subordinated in stress to "around":

(17)
There was movement at the station, for the word had passed around
ᴵ   o   I   o   ᴵ   o   I o   ᴵ   o I   o I   o I

One way of reducing the monotony of compound meter is to "modulate" it—that is, to vary the measure in some systematic or consistent way. The first three stanzas of Hardy's "The Voice," for example, all switch from triple to duple in the last measure. Since the number of syllables in a measure affects the tempo of reading—the more, the faster—this represents a meditative slowing-down, functioning also as a kind of stanzaic punctuation:

(18)
Woman much missed, how you call to me, call to me,
I o O I o o o I o o I o o

Saying that now you are not as you were
I o   o I o o I o o   o I

When you had changed from the one who was all to me,
I o o I o o I o o I o o

But as at first, when our day was fair.
ᴵ o o I   o o I o I
                                ("The Voice" ll.1–4)

This is very different from what happens in the last stanza, where the deflating realization that what he is hearing might be "only the breeze" causes the metrical structure to collapse like a balloon, from compound to simple meter and from sixteen ictus to thirteen (common meter):

(19)
Thus I; faltering forward,
I o I o o I o R

Leaves around me falling,
I o I o I o R

```
Wind oozing thin through the thorn from norward,
 I    o   o    I     o      o   I     o    I    o

And the woman calling.
 ɪ    o   I o   I   o     R
```

This rather neatly illustrates the principle of unity-in-variety that underlies all meter: strikingly different as this stanza is from its fellows, it remains like them a sixteen-beat structure. It illustrates another point worth emphasizing about meter in English: that it is not completely determined by the text, but something co-operatively created by the reader in performance (and to read a poem we must perform it, if only in the mind). Although my scansion of the last line conforms to the pattern (echoing line two), it is not the only way of realizing the line as a four-beat utterance: an unusual IRIR (extended dimeter) reading (found also in ballads such as "Edward, Edward") underscores the line's paradoxical stubborn insistence on the final reality of the apparitional voice:

(20)
```
     And the woman calling.
      o    o    I o R I   o     R
```

The prosodic structure of a line—the distribution of stress, accent, and syntactic breaks—is a map of potential: it will rule out some metrical patterns but it may allow more than one, and our choice among those possibilities is an act of interpretation (some readers, for example, would accent "I" in the first line of (19), rendering the pattern *oI Ioo Io*). You may prefer (19) for its greater fidelity to the underlying pattern or (20) for its greater complexity and contextual appropriateness: the choice is yours.

Complex Meters (Including Iambic Pentameter)

Most accounts of English meter conflate the categories of compound and complex meter into something called "accentual-syllabic" or "syllabotonic" meter, but as we shall see the two are very different. Simple or isoictic meter is lively, but disordered; compound or ictosyllabic meter is ordered, but not particularly lively (though it might have a kind of mechanical vigor); complex (also called "ictothetic" or "footed") meter, in the form of (say) iambic pentameter, is both ordered and lively, and for this reason closer to the rhythms of English speech than either of the others. This is why most of the canonical poets of English literature from Spenser to Yeats make relatively little use of simple and compound meters (though Blake is a notable exception). Shakespeare, for example, uses compound meters only for special purposes (e.g. the chanting of the witches in *Macbeth*) and simple meters for occasional doggerel passages, like the Fool's prophecy in *Lear* or this senary couplet in simple meter from the very early *Comedy of Errors* (there are a few other ways of scanning it):

(21)

```
     Mome, malt-horse, capon, coxcomb, idiot, patch!
      I      I    O     I o R I   o    I oo    I    R

     Either get thee from the door, or sit down at the hatch.
      O  o I   o    ᴵ    o  I R o I  I    I   o   o  I    R
```
                                                    (3.1.32–33)

It's vigorous, bouncy stuff in the manner of the older comedies such as *Gammer Gurton's Needle* (1575), but it's hard to imagine the subtler parts of *Hamlet* in such a meter. Shakespeare's plays, like the major poems of Milton, Pope, Keats, and Larkin, are written in a metrical form that manages to avoid both the insistent sing-song of simple meter and the deadening regularity of compound meter by specifying two different kinds of regulation but permitting a certain degree of slippage between them. Complex meter specifies both a certain number of beats, that is, and a grid of syllable-positions, allowing the placing of the beats to vary to some extent along that grid of positions. The price paid for this flexibility, incidentally, is that unlike simple and compound meter its form is not automatically obvious, even to native speakers: it has to be acquired, albeit unconsciously, as a kind of skill, through reading and listening, and not everyone succeeds in acquiring that skill, as teachers of English literature and patrons of amateur Shakespeare can testify.

So how does it work? I shall deal with iambic pentameter because of its importance in the tradition, but *mutatis mutandis* the same remarks apply to iambic trimeter, tetrameter (as in Marvell's "To his Coy Mistress") and hexameter (the "alexandrine"). The prototypical pentameter can be mapped directly onto a grid of ten syllable-positions, alternately w(eak) and S(trong): wS wS wS wS wS, where every S-syllable may carry a beat. This is traditionally, economically and conveniently (though not *necessarily*) thought of as a sequence of five similar "feet," each consisting of a w[eak] and a S[trong] syllable; such feet are often referred to as "iambs" (hence "iambic pentameter," where *penta* derives from the Greek for "five"): "The cur|few tolls| the knell| of par|ting day|" (Gray, *Elegy* 1). The division of the line into feet, it should be emphasized, is purely notional: feet are a kind of scaffolding, irrelevant to the performance of the verse. They do not necessarily correspond to pauses or boundaries of any kind (we don't say "cur, few" or "par, ting"), nor need they coincide at all with punctuational or syntactic cuts, any more than the lines on an architect's blueprint need correspond to cracks or fissures in the fabric of the building.

Each position is usually occupied by one syllable, but under certain circumstances may be occupied by two or by none.[1] For a line to be metrical, each S-position must be occupied by an independent syllable—that is, one capable of carrying a beat, by virtue of being either (a) a fully stressed syllable, (b) an accented syllable, or (c) an unstressed syllable that is not dominated by a neighboring stressed syllable (that is, it is protected by an intervening syntactic break). An Elizabethan critic, George Gascoigne, remarked of the following two lines that the first would "pass the musters" but that the second was "neither true nor pleasant," the reason being that in each of the middle three feet the unstressed syllables in S-position (italicized) are dominated by stressed neighbors:

(22)

```
I  ùnderstánd  your  méaning  by  your  éye
w  S    w    S      w      S   w   S   w    S
```

```
*Your  méaning  I  ùnderstánd  by  your  éye
 w      S  w    S  w  S    w    S    w    S
```

If this were all there were to it, then iambic pentameter would simply be another kind of compound meter, albeit with an anomalously odd number of beats. This in itself would make it a more naturalistic form, however, in that it "escapes the elementary four-beat rhythm, with its insistence, its hierarchical {dipodic} structures, and its close relationship with the world of ballad and song" (Attridge, *Rhythms of English Poetry* 124). Another interesting consequence of the "fiveness" of pentameter is that it has a kind of completeness in itself and is not required to enter into pair-bonding with another line (in theory a poem could consist of one pentameter) and so it is the one form of English meter that does not require rhyme (poets have experimented with unrhymed trimeters and tetrameters but these have never become naturalized in the tradition). Unrhymed pentameter is known as "blank verse."

What makes a complex meter markedly different from a compound one is that it is not confined to one template. From the original or matrix template we can derive others: the simplest way of producing a new template is to add an extra weak position——a tail—to the end of an existing template, indicated here by a "{" or opening brace functioning as the final foot-marker: *Resem|bling sire|, and child|, and ha|ppy mo{ther* (Shakespeare, *Sonnets* 8.11). Tails were traditionally called "feminine endings"; they make a line a little less formal, and in broad terms their frequency tends to increase as Shakespeare's career progresses, from less than 1 percent in at the start of his career to over 20 percent in the last plays.

More interestingly we can reverse any wS foot in the original template to Sw (sometimes called a "trochee," rhyming with "poky"), provided it is followed by a w-position (which rules out consecutive or final reversals). The odd thing about a reversal is that we perceive not just a beat but a beat *where we expect an offbeat*, and an offbeat where we expect a beat. The result for one who has internalized the meter is an interesting doubleness of effect, a sense of two things happening at once that Hopkins described metaphorically as 'counterpoint'. In what follows reversals will be enclosed in angle brackets (when both syllables in a foot are independent we have a reversible foot, one where the reader or performer must choose one option or the other, indicated by "<Foot|": *<Trees cut| to Sta|tues, Sta|tues thick| as trees|*, Pope, "Burlington" 120). To illustrate with examples from each century from the fourteenth to the twentieth:

(23)
```
    <Redy> to wen|den on| our pil|grimage|
    S  w    w  S    S  w    S   w  S
```
(Chaucer, General Prologue 1.21)

```
    <Done is> a ba|ttell on| the dra|gon blak|
    S   w     w  S    S  w    S   w    S
```
(Dunbar, "Done is a battell" 1.1)

```
    <Wanton> as youth|ful goats|, <wild as> young bulls|,
    S   w    w  S      w   S        S   w     w     S
```
(Shakespeare, 1 Henry 4 4.1.103)

Since the second tier of scansion adds no extra information I shall scan the remaining examples without it: *<Abject> and lost| lay these|, <cov'ring> the flood|*, (Milton, *Paradise Lost* 1.312); *<Woman's> at best| a con|tradic|tion still*, (Pope, *To a Lady* 270); *<Season> of mists|, and me|llow fruit|fulness|*, (Keats, "Ode to Autumn" 1); *My swi|vel eye| <hungers> from pose| to pose|* (Larkin, "Lines on a Young Lady's Photograph Album" 3). Reversals lend energy to the verse, because they carry an element of surprise—a beat where we expect an offbeat—and in consequence can have a button-holing, attention-grabbing effect: *<Hung be> the hea^{ve}ns| with black|, <yìeld day| to night|!* (*1 Henry 6* 1.1.1); *<Cromwell>, I charge| thee, fling| away| ambi{tion!* (*Henry 8* 3.2.440); *<Batter> my heart, <three-per|son'd God|, for you|* (Donne, "Holy Sonnets" 14.1; compare "Assault| my heart|"); *'<Courage>!' he said|, and poin|ted t°ward| the land|.* (Tennyson, "The Lotos-Eaters" 1).

Whereas reversals apply to feet (odd-even pairs like syllable-positions one and two), a swap is a switching of properties between even–odd pairs of positions (two and three, four and five, etc.), so that the sequence w-S w-S becomes w-[w S]-S (we write this as "w-[W s]-S" to reflect the fact that only certain kinds of syllable may form part of a swap: the s-syllable, for example, is always a stressed syllable that is subordinated syntactically to the following S-syllable, as indicated in the following examples—we begin with Shakespeare because swaps are a sixteenth-century development):

(24)
```
    The per|fect ce|remo|ny [of lòve's] ríte|
    W  S    w  S  w S  w  W    s         S
```
(Shakespeare, Sonnets 23.6)

```
He trus|ted to| have e|qual'd [the mòst] Hígh|
  w     S    w    S    w    S    w      W   s    S
```

(Milton, Paradise Lost 1.40)

Swaps are less common than reversals, but commoner then you might think (from about 1.5 percent of lines in Pope to nearly ten times that number in late Shakespeare). Later examples: *A youth| of fro|lics, {an òld} áge| of cards|*, (Pope, *To a Lady* 244); *To vi|sit dol|phin-co|ral {in dèep} séas|*; (Keats, "To Homer" 4); *The fa|thers {with bròad} bélts| <under> their suits|* (Larkin, "The Whitsun Weddings" 36). Whereas in a reversal the beat occurs a little earlier than expected, in a swap the beat on the subordinated stress is momentarily delayed, because that syllable is closely bound to the following word: the effect is that of a slightly deferred beat, a little like a syncopation in music. At the same time, the s-syllable or subordinated beat will be slightly prolonged and more prominent by virtue of carrying a beat (we may even, as readers, consider the possibility of accenting the s-syllable:—"the *most* High," "an *old* age," "in *deep* seas").

Another feature of the engaging complexity of iambic pentameter is the fact that since we perceive each syllable in terms of its position while keeping aware that those positions may slide around in the template from line to line, we are much more aware of the prosodic values of beats and offbeats than we are in compound or simple meter. Heavy mappings (stressed syllables in offbeat positions), for example, offer a felt resistance to the meter: in the following lines Milton uses heavy mappings (underlined) to suggest the effort of Satan's journey through Hell: *O'er bog| or steep|, through strait|, <u>rough</u>, dense|, or rare|, / With head|, <u>hands</u>, wings|, or feet| pursues| his way|* (*Paradise Lost* 2.948–49); Hamlet contrasts the efforts of this world to the fluid ease of heaven in a transition from a dipodic line with two light mappings (non-stresses in beat position, indicated here by Roman type) to an awkward line with two heavy mappings: *Absent| thee* from| *feli|city| a while|, / <And in <u>this</u> harsh| <u>world</u> draw| thy breath| in pain|* (*Hamlet* 5.2.346–47). In simple and compound meter light mappings are often performed rather heavily and insistently; in pentameter, they co-opt the procedure of Beat Addition (see above), which satisfies the demands of the meter with minimal disruption to naturalistic speech-rhythms.

A Note on Traditional Terminology

The traditional terminology for discussing meters in English is frequently unhelpful, because it is based not on an analysis of English but on the terminology of classical Latin and Greek verse, as a way of attempting to dignify by association the (very different) home-grown variety. To begin with, it only applies fully to compound and complex meters, which it fails to distinguish (simple meters are beneath its notice and beyond its analysis). Metrical labels consist of a two-term phrase like "iambic pentameter": the first term refers to the typical number of offbeats per beat and the second to the typical number of ictus in the line (not beats: rests are ignored). To make the second term you count the ictus—one ictus (*mono-*), two (*di-*), three (*tri-*), four (*tetra-*), five (*penta-*), six (*hexa-*), seven (*hepta-*), or eight (*octo-*)—and add the appropriate prefix to -*meter* (the stress falls on the third last syllable). Thus (12) and (18) above are tetrameter, (16) a combination of tetrameter and trimeter, (9) hexameter, and so on; in ignoring rests, incidentally, such a taxonomy is unable to discover or demonstrate the underlying relatedness of (18) and (19).

Traditional terminology sees compound meters as composed of classical "feet" such as the iamb (*oI*), the trochee (*Io*), the anapest (*ooI*), the dactyl (*Ioo*), and the paeon (*oooI*). Thus (12) is supposedly "anapestic tetrameter" and (15) "dactylic tetrameter." Where there are fewer syllables in the head or the tail (as appropriate) than in the measure, as in (14–16) or the even-numbered lines of (18), the line is traditionally called "catalectic." But consider the even-numbered lines of (18): traditionally they would be called "dactylic tetrameter catalectic" (*Ioo Ioo Ioo Ioo*), but if the first line had had a head and no tail (e.g. "O /Woman much /missed, how you /call to me /so,") we would be obliged to describe exactly the same second line as something quite different: "*anapestic* tetrameter catalectic" (*ooI ooI ooI ooI*). Or consider that very common meter of Elizabethan drama, the four-beat duple. Traditional terminology requires us to specify it as either "iambic" or "trochaic":

(25)

```
Now the hungry lion roars,
 I   o I  o  Io   I
```

```
And the wolf behowls the moon;
ᴵ    o I  o I    o I
```

(Shakespeare, A Midsummer Night's Dream 5.1.371–72)

Metrically it is neither, though rhythmically we may find falling sequences ("<hungry><lion>") as well as rising ones ("the wolf/ behowls/ the moon/"); for further discussion see Attridge (*Rhythms of English Poetry* 108–14).

Finally, it should be pointed out that the terminology not only creates meaningless distinctions but conflates a crucial distinction in (for example) using the same term ("iambic hexameter") for a compound meter (duple senary—e.g. the odd-numbered lines of Poulter's measure, 13)—and for the six-footed complex meter called the "alexandrine." Pope writes of the alexandrine as something <*That, like| a woun|ded snake||*, <*drags its*> *slow length| along*" ("Essay on Criticism" 357; the double solidus indicates an obligatory word-break to accommodate the necessary—though somewhat attenuated—rest).

Pseudo-Meters

So far I have dealt only with overt meter—that is, metrical regulation that can be perceived by a listener or apprehended during the process of reading. There might seem to be little point in any other kind, but some Modernist poets (such as Marianne Moore and W.H. Auden) have experimented with forms of linear regulation that are covert, in the sense that they cannot be directly perceived or experienced, only discovered by examination; the main example would be isosyllabics, the regulation of lines solely by the number of syllables. Because syllables in English vary so grossly in length and complexity they cannot be subitized, and so isosyllabic meter is impossible to perceive directly. Covert meter of this kind is not easily distinguishable from free verse to the reader or listener, and is probably more useful to the poet in the process of composition as a form of ludic constraint to work against.

Finally I will say a word about imaginary meter: meter that is based on more or less imaginary qualities of syllables. The major example of this is a product of the dream that has haunted English-language poets since the sixteenth century, that of writing poetry in the quantitative meters of classical Greek and Latin. Those meters are based on the opposition between two kinds of syllabic structure, "heavy" (or "long") and "light" (or "short"), and though this distinction also obtains in English phonology (and, as in Latin, in part governs stress-placement in words) it is less obvious in English and unsuitable for quantitative meter in generating too few light syllables. For a full account of imaginary quantitative meter in Elizabethan poetry see Attridge (*Well-weigh'd Syllables*). The quest was renewed by nineteenth-century poets such as Longfellow; perhaps the best solution to this self-imposed "problem" was that of A.H. Clough, whose hexameter gives the appearance of adhering to classical rules but is in effect simply a headless tailed dolnik senary. In the following example, I indicate the actual scansion on the second row, and the imaginary Latin scansion within the line, with "|" for foot-divisions and "/" for caesurae; it will be seen that the actual scansion partly reflects the imaginary one, in that each pseudo-foot begins with an ictus (as Teutonic scholars claimed of the Latin hexameter) and the caesura (in Latin merely a word-break) coincides with the first rest in the senary:

```
(26)
Rome disa|ppoints me| much; / I| hardly as |yet under|stand, but
  I    o o   I      o   I R o  I o o    I   O  o   I     o R


Rubbishy|  seems the| word / that| most ex|actly would| suit it.
  I o o   I    o    I R o   o   I o I o o      I o R
```

(Clough, Amours de Voyage 1.1.9–10)

I have underlined the most outrageous violations of classical scansion. Notice the way in which the final rest of line 9 encodes Claude's typical finicky hesitation over the exact word.

Meter and Genre

Some connections between meter and genre are almost natural, such as that between folk-poetry of all ages and simple meters. Meters also become generic markers or signals because they get used for particular genres and thus acquire associations that subsequently connect them to those genres. For example, one important reason that verse drama from Dryden to Browning (and the nineteenth-century dramatic mono-logue) is written almost entirely in iambic pentameter is that Shakespeare wrote his plays in iambic pentameter; this is equally the reason that twentieth-century verse dramatists like late Yeats, Eliot and Fry chose *not* to use iambic pentameter. But this doesn't mean that the original choice was purely arbitrary: there can be little doubt that blank verse took over as the language of drama in the 1580s because as a complex meter it represents a genuine improvement in both subtlety and lifelikeness over the simple four-beat and senary couplets of the medieval and late Tudor stage. One meter may acquire more than one association: Milton in the seventeenth century made blank verse the vehicle of epic poetry, and Thompson in the eighteenth of meditative anec-dotal poetry. A different use of iambic pentameter developed in the same century in the form of the endstopped heroic couplet, with its cultivated antithetical balances within and between lines, which tend to reinforce a conservative ideology in which apparent superficial contests and contradictions are evidence of an underlying political harmony that shouldn't be disturbed by innovation or reform:

```
(27)    <Here hills| and vales|, the wood|land and| the plain|,
            <Here earth| and wa|ter seem| to strive| again|,
        Not Cha|os-like| toge|ther crush'd| and bruis'd|,
        <But, as| the earth|, harmo|nⁱously| confus'd|:
        Where or|der in| vari|ety| we see|,
        And where|, though all| things di|ffer, all| agree|.
```
                                    (Pope, *Windsor Forest* ll.11–16)

In this way a metrical form can become a way of encoding ideologies, which can make it difficult to say anything new or subversive in the form: this is why William Blake, in trying to make poetry say new and radical things in the late eighteenth century, felt obliged to abandon complex meter altogether (juvenilia notwithstanding) and return to simple and compound forms in the *Songs of Innocence* and *Songs of Experience*. It is interesting to note, incidentally, that whereas medieval and early modern folk-poetry is almost all in simple meters, eighteenth- and nineteenth-century revivals of those genres ("The Rime of the Ancient Mariner," "Mary Had a Little Lamb") are almost always in compound meters (Coleridge's "Christabel" was an early and interest-ing exception).

NOTE

1   A position has double occupancy when it includes an unstressed syllable that doesn't count in the metrical tally, like the eighth position in the following line: "These vi|olent|

delights| have vi°l|ent ends|" (*Romeo* 2.6.9). Zero occupancy is very rare, confined to early pentameter like Chaucer and Wyatt, late pentameter like Larkin, and Renaissance dramatic blank verse: "^ Whan| that A|pril with| his shou|res soo{te" (Chaucer, *General Prologue* 1); "^ Come|, my lord|, I'll lead| you to| your tent|." (Shakespeare, *1 Henry 4* 5.4.9); "Ano|ther church|: ^ ma|tting, seats|, and stone|" (Larkin, "Churchgoing" 3); for a fuller account see Groves, "Shakespeare's Pentameter."

REFERENCES AND FURTHER READING

Attridge, Derek. *Poetic Rhythm: An Introduction.* Cambridge: Cambridge University Press, 1995. [*A simpler introduction to the topic*]

Attridge, Derek. *The Rhythms of English Poetry.* London: Longmans, 1982. [A comprehensive account of English meter.]

Attridge, Derek. *Well-weigh'd Syllables: Elizabethan Experiments in Quantitative Verse.* Cambridge: Cambridge University Press, 1974.

Auden, W.H. and John Garret. (eds.). *The Poet's Tongue: An Anthology.* London: G. Bell & Sons, 1935.

Brogan, T.V.F. *English Versification 1570–1980: A Reference Guide with a Global Appendix.* Baltimore: Johns Hopkins University Press, 1981. [Invaluable reference and introduction to the historical range of metrical theory.]

Cureton, Richard D. *Rhythmic Phrasing in English Verse.* London and New York: Longman, 1992.

Groves, Peter L. "Shakespeare's Pentameter and the End of Editing." *Shakespeare* (Journal of the British Shakespeare Association), 3 (2007): 126–42.

Groves, Peter L. *Strange Music: The Metre of the English Heroic Line.* ELS Monograph Series 74. Victoria, B.C.: University of Victoria, 1998. [A full account of the complexity of iambic pentameter.]

Tarlinskaja, Marina, "Beyond 'loose iamb': the form and themes of the English 'dolnik.'" *Poetics Today* 16 (1995): 493–522.

4

The Stanza

Echo Chambers

Debra Fried

Not a genre, but a marker for many poetic genres, the stanza is a workhorse not much written about aside from its labor within individual genres and poems. Any grouping of poetic lines can be loosely called a stanza. Some stanzas have a long history and travel through languages; others are invented on the spot, just for one poem. Traditional stanzas obey the pattern set up by the pattern of end-rhymes. Rhyme scheme provides a shorthand to identify set stanzas such as the hymn quatrain (*abab*), the envelope stanza (*abba*), *rime royal* (*ababbcc*), *ottava rima* (*abababcc*), or the Spenserian stanza (*ababbcbcc*). If the stanza's lines have assorted lengths, that pattern may be indicated by adding the number of beats per line. Even thus enhanced, these alphabet blocks provide only the simplest model of this most versatile of poets' toys.

Divider and connector, trellis and climbing vine at once, the stanza is as subject to the individual poet's crafting as the line, as freighted with the history of its uses and as ripe for reinvention. In any particular poem, the stanza may hand off the sense to the succeeding stanza, take a stand and stop the sense, or nonsense, in its tracks, take a breath for a brief aria, murmur an aside, or look at itself in a mirror (momentarily finding a figurative slant in its own schematic design). Poets construct stanzas as readily for a poised vignette as for an unfolding narrative. Some stanzas seem built for the long haul, while others accrete in shorter poems. The stanza is both richly taxonomized, and under-described. English has terms for stanzas of from two to nine lines, some very rare, but none for the vast numbers of *poems* two to nine stanzas long; no term is attached to stanzas that dwindle in line length, or to those that expand. The same word must serve for the continuation of syntax over line breaks and over stanza breaks; *enjambment* names the straddling in "man's first disobedience and the fruit / Of that forbidden tree" (*Paradise Lost* ll.1–2) or a storm-tossed ship's "awkward rift" that "shattered the / Whole of her stern-frame" (*Don Juan* 2. 211, ll.212–13), or

A Companion to Poetic Genre, First Edition. Edited by Erik Martiny.
© 2012 John Wiley & Sons, Ltd. Published 2012 by John Wiley & Sons, Ltd.

such celebrated twentieth-century slicings (or splicings) as "shafts of the / / sun" in a syllabic poem:

> The barnacles which encrust the side
> of the wave, cannot hide
>   there for the submerged shafts of the
>
> sun,
> split like spun
>   glass
>
> (Marianne Moore, "The Fish," ll.8–13)

Perhaps we rest content with a small vocabulary because we'd need such a big one, were we to name everything the stanza can do and be.

The division between non-stanzaic (stichic) and stanzaic (strophic) poems is not sharp and absolute. Blank-verse epics can modulate into quasi-stanzaic sub-sections signaled not by white space but by a new cadence, a shift in idiom, or occasional echoic effects, even irregular end-rhyme. Occasional sonnets and near-sonnets lurk in the blank verse of Wordsworth's *Prelude*; melodic setpieces punctuate *Paradise Lost*. It would be hasty to say that stichic verse is born of writing and strophic verse of music, for each may take on the features of the other's parent, as when Adam and Eve invent music in the blank verse of *Paradise Lost*, or a written letter conveniently fills three stanzas in *The Faerie Queene*—except for the metrical excrescence of Duessa's false signature as "*Fidessa*" (1.12.26–28; 28. 9).

A rhyming, metered stanza stands in for, stands out as, poetry against unrhymed lines or prose. In a prose love letter to Ophelia, Hamlet includes an *abab* stanza ("Doubt thou the stars are fire / Doubt thou the sun doth move / Doubt truth to be a liar / But never doubt I love"), confessing he is "ill at these numbers" (unskilled at writing in meter). Elizabethan poets prized stanzas with interlinked rhyme schemes, finding in such intricate "intertangled" patterns an admirably tight bond, as in sturdy walls in which bricks are alternately laid length-wise and width-wise, yielding what George Puttenham calls good "band." Stanzas that strike modern eyes as bristling contrivances or arbitrary grids may figure to earlier poets works of fine masonry, crafted for strength (Puttenham 157, 155). Whether like barrel staves or ladder rungs, the English "staff" or the Italian "stanza" (room, stopping place) is a scaffold that helps a poem to be built. Stanza constraints can prompt poetic invention, suggest turns of plot, open the door to unexpected images or even uninvited characters. The needs of building stanzas nudge poets down new paths at every level of composition. The tussle of individual poetic idiom with inherited forms, the nurturing of voice by the demands of stanzaic composition as a crucible for sustained practice: some of these mutualities are irredeemably local—acts of verbal tinkering and substantial thinking are linked. Stanza constraints in turn corral and categorize magpie miscellanies. In the "kaleidoscopic" accrual of images in some stanzas of Byron's *Don Juan*, "we are supposed to watch the pranks in texture and structure, not to assess congruities" (West 29); congruity with the *ottava rima* of the poem is enough.

Stanzas are perhaps the most legible markers of poetic contrivance, but they can also be the subtlest forms of its prophesying and ancestral voices. Stanzas divide poems, tally poems, organize them, rally them along, chart their progress, link them to poems similarly shaped and sounded. Repeated tune, blocky or bristly, silhouettes or husks, stanzas can figure ghostly remains of departed voices or material solidities beyond utterance. Poets can pretend to be taken for a ride by the stanza, or to rein the stanza in, or to let the stanza jog its own way home. A complex stanza is a show-case for a poet's syntactic dexterity, an abacus on which we watch the poet do a lightning-quick sum that always comes out even, a borrowed lyre that plays a new music. The stanzaic frame houses subpatterns not visually mapped in its lineation that help the poet realize, and make seem natural or inevitable, the strophic unit. The sequence of stanzas includes some linked sub-groupings, clusters that in turn are not revealed as such except by reading, others that the typesetting signals. While many traditional stanzas are knit together by rhyme scheme, a stanza's visual cohesion may lock a group of lines together in the absence of rhyme.

The framer of stanzas is more than a special kind of verbal artisan. The stanza of any length—even the couplet—affords an arena in which basic features of poetic form can be highlighted with particular clarity. The relation of norms and significant devia-tions; the power of structural grids to stage the poem's play with chance, invention, and necessity; the shifting status of the poem's competing appeals to ear and eye; the status of the page as a site for musical or visual units; the partitioning of a long poem into overlapping zones; the portioning out of the work of the poem's syntax line by line; the poem's way of keeping or spending its bequests from past poems: all of these things come into focus with a close look at stanzas.

Stanzas long predate writing. Yet we should use caution in assuming that these recurring measures are a relic of dance, or of the ancient tragic chorus's turns in per-formance, or of singing a long story to a short tune, as Ezra Pound quipped. To be sure, part of the charm of stanzas is that they are rooms haunted by cultural specters of forms that predate the printed page. But perhaps a more significant part of their appeal is their chameleon capacity to take on a figurative coloring of almost any kind. As essays in this collection attest, some stanzas are themselves particular poetic genres (limerick, haiku), while others shape a range of genres (three-line groupings in *terza rima* and villanelle). Some stanzas accrue in chains or sequences; others stand alone (as there is no tradition of limerick sequences or triolet coronas). When stanza breaks don't chart predictable divisions of syntax, they nonetheless allow us and the compos-ing poet to keep track of how much work the syntax is doing per stanza. Different kinds of meter may enforce different relations to the stanza. Strictly syllabic poems, where line length depends on syllable count alone, may require at least two matched stanzas to be recognized as such.

In the tendentious, often loopy treatise, "The Rationale of Verse" (1848), Edgar Allen Poe rehearses a parable of how poetic forms and meters emerge from the "satisfaction in equality of sound" working in tandem with the always renewed impulse to avoid monotony by devising increased complexity. He demonstrates this principle up to a four-line grouping in which he finds fourteen levels of sound ratios, the last being "the proportional equality, as concerns number, between all the lines, taken collectively, and any individual line—that of four to one." Fiat stanza: "The consideration of this last equality would give birth immediately to the idea of *stanza*—that is to say, the insulation of lines into equal or obviously proportional masses" (Poe 39).

A matching array of stanza shapes may belie the sequence's robust variety, the mix of the poem's enactments of the stanza's potentialities. In some unmetered verse, an irregular batching of lines may jar with the poem's uniformity in idiom or syntax. Until you visit and traverse each island, there is no predicting the climate or flora of the archipelago. Couplet niches and quatrain crannies in one stanza may flatten into discursive plains in the next. To compare styles of Spenserian stanzas is to note Byron's management of the medial couplet or Keats's way with the closing alexandrine. The printed outline of the stanzas of Moore's "The Fish" promises seriality and balance as well as craggy intricacy, but the roving syntax that builds the stanzas defies their visually matched contours. No matter how eye-catching their outline, you must *read* poems in stanzas, not just look at them, to judge how, or if, the stanzas' shape is fashioned to signify.

John Dryden distinguishes the craft required to write well in the heroic couplet and in the pentameter *abab* stanza—the form of Dryden's *Annus Mirabilis* Gray would later adopt for "Elegy Written in a Country Churchyard" (hence the *elegiac quatrain*). Defending the stanza of *Annus Mirabilis* (1666), Dryden links the form's nobility to the planning it requires:

> I have chosen to write my Poem in *Quatrains* or *Stanza's* [sic] of four in alternate rhyme, because I have ever judg'd them more noble, and of greater dignity, both for the sound and number, then [*sic*] any other Verse in use amongst us . . . for there [in couplets] the work is sooner at an end, every two lines concluding the labour of the Poet; but in Quattrains he is to carry it farther on; and not onely so, but to bear along in his head the troublesome sense of four lines together. For those who write correctly in this kind must needs acknowledge, that the last line of the Stanza is to be consider'd in the composition of the first.
>
> (Dryden 44–45)

One way to test the difference between these two forms is to begin with three consecutive heroic couplets from *The Rape of the Lock*:

Oh, had I rather unadmir'd remain'd	a
In some lone isle, or distant Northern land;	a
Where the gilt Chariot never marks the way,	b
Where none learn *Ombre*, none e'er taste *Bohea*!	b
There kept my charms conceal'd from mortal eye,	c
Like roses, that in desarts bloom and die.	c

(4.153–58)

If I reshuffle these lines from Belinda's outburst into an interlocking six-line stanza, I can further show the stanza's interlocking armature by indenting to chart the rhyme scheme, (*abcbac*), a graphic practice whose fortunes Rosemary Huisman chronicles from Latin and medieval verse beginnings through to the nineteenth century. Without the couplet's snap and dispatch, the resulting stanza takes on a melancholy inapt for Pope's purposes:

Oh, had I rather unadmir'd remain'd	a
Where the gilt Chariot never marks the way,	b
There kept my charms conceal'd from mortal eye,	c
Where none learn *Ombre*, none e'er taste *Bohea*,	b
In some lone isle, or distant Northern land,	a
Like roses, that in desarts bloom and die.	c

What gives this stanza-of-scrambled-couplets its flavor is that each of the three rhyming pairs delays a different interval before its completion. The a-rhyme waits three intervening lines before it recurs; the b-rhyme recurs first, creating an *abcb* quatrain; the c-rhyme finds its partner only when both b and a rhymes have found theirs, after two intervening lines. *The Rape of the Lock* is unthinkable in stanzas like these because its mocking nod to epic requires classical epic, hence non-stanzaic (stichic) form, like that of Homer and Virgil. The joke of Belinda's burst of angry regret stems from its reductive updating of Achilles' lament for the death of Patroclus, addressed to his mother, the goddess Thetis. The idea of an experimental, interlaced stanza form derives from post-classical troubadour traditions; pressed into service for mock-epic, such a stanza is like a mixed metaphor. Its prosodic pedigree is wrong for the gag underlying Pope's choice of heroic couplets.

Alternately, we can undo some of Gray's antitheses, as displayed in the famous lines which have Pope's (and Pope's sources) as a source:

Full many a gem of purest ray serene	a
The dark unfathomed caves of ocean bear:	b
Full many a flower is born to blush unseen,	a
And waste its sweetness on the desert air.	b

(ll.53–56)

To give the lines syntactic symmetry yields an envelope stanza (*abba*); that is, to place the flower and gem side by side in the a-rhymed lines, requires a reversal so that both the statement about the flower and the gem are structured subject–verb–object/complement:

The dark unfathomed caves of ocean bear
Full many a gem of purest ray serene;
Full many a flower is born to blush unseen,
And waste its sweetness on the desert air.

Clearly, something has changed, though only the order and not the wording of the lines has been tampered with. A crucial stylistic distinction of the "Elegy" has been erased, which one commentator describes as "the great suspended chords that sound through the poem and give it its characteristic inevitability."

Do stanzas mean anything? To approach this question, we'll need to think about how we perceive stanzas—through ears, eyes, or both? Stanzas of metrical design appeal to the ear with an audible rhythm, often marked by rhyme at line endings. The shape on the page diagrams how the sounds are organized, but that diagram's silhouette represents nothing beyond that. The poem is simply poem-shaped. This disconnection between sense and the visible shape of lines organized into stanzas suggests that we are likelier to understand how stanzas come to bear meaning if we cease to expect sound reliably to echo sense. When we pronounce "dog" to mean our four-legged pet, the "d" does no work beyond specifying that we didn't mean "hog" or "frog." But when we say "dirty dog" or "dirty diggy dog," we are springing the "d" of "dog" into prominence through repetition (*alliteration*). "Dirty diggy dog / Happy piggy hog" combines meter, rhyme, and alliteration into an elementary couplet, the most basic kind of stanza. Like other sound-organizing structures in poetry, stanzas marshal features of language left over from the work of meaning. Writing of rhyme in Medieval verse forms, James I. Wimsatt notes, "In ways beyond the support of the sense, prosodic patterns in poetry capitalize on the leftover qualities that ordinary language neglects. By imposing an independent system of sound that has only 'musical' import, the prosody provides an organizing framework for the material qualities of sound" (Wimsatt 22). In that way, the stanzas we hear are markers of poetry or signals for readers to use the interpretive procedures they bring to poetry. Bear in mind that "Formal relations do not have meanings as words have meanings" (Nowottny 121).

What about the stanzas we see? What does it mean to ask this question? Is it like asking if the length of a poem means anything, or if the wide-screen format of a movie means anything? Are stanzas parts of poetic *form*, or features of *format*? Are they suggestive shapes or orders, implied cogencies that transcend a poem's chaoses? Stanzaic gatherings display the writer's virtuosity as an arranger and dovetailer of words in measured patterings, but mere poetic craftsmanship can give stanzas a banal bad name as tinkly jingle or hokey verbal tinkering. Like verse in meters, nonmetered verse has had its own more and less successful styles of gathering lines into groups. Sometimes the visual appeal of a stanza's graphic design can mute its phonetic patterning, sometimes amplify it. Stanzas in the eye can figure for one poet a robust saliency, an out-thrusting of the world's substance, an insistent making-present. For another poet, the visual stanza shape can drift into obliteration, marking a last spectral dwindling or trace overlaid by time. Thomas Hardy, an inveterate inventor of complex stanza forms, often shows an "epitaphic sense" of stanza form. Imagining poems as surfaces chiseled with memorial words, now decayed, he figures the resulting printed stanzas as leaving "only the husk of their inscriptions, the versified impression" (Taylor 177).

Some poems display local heightenings of meaningful suggestion within a stanza's designs. This third kind of meaning might be called iconic. If we think of a stanza as a poetic "scheme" or surface design, an iconic use of it slants a stanza into a "trope" or metaphor, momentarily in a long poem or sometimes throughout a shorter one (Hollander 1–17). Here the possibilities are endless, and so is the need for readerly tact, as in the construal of any figurative language. The clustering of lines into regular strophes can be perfectly unself-regarding for sustained stretches of a poem, until the run is broken by a stanza that brings attention to its status, wittily or plangently. The blank-verse poet has to marshal different resources to set off a particular set of lines as a sub-grouping, while stanza divisions make any stanza ripe for salience at the poet's will. Catherine Addison notes that in long stanzaic narratives, a particular stanza "full of little surprises of virtuosity will wake up its reader to consciousness of form more regularly than a less stylized, more prose-like form such as blank verse" (Addison 131). Stanzas are rarely continuous icons in a poem. Instead, at distinctive, sometimes surprising nodes, the poem's sturdily instrumental latticework may flash into self-regarding significance—may become a meaningful trope or metaphor rather than a scheme or surface design. Poets may elicit any number of figurative possibilities even from a simple stanzaic pattern. While Pope exploits the double pull of antithesis throughout the heroic couplets of *The Rape of the Lock*, he wittily dramatizes the saving grace of that rhetoric at particular junctures. Explaining how the sylphs keep young women from straying by guiding them through "mystic mazes" (1.92), Pope's Ariel reveals the mechanism of constant competing temptations that alone prevent them from yielding to any single allure:

> What tender maid but must a victim fall
> To one man's treat, but for another's ball?
> When *Florio* speaks, what virgin could withstand,
> If gentle *Damon* did not squeeze her hand?

> (1.95–98)

Rivals Florio and Damon here stage the antithetical symmetries of the heroic couplet. Because their force is evenly balanced, neither prevails: chastity is preserved, thanks to the poise engineered in Pope's couplet design. Equal tugs in opposite directions keep things stable and maids safe.

Moments of stanzaic self-mirroring need not be witty. In 1863, Emily Dickinson writes a poem of four four-line stanzas about four trees on their own "Acre," randomly placed and answering to no grand plan, yet maintaining a lively reciprocity with their surroundings. This is the poem's third stanza ("them" is the four trees; "Him" is probably the "Acre," though residually may include "God" mentioned in the preceding stanza):

> The Acre gives them—Place—
> They—Him—Attention of Passer by
> Of Shadow, or of Squirrel, haply—
> Or Boy—

> (["Four Trees"] ll.9–12)

What accounts for the capacity of this small stand of trees to bestow on the land they occupy the "Attention" not just of a passing observer but of "Shadow"? If the four trees are a figurative shadowing-forth of the four lines of Dickinson's stanza, the curiosity squirrel and boy confer (tree-climbers both) is as mobile and brisk as shadow's is mobile and gradual. There is an "or" sounding in "four," quatrain constraints leaf into options, and the stanza's narrow plot of ground gives place and takes place. This stanza is not a discrete troping of the hymn stanza's schematic foursomes; rather, the whole poem is a meditation on the mobile mutalities of a created world, the stanza being another instance of these qualities. The phenomenal world has for Dickinson a strophic texture of the random and the interlocking. It is not one thing after another, sense variously drawn out.

In a long stanzaic narrative, a poet can use the "iconic" power of the stanza to see if we're paying attention. A famous "freeze frame" of a stanza early in *The Faerie Queene* ends by snapping a picture of the Redcrosse Knight and composing a tidy caption for it. The Knight is battling with the snaky monster Error, and has just struck her a glancing blow with his sword:

> Much daunted with that dint, her sence was dazd,
> Yet kindling rage her selfe she gathered round,
> And all attonce her beastly bodie raizd
> With doubled forces high above the ground:
> Tho wrapping up her wrethed sterne arownd,
> Lept fierce upon his shield, and her huge traine
> All suddenly about his body wound,
> That hand or foot to stirr he strove in vaine:
> God help the man so wrapt in Errours endless traine.
>
> (1.18.1–9)

The Spenserian stanza here stops to read itself. But the poem will soon give us reason to distrust this tidy use of its final, six-beat line to label this picture of the knight rendered immobile by the coils of Error. The clarity of the picture and its tidy allegorical meaning is itself a trap, an immobility we should be cautious about endorsing. We're fixed, like Redcrosse himself. Patricia Parker describes our interpretive fix: "The picture is frozen in its stanza-frame, at the very point where 'Errour' the monster is made coequal with her abstract allegorical sense." Even as the stanza invites us to pause over its neat explication of its own structure, there's "the danger of a premature or false reading. Spenser's 'Errour' disappears, leaving her trace in the serpentine progress of the poem itself" (Parker 69). This false closure of a premature caption arouses us to do a double-take at other stanzaic closures in *The Faerie Queene*, whether cliffhangers or conversation-stoppers, meanwhiles, or meanderings, or knots that ensuing stanzas prove to be slip-knots.

A fourth, important way that stanzas mean, whether their appeal is chiefly to sound or vision: as allusions to other poems in that stanza, or similar stanzas. In nineteenth-century uses of the Spenserian stanza, cavalier *enjambments* make rhyme easier, while tagging more legibly the rhyme scheme's constructedness.

The force stanzas can exert on literary allusion in prose deserves a brief reckoning. Stanzas can weld a set of words or sentences together so tightly that citing a snippet of a stanza brings the whole stanza to bear. In Jane Austen's *Emma* (1816), a character who exacts another's hearing of Gray's gem-flower quatrain is rendered both comic and suspect. Mrs. Elton rattles on to Emma about the "absolutely charming" Jane Fairfax:

> "We must bring her forward. Such talents as hers must not be suffered to remain unknown.—I dare say you have heard those charming lines of the poet,
>> Full many a flower is born to blush unseen
>> And waste its fragrance on the desert air.
> We must not allow them to be verified in sweet Jane Fairfax."
>
> (Austen 221)

Austen allows us to hear the egoism of Mrs. Elton's self-satisfied ramblings amplified against the chaste rhythms (slightly misquoted, and sadly misapplied) of Gray's well-known lines. A tag from the same stanza flavors an auctioneer's pitch in George Eliot's *Middlemarch* (1872):

> Suppose it should be discovered hereafter that a gem of art has been amongst us in this town, and nobody in Middlemarch awake to it. Five guineas—five seven-six—five ten. Still, ladies, still! It is a gem, and "Full many a gem," as the poet says, has been allowed to go at a nominal price because the public knew no better.
>
> (Eliot 656)

Pilfered for sloganeering, Gray's famous opening chords are now followed by a tune hilariously mercenary in rhythm and diction. The stanza-conjuring phrase is cut adrift from the antitheses that animate what's missing but allusively heard and tie it to what the stanza's integrity helps us recall "the poet says" of worldly vanity and poverty's anonymity. By testing Gray's "Full many a gem" against the huckster's "nominal price," Eliot heightens the scene's cynical comedy.

So firmly does Gray's stanza carry its melody, a few borrowed notes can awaken complex echoes in an invented pattern of freshly different design. In Henry David Thoreau's "Sic Vita" (1841), a "nosegay" of violets looped with straw speaks of itself as "a parcel of vain strivings tied / By a chance bond together" (13, ll.1–2). This hastily gathered bouquet, "dangling this way and that," with "links . . . loose and wide" (ll.3–4), almost at random plucks up a strand of Gray's durable quatrain:

> And here I bloom for a short hour unseen,
>> Drinking my juices up,
> With no root in the land
> To keep my branches green

> But stand
> In a bare cup.

(ll.19–24)

Gray's flower born to blush unseen—in the "Elegy," a figure for the isolated poor unable to invest their unrecognized talents—enters Thoreau's imagination as a short-lived offering of wildflowers. The flowers and the loose, openwork stanza figure his own young life for which he imagines no long future, as well as a wild intermixture of American song uncoiled from English roots. His nonce-stanza opens with a five-beat line, but from there follows no inherited pattern, troping its rough-cut but regular design as an unconsidered randomness. The poignantly dwindling silhouette of Thoreau's stanza shadows forth a raggedly splayed bouquet, fed by allusion's power to hint at a shredding and loose rebinding of Gray's "Elegy" stanza, releasing a new sweetness in the American air.

Poets today who have forsaken meter have not abandoned the stanza. Lines tidily batched in twos, threes, and fours may be just as common in new books of poetry as stichic poems with no interruptions or divisions or poems grouped in irregular verse paragraphs. Revising a free-verse poem may involve rebatching lines, relocating white space between linear groupings. Allusive power adheres even to free-verse stanzas: for instance, some unmeasured and unrhymed tercets will read as quatrains missing a line, others as revenants of *terza rima*. Poets who have returned to measured verse designs, inherited or invented, craft stanzas any Elizabethan would recognize as of skilled masonry. Stanzas serve as muse, blueprint that gets the poem built, as when A.R. Ammons ends "Hibernaculum," an unmetered, unrhymed poem in 112 groups of three tercets, with a nod to the stanza as structuring convenience:

> . . . I'm reading Xenophon's *Oeconomicus* "with
> considerable pleasure and enlightenment" and with
> appreciation that saying so fills this stanza nicely.

(Ammons 388)

In twenty-first-century verse, the stanza's lattice keeps the line under control, as when Rachel Wetzsteon repeats, and invokes, a five-line scheme, half-lax, half-leashed, in "Commands for the End of Summer":

> Make me
> spontaneous,
> gathering winds, but don't
> blow so giddily, I teeter
> too much.

(ll.6–10)

Batched lines continue to manage the printed page's impact, hint at style or pacing of performance, and imply fables about the poem's larger orders. The stanza remains elemental in poetry's house of possibility.

References and Further Reading

Addison, C. "Little Boxes: The Effects of the Stanza on Poetic Narrative." *Style* 37: 2003. 124–43.

Ammons, A.R. *Collected Poems 1951–1971*. New York: W.W. Norton. 1972.

Austen, J. *Emma* (1816), ed. J. Kinsley, intro. A. Pinch. Oxford: Oxford University Press, 2003.

Bradford, R. *The Look of It: A Theory of Visual Form in English Poetry*. Cork: Cork University Press. 1993.

Cushman, S. *Fictions of Form in American Poetry*. Princeton: Princeton University Press. 1993.

Dryden, J. *The Poems and Fables of John Dryden*, ed. James Kinsley. Oxford: Oxford University Press. 1970.

Ferry, A. *By Design: Intention in Poetry*. Stanford: Stanford University Press. 2008.

Hall, J.D. *Seamus Heaney's Rhythmic Contract*. Basingstoke: Palgrave Macmillan. 2009.

Eliot, G. *Middlemarch* (1872), ed. W.J. Harvey. Harmondsworth: Penguin. 1965.

Häublein, E. *The Stanza*. London: Methuen. 1978.

Hollander, J. *Melodious Guile: Fictive Pattern in Poetic Language*. New Haven: Yale University Press. 1998.

Huisman, R. *The Written Poem: Semiotic Conventions from Old to Modern English*. London: Cassell. 1998.

Mitchell, D. *Measures of Possibility: Emily Dickinson's Manuscripts*. Amherst: University of Massachusetts Press. 2005.

Nowottny, W. *The Language Poets Use*. London: Athlone. 1962.

Parker P. *Inescapable Romance: Studies in the Poetics of a Mode*. Princeton: Princeton University Press. 1979.

Poe, E.A. *Essays and Reviews*, ed. G.R. Thomson. New York: Library of America. 1984.

Puttenham, G. *The Art of English Poesy: A Critical Edition* (1589), ed. F. Whigham and W.A. Rebhorn. Ithaca, NY: Cornell University Press. 2007.

Smith, B.H. *Poetic Closure*. Chicago: University of Chicago Press. 1968.

Taylor, D. *Hardy's Metres and Victorian Prosody*. Oxford: Oxford University Press. 1988.

Thoreau, H.D. *Collected Poems of Henry Thoreau*. Enlarged edition, ed. Carl Bode. Baltimore: Johns Hopkins University Press. 1964.

Voigt, E.B. *The Art of Syntax: Rhythm of Thought, Rhythm of Song*. St. Paul, MO: Graywolf. 2009.

West, P. *Byron and the Spoiler's Art* (1960), 2nd edn. New York: Lumen. 1990.

Wetzsteon, R. *Sakura Park*. New York: Persea. 2006.

Wimsatt, J.I. "Rhyme/Reason, Chaucer/Pope, Icon/Symbol," *Modern Language Quarterly* 55 (1994): 18–46.

Wolfson, S.J. *Formal Charges: The Shaping of Poetry in British Romanticism*. Stanford: Stanford University Press. 1997.

5

Trying to Praise the Mutilated World
The Contemporary American Ode

Ann Keniston

Unlike sonnets, villanelles, elegies, and the like, odes are often hard to identify and harder to define. An ode, virtually all scholars agree, is a poem of praise or celebration; it generally addresses rather than describes its subject; it employs a formal and often public tone and is often extended in length. But these criteria do not apply to all odes, and they are so broad that they can be applied to poems that aren't odes at all. Odes also present tonal problems for both readers and poets. Because they are often occasional, their acts of praise can seem forced; in fact odes are notorious for their tendency to verge on bathos, ridiculousness, or what *The New Princeton Encyclopedia of Poetry and Poetics* calls "burlesque." Odes nearly always balance a sincerity that risks cloying with an ironic self-consciousness that risks obliterating the work of praise.

Odes in fact have generally been defined in terms of dichotomies and conflicts. Most readers define the ode in English in terms of a double and conflicted lineage. The odes of the Greek poet Pindar (c. 522–443 BC) celebrating the feats of athletes and statesmen are formal, detached in tone, and divided into three repeating sections, corresponding, according to most scholars, to the moves of dancers to which odes were sung.[1] This tripartite structure invites different approaches to and perspectives on a central topic; Pindaric odes generally move toward an integration of their opposing viewpoints, although this movement is sometimes difficult to discern. The odes of the Latin poet Horace (65 BC to 8 BC), often seen as antithetical to the Pindaric, are for the most part private, colloquial, intimate, and nondidactic, and they employ regular quatrains instead of the irregular long stanzas characteristic of Pindaric odes. Indeed, it is sometimes argued that Horace's poems are known as odes only because of an error in translation (Curran 63).

Because of the near-universality of this way of reading, subsequent odes have often been understood in terms of their capacity to balance public with private subject matter and the didactic tone of the Pindaric with the intimacy and irreverence of the Horatian.[2]

A Companion to Poetic Genre, First Edition. Edited by Erik Martiny.
© 2012 John Wiley & Sons, Ltd. Published 2012 by John Wiley & Sons, Ltd.

Such a mode of criticism is useful in reading contemporary odes insofar as they, like contemporary American poems more generally, are indeed often concerned with joining public and private modes of utterance. Yet this critical framework is also limited: it sometimes focuses too exclusively on locating the Pindaric and Horatian strands of given poems and can lead to inconsistent or even illogical conclusions.[3] Not only does it disregard other, less often discussed modes of classical ode, it ignores more urgent and critically useful oppositions and conflicts that recur in odes of different kinds.[4]

A more flexible mode of reading, and one especially useful to contemporary American odes, dispenses with such questions of taxonomy to focus on the ways odes engage with fundamental lyric problems of animation and knowledge. Paul H. Fry's important 1980 study locates two essential and contradictory features in what he calls the Pindaric tradition in English poetry: odes rely on invocation—the attempt through language to make present something absent—but they are also proleptic, anticipating and repeating what is already known in ways that prevent the embodiment of the invoked other (10–12). Odes thus involve both faith and doubt, but because in odes, the "burden of doubt" ultimately "subverts the assertion of knowledge" (8), odes are for Fry irremediably ironic (1). Like Fry, Susan Stewart has more recently maintained that praise poems, which she also calls odes, paradoxically "make absent things present *by recalling them* rather than by manifesting them" (237, emphasis mine). But Stewart emphasizes that because odes insist on rebirth, they reveal not irony but instead the poet's "mastery of lack or suffering" (236). In the process, they also evoke, in Stewart's terms, "the abyss of darkness underlying all creation, the materiality of matter, and the fact of death" (243).

Odes in this way express two fundamentally competing impulses. They yearn toward the possibility of animation, proximity, and presence; yet they also already know that such gestures cannot be fulfilled. This conflict is especially useful in reading contemporary American odes, which are acutely conscious of the tonal risks—the danger both of hypersincerity and of self-defeating irony—that I associated above with all odes. Unlike earlier classical and earlier English odes, whose praise is often indirect, contemporary odes explicitly praise, and they also interrogate the project and nature of praise. Anne Carson has defined as particularly modern the conviction that "all epistemological authority to define a boundary between blameworthy and praiseworthy action has been withdrawn" (126). Contemporary ode writers acknowledge the loss of this authority by insisting that contemporary experience is compromised or broken even as they attempt, at times forlornly, halfheartedly, or overzealously, to praise it. Adam Zagajewski's influential "Try to Praise the Mutilated World," published in *The New Yorker* just after the attacks of September 11, 2001, is in this way exemplary. The poem moves from the assertion "Try to praise the mutilated world" (l.1) through "You must praise" (l.6) to "You should praise" (l.12) to the imperative "Praise" (l.18) as it catalogs a series of mutilated objects, from "The nettles that methodically overgrow / the abandoned homesteads of exiles" (ll.4–5) to "the refugees heading nowhere, / . . . the executioners sing[ing] joyfully" (ll.10–11) to the simple "grey feather a thrush lost" (l.19). Contemporary American odes do something similar:

they bind the knowledge of mutilation to the compulsion to praise, insisting that they must praise *because* praising is so difficult. While Fry and Stewart juxtapose the thematics of hopeful ignorance with painful foreknowledge, contemporary poets often enact this conflict tonally, by forcing together the sincere and the ironic.

In this way, contemporary odes intervene in a conflict central to and divisive in American poetry. Over at least the past forty years, American poetry can be plausibly read as having split into two camps: one (including the postconfessionals) values truth-telling or sincerity, while the other (including the Language and "experimental" poets) emphasizes a linguistic surface that resists transparency in ways that are fundamentally ironic. (Indeed, recent calls for a "new sincerity" in experimental poetry reveal the dangers of a poetics based entirely on what is sometimes explicitly called irony.[5]) Contemporary odes acknowledge this problem, and they also attempt to resolve it. By insisting on both the fact of mutilation and the need to praise, they impel the ironic against the sincere. In the process, they keep readers on their toes: contemporary odes are often funny and parodic, but they do not shirk abstract language or disjunction. This capacity to elide elements of accessible and difficult poetry offers a resolution, or perhaps a circumvention, of recent controversies about the extent to which recent poetry's difficulty has caused a catastrophic decline in poetry readership and about how to reverse this decline.[6]

American odes, it can therefore be argued, have continued to proliferate because they are positioned at a crucial nexus: they help resolve urgent contemporary conflicts about poetic voice and audience. Pablo Neruda's several volumes of *Elemental Odes*, published in the 1950s and first translated into English in 1990, are sometimes seen as the origin of the recent spate of ode-writing, but Neruda's simple odes to ordinary objects, relying heavily on simile and written mostly in a sense of quiet wonderment, are quite different from most recent American odes. Indeed, one feature of such odes is that they are hard to identify as such; they frequently excise the term "ode" from their titles and thus renew old questions of classification. At the same time, recent odes tend to contain several linked features:

1. Contemporary odes celebrate not just ordinary but often unlovely things or experiences. Considering topics including a maggot, a boll weevil, public bathrooms, an episiotomy, stammering, and the like, they undertake an often difficult, strained, or impossible project of reclamation: they celebrate what is normally reviled.[7]

2. Contemporary odes often exploit tonal discrepancies. Sometimes they employ a highly formal, self-consciously archaic voice in relation to something apparently insignificant; at others, they veer between formal and highly vernacular speech. The effect is both to mock praise and to insist on it; these poems acknowledge praise to be archaic, stuffy, and artificial, yet they also reveal their speaker's devotion to praise and the importance of praise more generally.

3. Contemporary odes explore and exploit the problematics of address and animation. Almost without exception, they address their objects and in the process

draw attention to the difficulty of turning an object into a subject.[8] Often the addressee is indifferent to the poem or unable to hear it; sometimes the "you" is partially or excessively personified; sometimes address occurs only sporadically in the poem, reminding the reader of its awkwardness and artificiality.

4. Contemporary odes complicate traditional distinctions between praise and lament. Loss persists in these odes, partly because they often include passages of past-tense narration seemingly at odds with the ode's immediacy. These poems ask whether the act of remembering—enacted through the writing of the poem—can mitigate the losses effected by time.

Contemporary odes of all kinds, as these features suggest, poke fun at their subjects and by implication at themselves, but they also affirm the project of praise and thus their own legitimacy as odes. In the remainder of this chapter, I will explore the implications of this double aim in relation to several odes, which exemplify the tendencies of contemporary ode writers more generally. First I will juxtapose two odes from Robert Pinsky and Bernadette Mayer, poets of quite different "schools," to argue that, by refusing to distinguish ironic from sincere discourse, odes help break down the common opposition between the "mainstream" and "experimental" strands of contemporary poetry. Then I will turn to two recent volumes—by Kenneth Koch and W.S. Merwin—which elaborate in quite different ways the ode's concern not only with tonal play but with loss and memory.

Past U.S. Poet Laureate Robert Pinsky stands firmly within the mainstream of contemporary poetry, as his numerous honors reveal.[9] Bernadette Mayer's reputation is more strictly local, and her aesthetic is more experimental; her work has been associated both with the Language and New York School movements, and her poems reveal the influences of surrealism and of her experience as a performance artist ("Bernadette Mayer"). Certainly Pinsky's "To Television" and Mayer's "Ode on Periods" differ in many ways. Pinsky's poem focuses on its addressee; despite the lack of the identifier "ode" in the title, it directly thanks its addressee. Mayer's focus, perhaps partly because her ode is "on" rather than "to," is less about periods than about poetry itself, although it also insists that it isn't "a real poem" (25), much less the kind of ode that would

> call on the moon . . .
> or anthropology or the bible or talk about being untouchable
> or power etc
>
> (ll.25–27)

The poems read very differently as well: while Pinsky's focuses on the features of television, Mayer's contains a zany and sometimes disturbing free association, including a discussion of a dream in which

I had a deep cut on my finger
filled with delicious tofu cake
and when you took off your clothes your penis
was among them hanging by a cord on a hook.

(ll.10–14)

Despite these differences in tone, both poems praise entities seldom deemed worthy of praise, and both do so by juxtaposing high with colloquial language. One of Pinsky's catalogs includes these lines:

A box a tube
. . .

Coffer of shades, ordained
Cotillion of phosphors
. . .

Homey miracle . . .

(ll.3–8)

This list joins the polysyllabic and scientific "phosphors" and the old-fashioned "cotillion" with the far more familiar "box," "tube," and "homey" in a way that reveals the poet's virtuosity, as the aural transformation of "coffer" to "phosphors" and "cotillion" to "homey" reveals. This juxtaposition is central to the poem's argument: television undermines elitism (the pretentious speaker once "scorned you" but no longer does) because it refuses to distinguish between high and low culture. Pinsky also shifts without transition between the idea of television, its physical composition, and an actual TV set "in a hotel room" (l.18). Mayer's tone shifts are if anything more extreme:

I think the world is all fucked up in many ways (see footnotes)
and one of these is the apparent interdiction in dumb poetic tradition
of speaking of and being heard on the glories of sublime menstruation.

(ll.18–20)

Interrupting her rant with a scholarly reference to footnotes, Mayer embraces, then shifts away from polysyllables, ending not with sublime beauty or truth but sublime menstruation. Both poems in this way recall Zagajewski's juxtaposition of mutilatedness with praise: both acknowledge that the ode is too elegant or archaic for their mundane or unpleasant subject matter, yet both celebrate their topics by bringing together overt, at times exaggerated praise and self-mockery, to comic effect. Both are simultaneously sincere and ironic, exploiting the disjunction between their extreme praise and its humble object partly by deflating—through shifts to ordinary or "low" language—the pomposity of their own undertaking.

Invocation in odes, according to Fry, always articulates concerns with poetic vocation (2): odes, to put the matter more simply, originate in and articulate anxieties about whether the poet's speech can in fact be heard. Such issues are central to both Pinsky and Mayer: both odes celebrate but also express doubt about poetry's capacity to reach its audience. Pointing out that menstruation has never been a subject for poetry, Mayer's speaker attempts to correct this imbalance, justifying the attempt by insisting that "now . . . poems've got everything in them" (1.29). This wish to enlarge poetry's capacity, though, leads to an indirectly expressed anxiety about whom such a poem is for. In the last lines, Mayer addresses a reader, probably male and certainly ignorant:

> if you really wanna know
> most of us you know
> all get ours on the same day no kidding.
>
> (ll.38–40)

The poem ends with an appeal to a quite different, collective, female addressee: "So Friends! Hold the bloody sponge up! / For all to see!" (ll.44–45). The gesture is ridiculous and also poignant: it mocks the possibility that the poem, like a political speech, can inspire its readers to action even as it makes that wish explicit. The inconsistency of this late-appearing address thus expresses both desire for and doubt about the poem's audience in ways that engage with particularly contemporary anxieties about readership.

Pinsky's poem ends with a less overt attempt to locate and define an audience. Turning from the attributes of the television to what is seen on it, the speaker invites a stream of characters into the brief solitude of the hotel room (he often, he says, turns on the television for a few moments before going out to meet an audience [ll.19–20]). The final image of seeing Jackie Robinson on television (ll.27–29) reveals the ambivalent capacity of television to fulfill our wishes. Robinson's appearance is "live" but only euphemistically: the TV recreates him but doesn't make him actually present, just as the image of him "stealing / Home" has particular power for the traveler far from home. The moment reveals television's capacity both to foster and undermine the illusions of animation and reciprocity central to Fry's conception of the ode. And indeed Pinsky makes the analogy between television and the work of the ode explicit at the poem's end when he turns from the "image" of Robinson to that effected by his own poem:

> . . . the image—O strung shell—enduring
> Fleeter than light like these words we
> Remember in, they too winged
> At the helmet and ankles.
>
> (ll.29–32)

Like remembered TV scenes, poetry embodies a paradox: it makes "enduring" what is "fleet," brief, already vanished. Like the flickering images on TV, the poem's images and complex music—the strung shell in another of Pinsky's poems refers to a primitive musical instrument[10]—attempt to compensate for absence both by unmaking and acknowledging it.

The ending of Pinsky's poem celebrates the capacity of the ode, like television, to embody the paradoxes of vanishing and permanence. Although Mayer's parodic tone carries through to the last lines, "Ode on Periods" praises, even as it enacts, its speaker's "freedom to speak about everything." In both poems, praising occurs not despite but through mockery; both acknowledge disgust, loss, temporal change, and mutilatedness (an idea made queasily literal by Mayer's dream of the severed but still functional penis) as both celebrate the capacity of poetry to fuse opposites, to render the fleeting permanent, and to play. My claim is not that these poems in particular echo each other but that such patterns can be traced in virtually all contemporary odes; the ode form tempts American poets of different schools and aesthetics to write in a mode that is at once comic and poignant, funny and wistful, exaggerated and subtle. In the process, odes advance a self-conscious poetics that considers explicitly "what praise poems" themselves, in Stewart's terms, "are for."

Among the evidence of the continued viability, if not resurgence, of the ode in American poetry are two recent volumes, both by prolific and much-honored poets at the end of their careers. Both Kenneth Koch's 2000 *New Addresses* (published when he was approximately 76) and W.S. Merwin's 2008 *Present Company* (published when he was 81) entirely comprise poems whose titles begin "To." Both volumes forego "Ode," although both praise their addressees, sometimes indirectly.[11] Both emphasize, as their titles suggest, the extent to which what is evasive, invisible, or fleeting can be made "present" through address. They do so quite differently: the addressed object is often, in Koch's case, both ridiculous and sublime while, in Merwin's, it is simultaneously imperceptible and omnipresent. Although the volumes differ in tone and sensibility, both consider the paradoxes I have associated with the ode, even as both impel the ode toward a province usually associated with elegy, asking to what extent poems can recover or compensate for what is lost.

The poems of *New Addresses*, perhaps in keeping with Koch's lifelong interest in comedy, are among the funniest of contemporary odes.[12] This is an effect partly of their subjects: Koch's addressees include the kinds of abstract qualities that odes have seldom celebrated ("Carelessness," "Kidding Around," "Jewishness") as well as entities that are not generally seen as discrete ("My Twenties," "Living in the City," "Some Abstract Paintings"); several combine a series of unlike entities ("Walking, the French Language, Testosterone, Politics, and Duration"). As Pinsky startles by addressing the television in all its thingness, Koch physicalizes his addressees, often via prepositions of place: in "To the Ohio" (5) he claims "In my teenage years / I drove *over you*" (ll.5–6); "To my Twenties" (18) includes the lines "*With* / *You* I race down to get [a dropped nickel]" (ll.16–17), and "*In you* I marry" (l.23); in "To Psychoanalysis" (20), the speaker takes "the Lexington Avenue subway / To arrive *at you*" (ll.1–2, all emphasis mine). In several poems, addressees speak (the bossy Testosterone [22–23], for example, generally begins each sentence, "Let's," while Jewishness [28] argues against the speaker's Eurocentric aesthetic); in at least one poem, the addressee (in this case World

War II [15]) dies ("of a bomb blast in Nagasaki"). These strategies make comically visible the problematic assumptions behind poetic address, which generally assumes a potentially responsive other but does not explore what such a response might look like.

Koch's address is often in this way parodic, but its parodic tone enables the expression of authentic feelings. In some poems, Koch at first insults his addressees, then shifts to praise, as in "To Kidding Around" (10), which begins, "Kidding around you are terrible sometimes" (l.1), then claims toward the end, "Yet sometimes you are breathtaking, / Kidding around!" (ll.24–25). The brief "To Carelessness" (11) is structured similarly, though here the negative enables the positive, since carelessness, which leads to the speaker getting attacked by hornets, also saves his life:

> . . . I stepped on a booby trap
> That was badly wired. You
> Had been there too.
> Thank you. It didn't explode.
>
> (ll.7–10)

Other poems bind castigation to praise through the poet's manipulation of imagery. In the punningly titled "To My Old Addresses" (45), following a list of the various places the speaker has lived, the poem becomes hyperbolic:

> . . . O
> My old addresses! O my addresses! Are you addresses still?
> Or has the hand of Time roughed over you
> And buffered and stuffed you with peels of lemons, limes, and shells
> From old institutes?
>
> (ll.11–15)

The shift from exclamations to questions leads to a dense, rhyming ("roughed... buffered... stuffed"), somewhat out-of-control chain of imagery in which the quasi-Shakespearean personification of Time's rough hand yields to a description of an actual hand stuffed with citrus peels. As Pinsky insists that TV is both an idea and a thing, both exalted and low, the old addresses are both ideas and actual places, which uncomfortably coexist, rendering the poem's use of the high "O" of apostrophe excessive and poignant. As in fellow New York School poet Mayer's extreme chains of images, the poignancy—the sincerity—here derives from and is expressed through the comically hyperpoetic language.

For Carson, praising in poems invents a community that "will complete [the poem] . . . by presuming it already exists" (133). Such an assertion cogently summarizes the work done by Koch's odes. Many of these poems reanimate long-past events, characters, and scenes. "To Jewishness, Paris, Ambition, Trees, My Heart, and Destiny" (31–32), which begins by asserting

> You have all gathered here to talk with me,
> Let's bring everything out into the open.
> It's almost too exciting to have all of you here—
>
> (ll.1–3)

And indeed, after some initial awkwardness ("Who would like to ask the first question? / Silence" [ll.7–8]), the poem, like many others, devolves into a kind of picnic or party, in which side conversations occur ("Jewishness and ambition go off to a tree-greened-out corner / And start their confab. Destiny walks with Paris and me / To a house where an old friend is living" [ll.24–26]). One might expect odes to express anxiety about such patently artificial social groupings, yet anxiety is absent from Koch's poems, which delight in their capacity to conjure and juxtapose, to turn seeming irritants into occasions for gratitude.

One explanation for the absence of sadness may lie in Duration's assertion (59) that "'You don't have me but you partake of me'" (l.4). These poems are preoccupied with their own act of conjuring what is both ubiquitous and intangible. "To Breath" (72), for example, shifts between time frames and characters. The poem begins in the present tense with Breath's existence "in me" on a weekend morning, then chronicles its arrival at the moment of the speaker's birth, then turns to the youthful mother's capacity to "warm" the speaker while he continues to breathe (ll.1–4). Part of the praiseworthiness of breath, Koch implies, is its disregard for history, for the fact that neither mother nor speaker are now young. Yet breath also evokes mortality: "Without you, the millions of joys would be nothing." This tension impels the ars poetica expressed in the last lines, in which the speaker asks breath to do one thing, after which it can abandon him:

> I want to understand certain things and tell them to others.
> To do it, I have to get them right, so they are hard to resist.
> Stay with me until I can do this.
>
> (ll.13–17)

More forthrightly than Pinsky and Mayer, Koch here links invocation with vocation: he commands breath to stay so he can complete his work as a speaker and by implication as a poet. Breath, according to Koch, forestalls death via animation, and "To Breath" similarly animates by personifying breath even as it acknowledges that breath already animates us. The poem in this way reiterates what breath already does, yet implicit in this excess is the speaker's knowledge of the future cessation of breath. In this way, the poem cogently enacts what Stewart calls a fundamental paradox of ode: it "give[s] birth to, and animate[s,] . . . the fact of death" (243).

While *New Addresses* jams the ironic and self-mocking up against the sincere and deeply felt, the tone of W.S. Merwin's *Present Company* is more muted: Merwin's poems seldom directly praise or condemn. Instead, their concern is with knowledge and presence, terms that recur throughout the volume. And these *are* questions in the volume; questions, unpunctuated as in all Merwin's recent volumes, replace Koch's often antic exclamations. While Koch's poems often end in bemusement, their praise both curtailed and enabled by loss, Merwin's volume more directly presses ode against elegy, insisting on the ubiquity of absence by interrogating the assumption of presence that underlies his poems' acts of address. As Zagajewski finds in mutilatedness the need to try to praise, praise offers Merwin a way to comprehend loss.

Like Koch's "To Breath," Merwin's "To the Air" (44–45) considers the extent to which breath cannot be commanded. But while Koch assumes breath's ubiquity, Merwin's poem is filled with doubts, especially about his act of address. When the speaker asserts, "I cannot say / how long you had been / present" (ll.3–5), he articulates a temporal uncertainty, intensified by the use of the past perfect, which implies that the presence has now ended. Moreover, air cannot be possessed:

> never
> could I live without you
> never have you
> belonged to me
> never do I want
> you not to be with me.
>
> (ll.15–20)

This paradox—air is necessary but evasive—echoes Koch's more strained attempt to command the uncommandable breath. But Merwin's poem does not struggle to master air as Koch's does, partly because his concern is with his position not as writer but as listener:

> invisible friend
> go on telling me
> again again.
>
> (ll.35–37)

Part of the telling has already occurred, and its cessation seems imminent, since otherwise the command would be unnecessary. The poem, like many in *Present Company*, represents what is "invisible," what evades sensation, what is partly but not entirely real. (Other poems in the volume address a reflection, a face in the mirror, the corner of the eye, and a shadow, all contingent, not fully perceptible entities that occupy an intermediate position between self and world.) "To the Air," like many poems in the volume, subverts the explicit tensions between the sincere and the ironic in Koch's poems by revealing not only the proximity of presence to absence but often the impossibility of distinguishing them.

A particularly dramatic enactment of this dynamic, one in which, in the terms of "To the Present" (43), "you come [while] . . . / you are disappearing / without making yourself known" (ll.17–20), comes in a sequence of dated poems midway through the volume, all of whose other poems are undated. These poems, written between

September 10, 2001 and October 2, 2001, do not comment directly on the attacks of September 11, yet their descriptions of mostly seasonal cycles of loss and diminishment both evoke the human events of that time and offer an alternative to them. "To Words" (80) begins, "When it happens you are not there" (l.1) and argues that words can "say what could not be said" (l.20). But the referent of "it" remains unidentified, and the poem enacts the fundamental incapacity of words to exceed language. Like Zagajewski's poem, also associated with the 9/11 attacks, Merwin acknowledges mutilation without elaborating on it. The dates following these poems reveal the difficulty of Merwin's book-long project of praise and also his commitment to it.

It is in this context significant that these poems dispense with the dynamics of hearing and response that are crucial to Koch's odes. Sometimes the poet's words aren't meant to be heard; sometimes there is a gap between intention and language; sometimes the problem is in the mechanism of transmission, as in "To a Friend Travelling" (28), which describes "one of those letters / . . . / unsigned and never sent" (ll.17, 25). The poems of *Present Company* are similarly unsent letters: address is for Merwin a necessary fiction, an artificial realm of solace amid the knowledge of absence. More exactly, it represents a particular response to the problem of foreknowledge or prolepsis. Address does not mitigate the reality of absence, forgetting, and disappearance but instead offers a way to evade loss's power through a wholly textual mode of presence enabled and circumscribed by memory. "To the Afterlife" (113) addresses an entity that exists, by definition, in the future:

> if you do not hear us
> we can ask anything of you
>
> listen
>
> now in the still night
> the sound of breathing
> remember it
> whether you hear it or not.
>
> (ll.16–22)

Paradoxically, the capacity to anticipate enables both memory and address, allowing the speaker to "ask anything." Prolepsis is here not associated, as in Fry, with irony or futility but with freedom.

The odes of Koch and Merwin are in some ways atypical not only in their quantity—few other contemporary American poets have written a full volume of odes—but in their preoccupation with the past: these are very much late poems. Yet these volumes also exemplify the kinds of experiments in tone and subject matter that typify contemporary American odes. Both volumes pull away from the formal, public tone associated with Pindaric praise and thus with the pressures that often accompany the project of ode-writing. As both explore the relation of remembering and loss to praise, both avoid the defensiveness that risks opening odes what has sometimes been called an excess of embarrassment (Burrow 4). Relying on a variable tone that allows humor, wistfulness, stridency, and detachment to coexist, these volumes, like many recent odes, reclaim sadness in a way that leaves the poet paradoxically freer to praise.

Why, then, has the ode persisted and even flourished among contemporary American poets? Certainly the poems I have discussed, like all postclassical odes, consider the relation of private feeling to public utterance in ways that recall the central opposition between Horatian and Pindaric ideas of ode. But what is more striking is that all these odes in different ways exemplify poetry's capacity to scrutinize what we might otherwise ignore and to celebrate what we might otherwise revile. In the process, contemporary odes insist that poetry is relevant to contemporary culture. I began by describing the difficulty of defining the ode, but this difficulty has ensured poets' continuing interest in the ode and the ode's continuing relevance. Because odes are so hard to identify and classify, they do more than repeat or vary the form's previous iterations. The ode in contemporary hands tries out different ways of resolving the concerns most pressing to contemporary poetry. It seems likely that future odes will do something similar for their own poetic and cultural moment.

NOTES

1 The opposing nature of the ode's different sections is apparent in their names: these sections are generally called the strophe, the antistrophe, and the epode or, following Ben Jonson's Pindaric ode "To the Immortal Memory and Friendship of That Noble Pair, Sir Lucius Cary and Sir H. Morison," the turn, the counterturn, and stand.

2 Curran claims, as do several other critics, that the English ode involves the imposition of a "Horatian voice" onto "a Pindaric form" (71), an argument that is sometimes made about Romantic odes in particular.

3 Critics have disagreed about the extent to which different odes by Wordsworth, Keats, and others, adhere to one more than the other camp. Lynne McMahon paradoxically argues that J.D. McClatchy's "Late Night Ode," a loose translation of an ode by Horace, is also Pindaric (369).

4 Among the Classical traditions of ode not accommodated by this framework, though referenced in unsystematic ways by several readers, are the private odes of Sappho and the odes celebrating of ordinary life, including drinking, of Anachreon. Some readers also see Biblical psalms as a distinct ode tradition.

5 Jason Morris claims that the "New Sincerity" movement grew from a sense of the dead end confronting an experimental poetics overly reliant on irony. Yet New Sincerity is not about refusing but redefining irony: "irony is the event the New Sincerity proposes to write the end of, even while struggling within it, as part of its history."

6 For a discussion of the controversies surrounding the Poetry Foundation's recent attempts to widen the audience for poetry, see Goodyear.

7 These poems are, respectively, by Yusef Komunyakaa, Timothy Krcmrik, Barbara Hamby, Kimberly Johnson, and Kenneth Koch (*New* 9).

8 The exception is odes "on" rather than "to" their subjects, although such odes sometimes address other entities.

9 Poet laureate from 1997 to 2000, Pinsky was director of the "Favorite Poems Project." His translation of *The Inferno of Dante* won several awards, as have his volumes of poetry; he has also published several volumes of criticism.

10 Pinsky's "Last Robot Song" describes "a little newborn god / that made the first instrument . . . / He scooped out a turtle's shell /

And strung it with a rabbit's guts" (ll.1–2, 6–7).

11   Koch has claimed in an interview that the volume's poems are not odes (Hilbert) though most reviewers, including Ken Tucker, have disagreed.

12   Koch wrote a book entitled *The Art of the Possible!: Comics Mainly without Pictures* and also taught a class in twentieth-century comic literature at Columbia (Padgett 41).

REFERENCES AND FURTHER READING

"Bernadette Mayer (1945–)." *Poetry Foundation.* August 10, 2009. www.poetryfoundation.org/archive/poet.html?id=81141.

Burrow, J.A. *The Poetry of Praise.* New York: Cambridge University Press. 2008.

Carson, Anne. *Economy of the Unlost: Reading Simonides of Keos with Paul Celan.* Princeton: Princeton University Press. 1999.

Curran, Stuart. *Poetic Form and British Romanticism.* New York: Oxford University Press. 1986.

Dunn, Douglas. "Ode to a Paperclip." *New Selected Poems 1964–2000.* New York: Faber. 2003. 109.

Fry, Paul H. *The Poet's Calling in the English Ode.* New Haven: Yale University Press. 1980.

Goodyear, Dana. "The Moneyed Muse." *The New Yorker.* February 19, 2007. www.newyorker.com/reporting/2007/02/19/070219fa_fact_goodyear.

Hamby, Barbara. "Ode to Public Bathrooms." *The Alphabet of Desire.* Washington, DC: Orchises. 2006. 80–1.

Hilbert, Ernest. "A Conversation with Kenneth Koch." Random House.com. April 24, 2008. www.randomhouse.com/boldtype/0400/koch/interview.html.

Johnson, Kimberly. "Ode on My Episiotomy." *A Metaphorical God.* New York: Persea. 2008. 24.

Jonson, Ben. "To the Immortal Memory and Friendship of That Noble Pair, Sir Lucius Cary and Sir H. Morison." *Works.* Vol. 1. Ed. C. H. Herford and Percy Simpson. Oxford: Clarendon Press. 1925. 188–89.

Koch, Kenneth. *The Art of the Possible!: Comics Mainly without Pictures.* New York: Soft Skull. 2004.

Koch, Kenneth. *New Addresses.* New York: Knopf. 2000.

Komunyakaa, Yusef. "Ode to the Maggot." *Talking Dirty to the Gods.* New York: Farrar. 2000. 10.

Krcmrik, Timothy. "Boll Weevil Ode." *Iowa Review* 35.1 (2005): 41.

Mayer, Bernadette. "Ode on Periods." Poets.org. August 10, 2009. www.poets.org/viewmedia.php/prmMID/16179.

McMachon, Lynne. "The Next New Thing?" *Literary Imagination* 4.3 (2002): 353–85.

Merwin, W.S. *Present Company.* New York: Knopf. 2007.

Morris, Jason. "The Time between Time: Messianism & the Promise of a 'New Sincerity.'" *Jacket* 35 (2008). http://jacketmagazine.com/35/morris-sincerity.shtml.

"Ode." *The New Princeton Encyclopedia of Poetry and Poetics.* Ed. Alex Preminger and T.V.F. Brogan (co-editors), and Frank J. Warnke, O.B. Hardison, Jr., and Earl Miner (associate editors). Princeton: Princeton University Press. 1993.

Padgett, Ron. "The Pleasure of Fried Shoes." *Writers and Teachers Talking.* Ed. Judy Kravis. Cork: Cork University Press. 1995. 35–44.

Pinsky, Robert (trans.). *The Inferno of Dante: A New Verse Translation.* New York: Farrar. 1994.

Pinsky, Robert. "Last Robot Song." The New Yorker. January 26, 2009. June 5, 2009. www.newyorker.com/fiction/poetry/2009/01/26/090126po_poem_pinsky.

Pinsky, Robert. "To Television." *Jersey Rain.* New York: Farrar. 2000. 31–32.

Stewart, Susan. "What Praise Poems Are For." *PMLA* 120.1 (2005): 235–45.

Tucker, Ken. "You Talking to Me?" Review of *New Addresses* by Kenneth Koch. New York Times Book Review. June 4, 2000. www.nytimes.com/books/00/06/04/reviews/000604.04tuck.html.

Zagejewski, Adam. "Try to Praise the Mutilated World." Trans. Renata Gorczynski. *Without End: New and Selected Poems.* New York: Farrar. 2002. 60. Orig. pub. *The New Yorker.* September 24, 2001.

6
English Elegies

Neil Roberts

Elegy has been the subject of intense and theorized debate in contemporary criticism, largely under the influence of psychoanalysis. Peter M. Sacks's *The English Elegy* maps the poetry of mourning from Sidney to Yeats, in the light of the "significant similarity between the process of mourning and the oedipal resolution" (8). Jahan Ramazani's *Poetry of Mourning* carries the argument into the modern period, covering British, Irish, and American poetry up to Heaney. In the process Ramazani challenges the normative Freudian distinction between mourning and melancholia, largely accepted by Sacks, and portrays modern elegy as often violently agonistic, in the context of both familial mourning and the commemoration of literary precursors.

In this essay I shall be looking at poetry from the latter end of Ramazani's period and beyond, and concentrating on work by English poets. This is partly to complement Ramazani's account, which ignores English poetry after Auden, partly to avoid historical complications, and partly because, in some respects, an intriguingly different picture emerges. I shall be concentrating on three areas: elegy for the father, for poetic partners, and self-elegy.

The Death of the Father: Tony Harrison, Ted Hughes, Peter Redgrove

The most dramatic way in which modern elegists, in Ramazani's account, are more agonistic than their precursors is in their mourning of the father. His account of this development concentrates almost entirely on American poets, especially of the "Confessional" period, whose family elegies he describes as "curses, condemnations,

A Companion to Poetic Genre, First Edition. Edited by Erik Martiny.
© 2012 John Wiley & Sons, Ltd. Published 2012 by John Wiley & Sons, Ltd.

and exorcisms." American elegists radicalize the genre by "denouncing, mocking, ravaging and exposing their parents in stunning acts of confrontation." His star exhibits are Plath ("there's a stake in your fat black heart"), Berryman, whose father "wiped out my childhood" by killing himself, and Lowell who "uses his memoir and elegies to humiliate his father" for his "impotence and self-delusion" (221, 233, 237, 244).

Ramazani's account of American elegy is incontrovertible but it elides (as psychoanalysis tends to) a factor which makes a marked difference when we consider some of the English poets of the same or slightly later period: class. The Confessional poets are all from middle-class backgrounds and while, at least in the cases of Plath and Berryman, the mourning of the father is energized by trauma that has nothing to do with class, for a person of working-class parentage, especially in an age of social mobility, the Oedipal scenario is significantly class-inflected.

Two of the most important English poets of the later twentieth century, Tony Harrison and Ted Hughes, wrote elegies for working-class fathers. Harrison and Hughes are ideologically and stylistically very different writers, but it is in these elegies for their fathers that they have most in common. In Harrison's case these poems are central to the ideological project of his *oeuvre*, and among his best known and most admired. Hughes is commonly regarded as an asocial and apolitical writer to whom nature is more important than any social concerns, but his poems about his father reveal something about class, history and shared social experience that is fundamental to his identity. The fathers of both poets are represented above all as victims, and although there is, especially in Harrison's case, conflict in the relationship, the anger in the poems is mainly directed at the causes of their victimization. Harrison's focus is on the cultural oppression that made his father "feel like some dull oaf" ("Marked with D." 14); Hughes's is entirely on the trauma that his father suffered in World War I. This may not seem like a class-specific trauma, but to Hughes his father's fate was paradigmatic of the West Yorkshire towns and villages that were "sacked" and "bled" to death through "the bottomless wound of the railway station" ("First, Mills," 12, 4–5); and he confessed that much as he admired Wilfred Owen he felt a reservation about him because he was an officer (*Letters* 594). He once wrote that "For England the Great War was, in fact, a kind of Civil War" (*Winter Pollen* 43). The most distinctive thing about the paternal elegies of both poets is that it is not the father's death but his life that is mourned; indeed, Hughes's most powerful elegy for his father was written many years before he died.

The orthodox psychoanalytic account of the "work of mourning" is that the bereaved person withdraws libido from the lost loved one and invests it elsewhere. Melancholia results from the failure to make this substitution. Accordingly, writes Peter Sacks, "few elegies or acts of mourning succeed without seeming to place the dead, and death itself, at some cleared distance from the living" (19). This account does not fit Tony Harrison's elegies for his father. Harrison is mourning not his father's death but limitations imposed on him in his life and, more personally, his own failure, in life, to heal the breach caused by his education and removal from the working class: "what's still between's / not the thirty or so years, but books, books, books" ("Book-Ends" ll.15–16). The young Harrison won a scholarship to an independent school, read classics at university and not only became a poet but made a living out of writing for the theatre. In the "School of Eloquence" sequence that includes his elegies for his parents he represents this progression as a Faustian pact: one of the poems concludes, quoting Marlowe, *"I'll burn my books"* ("Aqua Mortis" l.16, quoting *Doctor Faustus*, V.ii.184). The "soul" that he has sold is the bond with his origins and especially his family.

In these poems Oedipal conflict is tangential and compromised. In "Currants" the father takes his adolescent son to the bakery where he works "to be 'wi' t'men'." Appropriately to the implied rite of passage, the poem is charged with the sexual imagery of the boy's fantasies: an Eccles cake needs "the currants you could take / in a hand imagined cupped round a girl's breast." The father sweats into the currants then offers some to the boy, who fastidiously rejects them. The father retorts: *"Next Sunday you can stay 'ome wi' yer mother!"* However, unlike Paul Morel in *Sons and Lovers*, the son is not feminized by this failure to identify with the father. He goes on to imagine "grapes, each bunch the weight of a man's balls," and contrast them with the "blackened currants" of his father's cakes (ll.3, 4–5, 16, 27, 31). In "Turns" the son tries on his father's flat cap in the fond hope that it makes him look more "working class" and his mother tells him that the cap suits him. But the poem cuts to his father's death, "sprawled" in the street with his cap "turned inside up beside his head . . . so folk might think / he wanted charity for dropping dead" (ll.1, 8, 9, 11–12). The symbols of paternal (the word "patriarchal" would be absurdly out of place) identity turn out to be signs of emasculation.

Harrison once said in an interview that metrical verse (in which he almost invariably writes) is meaningful to him both ideologically—an "occupation" of the discursive territory of the ruling class—and organically, because it is associated with the rhythms of the body such as the heartbeat (Astley 236). His work is riven by conflict deriving from the question whether he "occupies" poetry on behalf of people like his father or only for himself. Hence self-lacerating lines such as "You're lost in this sonnet for the bourgeoisie" ("Working" l.8), "I'm opening my trap / to busk the class that broke him" ("Turns" ll.14–15) and "I've come round to your position on 'the Arts' / but put it down in poems, that's the bind" ("A Good Read" ll.11–12). Although precursors such as Thomas Gray (whose quatrains in the "Elegy Written in a Country Churchyard" he indefatigably imitates) are important presences in his poems, what they are most haunted by is the language of his origins, and above all his father. The most productive act of "mourning" in the elegies is to bring this language and his own into a relationship that is not merely juxtapositional or even confrontational but creatively dialogic.

Harrison accomplishes this task in a number of poems, perhaps most effectively in "Book Ends," a poem about the friction between father and son when they join in mourning Harrison's mother. Harrison struggles to find words to put on his mother's grave:

> The stone's too full. The wording must be terse.
> There's scarcely room to carve the FLORENCE on it—
>
> *Come on, it's not as if we're wanting verse.*
> *It's not as if we're wanting a whole sonnet!*

(ll.17–20)

The italicized words, attributed to the father, are plausibly vernacular but also consonant with the lexis of the poet in his own person. Most importantly they are iambic pentameter with full rhymes: the father continues the son's meter and completes his rhymes, as he does again with *"You're supposed to be the bright boy at description / and you can't tell them what the fuck to put!"* (ll.27–28). In the immediately following poem, "Confessional Poetry," Harrison asserts that his father's words often did scan, but this isn't really the point (l.8). These are words in which the voices of son and father meet. The son "grants" the father poetic utterance and at the same moment the father grants the son his vigorous vernacular. In contrast to Sacks's model of elegy there is no "cleared distance" between the mourner and the mourned but the closest possible identification (which encompasses conflict) because the "work" of the elegy is less to "decathect" from the dead than to compensate for a failure of connection in life.

In Ted Hughes's elegies for his father the trauma is not the loved one's death but has always been there, and is constitutive of the son's subjectivity. In "Dust as We Are" he calls himself his father's "supplementary convalescent" (l.15) and in "Out" his "luckless double" (l.14). "Dust as We Are" takes its title from the passage in the *Prelude* where Wordsworth celebrates the growth of "the immortal spirit . . . / Like harmony in music" (Book I, 340). Hughes's own soul, by contrast, grew in the shadow of his father's trauma, "A strange thing, with rickets—a hyena. / No singing—that kind of laughter" (ll.37–38). As Harrison finds his most authentic poetic voice in dialogue with his father, so Hughes seems to imply that he is indebted to his father for what he considered his own most authentic voice, that of *Crow*—"songs with no music whatsoever" (Faas 208). The father's actual death doesn't figure in these poems at all, because he was "killed but alive" ("Dust as We Are" l.29), "Dragged bodily from under / The mortised four-year strata of dead Englishmen / He belonged with" and "reassembled" but mentally still "Gripped" to "a time // He no more than they could outgrow" ("Out" ll.10–12, 34, 44–45). Consequently there is no essential difference between "Dust as We Are" and "For the Duration," the formal elegies published in 1989 after the father's death, and "Out" published in 1967.

Oedipal conflict figures even less in these poems than in Harrison's elegies. Nor is there much evidence of the traditional effect of elegy, consolation. There is little if any movement: the poet like his father is "Gripped" by the trauma of the war, his "mind / Stopped with numbness" ("For the Duration" ll.36–37), "nobody / Can ever again move from shelter" ("Out" ll.18–19). "For the Duration" ends with a recollection of his father shouting in nightmare, uttering the horror about which his waking self remained silent:

> The whole hopelessness was still going on,
> No man's land still crying and burning
> Inside our house, and you climbing again
> Out of the trench, and wading back into the glare
>
> As if you might still not manage to reach us
> And carry us to safety.
>
> (ll.41–46)

Ending on this note, with the sequence of present participles, strongly suggests an uncompleted action, just as the title suggests more than the duration of the war itself: certainly the duration of the father's life, perhaps also the son's.

In "Out," the elegy that Hughes wrote when his father was still alive, there are "curses, condemnations, and exorcisms," but the object of these is not the father. The third part of the poem sets the inherited trauma in the context of national mourning on Remembrance Day, and is a vehement rejection of institutionalized mourning and the poppy that is its symbol:

> So goodbye to that bloody-minded flower.
>
> You dead bury your dead.
> Goodbye to the cenotaphs on my mother's breasts.
>
> Goodbye to all the remaindered charms of my father's survival.
> Let England close. Let the green sea-anemone close.
>
> (ll.53–57)

These lines lend themselves to a powerful political reading: rather than putting the war behind us, the custom of Remembrance perpetuates the "bloody-minded" sense of national identity that brought it about in the first place. The final line, with its echoes of Blake's "green and pleasant land" and John of Gaunt's "this England" speech in *Richard II*, is a startling utterance by the future Poet Laureate. But they could equally be an expression of despair at the inefficacy of mourning, a cry of rage and anguish whose hyperbole only betrays the hopelessness. Just as Harrison is attempting to speak on behalf of a whole class, so Hughes's *oeuvre* doesn't represent this hopelessness as a merely personal matter. I have already drawn attention to the way that poems in *Remains of Elmet* show his father's trauma to be paradigmatic of the towns and villages of West Yorkshire where he grew up, and in a broadcast roughly contemporary with the poem "Out" he said, "I can never lose the impression that the whole region is in mourning for the first world war" ("The Rock").

My third example of English paternal elegy, Peter Redgrove's sequence "My Father's Trapdoors," is, like his American precursors, set in a middle-class family, but more closely resembles Harrison's elegies in its compensatory rather than confrontational tendency. In Redgrove however the Oedipal scenario is blatantly, even parodistically on display:

> He could wave his wand casually
> And I would reappear elsewhere;
> Once in bed at ten cuddly with mother
>
> He waved a wand in his voice
> And I got out of the silken double-cabinet
> For ever.

(ll.67–72)

The phallic imagery has both Freudian and Lacanian reference, but it is generated by the central image of the father as a conjurer, who has the ability to transitively "disappear" his son by besetting him with "trapdoors" like those used to engineer disappearances on a stage. This oppressive power is, in the poem, the defining characteristic of masculinity, which the poet has resisted during his father's life but tries to make his peace with in mourning.

The poem's middle-class context is made clear in the first section, which narrates the father seeing the son off to boarding school at the station, and surprising him by taking him "behind the newsprint" to "kiss me hard . . . his kiss was hungry and a total surprise." The son has already been feminized by his grief at being sent away—"I was a vase of flowing tears"—and the sudden expression of love from the stereotypically masculine father—"He wore a hard white collar and a tight school tie / And a bristly moustache"—only confirms his feminine identification, which is asserted with three emphatic negatives: he "did not belong / Not to father, no" (ll.1–11).

In the second section the rejected masculinity is exemplified by the father's "magical" and socially inscribed powers of playing golf, winning at cards and accumulating trophies for sport and public speaking. They signify powers that the son cannot aspire to emulate but also, by implication, inauthenticity: the father's "magic" is a matter of conjuring tricks and when he dies he leaves "Only material for a funeral" (l.26). The bereaved son wanders around the father's house looking for traces of him but finds only poignantly contingent objects: fluff and dust, obsolete sixpences, a corroded watch and a dental plate. The father has "disappeared" himself just as he used to disappear his son, but the son is "not a woman or a little boy," he gives "rough kisses" himself and needs to make peace with the idea of masculinity by imaginatively resolving his relationship with his father (ll.74–75). Thus, though the ideological and social context is completely different, the structure of mourning is the same as in Harrison's elegies. The poem ends with an image of this resolution, when the resurrected father emerges from the conjurer's magic cabinet, not in the hard collar and school tie, nor in the conjurer's evening dress, but

> in the buff and happy as Jesus save that
> His lean rod is floating out just as it should,
> Floating like my own, pleased to be like him.

(ll.120–22)

Poetic Partners: Ted Hughes, Penelope Shuttle

The paternal elegies I have discussed suggest that elegizing—and the mourning that it represents—is not necessarily, in Peter Sacks's words, a "withdrawal of affection . . . and a subsequent reattachment . . . to some substitute" (6). Hughes's *Birthday Letters* is an even more striking case in point: this sequence, written over a period of thirty-five years, reads like a deliberate commitment to Freudian "melancholia." The cases have something in common: Harrison and Redgrove are trying to make a connection with their fathers that they feel was lacking in life, and in Harrison's case there is an element of guilt in the estrangement for which he is compensating. This is *a fortiori* the case with Hughes's elegies for Sylvia Plath. Sacks writes that elegy often staves off self-directed anger and deflects guilt "which if unalleviated would drag him towards melancholy. The so frequent formulaic Where were you? may thus mask the more dangerous Where was I?" (22) There is no such masking in *Birthday Letters*. The poem "The Machine" takes its title from an entry in Plath's journal, written at Cambridge in 1956, after her first meeting with Hughes, when she knew he was in town, recording her anguish at waiting for him to call on her

> While I was just sitting,
> . . . no more purpose in me
> Than in my own dog.
>
> (ll.10–12)

The sequence never directly confronts the moment of Plath's death, but this poem's conclusion implicitly conflates his (in reality innocent) absence from Plath in Cambridge with his absence when she took her life, acknowledging guilt but displacing it:

> my life
> Forever trying to climb the steps now stone
> Towards the door now red
> Which you, in your own likeness, would open
> With still time to talk.
>
> (ll.25–29)

The steps of her student lodgings in Cambridge are silently transmuted to those of the London flat in which she took her life seven years later. "Forever" makes clear the melancholic nature of the poem.

Elegy as recently theorized is a genre in which contests rage on or beneath the surface. Ramazani speaks of "the poet's aggressive bid for literary ascendancy" (228) and Sacks writes that "Few elegies can be fully read without an appreciation of their frequently combative struggles for inheritance" (37). While Hughes, who claimed that *Birthday Letters* was a way of making "direct, private, inner contact" with Plath, would deny that either kind of contest is in play, the intensely agonistic context of Plath biography into which it was launched almost forces the book into a contestatory role (Wagner 22). The literal inheritance of Plath's literary estate is one obviously relevant issue; ownership of what Hughes called "the facts of . . . his own life" is another (Hughes, *Independent* 19). Linda Wagner-Martin, for example, described *Birthday Letters* as an "affront" because in it Hughes had "argued with the narrative [Plath's] poems had created; he had set himself the task of correcting the story her writing had told" (148).

Hughes believed that his own poetic development had been blighted by his failure to write an account of his relationship with Plath earlier in his life. Plath's own celebrity as a poet is critical to this failure. As her fame grew Hughes's own role in her life, death, and literary career came under increasingly hostile public scrutiny. From literal accusations of murder to questioning of his right to her literary estate, the context in which such an account might be written and published came to resemble a courtroom. A relationship which had been, for most of its existence, a personal and literary partnership, was publicly construed as one of mutual hostility. All of this happened, of course, in the wider context of gender politics. Whether he wished it or not, anything Hughes wrote about Plath would be interpreted as an intervention in a debate which he mostly despised. Whether or not Hughes might have written earlier and differently if he had not been placed in this bind, the style and manner of *Birthday Letters* respond in obvious ways to this agonistic context.

Another way in which elegy has been construed as a contest is what David Kennedy describes as "self-conscious performance in which the elegist asserts his own poetic skill and becomes a part of a pre-existent tradition or lineage of similarly skilled poets" (13). The frequent use of Plath's titles and quotation from her poems might make *Birthday Letters* seem an example of such a contest, but as Edward Hadley has argued this is not so. Hughes deliberately withdraws from emulation, aiming at a style that is "so raw, so vulnerable, so unprocessed, so naive, so self-exposing & unguarded, so without any of the niceties that any poetry workshop student could have helped me to" (*Letters* 72). This style serves a number of functions. Lack of literary finesse has the rhetorical effect of sincerity, conforming to Hughes's notion of "direct, private, inner contact." It also absolves Hughes from the suspicion of competing with Plath, of attempting to break the control that her celebrity has over his life by proving himself the better poet. The use of direct apostrophic address in most of the poems also has an implicitly polemical purpose. To refer to Plath in the third person would be to address his words to an audience composed partly of his antagonists. There is the occasional outburst against these antagonists, in the manner of Milton's "blind mouths" ("Lycidas" l.119), in poems such as "The Dogs Are Eating Your Mother," but such poems seem out of place in the predominant atmosphere of rapt communion and memory. The polemic is more effectively conducted by means of the closed circle of communion, with results such as, "Remember how we picked the daffodils? / Nobody else remembers, but I remember" ("Daffodils" ll.1–2). What I have called a deliberate commitment to melancholia may also be seen as a response to this context.

What is perhaps more at stake than anything else in *Birthday Letters* is the right to mourn Plath. This could hardly be established by a text that enacted the withdrawal and reinvestment of libido.

If Hughes doesn't attempt to emulate Plath poetically, *Birthday Letters* is of course dense with allusions to and quotations from her writing. What do these engagements signify about *Birthday Letters* as an act of mourning? I will focus on what is perhaps the most highly charged example, "The Rabbit Catcher."

Plath's poem of this title is itself an engagement with an earlier poem by a writer admired by both herself and Hughes: D.H. Lawrence's "Love on the Farm." Lawrence's poem is a dramatic monologue in the voice of a farmer's wife awaiting the return of her husband, who arrives with a dead rabbit that he has snared. It culminates in a highly eroticized self-identification of the speaker with the dead rabbit. Several details of Plath's poem clearly allude to this precursor: "Tight wires between us" and "a mind like a ring / Sliding shut on some quick thing" to "the wire ring / Her frantic effort throttling" and "what fine wire is round my throat"; and above all "How they awaited him, those little deaths! / They waited like sweethearts. They excited him" to "so I drown / Against him, die, and find death good." As the final example makes clear, Plath's poem is a critique of rather than an indulgence in the identification of sex and death, but it would be natural, in this intertextual context, to read it as also a dramatic monologue (Plath ll.26–28, 24–25; Lawrence ll.40–41, 59, 67–68).

However, Plath's "Rabbit Catcher" is in several ways one of the most highly charged of her poems in the biographical and textual narratives that haunted Hughes. It is one of the poems in Plath's original *Ariel* that Hughes omitted on the grounds of being too "personally aggressive." Clearly he didn't read it as a dramatic monologue. It was one of only two poems (with "Event") that he said he resented for taking "her sudden discovery of our bad moments" as subjects (Malcolm 143). It was written the day after the visit of Assia and David Wevill to Court Green, the occasion when, according to another *Birthday Letters* poem, Hughes fell in love with Assia. It was also the subject of a bizarre public quarrel with Jacqueline Rose, who read suggestions of lesbian sexual activity into Plath's lines about hair gagging the mouth and tasting the gorse: "such fantasies, such points of uncertainty, are the regular unconscious subtexts—for all of us—of the more . . . obvious narratives of stable sexual identity" (138). Hughes was so outraged by this that he took the, for him, unusual step of writing a letter of protest to the *Times Literary Supplement*: "Professor Rose distorts, reinvents etc Sylvia Plath's 'sexual identity' with an abandon I could hardly believe— presenting her in a role that I vividly felt to be humiliating to Sylvia Plath's children."

All of these occasions concerning Plath's "Rabbit Catcher" are revealing of Hughes's way of engaging with Plath's poetry in *Birthday Letters*. As a poststructuralist critic Rose had no notion of speculating about Plath's actual sexual identity. She is insistent in her book that the "Plath" and "Hughes" of whom she writes are textual, not biographical entities. But Hughes was no more capable of seeing the poem in that way than he was of seeing it as a dramatic monologue. He was upset by the poem because of the way it used a "bad moment" between them and excluded it from *Ariel* presumably for this reason. His own "Rabbit Catcher" consists mostly of a narration of the incident that prompted Plath's poem, a day that began with Plath in an inexplicably bad mood: "What had I done?" (4). To the reader who knows when Plath wrote the poem this seems astonishingly dishonest, until we reflect that he is focusing not on the poem but on the incident, which presumably occurred sometime earlier. For him the poems are not merely texts but the (often highly problematic) creative outcome of life-events that were also events in his own life. Thus he sets himself apart from readers for whom the poems can *only* be texts.

There are moments in *Birthday Letters* when Hughes figures poetry as a destructive element in Plath's life and their marriage. "Flounders" for example narrates a day of boating adventure in New England which was "a toy miniature / Of the life that might have bonded us":

> It was a visit from the goddess, the beauty
> Who was poetry's sister—she had come
> To tell poetry she was spoiling us.
>
> (ll.48–53)

The allegorical personification is rather dusty but the implication that, as Keith Sagar puts it, "the imperatives of poetry and those of survival, or at least of a successful marriage . . . are . . . mutually exclusive" (71) is, for a writer so apparently dedicated to poetry as Hughes, startling. This implication is also at work in "The Rabbit Catcher."

Hughes's poem focuses on a family day out, when Plath discovered snares that had been set for rabbits and tore them up in rage, crying "Murderers!" Hughes in turn is appalled by this destruction of what he calls

> precious saplings
> Of my heritage, hard-won concessions
> From the hangings and the transportations
> To live off the land.
>
> (ll.59–62)

To the reader of Plath's poem however this background is likely to be irrelevant. The response to Lawrence, and the metaphor of the noose for an oppressive sexual relationship, are much more important than any judgment about the actual morality of snaring rabbits. The most startling move in Hughes's poem is that he represents Plath's poetry as *itself* predatory: "In those snares / You'd caught something" (ll.67–68). What it was she had caught seems comparatively unimportant: Hughes is uncertain whether it was something in himself, unknown to him, or her own "doomed self." "Whichever…" he continues, implying that the identity of the victim is less important than the predatory activity itself:

> Those terrible, hypersensitive
> Fingers of your verse closed around it and
> Felt it alive. The poems, like smoking entrails,
> Came soft into your hands.
>
> (ll.71–74)

In this strange metaphor the "verse" is figured as the predator, like a bird of prey drawing from the body of its victim the "entrails" which are the poems. The poems are thus implicitly pre-existing entities devoured by the verse. Hughes's poem thus places the readers of Plath's poetry in the position of witnesses of a macabre death-ritual, while he has unique access to the lived reality of their relationship. As a guide to reading Plath this is intolerable, but as the maneuvering of someone who has to battle for his own right to mourn it is compellingly moving.

The combination of circumstances that make *Birthday Letters* such an embattled melancholic text is unique and unlikely to be repeated, but as an elegy for a poetic partner it is not unique. Penelope Shuttle's *Redgrove's Wife* consists mainly of a sequence mourning Peter Redgrove, her partner for thirty-three years, who died in 2003. Like Hughes's mourning for Plath, Shuttle's for Redgrove has a public as well as a private aspect, but in this case, though the public may intensify the private, it doesn't conflict with it or, as it does with Hughes, enforce a melancholic text. Much of the volume's engagement with the mourning of poetic partnership is encoded in the startling title, which has a number of subtle facets. Shuttle was indeed Redgrove's wife for many years, but she had also as a feminist resisted marriage and had only become a legal wife for the convenience of shared property ownership. There is thus a certain doubleness about the title, a shimmer of irony: who is "Redgrove's Wife" (Shuttle 10)? Is she identical to Penelope Shuttle, and to the author of these poems? The question is emphasized by the double-voiced, question-and-answer form of the title poem:

> Pity Redgrove's Wife?
> I think not.
>
> Praise Redgrove's Wife?
> Why not? . . .
>
> Publish Redgrove's Wife?
> I shall not.
>
> (*But I shall.*)
>
> (ll.1–12)

In this poem the speaker wryly negotiates various aspects of her relationship not only to Redgrove but to the person signified by the title. She was not only the private married person but also partner in a number of public enterprises including several jointly authored books. Though she was an equal partner in these enterprises she was somewhat in the shadow of Redgrove's more flamboyant literary personality: another flicker of irony in the title. The poem was written when Redgrove was still alive, but its publication in a collection of elegies points up the difference between Redgrove's wife and Redgrove's widow: a third category of difference.

Most of the elegies, in stark contrast to *Birthday Letters*, make little reference to the specifics of the relationship. One way in which they might be said to do the work of mourning is by articulating grief as commonplace, so that a reader who was him- or herself also grieving could *identify* with the speaker, in a way that would be out of the question with Hughes's poems:

> I wept in Tesco
> Sainsburys
> and in Boots

> where they gave me
> medicine for grief

> But I wept in Asda
> in Woolworths
> and in the library

> where they gave me
> books on grief.
>
>   ("Missing You" 2, ll.1–10)

Even though many of these poems are addressed to the lost loved one, they do not, like Hughes's, construct an exclusive dialogue, but invite the reader to recognize that he/she has been or will be in exactly the same situation. Nevertheless, the fact that Shuttle has lost more than a privately loved partner, that she is also bereft of part of her poet self, is implied in lines such as these:

> Think of me without you,
> stuck here forever between rainless May
> and the drought of June.
>
>   ("Missing You" 16, ll.12–14)

Even though the title may nod towards a rueful sense of being known as the secondary member of a partnership, there is no sense of poetic rivalry in *Redgrove's Wife*. One poem can however be construed as a stylistic image of Redgrove, and a reaccentuation of his gender ideology. The poem "Dukedom" is written in a more luxuriantly sensuous style than Shuttle's norm, which sounds like a conscious or unconscious imitation of Redgrove poems such as "The Case" and "Six Odes":

> He folds me in his septembers worked
> in ivory silk, in his seascapes of living memory.
> He wraps me in his dukedom
> of windfall, godfinch and peach.
> He inflicts his dukedom on me like dew on a fountain,
> like a year of consents,
> like a lily merchant.
>
> He brings me a list of colours ranked in order of sleep.
>
> (ll.5–12)

Redgrove was known as a celebrator of the feminine in humanity and nature: of nature as the "Goddess," in poems such as "The Idea of Entropy at Maenporth Beach," "Six Odes," and "The Quiet Woman of Chancery Lane." In this poem Shuttle takes one of most traditional motifs of elegiac poetry, the rebirth of the vegetation god, and identifies it with Redgrove both stylistically and by a knowing reversal of his gendering of nature. This is perhaps the poem in which the work of mourning is most creatively performed.

Self-Elegy: Peter Reading

An important sub-genre to which Ramazani pays a lot of attention is self-elegy. In poets as varied as Wallace Stevens, Langston Hughes, Auden, and Plath, he finds modern self-elegies to be "often more compensatory than elegies proper, stemming no doubt from a salutary residue of narcissism yet also suggesting an important exception to the [dominant] melancholic tendency" (30). One late twentieth-century poet, Peter Reading, has almost made self-elegy his definitive genre (he has published books titled *Final Demands*, *Last Poems*, and *Ob.*) but fewer poets have more strenuously resisted compensation, above all the compensation of poetry itself: "Medic and poetaster glibly / (equally impotent platituders) / tender inadequate barbs" (*Final Demands*, in Reading 142). Reading's persona is someone who obsessively consoles himself by writing poetry, in the full knowledge that the consolation is empty. He fills books with meticulous imitations of classical meters and, in his most impressive middle period, elaborately constructed narratives, that are dedicated to their own futility. The death of the poet in books such as *Final Demands* brooks no consolation because it is itself a trope for the death of humanity. His whole *oeuvre* can be seen as a prolonged elegy for the idea of humanity as anything other than a destructive organism (which he sarcastically refers to as "*H. sap.*") wreaking havoc in a brief moment of geological time:

> Love it, love its fossil skull-splitting cudgel,
>   love it, love its anti-tank-grenade launcher,
>   love it, love its neo-pongoid theological tenets.
>   (*Going On*, in Reading 78, ll.893–95)

At one point the persona claims that his poetry is beyond elegy:

> What after Elegy? Callous de-
> tachment feigning concern for
> Post-Elegiac and Post-
> Post Elegiac *H. Sap.* . .
>
>   (ll.531–34)

However, the dominant tone of the poetry is not "callous detachment" but alternating rage and despair, usually expressed in grimly comic terms, what he calls the "slick prestidigital art of Not Caring / Hopelessly Caring" (*Going On*, epigraph, 5). "Not Caring" is an intellectual attitude consistent with the recognition that *H. sap* is a temporary organism; "Hopelessly Caring" is the inescapable consequence of being a member of the species.

Reading's poetry is mostly written in imitations of various classical meters. Appropriately enough his favorite meter is the elegiac distich. This practice compares interestingly with Harrison's devotion to traditional English meter. Harrison's practice, as mentioned above, combines a conscious and ideologically motivated allusion to the canon of English poetry with a humanist belief that poetic rhythm is inherently valuable because it echoes the rhythms of the human body. Neither Reading nor most of his readers are directly familiar with Latin and Greek poetry, so his meters have no direct intertextual force, in the way that Harrison's iambic quatrains do. Their most overt function is to emphasize what he calls the "ludic" character of poetry, one of the central tropes of his *oeuvre* being the idea that, even as the poet refers obsessively to war, social breakdown, environmental catastrophe, and his own inevitable death, the writing of poems about such matters is a distracting game.

However, in the most elaborate and coherent of his elegiac works, *Final Demands*, Reading makes striking use of Harrison's "humanist" sense of meter to produce a text that is an elegy for itself as well as its author and humanity at large. The central device of this book is the discovery of old letters by dead writers who "survive" only in the fragmentary narratives of this correspondence. Reading emphasizes the fragile materiality of these letters by printing them in a cursive script and attributing gaps in the text to "foxing"—a device that he takes further in texts such as *Perduta Gente* and

Evagatory, which include reproductions of actual handwriting and found material, sometimes illegibly smudgy. *Final Demands* opens with the author/protagonist experiencing "Crapulous death-fright" and, via an extended comparison with Homer's Odysseus landing on the Phaeacian coast and covering himself with dead leaves, he "sinks in the lines of the dead" (119). The author is half-erased from the text by the uncertainty about how much of it is "found," and the Homeric comparison inaugurates a parallel between the "dead leaves" of old writing and literal fallen leaves, in the recurring hemistiches, "frail wisps of dead bestraked leaves," "crackle of anhydrous bay" and "Croxley papyrus and bond." On the final page of the text these phrases are repeated, detached from context, like fallen leaves themselves, with the metrical pattern of the hemistich marked (a familiar way of Reading "laying bare the device"), followed by the pattern on its own, the borrowed structure that has sustained so much of Reading's poetry, devoid of words, like Harrison's heartbeat going on after speech has failed; finally the pattern is repeated and struck out, as if not only the poet but the poem has died (158).

This examination of some notable English practitioners of elegy has reinforced some established critical positions on the subject, such as the dubious value of Freud's normative distinction between mourning and melancholia (the "melancholic" character of Hughes's, Harrison's, and in a different way Reading's texts is necessary to the end these poets wish to achieve) and the tendency of modern poets to resist compensation. However, we have seen that compensation is still a possible element even in the most Oedipal of elegies such as Redgrove's "My Father's Trapdoors," and that the aggressive characteristics of American paternal elegists are not imitated by their English counterparts, especially when it is the life rather than the death of the father that is being mourned, above all in a working-class context. One matter on which all critics agree is that elegy is a genre which answers to one of the profoundest and most permanent human needs, and as such is it likely to continue to challenge any totalizing account of it.

REFERENCES AND FURTHER READING

Astley, Neil (ed.). *Bloodaxe Critical Anthologies I: Tony Harrison*, Newcastle upon Tyne, Bloodaxe. 1991.

Faas, Ekbert. *Ted Hughes: The Unaccommodated Universe*, Santa Barbara, Black Sparrow Press. 1980.

Hadley, Edward. *The Elegies of Ted Hughes*, Basingstoke, Palgrave Macmillan. 2010.

Harrison, Tony. *Selected Poems*, Harmondsworth, Penguin. 1984.

Hughes, Ted. "First, Mills," *Collected Poems*, London, Faber. 2003. 462–63.

Hughes, Ted. Letter to editor, Times Literary Supplement, April 24, 1992. 15.

Hughes, Ted. "The Rock," *The Listener*, 70, September 19. 141–43. 1963.

Hughes, Ted. "Sylvia Plath: The Facts of Her Life and the Desecration of Her Grave," *The Independent*, April 22, 1989. 19.

Hughes, Ted. *Winter Pollen: Occasional Prose*, London, Faber. 1994.

Hughes, Ted. *Letters of Ted Hughes*, ed. Christopher Reid, London, Faber. 2007.

Kennedy, David. *Elegy*, Abingdon, Routledge. 2007.

Lawrence, D.H. *The Complete Poems of D.H. Lawrence*, Vol.1, London, Heinemann. 1964.

Malcolm, Janet. *The Silent Woman: Sylvia Plath and Ted Hughes*, London, Picador. 1994.

Plath, Sylvia. *Collected Poems*, London, Faber. 1981.

Plath, Sylvia. *The Journals of Sylvia Plath 1950– 1962*, ed. Karen Kukil, London, Faber. 2000.

Ramazani, Jahan. *Poetry of Mourning: the Modern Elegy from Hardy to Heaney*, Chicago, Chicago University Press. 1994.

Reading, Peter. *Collected Poems II: Poems 1985– 1996*, Newcastle upon Tyne, Bloodaxe. 1996.

Redgrove, Peter. *My Father's Trapdoors*, London, Cape. 1994.

Rose, Jacqueline. *The Haunting of Sylvia Plath*, London, Virago. 1992.

Sacks, Peter. *The English Elegy: Studies in the Genre from Spenser to Yeats*, Baltimore, Johns Hopkins University Press. 1985.

Sagar, Keith. *The Laughter of Foxes: A Study of Ted Hughes*, Liverpool, Liverpool University Press. 2000.

Shuttle, Penelope. *Redgrove's Wife*, Newcastle upon Tyne, Bloodaxe. 2006.

Wagner, Erica. *Ariel's Gift*, London, Faber. 2000.

Wagner-Martin, Linda. *Sylvia Plath: A Literary Life*, 2nd edn., Basingstoke and New York, Palgrave Macmillan. 2003.

7

The Self-Elegy

Narcissistic Nostalgia or Proleptic Postmortem?

Eve C. Sorum

The self-elegy has functioned as the implicit, but often elided, younger sibling of the elegy. Unlike the elegy, it does not suggest the same ethical high-ground of mourning for a lost other, providing order to sorrow and a path towards consolation, even if unresolved. Instead the self-elegy is often seen as a deeply narcissistic poetic form, one that requires the poet to take the place of both mourner and mourned, foregoing that essential element in an ethical relationship: imagining yourself in relation to an other (Spargo 7). And yet we can also see this form as exemplifying the ultimate act of poetic imagination, one in which the poet must make the terrifying leap to think him or herself dead (Vendler 35). The struggle between these two responses to the form is, in fact, at the heart of the tension that is most defining within self-elegies— what Jahan Ramazani calls the "form's central perplexity" (*Yeats* 136)—that the poem must exist in a state of self-reflexivity in which the poetic voice always grapples with its predicated absence. Some central elements of the self-elegy emerge from this tension. First, self-elegy always foregrounds, whether implicitly or explicitly, the question of the relationship between the poet and his or her poems. That relationship is not fixed: the poem may attempt to divorce the (imagined dead) poet from the texts that remain, or it might envision the merging of the two—the poet living on through the poetry. Similarly, self-elegies often grapple with two conflicting desires: the wish to be remembered and missed, versus the hope that those left behind will not suffer. Unlike with the traditional elegy, which functions as a monument and a sign that the mourned is *not* forgotten, self-elegy is always proleptic and, therefore, uncertain about its status as memorial.

While this essay will focus on examples from the Anglo-American poetic tradition, the genre has its roots centuries back; indeed, we could locate some of the most powerful lyric passages of self-elegizing in Sappho's fragments: "Someone, I tell you, / will

A Companion to Poetic Genre, First Edition. Edited by Erik Martiny.
© 2012 John Wiley & Sons, Ltd. Published 2012 by John Wiley & Sons, Ltd.

remember us" (ll.1–2), she reassuringly writes. If we turn to a seminal poet in the Anglophone tradition, William Shakespeare, we see an elaboration on this theme of continuance through verse, though now infused with an element of unease. Standing at the center of Shakespeare's sonnet sequence, sonnets 71–74 perform a self-elegiac function within the larger narrative of the love story. In this set of four poems, the poet traverses the two trajectories central to the self-elegy: one that charts the kinds of relationships that might exist between poet and poem, and the other that maps the movements between remembrance and forgetting. Sonnet 71, the most famous of the four, appears to set us firmly on one end of the spectrum, both forbidding mourning ("No longer mourn for me when I am dead" [l.1]) and distancing the poet from his poem ("remember not, / the hand that writ it" [ll.5–6]). Yet ambivalence about these imperatives is built into the very lines that present them: with his reiteration of first-person pronouns—there are ten combined uses of "I" and "me" in this fourteen-line poem, alongside the use of "my" twice—Shakespeare does not, in fact, let the reader forget about the presence of the poet. Such rhetorical protestations emerge most playfully in the parenthetical asides of lines 9 and 10. In the first instance, the speaker uses the interruption to insert himself and, even more importantly, his voice into the reader's consciousness, adding the "(I say)" (l.9) just before he imagines the reader looking at this poem. The second aside goes even further in asserting the poet's presence, with a "perhaps" inserted into a line that imagines the poet merging with the earth. Not only does the poet suggest his continued life in the words on the page, but he also questions the inevitability of his own bodily decay.

This movement towards asserting the presence of the poet and the power of his verse as legacy continues in the sonnets that follow. While sonnet 72 elaborates upon the same theme of urging the beloved to forget the poet after death, it still inserts the idea of the inverse occurring: the beloved engaging in a hyperbolic praising and lauding of the dead poet. Sonnet 73, which famously begins "That time of year that thou mayest in me behold" (l.1), changes the focus slightly, instead arguing that the very idea of the poet's death increases the beloved's love. The terms of Shakespeare's self-elegies transform at this point, for death becomes the source of deepened and renewed love, rather than of potential decay of that love. This move leads the way, therefore, toward the final self-elegy in the cycle, sonnet 74. Here the body of the poet gives way to the body of the poem, which thereby becomes part of an economy of memory and recognition. Within this value system, "my life hath in this line some interest" (l.3), and this double form of interest—both intellectual concern and economic payment—will remain with the beloved and the reader "for memorial" (l.4). The complicated switching of worth between body and verse is signaled by the tongue-twistingly alliterative impersonal pronouns in the final line, which enact the complex merging of poet's body, poem, and beloved: "And that is this, and this with thee remains" (l.14). "That" here refers to the poem ("this"), which is contained in the "that" of the preceding lines—the poet's wretched and rotting body. Shakespeare's poem is what stays with the beloved, the pun in the final word suggests, as the ultimate remains of the poet's body.

With this move into self-elegy as a literalization of the poetic corpse, we can sense two possible tonal endpoints for the form: parody or anguished lamentation. The first is carried to its extreme in Jonathan Swift's "Verses on the Death of Dr. Swift" (written 1731; published 1739), which addresses one of the more troublesome issues of the self-elegy—the inherent egotism involved in making oneself the subject of the elegy. At first the poem seems simply to parody the genre, as the poet imagines his friends mourning more because of their fear that his death portends their own demise, than from any great sadness. Insouciantly, Swift writes, "Why do we grieve that Friends should dye? / No Loss is more easy to supply" (ll.243–44), and he proceeds to imagine the disappearance of his books from shops and his memory from the public's mind—closely linking the life of the body with the life of the text. Yet this critic of mourning points to a different function for the parodic and anticipatory self-elegy: that of setting the record straight. Swift uses the device of the impartial observer who, as "One quite indiff'rent in the Cause, / My Character impartial draws" (ll.305–06). For the remaining lines, almost two hundred of them, this authorized voice paints a much more sympathetic picture of Swift, a version that implies how Swift would, in fact, like to be remembered. In particular, Swift's inclusion of footnotes that both explain his reference to contemporaneous events and excoriate his attackers gesture to the kind of control (ostensibly posthumous, though it was actually published before his death) that he hoped to exert on future readers.

Nineteenth-century poets move to the other end of the tonal scale by infusing the self-elegy with a more overt anguish and eschewing the satiric self-fashioning seen in Swift. One such adaptation of the form can be seen in Keats's sonnets, which anticipate and reflect on his own death. Tellingly, we see these moments of self-elegy often when Keats is reflecting on an encounter with a work of art or literature. In these cases, in fact, experiencing the sublimity of the artwork directly leads the poet to an alternate catalyst of the sublime—fear of death. Manifesting more awareness of the impact of great art than anxiety about his own poetic legacy, Keats's lines "On Seeing the Elgin Marbles" suggest that viewing these freizes inspires thoughts of impending death: "each imagin'd pinnacle and steep / Of godlike hardship, tells me I must die" (ll.3–4). Similarly, in "On Sitting Down to Read King Lear Once Again," the experience of reading the play, described by Keats as "the fierce dispute" (l.5) that "Must I burn through" (l.7), provides an analogy for his own death: "when I am consumed in the fire" (l.13). The transformative encounter with Shakespeare's drama mirrors what Keats hopes will happen in death, as he imagines how the consuming fire might "Give me new Phoenix wings to fly at my desire" (l.14). Keats's sensuous exploration of the relationship between these two sublimes—his own death and an encounter with art—leads us to feel, as Marjorie Levinson writes, that "we are watching a man fondle his own mortality" (l.250). By presenting these ecstatic links between aesthetic experience and his own mortality, Keats is able to transform his death into a final poetic act. Questions of memory and recognition fade, therefore, since the act itself proves unforgettable and transformative. Of course, the pleas at the end of "On Sitting Down to Read King Lear Once Again" ("Let me"; "Give me," Keats implores) remind us that such a transformation is not guaranteed. The somber inverse of this aesthetic and corporal merging comes out in the sonnet "When I have fears that I may cease to be," in which the poet confronts leaving work unfinished, love unfulfilled. Keats tempers his quiet despair through an act of imaginative immersion: "on the shore / Of the wide world I stand alone, and think / Till love and fame to nothingness do sink" (ll.12–14). The ambiguity of where this thought-act resolves suggests the mental torture involved in confronting one's own death; instead of thought leading to creation or transcendence, it leads here to submersion, sinking, and disappearance of the self from the "wide world."

Such evaporation of the self reaches its apotheosis in Christina Rossetti's "Song" ("When I am dead, my dearest" [1848; first published 1862 in *Goblin Market and Other Poems*]). Along with the sonnet "Remember" (1849), also in *Goblin Market*, "Song" presents a version of self-elegy that evades the writerly anxiety evinced by Keats, Swift, and Shakespeare. Instead, in "Song" the poet renounces her claim on memory, telling the reader to "Sing no sad songs for me" (l.2). While "Remember" begins with a plea against being forgotten—"Remember me when I am gone away" (l.1)—it ends by reassuring the reader that it is "Better by far you should forget and smile" (l.13). Of course, to take both of these calls for amnesia simply at face value would belie the ambivalence and self-reflexivity that we have seen as inherent to the self-elegy form thus far. Indeed, the last lines of "Song" reveal that this process of forgetting is one anticipated for both reader *and* poet: "Haply *I* may remember / And haply may forget" (ll.15–16, my emphasis). Despite the seeming insouciance about memorialization, Rossetti's use of the conditional "may" in the last lines points to an implicit uncertainty about the issue of memory after death. While Rossetti's faith allows for a poetic power that emanates from the "omniscient view of a hypothetical afterlife" (Raymond 174), she still struggles with the effects of such absence. Thus, although she tells her mourners to abstain from "sad songs," she imparts this order through her own final sad song about all that she will not experience. That central self-reflexive tension of the self-elegy reemerges even in the face of a belief in a desirable afterlife.

While Rossetti's lyrics, despite their latent struggles with absence, still work to familiarize the experience of death, Emily Dickinson's contemporaneous pieces portray a destabilizing and unfamiliar afterworld that radically contrasts with the domesticated version in American sentimental poetry of the period (Farland 369). In poems like "Because I could not stop for Death" (poem 712) and "I died for Beauty" (poem 449), Dickinson neither exults in the omniscience that death provides (like Rossetti in "Remember") nor reads loss in light of a particular relationship (like Shakespeare, for example). Instead, the posthumous voice in Dickinson exists in an anonymous world, dwelling upon the alienation inherent in mortality. Thus "Because I could not stop for Death," which at first seems to describe the experience of death as a pleasant excursion for which the speaker "had put away / My labor and my leisure too" (ll.6–7), becomes unsettling in the movement from the third to the fourth stanzas, when the speaker realizes that her sense of time has been radically upended: "We passed the

Setting Sun // Or rather—He passed Us—" (ll.12–13). Following this insight, the tone shifts, and we become aware of the lack of solace in the death that Dickinson envisions. Instead of ending in a celestial paradise, death here leads to internment underground. The process of death—that moment of realization that the journey was "toward Eternity" (l.24)—is equally demystified and characterized by its excruciating duration, rendering it an experience too much in time, even while on the way to the timelessness of afterlife.

In many ways Dickinson can be seen as ushering the self-elegy into its modernist phase, in which the form, with its exploration of the breakdown between subject and object, mourner and mourned, melds self-reflection and self-annihilation. The modernist self-elegy both emerges from and illuminates contemporary concerns about rituals of mourning and the authority of the poetic voice. Such problems are fully explored in the poems of Thomas Hardy. In "Afterwards" (1915), for example, Hardy directly asks how he will be remembered, most stanzas functioning as a variation on the same question: "will the neighbors say, / 'He was a man who used to notice such things'?" (ll.3–4). Hardy roots this questioning in the idea of perception—how he was perceived before death, how he perceived the world, and how he will be perceived after death. Each stanza begins with the moment of Hardy's death—asking, for example, "And will any say when my bell of quittance is heard in the gloom" (l.17) at the start of the final stanza. This repetition initiates a cyclical return to the moment of death when self-elegy becomes the only viable poetic mode. Yet it is not simply a preoccupation with an original point of loss that defines this poem; it is also deeply concerned with the different ways that his death might be described, all different rhetorical variations on the event: "When the Present has latched its postern" (l.1), "in the dusk when, like an eyelid's soundless blink" (l.5), "If I pass" (l.9), "I have been stilled at last" (l.13), and that "bell of quittance" (l.17). With these rehearsals of the appropriate poetic language for his own end, Hardy transforms his death and memorialization into linguistic and poetic acts, and signals his anxiety about the form such language should take. Here, once again, we confront the tension between narcissistic and transcendent versions of self-elegy.

Ramazani notes, "all modern writing may be covertly self-elegiac" (*Poetry* 215), and both Hardy and W.B. Yeats's poetry substantiates this pronouncement. Where Hardy is interrogative, however, trying to shape our memory of him without such shaping becoming clear, Yeats is aggressive, staking his claims in his self-elegies and confronting head-on the issue of memorialization. Ramazani has discussed in depth the different versions of self-elegy that Yeats wrote throughout his career, beginning with versions that enact the deaths of earlier poetic selves in order to bring the latest poetic persona to the fore (*Yeats* 137–45). Later in life, Yeats adopted a more definitively self-elegiac mode, using the imperative voice in poems like "Under Ben Bulben" (1938) to challenge the supremacy of death over poetic authority. This poem, which he put first in his last collection (published posthumously, first in another order and then restored to his desired sequence), presents a series of commands—"Swear by what the Sages spoke" (l.1), "Know that when all words are said" (l.27), "Irish poets learn your trade" (l.68)—that gesture to Yeats's overwhelming urge to thrust himself and his poetry "Back in the human mind again" (l.24). The poem asserts the power of art to "Bring the soul of man to God / Make him fill the cradles right" (ll.40–41), and it goes even further in the final stanza by making the poem into a literal inscription from beyond the grave. Here the poet appears in the third person, being acted upon ("Yeats is laid" [l.85]), but his power over the poetic language only strengthens in this posthumous position. His final order, though distanced by the third person, is given in the present tense: "By his command these words are cut" (l.91). The words that he wills into being place Yeats in a position of authority over death, for they focus on how we perceive death, ordering us to "Cast a cold eye / On life, on death." (ll.92–94).

Such bombastic certitude about the ability of the poet to look equally on life and death resonates with the project of modern poetry as defined by writers like T.E. Hulme and Ezra Pound, who argued for a spare and clear-eyed version of verse. And yet Yeats does not end there. While he begins his last collection with "Under Ben Bulben," with its arrogance in the face of death, he ends with two poems that gesture to a slightly different attitude. In the penultimate poem, "The Circus Animal's Desertion," Yeats laments how his poetry separated him from the reality from which it emerged, admitting that "It was the dream itself enchanted me" (l.28). Now, facing death, the poet returns to the roots of all such poetic dreams, "the foul rag and bone shop of the heart" (l.40). In this version, the self-elegy involves a return to the roots of poetic inspiration, roots that are defined by their gritty nature. And yet Yeats follows this poem with "Politics," the final poem in the collection, which suggests return to a different origin. The final lines of the poem, "But O that I were young again / And held her in my arms" (ll.11–12), bring us not to the "rag and bone shop of the heart," but, with their reference to the sixteenth-century poem, "O western wind, when wilt thou blow," to the roots of Anglophone lyric.

These series of movements in Yeats's late self-elegies from poet as ultimate observer and legislator, to poet as conduit of real experience, to poet as romantic lover, point to tensions about the role of self-elegy that define its resurgence as a form in the modernist period. At the heart is the question of the relationship between the modernist poet and his predecessors, a question made more pressing because of the simultaneous desire to reject the poetic canon and to rewrite its trajectory so that it includes the poet in question. In other words, one feature we will see emerging in modernist elegies is the question of how to secure one's place as a poet in a tradition that one may, in fact, want to deny.

Disastrously inserting itself into this aesthetic debate, World War I presents a counterpoint to the narrative of self-creation and realization that we see in Yeats's self-elegies. Since the assumed egotism of imagining one's own death loses credence in the face of mass slaughter, the poems produced by the "trench poets" who fought in the war present different relationships between poet and tradition, death and poetic memory. We can see two versions by looking at the self-elegy by Rupert Brooke, "The

Soldier" (written in 1914), which was published early in the war and before Brooke
had actually seen much fighting first-hand, and the later poem by Wilfred Owen,
"The Show" (written in 1918). Brooke's poem immediately sets itself within a specifically national heritage, staging both the poet and the poem as inherently and irrevocably English. Even the land where the dead soldier-poet's body will be buried takes
on this national flavor, Brooke reassures us: "there's some corner of a foreign field /
That is forever England" (ll.2–3). Continuity is the central feature of this proleptic
self-elegy; through death and through this poem, written in the form of a Shakespearian
sonnet, Brooke places himself in an aesthetic and a national tradition that assures not
simply his own membership in that heritage, but also the beneficial expansion of that
tradition, as the poet's death becomes part of the project to claim more land for
England. Thus even in death the soldier-poet can fulfill his martial and literary duty;
those two projects become one.

   If Brooke's popular poem suggests that the death of the poet will both continue
and promote the British poetic tradition, Owen's poem occupies that tradition only
to challenge it. Like Dickinson, Owen uses the posthumous voice in this poem,
speaking from beyond the moment of death. We begin with a panoramic view of
a world that seems unrecognizable, both to the dead speaker and to the reader: "My
soul looked down from a vague height, with Death / As unremembering how I
rose or why" (ll.1–2). In this poem, unlike in Brooke's, neither the terrain of war nor
the poetic form are made familiar; instead the dead speaker hovers above, trying to
parse both the space and the actions, while the verse, which relies on a slant rhyme
that gestures to the disrupted and partial nature of any kind of movement in this
world, breaks down into shorter and shorter stanzas as the speaker gets closer to
understanding his own place in the horrific scene. Both speaker and reader only learn
in the final words that the speaker's own beheaded body is on this unearthly
battlefield.

   By making the speaker an unknowing observer of the carnage below, Owen foregrounds the haunting question implicit in war self-elegies: whether the soldier-poet
is always both murderer and murdered, guilty even when the victim. In another poem,
"Strange Meeting," Owen states this assumption directly, with a shade informing the
speaker, "I am the enemy you killed, my friend" (l.40). The self-reflexive and self-
incriminating nature of wartime self-elegy is made manifest; mourning one's own
likely death involves recognizing your role in the death of others. Such knowledge
creates a conflicted relationship between poet and poem. Unlike in Brooke's "The
Soldier" or the more infamous "In Flanders Fields" by John McCrae, both of which
use the voice of the dead poet to inspire other soldiers and suggest both poetic and
material continuity, Owen's "The Show" and "Strange Meeting" point to the impossibility of continuing the poetic project from the conflicted perspective of killer and
killed. Thus "The Show" ends as soon as the speaker realizes that on the field he has
been viewing with such dispassion lies his body and, next to it, "the fresh-severed
head of it, my head" (l.29). Owen puts the lie to the most reassuring fantasy of the
self-elegy—the sense that one can continue to narrate from the grave.

For non-combatants, of course, self-elegy could continue to have a more traditional leaning. In Ezra Pound's post-World War I poem, *Hugh Selwyn Mauberley*
(1922), which mourns everything from the destruction brought about by war to the
loss of authenticity in contemporary society, we see a return to both a Swiftian mode
of satiric self-elegy and a more egotistical anxiety about longevity. The poem begins
with a self-elegy for a Pound persona, *"E. P. Ode pour L'Election de son Sepulchre."* Here
Pound offers one solution to the problem of how to both situate oneself in a poetic
tradition and signal a break. The *Ode* elegizes the poet who, "out of key with his
time" (l.1), "strove to resuscitate the dead art / Of poetry" (ll.2–3). E.P. fails in this
project, but the poem proclaims it the fault of the country and the age, "half savage"
and "out of date" (l.6). An elegy for the past poetic self becomes a condemnation
of the culture that killed him, and Pound can simultaneously signal his position
among the great poets of the past and his break from them through this act of
commemoration.

Such confidence is absent in Mina Loy's "An Aged Woman," which Loy deliberately
identifies as an epitaph, prospectively dating it "Mina Loy / July 12th / 1984." Instead
of focusing on the poetic corpus to be buried, Loy's poem turns its attention to
the physical body and brain of the poet. The poem laments the lost "precision" (l.5)
that characterized Loy's youthful body and brain, yet it does so from a not-yet-aged
state. Thus the voice of the poet asks her future older self, "Does your mirror Bedevil
you" (l.11), as the still-living Loy imagines that it must. This schizophrenic poetic
disassociation of poet from her imagined dying body is possible, we learn in the
final lines, because "Dilation has entirely eliminated / your long reality" (ll.20–21).
This complicated balance between retrospective and prospective positions means
that Loy cannot simply shed the past. Instead, she views the trajectory towards
death as a process of disintegration, an erasure of past events through the unraveling
of memory. In so doing, Loy departs from the self-elegy as a mode of consolidating
both poetic and personal identity, instead using it to identify the process of aging
as a coming into self-alienation—a move into a radical otherness. Death, however,
will allow her to reassert control, as the only act that will take the "excessive incognito" (l.17) of the aged woman out of the "Mina Loy" that exists in the epitaph. By
ending with the future date of anticipated death, Loy counteracts the "dilation"
of aging and brings the poem back to a precise, even if imagined, point of
self-definition.

The figurative killing-off of the self in Loy's poem becomes both more literal
and more satiric in British poet Stevie Smith's self-elegies. Smith, like Keats and
Dickinson, was deeply preoccupied with death in her poetry, but her self-elegies
work from the assumption that death is a manifestation of agency, rather than a
potential threat to it. In "Death Came to Me" (1937), Smith presents the moment
of death as one of ultimate control, defined primarily by the choice of how to enact
it. Rejecting both knife and poison, destroyers of the flesh and the heart, respectively, the poem's "I" chooses the revolver: "I put it to my head / And now I'm
dead" (ll.45–46). The eerie playfulness of Smith's rhymes is coupled with moments

in which internal and end rhymes merge in provocative ways. Her rhythmic flour-ishes—the rhyming of "quickening," "thickening" (l.27), and "strychnine" (l.28), or of "distinction" (l.36) and "extinction" (l.37)—point to the more subtle way that Smith positions her poetic persona's choice of death: it is in this act of extinguish-ing oneself that you achieve distinction, and the very poison that can kill will also excite and make substantial. The terms of the original tension between egotism and selfless poetic imagination become blurred in the suicide self-elegy, therefore, because death becomes the necessary catalyst for lyric inspiration and, therefore, poetic memorialization.

The suicide self-elegy reaches a pinnacle in Sylvia Plath's verses, which merge the art of poetry and the act of death to create what Ramazani calls a "thanatological muse" (*Poetry* 284). The self-elegy dominates Plath's later poems, and she translates the genre into a performance of self-immolation and recreation. Most famously, "Lady Lazarus" (1962) anatomizes both the newly risen Plath and the viewing/reading public. "There is a charge" (l.57), she reminds the reader, for "a word or a touch / Or a bit of blood" (ll.62–63), and this toll on the reader gives, in turn, the poet her own "charge"—that electric shock that transforms her into "your opus" (l.67) that will "turn and burn" (l.71). A material and metaphorical phoenix, Plath's self-elegy ends with her rising from the ashes, nourished by the very destruction she narrates, as a newly ravenous and dangerous being who will "eat men like air" (l.84). In its powerful transformation of self-negation into self-creation, Plath's poem lays bare the aesthetic-masochistic impulse that governs many acts of self-elegy. Ambivalence or insecurity about the fate of one's poetry after death disappears in the face of this imbrication of bodily annihilation and poetic creation.

While Plath presents one later twentieth-century view on the merging of poetic and material bodies, another, less apocalyptic version can be seen in the self-elegies of W.H. Auden, in which thoughts of death lead to an embrace of the elements that have made up his poetic persona and material body. Thus in "Lullaby" (1972), Auden looks with appreciation on his aging body (contra Loy), which has returned to a fetal state with "licence to lie, / naked, curled like a shrimplet" (ll.11–12). What character-izes this lullaby to a "Big Baby" is Auden's sense of deep satisfaction; his "last thinks all be thanks" (l.31) to those people and places that shaped his life. Unlike Yeats's struggle against ending, Auden seems to welcome it, calling out "Now for oblivion" (l.46) in the last stanza. Auden's catalog of his past influences in this poem and others ("Prologue at Sixty" [1967] and "A Thanksgiving" [1973], for example) implies that he understands himself as an accretion, a being who gains in meaning and resonance because of these influences. In this formulation, death does not sever the poet from his poems. Instead, Auden's list of poetic influences reveals the endurance of poetry beyond the poets' lives. Auden achieves the goal of maintaining his poetic legacy precisely by *not* attempting to consolidate his position. The poet survives as part of a community and a continuum. Auden places human endurance within a more cosmic scale, calling humanity the "anxious species to which I belong" ("Prologue at Sixty" 20). The movement into death becomes a passage through language to the body, the site of a democracy of urges, and Auden asks only that, "Giver-of-Life, translate for me / till I accomplish my corpse at last" (ll.109–10).

Wallace Stevens also looks for a way out of the singular ego when he confronts his own death in his self-elegies, but he turns not to the body or to a continuum of influences, but to an impersonal natural world. In "The Planet on the Table" (1954) Stevens argues that his poems' longevity is less important than their successful reflection of "the planet of which they were part" (l.15). His poems are like the other natural elements that inevitably move towards "waste and welter" (l.5), frangible and subject to decay. At the same time, however, the poems function in their very mutability as real markers of the world, forming together the "planet on the table" that the title indicates. Likewise, the poet and the sun are placed in apposition—"His self and the sun were one" (l.7)—making the poems as much a product of the natural world as of the poet's mind and, at the same time, transforming the poet into something as pervasive and enduring as the sun. The self-elegy here functions to naturalize and memorialize both the poet and the poetry, suggesting that the poetic project will last even as individual examples fade.

The self-elegy remains a viable form for contemporary poets, and the same questions of poetic inheritance and methods of memorialization haunt these more recent versions. In the poem "Summer Night" (2001), for example, Louise Glück's sense of her own mortality directs her attention to the poetic tradition and to the realization that poetry's imitation of life may lead to "not the apotheosis but the pattern" (l.13). This is a turn that mirrors, in some ways, Stevens's take on poetry as a manifestation of the everyday world, but Glück does not transform this metaphor into one that suggests the naturalization of the poet. Instead, like Auden, she places herself in a tradition, within a line of "predecessors" (l.17) whose work provides the template for hers, even as they are "disguised as convention" (l.18). A transformation does, however, take place in her final stanza, where the "balm of the ordinary" (l.19) is placed in apposition to "imperial joy and sorrow of human existence" (l.20). It is through the ordinary pattern, Glück suggests, that we will have some access to human drama and emotion, and it is the "closeness of death" (l.22) that provides this insight. The revelation is a quiet one, and the place that the poet takes is not one as a radical innovator, but as a member of a community.

Stephen Dunn, in contrast, returns us to a Swiftian imperative tone in "A Postmortem Guide" (2000). Yet this poem is without the self-aggrandizement we saw in Swift; instead, it functions in the pragmatic way that it promises by presenting both what should be said, and how the mourners should feel. Dunn warns his eulogist that "there's nothing definitive to be said" (l.6) and embraces the paradoxes that define human life—the ability to "live without hope / as well as I could, almost happily, / in the despoiled and radiant now" (ll.40–42). With its unsentimental perspective on his past life, Dunn's poem evades the nostalgia that the self-elegy can fall prey to and presents the poet much in the way that Stevens presented his poems—as a product of a flawed, yet beautiful world. Together, Glück and Dunn present two contemporary trajectories for the self-elegy that focus on continuity within traditions, both poetic and personal. Rather than functioning as the most narcissistic of poetic forms, therefore, the self-elegy now seems a vehicle for promoting a clear-eyed look at the poet as product of place and age.

REFERENCES AND FURTHER READING

Armstrong, Charles I. *Figures of Memory: Poetry, Space, and the Past.* New York: Palgrave Macmillan, 2009.

Auden, W. H. *Collected Poems.* Ed. Edward Mendelson. New York: Vintage, 1991.

Brooke, Rupert. *The Penguin Book of First World War Poetry.* Ed. Jon Silkin. 2nd edn. New York: Penguin, 1996.

Dickinson, Emily. *Final Harvest: Emily Dickenson's Poems.* Ed. Thomas H. Johnson. New York: Little, Brown and Co., 1961.

Dunn, Stephen. *Different Hours.* New York: Norton, 2000.

Farland, Maria Magdalena. "'That tritest/brightest truth': Emily Dickinson's anti-sentimentality." *Nineteenth-Century Literature* 53.3. 1998: 364–89.

Glück, Louise. *The Seven Ages.* New York: Ecco Press, 2001.

Hardy, Thomas. *The Complete Poems.* Ed. James Gibson. New York: Palgrave, 2001.

Keats, John. *Poems.* Ed. Gerald Bullett. London: Everyman, 1990.

Levinson, Marjorie. *Keats's Life of Allegory: The Origins of a Style.* New York: Blackwell, 1988.

Loy, Mina. *The Last Lunar Baedecker.* Ed. Roger L. Conover. New York: Farrar, Straus and Giroux, 1996.

Owen, Wilfred. *The Penguin Book of First World War Poetry.* Ed. Jon Silkin. 2nd edn. New York: Penguin, 1996.

Plath, Sylvia. *The Collected Poems.* Ed. Ted Hughes. New York: Harper & Row, 1991.

Pound, Ezra. *Selected Poems.* New York: New Directions, 1975.

Ramazani, Jahan. *The Poetry of Mourning: The Modern Elegy from Hardy to Heaney.* Chicago: University of Chicago Press, 1994.

Ramazani, Jahan. *Yeats and the Poetry of Death: Elegy, Self-Elegy, and the Sublime.* New Haven, Yale University Press, 1990.

Raymond, Claire. *The Posthumous Voice in Women's Writing from Mary Shelley to Sylvia Plath.* Burlington, VT: Ashgate, 2006.

Rossetti, Christina. *The Complete Poems of Christina Rossetti: Volume I.* Ed. R.W. Crump. Baton Rouge: Louisiana State University Press, 1979.

Sappho. *A Book of Women Poets from Antiquity to Now.* Ed. Aliki Barnstone and Willis Barnstone. New York: Schocken Books, 1992.

Shakespeare, William. *Shakespeare's Sonnets.* Ed. Stephen Booth. New Haven: Yale University Press, 2000.

Smith, Stevie. *Collected Poems.* Ed. James MacGibbon. New York: New Directions, 1983.

Spargo, R. Clifton. *The Ethics of Mourning: Grief and Responsibility in Elegiac Literature.* Baltimore: The Johns Hopkins University Press, 2004.

Stevens, Wallace. *The Collected Poems of Wallace Stevens.* New York: Vintage, 1990.

Swift, Jonathan. *The Poems of Jonathan Swift: Volume II.* Ed. Harold Williams. Oxford: Clarendon Press, 1937.

Vendler, Helen. *Wallace Stevens: Words Chosen out of Desire.* Cambridge, MA: Harvard University Press, 1986.

Yeats, W.B. *The Collected Poems of W. B. Yeats.* Ed. Richard Finneran. Rev. 2nd edn. New York: Scribner, 1996.

8

Free Verse and Formal

The English Ghazal

Lisa Sewell

The Form

Ghazal (pronounced *ghuz*-zle *not* gah-*zall*) is an Arabic word that means "talking to women" (Kanda 4) or "whispering words of love" (Ali, *Rebel's Silhouette* ix); it also refers to "the agonized wail of the wounded deer," pointing toward the etymological origins of the English name for the gazelle (Kanda 4). This ancient form is associated with love and in particular with the torment of frustrated, unfulfilled desire—as the two definitions suggest. The ghazal is often compared to the sonnet—an analogy that annoys some prominent scholars of Persian and Urdu poetry because it suggests that the two forms evolved contemporaneously when the ghazal is at least six hundred years older than the sonnet.[1] But the correspondences are nevertheless quite striking: both are brief lyrics that adhere to strict metrical patterns and rhyme schemes and are central to the lyric traditions of their respective cultures. Like the sonnet, ghazals are generally untitled, though they do not necessarily appear in strict sequences, and as I've already suggested:

> Within the ghazal, the poet . . . presents himself as a solitary sufferer, sustained by brief flashes of ecstasy, defined by his desperate longing for some transcendent object of desire . . . Human (female or male), divine, abstract, or ambiguous: its defining trait is its inaccessibility.
>
> (Faruqi and Pritchett 7)

A Companion to Poetic Genre, First Edition. Edited by Erik Martiny.
© 2012 John Wiley & Sons, Ltd. Published 2012 by John Wiley & Sons, Ltd.

As in the sonnet tradition, the frustrated lover and unobtainable beloved are conceits that are available to the poet to manipulate and play on. Traditionally, the ghazal tends to be "highly condensed, reflective verse, with an abundance and variety of lyrical effects, verbal complexity, and metaphorical abstraction" (Ahmad xv). The great poets of the ghazal are often compared to the metaphysical English poets like Donne and Herbert, with their focus on liminality and the desire to transgress the boundaries of ordinary, worldly existence. Over time a set of common images and motifs that convey liminality and irresolvable emotional states developed—the mirror, the self-consuming candle, the blossoming rose.

The ghazal is also distinct from the sonnet in ways that make it surprisingly contemporary. Unlike the sonnet, which is structured around a logical progression, the ghazal is composed of a series of between five and twelve autonomous or semi-autonomous two-line verses called *shi'r*.[2] Each verse displays formal continuity and thematic independence, and can stand on its own, evoking disparate subjects and a wide range of moods: "One couplet may be comic, another tragic, another romantic, another religious, another political" (Ali, *Ravishing* 3).[3] There is never enjambment between verses, and typically, there is no development or elaboration as the poem progresses. Thus, the ghazal is a capacious form, allowing differences and inconsistencies to reside within its structure without striving toward resolution. As Robert Bly has suggested, the ghazal "invites the reader to discover the hidden center of the poem or the hidden thought that ties it all together, a hidden center unexpressed by the poet himself or herself" (6). This aspect of the ghazal, which approaches the postmodern "openness" of parataxis, helps explain its appeal within contemporary North American poetry, which often valorizes the open-ended, experimental, and self-reflexive. In "The Resistance to Closure," Language-poet Lyn Hejinian describes a "closed" text as one "in which all the elements of the work are directed toward a single reading . . . [without] any lurking ambiguity" (368). In contrast, in an "open" text, "all the elements of the work are maximally excited." An open text can be interpreted in multiple ways, inviting the reader's participation, "and rejecting the authority of the writer over the reader and thus, by analogy, the authority implicit in other (social, economic, cultural) hierarchies . . . often emphasiz[ing] or foreground[ing] process . . . and thus resist[ing] reduction and commodification" (369). The ghazal, with its disconnections and provocative white space between verses, can be understood in similar terms.

Traditionally, the unifying aspects of the ghazal are equally distinctive of the form, and are as strict and demanding as the meter and rhyme-scheme of the sonnet; the disconnection between verses is balanced by rhyme, meter, and refrain, creating what Kashmiri-American poet Agha Shahid Ali has referred to as a "stringently *formal* disunity" (*After New Formalism* 124, my emphasis). In the late 1990s Ali helped popularize the traditional ghazal form in the United States; here are the first few verses from one of Ali's ghazals:

> In Jerusalem a dead phone's dialed by exiles.
> you learn a strange fate: you were exiled by exiles.

You open the heart to list unborn galaxies.
Don't shut that folder when Earth is filed by exiles.

Before Night passes over the wheat of Egypt,
let stones be leavened, the bread torn wild by exiles.

(*Ishmael* 28, ll.1–6)

As this example illustrates, there is no development between the verses. The first verse, or *matla*, establishes the metrical pattern and alerts the reader to the other key patterns the poem will follow: the *qafiya* (root rhyme) immediately precedes a one or two word *radif* (refrain) that will complete each two-line verse. In the *matla*, the *qafiya* ("dialed," "exiled," "filed," "wild") and the *radif* ("by exiles") sound in both lines, but for the rest of the poem they only recur in the second line of each verse. As Ali suggests, once the poet establishes this pattern, "she or he becomes its slave" (*Ravishing* 3); in this case the *qafiya* ("dialed") also rhymes with the *radif* ("by exiles"), giving the poem an additional musicality, and giving Ali an especially demanding master.

The demands of the *radif* present significant challenges to any poet. As John Hollander has suggested, a refrain cannot merely repeat the same words over and over again, but must "accrue new meaning" as it is imported across the boundaries and borders of discreet verse units (77). The *radif* is especially important because the ghazal was originally composed to be recited or sung. As Ali explains:

At a *mushaira*—[a] traditional poetry gathering . . . when the poet recites the first line of the couplet, the audience recites it back to him, and then the poet repeats it, and the audience again follows suit. This back and forth creates an immensely seductive tension because everyone is waiting to see how the suspense will be resolved.

(*Ravishing* 8)[4]

In other words, if Ali were to recite his ghazal at a *mushaira*, by the time he arrived at the fifth verse, "By the Hudson lies Kashmir, brought from Palestine— / It shawls the piano, Bach beguiled . . . ," the audience would join him in reciting the *radif*: "by exiles"! (*Ishmael* 28, ll.9–10).

Another convention of the ghazal, though one that is not compulsory, is the author's incorporation of his or her name or pen name into the final couplet or *maqta*. A poet may wish to "express his own state of mind or describe his religious faith, or pray for his beloved, or indulge in poetic self praise" (Kanda 3). Ali's *maqta* is especially impressive: "Will you, Beloved Stranger, ever witness Shahid— / two destinies at last reconciled by exiles?" (29, ll.23–24). Ali trebles the self-referentiality of the *maqta*, referring to himself directly as "Shahid," but also indirectly in two different ways for "Shahid" means "witness" in Urdu, and "beloved" in Arabic. Ali spells out the multiple meanings of his name in another ghazal "Arabic," which is also included in *Call Me Ishmael*. Punning and word-play of this kind is also typical of ghazals written by the great Persian and Urdu poets.

Historical Background

The *ghazal* has origins in sixth-century pre-Islamic Arabic verse and has been adopted by an even wider range of cultures and languages than the sonnet. It evolved from the *qasidah* (ode), a highly stylized long poem in two-line verses "written in praise of the emperor or his noblemen." The amatory opening of the *qasidah*, called *nasbib*, developed into the ghazal, but while the *qasidah* could be over a hundred two-line verses in monorhyme, the ghazal rarely exceeds twelve (Kanda 2). In the eleventh century, the form arrived in Persia and soon eclipsed the *qasida* and became the canonical standard in Iran. The ghazals that are best known in Western cultures were written by Persian mystics and poets, including Jalal al-Din Muhammad Rumi (thirteenth century) and Hafez (fourteenth century). The form reached India with the Moguls and became an important vehicle of expression of a new language, Urdu, which developed out of the commingling of Arabic, Persian, and Hindi.

In the nineteenth century, the ghazal became the most popular form of Urdu poetry, comprising seventy-five percent of the poetry written during that time (Kanda 1). Mirza Asadulla Khan Ghalib (1797–1869) and Muhammad Iqbal (1877–1938) are the best-known and most revered practitioners from the period. During this time, the ghazal also began to disseminate into Western poetry. It became very popular among the romantic poets in Germany, primarily through the influence of Goethe who imitated Persian models of the ghazal in his *West-östlicher Divan* (1819). In the early twentieth century, Federico García Lorca published a number of ghazals—he called them *gacelas*—seemingly paying homage to his native Andalusia's Moorish heritage, though his *gacelas* do not follow the rhyme scheme of the form (Werner 31).

The Ghazal in North America

Because of the difficulty of translating the rhyme scheme and refrain as well as the meaning of the Persian or Urdu ghazal, for the most part, readers in English-speaking countries have encountered Rumi, Hafez, Ghalib, and Iqbal in free verse.[5] Aijaz Ahmad's *Ghazals of Ghalib* (1971) helped introduce the form to North America, leading to early explorations of the ghazal in English by American and Canadian poets. Ahmad asked a number of American poets—including W.S. Merwin, Adrienne Rich, William Stafford and Mark Strand—to produce English versions of Ghalib's poems based on his own literal translations. Although it doesn't convey the formal aspects of the ghazal, Rich's translation of the following verses from one of Ghalib's poems suggest why this book inspired so much excitement—about Ghalib as a poet and about the ghazal:

> I'm neither the loosening of song nor the close-drawn tent of music;
> I'm the sound, simply of my own breaking.
>
> You were meant to sit in the shade of your rippling hair;
> I was made to look farther, into a blacker tangle.
>
> No wonder you came looking for me, you
> who care for the grieving, and I the sound of grief.
>
> (58, ll.1–4; 8–10)

Here, Rich conveys the non-linear, associative power of Ghalib's verses, as well as themes that are common to the form: grief, longing, and feelings or situations that are impossible to resolve: the paradox of being unable to distinguish between the single note or song and the whole composition, or between the speaker and the sound of his "own breaking." Though the verses do not adhere to a metrical pattern or rhyme scheme, the recurrence of participles ("loosening," "breaking," "rippling," "looking," and "grieving") creates a loose net of sound and meaning. The verses mirror each other in this way, while also glancing off in different directions.

The translations in *Ghazals of Ghalib* made the ghazal accessible, available and exciting to a reading public that went beyond scholars of Urdu poetry. What readers took away from Ahmad's collection was the possibility of a *form* that could resolve the "conflict between the desire to satisfy a demand for boundedness, for containment and coherence, and a simultaneous desire for free, unhampered access to the world" that Hejinian identifies in "The Rejection of Closure" (368). The ghazal seemed capable of containing the irrational, disjunctive, and atemporal, emphasizing contiguity and juxtaposition over relationships of hierarchy. The white space between the verses of the ghazal mark gaps in knowledge, absences that invite the reader's participation in the production of meaning, both expanding with possibility and contracting into the unsayable and unrepresentable. At a time when American poets were rejecting the strictures of impersonality and formality dictated by the New Criticism, the ghazal gave them permission to resist the logic and rationality of the Western tradition, and at the same time pay homage to a long-standing, much beloved, non-Western form.

But for some, this was the beginning of a dark period for the genre because it led to *free-verse* ghazals in English—a heresy for those who appreciated the intricacies of the traditional ghazal. Agha Shahid Ali literally went on a campaign "to take the gift back," publishing a polemic against free-verse ghazals in several different versions. In "The Ghazal in America: May I?" he complains that "the Americans have got it quite wrong" (123). Adrienne Rich, who published her own ghazal sequence in 1968, seems to have been the main culprit: "[she] and so many others have either misunderstood or ignored the form and those who have followed them have accepted their examples to represent the real thing" (123). Ali admits that these Western practitioners did grasp the imposed disparity between verses, but he insists that these free-verse versions lack the "technical context [and] formal unity" that saves the ghazal from seeming completely random and arbitrary. Concern that even with a strict contextualizing rhyme scheme, the ghazal may be completely arbitrary has been a concern in Western scholarship on Persian and Urdu ghazals for the last half-century. The qualities that have been said to give the ghazal unity range from themes and motifs to "psychological associations" (Pritchett 121). Pritchett observes that this quest for unity troubles Western scholars and not scholars, poets, and readers in India, where the Urdu ghazal is still alive and well. In his experience, "their deep enjoyment of ghazals was obviously not founded on any quality dependent on the ghazal as a care-fully arranged whole" (125). The important unit in the ghazal is the verse, not the whole ghazal in which it appears—making the question of arbitrariness completely irrelevant.

In "The Ghazal: A Poorly Adapted Form in English," Pariksith Singh also con-demns Rich for introducing a bowdlerized version of the ghazal to Western readers:

> Adrienne Rich and many others have written free verse ghazals. They have used a string of couplets in vers libre . . . unrelated in content, as their criteria for a ghazal. To me, this is like calling a fourteen line poem a sonnet. While I do not contest a poet's freedom to modernize and improvise . . . One should know the rules before deciding to break them.
>
> (51)

The remainder of this essay will interrogate these criteria for the "real thing" by exploring examples of both the "real" and "free-verse" ghazal in English. While formal ghazals in English can work beautifully to emphasize disjunction within structure, many of the poets who have chosen to work in free verse find ways to create resonances and connections that convey the simultaneous unity and disunity of the form. Certainly some so-called free-verse ghazals seem to have no connection to the form, but many formal ghazals in English fail for the reasons other poems in form fail: "predictability" and "monotony" (Lorna Crozier, quoted in Woodland 251). But the successes in each style suggest that the ghazal can be vital in English in both manifestations, offering a forum for discontinuity and disjunction that perfectly suits a twenty-first-century poetic sensibility.

Ali's own ghazals in English provide some of the finest examples of how the rhyme-scheme and refrain can provide a fluid container for divergent ideas, emotions and themes that point toward an unarticulated central idea. During the period before his death, Ali devoted himself to the ghazal form; *Call Me Ishmael Tonight*, which was published posthumously, is composed entirely of ghazals. Ali was born and educated in India, and lived much of his adult life in America, where from afar, he witnessed the political violence and upheaval that constantly plagued India and devastated

Kashmir, where he lived as child, in particular. The poem cited above, "By Exiles," clearly suggests that cultural and geographical displacement are concerns that inform his work. As the verses cited above demonstrate, "By Exiles" touches on a number of different subjects, but the situation of exile returns—like the refrain—in myriad shapes and guises. As Malcolm Woodland has argued, in *Call Me Ishmael Tonight*, Ali uses the ghazal form to construct a "postcolonial thematics of cultural trauma, loss, memory, return and cultural identity" (249). But in this poem, and in many others, these "thematics" extend to all of humanity.

The poem is framed by the specific exile of the Palestinian people: it takes its epigraph from Palestinian poet Mahmoud Darwish and is dedicated to Edward Said. The first verse establishes a theme of multiplying displacement, noting the bitter irony of the Palestinians being "exiled by exiles"—where the founders of the state of Israel are the exiled who then exile others. But here and in many other poems, Ali presents exile and dislocation as an almost universal fate and "metaphysical given" (Woodland 261), as the poem ranges across continents—naming Jerusalem, the Hudson, Egypt, Kashmir—and identifies with a diverse group that includes Bach, Oscar Wilde, Majnoon, Saqi (one of Iqbal's pen names) and of course, himself. The poem proposes that estrangement and dispossession are fundamental to the human condition; in one way or another, we are all exiles.

These ideas work at the level of form as well as content, especially through the refrain. As Woodland suggests Ali is able to "heighten the sense of loss and displacement . . . because the refrain itself seems to be continually displaced" (260). It also powerfully conveys two distinct and contradictory meanings: because it keeps changing contexts and shifting terms as it appears in each successive and disparate verse, "by exiles" suggests endless mutability and the possibility for change, but at the same time it returns each verse to the same bleak phrase, pointing toward the difficulty of altering the outsider status and loss associated with exile. Here, and in many of his ghazals that address political subjects, Ali also engages in an intertextuality—for example the phrase "exiled by exiles" is one he borrowed from an article by Edward Said—incorporating numerous borrowed images, phrases, and even lines into the poem. Thus the poem, like the speaker, has multiple origins and in its hybridity creates a home of sorts for these textual and actual exiles.[6]

Ravishing DisUnities, the collection Ali edited, is an excellent resource for ghazals that adhere to the traditional structure. Craig Arnold's "Ghazal for Garcia Lorca" stands out as one of the finest. Perhaps Arnold chose the form to pay homage to Lorca's own interest in the ghazal, but the poems conforms to the requirements of the form on many levels. Arnold's poem has an evocative, and haunting ambiguity, as well as the paradoxical quality that is appropriate to the ghazal form: Granada seems to be a city of great possibility and utter cruelty—"I felt at home, how home is hard with cruel people" (17, l.19). Several underlying, only hinted-at concerns infuse the space between the verses: Lorca's fate as a martyr during the Spanish-American war, the sexual politics of Lorca's homosexuality, and Arnold's own situation as a tourist in Granada. He also manages to make the form seem effortless. The *qafiya*, established in the *matla* by "die" and "prying," sounds throughout but unobtrusively. The *radif* forces everything that is described to take place "in Granada," but Arnold allows a disjointed range of ideas to circulate, including the Arabic/Moorish origins of the architecture and culture in Granada, the circumstances of Lorca's murder, the oppressive sexual politics of Spanish culture, and the beauty of Andalusia.

Before Ali, Adrienne Rich was the poet who introduced the ghazal in English to North America.[7] In an interview, Rich explains that through her work on the Ghalib translations, she found a form that allowed her to deal with her own sense of "fragmentation" at the time: "I found a structure which allowed for a highly associative field of images . . . [a]nd . . . felt instinctively, this is exactly what I need, there is no traditional Western order that I have found that will contain these materials" (*Collected Early Poems* 426). Soon after working on the translations of Ghalib, Rich composed two ghazal series: "Ghazals: Homage to Ghalib," *Leaflets* (1969) and "Blue Ghazals," *The Will to Change* (1971). Both collections address her anti-war activism, civil rights work and dawning feminist consciousness, and her insistence that personal disturbances and disruptions are inseparable from those occurring in the world around her. These are love poems, but the beloved is a society that has lost its way, and must find its potential to reject "the order of the small town on the riverbank, / forever at war with the order of the dark and starlit soul" (108, ll.1–2). David Caplan suggests that Rich used the ghazal form and its association with non-Western culture to give a shape to her own resistance to Western logic, power, and hierarchy, "to mitigate the more immediate pressures of contemporary American literary and political culture. She employs a motif, a non-Western gesture, not a prosody whose requirements she must fulfill" (49).

Rich's poems evoke the ghazal on several levels: most obviously through the accretion of disparate verses that are whole and complete in themselves and her exploration of paradox. In "7/12/68," the first ghazal in "Homage to Ghalib," Rich moves from "electric clouds" and tractor-riding lovers in the first verse to a bare wall in the second to an observation in the fourth that could describe her experience of reading Ghalib's poems: "the vanishing-point is the point where he appears. / Two parallel tracks converge, yet there has been no wreck" (104, 1, ll.8–9). She also creates repetition and connection within and between verses through images and through consonance, alliteration, and assonance. In the other verses from this ghazal the alliteration of "paint," "pain," "point," "parallel," and "privacy" creates subtle linkages, and the exact repetitions of "point" and "point" further evokes original form. The parallel lines and vanishing points recur in a different form in the next ghazal: "These words are vapor-trails of a plane that has vanished; / by the time I write them out, they are whispering something else" (105, ll.4–5). Here the connection between the two-line verses of the ghazal and the sense of disaster and loss in the strife-torn world that surrounds Rich is made explicit.

Though she does not use a refrain or root rhyme, Rich often pays homage to the "signature" of the *maqta*, as she does in the final verse of "7/12/68": "When you read these lines, think of me / and what I have not written here" (104). The poems also gain power from residing in sequences—images and sounds continue to appear in different contexts, creating resonances that do not suggest closure but further possibilities and associations. In "Homage to Ghalib," references to vanishing points, the stars, burning, eternity, writing that appears and disappears, and various short-lived insects forge subtle connections within and between the poems in the sequence.[8]

American poet Galway Kinnell's "Sheffield Ghazals" are even further from the traditional form than Rich's ghazals—he often ignores the two-line verse structure, though many lines seem to come in pairs. Nevertheless, Kinnell finds structural ways to evoke the form and through the concentration of language and intensity of insight he conveys the same essential, unnamable quality that we find in Ghalib. On the surface, "Driving West," describes a car journey but doesn't tell the story of the journey. Instead, Kinnell contemplates travel and its effects, from the economic to the emotional: "A tractor-trailer carrying two dozen crushed automobiles overtakes a tractor-trailer carrying a dozen new. / Oil is a form of waiting" (38, ll.1–2). In addition to repeating the phrase "tractor-trailer carrying" twice to gesture toward the monorhyme of the ghazal's refrain, this observation sets off a chain of associations. Contemplating oil leads to a consideration of "the internal combustion engine" and "airplanes [that] rise through downpour and throw us through the blue sky" (38, ll.3, 5). Car models are juxtaposed with lightning, computers, windshield wipers and lovers who are also "driving west." The associations are clear—he moves from contemplating "the idea of the airplane [that] subverts earthly life" to "computers [that] can deliver nuclear explosions to precisely anywhere on earth" and subvert life in an entirely different way (6–7). But the logic is not narrative and the significance of the connections are implied, but never spelled out. Asking the reader to contemplate the spaces between verses as much as the verses themselves, Kinnell intimates the linking repetitions of the ghazal through subtle connections between verses that are based on syntax and sound. Longer, contemplative sentences are juxtaposed with short, declarative statements; alliteration gives the verses musicality: "The windshield wipers wipe, homesickness one way, wanderlust the other, back and forth" (11). Kinnell also always concludes by addressing himself, in the tradition of the *maqta*, connecting the indecisiveness of the windshield wipers to the human condition: "This happened to your father and to you, Galway—sick to stay, longing to come up against the ends of earth" (12). And though mortality is never addressed directly, the final human journey toward death seems to be the underlying theme of this ghazal.

English-Canadian poet John Thompson is credited with introducing the ghazal to Canadian readers during 1970s through his undergound classic, *Stilt Jack* (1974). The poems were written during a very difficult period in Thompson's life—his house and all his belongings had been destroyed in a fire, he had barely received tenure at the university where he worked, and his wife had left him—and he died before the book was published. Thompson's poems beautifully articulate loss, disconnection, and a sense of unsettledness and though unconventional, they also earn their status as ghazals. In a brief introduction, Thompson explains that he was attracted to the ghazal because the verses "have no necessary, logical, progressive, narrative, thematic (or whatever) connection" and "the poem has no palpable intention upon us. It breaks, has to be listened to as a song: its order is clandestine" (5). This clandestine, underlying logic of association is quite evocative in the poems:

> Now you have burned your books: you'll go
> with nothing but your blind, stupefied heart.
>
> On the hook, big trout lie like stone:
> terror, and they fiercely whip their heads, unmoved.
>
> Kitchens, women and fire: can you
> do without these, your blood in your mouth?
>
> (8, ll.1–6)

Without books, without language, the speaker is blind, a blindness that is underscored in the second stanza by the trout who lie "like stone" but also presumably on stone, waiting to be prepared for consumption. The trout are both "fiercely" active and "unmoved," a melding of opposites and impossible, irreconcilable states that seems to take its inspiration from the traditional ghazal. Each verse is evocative and could stand on its own but the spaces between point the reader toward a range of associations. Like Rich, in *Stilt Jack* Thompson returns again and again to the same images—books, a fish hook, the eyes, women, and fire all return—but the context changes. They evoke their previous incarnations but also present new resonances, enriching the entire sequence.

Canadian poet, Phyllis Webb seems to have been influenced by her reading of Ahmad's volume of Ghalib and also by Thompson's *Stilt Jack*. Webb published a chapbook, *Sunday Water: Thirteen Anti-Ghazals*, and extended her exploration of the form in *Water and Light*. The first poem in *Sunday Water* explicitly evokes Thompson:

> I watch the pile of cards grow.
> I semaphore for help (calling stone-dead John Thompson).
>
> A mist in the harbour. Hydrangea blooms turn pink.
> A game of badminton, shuttlecock, hitting at feathers!
>
> . . . . . .

> Four or five couplets trying to dance
> into Persia. Who dances in Persia now?
>
> A magic carpet, a prayer mat, red.
> A knocked off head of somebody on her broken knees.
>
> (143, ll.1–4, 7–10)

In the preface to *Sunday Water*, Webb notes that while in the ghazal tradition, "the Beloved represents . . . not a particular woman but an idealized and universal image of Love," her own ghazals resist such idealization, favoring "the particular, the local, the dialectical, the private" (quoted in Butling 46). For this reason she names her own poems anti-Ghazals. Although Webb certainly rejects the theme of idealized love here, this "anti-ghazal" is connected to the form in other ways. Following another aspect of ghazal tradition, Webb calls attention to her project of writing ghazals—the stack of cards, the lines that refer to trying to make "four or five couplets . . . dance / into Persia" (7–8). Each verse shifts gear, addressing or describing very different subjects, but through assonance, consonance, full- and half-rhymes, the poem also retains a relationship to the formal aspects of the ghazal, creating links through pure sound: the "o" of "semaphore for" in the first verse seems to provoke the "harbour" that appears in the second as well as the "four or five couplets" in the fourth.

In addition to acknowledging the origins of the form, Webb voices concern about her appropriation of it, and also allows the suffering of women in contemporary Iran under the Ayatollah Khomeini into the poem. Although she doesn't date her poems like Rich, in a note included in the chapbook, Webb explains that she wrote the poems in 1981, soon after the 1979 Iranian Revolution. Pauline Butling has suggested that the ghazal form also offered burgeoning feminist poets like Webb and Rich a way to reject "oppressive discursive patterns" (65). As she notes, although the ghazal evolved within a culture that was just as patriarchal (if not more) as the culture that invented the sonnet, "Webb's outsider position in relation to Urdu culture enables her to . . . use the disjunctive form as a way of creating gaps in Western thought" (65).

Clearly the ghazal has come into its own in English. Whether strictly following the form or creating connections between disparate verses through other means, these contemporary ghazals are distinct from the great works in Persian and Urdu, but they do retain a focus on forms of love and devotion, and on the terror and grief of the human condition. Toward the end of his essay on the problems of the free-verse ghazal, Singh insists that "all the [formal] rules [of the ghazal] . . . are only on the surface. The true measure of a ghazal is its *saleeqah* or the way a certain thing is said or not said, or what is left unsaid" (51). It is this quality that has been conveyed to Western readers, even through translations that ignore those rules, and it is what informs many ghazals.

NOTES

1   In his introduction to *Ravishing DisUnities: Real Ghazals in English*, Agah Shahid Ali writes of needing "to register a protest, an irritation at Paul Oppenheimer's assertion that the sonnet is 'the oldest poetic form still in wide popular use'" (1). Shamsur Faruqi and Francis Pritchett also bristle at Oppenheimer's ignorance that "the ghazal antedates the sonnet by about six hundred years" (7).

2   Many writers and scholars refer to the *shi'r* as a couplet, though this is technically incorrect since except for the first one, the verses within a ghazal do not rhyme.

3   Ali even goes so far as to suggest that each verse can be treated as a separate poem in which "the first line serves as the octave of a Petrarchan sonnet and the second as the sestet" (*Ravishing* 183).

4   Louis Werner provides an extended description of the mushaira in "A Gift of Ghazals."

5   Coleman Bark's translations of Rumi have made him a best-seller, but it is not at all clear from Bark's versions that Rumi even wrote in the form of the ghazal.

6   David Caplan's chapter on the ghazal in *Questions of Possibility: Contemporary Poetry and Poetic Form* includes a more elaborate discussion of this connection.

7   Rich's ghazals have earned praise from many corners. Ali actually praises them in the introduction to *Ravishing DisUnities,* but he did not include her in his anthology.

8   Another notable free-verse ghazal sequence is Spencer Reece's "Florida Ghazals," *The Clerk's Tale*, New York: Mariner Books, 2004.

REFERENCES AND FURTHER READING

Ahmad, Aijiz, ed. "Introduction." *Ghazals of Ghalib*. New York: Columbia University Press, 1971. vii–xxviii.

Ali, Agha Shahid. *Call Me Ishmael Tonight*. New York: W.W. Norton, 2003.

Ali, Agha Shahid. "Introduction." *Ravishing DisUnities: Real Ghazals in English*. Hanover, NH: Wesleyan University Press, 2000. 1–14.

Ali, Agha Shahid. "The *Ghazal* in America: May I?" *After New Formalism: Poets on Form, Narrative, and Tradition*. Ed. Annie Finch. Ashland, OR: Story Line. 1999. 123–32.

Ali, Agha Shahid. "Introduction." *The Rebel's Silhouette: Selected Poems of Faiz Ahmad Faiz*. Amherst: University of Massachusetts Press, 1991. vii–xx.

Bly, Robert and Sunil Dutta, eds. *The Lighting Should Have Fallen on Ghalib: Selected Poems of Ghalib*. New York: Ecco Press, 1999.

Butling, Pauline. *Seeing in the Dark: The Poetry of Phyllis Webb*. Waterloo, Ontario: Wilfrid Laurier University Press, 1997.

Caplan, David. *Questions of Possibility: Contemporary Poetry and Poetic Form*. New York: Oxford University Press, 2005.

Faruqi, Rhahman Shamsur and Frances W. Pritchett. "Lyric Poetry in Urdu: The Ghazal." *Delos* 3:3–4 (Winter 1991): 7–12.

Hejinian, Lyn. "The Rejection of Closure." *Twentieth-century American Poetics: Poets on the Art of Poetry*. Ed. Dana Gioia, David Mason, and Meg Schoerke. New York: McGraw Hill, 2004: 367–76.

Hollander, John. "Breaking into Song: Some Notes on Refrain." *Lyric Poetry: Beyond New Criticism*. Ed. Chaviva Hosek and Patricia Parker. London: Ithaca Books, 1985. 73–89.

Kanda, K.C., ed. *Masterpieces of Urdu Ghazel: From the 17th to the 20th Century*. London: Sterling Publishers, 1990.

Kinnell, Galwy. *Imperfect Thirst*. Boston, New York: Houghton Mifflin, 1994.

Rich, Adrienne. *Collected Early Poems, 1950–1970*. New York; W.W. Norton, 1993.

Rich, Adrienne. *The Fact of a Doorframe: Poems Selected and New 1950–1984.* New York: W.W. Norton, 1984.

Pritchett, Frances W. "The Word Ghazal." A Desertful of Roses: The Urdu Ghazals of Mizra Asadullah Kahn "Ghalib." www.columbia.edu/itc/mealac/pritchett/00ghalib/about/x_genre_overview.html?

Pritchett, Frances W. "Orient Pearls Unstrung: The Quest for Unity in the Ghazal." *Edebiyat* 4 (1993): 119–35.

Thompson, John. *Stilt Jack.* Toronto: Anansi, 1978.

Weaver, Andrew. "That Bastard Ghazal." *Poetics.ca.* 1. http://wordsters.net/poetics/poetics01/01weaverprint.html.

Webb, Phyllis. *The Vision Tree: Selected Poems.* Vancouver: Talonbooks, 1982.

Werner, Lois. "A Gift of Ghazals." *The Annual of Urdu Studies*, 17 (2002): 28–35.

Woodland, Malcolm. "Memory's Homeland: Agha Shahid Ali and the Hybrid Ghazal." *English Studies in Canada*, 31:2/3 (June–September 2005): 249–72.

9

On "the Beat Inevitable"

The Ballad

Romana Huk

From the first it had been like a
Ballad. It had the beat inevitable. It had the blood.
A wildness cut up, and tied in little bunches.
Like the four-line stanzas of the ballads she had never quite
Understood—the ballads they had set her to, in school.
                     Gwendolyn Brooks, "A Bronzeville Mother"

CLOWN What hast here? Ballads?
MOPSA Pray now, buy some. I love a ballad in print, alife,
for then we are sure they are true.
                     William Shakespeare, *The Winter's Tale*

Backdrop: Ballad Studies

A sign for one of modern culture's earliest, most formative and collectively produced *ur*-genres—like the once anonymous epic or romance—the word "ballad," loosely defined, has been snatched up by a variety of research realms, including those devoted to folklore and narrative theory as well as oral literature and performance studies. And many have, over time, generally agreed that it is "the common ancestor of all varieties of verse" (Graves 8). Some more pointedly question whether its ancestors not only predate the epic, but served as materials from which epics were "stitched together"; others maintain that what we now know as ballad "evolved, very simply, from the decomposition of the literary romance" (Nygard 12), and that it might therefore be called "the literary débris of the Middle Ages."[1] Some argue that the ballad's very "ontology is song" (Newman 3), so that minus its music such a poem, be it a ha'penny broadside or a Bob Dylan lyric, is not true ballad; others like Mopsa above—an early

A Companion to Poetic Genre, First Edition. Edited by Erik Martiny.
© 2012 John Wiley & Sons, Ltd. Published 2012 by John Wiley & Sons, Ltd.

product of the age of print—profoundly disagree. Some take for granted the ballad's debt to the songs sung by wandering minstrels in medieval Europe, particularly France (the word "ballad" deriving most obviously from French dance songs, or "bal-lares," from which we also have "ballet"); others, like mid-twentieth-century ballad scholar William J. Entwistle, have argued that "we now know there was an active Asian focus in the tenth century . . . enjoying far greater resources of style. It was, moreover, in a far better position to influence Russian and Balkan folksong, and coin-cidences between eastern and western balladry assume a fresh significance" (380). Indeed, twenty-first-century genre studies—in the hands of, say, Wai Chee Dimock or Marleen S. Barr—revel in the promiscuous intercourse that they argue has linked continents as well as their lyric, epic and narrative modes from the outset, wishing to render moot all such attempts to pin down genealogies or sited histories for this or any other poetic form.[2]

But what I'm most interested in are what newly explosive and globalizing theories rarely account for in their tales of ancient and modern "genre fission":[3] the uses that both poets and critics have made of their *assumptions* about the origins and properties of this most elusive of forms. I'll want to argue that its longevity has, ironically, in the Anglo-American tradition at any rate, been ensured by the very fact that it remains difficult to historically tag or even define.[4] (Most editors of ballad anthologies depend on this, claiming it's easier to collect the anonymous ballad than date or describe it.) Although readers assume they can recognize it by its repetitive rhythms and rhymes, it really needn't adhere to any common metrical disposition; one "knows it when one sees/hears it," its collectors often explain, offering examples of the most famous ballads from the British Isles—like "Lord Randal," "Sir Patrick Spens," and "The Twa Corbies"—that vary widely in stanza form. The ballad's themes also range from (and often combine) the spiritual, supernatural, eternal, or comic to the political, revolu-tionary, topical, or tragic. And though in theory it tends toward borderlessness, borders—particularly contested ones—have made fine breeding grounds for ballads; take the ancient one between Scotland and England, with its oft-collected "Border Ballads," or the more recent one between Mexico and the U.S., with its border *corrido.* And though for some the bottom line is that a ballad is "a song which tells a story," these same theorists will often claim that "[h]owever, not all story-songs are ballads" (McAlpine 309). The problem with *that* theory is that it censors the topical and political ballad or broadside, and some of the most familiar poems in "ballad stanza" by, say, William Blake or P.B. Shelley, are most decidedly *not* stories but cries and incitements against the state of things, or the state—like Blake's "London" or Shelley's "Song to the Men of England."

Protean and beguiling, perhaps the one thing that might be said for all ballads since their great "revival" in the Romantic era is that they turn on their belatedness; the ballad's simple, once-communally-produced sounds cannot *but* bear the mark of an absence: an earlier and unclear if certainly collective and complicit history.[5] Inevitably anachronistic, used by noted or "elite" poets as "the lesser lyric" (Newman 1 and *passim*)—a mode that, unlike signature work, responds to "the call of the popular" in culturally owned rather than inventive phrasings and imagery formed through "a process of textual transmission and interpolation" (McGann 59)—ballads both beckon alluringly back to the roots of the genre in communal song *and* recall their own demotion by print poets and critics who, by the early modern period, preferred the more intricate sonnet and other virtuosic modes. Indeed, its one-time relegation to categories outside "civilized literature" (Graves 9)—due to assumptions that, as Robert Graves argues, the centralization of a culture signals the end of its true life on peripheries, outside national or otherwise institutionalized, codified discourse—has made the ballad peculiarly attractive even to postmodernism's most recent and most radical poets. It has become a form for not only sniping at discursive centers of power, but also for rethinking the rise of the "bourgeois individual," which Marx and others dated back to the 1700s: the precise moment when ballads began to be energetically collected and archived. Something indefinable, elemental, to be both loved and feared, was being lost in that transition; therefore even figures like Lord Macaulay, not given to radical criticism of his national culture (and indeed, called a "systematic falsifier of history" by Marx[6]), wrote with strange passion and nostalgia in his *History of England* about the ballad's place in 1685:

> No newspaper pleaded [the common people's] cause. It was in rude rhyme that their love and hatred, their exultation and their distress found utterance. A great part of their history is to be learned only from their ballads. One of the most remarkable of the popular lays chaunted about the streets of Norwich and Leeds . . . is the vehement and bitter cry of labour against capital. It describes the good old times when every artisan employed in the woolen manufacture lived as a well as a farmer. But those times were past. Sixpence a day was now all that could be earned by hard labour at the loom. . . . For so miserable a recompence were the producers of wealth compelled to toil, rising early and lying down late, while the master clothier, eating, sleeping, and idling, became rich by their exertions. A shilling a day, the poet declares, is what the weaver would have, if justice were done.
>
> (371)

Women too are depicted and recorded as partaking in balladry's street presence—for example, in great eighteenth-century engravings like Hogarth's "Beer Street" (1751), which gives us two fishwives excitedly reading a broadsheet together, or in Chambers' *Book of Days* (1863–64), which recalls two women being sent to jail "for "singing political ballads" in duet before Lord Bute's door in South Audley Street (Palmer 7). Although critique of street balladeers at the time was sharp, informed by state legislation since 1597 that "minstrels wandering abroad" were to be considered "vagrant and vicious," "rogues," and whipped (6), and although such depictions as Hogarth's were roundly critiqued as idealized, Blake famously and passionately integrated even the most workaday Cries of London—"a centuries old genre textualizing the songs of those hawking their wares in the city streets" (Newman 139)—into his eighteenth-century poetry. His influence alone on a variety of transatlantic twentieth-century poets, from Stevie Smith to the Beats, would have been enough to ensure the echoing continuance of that once ubiquitous if contested and finally extinct sound.

Yet ballads, more powerfully than their richer cousins the sonnet, sestina, villanelle, and other well-defined (and "refined") forms, come haunted by what they no longer *can* be; they remain paradoxically occupied—*especially* in updated, single-authored, printed "literary ballad" versions—by their collective past. So that even when the ballad's "beat inevitable," as Gwendolyn Brooks puts it in my first epigraph, serves what we think of as "private" experience, like love, the form's traditional objectivity, or "absence of subjectivity" (Andersen 18) as some have put it, and its metonymic rather than metaphoric tendencies, can surprisingly function with almost postmodern force to render such intimacies with internal distances that shock as well as fascinate. It might, perhaps, even be said (without delving, for lack of time, into Freud's, Lacan's, or Kristeva's theories of the "uncanny," though they would be fruitful here) that the ballad becomes modern poetry's form *for* the forgotten/familiar, or perhaps the "cultural uncanny": a deeply resonant, sonically material, and rhythmically repetitive mnemonic for the mobilization of a lost communal impulse that, with the rise of individualism (as well as the lyric poet), takes its place alongside other modes of knowing and desiring that have become for us very nearly unrecognizable or suppressed (and thus riveting).

And as such, of course, the ballad can be dangerously deployed in cultural projects at *both* ends of the sociopolitical spectrum; its status as indefinite "relic" has been used to construct chauvinistic nationalist visions of identity and community as well as explode them. For although we assume one "knows ballad when one sees/hears it," in reality, as Michael Cohen argues, "[t]he socio-political value of ballads is derived from their association with the idealized oral cultures of imagined folk communities, rather than from qualities inherent in the individual objects themselves" (4). In other words, another way we continually "lose" the ballad is through the cracks between ideology and phenomenology in reading practices, whatever collectors may say about their enabling us to simply encounter it. We *may* assume ballad's role in the modern era was best defined by that famous experiment in cultural renewal that William Wordsworth and S. T. Coleridge conducted just after the French Revolution by recalling the ballad's "language of the common man" for the writing of their own *Literary Ballads* (1798). Or we may value most the way ballad "songs of innocence" can back the progressive purposes of, for example, abolitionist poetry like Blake's "The Little Black Boy." But the form has also been policed towards very different ends in, say, the case of John Greenleaf Whittier, one of the most popular of nineteenth-century American balladeers. As Cohen explains, postbellum American critics "argued for a basic distinction between Whittier's antislavery poems and his [later] 'ballads'"—"all poems of 'eastward [New England] regionalism,' 'supernaturalism,' or folklore" (2). "Through poems like these," Cohen continues, quoting postbellum critic R. H. Stoddard, "Whittier became 'one of the few American poets who have succeeded in obtaining the suffrages of the reading public and of the literary class' . . . [which] made [him] the 'most American of all American poets'" (3). The term "ballad" was thus divorced from *political* writing, and Whittier's antislavery works dismissed as "productions":

> Antebellum readers had understood Whittier's antislavery poems to be ballads, and they identified the "balladic" form as inhering in the political relations that these poems established among readers. . . . [T]o name as ballads [which American scholars would define as "a truly national or popular poetry" (Child 214)] those poems on New England folklore, on the other hand, helped to centralize New England regional history in emergent concepts of American identity.

Such reverence for the site of America's beginnings—promoted too by the infamous Francis James Child's students and descendants in ballad collections, like Katharine Lee Bates—depended on reverence for what she called without compunction "[o]ur own Anglo-Saxon ancestors" (ix). This taught readers that "being American means having Anglo-Saxon or Teutonic or northern European blood, in contrast to those of African, Asian, Jewish, or southern European descent" (Newman 189), among others.

And of course, as Steve Newman explains, "many have pointed out [that] it is elite literature and not the traditional ballad itself that is 'revived' . . . in the phenomenon scholars have named the Ballad Revival" (3). Because

> [b]y the time we reach the New Criticism, the ballad, though often explicitly contrasted with lyric, is also enshrined as the genre that initiates readers *into* lyric . . . This is the culmination of a dual narrative of personal and national development emergent in the Long Eighteenth Century in which the ballad gains definition as the favored text of childhood and the nation's early days.
>
> (Newman 4)

For prominent New Critics Cleanth Brooks and Robert Penn Warren, ballads led students from, in the latter's words, the "non-bookish" to the "bookish" (Newman 14). Or toward what Newman argues was, once, the kind of "elite consciousness" that supposedly could, through "nostalgia often informed by a complacent scheme of personal and national development" (4), contemplate culture's progression toward a more democratic society. Thus ballad is caught up in a debate that, as Newman puts it, "continues to this day [2008], over who has and has not been included in [that] supposed progression . . . so sorely unrealized in practice" (4).

I'll end below with some new contributions to that debate by poets who occupy the extreme edge of radical experiment—like American "Language" poets Charles Bernstein and Harryette Mullen, as well as British and European performance writers cris cheek and Caroline Bergvall—thereby disproving the old argument that the ballad's use-value petered out after the nineteenth century (or after Poe, Dickinson, and Hardy). The ironic fact is that it was precisely due to the atomizations and alienations of the twentieth century that poets have found non-ironic use for it, and that the postmodern avant-garde have in their turn recalled it despite abandoning most other traditional modes. In conclusion I ponder the possibly surprising future of the ballad in the hands of twenty-first-century writers whose goals differ very little from those street criers of over half a millennium ago. But first, let me illustrate points made above by moving to the poems themselves, starting with examples of the modern ballad's oldest ancestors and focusing on how twentieth-century invocations of their powers contribute to what we now, in the twenty-first, make of this ancient but intimate form—both its strengths and its dangers.

From Orality to "(Inter)textuality": Ballads Ancient to Postmodern

One need only flip through English-language anthologies to see that no particular stanza form holds for all ballads—though students of literature learn the term "ballad stanza," defined as quatrains that alternate four- and three-beat lines rhyming *abcb*. *The Cambridge Guide to Literature in English* (2006) explains that the marked preponderance of this pattern may suggest that ballads were once made up of fourteen-syllable rhyming couplets (66); such arguments often have subtle regional and national politics involved—such as Graves' claim that "[t]he ballad stanza is itself from the South [of England]; it occurs first, it is said, in the camp songs of the Roman Legionaries" (36). Whatever one might argue about one favorite border ballad, "Sir Patrick Spens" (Sir Walter Raleigh, for example, argued that it was too good to have been composed communally) it certainly is in ballad stanzas, with extra syllables giving its inevitable beat a frequent lift and twirl. Its subject also doesn't disappoint those who value most the socially carnivalesque nature of ballads. This one recalls "the best sailor that ever sailed the sea" being sent out during the most inhospitable season to retrieve, on a whim, the "King's daughter of Noroway" for his own King, who "sits in Dunfermline town, / Drinking the blude-red wine" (ll.1–2). What the latter is doing, more to the point, is wondering in his boredom where he can find a "skeely [skillful] skipper" (3) to sail his brand new ship. Spens, who first laughs and then weeps upon the letter from his King, has no choice but to agree to his own near-certain demise:

> 'O wha is this has done this deed,
> And tauld the King o' me,
> To send us out, at this time of year,
> To sail upon the sea?
>
> (ll.21–24)

The ballad makes clear how cruel feudal power relations can be from the point of view of common folk similarly subject to them. But as in most ballads, the moral isn't exactly clear—because Spens, too, then subjects *his* crew to almost the same dilemma, after a scuffle with hosts in Norway drives him back out to sea against the advice of his men:

> They hadna sail'd a league, a league,
> A league but barely three,
> When the lift grew dark, and the wind blew loud,
> And gurly grew the sea.[7]
>
> (ll.53–56)

The rest is inevitable: their many wives lose "their ain dear loves" for the sake of one King's lust for vicarious adventure and for one royal daughter. The image at the end is of the sailors lost to sight: "Half owre, half owre to Aberdour, / . . . fifty fathoms deep"—the latter a sign in ballad semiotics for the culturally repressed and the potentially forgotten that its singing remembers. The final image, of "gude Sir Patrick Spens / Wi' the Scots lords at his feet" is multivalent in its love and critique; Spens has tragically taken the King's place at sea, but this dignified burial also expresses a desire to leave him there, upending the hierarchy on dry land.

Images of sunken subjects for balladry surface in not only, say, Shakespeare's *Tempest*, but in much later poetry inspired by it—such as Sylvia Plath's "Full Fathom Five" (1958), which recalls the first line of Ariel's song about the drowned sailors due to reappear by the play's end. Plath's version can be seen as a modern, privatized "border ballad"—full of the sub-genre's traditional "antagonism . . . disquiet and tension" (McAlpine 313)—directed not at neighbors but at her fearsome father, re-arising like a watery rival territory:

> Old man, you surface seldom.
> Then you come in with the tide's coming
> When seas wash cold, foam-
>
> Capped: white hair, white beard, far-flung,
> A dragnet, rising, and falling, as waves
> Crest and trough. Miles long
>
> . . .
>
> I walk dry on your kingdom's border
> Exiled to no good.[8]
>
> (ll.1–6; 41–42)

Translated from narratives of feudal injustice and collective border rants to a personal narrative of loss and postwar cultural trauma, ballad's ancient image of the submerged/ remembered culminates in Plath's final pun of the poem: her German father's "shelled bed." Not that he died *in* the war, only during it, but she famously linked his daunting authoritativeness to Nazi violence in a number of her poems. I read this one as a ballad whose "form suffers," she tells us—like that of the father she hopes/fears to "re-member"—because it's actually about the dangerous faultline present in any such project of preservation. Especially when it involves dipping into balladry's cultural cache of sound, memory, and language, fleshing out what she calls "muddy" visions of origins by returning a beat to the dead and gone (as Frankenstein did to his monster). "All obscurity," as an earlier stanza puts it, "Starts with a danger: // Ages beat like rains / On the unbeaten channels"—"of the ocean" here, as the next line continues, but also of the "time in runnels" that the "archaic trenched lines of [his] grained face shed," like the archaic lines of balladry (en)trenched in cultural memory. The latter remain "unbeaten": open channels for the submerged, forgotten, or repressed to rhythmically return. And while such preservation lay at the heart of many ancient ballads, in modern ones like this "the old myth of origins" becomes more dangerous freight, transformed by its very loss and submergence into not only the rich and strange but also, potentially, rechanneled violence—or even, as history has proven, genocidal desire—because what's murky becomes a screen for two-way projection, and here we're told quite explicitly: "this *thick* air is murderous" (my emphasis). Plath contemplates how it is that the all but tidal beat of poetry, its "rising and falling as waves," brings up her father and all he metonymically drags back with him but only unclearly—making him prey for her, as well as her for him. In other words, any such conjuring through "the old myth of origins"—Aryan or otherwise—is dangerous, "no good," and daughter like father treads that border in this piece.

I realize that Plath's slimmer, all but Dantesque tercets (as the rhymes in my excerpt suggest) with their rigid 7–9–5 syllable count, their off-rhyme and highly signature imagery may not be seen by all as clearly balladic; I read them as such because of their approximations of trimeter in their final lines and their allusions to balladic symbols and songs. Though the most tenuous ballad I treat here, its inclusion might be justified by recalling how widely ancient ballads varied in their form. For example, a close cognate of continental versions, "Lady Isabel and the Elf-Knight," opens with a ballad stanza depicting this particular king's daughter sewing in her bower, a familiar balladic image—until she hears the elf-knight "blawing his horn" and faster couplets take over the action in a very differing portrayal of female balladic character:

"If I had yon horn that I hear blawing,
And yon elf-knight to sleep in my bosom."

This maiden had scarcely these words spoken,
Till at her window the elf-knight has luppen.

"It's a very strange matter, fair maiden," said he,
"I canna blaw my horn but ye call on me.

"But will ye go to yon greenwood side?
If you canna gang, I will cause you to ride."

He leapt on a horse, and she on another,
And they rode on to the greenwood together.

(qtd. in Snydergaard 36–37, ll.1–14)

Within a line, the elf-knight turns out to be a serial killer of seven king's daughters, intending to make our heroine the eighth. But she, in a familiar ballad move, invites him to lay his head on her lap and rest before she dies—i.e., "sleep in her bosom"— and when he does, she slays him with his own sword, getting the last word: "If seven king's-daughters here ye hae slain, / Lye ye here, a husband to them a'." The blade-like force of the four-beat rhyming couplets in the above variation on the ballad meter is something that later poets like e. e. cummings, for example, would make good use of in his own wonderfully arrow-like ballad of love turned prey, "All in green went my love riding":

> All in green went my love riding
> on a great horse of gold
> into the silver dawn
>
> four lean hounds crouched low and smiling
> my heart fell dead before
>
> (1923; ll.31–35)

Many readers assume that cummings' poem references the mythic story of Actaeon's death before huntress Diana's hounds—a favorite of other high modernists such as Ezra Pound—since ballads often recall mythic narratives. Yet cummings, unlike Plath, employs perfectly standard ballad images that lift this story out of any specificity and into the ballad's fantastic dream domain with its uncanny sense of foreboding and familiarity. cummings' heart-stopping success here is in transforming the "red rare deer"—"fleeter . . . than dappled dreams" (ll.6, 8)—from the "harts" that they literally are in the poem into the speaker's own currently beating, modern one by the end. His final "before" thus fades without end-stop into *all* its meanings, including "in the past" as well as "in front of"; therefore the "famished arrow [that strangely and anachronistically] sang *before*" the "four fleet does" in one couplet suggests it sings most importantly before *him*, in ballad, through the ages, zinging into his own century and straight into his "heart." Perhaps the number "four" that repeatedly informs the poem's images recalls the loose tetrameter of ballad and its quatrains even as this modern descendant streamlines their power. In any case, cummings' experiment is certainly with the *sound* of ballad: the permission it affords to pull up near-chant-like beats sped by rhyme—here through a preponderance of monosyllabic words that become swift footfalls in this race to the finish. And while ballad forms like "The Elfin Knight" have been associated with protective incantations (McAlpine 313), cummings seems most interested in the "famished" danger of it: its startling accuracy of a/effect coupled with its licensed vagueness of moral, its ravishing sound that wins accord from readers prior to their contemplation of its words.

Ballads like "Lady Isabel" also deploy potent metonymic images of gendered economies (sequestered spinning, bowers, female "laps," riding, the "horn," the wild-card freedoms of the "greenwood," etc.) that course through ancient balladry to inspire poets as various as Alfred Tennyson and Stevie Smith. Tennyson, in "The Lady of

Shalott," combines such images with characters from a thirteenth-century Italian novella, *La Donna di Scallota*, as well as from the same century's version of *Morte d'Arthur*, to give us a spinning, cursed, but willful protagonist doomed to die of desire for love. Tennyson expands the ballad stanza to nine lines rhyming *aaaabcccb*—the "b" lines all ending in "Shalott," "Lancelot" or "Camelot," which sonically aids the ballad's "beat inevitable" to bring these three tragically together. For although "She has heard a whisper say / A curse is on her if she stay / To look down to Camelot,"

> She left the web, she left the loom
> She made three paces thro' the room,
> She saw the water lily bloom,
> She saw the helmet and the plume,
> She look'd down to Camelot.
> Out flew the web and floated wide;
> The mirror crack'd from side to side;
> "the curse is come upon me!" cried
> The Lady of Shalott.
>
> . . .
>
> And at the closing of the day
> She loosed the chain, and down she lay;
> The broad stream bore her far away,
> The Lady of Shalott.
>
>   (III.37–45; IV.19–27)

Tennyson's Lady, like Lady Isabel, suffers the fate (soldered here to its ubiquitous Greek image as a "web") of obeying her own lusty desire—imaged above in that blooming water lily, an orgasmic feminine response to the helmet and "plume." But their ends communicate rather startlingly different things. Loosing the chain and lying down is an unmistakable reference to loosing the medieval chastity lock, and that sends this lady downstream (alongside that ill-fated dallier with royalty, Ophelia, an image much loved by Victorian artists such as John Millais). Musing that "the Lady of Shalott is evidently the Elaine of the *Morte d'Arthur*, but I do not think that I had ever heard of the latter when I wrote the former," Tennyson connects the inevitable travel through time of such balladic images to the very story he tells, as though this figure was foredoomed to appear at the dock of his own imagination, which is his own and not his own.[9] Yet his reworking is neither inevitable nor innocent, nor indeed true to all the possibilities that ballad tradition offers him. Still, his is a wonderful demonstration of the ballad refrain's capacity to create a kind of train-wreck effect, to make things converge (as do Thomas Hardy's *Titanic* and iceberg, for example, in "The Convergence of the Twain").

Twentieth-century ballads by women like Stevie Smith often deconstruct what balladeers before them (re)channel as inevitable. Not things like repressed knowledge of *death*'s inevitability, indisputable as it is (and one of ballad's as well as Smith's favorites), but rather stories of what, for example, is common within female experience, transmitted though fairytales and other "trenched" (as Plath put it) pathways of early learning to become, paradoxically, an index of the real. Smith often probes those beloved nineteenth-century images of female ruin and beautiful death that we find in Tennyson's poem—coupled dangerously as they are with nationalizing myths of origin and nostalgia for heroic British lore which renders them anachronistically archetypal, and thus potentially prescriptive—yet she does so knowing full well that she has, nonetheless, been helplessly composed of them. Therefore hers is a form of belatedness that nevertheless *is* in the ballad spirit, in a sense, because her self-conscious use of the form—which I see as deeply related to that of a poet she loved, Emily Dickinson—points up her *own* formation by collective history despite its vanishing points, leaving her in a position of displacement from lyric autonomy into the cultural uncanny. (Indeed, the fact that Smith often sung her poetry tells us much about her conception of its cultural work; she utilized common and ancient tunes just as street balladeers had done, suggesting the collective nature even of her own beguiling voice which so many have misinterpreted as pitched at idiosyncrasy.) In "I rode with my darling," Smith takes up the trope of riding off dangerously with a potential lover—as in Lady Isabel's story—but derails her own narrative with the "reasonable" response of said lover, recognizable from the "real" realm of gendered discourse in her own time. She thus breaks the ballad's spell only to cast rationality itself back into it, pondering customary allegiances through a process of defamiliarization that is quintessentially balladic by the end:

> I rode with my darling in the dark wood at night
> And suddenly there was an angel burning bright
> Come with me or go far away he said
> But do not stay alone in the dark wood at night.
>
> My darling grew pale he was responsible
> He said we should go back it was reasonable
> But I wished to stay with the angel in the dark wood at night.
>
> . . .
>
> Loved I once my darling? I love him not now.
> Had I a mother beloved? She lies far away.
> A sister, a loving heart? My aunt a noble lady?
> All all is silent in the dark wood at night.
>
> (ll.1–7; 23–26)

A devotee of Blake's ballads, Smith deploys his "Tyger, tiger, burning bright" as her speaker's *chosen* tutelary spirit—thereby suggesting that she, like him, meant to upend stereotypes and encounter the fearful minus the impulse to read it as "evil."

This angel seems to take her down a proto-deconstructive path, an apocalyptic *via negativa*, because what her sojourn far from civilized centers and their centripetal pull brings her to is a "pale tower" of no "consolation," an anti-structure of bare-stone "resisting without belief" all the cultural and familial myths that "once" supported her. (Even the "darling" of the ballad's title has "r[idden] off angrily," imploding any romance that may have arrived in the poem with *him*.) But whereas Tennyson gave us the ominous image of the mirror "crack'd" upon Lady Shalott's arousal—the shattering of her one and only tenable identity—Smith portrays such revelation in line with the breakout from character accomplished by Lady Isabel. As Larry Snydergaard writes of the latter: "Her center has not been shifted to a beloved; she has instead shifted her own center and . . . established a certain erotic independence [through] neither a return to the family seat nor a transfer to the home of the beloved" (28). Fantastic yet familiar, the similarly de-centered state Smith's speaker describes at the end above through her embrace *not* of her darling but of the *unheimlich*, is one Smith often revisited in her discomfiting ballads and valorized as revelatory of the *real* real: our *non*-autonomous (lyric) subjectivities caught in webs woven and rewoven of textual imperatives no less imprisoning than the Lady of Shalott's. The difference is that in Smith's modern version triumph is less shrill because she, like others in her postwar era, was beginning to suspect "disconsolately" that there is nothing beyond that cultural text: "All all is silent in the dark wood at night."

The deconstructive force of ballads such as Smith's—connectable in many ways to those of her contemporaries, like W.H. Auden[10]—might be seen to culminate in, say, what recent critics have called Gwendolyn Brooks' "anti-ballads": particularly her two poems written about a fourteen-year-old Chicago (Bronzeville) boy, Emmett Till, who in 1955 while visiting his great-uncle in Mississippi was lynched for allegedly whistling at a white woman.[11] The event and its aftermath were full of precisely the sort of sanctioned inhumanity that ballads often translate into metonymic dreamscapes, in order to "cry out" what *does occur* yet remains repressed as unthinkable. The ensuing trial—which some view as the first great media event of the civil rights movement in the U.S.—brought out all the submerged racial assumptions about "American" culture I alluded to earlier; the state-appointed defense attorney, for example, assured the jury in his final appeal that "every last Anglo-Saxon among [them had] the courage" to acquit the two men responsible of murder (Pollack and Metress 6). And they indeed did, after a deliberation that lasted only a little over an hour. (A grand jury subsequently acquitted them even of kidnapping, though the men had themselves publicly confessed to that much.) Journalists and artists alike afterward "took up the cause of finding out the 'real story'" because, as with Macaulay's street balladeers, it was felt, particularly by the African American community, that "no newspaper pleaded [their] cause"; over 140 literary and popular retellings of the incident and its significance have to date been collected (7). This, again, is the traditional ground of topical ballad—but Brooks' strategy of employing it highlights its effectiveness not for those in danger of losing their voice, but for those "Anglo-Saxons" privy to its language.

She does so by, however, making use of that language, particularly its metonymic reference—"hence the namelessness of all characters in the first poem" (May 102). Yet we know very well who's speaking in "The Bronzeville Mother": the "revenged" white woman, with significant irony, in that the poem's frequently shortened title refers to the mother of the murdered boy. (The full title is "A Bronzeville Mother Loiters in Mississippi. Meanwhile, A Mississippi Mother Burns Bacon"—because repressed thoughts begin to undermine business as usual.) Yet Brooks gets revenge in turn by causing Carolyn Bryant's historical reality to fade into what the speaker herself identifies, in the first stanza (also my first epigraph), as "a ballad," though she claims couldn't really understand them at school; the suggestion of course is that this speaker is caught up in a "text" that has written *her*, in effect—a very postmodern idea housed in a very, very old story. Indeed, Brooks explicates what ballad scholars have long found uncanny about the form; for example, G.L. Kittredge, in his 1904 introduction to Child's collection of ballads, sounds like he's providing a preamble to "structuralism and its aftermath: 'a ballad has no author . . . ; [it is] 'a tale . . . *telling itself*, without the instrumentality of the speaker . . . There are *texts*, but there is no *text*'" (Harris 9). Brooks' speaker, indeed, ventriloquizes such a text, informed by heroic ballad language—but only in the sense of its tragic narrative predictability, for her "form suffers," as did Plath's. Though she begins to unfold her tale as one of feudal valor, casting herself as a "maid mild" whose honor has been saved by her "Fine Prince," Brooks pointedly produces *not* the four-line stanzas her speaker invokes at the start but ungainly five-, six-, and seven-liners before degenerating into extended and unformed verse paragraphs which lose the plot altogether when Bryant can no longer remember what "that foe had done / Against her," and thus "could think / Of no thread capable of the necessary / Sew-work" to bind present to ballad experience. We become most uncomfortably aware at this point that there is no role available in the story at all for the titular but silent Bronzeville mother "loitering" on its edge. *Her* poem, this one's companion in two proper ballad stanzas, is indeed a thin and desolate "Last Quatrain"—its title provided by its companion poem. Its frightening vacancy seems to recount only her untranslatable experience. But the uncontrolled verbosity of the Mississippi woman's story falls apart precisely upon recalling her *look* at court: those "[d]ecapitated exclamation points in that Other Woman's eyes." With the recollection of this "Other," and photos of the boy's "mouth too young to have lost every reminder / Of its infant softness," her husband Roy Bryant's advances—"*His* mouth, wet and red, / So very, very, very red" (my emphasis)—suddenly also appear, like that look, outside her heroic narrative, their redness linked not to royalty but to the bloody "real." The ballad scaffolding therefore suddenly collapses: there is "no hoof-beat of the horse and . . . no flash of the shining steel":

> She did not scream.
> She stood there.
> But a hatred for him burst into glorious flower,
> And its perfume enclasped them—big,
> Bigger than all magnolias.

The last bleak news of the ballad.
The rest of the rugged music.
The last quatrain.

(ll.124–31)

These final lines are mutely multivalent: that last bit of "news" told above might be the truth in Brooks' view—i.e., of the murder—*or* of the self-compromising cultural work balladry has been used to do in her time. Yet it may also be the news, in surprisingly balladic language, of emotion bursting open, if we recall the Lady of Shalott's orgasmic flowering. If certainly *anti*-orgasmic here, it similarly portends a demise— not only of the ballad itself, but of this speaker's life as lived in the kind of dreamy, bacon-burning self-delusion that ballads *can* be employed to maintain.

I want to consider in conclusion ways in which the ballad tradition has, more recently and against the odds, been recalled to use by postmodern poets even after such expositions and demolitions of its darker powers. It has much to do, as I suggest above, with recent literary theory's resistance to belief in self-actualizing individuals and lyric expressiveness; recognizing that we are each helplessly formed by a collectively owned, linguistically fueled "imaginary" reintroduces the ballad's relevance— and its supposedly fantastic realm as, more frighteningly, the place of our uncanny incarceration (alongside Brooks' speakers). Yet if language in its most enculturating forms does, as Brooks and Smith feared, construct collective reality, then it also becomes the space for *reconstructions* of the same—not as new repositories of *ur*-knowledge and chauvinistic, even violent, cultural wisdom, but as newly provisional and pluralized "realities" for poets writing beyond the *aporias* of poststructuralist thought and toward new ways of thinking about positive, democratic (and thus revisable) collectivity.

For example, Harryette Mullen's 1995 book-length poem, *Muse & Drudge*, may have surprised some in the Language poetry community by being in balladic quatrains, and bluesy, if also linguistically innovative and unruly in its rhymes and meter. Wary like her contemporaries of both narrative and lyric "self-expression," Mullen *therefore* turns to the ballad, I would argue, in order to reconstruct a story of personal identity in a fully updated way, recognizing as she does that lyric expression is helplessly formed *through* collective processes in language—though that's something she, unlike Smith or Brooks, regards as potentially fruitful as well as frightful. An African American who "[learned her] oral tradition in textbooks" (2), records, tapes and films, Mullen is interested here in remaking her own black female identity not "from the inside" but from collective materials—i.e., *not* "romantically" but *as* a "text," finding even her own long-compromised ancestral memory buoyant and resident in language use and its sounds. Though she knows they grow out "sorrow's home" (80), or language built to defile those oppressed and suppressed within it, she nonetheless finds in texts not only the silences that loiter helplessly outside Brooks' "Last Quatrain" but also black ingredients that merge with their white containers to come out "bluish":

> white covers of black material
> dense fabric that obeys its own logic
> shadows pieced together tears and all
> unfurling sheets of bluish music
>
> (32)

Reading those "sheets" (which just above these lines went with "quilts," with the balladic dream-life of her culture) as *revisable*, be they text or music, she gently torques their sounds—as blues and jazz did to hymn-sheets, as well as popular ballads—and thereby finds even her title by signifying on various words associated with darkly liminal behavior, like "mules and drugs" (74). And if "drugs" gives way to "drudge," defined as both "slave" and, by connotation, hard work, Mullen accepts both here, not changing the sad aspects of her linguistic inheritance but just reworking it, hard. Yet the poem is anything but vituperative or accusatory; instead, its exuberant language play seduces us by simply retuning it, asking our indulgence "while [she] slip[s] into something more funkable" (73)—suggesting that identity must to some extent be fungible if language is indeed our writing on the wall. Such moves in balladry revise both Language poetics' "line" on form *and* the mainstream's traditional one, using the "brash insistence of tetrameter" (Damon 331) to set deconstructed fragments of iden- tity to new music as well as once again "break down the pentameter," as Kamau Brathwaite put it (after Pound): that "civilized" Anglo-American normative line with its long near-monopoly on individual, rational reflection in poetry (466). Both mainstream and radical "elite traditions" repress what informs them nonetheless at subliminal linguistic levels that tune American English, for good or ill; therefore Mullen sets out to address what she calls (via gallows humor) the "endemic mnemonic plague" (28) by recollecting, *re-tuning* and *remaking* that collective text. For her the cost of not doing so, and with a fuller cast this time, rhymes with that of "bubonic plague"—which in the Middle Ages was, if we remember, called "black death."

"Recasting" ballads for twenty-first-century culture might be done as simply as that—in the hands of, say, cris cheek, the British performance poet. His project "Coleridge's Rime of the Ancient Mariner" makes no change to this most famous of ballads, but records it as recited in 2005 by school-age children, staff, canteen- workers, and cleaners at Coleridge Community College: a Cambridgeshire school (then in danger of closure) serving students speaking seventeen different languages and sport- ing numerous postcolonial and international backgrounds. The ballad as a social/liter- ary form comes to a special kind of apotheosis in this work, which renders Coleridge's "literary" ballad even more true to the genre's roots than the original managed to be by reviving it via a new kind of "oral tradition," by allowing it new "re-composition" *not* by cheek but by the community—particularly the near-disenfranchised within it. It thereby takes on a socially transgressive dimension as well: that of interrogating *falsely* unifying categories, such as "Englishness," in what has always and increasingly been a multicultural and polylinguistic "united kingdom." At the heart of Coleridge's poem is, of course, instigation to value "otherness"; what returns the wind to the mariner's sails—after he's killed the albatross, a benign immigrant on board—is his response to the water snakes below his ship: without recoiling, as is our wont, he thinks them "beautiful," even "bless[es] them unaware." A typical Romantic, Coleridge (like Blake) *recasts* the Edenic *out*cast, the all-but primordially fearful snake, as being in need of reintegration into the whole, for as the ballad's most famous lines have it, "He prayeth best, who loveth best / All things both great and small; / For the dear God who loveth us, / He made and loveth all." Even cheek's form of balladic belatedness may take its cue from Coleridge's poem; as Jerome McGann has argued, the "Rime's" studiously implanted archaisms and diverse textual layers "imitate a transmitted ballad" (59) because Coleridge wished to foreground the continual re-interpretive process over time that constituted, for him, not "universal" meanings but *transhistorical* ones (54). He saw even the "truth" of the Bible as the product of such evolutionary processes: inspiration preserved over time by successive communities out of their—dare we say it—ballads and lore continually revised to remain "true." Coleridge's ballad is therefore very simply remade by cheek through its being re-sited/recited in this twenty-first-century school—proving that the music, or sound of the ballad, cannot and will not remain the same in future constituencies but that this fact paradoxically ensures its life, even as the life of balladry, remembered communally, provides a pivot, a text, for re-imagining one's context *through* community.

Therefore what Brooks refers to with understandable ambivalence above as ballad's "rugged music" now finds itself reformed for new kinds of cultural work. Not only demographic shifts but also new global formations and culture-altering catastrophes have called it back, alongside emerging trends in philosophy and theory, to re-conceive what "community" might mean in the future—particularly given our loss of faith in the eighteenth century's conception of the "individual." For example, the 2001 attacks on the World Trade Center produced a palpable shift in consciousness for scattered communities across the world—including those of artists. As poets on both sides of the ocean have suggested, it was hard afterward to simply continue with the same forms of radical writing because—as is often true in ballad's precincts, too—suddenly all seemed de-centered and strange: the target of critique, what was at stake, and the way forward all seemed to have irrevocably shifted. A new mode of more "popular" address seemed needed in order to sympathetically occupy, and listen to, the moment with others, as well as invoke new kinds of community in response. This was particularly true for Charles Bernstein, a New Yorker whose post-9/11 book of poems, *Girly Man* (2006), responded to the "cries" of his local environment and the exigencies of "these daze," as one section has it, even more immediately than his previous collections had done—and with, more to the point, numerous balladic poems. The ballad's power for him is not only attached to its potent history of revolt and subversion of the "official line" at any given time, but also to its sonic force, its simplicity and repetition which invoke community and change just as it always did: by creating the rhythm for participation, and therefore social interaction; as he puts it, "the heavily-stressed poetic rhythm creates the 'public' space in which the social work can take place" (Damon 331[12]). In other words, here is space for revival of that "debate that continues to this day," as my quote from Newman put it earlier, about our supposed progression towards a democratic society. Bernstein's titular poem, "The Ballad of the Girly Man," as well as the whole of the book it concludes offers, in my view—alongside emerging work in balladic mode by Caroline Bergvall, focused as it is on the recent banking crisis—the most intriguing place for me to end this essay. Both take us back to the streets for information, broadside-like interventions and popular interpretations of topical events, making a music of what they hear—updated "cries of London" *and* New York, one might say—in a newly pluralized, non-atavistic yet politically engaged, meta-balladry that addresses global as well as local communities.

Bernstein's book at times simply transcribes, in a surprisingly traditional way, those cries of New York as he hears them, some of them unrelated to the attacks but forever ongoing—like "Wherever Angels Go," a street beggar's importuning of passers-by. Set to a tune by Ben Yarmolinsky,[13] it manages, though repetitions of clichéd language suddenly given an ancient shadow by balladic form, to recall a backdrop of unresolved misery to the city's topical tragedy:

> Oh, hey, buddy, can you spare me a dime?
> I've been searching for you so long
> Yeah, hey, sister, I ain't into no crime
> Won't you show me the way to go home
> Won't you show me the way to go home.
>
> (167)

Like a sign for the whole city's sudden sense of homelessness, of displacement from what it thought it was, and entry—even through its own familiar streets—of the *unheimlich*, this ballad, an enduring bit of that ever-veiled yet complicit "real," stands in the heart of the book's final, titular section. Earlier in the book's surprisingly epistolary prose sections the poet made clear that delivering the "reality" of the moment was impossible; describing what he saw as walked home on "9/11," like people rollerblading as normal, five miles from ground zero, a scene "almost serene" (19), would produce nothing but a sense of—well, as our speaker puts it in one solitary line, "Uncanny is the word." Ballad seems suddenly relevant as a distancing yet emotive, *un*realistic form that nonetheless binds people in real, shared experience, calling up what Newman describes as its "doubleness of lyric" (3), its "unusual blending of individual and communal language," to address a city "overwhelmed by explanations for things that, at the visceral level, can't be rationalized" (Bernstein 28). Therefore balladic elements like refrain, even in these prose sections, punctuate what the poet records, days later, "walk[ing] on Liberty Street" (26)—which is a real street, but in this book also a song-like reference to the state of the nation, its "democracy." We follow, as we might a street balladeer, taking in what he sees and hears as he goes: what appears on T-shirts, in Battery Park, or in the subway, where homemade signs lamenting someone missing become "secular shrines" (27)—i.e., new forms of communal communication and commiseration. We also get an alarmingly multivalent refrain: *"They thought they were going to heaven"*—which, as in many ancient ballads here applies, without clarifying moral, to every one of the actors behind and in the tragedy, terrorists and trade center victims alike, as well as those that side with terror (*within* the U.S., too—"KKK or Timothy McVeigh, Lt, Calley or Dr. Strangelove" [30]) and those that side with imperial capitalism ("'We got what we deserved,' a shrill small voice inside some seems to be saying. But surely not *this* person, nor *this* one, not *this* one . . ." [29]). As in "Sir Patrick Spens," the result is a picture of the real waste of "gude" lives caught in fantastical webs of opposed cultural visions become fateful for the innocent in the hands of the powerful—be they powerful due to public office, wealth, or charismatic wielding of words and their followers' continuingly feudal instincts for loyal, even heroic, self-sacrifice.

Indeed, "The Ballad of the Girly Man" depends on a word that the *Oxford English Dictionary* dates back to "Spens": "gurly," which means not only the boisterous weather and rough seas we encountered in the ancient ballad but also, in its verb form "gurl," to *growl*, or, more importantly, *howl*—as Bernstein's forerunner in political, topical protest, Allen Ginsberg, did in his most famous of poems by that title. So when our speaker in this ballad takes a "girly man" stance—signifying on California Governor Arnold Schwarzenegger's 2004 taunting of opponents of the Republican Party agenda as "girly men"—he does indeed mean to be "Sissy & proud" but also to make a radical politics of it, through paradoxically aggressive crying out against aggression that is *not* balladic in his sense of being collectively and continually reformed and therefore democratic. The form instantly accuses his opposition of being of "ancient" provenance itself, but in the worst sense of maintaining greedy power and opportunism through age-old tools like xenophobic, scapegoating hatred and war:

> The truth is hidden in a veil of tears
> The scabs of the mourners grow thick with fear
> A democracy once proposed
> Is slimmed and grimed again
> By men with brute design
> Who prefer hate to rime
>
> Complexity's a four-letter word
> For those who count by nots and haves
> Who revile the facts of Darwin
> To worship the truth according to Haliburton
>
> . . .
>
> We girly men are not afraid
> Of uncertainty or reason or interdependence
> We think before we fight, then think some more
> Proclaim our faith in listening, in art, in compromise
>
> So be a girly man
> & sing this gurly song

> Sissies & proud
> That we would never lie our way to war.
>
> (179–81, ll.1–10; 23–30)

Ending with the couplet that begins my excerpt above and reappears as refrain throughout, Bernstein suggests, in part—and in some ways like Plath—that the "thickness" of those scabs is dangerous, allowing for the kind of "obscurity" with regard to what happened and a forgetting of the complexity of the event that lends itself to the fear-mongering that followed it and underscored the Iraq War. Veiled by the tears and their homonym—tears in the veil, the rent fabric of a more complex whole—is a truth that was encountered as the "uncanny" in the disordered yet communal responses to the initial event; such profound recognitions, like those that happen through reversal of fortune in ancient tragedy, are easily galvanized into bellicose blaming of others by the publicly powerful. Bernstein seems to want to produce a more public role for poetry too, therefore—even though, as one couplet has it, "Poetry will never win the war on terror / But neither will error abetted by error" (ll.21–22). Nonetheless, this poem incites its readers to *do* and *be* something, in what it imagines to have been the street balladeer's very style; it also, like the ballad Macaulay recalled against early industrialism's injustices, points up one politically sanctioned route toward inhumanity in culture's "progress": criminal forms of capitalism which have religious support, too, and global ramifications. Though the poem stumbles in its rhythms, its very meta-balladic awkwardness remembers, for me, poets like Smith—that other sad clown caught in the cultural ring, attempting to shift fates sealed by the unexamined moral violence of the powerful. The breaks in rhythm above sign Bernstein's belatedness as a balladeer, but also his awareness of the *dangers* of balladry if it doesn't embrace culture's new forms of "complexity" alongside its beguiling beat inevitable that drums up communal response with the participatory space its invites us to co-produce and share.

On this argument, the future for returns of the ballad form may be ensured for some time, sadly, given our continuing global crises of all kinds. I encourage readers to look for how ballad is informing eco-poetries, for example; or look ahead to the forthcoming work of even poets as non-traditional and as generically and linguistically adventurous as Caroline Bergvall, as they use balladry to interrogate world disasters such as the banking crisis. Long interested in public art, Bergvall, like Bernstein, has taken to the ancient/modern streets—picking up, in part, on responses to the crisis in the rap, grime, dub-step, and ragga of artists like "The Bug," a London musician/producer whose emblem as a noisy insect communicates his sense of being dwarfed by big business and other power brokers even as he cries out against sanctioned crimes that "make him mad" in *London Zoo* (2000), a multivocal, spoken-sung, collaborative album which has enjoyed recent cult-success. As part of a larger work due for exhibition this year in the John Hansard Gallery, her interpolations (in good ballad tradition) of these pre-existing songs within her verse will appear, quite literally, in the form of broadsides; unlike Bernstein, Bergvall's use of balladry involves not its traditional form so much as its material history: "the social technologies of the writing" and "the whole business of selling songs by the sheet in the street."[14] Thus a "yard of slip ballads" will be sown one into the other as a length and hung from a pole in the exhibition space—one of the ways in which broadsides were sold; a few hundred sheets will be printed up and distributed free at the exhibition, reminding those who wander in of the current price involved in acquiring access to literature, and of balladic street art's ancient, alternative literary economy of quick and unofficial circulation, social leveling and targeting of the near illiterate and the poor. Her concern is, also, that the broadsides exhibit all the messy "technologies" of printing that original street ballads did: bad letter blocks, mixed and often battered letterings, appropriated and often derivative illustrations, cheapest paper, presentation in up to five columns according to the size of the sheet itself, and spellings made more extreme to emphasize—like Mullen—the malleability of language, and the socially transgressive power of messing publicly with "official," standard spellings and proper pronunciations which Bergvall has interrogated for their historical interventions as shibboleths.[15] Excerpted from a longer work, "The Fried Tale (London Zoo)," these broadsides also become part of her ongoing tribute to Chaucer, particularly what Bergvall conceptualizes as "Middling English" (the title of the show) based around Chaucer's "decision to write in a spoken Southern English idiom [that] helped confirm the richness and versatility of a linguistic region that was starting to de-frenchify its cultural language, and de-latinate it" as well. Recalling such centuries-old examples of writers shifting national and other kinds of identity by communicating to differing constituencies and thereby forming new collective caches of resources and materials for social expression, Bergvall creates what she thinks of as a "synthetic yet also historically aware" intervention with the help of the ballad tradition. Collecting energy and materials from street songs as well as from more "academic" texts (including quoted passages from such figures as economist James Galbraith, who recently warned against disabling assumptions that the world's wealth is in capable hands), Bergvall invokes poetry's ancient power to play midwife/middleman for emergent forms of, *not* self-expression but cultural expression in the dialogue between increasingly distanced sectors of twenty-first-century society.

If the great Ballad Revival of the eighteenth century was a complicated response, in part, to the rise of the individual (and the "rational") in western culture and the arts, one might say, in conclusion, that descendants of the genre so revived have come full circle to accompany the demise of the same. No longer "belated" in quite the same sense, the form has new work to do; we are experiencing, as I write this, new collectively-encountered realities that, being beyond individual comprehension, join us at a "choral" level that ballad remembers very well. As Bergvall puts it in her forthcoming essay, "Middling English," we are in need of facing the uncannily familiar feeling, intimated by so many of the poets I've recalled here, that we've lost our tongue in every sense, individual as well as collective—that ours is the "Anonymity of the traveler whose masks have fallen deeply into the pits and currents of language." Her answer, like theirs: "Rebirth of the songer."

NOTES

1   "Stitched together" is a quote by Entwistle from F. A. Wolf's late-eighteenth-century thesis about the ballad origins of the *Iliad* and the *Odyssey*, *Prolegomena ad Homerum*; it was debunked near the end of the century by figures like Matthew Arnold (see the latter's essay, "On Translating Homer," for what Entwistle calls his "thundering against the philistines who dared to equal the 'ignoble' ballad manner with the 'noble' language of Homer" [375]). Entwistle of course casts a new Wolfian light on this "epic-ballad problem." I haven't time here to recount the battles that have arisen over the fact—no doubt true—that some ballads "laid hold," as T. F. Henderson claimed, of the romance's dying "essence"—but the class snobbery surrounding them is interesting; Henderson goes on to argue, in his *Ballad as Literature* (1912), that the form went inevitably downhill when it fell into common hands: "it was beyond it to produce anything that could properly be regarded as a new literary creation, but only a kind of mongrel debasement" (qtd. in Nygard, 13).

2   See Wai Chee Dimock's Introduction as guest editor of *PMLA*'s special issue on "Remapping Genres" (2007), which explodes all traditional notions of genre in a virtual *jouissance* of collapsing boundaries, viewing genre developments as displaced from particular national or historical continua by "a runaway reproductive process: off-beat, off-center, and exogenous . . . open sets endlessly dissolved by their openness . . . the result of accidental matches between the coordinates of literary history and the distribution of human populations across the globe" (1379).

3   See Barr's feisty *Genre Fission: A New Discourse Practice for Genre Studies* (Iowa City: University of Iowa Press, 2000).

4   I apologize for the fact that this essay's space limits disallow pursuing the ballad into other languages and cultures. I must explain, too, that I treat no Irish work out of respect for the complicated issues involved; as ballads are actually "scarce within the Gaelic tradition" (McAlpine 306), modern Irish ballads are

"belated" in a sense different from the one I'll define here.

5   It's important to note that I do not refer here to continuing traditions of balladry in, say, the Appalachians, or the longer surviving traditions in some parts of Scotland (where, due to lower literacy levels and other factors, ballads resisted print for longer than their counterparts in England [McAlpine 306]).

6   See *Das Kapital*, Volume One, Chapter 27, footnote 1.

7   From William Beattie's edited selection of *Border Ballads* (London: Penguin Books, 1952), p. 27. Gloss: "lift" = sky; "gurly" = growling.

8   Quotes from poetry unless otherwise indicated come from the electronic source, *Literature Online* (LION).

9   This quote from Tennyson appears unattributed in a footnote on *Literature Online*. In *Morte d'Arthur*, Elaine, who dies of love for Lancelot, similarly floats downriver to Camelot.

10 I refer most particularly to Auden's early political work. His balladry as a whole unfortunately becomes synonymous with "light verse" in the hands of his editor Edward Mendelson in *As I Walked Out One Evening: Songs, Ballads, Lullabies, Limericks and other Light Verse* (London: Vintage, 1995).

11 See Hughes in Wright (193). The poems I reflect on here can be found in Brooks' 1963 *Selected Poems*.

12 The quote comes from an email discussion between Bernstein and Damon. Damon's project of recovering the ballad tradition as informative of recent trends in rap, slam, and open-mike poetries is one very fruitful way to re-open study of balladic genres.

13 Yarmolinsky has been described as *The New Yorker* as "a kind of court jester among New York composers" (November 2005), one who brings folk sound together with classical and other influences.

14 Email to the author, 13 June 2010.

15 See *Say Parsley*, which recalls the 1937 massacre of Creole Haitians on the border of the Dominican Republic; victims were identified by their inability to pronounce *perejil* (parsley) in the accepted Spanish manner.

REFERENCES AND FURTHER READING

Andersen, Flemming G. "Technique, Text, and Context: Formulaic Narrative Mode and the Question of Genre." In Joseph Harris, ed. *The Ballad and Oral Literature*. Cambridge, MA: Harvard University Press, 1991. 18–39.

Bates, Katharine Lee. *Ballad Book*. 1890. Freeport, NY: Books for Libraries Press, 1966.

Bernstein, Charles. *Girly Man*. Chicago and London: University of Chicago Press, 2006.

Child, Francis James. "Ballad Poetry." *The Journal of Folklore Research* 31. 1994 (reprinted from 1874): 214–22.

Cohen, Michael. "Whittier, Ballad Reading, and the Culture of Nineteenth-Century Poetry." *Arizona Quarterly* 64: 3. Autumn 2008: 1–29.

Damon, Maria. "Was that 'Different,' 'Dissident,' or 'Dissonant'? Poetry (n) the Public Spear— Slams, Open Readings and Dissident Traditions." In Charles Bernstein, ed. *Close Listening: Poetry and the Performed Word*. New York and Oxford: Oxford University Press, 1998. 324–42.

Entwistle, William J. "New Light on the Epic-Ballad Problem." *The Journal of American Folklore* 62: 246. 1949: 375–81.

Graves, Robert. "Introduction." In Robert Graves, ed. *The English Ballad: A Short Critical Survey*. London: Ernest Benn, 1927. 7–36.

Harris, Joseph. "Introduction." In Joseph Harris, ed. *The Ballad and Oral Literature*. Cambridge, MA: Harvard University Press, 1991. 1–17.

Kamau Brathwaite, Edward. "(From) History of the Voice: The Development of Nation Language in Anglophone Caribbean Poetry." 1984. In Dohra Ahmad, ed., *Rotten English: A Literary Anthology*. New York and London: Norton & Co., 2007. 459–68.

Macaulay, Lord Thomas Babington. *History of England: From the Accession of James the Second to the Death of William the Third*. 8 vols. London: Longman, Brown, Green, Longmans and Roberts, 1858–1862.

May, Vivian M. "Maids Mild and Dark Villains, Sweet Magnolias and Seeping Blood: Gwendolyn Brooks's Poetic Response to the Lynching of Emmett Till." In Harriet Pollack and Christopher Metress, eds. *Emmett Till in Literary Memory and Imagination*. Baton Rouge: Louisiana State University Press, 2008. 98–111.

McAlpine, Kaye. *The Traditional and Border Ballad*. Edinburgh: John Donald, 2007.

McGann, Jerome J. "The Meaning of the Ancient Mariner." *Critical Inquiry* 8:1. Autumn 1981: 35–67.

Mullen, Harryette. "Harryette Mullen: In Calgary, Alberta," an interview compiled by Louis Cabri. *Boo* 7. July 1996: 2.

Mullen, Harryette. *Muse & Drudge*. Philadelphia: Singing Horse Press, 1995.

Newman, Steve. *Ballad Collection, Lyric, and the Canon: The Call of the Popular from the Restoration to the New Criticism*. Philadelphia: University of Pennsylvania Press, 2007.

Nygard, Holger Olof. "Popular Ballad and Medieval Romance." In E. B. Lyle, ed. *Ballad Studies*. Cambridge: D. S. Brewer for the Folklore Society, 1976. 1–20.

Palmer, Roy. *A Ballad History of England from 1588 to the Present Day*. London: Batsford, 1979.

Pollack, Harriet and Christopher Metress, eds. *Emmett Till in Literary Memory and Imagination*. Baton Rouge: Louisiana State University Press, 2008.

Snydergaard, Larry. "Traumatic Transformations: Villy Sørensen's Interpretive Schema and Four English-Scottish Ballads." In Susan Brantly and Thomas A. DuBois, eds. *The Nordic Storyteller: Essays in Honor of Niels Ingwersen*. Newcastle-upon-Tyne: Cambridge Scholars Publishing, 2009. 20–41.

Wright, Stephen Caldwell. *On Gwendolyn Brooks: Reliant Contemplation*. Ann Arbor: University of Michigan Press, 2001.

10
Oddity or Tour de Force?

The Sestina

Nicole Ollier

The sestina is a most singular and resilient poetic form whose invention is attributed to the French troubadour Arnaut Daniel. Jacques Roubaud describes his sestina as one of the most spectacular achievements of the *canso*, itself one of the most ancient and noble genres in the Old Provençal lyric repertoire. The *canso* consisted of forty to sixty lines, divided into stanzas, or *coblas*, built on a common pattern and generally ending with an *envoi*, or envoy, often referred to as the *tornada*.

The sestina uses six sixains, a prolific form of stanzas in English poetry; it was most popular, and highly recommended, deemed suitable for solemn themes as well as for amorous and extended narratives. The use of repeated words at the ends of lines instead of a rhyme-scheme is unique: the line-endings of the first stanza are repeated in the subsequent five stanzas, each one in a different order. The first line of each stanza begins with the last line of the preceding stanza: five words will end no fewer than sixty-five lines (Häublein 172). Häublein deems the sestina "the most fascinating stanzaic poem, with a fixed numerical order, usually *retrogradatio cruciato*, until repeated in original sequence in the envoi" (41).

In the *cobla*, Roubaud remarks, all six rhymes are "estramps," refrain-words. The *canso* rests on the chain of stanzas, achieved by a rotation of the intricately alternating rhyme-words. Preminger gives options for the *tornada*: "ABCDEF / FAEBDC / CFDABE / ECBFAD / DEACFB / BDFECA /ECA or ACE" (764–65).

Hobsbaum describes the *tornada* as a truncated concluding stanza, a summary that is further complicated by the fact that the remaining three end-words, BDF, must occur in the course of the lines, so that the three-line envoy will contain all six recurrent words (Preminger 764). Should the permutation be pursued beyond the six stanzas, Roubaud notes, the poem would fall back into the initial order. Yet the

A Companion to Poetic Genre, First Edition. Edited by Erik Martiny.
© 2012 John Wiley & Sons, Ltd. Published 2012 by John Wiley & Sons, Ltd.

permutational cycle does not come full circle, so that the *canso* remains suspended in an unfinished aural gesture (Roubaud 37).

The European Journey of the Sestina

The sestina has always excited the minds of theorists and practitioners alike, Haüblein muses: it started as a European phenomenon. The form was widely cultivated both by Arnaut Daniel's Provençal followers and by Dante and Petrarch in Italy. Their innumerable imitators were Michelangelo, Sannazoro d'Annunzio; the Spaniards Montemaya, Herrero, Lope de Vega, Cervantes; the Portuguese Lois de Camoes; the French poets Pontus de Tyard—a member of the Pleiade, who first constructed rhyming sestinas (*abcbca*) generating different stanzas, within the sestina—, the Comte de Grammont who produced an astonishing number; in the seventeenth century, the Germans Weckerlin, Opitz, von Abpclietz, Gryphus, Von Zegen, Eichendorff, and Borchardt (Preminger 764–65).

The first English sestina was composed by Spenser in the "August Eclogue" of his *Shepherds' Calender* (1579). William Drummond of Hawtornden (1585–1649) is known for his fine sestina, "Sith gone is my delight and only pleasure." English sestinas reappear towards the end of nineteenth century; A. Mary F. Robinson (1857–1944) attempted it and they are quoted by G. White in *Ballads, Rondeaus, Chants Royals, Sestinas, Villanelles, etc.* (1887). Swinburne wrote stanzas with varied verse patterns, and even with a unique rhyme in *Complaint of Lisa*, a double sestina. In the twentieth century, the form regained a certain popularity with Ezra Pound, T.S. Eliot, W.H. Auden, who all wrote sestinas of distinction. More recent poets such as Merwin, Ashbery, Kipling, Bishop, Roy Fuller, George Barker, Donald Justice, Diane Wakoski, and many others have tried the form.

Scope, Merits, and Limits of the Sestina

Sestinas have been used for amorous, pastoral, reflective, philosophical, meditative, didactic, and political subjects. They appear as single poems as well in epic and dramatic contexts. The sestina is one of the most exacting and controversial forms, which has challenged the technical potential and the supreme sense of artifice in the best poets. It enjoyed a great amount of prestige among Renaissance poets. Though its highly intellectualized structure has been deemed an obstacle to clarity, strength of metaphor, and lyric inspiration, it has been granted a distinctive aesthetic effect, arising from a fundamental tension with the structure itself. W.H. Auden is said to have "exploited its peculiar, though limited, qualities" (Spanos 551). It appears to some as a strange species which can be visited on occasion. Indeed Hobsbaum maintains that "the genius of poetry" evades it: "Forms like the villanelle and the sestina

. . . belong to the category of special effects. Individual poets have produced master-pieces in such set forms as these" (172).

The ungainliness of the sestina

To Cummins, the "metrical pattern is what holds the awkward, elliptical sound of the sestina together . . ., gives it the polish and sheen of a lyric." However he denies it is a lyric form, but rather sees it as "a meditative, narrative, dramatic form" (2). Because of its mathematical constraints and extreme complexity, he describes it as ungainly, too tricked out, it "mocks you, mocks itself," as it also mocks "formalists" by its "obviousness and lack of subtlety" (3). This of course might be verified with Louis Zukofsky's "Mantis," in which the remotely medieval theme of fatal love (embodied here by the mythical insect) runs the risk of getting lost in the convoluted abstractions of the poem. Cummins discourages any further analysis by adding that "the sestina never gets anything interesting said about it," critics using it to target bad writers or those writing unmetrical or non-metrical sestinas. He quotes Richard Wilbur to whom sestinas can be the ideal form if you need to write out of obsession. Because of the famous virtuosos that it is remembered by, such as Petrarch or Dante, trying one's hand at it may reveal a desire for permanence and perfection.

English Adaptations

One of the English precursors was Sir Philip Sidney (1554–86) who gave a couple of notable examples. In his prose work entitled *Arcadia*, Sidney inserted three sestinas, and as if to magnify the exploit, he made one into a double sestina. The effect has been likened to a knell of chimes, and highly suitable for threnody, or mourning-verse. Earlier than *Arcadia*, he produced a double sestina entitled "Ye Goat-herd Gods" which certainly sounds like a threnody; line-endings wind through them in varying permutations. When they come to stanza seven, they start up over again for a further six stanzas, maintaining the previous pattern, in the same order. The ensuing permu-tations are an exact repeat of the previous order of line-endings, so that stanza eight is symmetrical with stanza two, and stanza nine is symmetrical with stanza three. Here is William Empson's comment upon it: "The poem beats, however rich its orchestration, with a wailing and immovable monotony, for ever upon the same doors in vain" (Hobsbaum 172). In his "Paysage Moralisé," W.H. Auden seems to have consciouly derived inspiration from Sidney. More recently, Donald Justice composed with "Sestina: Here in Katmandu" a reminder not only of "Paysage Moralisé," and of Sidney's sestina, with conscious echoes of Swinburne's end-words, but also of the arch-text, Bunyan's *Pilgrim's Progress*. In his "Sestina d'Inverno," Anthony Hecht parodies Sidney's mournful Arcadia. The same dystopia migrates into Ezra Pound's "Sestina Altoforte," a dramatic monologue.

Love being a flood-theme, as Emily Dickinson would put it, it naturally occurs in Algernon Charles Swinburne's "Sestina" beginning "I saw my soul at rest upon a day," which is self-referential, metapoetic, and concerned with loss of permanence and mortality. The *tornada* ends with "Sing while he may, man has no long delight." This metaphysical reflection begins with an objectification of the soul as a bird and contemplation is the incentive to a hedonistic philosophy of life. To push the challenge further, Swinburne too invented a double sestina, "The Complaint of Lisa." Instead of composing a sestina and starting all over again with the same end-words once he has completed the sixth sixain, he composes twelve-line stanzas with twelve different teleutons. Another singularity is his choosing teleutons that rhyme. The conceit is a flowery one, the unhappy lover deems herself a plebeian flower, "I am the least flower in thy flowery way" (l.21), while the loved one is magnified, "O Love, Love, Love, the kingly sunflower!" (l.25). The more modest one is cosmically humbled by the heliotrope, and steeped in darkness: "So the white star-flower turns and yearns to thee" (l.3).

The *tornada* here becomes a six-line stanza which repeats the end-words three times instead of two, as is the case regularly. The sunflower is the symbol of the loved man, and the girl who loves him without any hope of fulfillment calls for death, and ends the sestina in the third person, as an elegy for herself, having died in her quest for the sunflower, a kind of Holy Grail. The sunflower, which stands for the indifferent beloved, saturates the *tornada* and closes it.

Architects, Houses, Home, and Homecoming

The cross-stitch and the braid

There is something in the building of a sestina that is reminiscent of the architecture of cathedral masons, astrologists, mathematicians, or esoteric magicians; the patient, careful crafstmanship of medieval tapestry, the regular and tidy duty of a woman's hairdressing. Something intimate, domestic, related to the inner sphere of home. The pattern used follows the gesture of the braider who crosses the strand in the center with a strand from the left, then from the right. This is called *retrogradatio cruciata*, from *retrogradatio*, moving backward (still used for backing up a car, *rétrograder*, or demoting someone), and cruciate, (from *crux*, signifying cross), as the cross-stitch on the canvas, in which the gesture is associated with the Christian sign of the cross—the canvas stitch, indeed stitching of any kind, also involves the disappearance and reappearance of the needle and thread, like the teleutons in the sestina. Sylvia Plath, who wrote a villanelle but no sestina, braids three voices in "A Poem for Three Voices." Backward crossing, or crossing backward, makes up the step of this dance, and for Marilyn Krysl, this "dyadic movement enacts a cathartic rite," its delivery of effects depending "utterly on counterpointing long against short duration is unique and uniquely suited to deliver its metempiric effect."

Drawing another inscrutable house

The charm of Bishop's "Sestina" lies in its fairy-tale atmosphere, its slant telling, the oblique way in which the protagonists remain anonymous, become archetypal, "the grandmother," "the child," and the objects—the "Stove" and the "almanac" are personified—the book is compared to a bird. All four words provide the teleutons, the remaining two being the "house" in which woman and child dwell, or that which the child draws, imagining another world, or perhaps re-membering a phantasized past which might explain or replace the present, and the "tears," which are at the core of the mood of the poem, and prove metamorphic. First shed by the grandmother, who hides them beneath laughter—not unlike the old black men we shall see telling lies in the "Cotton Sestina," "their good deep laughter in the gut" (l.22)—they are accompanied by those of the rain falling on the roof, as in a season for tears, turning "equinoctial," they are relayed by the sputtering of the singing kettle which pours those madly dancing tears into the grandmother's teacup, from where they imperceptibly wind their way into the child's drawing, in the same fashion as the "winding pathway" she draws, leading up to the house, a house as "rigid" as the poetic form chosen. The tears take the shape of buttons on the suit of the absent father introduced in the drawing, expressing the sadness of the daughter's longing, then the shape of moons shed by the almanac—acting as book of dreams, book of prayers, of prophecies, recipes, as Testament—into the flower-beds of the drawn house, which becomes the object of transference through which those mysteries are expressed, helping the child to make out the meaning of life; the house serves as the medium for the repressed mourning disguised under the dancing, the singing. Thus the child goes on drawing "another inscrutable house," since the mystery repeats itself, esoterically, in compulsively reiterated innuendoes. The dedication of the child to her drawing is matched by the careful tetrameters for which the poem is also notable. Not one teleuton is missing in the envoy, when many poets choose the lighter option of half:

> Time to plant tears, says the almanac.
> The grandmother sings to the Marvelous stove
> and the child draws another incrutable house.
>
> (ll.37–39)

The mad mother whom Elizabeth Bishop stopped seeing from the age of five because she had been put away in an institution is not placed in the drawing, only her madness merges in the "mad dance" of the tears on the hot kettle stove. What makes this sestina so hauntingly moving and so immortal is probably the fact that the constraint of concentrated repetition of the form perfectly espouses the sense of claustrophobia and repression of the short narrative: each word is necessary, elemental, respecting the secret of understatements. The childish simplicity of the words, the elliptical, pared-down form, the well-known reticence of the author, give a sense of magic to this unforgettable sestina which, in its consummate art, will forever become the reference for all modern versions.

In Bishop's wake

Bishop's other sestina, "A Miracle for Breakfast" does not achieve the same effect. Inspired from a painting by the surrealist de Chirico, it creates a strong visual impression. The poem describes a contemplative wait associated with a mock-investigation, and is therefore half-narrative, half-static, the expectancy—"waiting for the miracle" (l.24)—is meta-artistic, telling about the patience of art, the quest for a beauty that surprises in the quotidian ordinariness of common sights. Bishop painted, and this sestina, like the painter's eye, runs through all corners of the frame, drawing our attention to the change of light, to what can be seen in the mind's eye.

John Ashbery chooses a title resembling that of a painting for "Farm Implements and Rutabagas in a Landscape" but the prosaic elements in it announce the juxtaposition of ostentatiously literary language with proletarian heroes of the *Popeye* cartoon series; the poem reads like a post-modern film scenario, curiously disturbing in its parodic, heterogeneous style, and its hybrid genre. The domestic scene might be an antithetical example to the tableau Bishop creates; nevertheless, it appears as a stylistic experiment.

Supposedly one of Bishop's former students in Boston, or a poet imagining himself in that position, David Ray represents the writing of a sestina as an assignment the renowned poet gave to her class, and which defeated the unfortunate would-be author of the sestina-in-creation: "I made a chart but still screwed up the sequence" (l.5). He pauses to wonder at the goal:

> it's absurd, a fixed sequence
> Of six words weaving in and out, not even a leap
> Into chaos or free verse.
>
> (ll.18–20)

As he states his former incapacity to produce the clever deed in fifteen minutes, he manages to redeem himself after the fact with this metapoetic, metasestinesque act.

Secrecy

The intimacy of a parent and child having a conversation, or simply sharing silence in a house finds an echo in Robin Becker's "Sad Sestina," which might well be informed by Bishop's, with its guise of a kitchen, the "living room, where secrecy turns to habit" (l.9); instead of the mad dance of the kettle tears, we are given the father's precepts when he was "mad." As in Jeffers' "Cotton Sestina" which we shall see further down, the poet acknowledges his blues, and his temptation to evade reality:

Most days, I'd trade anything
to be rid of the blues, accustomed to flight and departure,
strategies that saved my life.

(ll.20–22)

The end-word "foot" is used now as a noun, now as a verb (to foot the bills), so that
a sense of sameness and instability, of recurrence and alteration is conveyed. The conflation of awful and cheerful in "December's awful / cheerfulness" (ll.33–34) is also
reminiscent of Bishop in the poem "The Bight"; "yesterday's," the first of the end-
words in Becker's sestina, betrays the obsession with time so common in this form,
and announces the final line in the envoy, concerned with flux, mutability, loss,
breaking-up, with the polysemy of the word "date": "a standing date with change, a
season of departures" (l.38).

Moving houses

Another poem spawned, it seems, by Bishop's sestina is "Sestina for the House" by
Ronald Wallace. A father and his young daughter chat in a house; the father, out of
love for his child and family at large, wants to move house. But the child loves her
house as she loves the doll's house she makes from leaves which understand it is time
for them also to accomplish the cycle of nature by falling lovingly, so as to be recycled
into a doll's house; she does not want to lose the house, as she can hardly imagine her
birds would pack up to follow her. Grief makes her voice her hatred to her father.
Both father and child experience the hurt that thwarted love can cause. The reciprocity
as well as the criss-crossing of feelings, the stubborn misunderstanding are heightened
by repetition, especially when the words resemble each other, "move" and "love" and
"leave" uniting the incompatible for the daughter who feels her father cannot understand a child. The pipe smoked by the father turns into Indian pipes in the garden
and the piping of the birds to the father: "Don't move. Don't move" (37), making
the father much less unmoved or immovable than he first seemed. The sestina sounds
like a threnody, an act of contrition, or a plea for mercy.

Blues and impossible homecoming

To use another textile metaphor, we might say that the sestina uses the teleutons as
shuttles plying back and forth to weave the cloth, although they do it in an inordinate
backward crossing fashion. The waning and fading of the colored threads gains interest
from the choice of polysemic *repetends* in which meaning can fluctuate, and create a
surprise. Some poets keep the radicals of the words and modify their endings as syntax
and meaning will have it. In "Cotton Field Sestina," Honorée Fanonne Jeffers takes
some liberty in superimposing the resort to all those possibilities: she changes "lies"
into "lying" and "liars," and, as is to be expected, uses the term as a verb or a noun,

and both in the sense of deceptiveness and that of reclining. "Dust" can also be "dusty," it turns into "grave dust," where "grave" is both mortuary and serious. As for the repetend "water," it now signifies the ocean of the Middle Passage, "salt water" (l.11), "the big water" (l.24), now sweat, "so much water / down my neck" (ll.4–5), now amniotic fluid, "denies me her waters" (l.32), now the boiling water in the saucepan where rice is cooking, with prophetic sybilline vocality, "thus speaks the guilty water / chattering down my rice" (ll.15–16), until it acquires a more abstract, symbolical meaning, "truth's water" (l.38) in the *tornada*. In the same fashion, the word "gut" is now "my gut" (l.6), meaning my archaic memory and instinctual feeling, now supposedly that of a cat, out of which cord is made (the use in actual fact is or rather used to be for surgery), "the song plucked on a gut / string" (ll.7–8), now the mother's matrix, "my mother's gut" (l.29), "her sweet gut" (l.33). "Blues" signifies the music of the black folks in the fields, "original blues" (l.12), or the blues of the poet coming back home to a cotton field, experiencing the nostalgia of a whole heritage of former generations of cotton-picking slaves: "ancestry: copper folks gone" (l.11).

The young woman forces herself to "reconcil[e]" (l.14) with home-coming in a sestina which is her own form of blues music—the repetitions, enhanced by the anaphoras, making it sound like a negro spiritual. The summoning of the picture of ancestry becomes a memory: "I remember . . . ," "I remember . . ." (ll.19, 21); the "road" (the teleuton in the first line) past the cotton-field is the road of memory, back to the time before birth in the uterus. The *tornada* sounds like a refrain, where all repetends seem polyphonic, carrying the several meanings they have engrained, adding the significance created in the confluence of those: the girl does not seem inclined to "trot behind her [mother] on her smooth road" (l.36), so that this particular end-word disappears in the envoy, except when it is embedded in the word "roadside." In spite of a haunting desire to "go home," the negations seem to preclude any welcome, or possible homecoming, when there is no longer a home, even in the persona herself, who is existentially estranged from her mother, and alienated from her motherland of Georgia.

This most moving sestina manages to incorporate the "rhythm an' blues" in a forceful fashion. The form of the sestina seems ideally suited to its mood, its nostalgia, its confessed guilt, its explicit desire for "reconciliation" rather than "escape," and ultimately its unresolved tension between a longing for love and the feeling of having been rejected. All those elements, and the presence of two women, mother and daughter, seem to claim a kinship with the arch contemporary reference in the matter of sestinas, Elizabeth Bishop's unadornedly titled "Sestina."

The prodigal

At a far remove from Bishop, yet inspired by the same economy of means, is a sestina which belongs to the sphere of home and homecoming, Miller Williams' "The Shrinking Lonesome Sestina." This poem revolves around the idea of subjective time that goes fast or slowly, the rapidity of it is symbolized by the steadily diminishing length of each successive stanza, until the sixth, which holds nothing but the end-words, falling into two sentences, like the signals of an SOS from a sinking ship:

> Time
> goes
> too
> fast.
> Come
> home.

(ll.31–36)

There follows the *tornada*, recalling the once not-so-fast time, and anticipating the time when the missed person will come home: "Me, I'll still be home" (l.39), the poet asserts in characteristically oral language. Home, which was the first teleuton, and which is the one obsession, the place to which the bubble in the compass points, where the lonely parent waits.

We have seen that the temptation is great, to take more and more freedom with the rules, the rhythm, to use parody, to debunk the learned medieval heritage, to tamper with the formula, and to exploit to the full the possibilities of the polysemic teleutons. This needs to be done within the iron vice of the form, be it through the length of the lines, the tone of discourse, but also the syntax, the repetends, and in a dialogic fashion. The troubadour reference remains in the memory of the sestina-writer, who is conscious of the orality of his speech, the musicality of the original melody, the addressees, the performative or illocutionary act of the song, and the initial solemnity of the occasion, as well as the prestigious lineage, and the call for immortality. Among the poets who go astray, comically, in a picturesque fashion, are some of the greater writers in the English language. The mirror effect of the sestina form makes them well aware of the act of writing, and the sestina reflects and incorporates their activity.

Tampering with the Rules and Other Liberties: Metasestinas

Vernacular encoding

The troubadour is undoubtedly the model for the tramp for Rudyard Kipling when he uses oral language with truncations in "Sestina of the Tramp-Royal," a poem in which the missing consonants mimick the neglectful pronunciation of the modern-day wanderer: h's are dropped as in *My Fair Lady*, as well as final g's in gerundive forms, or dentals, voiced or unvoiced, at the end of words. Pronunciation slackness or an accent is rendered by "Gawd," slang phrases can be used, "unless you . . . drew your tucker some'ow from the world" (l.17). A few grammatical sub-standard slips in conjugated verbs, "What do it matter" (l.7), "it aren't no good" (l.13), coexist with archaic niceties "she [the world] 'ath done" (l.37). Yet the French construction of the compound name, "Tramp-Royal" in the proleptic title announces elements of an aristocratic mind, paving the way for the meditation on life and death, even to the reflection on the brevity of our life-span on earth,—"life's none so long" (l.24), which goes along with the poetic choice of the metaphors ("my mate—the wind that tramps the world" [l.30]), some biblical archaisms, the elegant and often learned phrasing. The sestina is metaliterary since life is compared to a book which must be read from cover to cover. The tramp royal completes the sestina with a *tornada* which is the composition of his own elegy, voicing the turning of the last page, with a blessing for the world, and a satisfaction for having known it as fully as the choice of a free tramp's life allowed him. This sestina belongs to the genre which Gérard Genette calls "écritures sur le seuil," writing on the threshold of death.

Variations in teleutons: loosing the fetters

"Want a fun poetic challenge?": that is Marilyn Taylor's invitation in her amusing paper illustrated by a sestina titled "How to Write a Sestina" by New Jersey poet Edmund Conti; she suggests that "small variations are absolutely legitimate. In fact, playing a little fast and loose with your repetends often adds variety and freshness to a form that runs the risk of becoming monotonous." In Conti's sestina, "body" may turn into "somebody" or "lines" into "line's," "long" into "headlong." Those minor changes which we have already witnessed are sometimes less modest, both in frequency and nature.

On the threshold, father and son

Variation can be transformation: David Wojahn's persona in "Floating Houses" speaks in the voice of a father to his son whom he remembers as a boy, and to whom he talks about his own son, whose precarious health seems an augury of poor longevity. The poet uses the end-word "sound," first in the sense of a bay, "across the sound," then the word turns into the verb to sound, later a noun, until it reaches the meaning of health, "body unsound." The end-word, "houses" becomes "housed"; "location" becomes "locate" and the word "timber" once turns into "timbre," meaning pitch of voice; "stationary," or "unstationary," is once cut into "radio station"; more unexpected, the word "boy" becomes "buoy," or "buoyed," the last meanings merge together in the last line: "And there his papa's lantern, a light the boy can locate" (l.39). The three generations are looking for landmarks and signs to read their destiny. The sick boy needs his father as a buoy; and hope in the health of the son is like a buoy to the boy's father. The impermanence, instability of ever-moving signs may illustrate what the title announces, "floating houses," fluctuating envelopes, containers, which urge the reader to flexibility to adapt, as the fathers need to be prepared for what the future may have in store for them or their progeny.

Squaring the circle: unique teleuton

The formula is altogether modified in a very amusing sestina, "Bob" by Jonah Winter. The name Bob serves as end-word for each of the thirty-nine lines. The position, true to the tradition of courteous love in the medieval *canso*, is that of a lover whose love is unrequited. He has a rival, by the name of Bob. The shortness of the name, its reversibility, the way it can be turned into a verb, the plosive consonants it contains, which make it sound like the opening of a cork in a champagne-bottle, turn it into a metamorphic syllable, pliable to every intonation. First the subject of the third-person narration, Bob is addressed personally before dropping into history. Soon after trying to be fair with his rival, the poet falls into some petty chanting: "Bob / also, does not have tenure—ha ha ha—*and* Bob / cannot cook as well as I can" (ll.30–31); "what I can't understand , Bob— / yes I'm talking to you again, is why you, Bob, / could be more desirable than me" (ll.34–36).

The poet tries to exact a vengeance on the man who stole his girlfriend, to belittle him through his derogatory remarks, but his pillorying falls short, and after an ellipsis, the *tornada* functions as a coda, "[M]onths later," which blocks any hope of ever recovering the girlfriend, now married to Bob. As for the poet, he ironically has incorpored the object of his jealousy and endlessly mimicks his rival, agitated by the reeling movement of his incantation, "Me? On a dark and stormy sea of Bob-thoughts, desperately, I bob" (l.38). So that the two rivals are united in a single predication. The poet does what the other is. Loving the same girl, being haunted by the rival, has literally and comically superimposed the two.

Metapoetry, *rigor mortis*, the grave sestina as coffin

One feature of a number of sestinas is self-referentiality, the mirror-effect, and the poet's consciousness of writing a sestina, publicizing the attempt, convoking an audience to witness the exploit: hence a strong metapoetic, metasestinesque strand. The sestina appears as such a constraint to Ronald Wallace in an elegiac poem to a dead friend that he compares the form to a coffin in "The Poet, Graveside" where one of the teleutons is the word "poem." The poet talks to the deceased

> in this stark, symmetrical place more
> rigid than the most restrictive poem.
>
> (ll.4–5)

He wonders where God's mercy worked, which ought to have given "more solace than the most respected poem," naming the sestina presumably, since he is writing to perform this divine gesture. Abruptly, the performance of sestina-writing in action fires off like a wet petard, with a rickety quatrain by way of envoy, ending:

> *God, don't let us be*
> *cut off, incomplete, like a sestina, ending here.*
>
> (ll.27–28; emphasis in the original)

The defeat in the form of a prayer to God may be a refusal to comply with the deadly shape of the coffin-like form invoked at the beginning, just as it is a refusal of the friend's loss.

Ungainly revolution

The title "How the Sestina Works" appears as a recipe to write a sestina: indeed, with it, Anne Waldman also writes a metasestina, choosing as a teleuton the word "poetry," and as another, the impossible "methedrine," whose lack of pliability narrows down the possibilities to almost naught; still another is "yawn." So that the poem is bound to revolve around itself and the tension is between medicine and weariness, the first line running: "I opened this poem with a yawn." Since the poem is an activist exhortation to revolution, it is no wonder that the ending should skid off the rails, and the *tornada* add an extra line after an invocation without verbs, using the end-words as a series which appears to have been thrown pell-mell into the pot to suit the purpose of that envoy, leaving no room for articulation except outside the tight imposed format: "I choose all of you for my poem personally" (l.40). The gesture is a form of incommunicado, failing to communicate externally, choosing the personal, rather than the social sharing.

The dummy element, *post-mortem* communion

Pushing further the hermetic choice of end-words, a curious sestina by James K. Baxter selects a setting in a faraway culture, described as "on its deathbed," and the setting is "a Maori house." Some pidgin English is included, presumably uttered by the "pakeha farmers" or the "marae," and one teleuton does not belong to the English vocabulary: "kai," which could be interpreted as a local name, along with the other linguistic exoticisms. The different contexts define it as meaning "food" or "dish," but the title "Sestina to Frank McKay" motivates its choice as a tribute paid to a poet. The recurrence of the opaque teleuton woven into the fabric of the poem in a numerological fashion as a magical strand works in the tradition of keening, of the threnody which Greek hired mourners used until recently to improvise, borrowing set frames and incorporating the name of the deceased and some biographical elements they had collected.

Metalexical, un-romantic courtship

Tension between tradition and innovation, faithfulness and deconstruction can be found in a form of carnivalization of the genre, when the *amour courtois* is inverted into a courtship voiced in a loathsome jargon by an obnoxious wooer who seems innocent of Ronsard's poem "Mignonne, allons voir si la rose qui ce matin avait éclose . . .": Karl Jay Shapiro uses the highly repetitive form in "Sestina of the Militant Vocabulary," as a sheath to line up like teleutons the words a militant might use for indoctrination, namely opaque, boring abstractions, some rather meaningless, such as "power structure," "Establishment," or radically simplistic and scornful, "pigs." The empty rhetoric turns round and round, with a parallel between war and love until the *tornada* allows the reader to understand a man is trying to ideologically intoxicate a prospective girlfriend into experiencing the sexual revolution with him—making of himself a perfect bombastic obnoxious fool in the process. This performative sestina, supposed to persuade, is pleasantly parodic and self-destructive in its counterproductive effect. Yet its comical impact derives greatly from its dialogism with the original medieval tradition, which enhances the ruthlessness, the machism of a brutish prospective lover, whose totalitarian ideas leave no room for the respect of the female or of the poetic genre he tackles.

Formulaic Poetry

Circularity, cyclical time, uroboros

When James Cummins tries to figure a sestina placed in the epoch when it thrived, what he sees is "the sense of circularity and completion," "a ritual" (3). The number mysticism of the medieval mind gives him an insight into the fascination for the sestina, that stops short of the seventh stanza, which would signify wholeness and make it go back to the initial numerical pattern, creating a mirror stanza to the first, and a closing of the circle. This figure of the serpent biting its tail is refered to as uroboros, symbolizing the endless cycle of time.

Marianne Shapiro sees the sestina as a poetic form deeply concerned with time as a structuring principle rather than with metrical virtuosity. The sense of time, "a structural component of the form" for Cummins, is to be thought of as Heraclitean, the repetition of end-words being both the same and different, since they are used in an ever-changing context. Each teleuton must develop and acquire some added or slightly different meaning, thus voyaging through the poem and modifying its own echo. Repetition plus variation, he recalls, quoting Frank Baldanza evoking Proust, and Huckleberry Finn, create rhythm, similar to the "little phrase" by Vinteuil, and not unlike conversation.

He reminds us that the sestina "is a relic from an age of faith," with a "meditative voice" in dialogue with God, and with the "adornments" of the Catholic faith. Indeed,

Marilyn Krysl develops this idea of "the sestina as rite" and takes up David Rothman's emphasis on "the greatest possible sequential displacement and juxtaposition" that come from the repetition next to each other of two words which were furthest apart previously. The sense of order created by repetition, and even concentration, as Krysl maintains, goes along with a sense of magic, the power of things, "Safety and magic on one side, freedom and movement on the other."

Numerology and metaphysics, mathematical completeness

The practice of the sestina has been described as equivalent to "squaring the circle" (Spanos 551), since the poem is a "squared form" made up at the core of six sixains. It therefore superimposes squared forms upon a circular form since the pattern of permutations drives back towards the initial figure. This superimposition creates a tension, which the fluidity of the sixains strung together denies. The poem is informed by "a connective logic working toward a smooth and orderly transition from stanza to stanza, creating an easily perceived and formally perfect unity" (Spanos 549). The reader perceives two antithetical thrusts at the same time as he intellectually grasps the whole: "The dynamics of squared forms, the *retrogradatia cruciata*, works toward a logical and mathematical completeness, by a process of repeated and systematic destruction of a previously perceived order in the recomposition of that order according to principles which are impenetrable in the act of reading" (Spanos 549).

Tension drives towards a resolution which is sometimes a state of irresolution, the *sofrirs* engendered by *dezir* must be tempered by the *mezura* of writing, a performance which Bishop for one perfectly perpetuates. "Singing poems was a way of mediating desire with time's flux" (Krysl 3). In this *mezura*, numbers signify, symbolize, conjure up. Six represented "the highest state of union attainable in the profane world," and also appears in geometry as the double triangle: it is the figure of the Seal of Solomon, or the Star of David, the middle sephiroth of the Kaballah tree, joining heaven and earth, as the Greek pillar joins the uranian and chthonian forces. The end-word sequence therefore matches the solar and lunar zodiacal signs (two stars which are so present in some of the sestinas we have examined), and the stanzaic structure could be seen as rendering the sun's annual course round the ecliptic. Six represented the "perfect marriage" of polar opposites in earthly life and temporal time. Six also represented perfect harmony in the realm of sound, enabling you to hear the music of the spheres, which the love-lorn Klaius praised in his beloved in Sir Philip Sidney's "Ye Goat-herd Gods," "She, whose least word brings from the spheres their music" (l.68). Klaius laments over his own discordant music, yet the sestina attempts to conjure up some magic assistance, thanks to its formula.

A specificity of the number six is its lack of a centre, and it stops just before the sacred number seven is reached. For Krysl, "The symbology of six and seven resonates subliminally, bodily, when we hear them in the formal structure of music and poetry" (4). For Cummins, quoted by Krysl, the formula gives the reader "the sense of circularity and completion—of Eliade's sacred and profane time—that resonated in the medieval mind, and resonates still."

That sense of permanence in spite of eclipses, the rhythm of disappearance and re-apparition, are not alien to Freud's *fort und da*—the small child's playing with an object hung from a spool, thus making the apprenticeship of presence and absence, that of his mother for the psychoanalyst, and symbolically, the cycle of life and death. The flux of time, and the fluctuation of the teleutons that come and go, may symbolize the river of life, the passing of time which, in its cyclicity, repeats itself, in the shape of a spiral, each closing of the cycle slightly open and bringing back the same in a slightly different guise. As in Milan Kundera's *Unbearable Lightness of Being*, where a hat carries layers of meanings when it is used for different occasions, as in Flannery O'Connor's short-story "God Country People" where a wooden leg becomes loaded with meaning by the end of the story, each return to a teleuton adds another nuance, until they all accumulate by the end of the sestina so that anticipation and retrospective hindsight, or reminiscence, go together. After the teleutons have played their little dance on the ring of the sestina, or the needle has completed its final stitch, they are taken up by the tailor who calls them back in half the number of lines, the echo reverberating louder from this accrued concentration.

Arithmetics and other unholy fragmentations

A thorough re-interpretation of the sestina to render it indigenous to the New World is attempted by Florence Casseen Mayers who drives the formulaic origin of the form to its limit, choosing figures as repeat-words, which she places in the initial position of the lines rather than as teleutons, which she only occasionally replaces with rhymes. Her "All-American Sestina," announces the divorce with the European tradition, and a radical change of the formula. It uses no sentences—only one verb in an idiomatic aphorism—but instead a litanic list of elements that render a vision of a modern, industrial, automated, materialistic, very much disembodied American life, reminiscent of "A Supermarket in California" by Allen Ginsberg (*Howl*). The first stanza begins in the numerical order of a child learning to count and after the creed of the nation, names a few staples of everyday life in the United States.

> One nation, indivisible
> Two-car garage
> Three strikes you're out
> Four-minute mile
> Five-cent cigar
> Six-string guitar
>
> (ll.1–6)

The formula is then carefully applied, with one rare variation, when the figure is a multiple, and comes second, "sweet sixteen"; sometimes as in an advertisement for real estate, "four rms, hi flr, w/vu." The poem also brings the summary of American life to the tomb in the *tornada*, the juxtaposition of the vanities of earthly possessions enhanced by their closeness to what awaits the owner eventually: "Six feet under, one-horse town" (l.39).

Quoted as a modern sestina-writer is Diane Wakoski, noticed for her fluid syntax and difficult end-words in "Sestina from the Home Gardener" (1968). She manages to give flexibility to her sestinas by lengthening her lines, which fluctuate between pentameters and heptameters, creating more distance between the repetitions. Those serve the purpose of a floral confusion between the young California wife of a gardener and a gipsy flower for instance, the woman metamorphoses into a gardener tending sunflowers, which are in fact blackjack players. Husband and wife show their incompatibilities through their antagonistic tastes for quite different hours of the day. The floral *parabola* does smack of a faintly medieval flavor.

Sestinas have become a reference, a legend, almost a myth: some oddity that belongs to the theory and didactics of poetics. The idea remains, of a form which is disciplinary, in the sense of its dogmatism, existing as an exercise, and at the same time formulaic, and therefore liable to bring into communion with the sacred and the divine. Just as the esoteric numbers were a ladder to mysticism in medieval times.

Conclusion, or Envoy

Our exploration of the journeys and transformations of the sestina from its creation by the *troubadour* Arnaut Daniel in Southern France in the early twelfth century to the contemporary poets who emulate him in the English language in Europe or in the United States cannot but leave a lot of authors on the roadside. An exhaustive collection of all recorded sestinas in the English language could result in an interesting anthology. Translating sestinas from another language would create constraints which a translator might not find more of a challenge than rhymes. This journey had to limit its ambitions about a genre, the "limited" qualities of which it is not for us to judge. What has the sestina lost or acquired over the centuries? First, it has lost the music: it no longer is a song, even though the accents and rhythms of blues can occasionally be heard, so that this special form of *canso* somehow is faithless to its origins. What it has partly carried through the centuries is the tradition of *amour courtois*, even though the result is, parodically, a sometimes unromantic, discourteous, form of courtship, proffered with a vindicative tone, by the lady instead of the man. Love certainly is at the core of many sestinas, but the archaic pastoral form of Sidney's times, and the celebration of *eros*, have yielded to a kind of *agape* between parent and child. This unfulfilled, unhappy, or grieving love, is linked to impermanence, loss of the loved one, past and effective, or feared in the future. Whatever the cause of the loss, it is inevitably linked with death, real or symbolic, and to ephemerality. Yet a dialogism with the original creation is occasion for mirth, just as the extreme formality of the sestina clashes comically with a faulty, colloquial, even slangish language, the troubadour singing in the voice of a tramp, a modern-era replica of the wandering knights of bygone days or haranguing with the vocabulary of a political activist. The sixteenth century created its masters, whose disciples seem to have formed a brother-hood, recognizable through the choice of similar themes and/or the resort to identical teleutons. However the twentieth century also created the arch-reference with Elizabeth Bishop who certainly wins the prize, as no other poet seems quite so successfully to make the most of the constraints of the sestina, not only transcending its limits, but using them to work towards what she purports to convey, a grammar of secrecy and reticence, a mystery of repressed confidences, and the oppression of a grief which has been incorporated and can only be objectified through a catharsis of words, art serving to mourn a loss which propriety and the contingencies of a family forbid to voice, in a perpetual avoidance and masking of truth. Unlike her, many other artists put their special imprint in the practice of the exercise by modifying the rules in all kinds of imaginative ways, the rigidity of the sestina-form appearing to some as a coffin. Going back to the troubadours' time, the number symbolism, and the squaring of the circle of a form which pulls in two antagonistic directions, result in a race for emulating the difficulties and finding parodic, sometimes riddlesome modern equivalents of the esoteric, sacred, numerology of the Middle Ages. Some poets insist on trying their pens at the sestina, seldom failing to fall into the temptation of metapoetry; some prefer to sneer at this difficult challenge and dismiss it with a turn of the heel, few remain indifferent to the existence of a genre which, like the tree, or pillar of poetry, sends its roots deep into the unenlightened eras, and reaches into modern times, so that its revival is probably but beginning.

References and Further Reading

Ashbery, John. The Double Dream of Spring, 1966, 1979, The Morning of Starting Out: the First Five Books of Poetry, 1997, www.poetryfoundation.org/archive/poem.html?id=177258.

Auden, W.H. *Selected Poems*, ed. Edward Mendelson, New York: Vintage, 1989.

Auden, W.H. *Collected Shorter Poems 1927–1957*, London: Faber & Faber, 1966, 1977, pp. 57–58, "Paysage Moralisé," "Have a Good Time," http://escottjones.typepad.com/myquest/2006/08/paysage_moralis.html.

Baxter, James K. "Sestina to Frank McKay," also author of "Sestina of the River Road," "Sestina of the Makutu," "Sestina," http://sestinas.jelyon.com/2007/05/10/sestina-to-frank-mckay-james-k-baxter.

Becker, Robin. "Sad Sestina," *Selections from Bookgleaner*, Bookgleaner@gmail.com, http://inardboundpoetry.blogspot.com/2007/01/304-sad-sstina-robin-becker.html.

Bishop, Elizabeth. *Poems 1927–1979*, New York: Farrar, Straus and Giroux, 1983.

Cummins, James. "Calliope Music: Notes on the Sestina," *Antioch Review*, Spring 2007, 55: 2, 148–60.

Davidson, F. J. A. "The Origin of the Sestina," *Modern Languages Notes* 25 (1910): 18–20.

Häublein, Ernst. *The Stanza*, New York: Harper & Row, 1978.

Hecht, Anthony. "Sestina d'Inverno," http://sestinas.jelyon.com/2007/05/09/sestina-dinverno-anthony-hecht.

Hobsbaum, Philip Dennis. *Rhythm, Metre and Rhyme*, New York: Routledge, New Critical Idiom, 1996.

Jeffers, Honorée Fanonne. *American Poetry Review*, May/June 2004, 33:3.

Jeffers, Honorée Fanonne. "Cotton Field Sestina," *American Poetry Review*, May/June 2004, 33:3, http://web.ecscohost.com.haysend.u-bordeaux3.fr/ehost/detail.

Justice, Donald. "Sestina: Here in Katmandu," http://americanpoems.com/poets/donaldjustice/384, also author of "Hang it all, Ezra Pound, there is only the one sestina!"

Kipling, Rudyard. "Sestina of the Tramp Royal," http://daypoems.net/poems/1856.html.

Krysl, Marilyn. "Sacred and Profane: the Sestina as Rite," *American Poetry Review*, March/April 2004, 33:2, 7–12.

Lankford, Ryan. "Bishop's Sestina," *Explicator*, September 1, 1993, 52:1.

Maris, Kathryn. "Darling, Would You Please Pick up Those Books," runner up in 2008 *Troubadour Poetry* competition judged by Jo Shapcott and Stephen Knight www.guardian.co.uk/books/booksblog/2008/dec/15/sestina-maris-troubadour-arnaut.

Mayers, Florence Casseen. "All-American Sestina," *The Atlantic Monthly Company*, July 1996, 278:1, 86, www.theatlantic.com/unbound/poetry/antholg/mayers/sestina.htm, the poem can be heard read by the author in RealAudio.

Miller, Williams. "The Shrinking Lonesome Sestina," http://geocities.com/bjlandry_00/williamsshrinkingsestina.html.

Pound, Ezra. "Sestina Altoforte," http://homepages.wmich.edu/~cooneys/poems/Pound.altaf.html.

Preminger, Alex (ed). *Princeton Encyclopedia of Poetry and Poetics*, Fran J. Warnke and O. B. Hardison, Jr., associate editors, enlarged edn. 1965, reprt. 1979, 764–65.

Ray, David. "Miss Bishop's Sestina," http://sestinas.jelyon.com/2007/05/10/miss-bishops-sestina-david-ray.

Roubaud, Jacques. *Les Troubadours*, bilingual anthology, Paris: Seghers, 1971.

Shapiro, Karl Jay. "Sestina: of the Militant Vocabulary," http://sestinas.jelyon.com/2007/05/10sestina-of-the-militant-vocabulary-karl-jay-shapiro.

Shapiro, Myriam. *Hieroglyph of Time: The Petrarchan Sestina*, Minneapolis: the University of Minnesota Press, 1980.

Sidney, Philip. "Ye Goat-herd Gods," http://homepages.wmich.edu/~cooneys/poems/Sidney.sestina.html.

Sot, Michel, Boudet, Jean-Patrice and Guerreau-Jalabert, Anita. *Histoire culturelle de la France*, ed. Jean-Pierre Rioux and Jean-François Sirinelli, vol. I: *Le Moyen-Âge*, ed. Michel Sot, Paris: Seuil, 1997.

Spanos, Margaret. "An Exploration of the Dynamics of Poetic Structure of the Sestina," *Speculum*, Mediaeval Academy of America, 53:3, July 1978, 545–57.

Stillman, Frances. *The Poet's Manual and Rhyming Dictionary*, New York: Thomas Y. Crowell, 1965.

Swinburne, Algernon Charles. "Sestina," http://sestinas.jelyon.com/2007/05/17/sestina-algernon-charles-swinburne, "The Complaint of Lisa," http://sestinas.jelyon.com/2007/05/17/the-complaint-of-lisa-algernon-charles-swinburne.

Taylor, Marilyn. "Want a Fun Poetic Challenge?" *Writer*, June 2008, 121:6, 15–16.

Wakoski, Diane. "Blackjack Sestina," http://sestinas.jelyon.com/2007/05/10/blackjack-sestina-diane-wakoski, "Sestina from the Home Gardener," http://sestinas.jelyon.com/2007/05/10/sestina-from-the-home-gardener-diane-wakoski.

Wallace, Ronald. "Sestina for the House," http://sestinas.jelyon.com/2007/05/10/sestina-for-the-house-ronald-wallace; "The Poet, Graveside," http://sestinas.jelyon.com/2007/05/10/the-poet-graveside-ronald-wallace.

Winter, Jonah. "Sestina: Bob," *Poetry*, Spring 1999, 2000, *Ploughshares*, Cohen Award, Boston: Ploughshares, Emerson College.

Wojahn, David. "Floating Houses," http://sestinas.jelyon.com/2007/05/09/floating-houses-david-wojan.

Woloski, Shira. "Representing Other Voices: Rhetorical Perspective in Elizabeth Bishop," Hebrew University of Jerusalem, Style, Northern Illinois University. http://web.ecohost.com.haysend.u-bordeaux3.fr.ehost.

Zink, Michel. *La Prédication en langue romane avant 1300*, Paris: Honoré Champion, 1976.

Zukofsky, Louis. "Mantis," www.poemhunter.com/best-poems/louiszuzofsky/mantis.

11

The Rondeau

Still Doing the Rounds

Maria Johnston

> *Now that we all get laid and everyone swings,*
> *who needs the formal continence of* l'amour
> courtois *and the hang-ups of a provincial clique?*

Derek Mahon, the pre-eminent aesthete of contemporary Irish poetry, asks in the
opening lines of the "Domnei" section of his 1995 poem *The Hudson Letter*, only to
then concede how, "Still . . . in a star-lit corner of the soul there sings / to an enclosed
loved one the intense troubadour / in his quaint language, and his rondeau rings /
resiliently on the vineyards" (ll.1–9). Despite being too often thought of as a diminu-
tive, and even an inconsequential, merely decorative, form—Thomas M. Disch has
observed how it is generally regarded as "the effetist fop of formalist poetry" (279)—
the rondeau has nonetheless proven to be a thoroughly resilient one. Indeed, such is
the power of its charms that certain contemporary poets have attested to writing
rondeaux almost against their will, as evidenced here in Richard Wilbur's account of
his grudging submission to the form: "I'm not much attracted to the rondeau sort of
thing—to those doilies of poems. I would only write them if I had to. I woke up in
the middle of the night the other night and wrote a rondeau, but I didn't know I was
doing it until I was half way through" (Butts 74–75). Thus, when Anthony Hecht
posits the question to readers of contemporary American poetry: "Where are the
stately, measured forays / Of ballade, villanelle, rondeau?," the answer confirms both
the endurance of French fixed forms across the centuries and across national boundaries, as well as Wilbur's position as the most prominent living American new-formal-
ist: "They're all in Richard Wilbur's verses" (175). The rondeau's stubborn endurance
is owed to its ability to travel and adapt. First developed in France in the fifteenth
century by troubadour poets such as Charles d'Orléans—his "Le Temps a laissé son

A Companion to Poetic Genre, First Edition. Edited by Erik Martiny.
© 2012 John Wiley & Sons, Ltd. Published 2012 by John Wiley & Sons, Ltd.

manteau" is one of the best known from this time—and then revived there in the seventeenth century by Vincent Voiture and Isaac de Benserade, it was brought to England by Thomas Wyatt in the sixteenth century but did not take hold there until the end of the nineteenth century when it was taken up by poets such as Algernon Charles Swinburne, Austin Dobson, Edmund Gosse, W.E. Henley, Ernest Dowson, Thomas Hardy, and Robert Bridges, whose poetic sensibilities were seduced by this exotic and elaborate form and who found a necessary guidebook to it and other French forms in Théodore de Banville's *Petit Traité de poésie française*.

Austin Dobson, himself a hardy practitioner of the form in the nineteenth century, penned this self-reflexive rondeau—an adaptation of one by Voiture—on the particular challenges that the form with its hard-to-master intricacies posed to even the most ardent versifiers:

> You bid me try, blue eyes, to write
> A rondeau. What! Forthwith?—To night?
> Reflect some skill I have, tis true;
> But thirteen lines!—and rhymed on two!—
> 'Refrain', as well. Ah, helpless plight!
>
>   (ll.1–5)

As Dobson illustrates, the rondeau, derived from the French for "little circle"—an etymology that highlights the roots of this most musical form in dance and song—is usually made up of thirteen lines, with the first two feet of the first line sounding at the end of both the second and third stanzas as a refrain or *rentrement*, to total fifteen lines in all. Only two rhymes are used throughout making for a tight rhyme scheme: *aabba aabR aabbaR*. Gleeson White in his anthology *Ballades and Rondeaus* (1887) emphasized the complex and often concealed artistry that marks out a successful rondeau: the form "may be so deftly wrought . . . that those who read it simply as a dainty poem never suspect the stern laws ordering the apparent spontaneity of the whole" (lxii). Indeed, the refrain is the crucial attribute of the form in measuring its achievement and in generating the "dainty and spontaneous wit" that is "the secret of the rondeau," as White professes:

> If, like an 'Amen' to a hymn, the refrain comes merely as an extraneous comment on the preceding lines, it is no true rondeau . . . In the refrain the sound must reappear exactly, but the sense may be altered; in fact, this playful variation of its meaning is one of the charms of the verse.
>
>   (lxi–lxii)

From this then it would appear that it was precisely the exigencies of the form that have long attracted poets.

Tracing the rondeau's development into the present moment is an involved task. For a detailed and authoritative overview of its evolution and its close relation to the forms of the triolet, the rondel, the roundel, and the *rondeau rédouble* (devised by the seventeenth-century poet Jean de La Fontaine, but, as Helen Cohen tells us with a dismissive flourish, only remotely related to the rondeau proper and "has never enjoyed the slightest popularity in France"), I would point the indefatigable scholar to Cohen's study *Lyric Forms from France* (1922). Intimately related as it is to these other French fixed forms for which, as *The Princeton Encyclopedia of Poetic Terms* tells us, "rondeau" was once a generic term, the degree of overlapping between these fluid, even interchangeable, forms can make for problems of definition. In modern usage, the distinctions between rondel and rondeau often blur. Even the arch-formalist Wilbur has himself fallen into this trap. Questioned in a 1974 interview over his use of the title "Rondeau" for what was in fact, strictly speaking, a rondel, his explanation is telling: "No two authorities—Saintsbury, et al.—appear to agree at all points. However, I should judge that by most contemporary "rules" the poem I translated is a rondel. Charles d'Orléans evidently believed himself to be writing a rondeau and Babette Deutsch clears him of irregularity by noting that rondel and rondeau were at one time synonymous (Butts 120). Wilbur thereby uncovers the semantic quagmire that can open up when these slippery French forms are brought into play. Swinburne, in the nineteenth century, may be seen to have confused matters further by devising a variation on the rondeau which he termed a "roundel"—he published his *Century of Roundels* in 1883—and even took care to celebrate its technical qualities in his manual-poem "The Roundel": "A roundel is wrought as a ring or a star-bright sphere, / With craft of delight and with cunning of sound unsought" (ll.1–2). Despite the appeal of Swinburne's enthusiasms, this essay must limit its focus to the rondeau proper and its wide-ranging presence in poetry in the English language.

Although, as Mahon's lines indicate, the rondeau was traditionally used by the troubadours to treat the theme of love, or *amour courtois*, it has by no means confined itself to this theme exclusively as it has developed. Its range extends far beyond any one subject or mode as it has been used to express both light and serious matters by poets of a diversity of standpoints in terms of nationality, language, race, gender, and school. Often, it addresses the subject of death, war, and oppression. Indeed, as Cohen points out with reference to John McCrae's "In Flanders Fields": "the most frequently quoted and widely known of all the poems produced during the Great War, is a rondeau" (4). Its transnational reach, the fact that a rondeau can transcend linguistic boundaries to exist simultaneously in different versions, has long been one of its distinguishing features. Included in his 1870 collection *Poems*, Dante Gabriel Rossetti's translation of François Villon's "To Death, of his Lady" into English is exemplary in this regard. Villon's is a shortened rondeau which follows the rhyme scheme *abbaabR abbaR* and this truncation makes it more appropriate to the theme of premature death, of the life cruelly cut short. Perhaps because of his own life's circumstances, Rossetti's rendering is decidedly darker in tone than Villon's original. As the first stanza opens:

> Death, of thee do I make my moan.
> Who hadst my lady away from me,

> Nor wilt assuage thine enmity
> Till with her life thou hast mine own;
> For since that hour my strength has flown.
> Lo! what wrong was her life to thee,
>   Death?
>
>   (ll.1–7)

This strongly worded cross-examination of death makes effective use of the rondeau's rhyme scheme and effects of repetition to intensify the interrogative nature of the tone. Hanging off the end of the stanza in the silence of the blank space and finished with a question mark, this forceful rentrement—"Death?" becoming a tortured ejaculation in the poem's final line, "Death!"—has a powerful impact. The form of the rondeau thereby greatly enhances the content of the poem, the vigorous heft of the refrain making for an intense emotional resonance.

Published in *Lyrics of Lowly Life* (1896), Paul Laurence Dunbar's "We Wear the Mask" has been hailed as a "landmark of black expressivity" (Baker 39). Dunbar cast the poem as a rondeau and so puts this fixed form to a more pointedly public and political use in confronting the subject of racial injustice in the United States and the brutal, double reality of African-American existence, as the poem's commanding opening lines declaim: "We wear the mask that grins and lies, / It hides our cheeks and shades our eyes,— / This debt we pay to human guile" (ll.1–3). The concluding lines hammer the point home:

> We smile, but, O great Christ, our cries
> To thee from tortured souls arise.
> We sing, but oh the clay is vile
> Beneath our feet, and long the mile;
> But let the world dream otherwise,
>   We wear the mask!
>
>   (ll.10–15)

Dunbar, who was himself the son of slaves, studied both the poetry of the canonical white male poets—Keats, Coleridge, Wordsworth—early in his career as well as negro folk literature and songs; accordingly, he wrote poems in standard English and in negro dialect. Here, in keeping with this duality, the rondeau, a traditional form devised by white male poets, seems the ideal form in which this black poet may express the doubleness of African-American experience and register the deeper ambivalence that informs Dunbar's poetic project; Dunbar famously described himself as a "black white man." Following the rhyme scheme *aabba aabR aabbaR*, the rigidity of the rondeau's well-wrought bind becomes the poetic equivalent of the mask as the black poet, representative of his race, must restrain his emotion (his "cries"), and his song and that of his people, must be held in check in the face of the overpowering social reality. In the first line above, the "smile" and "cries" that denote the tragic but necessary proximity of forced-happiness and unbearable pain—this "double consciousness"—are linked through sound as they chime assonantally, while "Christ" carries forward into the almost identical sounding "cries" in the same line to amplify the cruel irony which has a Christian society founded on such depravity. Furthermore, the weighted movement of the lines between the two rhymes, *a* and *b*, is mimetic of the balancing of oppositions that comprises this double consciousness and conveys too the circumscribed expression of the black speaker. The rondeau's unrelenting, deadening rentrement is the appropriate vehicle for the registering of such a statement: the awful logic that directs this speaker's survival strategy is matched by the logic of the rondeau's strict form, its unyielding rhyme scheme and clamping refrain.

Moving into the twentieth century, Thomas Hardy composed a number of rondeaux including "The Roman Road," "Midnight on Beechen," and "The Skies Fling Flame" from *The Dynasts*, all of which represent, as Dennis Taylor has pointed out, "interesting variations in the history of the form" (253). Hardy had been given a copy of White's *Ballades and Rondeaus* by Florence Henniker and also owned George Saintsbury's *French Lyrics* (1882) from which he learned about the development of the tradition—Saintsbury outlines how the rondeau separated by degrees into the triolet, the rondel, and the rondeau proper—and would have been alerted to what Saintsbury promotes in these French forms as the "musical effects of their rhymes and refrains" (xx). Aware of the degree of intersection between these French fixed forms and the possibilities for variation therein, Hardy described his "When I Set Out for Lyonnesse" as "one of the many varieties of Roundelay, Roundel, or Rondel" (Taylor 253). Published in *Time's Laughingstocks and Other Verses* (1909), Hardy's "The Roman Road," hailed by Louis Untermeyer as "as neat a rondeau as Austin Dobson ever fashioned" (25), is a fine example of his workings with the form. Traditionally, the Roman Road, as part of the network of roads constructed during the Roman Empire, holds great import for scholars of history and military history, as they "delve, and measure, and compare" in their endless researches (5). As the poem progresses, it too may be seen to become a road or route and one, unlike the seemingly "straight and bare" Roman Road, that is marked out by swerves and stops over the line-breaks ("hair / across the heath") and across the stanza breaks ("and compare // Visioning on the vacant air") (ll.2–3; 5–6). Through the digressive workings of memory, the poem arrives in its final stanza into another, more immediate, realm that the road grants access to for this wistful speaker:

> But no tall brass-helmeted legionnaire
> Haunts it for me. Uprises there
> A mother's form upon my ken,
> Guiding my infant steps, as when
> We walked that ancient thoroughfare,
>   The Roman Road.
>
>   (ll.10–15)

The "ancient thoroughfare" is haunted with the history of human civilization to the general eye, but for this remembering speaker it is overlaid with a more vital, personal meaning and stands thereby as a route that leads back to family origins, to formative memories of a mother guiding her growing child along its extending path. This veering off into a more private history is enacted through the syntax that, as it turns abruptly on the line-end, creates an interruptive disturbance: "uprises there / a mother's form." Here, "legionnaire" in the preceding line must find its rhyme in the next and in this way the particular dictates of the rondeau's fixed rhyme scheme make possible a dramatic tension that lays emphasis on the turn into the speaker's ruptured past. By the end, the meanings of the rentrement have proliferated and so it may be seen to function as a signpost that marks out how far we have traveled along this endless route; "The Roman Road" may be seen to have more than one destination. In this way then, the "Roman Road," through the divining force of the rondeau itself of the same title, has truly had its "measure" extended.

The continuance of the rondeau into the twentieth century has been characterized by an extensive opening-out of its uses. John McCrae's rondeau "In Flanders Fields" is one of the landmark poems of the Great War. Spoken by a posthumous collective of the war dead, it opens on what appears to be a scene of pastoral beauty in the first line, but which, with the turn of the line-break is revealed as a mass war-grave: "In Flanders Fields the poppies blow / Between the crosses, row on row" (ll.1–2). As the site of Flanders Fields is transformed from a pastoral setting into one of systematic carnage, the rentrement reinforces this stark unveiling, as the second stanza declaims: "We are the Dead. Short days ago / We lived . . . and now we lie, / In Flanders fields" (ll.6–7, 8–9). In what is by now a familiar trope in war poetry, the larks' music soaring defiantly over the battlefield contrasts with the jarring mechanical noise of the "guns below" and, with this in mind, the rondeau itself, with its ear-delighting rhyme harmonies and musical design may be seen to be the poetic equivalent of the larks' continuing song. Thus, the poem gives way to the living voice of the dead as they instruct those who are left to maintain the struggle:

> Take up our quarrel with the foe:
> To you from failing hands we throw
> The torch; be yours to hold it high.
> If ye break faith with us who die
> We shall not sleep, though poppies grow
>   In Flanders fields.

> (ll.10–15)

The dead will persist and will not be quiet—"we shall not sleep"—until the fight has been won and the world set to rights. The last utterance of the rentrement returns us to the image of the frail poppies with which the poem innocently opened but by now these blood-colored blooms have taken on a larger symbolic meaning as markers of the still-flourishing continuing presence of the wounded dead in life. The rondeau form itself speaks of continuance through its repetitions and refrains.

The rondeau is often regarded as a light-verse form and its roots in song are appropriate to its twentieth-century usage by a song lyricist such as Ira Gershwin. Gershwin himself trained first as a poet, and as a lyricist he displayed the poet's lapidary approach to his craft. As a self-styled apprentice to his art, he had as a teenager dedicated himself to poetry and set about training himself in verse forms, as he later recalled: "In my late teens I fooled around with French verse forms, such as the triolet, villanelle, and especially the rondeau— with its opening phrase taking on new meanings when repeated" (215). Gershwin's lyric "Rondeau to Rosie" is alive to the playful possibilities that the form presents with its sly variations of meaning through repetition from stanza to stanza. Rosie, the beloved, is cherished for the way that, with a mere wink of her eye, she can procure tonic (in the form of "a bottle of a vintage rare . . . / and potent beer") for her man from the covert "magic lair" of any café establishment in prohibition-era America (ll.6–8). "My Rosie knows the places where / One goes to lose all trace of care," the speaker declares in the opening lines (ll.1–2). It ends with the following ode to Rosie and her innumerable gifts:

> To her I dedicate this lay;
> To her I owe my spirits gay,
> My smiling mien, my cheerful air,
> My rosy nose.
>
> (ll.12–15)

Rosie's wiles are matched by the same sleight of hand of the form itself. Gershwin's climactic homophonic pun on "nose / knows" (the sound is the same but the sense has been utterly overhauled) tops off the comedic aural effect of this witty, punch-drunk love song.

Like Gershwin, the American poet Louis Untermeyer committed himself to learning the craft of poetry by mastering the French forms. As he explained to Cohen: "I practised them one whole year, for exercise—as one studies scales" (Cohen 85). His rondeau "A Father Speaks" also exults in the form as a release for punning and multiple meanings as the speaker-as-father's "son and heir"—"heir" suggestive of an inescapable mortality—develops miraculously as the poem goes on into a life-giving and growth-enabling "sun and air" in the final stanza:

> I know that he,
> Facing the world's perpetual ills,
> Must rise above its whims and wills.
> He is, more than mere life to me,
> Our sun and air!
>
> (ll.11–15)

As if to reflect the expansive growth that the son represents, this stanza stretches out to fill six lines. Untermeyer's other rondeau offerings include the enjoyable romp of mad love "A Burlesque Rondo" and "The Poet Betrayed."

Composed during World War Two, W.H. Auden's "The Hidden Law" employs the rondeau form for its repetitive force and the inevitability of its fixed schemes. The rondeau, with its own precepts, mirrors the "hidden law" that governs all human life. Nothing is random or free in life as in the rondeau. Thus: "The Hidden Law does not deny / Our laws of probability" (ll.1–2). With its hammering regular meter and enforced rhyme scheme, *aabba aabR aabbaR*, the statement is commanding, its logic strict and inflexible.

> When we escape It in a car,
> When we forget It in a bar,
> These are the ways we're punished by
> The Hidden Law.
>
> (ll.12–15)

As Rainer Emig has noted, the poem's "self-consciously artificial form, that of a French *rondeau* normally reserved for light erotic verse, hints at complication" (215). The rondeau's artifice opposes the vitality of language and life by enacting the rigidities of death and its decrees that seal our living existence. There is no escape from the law of fate; sex (the erotic) and death are irrevocably bound up in the rondeau's very form.

Up until now, this essay has charted the use of the rondeau by male poets but female experience has also found expression in the form. Barbara Howes in her "Death of a Vermont Farm Woman" in *Looking up at Leaves* (1966) uses the form to express longing for death which is reiterated in the rentrement's "Is it time now?" (Howes 81). In the first stanza the supple run-on lines are mimetic of the "long / green evenings" of summer that "keep death at bay" (ll.4–5). But summer is dying, the seasons signify flux. The speaker is preoccupied with time, with the movement of the seasons, with how "Last winter lingered," and then in the third stanza, recalls the whole trajectory of her life: "Six decades vanished in a day!" Both stanzas pivot on the rentrement-question: "Is it time now?" which by the poem's end has turned from being an innocuous question into the wish for death that is the result of having lived too long and outlived one's own children. This is a life that has worn itself out and seeks conclusion: "I have looked long / for these hills to show me where peace lay" (ll.13–14)—the ellipsis gesturing at what lies beyond language—but the speaker is ultimately left hanging on a question mark with the final supplication of the rentrement at the poem's end.

Interestingly, the rondeau has been used by a number of American women poets in writing of lesbian experience. Traditionally used by the male troubadour poets to express their *amour* for a female beloved, these women poets use the form to articulate the taboo subject of lesbian sexuality. Claiming the form for their own, they re-appropriate it for their own feminist agendas and thus challenge the conventions of love poetry. Marilyn Hacker is not only one of the most formally adept contemporary American poets but should be read more fully as a transatlantic, or transnational, poet. Since the 1970s she has lived between Paris and New York and as a fluent French speaker has written across the borders of language, translating the work of French writers such as Claire Malroux, Vénus Khoury-Ghata, and Marie Étienne. Her own poetry in English makes innovative use of this displaced, bilingual reality, drawing on the linguistic possibilities, and exposing the ambiguities and tensions, that are opened up through this studied engagement with other languages and cultures. "Rondeau after a Transatlantic Telephone Call" (1980)—the title of which indicates the poet's transnational status—summons the rondeau in its traditional *mode d'emploi* only to knowingly update it for contemporary usage; sexually turbo-charged for maximum impact:

> Love, it was good to talk to you tonight.
> You lather me like summer though. I light
> up, sip smoke. Insistent through walls comes
> the downstairs neighbor's double-bass. It thrums
> like toothache. I will shower away the sweat,
>
> smoke, summer, sound. Slick, soapy, dripping wet,
> I scrub the sharp edge off my appetite.
> I want: crisp toast, cold wine prickling my gums,
> love. It was good
>
> imagining around your voice, you, late-
> awake there. (It isn't midnight yet
> here.) This last glass washes down the crumbs.
> I wish that I could lie down in your arms
> and, turned toward sleep there (later), say, 'Goodnight,
> love. It was good.'

(ll.1–15)

The whole of this intense love poem must be quoted in full in order to show its intricate workings at the level of sound and structure, and, crucially, the way that the rentrement, "Love, it was good," is expertly manipulated throughout. Having just hung up after a telephone call, the speaker continues the conversation through the sound-conduit of the rondeau. Throughout the first and second stanzas, the sound quality of the words themselves seems designed to arouse and excite the body of the absent "you," with the chain of sensuous sibilants surging over the stanza break to send out an erotic charge: "I will shower away the sweat, // smoke, summer, sound. Slick, soapy" The speaker's own stimulated, naked body is foregrounded as she antici-pates the cold shower that might relieve her sexual urges, her appetite's "sharp edge." In the second stanza, Hacker displays cunning in her use of the rentrement, as that opening word "love," initially the term of endearment used in addressing the absent beloved, now modulates into an abstract noun and one of the cravings that calls out to be satisfied, along with the "crisp toast, cold wine" which are pure sensation and provide a cold antidote for the speaker's fired-up state. Love, like food, is sustenance, oral pleasure and bodily need. The acute hunger in this lusty poem is sexual, physical, and its effects are felt as a continuous dull pain exacerbated by the "thrums" of string music throbbing relentlessly below "like toothache," a lurching music which is amplified by the rondeau's own rocking pattern of hard end-rhyme. The mouth is not only a physiological but a sexual organ and as a site of desire, of sexual desire, it is matched by the orality of the poem itself—a rondeau that is depth-charged with sound and sensation—with its supple enjambments and use of assonance and alliteration; the sibilance and predominant "s" and "i" sounds vibrate on the teeth and tongue just as the cold wine is felt "prickling" the gums. That this all-consuming, tormenting hunger cannot be satisfied—the poem itself is an address to one who is absent, "there," far removed in a different time zone—is made more palpable through the shifts of the rentrement as it moves from being merely a polite platitude ("it was good to talk to you") into a wrenchingly poignant articulation of the bereft in the final stanzas. Cut in two by a full-stop ("love. It was good") the rentrement enforces the rupture between the lovers and their bodies which, cut off from each other in time and space, are unable to conjoin in the craved-for sexual act. "I wish that I could lie down in your arms" the speaker laments, and here, as she crosses over into fantasy, the rentrement gives voice to the sexual fulfillment that can only be imagined, the poem ending with the last words spoken before sleep in post-coital bliss (shyly signaled by that sly "later" in parentheses): "Goodnight, / love. It was good," "it" being the sexual act that cannot be enacted but only imagined in this way. In expressing themes of lesbian love and sexual need, of fulfillment and its lack, the rondeau with its sonic and structural insistence acts as a form, or mouth, that both conveys and contains the intense feeling that is always on the verge of spilling out.

Cheryl Clarke, a contemporary African-American lesbian feminist poet, has also employed the rondeau to express concerns that are explicitly female. As a black poet, Clarke approaches traditional poetic forms with ambivalence and even suspicion: "How can I reflect my black self in a form, how can I speak my contempt from inside the master's formula?" she has questioned (48). Despite these reservations she recognizes that form may also be used to more positive effect in allowing the poet a degree of creative latitude, enabling one "to be rebellious and sometimes to be reserved." Her "Rondeau," defined by her as a "feminist critique of the cult of romance," has her employing the form in order to "control the language of difficult emotions," for, as she notes, form, as well as having problematic ideological associations can also be used to "put pain at some distance." It is the "tightness" that Clarke values as a poetic technician, and, as we have seen, the rondeau is one of the tightest poetic forms. "Rondeau" fuses sex and death in its rentrement: "They are bodies." The poem opens dramatically on a death-ridden scene: "They are bodies left unburied. / Instead of roaming the underworld they've tarried" (50). Here, the "bodies" clearly denote corpses. We then move into the second stanza on a surreal journey as the speaker joins the corpses of dead women on a ferry ride in a liminal zone between life and death. The bodies of these soulless women are judged by the observing speaker, each objectified in turn: "This one's pretty, that one tall, her there, she's fair." In the final stanza, the observing consciousness shifts back to reality and to the contemporary moment where the beloved is addressed:

> I try to act modern, but still I'm worried.
> We sleep together every night but still I'm worried
> that she or she loves you more expertly sexually
> than me obsessed by her or her like voices of insanity.
> Provocative and sexy nonmonogamy in theory.
> But they are bodies.
>
> (ll.9–15)

Here, the interplay between the physical act of random sex and the emotional need for security in love come into conflict as the speaker anguishes over the psychological effects of a "modern" open relationship. These other lovers, it turns out, are not merely "bodies" despite the rentrement's mantra-like insistence to the contrary. Thus, the very contemporary reality of sexual relations in the modern world is explored and the body as a form of both desire and death examined through the controlling structure of the rondeau with its ability to hold multiple meanings and the multiplicity of human experience to the light.

In a lighter and more comical way, Thomas Disch's "Rondeau for Emporio Armani" and "Smashing China," are good examples of how the form continues to entice poets into our own time; Disch has admitted to having gone "on a bender of writing rondeaux" in order to test his poetic abilities. As Disch also comments in his short essay on the form: "The rondeau has a much wider expressive and discursive range than it has generally been credited with" and his own attempts exemplify this (281). Disch's "Rondeau for Emporio Armani" is a delightful meditation on consumer culture, laden with brand names, and executed with a flair for the surprises of enjambment and the ingenuities of rhyme: "What is Armani? What if not money / Made visible? So too, Dior, Gianni / Versace—even, in a sense / Reeboks and Nikes" (ll.1–4; 286). The rentrement is played with to comic effect as the speaker interrogates "Armani," its meaning and motives, making for a rondeau that is, appropriately, one line short of its usual fifteen:

> What is Armani
>
> Doing, though, that everyone in Cunning
> 101 doesn't do as well? Money

> Smells so good. We've no defense
> Against our appetites. It isn't funny.
>   What is? Armani.

                                                                (ll.10–14)

It seems fitting in an essay that deals with the rondeau, a form that pivots on repetition, to end where we began with the rondeau's presence in contemporary Irish poetry. Here, we see the rondeau being examined in more immediate political contexts in the late twentieth century, specifically in the context of the "Troubles" in Northern Ireland. In his "Lunch with Pancho Villa" from *Mules* (1977) Paul Muldoon invokes the rondeau at a charged moment which has politics pitted against poetry. Here, the speechifying "pamphleteer" Pancho Villa—who may be seen as the opposite of the "poet"—accuses the poet of inactivity and starry-eyed indifference in times of crisis:

> 'Look, son. Just look around you.
> People are getting themselves killed
> Left, right and centre
> While you do what? Write rondeaux?
> There's more to living in this country
> Than stars and horses, pigs and trees,
> Not that you'd guess it from your poems.

                                                                (ll.11–17)

"Do you never listen to the news?" the pamphleteer jibes, putting forth the long-held idea of the poet as being unconnected to life, and recalling William Carlos Williams' famous lines about the difficulty of getting "the news from poems." From the pamphleteer's point of view the "rondeau," a merely decorative form of self-consciously wrought artifice that lacks any relevance to the world of political action, becomes representative of all poetic endeavor in this context, and so important questions concerning the poet's role and responsibility in times of war and depredation rear their head. Later, as if in response to the accusations leveled at the poet over his lunch with Pancho Villa, Muldoon, in his collection *Hay* (1998) pens a rondeau of his own, "Aftermath," which meditates on the mutuality between art and violence. Reading the poem, Clair Wills has recognized how the "strict rondeau form of the poem sets up a disturbing contrast with its gruesome subject matter" and, more perceptively still, how, "the rarefied pleasures of the rondeau are shown to be intimately connected with violence." (Kennedy-Andrews 195; Wills 204). Muldoon divides the form into three distinct numbered sections or stations over which the lines are stretched out on the rack of the rondeau form. Thus, the poem opens:

> I
>
> 'Let us now drink,' I imagine patriot cry to patriot
> after they've shot

> a neighbor in his own aftermath, who hangs still between two
>   sheaves
> like Christ between two tousle-headed thieves,
> his body wired up to the moon, as like as not.
>
>   (ll.1–5)

The rural setting—aftermath refers to the second mowing of grass, a verb which chimes hideously with the mowing down of the "neighbor"—takes on a lurid aspect as the *patria* of the patriots becomes a site of spectacularly bloody martyrdom. This is further heightened by the end-rhymes in the next stanza—"To the memory of another left to rot / near some remote beauty spot"—which amplify, through the persuasive harmony of end-rhyme, the brutal *dis*harmony of civil conflict; the breach between sound and sense is unnerving. In a poem that has to do with commemoration, it is fitting that rhyme as a mnemonic device is utilized, and the repetition of the impelling rentrement ("let us now drink") reiterates this need to remember, to "drink" to the memory of those killed. That it is the poet's job to commemorate is clear. As so often occurs in the rondeau, the third stanza brings about a development and with it a shift in perspective:

> III
>
> Only a few nights ago, it seems, they set fire to a big house and it got
> so preternaturally hot
> we knew there would be no reprieve
> till the swallows' nests under the eaves
> had been baked into these exquisitely glazed little pots
> from which, my love, let us now drink.
>
>   (ll.10–15)

As Wills has pointed out, the "big house" of Anglo-Irish culture referred to here shows how the roots of sectarian violence in Northern Ireland lie in the Anglo-Irish war. Echoes of W.B. Yeats' "The Stare's Nest at My Window" speak of the relationship between atrocity and art and the poem, in its elaborate intertextual weave, also may be read as a response to Michael Longley's poem "Aftermath" on which Longley has commented: "I imagine the possibility of swallows breeding near a battlefield and using blood as well as mud to build their nests" (Goodby 139). Violence and destruction are sources of art, as here, the heat of the inferno makes possible the pots from which the poet of the rondeau and his love can now "drink." These pots, "exquisitely glazed," may be seen as analogous to the rondeau's contained sections, and its formal order attests to the poetic impulse to form chaos into art with the rondeau enduring as a vessel of sustenance and remembrance in the face of unending death. At once "binding and liberating" as Donald Hall has observed (34), the rondeau is a living form that continues to engage poets, to be "made new," and never fails to show itself as a dynamic, capacious and various form that is capable of sustaining great imaginative pressure and of a deep and compelling expressivity.

REFERENCES AND FURTHER READING

Auden, W.H. *Collected Poems*. Edward Mendelson (ed). London: Faber and Faber, 1994.

Baker, Houston A. *Modernism and the Harlem Renaissance*. Chicago: University of Chicago Press, 1987.

Banville, Théodore de. *Petit Traité de poésie française*. Paris: Librairie de l'Echo de la Sorbonne, 1872.

Butts, William, ed. *Conversations with Richard Wilbur*. Jackson and London: University Press of Mississippi, 1990.

Clarke, Cheryl. "Thoughts on Form and Formalism and My Uses of Them." In Annie Finch (ed.), *A Formal Feeling Comes: Poems in Form by Contemporary Women Poets*. Brownsville: Story Line Press, 1994. 48–50.

Cohen, Helen Louise. *Lyric Forms from France: Their History and Their Use*. New York: Harcourt Brace, 1922.

Disch, Thomas. "Rondeaux and Roundels." In Annie Finch and Kathrine Varnes (eds.), *An Exaltation of Forms: Contemporary American Poets Celebrate the Diversity of their Art*. Ann Arbor: University of Michigan Press, 2002. 279–89.

Dobson, Austin. *The Complete Poetical Works of Austin Dobson*. Oxford: Oxford University Press, 1923.

Dunbar, Paul Laurence. *Selected Poems*. London: Penguin, 2004.

Emig, Rainer. "Auden and Ecology." In Stan Smith (ed.), *Cambridge Companion to W.H. Auden*. Cambridge and New York: Cambridge University Press, 2004. 212–25.

Gershwin, Ira. *Lyrics on Several Occasions by Ira Gershwin, Gent.: Selection of Stage and Screen Lyrics Written for Sundry Situations; and Now Arranged in Arbitrary Categories To Which Have Been Added Many Informative Annotations and Disquisitions on Their Why & Wherefore, Their Whom-For, Their How; and Matters Associative*. New York: Knopf, 1959.

Goodby, John. *Irish Poetry since 1950: From Stillness into History*. Manchester: Manchester University Press, 2000.

Hacker, Marilyn. *First Cities: Collected Early Poems*. New York and London: W.W. Norton, 2003.

Hall, Donald. *Breakfast Served Any Time All Day: Essays on Poetry New and Selected*. Ann Arbor: University of Michigan Press, 2003.

Hardy, Thomas. *Thomas Hardy: The Complete Poems*, ed. James Gibson. Basingstoke: Palgrave, 2001.

Hecht, Anthony. *Melodies Unheard: Essays on the Mysteries of Poetry*. Baltimore and London: Johns Hopkins University Press, 2003.

Hollander, John. *Rhyme's Reason: A Guide to English Verse*. New Haven and London: Yale University Press, 2001.

Howes, Barbara. *The Collected Poems of Barbara Howes, 1945–1990*. Fayetteville: University of Arkansas Press, 1995.

Kennedy-Andrews, Elmer, ed. *Paul Muldoon: Poetry, Prose, Drama: A Collection of Critical Essays*. Gerrards Cross: Colin Smythe, 2006.

Mahon, Derek. *Collected Poems*. Oldcastle: Gallery Press, 1999.

Muldoon, Paul. *Poems 1968–1998*. London: Faber and Faber, 2001.

Preminger, Alex and T.V.F. Brogan, eds. *The New Princeton Encyclopedia of Poetry and Poetics*. Princeton: Princeton University Press, 1993.

Rossetti, Dante Gabriel. *Dante Gabriel Rossetti: Collected Writings*, ed. Jan Marsh. London: Dent, 1999.

Saintsbury, George, ed. *French Lyrics: Selected and Annotated by George Saintsbury*. London: Kegan Paul, 1882.

Swinburne, Algernon Charles. *Swinburne's Collected Poetical Works*. Vol. 2. London: Heinemann, 1924.

Taylor, Dennis. *Hardy's Metres and Victorian Prosody: With a Metrical Appendix of Hardy's Stanza Forms*. Oxford: Clarendon Press, 1988.

Untermeyer, Louis, ed. *Modern British Poetry*. Rev. edn. New York: Harcourt, Brace and World, 1969.

White, Gleeson, ed. *Ballades and Rondeaux*. London: Walter Scott, 1887.

Wills, Clair. *Reading Paul Muldoon*. Tarset: Bloodaxe, 1998.

12
Weaving Close Turns and Counter Turns

The Villanelle

Karen Jackson Ford

Until recently, the villanelle was thought to have been invented in sixteenth-century France (or even earlier) and standardized in the next century by prosodists who took Jean Passerat's (1534–1602) nonce form in a poem he called "Villanelle" (c. 1574) as the exemplar of a genre: a nineteen-line poem comprised of five tercets and a quatrain, whose first and third lines form an alternating refrain in succeeding stanzas and conclude the final quatrain together as a couplet. Passerat's poem contained only two rhymes, A_1bA_2 abA_1 abA_2 abA_1 abA_2 abA_1 A_2 (A_1 represents the first refrain line, A_2 the second, and a and b the changing lines), and employed that repetitive structure to express the speaker's unvarying grief for his absent beloved:

J'ay perdu ma Tourterelle:	I have lost my turtledove:	A_1
Est-ce point celle que j'oy?	Isn't that her gentle coo?	b
Je veus aller après elle.	I will go and find my love.[1]	A_2

Passerat's constant lover in his constantly insistent form was taken to embody the genre in structure and spirit: rustic, amorous, simple, and, above all, repetitive. The rhythmic repetitions also harkened to the peasant folk songs and dances that lay behind the literary villanelle.[2] In this version of its history, the folksy villanelle traipsed inconspicuously through the centuries, sporadically in some accounts and continuously in others, until it was noticed in France and Britain in the nineteenth century by various aesthetes. Once revived, it enjoyed steady if slight attention from twentieth-century poets. Indeed, as Clive Scott observed with some surprise, "the fortunes of the [villanelle] have prospered in the last hundred years."[3]

However, this received history of the villanelle as a fixed form invented in the late Renaissance carries its own curious burden of error and repeated error. Julie Kane has

recently demonstrated that "the fixed-form villanelle 'tradition' was a ruse manufactured by an eighteenth-century priest and popularized by a nineteenth-century
satirist, based on a single preexisting specimen" (428). Amanda L. French concurs
that Passerat's "Villanelle" "has come to represent a nonexistent tradition of which it
is the sole example" ("First villanelle" 17). In the discoveries of Kane and French, we
have a bewildering, amusing, and intriguing revision of the villanelle's development
and an instructive case history in the politics of poetic form.

Kane's scrupulous research reveals that the fixed-form villanelle was not established
in the late Renaissance—and it was certainly not a medieval invention as numerous
commentators have claimed (Kane 429). Passerat's defining poem was one of only
"eighteen sixteenth- and early-seventeenth-century French poems identified in their
headings as 'villanelle' or 'villanesque,'" and it alone employed the structure familiar
to us; in fact, "none of the others resembles this form even slightly" (430). Though
Passerat wrote his "Villanelle" about 1574, and though it was available in print by
1606, no other poem in its form appeared until two centuries later when Théodore
de Banville published a parody of "I have lost my turtledove" in 1845 (440). Various
prosody manuals, anthologies, and histories of poetry had kept Passerat's "Villanelle"
from oblivion until then—by citing it as an example of that (nonexistent) tradition
or including it in anthologies of poetry—but the scholars not the poets had established
the genre, and, again, based on just that poem. Finally, Banville's own poetic treatise,
Petit Traité de poésie française (1872), assured the future of today's villanelle, "popular-
izing the form in England by way of the poets Edmund Gosse and Austin Dobson"
(Kane 441; McFarland 61–81). British poets who took up the form in response to
Gosse's "A Plea for Certain Exotic Forms in Verse" (1877)—Dobson, Oscar Wilde,
Andrew Lang, W. E. Henley, John Davidson, and Ernest Dowson—adhered strictly
to Passerat's nineteen-line form. Ronald E. McFarland's exhaustive search turns up
"no early writers of the villanelle in English . . . [who] relaxed the standards of
Passerat" (63).

This rigid adherence to the supposed form, something apparently distinctive in
English, is perhaps the most intriguing aspect of the villanelle's history, revealing an
impulse to establish a tradition where there is none:

> Ironically, although the villanelle's poetic form was fixed in the eighteenth and
> nineteenth centuries by less-than-accurate "scholars" who created the myth of a
> long-standing fixed-form tradition, a *genuine* fixed-form tradition has been erected since
> then on the foundations of the false one by poets who believed that they were perpetuat-
> ing a poetic form of medieval or Renaissance heritage.
>
> (Kane 44)

This impulse seems even more urgent today than it was in the late 1800s. If the desire
to fabricate an ancient heritage motivated poets a century ago, such longing for
tradition has become even more complicated (and contradictory) in the postmodern,
free-verse age. French speculates about our contemporary fascination with the
villanelle:

> To my mind, the villanelle has become recently popular at least partly because it has connoted tradition without bearing the burden of one. . . . The villanelle has the cachet of an elitist form but the shape and rhythm of a popular or folk form . . . ; it has therefore become one of the forms of choice in a poetic culture that is schizophrenically split between a devotion to defiant originality and a desire for the kind of eminence that an antique European fixed form can grant.
>
> ("First villanelle" 28–29)

French's provocative claim that the villanelle evokes a tradition without actually being hampered by one recalls a similar, though not so polemical, observation made thirty years ago by Philip K. Jason in his essay on "Modern Versions of the Villanelle." Jason, too, concludes that "[l]iterary history doesn't seem to be an important issue here. Instead, there is something about the very form—and its variety of possible functions—that has caught the attention of many poets" (136). While French suspects that contemporary poets write villanelles merely for the cultural prestige of *having written* in a traditional form, Jason assumes that poets today are compelled by the challenges of *actually writing* villanelles. It will be useful to consider these two issues— the villanelle's cultural connotations and its formal demands—separately before turning to several contemporary poems that respond to the villanelle's meanings and structures in distinctive ways.

If the villanelle does not have a venerable tradition reaching back to the troubadours, it does have a century of poets writing as though it had. Jason may have been right in 1980 when he sensed that literary history wasn't important to villanelle writers, but French is probably equally right today that poets now try their hands at the form precisely because they want to grab hold of its imagined history. However, the villanelle has only recently had the "cachet" and "eminence" of "an antique European fixed form." As recently at 1993, Clive Scott's surprise in *The New Encyclopedia of Poetry and Poetics* at the modern interest in the form in part betrayed its rude origins. Though McFarland asserts that "the subject matter and the thematic range of the form are virtually unlimited" (7), he must also acknowledge that the villanelle has often been associated with triviality and comedy (45). The tendency to regard the form as crude and comic might be predicted from its name, which comes from the Spanish *villano*, a peasant (3); in fact, the villanelle "first had as its only distinguishing features a pastoral subject matter and use of a refrain" (Scott 1358), qualities that were associated with simplicity of subject and form. Moreover, the repeating structure—not just the refrain lines but the limitation to only two rhymes— encouraged monotony and redundancy of form and consequently triviality and burlesque in content (McFarland 1–25). Though the form came to be employed for serious poetry, it retained its association with triviality, sometimes with humor and parody, increasingly with French fussiness and poetical pretention. Most descriptions of the villanelle now reluctantly mention its persistent reputation as a light form: thus, it "became a vehicle for *vers de société*," it has been used "mainly, but not exclusively, for *light verse*," it "can lend itself rather easily to light verse," and "the villanelle seems to have been exceptionally vulnerable to the cliché" (Scott 1358, McDowell 149, McFarland 75).

The issue of whether the villanelle is serious or slight can be glimpsed in the critical debate about Stephen Dedalus's "villanelle of the temptress" in James Joyce's *Portrait of the Artist as a Young Man* (188). Stephen wakes from a dream at dawn to "a morning inspiration" (182) and composes a poem about a young woman for whom he feels both attraction and scorn:

> Are you not weary of ardent ways,
> Lure of the fallen seraphim?
> Tell no more of enchanted days.

(188)

Mary T. Reynolds is one of many scholars to take up the persistent questions surrounding Stephen's villanelle: "Does its presence in the novel identify Stephen as a serious young poet who will become a competent artist? Or is it a piece of inferior verse that marks its author as merely a callow esthete?" (19). Though Reynolds concludes that Stephen is "a young man who has passed through what Joyce called the 'two eras,' Aestheticism and the Decadence, and has come out on the far side" (45)—that is, that his poem gives promise of a serious, mature artist—the debate itself nevertheless expresses doubts about the modern villanelle, most especially that it is too "precious," as Wayne Booth famously termed it, for serious poetry (328).

Such suspicions about the villanelle only increased through the twentieth century, when the free-verse revolution put all traditional verse forms under interdiction; this was probably most forcefully articulated by poets involved in movements seeking political liberation from the dominant cultures that produced most of the West's traditional poetic forms. In 1975, African American poet Gwendolyn Brooks, for instance, heralded the influence of Amiri Baraka, a leader of the Black Arts movement, for his role in casting off these forms, the villanelle prominently among them: "Then came Baraka, rejecting all lovely little villanelles and sonnets—to Orpheus or anything else. Prettiness was out. Fight-fact was in" (7). Brooks and Booth are far apart in audience and purpose, yet her dismissive attitude toward "lovely little villanelles" echoes his toward the "precious villanelle" in Joyce's *Portrait*, and both suggest that villanelles must concern themselves with prettiness rather than portentousness. Yet even through the social turmoil of the 1960s and 70s, poets occasionally tried their hands at the villanelle until the New Formalist movement in the 1980s renewed interest in this and other verse forms. Indeed, as we shall see, poets have increasingly committed their fights facts to villanelles, and this is especially true today.

Discussion about the proper form of the villanelle has been less lively than the debate about its cultural connotations. As Kane and French have shown, when Passerat composed his turtledove poem, "villanelle" meant only "villanellesque"—a poem fashioned after Italian songs called *villanella*. Even once they were defined as a genre of poetry, villanelles were composed with more or fewer than Passerat's five stanzas and in varying line lengths and meters. Miller Williams remarks on the acquisition of a metrical standard for the villanelle in English, describing the form as a "poem of nineteen lines, originally syllabic as a French form but in English construed as iambic pentameter" (85). And Scott also notes the inclination to regulate the English villanelle: French poets reviving the form in the nineteenth century "treated it as a stanza type" (with no rule on the number of stanzas), but their British counterparts insisted on taking Passerat's poem as a fixed form and codified the villanelle we have today (1358). Another formal question that was settled quickly by English prosodists concerns Passerat's feminine rhymes. McFarland describes the villanelle's transition into English, a curious process that involved both imposing and ignoring supposed rules:

> division into tercets, the first and third lines using feminine rhyme, the second masculine; no fixed number of tercets; the first and third lines of the first tercet to alternate as refrain lines in succeeding tercets until coming together at the end of the poem in a quatrain. Later practitioners were to return to the rigid 19-line form of Passerat, and especially in rhyme-poor English, the feminine rhymes have been disregarded.
>
> (62)

Beyond the nuances of rhyme and stress are the possibilities generated by larger structures of the villanelle. Repetition, above all, marks the limits and potential of the form. Though all commentators obviously focus on the villanelle's refrains and rhymes, Jason offers a succinct schematization of this central aspect of the form. The villanelle's "power resides in the interplay of constant (repeating) and variable elements," and its challenge is to create unity without tedium (137). Jason finds the villanelle especially apposite for handling duality, dichotomy, debate, and obsession (141–44). Robert McDowell proposes that the form is "well suited to meditation on mystery, listening, forgiveness, grace, and goodbye" (149). And poets have certainly employed the villanelle for subjects that seem to call for formal repetition. But Jason's sensible point about the interplay of constant and variable elements offers a more supple description of the villanelle's potential than thematic categories like obsession or forgiveness because it avoids equating the form with a particular content. A good villanelle can expose the sometimes paradoxical unity and multiplicity in a subject, but it can also make fine poetical uses of apparent tedium. The form's great range of function and tone, as well as its responsiveness to modernity, was established at mid-century in the operations of the three most famous villanelles in English: Dylan Thomas's "Do Not Go Gentle into That Good Night," Theodore Roethke's "The Waking," and Elizabeth Bishop's "One Art."

Thomas's poem is the best-known villanelle in English. Written while his father was dying, the poem famously argues that we must not acquiesce to death:

> Do not go gentle into that good night,
> Old age should burn and rave at close of day;
> Rage, rage against the dying of the light.
>
> (ll.1–3)

Thomas employs the refrain lines to suggest the futile, desperate repetition of the son's admonition to his dying father. Though the succeeding stanzas attempt to demonstrate that different people—wise, good, wild, and grave men—resist death for different reasons, this variation in the changing lines does not actually vary the argument and cannot overcome the obstinate fact of death any more than do the repeated assertions of defiance in the refrains. Thus, the command to rage against death subsides to a plea in the final stanza, "I pray, / Do not go gentle into that good night" (ll.17–18). The villanelle structure simultaneously gives voice to the son's insistence on fighting the inevitable and to the very fact of that inevitability; here, the refrain lines do not accrue meaning over the course of the poem but rather ingrain the one bald truth, death, and the son's single, willful response to it.

Yet "Do Not Go Gentle" also mines the villanelle's opportunities for variation within this fixity. The opposition of light and dark (life and death) takes distinct forms in relation to different kinds of men:

> Though wise men at their end know dark is right,
> Because their words had forked no lightning they
> Do not go gentle into that good night.
>
> Good men, the last wave by, crying how bright
> Their frail deeds might have danced in a green bay,
> Rage, rage against the dying of the light.
>
> Wild men who caught and sang the sun in flight,
> And learn, too late, they grieved it on its way,
> Do not go gentle into that good night.
>
> Grave men, near death, who see with blinding sight
> Blind eyes could blaze like meteors and be gay,
> Rage, rage against the blinding of the light.
>
> (ll.4–15)

But what lightning, light glinting on water, sunset, and meteors have in common is their transience, and each image of light ultimately summons the darkness it would defy. Thus, though "the dying of the light" is meant, of course, to refer to the waning of life and "that good night" to the coming darkness of death, life is characterized by *dying light* all along. This is one of the many ways the poem draws life and death into relation despite the speaker's adamant need to keep them apart.

Seamus Heaney has explicated another source of the poem's paradoxical unity in the intricate work of the phrase "good night," calling it "a pun," which embodies both "salutation and farewell," "a perfect equivalent for the balance between natural grief and the recognition of necessity which pervades the poem as a whole" (138–39). As a salutation, "good night" (like "good day") draws the speaker's father to the living present; as a farewell, it is even more complex, suggesting "sleep well," with the expectation of a greeting on the morrow, and "good bye," with the connotation of finality.

Moreover, it is not merely the diction or the figures of the poem but the very structure of the villanelle that makes possible the son's address to his dying father; indeed, in Heaney's supple understanding, the genre itself embodies the complex patterns of life and death:

> One of the poem's strengths is its outwardly directed address, its escape from emotional claustrophobia through an engagement with the specifically technical challenges of the villanelle. Yet that form is so much a matter of crossing and substitutions, of back-tracks and double-takes, turns and returns, that it is a vivid figure for the union of opposites, for the father in the son, the son in the father, for life in death and death in life. The villanelle, in fact, both participates in the flux of natural existence and scans and abstracts existence in order to register its pattern. It is a living cross-section, a simultaneously open and closed form, one in which the cycles of youth and age, of rise and fall, growth and decay find their analogues in the fixed cycle of rhymes and repetitions.
>
> (139)

Heaney's reliance on the language of paradox to describe the formal workings of the villanelle—flux and abstraction, open and closed, fixed cycles—attests to the inbuilt capacity of the form to represent not just life's paradoxes but our paradoxical responses to them. In "Do Not Go Gentle" the poem is able to formulate a response to the "necessity" of death even though the speaker, in his "natural grief," rails against such a formulation.

Theodore Roethke's popular "The Waking" was published in 1953, just a year after Thomas's villanelle appeared, and it might well be read as a refutation of "Do Not Go Gentle." This speaker submits to fate with delight and reverence—the inevitable fact of death, described placidly (and obliquely) as "waking to sleep," is cause to savor life, to "take my waking slow," rather than to rage against death. While Thomas's poem richly works the villanelle's capacity for insisting on one thing, Roethke's poem makes magic of repetition with enigmatic refrain lines that seem to shift and shimmer, emitting different meanings with each reiteration. Indeed, every commentator on "The Waking" observes its ambiguity, especially in the refrain lines "I wake to sleep, and take my waking slow" and "I learn by going where I have to go" (ll.1, 3).

What "The Waking" seems to want from the villanelle structure is not to insist on the singularity of its opening declarations but rather to reveal their multiplicity. Each repetition turns a new facet of meaning to the light. The poem's premise of "waking to sleep" has been interpreted numerous ways, from *only in sleep (in unfettered imagination) am I fully awake* to *waking and sleeping (and living and dying) are one* to *I live only to die*. All these propositions make sense, and most readers agree that the poem views life and death, waking and sleeping, as parts of a cycle. In "The Waking," death is thus a natural part of life that the speaker simply "cannot fear"—even though such phrasing acknowledges that others do fear it. But his response to mortality is to take life as it comes (learning "by going where to go" is one way he has of taking his "waking slow") without taking it for granted. Indeed, his calm marveling at life's mysteries is one way he makes acceptance of his fate compelling. Thomas's poem also admits something appealing in death—it is "that *good* night," after all—yet each stanza expresses regret about life in the face of death (remorse over words that "forked no lightning" or deeds that "might have danced" but didn't [ll.5, 8]), and life and death remain utterly separate realms, the latter to be avoided as long as possible. "The Waking" offers wonderment rather than regret, fascination rather than fear, and repetition here suggests a rapt attention to the world.

Roethke's repetitions are never simply that. Gertrude Stein's redefinition of repetition as "insistence" can illuminate the workings of many villanelles but especially of "The Waking." In "Portraits and Repetition" Stein recalls discovering that "there can be no repetition" (170), something she learned, it turns out, when she began "to consciously listen to what anybody was saying" (169), that is, when she gave the world the exquisite attention Roethke's speaker advocates. Insistence "can never be repeating, because insistence is always alive and if it is alive it is never saying anything in the same way because emphasis can never be the same" (171). Roethke's poem discovers just this in its refrains. In fact, every device in the poem that produces unity— sound effects like alliteration, assonance, rhyme, and the refrains—simultaneously generates difference:

> I wake to sleep, and take my waking slow.
> I feel my fate in what I cannot fear.
> I learn by going where I have to go.
>
> We think by feeling. What is there to know?
> I hear my being dance from ear to ear.
> I wake to sleep, and take my waking slow.
>
> Of those so close beside me, which are you?
> God bless the Ground! I shall walk softly there,
> And learn by going where I have to go.
>
> Light takes the Tree, but who can tell us how?
> The lowly worm climbs up a winding stair;
> I wake to sleep, and take my waking slow.

(ll.1–12)

Assonance and alliteration at once align and divide the poem's terms: wake/take, wake to sleep/waking slow, feel/fate/fear, think/feel, hear/ear, God/Ground/go, Light/lowly, takes/Tree, lowly worm/winding stair. Thus, even before the refrains emerge in the succeeding stanzas, they are sounding out the differences within similarity. Variation of wording in the second refrain ("I learn," "And learn," "lovely, [you must] learn," and back to "I learn") generates subtle shades of meaning, as does the appearance of the refrains in the context of each new stanza. Easing from declarative to imperative, from God to nature, from ground to air, the compulsion of going where one *has* to go gives way to the nimble "going where to go," a lighthearted pun on what it refuses to say: *knowing* where to go.

In this atmosphere of casual discovery, even individual words give off multiple meanings. The speaker "takes" (approaches? accepts? savors?) his waking slow, light "takes" (illuminates? transforms?) the tree, and he and his love "take" (inhale? grasp? ascend?) the lively air; "shaking" paradoxically keeps him "steady" (l.16), and the negative connotations of "away" are subdued by the positive connotations of its near-homonym "always" ("What falls away is always. And is near" [l.17]). Doubt becomes curiosity when questions follow rather than precede answers, producing a sense of charmed uncertainty: "We think by feeling. What is there to know?" "Of those so close beside me, which are you?" and "Light takes the Tree, but who can tell us how?" Like the shaking that keeps the speaker steady, the villanelle structure balances variation and recurrence. While "Do Not Go Gentle into That Good Night" employs the villanelle's refrains to insist and resist, to shake a stubborn fist at death, "The Waking" makes use of the same structures to inquire and accept, each stanza's venture into variation discovers the steady if mysterious wisdom of the refrains. The cycle itself, both a philosophy of life and a poetic structure here, is what gives Roethke's speaker his equilibrium.

But despite the enthusiasm for villanelles generated by Roethke's alluring "The Waking," the poem that initiated the contemporary fascination with the form is unquestionably Elizabeth Bishop's "One Art" (1976). French argues that the "common, contemporary, emphatically postmodern villanelle was surely ushered in" by Bishop's poem because "it specifically and irrevocably demolishes the implicit modernist analogy between technical mastery of poetic form and psychological mastery of self and world" (181). Indeed, "mastery" is the key issue in the poem itself, and the pairing of "master" and "disaster" in the A_1 and A_2 rhymes might support French's idea that technical virtuosity can no longer manage psychological crisis. Yet one could also argue just the opposite, that if on one level the speaker reveals an increasing lack of mastery over her increasing misfortunes, on another level she pulls herself together precisely by ushering them into a tightly controlled form. If she can force herself to "*Write* it!"—to write the word "disaster" (and, hence, to write about her disasters), then she "shan't have lied," and it will be true that grief can be mastered through art, and not, finally, through the "one art" of losing but the other art of poetry:

> The art of losing isn't hard to master;
> so many things seem filled with the intent
> to be lost that their loss is no disaster.
>
> Lose something every day. Accept the fluster
> of lost door keys, the hour badly spent.
> The art of losing isn't hard to master.
>
> Then practice losing farther, losing faster:
> places, and names, and where it was you meant
> to travel. None of these will bring disaster.

I lost my mother's watch. And look! my last, or
next-to-last, of three loved houses went.
The art of losing isn't hard to master.

I lost two cities, lovely ones. And vaster,
some realms I owned, two rivers, a continent.
I miss them, but it wasn't a disaster.

—Even losing you (the joking voice, a gesture
I love) I shan't have lied. It's evident
the art of losing's not too hard to master
though it may look like (*Write* it!) like disaster.

                                                              (ll.1–19)

It is important to see "One Art" in its entirety to appreciate not just its technical
mastery but its technical innovations, innovations that rendered the form conducive
to postmodern poetry and appealing even to contemporary poets who were suspicious
of traditional verse forms.

Changes of diction and syntax in the A_1 and A_2 lines, enjambment, punctuation,
slant rhymes: these devices trouble the expected consistencies of the poem and generate variation within repetition. Though the villanelle form provides a structural figure
for the speaker's notion that one can master loss by constant practice (repetition),
the repetend (the irregular recurrence of a line, in contrast to a refrain) uncovers the
emotional turbulence just beneath her truism. Repeated loss does not inure her to
losing, and misplacing keys or even her mother's watch cannot prepare the speaker
for the disaster of lost love. Thus, the deepening sorrows of the varying *a* and *b* lines—
lost keys, lost time, lost places, people, plans, lost homes, even whole "realms" of
loss—have not after all trained the speaker for the loss of love. Enjambment in the
first stanza prevents the A_2 line from achieving the conviction of a refrain, and that
repetend roils through the poem exposing the anxiety in the speaker's bravado.
Subsequent enjambments ("the fluster / of lost door keys," "where it was you meant
/ to travel," "my last, or / next-to-last") increase the sense of dislocation by denying
the rhymes the resolve of an end stop; likewise, slant rhymes (fluster, gesture) are
another source of dissonance, and even the exact but awkward rhyme "last, or" jars
against its polysyllabic counterparts. Intrusive ejaculations ("And look!" "*Write* it!"),
the dash like a catch in the voice before mention of the beloved ("—Even losing you"),
and the parentheses around the griefs she can barely acknowledge are also disruptive
elements that gainsay the speaker's efforts to be cavalier.

Perhaps the most distinctive innovation in Bishop's villanelle is how the A_1 and
A_2 lines *evolve* rather than revolve through the poem, shifting from a comic to a tragic
register despite the speaker's efforts to make light of her losses. Her assertion that
"The art of losing isn't hard to master" is convincing enough in the context of mis-
placed keys and ill-spent time. Even losing track of people and places and plans (in
the third stanza) is not downright disastrous, though we begin to see that more is at

stake here than keys and watches (even so, the mother's watch carries more serious overtones than the keys; it may be an heirloom, and it certainly signifies time and casts a shadow back on "the hour badly spent"). As the speaker enumerates much greater losses, "disaster" accrues new connotations: in the first three stanzas, it reads as a hyperbolic colloquialism ("I lost my keys, but it's no disaster"). In the context of cities, rivers, and a continent, however, the word "disaster" raises the specter of major cataclysm—earthquakes, floods, tidal waves—and though the speaker claims her bigger losses are not disasters of that sort, the scale of comparison has shifted decidedly from the comic to the tragic. By the last stanza, the poem offers an eruption of evidence—again, the dash, the qualifications "*even* losing you" and "not *too* hard," the fond details painfully couched in parentheses, the stutter ("like . . . like"), and the parenthetical command to "*Write* it!"—that if something looks "like disaster," it is disaster.

Yet here at the end, the self command to *write* the word "disaster" reveals that the art of poetry rather than the art of losing is the thing to master—and evokes the linguistic self-consciousness and self-referentiality that will soon dominate contemporary literature. In Euro-American letters in 1976, writing will not produce a frank statement that "I have lost my turtledove" and an earnest resolution to "follow after her" but a poem that strains against the structures of Passerat's "Villanelle" and in its straining expands the capacities of the form for a twentieth century characterized by emotional complexity, psychological contradiction, cultural displacement, and formal dissonance. If the political upheavals of the century resulted in the rejection of all the lovely little villanelles, scrappier villanelles continued to appear and joined in the work of cultural reform. McFarland selects thirty-three contemporary villanelles, "including one prose villanelle" (121), for an appendix to his study (121–41), and French lists over twenty-five pages of villanelle authors in an appendix to her dissertation ("Refrain again" 199–227). She dryly observes that "[a]lmost everyone nowadays seems to have written one or two villanelles (not usually more) just to see if they can" (185), and this includes poets (not all in French's tally) as various as Julia Alvarez, Wendy Cope, Rita Dove, Martín Espada, Marilyn Hacker, Duriel E. Harris, Seamus Heaney, Richard Hugo, Donald Justice, Weldon Kees, Carolyn Kizer, Maxine Kumin, Marilyn Nelson, Sylvia Plath, Alberto Ríos, Gary Snyder, Richard Tillinghast, Lyrae Van Clief-Stefanon, Anne Waldman, C. K. Williams, and John Yau, just to take an alphabetical swipe at the legions of contemporary villanelle writers.

These and dozens of other poets have experimented with the form that Thomas, Roethke, and Bishop made modern. Roethke's iridescent lines have proven inimitable; his legacy is a villanelle that contemporary readers find beautiful, compelling, and intriguing, a poem in fixed form that demonstrates traditional verse need not be outdated or restrictive. Thomas's villanelle gives a distinctly modern tenor to repetition by way of a speaker who castigates, commands, and insists precisely because he has no authority over death. Bishop's speaker also uses the villanelle structure to protest too much; the repetend becomes the formal equivalent of her notion that repetition inures us to loss, though the strain and dissonance of her lines expose the emotional turmoil she would deny. Jason argues "that the villanelle is often used, and properly used, to deal with one or another degree of obsession" (141), and this is unquestionably one thing contemporary villanelle writers have learned from Thomas and Bishop. Jason offers Sylvia Plath's early "Mad Girl's Love Song" (1953) as an instance of the relationship between the villanelle form and "the psychology of obsession":

> I shut my eyes and all the world drops dead;
> I lift my lids and all is born again.
> (I think I made you up inside my head.)
>
> (ll.1–3)

More recently, Wendy Cope's "Lonely Hearts" (1986) cleverly joins the villanelle structure to the rhetoric of personal ads to suggest the futility and monotony of looking for love in all the wrong places:

> Can someone make my simple wish come true?
> Male biker seeks female for touring fun.
> Do you live in North London? Is it you?
>
> Gay vegetarian whose friends are few,
> I'm into music, Shakespeare and the sun.
> Can someone make my simple wish come true?
>
> (ll.1–6)

The desires of Cope's speakers are anything but simple; it is their involved expectations ("bisexual woman, arty, young" [1.8], "Successful, straight and solvent" [1.10], "slim non-smoker, under twenty-one" [1.14]) that doom them to loneliness. The villanelle structure suits the round of hopeless seeking and inevitable disappointment.

Cope's strategy of cycling the refrain through different speakers (to reveal their similarity) is a rarely utilized technique; as Jason's point about obsession implies, the repetitive structure of the villanelle has typically been employed for a single speaker with a singular fixation. Yet Jason also speculates about "the potential of the villanelle for handling duality, dichotomy, and debate" (144), and Charles Martin's "Terminal Colloquy" (1978) exemplifies the villanelle's capacity for dialogue. The poem stages a colloquy between its refrains and its changing lines:

> O where will you go when the blinding flash
> Scatters the seed of a million suns?
> And what will you do in the rain of ash?
>
> I'll draw the blinds and pull down the sash,
> And hide from the light of so many noons.
> But how will it be when the blinding flash

Disturbs your body's close-knit mesh,
Bringing to light your lovely bones?
What will you wear in the rain of ash?

I will go bare without my flesh,
My vertebrae will click like stones.
Ah. But where will you dance when the blinding flash

Settles the city in a holy hush?
I will dance alone among the ruins.
Ah. And what will you say to the rain of ash?

I will be charming. My subtle speech
Will weave close turns and counter turns—
No. What will you say to the rain of ash?
Nothing, after the blinding flash.

(ll.1–19)

The refrain speaker is appropriately given the script of adamant naysayer: he asks the optimist of the changing lines where he will go and what he will do when the nuclear apocalypse ends the world with "a blinding flash." Every response ventured by the naïve second speaker is countered by the cynic: first with a contradicting "But," then a condescending "Ah" and "Ah," and last an emphatic "No." Having rebutted all of the innocent's hopeful replies in relentless refrains, the doomsayer repeats the question that matters most: "What will you *say* to the rain of ash?" Speech will be impossible because life will be extinguished. There will be *"Nothing, after the blinding flash,"* and the villanelle enacts the end of colloquy in a dialogue between naïveté and cynicism. The contrasting structures of the poem—insistent refrains versus variable lines, regular font versus italics—distinguish the two sides of the debate until the last line when the second speaker concedes the argument and utters the first's repetend in his own italics, a visual termination of hope.

"What will you say?" is a critical question for any villanelle, whose structures of repetition give such emphasis to the utterance. But the genre has a special charge of *saying* after Bishop's "One Art." As we have seen, that speaker uses the repetitive form to harden herself to loss, and writing about personal disaster helps her compose herself even if it doesn't finally give her mastery over sorrow. Still, her concluding "*Write* it!" initiates the propensity of many contemporary villanelles to be self-conscious about the act of writing one. Even Martin's naïve second speaker is heir to Bishop's witty master of disaster, proposing to be "charming" and "subtle" in speech and to respond to disaster by "weav[ing] close turns and counterturns"—we might say, by writing a villanelle. There are enough silly poems about composing villanelles and enough poems self-consciously titled "Villanelle" to indicate a heightened concern with writing in the form, but there are also many serious villanelles that foreground the act of writing poetry, an emphasis that responds to "One Art" but also reveals an acute self-consciousness about the contemporary poet's relationship to literary tradition.

Julia Alvarez's "Woman's Work" concludes the "Housekeeping" sequence in her first volume of poetry, *Homecoming* (1984). The entire volume is keenly focused on the effects and efficacy of different verse forms, but "Mother Love" and "Woman's Work," poems on facing pages, reserve the villanelle for the related subjects of inexorable mother–daughter attachment and the unremitting round of domestic chores. In "Woman's Work," the poet-daughter considers her mother's defense of housework:

> Who says a woman's work isn't high art?
> She challenged as she scrubbed the bathroom tiles.
> Keep house as if the address were your heart.
>
> (ll.1–3)

The daughter complains that "Doing her woman's work was hard art" (6) and plans to escape the prison of her mother's "housebound heart" (9), yet she grows up to carry on her mother's work in her writing, "housekeeping paper as if it were her heart" (19). In "Women's Work" repetition embodies the speaker's struggle with her familial past just as the villanelle itself embodies her struggle with the literary past. Lyrae Van Clief-Stefanon's "Hum" (2002) also counters a consuming, distracting love with writing and also employs the villanelle to represent both the insistent "hum" of, in this instance, sexual desire and the form of writing that might master it:

> Sometimes the hum and pull keeps me awake
> all night: a low current, some faint desire—
> I'll write it down. I'll see what I can make.
>
> (ll.1–3)

The speaker of "Hum" housekeeps her heart precisely *by* housekeeping paper and changes the "dumb awe" of sexual attraction for "writing, God-like, [to] see what I can make // of longing" (ll.14–16). What she makes, of course, is a villanelle, and her godlike feeling comes not only from creating a poem but from the particular cultural authority of creating a poem in conventional form.

Duriel E. Harris's "Villanelle: for the dead white fathers" (2003) even more explicitly confronts the tensions and ambiguities of contemporary poets employing villanelles (and other conventional forms). Her speaker dresses down the dominant Anglo-European tradition but not by rejecting it; rather, she insists on her place, even on the priority of her place, in that tradition: "You're poets dead; I'm poet live," she asserts in the final quatrain, having demonstrated her poetic vitality and virtuosity in the preceding stanzas:

> I can write frontpocket Beale Street make you sweat and crave the blues,
> Dice a hymnal 'til you shout Glory! The Holy Ghost done sent me sin!
> BACKWATER, yeah, but I ain't wet, so misters, I ain't studin' you:

Signify a sonnet—to the boil of "Bitches Brew."
Rhyme royal a triolet, weave sestina's thick through thin.
I said God made me funky. There ain't nothin' I cain't do.

. . .

Shish kebab heroic couplets and serve 'em dipped in barbecue,
Slap-bass blank-verse lines, tunin' fork tines 'til you think I'm Milton's kin.
Indeed, God made me funky. There ain't nothin' I cain't do.

(ll.4–9, 13–15)

Harris is an award-winning slam poet with a bachelor's degree in English from Yale, a master's in Creative Writing from New York University, and a Ph.D. from the University of Illinois, Chicago; her lively black speaker's quarrel with the dead white fathers is as complex as her own cultural background. "I ain't studin' you" is not to say that she *hasn't* studied the Western poetic canon, as is immediately evident when that rebuff is followed by a litany of verse forms in the white tradition: sonnet, rhyme royal, triolet, sestina, heroic couplets, blank verse. But this expertise in the poetry of the dead white fathers is deeply entwined with the speaker's knowledge of African American expressive forms—spirituals, hymns, gospel songs, and most of all the blues.[4] "I ain't studin' you" alludes to the famous refrain from "Down By the Riverside"—"I ain't gonna study war no more"—and is less a denial of *learning* canonical forms than a rejection of the *value* of learning and emulating only them.

Harris's poem mixes the blues and the villanelle, in many thematic allusions to blues (in specific references like "Backwater Blues," Beale Street, "Bitches Brew," *While you were steppin' out, someone else was steppin' in*"), and in the shared structures of tercets and refrains. The classic blues stanza contains three lines, the first repeated in the second, the third different, but all three rhyming on a single sound (*AAa*). The variation in the villanelle's repetend finds its counterpart in the blues practice of "worrying the line," altering the second refrain line in performance by varying the phrasing, pitch, or including ejaculations, slurs, or growls.[5] Carolyn Beard Whitlow's description of her own blues villanelles, "Rockin' A Man, STone Blind" and "Local Call," provides a good account of Harris's hybrid poem:

Blues Villanelle. Blues in black and white. Touchstone of traditions, African-American and European, a fusion of form and content, embodiment of the influences of folk, blues, jazz, gospel, classical, harmonies of the musico-literary languages we speak. But this brew ain' bleach blon'. American black to its roots, even couched in the villanelle, this syncretion is poetry steeped in a folk tradition which lifts off the page in its orality. The languid eight-beat accentual-syllabic triplets with an AAa rhyme scheme [of the blues] . . . have been modified to fit the AbA2 structure of the standard villanelle stanza, form in both instances taking a back seat to the blusality of the content, voice dominant.

(66–67)

Whitlow concludes that writing a blues villanelle is like "creating an aesthetic pattern in a wall of bricks" (67), but Harris's poem does not distinguish between the wall and the pattern. "There ain't nothin' I *cain't* do" is a crucial revision of the fatalistic blues lament, "There ain't nothin' I *can* do," and Harris's speaker isn't studying Anglo-European poetic forms because they are already so thoroughly her own. However irreverent, the poem is, after all, a "Villanelle: *for* the dead white fathers," not against them, and we may take her to be "Milton's kin" because she *is* Milton's kin . . . as well as kin to Jean Passerat, Elizabeth Bishop, W. C. Handy, Miles Davis, and countless others. Like Alvarez's speaker who is reluctantly her mother's child, "a woman working at home on her art," Harris's speaker is her diverse parents' child, signifying sonnets and weaving sestinas.

French maintains that contemporary poets "have inadvertently constructed, not altered or demolished, a tradition," with the implication that villanelle writers today imagine themselves to be dismantling the very tradition they are in fact erecting (269). Yet when Martín Espada and Marilyn Nelson form the Third World Villanelle Society, or when Duriel Harris composes a villanelle for dead white fathers, they are quite deliberately entering the tradition in order to help shape its cultural meanings rather than proposing to demolish it—intervening and adapting, perhaps, but not destroying.[6] That the villanelle's tradition is relatively young and that it rests on a shaky foundation may explain why it is a form that "appeals to outsiders" (Fry 227). But, given that a single poem inadvertently inaugurated the tradition, perhaps there are no villanelle insiders. In its historical and formal close turns and counterturns, the villanelle is an unexpectedly open genre.

NOTES

1   French, "First villanelle" 7–8.

2   "The poetic villanelle originated in the Italian musical villanella, an early-sixteenth-century genre whose courtly composers imitated peasant songs of the oral tradition. Like the villanella, the earliest villanelles employed refrains and 'rustic' subject matter" (Kane 428).

3   Scott's remark appears in his entry on the villanelle in The New Princeton Encyclopedia of Poetry and Poetics, a definitive reference volume (1358). For thorough surveys of the history of the villanelle and its critics, see Kane's "Myth" and French's "Refrain Again."

4   W. C. Handy composed "Beale Street Blues"; Miles Davis wrote "Bitches Brew"; "I ain't gonna study war no more" is the famous refrain from the folk spiritual "Down by the Riverside"; "slap bass" is a vigorous string-plucking technique associated with early jazz performers; God Made Me Funky is a Toronto-based funk group and the name of their first album. Harris also quotes a line composed by Chicago blues artist Buddy Guy: "While you were steppin' out, someone else was steppin' in" (l.17).

5   For instance, Robert Johnson's "Kind Hearted Woman Blues" worries the line in the second stanza: "I love my baby, my baby don't love me / I love my baby oooh, my baby don't love me / I really love that woman, can't stand to leave her be."

6   Nelson thanks "the Third World Villanelle Society," an imaginary organization she and fellow poet Espada formed, in her acknowledgments to Fields of Praise: New and Selected Poems (xiii).

REFERENCES AND FURTHER READING

Alvarez, Julia. "Woman's Work." *Homecoming: New and Selected Poems*. New York: Plume/Penguin, 1996. 45.

Bishop, Elizabeth. "One Art." *Elizabeth Bishop: The Complete Poems, 1927–1979*. New York: Farrar, Straus, Giroux, 1979. 178.

Booth, Wayne. "The problem of distance in *A Portrait of the Artist*." *The Rhetoric of Fiction*. Chicago: University of Chicago Press, 1983 (Original work published 1961). 323–36.

Brooks, Gwendolyn. "Gwendolyn Brooks." *A Capsule Course in Black Poetry Writing*. Detroit: Broadside, 1975. 3–11.

Cope, Wendy. "Lonely Hearts." *Making Cocoa for Kingsley Amis*. London: Faber and Faber, 1986. 27.

French, Amanda Lowry. "The first villanelle: a new translation of Jean Passerat's 'J'ay perdu ma Tourterelle'" (1574). October 28, 2003. http://amandafrench.net/FirstVillanelle.pdf.

French, Amanda Lowry. "Refrain again: the return of the villanelle." http://amandafrench.net/Dissertation.pdf.

Fry, Stephen. *The Ode Less Traveled: Unlocking the Poet Within*. New York: Penguin/Gotham, 2005.

Harris, Duriel E. "Villanelle: for the dead white fathers." *Drag*. Minneapolis: Elixir, 2003. 53.

Heaney, Seamus. "Dylan the durable?" *The Redress of Poetry*. New York: Farrar, Straus and Giroux, 1995. 124–45.

Jason, Philip K. "Modern versions of the villanelle." *College Literature* 7.2. 1980: 136–45.

Johnson, Robert. "Kind Hearted Woman Blues." January 1, 2001. "Robert Johnson." June 11, 1999. Blues Lyrics On Line. http://blueslyrics.tripod.com/lyrics/robert_johnson/kindhearted_woman_blues_take_1.htm#top.

Joyce, James. *A Portrait of the Artist as a Young Man*. 1917. Oxford: Oxford University Press, 2000.

Kane, Julie. "The myth of the fixed-form villanelle." *Modern Language Quarterly* 64.4 2003: 427–43.

Martin, Charles. "Terminal Colloquy." *Starting from Sleep: New and Selected Poems*. Sewanee: Overlook, 2002. 182.

McDowell, Robert. *Poetry as Spiritual Practice*. New York: Free Press, 2008.

McFarland, Ronald E. *The Villanelle: The Evolution of a Poetic Form*. Moscow, ID: University of Idaho Press, 1987.

Plath, Sylvia. "Mad Girl's Love Song." *Mademoiselle* 37. 1953: 358.

Reynolds, Mary T. "Joyce's villanelle and D'Annunzio's sonnet sequence." *Journal of Modern Literature* 5.1. 1976: 19–45.

Roethke, Theodore. "The Waking." *The Collected Poems of Theodore Roethke*. Garden City, NY: Doubleday, 1966. 108.

Scott, Clive. "Villanelle." In Alex Preminger and T.V.F. Brogan (eds.). *The New Princeton Encyclopedia of Poetry and Poetics*. Princeton: Princeton University Press, 1993. 1358–59.

Stein, Gertrude. "Portraits and Repetition." *Lectures in America*. Boston, MA: Beacon, 1985 (Original work published in 1930). 165–206.

Thomas, Dylan. "Do Not Go Gentle into That Good Night." *The Collected Poems of Dylan Thomas*. New York: New Directions, 1952. 207–08.

Van Clief-Stefanon, Lyrae. "Hum." *Black Swan*. Pittsburg: University of Pittsburg Press, 2002. 17.

Whitlow, Carolyn Beard. "Blues in black and white." In Annie Finch (ed.). *After New Formalism: Poets on Form, Narrative, and Tradition*. Brownsville, OR: Storyline, 1999. 63–69.

Williams, Miller. "Villanelle." *Patterns of Poetry: An Encyclopedia of Forms*. Baton Rouge: Louisiana State University Press, 1986. 85–86.

13
Looping the Loop

Terza Rima

George Szirtes

Dante's terza rima is one of the supreme metrical inventions in the history of poetry. But in spite of several, if not very numerous, attempts, the metre has never been acclimatized in English.
Laurence Binyon, "Terza Rima in English Poetry" *English*, 1940

The one thing everybody knows about *terza rima* is that it was first used by Dante for the *Commedia*, invented by him for the purpose. The second is that there is a paucity of rhyme in English which is the reason it has not been much used by English-language writers, although Laurence Binyon himself did use it in his own translation of 1933.

Terza rima is essentially a narrative form whose rhyming structure is *aba bcb cdc* and so forth, for as long as it takes a story, an episode of a story, or even an anecdote to be told. The passage generally ends with a single line that rhymes with the middle line of the previous stanza.

Unlike, say, a sonnet—though some sonnets have employed passages of *terza rima* pattern, Shelley's "Ode to the West Wind" being the most famous example in English, the five sonnets comprising it each using *terza rima* until the final rhyming couplet—the nature of the *terza rima* is, generally, not to propose and turn over an idea but to propel the reader forward by constantly linking to the next three-line stanza.

We might perhaps picture the sonnet as a room with certain proportions. The furniture can be moved about, the curtains changed, the windows and door moved if one likes, but the dimensions of the room are given. The sonnet is a fully occupied space. The links of *terza rima*, on the other hand, may be compared to the way railway carriages are coupled, or to a chain stitch, or to a dance that takes you from one place to another (think of a Straight Hey in country dancing). It hardly matters which analogy we use providing there is enough energy or power to drive the movement.

A Companion to Poetic Genre, First Edition. Edited by Erik Martiny.
© 2012 John Wiley & Sons, Ltd. Published 2012 by John Wiley & Sons, Ltd.

There are various other metrical narrative forms, of course. Blank verse, rhyming couplets, and the ballad offer a range of possibilities for the poet, but *terza rima*, by virtue of its three-line structure and link across stanzas, is sometimes less tolerant of abstraction and passages of description than blank verse or heroic couplet and is a more subtle instrument than the ballad, whose short lines and close rhymes leave less room for expansion. In *terza rima* song and speech find a compromise. If song is about pattern then the pace of *terza rima* hurries it towards speech. And because it keeps moving it cannot afford too much digression. *Terza rima* is, therefore, as looked at from the viewpoint of a practicing poet, in many ways incident led.

The anecdotal bent of *terza rima* may of course develop into something longer, into a chapter, or series of chapters as in Dante, or indeed, into something of epic length. There is no immutable technical reason why it shouldn't launch on an epic voyage though it rarely does. The technical reasons that limit it are less the ear of the listener than the resources of the poet, since rhyming twice is clearly more demanding than rhyming once, and when done mechanically the rhyme does begin to nag at the ear. But the same might be said of any form or device in a long poem, and that includes poetry in rhyming couplets and blank verse. Rhythmic flexibility is the key and that means rolling over enjambments, supple use of stress and breath, and highly mobile caesuras.

Form might be regarded in various ways: as courtesy, as game, as ritual, as architecture, as engine, and as dance. Courtesy is a sophisticated, coded way of addressing another and establishing a set of social expectations. Modernity has tended to reject it, partly on the grounds that it might be over-constrictively hierarchical, only to replace it with its own codes, no less constrictive, no less hierarchical, but less willing to be codified in a book of poetic etiquette by an aspiring Emily Post of verse. The very word, *etiquette* is an object of suspicion, suggesting dishonesty and prissiness. Other cultures' courtesies are to be honored, but ours are to be reduced to a knowing minimum. We feel our way to the limits of our liberties and look askance at those who do not recognize them. One would have to be something of a prude to build a case for *terza rima*, or any other demanding form, entirely on grounds of courtesy.

We may, of course, regard courtesy as a game with all the functions of a game; that is, on the one hand, entertainment, and on the other the symbolic acting through of structured energies that might otherwise be employed in real conflict. Game depends on rule and surprise, pitting the fixed against an element of chance that may amuse or frustrate. The rules of a game don't produce uniform results or uniform development. No two games of football are exactly the same, though the rules that govern them are identical. Of course the rules themselves may be applied in various ways by the officials or the players. Games are fascinating because of the delicate balance between the structure and the variable. So games in poetry may amuse: the more demanding the rule the greater the amusement. Byron, for example, may amuse by rhyming "intellectual" with "hen pecked you all" in *Don Juan*, daring us with the polysyllabic then offering bathetic relief with an ingenious but distinctly unheroic resolution. But, on the symbolic level, the demands of form, serve as recognized sublimations of energy, much as in sport the beauty of the disciplined body in action enacts a desire.

Ritual, as most people recognize, carries enormous psychological significance, whether as superstition that jokes about itself as superstition yet continues in superstition, in terms of routine or of certain lucky items, or as a religious ceremony that conjures the deity or commemorates a sacred name. The meaning of ritual is almost independent of its magical object. It produces its own magic. Whispering a spell over and over again produces the expectation of miraculous change or illumination. Whatever I say three times is true. Weave a circle round him thrice. *Shantih, shantih, shantih.* The three of *terza rima* too is a form of ritual. It helps, of course, if you are a believer, for ritual otherwise is simply people behaving strangely.

Architecture in form offers a firm and, importantly, *indifferent*, structure that can take the weight of ideas, emotions, and events. It is indifferent because, once adopted, it is simply there, irrespective of mood or self. If the architecture is wrong the house falls down. Each poetic form imposes its own particular kind of architectural indifference. *Terza rima*'s begins with courtesy, runs through game and ritual and assumes the form of architecture. The structure of hell, purgatory, and paradise is itself an architecture that Dante must explore. The architecture of the verse provides the framework for the language of the poem; its staircases and corridors and rooms and halls. Architecture, as classically understood, depends on some kind of regularity. Goethe said architecture was frozen music.

But *terza rima* is also the engine that keeps us moving down the passages and chambers, always propelling the poem forward. Of all the formal devices available it is arguably the one with the greatest forward dynamic. Once the engine is engaged it wants to keep going and the reader too moves on, ever mindful of what has been left behind and what is to come, moving on towards the last of the useful metaphors: the dance, so that eventually, as Yeats put it, we cannot tell the dancer from the dance.

Dante and the Origins of *Terza Rima*

It is possible that Dante adapted the Troubador (Occitan) form known as the *sirventes* (the word derived from "servant" or "soldier") that was used chiefly for satirical purposes or, alternatively, to laud with praise. Bertrand de Born used it, as did Marcabru and Peire Cardinal. In the *sirventes*—essentially a song form—the rhyme scheme is *abacdde*, with the next verse repeating exactly the same pattern.

In Dante the groups of three lines are thought to be associated with the Trinity (the whole poem is, after all in three parts, and its subject is the Christian theme of redemption).

Despite this, *terza rima* was not associated with the high aristocratic style; as has been generally noted—by Dante himself in fact—it was, rather, famously vernacular, even racy, written in colloquial Tuscan rather than in Latin, but capable of great heights and depths.

In terms of meter Dante's poem works on regular hendecasyllables, that is to say with eleven syllables per line. In adopting the form, French poets tended towards the native alexandrine while, in English, pentameter or tetrameter have prevailed.

Terza Rima via Translation

Dante's *Inferno* begins with incident, *in medias res*:

> Nel mezzo del cammin di nostra vita
> mi ritrovai per una selva oscura
> che la diritta via era smarrita.

> Ahi quanto a dir qual era è cosa dura
> esta selva selvaggia e aspra e forte
> che nel pensier rinova la paura!
>
> (*Inferno*, Canto 1, ll.1–6)

Caroline Bergvall's poem, *Via: 48 Dante Variations*, is based on forty-eight variant translations of the first verse of Dante's poem, from the Rev. Henry F. Cary in 1805,[1] through to Armand Schwerner's *Cantos from Dante's Inferno* (Talisman House) of 2000. Forty-eight is just a fraction of the total number of translations, which is now reckoned in the hundreds, but of Bergvall's forty-eight only fifteen employ consistent *terza rima*. Among these is Charles Bagot Cayley (1823–81), whose 1851 version begins:

> Upon the journey of our life midway,
> I found myself within a darksome wood,
> As from the right path I had gone astray.

> Ah! But to speak hereof is drearihood;
> This wood so wild, so stubborn, and so keen,
> That fear is by the very thought renewed
>
> (*Inferno*, Canto 1, ll.1–6, tr. Cayley)

Three years later appeared Thomas Brooksbank's translation of the *Inferno* beginning thus:

> Midway upon the journey of my days
> I found myself within a wood so drear,
> That the direct path nowhere met my gaze.
>
> (*Inferno*, Canto 1, ll.1–3, tr. Brooksbanks)

Melville B. Anderson's often-quoted version of the same is:

> Midway the path of life that men pursue
>   I found me in a darkling wood astray,
>   For the direct way had been lost to view.
>
> Ah me, how hard a thing it is to say
>   What was this thorny wildwood intricate
>   Whose memory renews the first dismay!
>
>   (*Inferno*, Canto 1, ll.1–6, tr. Anderson)

Dorothy L. Sayers has:

> Midway this way of life were bound upon
>   I woke to find myself in a dark wood,
>   Where the right road was wholly lost and gone.
>
> Ay me! how hard to speak of it—that rude
>   And rough and stubborn forest! The mere breath
>   Of memory stirs the old fear in the blood.
>
>   (*Inferno*, Canto 1, ll.1–6, tr. Sayers)

And there are many others, following the form strictly, in their own way, most notably Robert Pinsky:

> Midway on our life's journey, I found myself
>   In dark woods, the right road lost. To tell
>   About those woods is hard—so tangled and rough
>
> And savage that thinking of it now, I feel
>   The old fear stirring: death is hardly more bitter.
>   And yet, to treat the good I found there as well
>
> I"ll tell what I saw . . .
>
>   (*Inferno*, Canto 1, ll.1–7, tr. Pinsky)

In Dante the individual verses tend to go with full stops or commas, bringing the forward movement to a brief elegant stop before continuing. The verses are units of sense. Sayers keeps to this though she loosens it a little by shifting the line breaks. Pinsky maintains it and brings a kind of ruggedness to the whole by not only running sentences over stanzas but by breaking the flow of iambics and starting new sentences at odd points in the line. So, as we go through these, we find the music giving way to speech, pattern to story.

Laurence Binyon and Peter Dale also produced *terza rima* versions of Dante, but Cary, for his part, dropped the rhyme scheme and worked through without rhyme. Many translations (Longfellow, W.G. Rossetti, Kirkpatrick, Musa, Sisson, Mandelbaum, Robert and Jean Hollander, Steve Ellis, and Heaney—the Ugolino episode) didn't try rhyme at all, except occasionally.

John Ciardi, in his version, established a half-way house, with:

> Midway on our life's journey I went astray
>   From the straight road and woke to find myself
>   Alone in a dark wood. How shall I say
>
> What wood that was! I never saw such drear,
>   So rank, so arduous a wilderness!
>   Its very memory gives a shape to fear.
>   (*Inferno*, Canto, ll.1–6, tr. Ciardi)

Ciardi keeps two thirds of the rhyme but moves sentences over stanzas and abandons the idea of hooking one verse to the next. In that respect the key element of *terza rima* is lost and all that remains is the reminder that a formal ordering device of echoes and courtesies was part of the meaning of the poem.

The preponderance of forms other than *terza rima* must testify to the difficulty of the project or, at least, a weighing-up of potential gains and losses. Josephine Balmer, in her review of Ellis's ultra colloquial translation, sums this up when she says:

> For Dorothy Sayers in 1949 it was "terza rima or nothing." Steve Ellis, in his excellent new version of Inferno, confesses that he has ignored Dante's tortuous scheme, noting that in his own verse he has always found rhyme difficult (an admission which will no doubt elicit sighs of relief from all those who, like Robert Lowell, prefer live poetry to "stuffed birds").

The Question of Rhyme

This is not an article on translation, or on the debates between translators, but the various translations do draw attention to "the other thing that is always said," that there is a paucity of rhyme in English. If that is the case there is a genuine difficulty, not only in translation, but in composition too.

We may, however, wonder whether the difficulty is not a little overstated. The cornerstone of the argument is that English is not a properly inflected language so the regularity of verb and noun endings deprives the poet of a wealth of possibilities. But inflection rhymes are thought to be rather cheap in many languages. In Hungarian, for instance, they are called *ragrím*, and mostly disdained by serious poets. It is as if a serious English-language poet were proposing to make substantial use of rhymes ending in *-ation*, or *-ness*, the first resort of the vocabulary-poor who need a bit of bling to make it swing.

A greater problem is the large range of English vowel sounds. Our five written vowels resolve into several more. The International Phonetic Alphabet points to thirteen distinct vowel sounds, to which should be added up to twelve diphthongs. That is without the regional variations. (It's not surprising that foreign speakers of English are more easily given away by their vowels than by their consonants.) Italian has but five.

But the problem is not insurmountable, because various departures from true and full rhyme are permitted, among them eye-rhyme, where it is the spelling rather than the sound that does the rhyming work. A number of eye-rhymes were full rhymes once. But we may allow ourselves greater or lesser consonantal variations, accentual variations, and licenses of many kinds. We might even think full rhymes a little childish, or a little too insistent. Many poets and translators of poetry employ half-rhyme. It may be that the gesture towards rhyme, the slightly distorted echo, is read as a distancing device to keep the childish hence, to prevent insistence or nagging, almost—as oddly appropriate in English—an act of due diffidence.

Milton, in his famous preface to *Paradise Lost*, said:

> The Measure is *English* Heroic Verse without Rime, as that of *Homer* in *Greek*, and of *Virgil* in *Latin*; Rime being no necessary Adjunct or true Ornament of Poem or good Verse, in longer Works especially, but the Invention of a barbarous Age, to set off wretched matter and lame Meeter.
>
> (Milton, "The Verse" *Paradise Lost*)

No doubt he is right in that rhyme is absolutely not a necessity in poetry, not even as adjunct or ornament, however, a defense of it might be made along lines less traditional, not as adjunct or ornament but as structure. In this defense the issue of ornamentation is unimportant.

This is not the place to develop such an argument, but since *terza rima* inevitably involves rhyme in its *rima*, a very brief attempt might be made. The defense would argue not by way of the final product but by way of process and the relationship between the user of language and language itself.

The proposer might argue that the act of finding rhyme is a different sort of negotiation from employing meter or, in fact, writing free verse. Finding rhyme is the constant deflecting of some possible intention. The poet may wish to say something then seek the words in which to say it, but rhyme constrains the process. Intention is necessarily modified. Out of that modification arise various new active possibilities. Language itself is more active as a result: its accidents, its demands, cannot be ignored or overridden. Thought must move differently and take a less directive role.

Since language in poetry is of primary importance—it is interesting how translations of Dante that depart from *terza rima* shift the reader ever further from verse as verse and closer to story, a story in which form plays a less active part—it might be argued that the active, volatile, aspects of language as sound beyond instrumental meaning are of particular interest.

Whether poetry is capable of being paraphrased (rather than summarized) or not is a moot question, but it could be argued that the effect of shifting Dante from *terza rima* into blank verse is to rewrite the poem as paraphrase with ornamental features, that is to say with local effects that heighten descriptions and moods. The story then is the real thing: its poetic qualities are the adjunct (the Sinclair translation is, in fact, prose).

The argument against rhyme also turns on the dangers of doggerel and cliché. Rhyming "moon" with "June" is certainly a cliché given the appropriate cliché context, but the art of rhyming—and English poetry is full of wonderful poems that do employ rhyme—lies in avoiding cliché, which is, essentially, easy closure.

The last major strand of the argument is based on the old antithesis between the *modern* as in Modernism and the *traditional* as in everything else. After over a hundred years of Modernism it may be the case that a device like rhyme need not insist on some pre-lapsarian, conservative caricature of tradition, but that it may take full cognizance of all that has happened and begin to define its function according to different principles.

Rhyme is not the life and soul of poetry by any means. But while it makes perfect sense to speak of an unrhymed sonnet, it makes no sense at all to speak of unrhymed *terza rima*.

Examples of *Terza Rima* in English Verse

What then can we say of the use by English language poets of *terza rima*? Chaucer is often credited as the first practitioner in the third part of his poem "A Compleynte to His Lady":

> Hir name is Bountee set in womanhede,
> Sadnesse in youthe and Beautee prydelees
> And Plesaunce under governaunce and drede;
> Hir surname is eek Faire Rewtheless
> The Wyse, yknit unto Good Aventure,
> That, for I love hir, she sleeth me giltelees.
>
> Hir love I best, and shal, whyl I may dure,
> Bet than myself an hundred thousand deel,
> Than al this worldes richesse or creature.
> Now hath not Love me bestowed weel
> To love ther I never shal have part?
> Allas, right thus is turned me the wheel,
> Thus am I slayn with Loves fyry dart!
> I can but love hir best, my swete fo;

> Love hath me taught no more of his art
> But serve alwey and stinte for no wo.

(III.2–17)

Chaucer was born only some twenty years after Dante's death and travelled to Italy as an ambassador in 1372 in his late twenties or early thirties, returning there six years later. His early work includes translations from the French, including parts of *Romaunt of the Rose* but after 1370 Italian literature, including the work of Dante, Petrarch, and Boccaccio, becomes very important to him, and much has been written about the relationship of Boccaccio's *Decameron*, and Chaucer's *The Canterbury Tales*. Lydgate talked of Chaucer's "Daunt [Daunt, referring to Dante] in English."

Clearly the adoption of a form so particular to an Italian poet signals the importance of Italian literature to English. The next, and vital, wave of Italian influence, after Chaucer, is by way of Sir Thomas Wyatt (c.1503–42) and, Henry Howard, Earl of Surrey (1517–47). Like Chaucer, Wyatt spent months in Italy and brought an Italian ordering influence to bear on English versification. Grierson and Smith's *A Critical History of English Poetry* tells us that in 1527 Wyatt returned from Rome "with an enthusiasm for Petrarch, and three measures new to English—*terza rima*, *ottava rima*, and sonnet." Wyatt, in fact, employs an adapted form of *terza rima* in a satire titled, *Mine Owne John Poyntz*, beginning:

> Mine own John Poyntz, since ye delight to know
> The cause why that homeward I me draw,
> And flee the press of courts, whereso they go,
> Rather than to live thrall under the awe
> Of lordly looks, wrappèd within my cloak,
> To will and lust learning to set a law:
> It is not for because I scorn or mock
> The power of them, to whom fortune hath lent
> Charge over us, of right, to strike the stroke.
> But true it is that I have always meant
> Less to esteem them than the common sort,
> Of outward things that judge in their intent
> Without regard what doth inward resort.
> I grant sometime that of glory the fire
> Doth twyche my heart. Me list not to report
> Blame by honour, and honour to desire.
> But how may I this honour now attain,
> That cannot dye the colour black a liar?

(ll.1–18)

As also in *Of the Mean and Sure Estate*, that begins:

> My mother's maids, when they did sew and spin,
> They sang sometime a song of the fieldmouse,

That, for because her lyvelood was but thin,
Would needs go seek her townish sister's house.
She thought herself endured too much pain:
The stormy blasts her cave so sore did souse
That when the furrows swimmèd with the rain,
She must lie cold and wet in sorry plight;
And worse than that, bare meat there did remain
To comfort her when she her house had dight—
Sometime a barley corn, sometime a bean,
For which she laboured hard both day and night
In harvest time whilst she might go and glean.
And where store was 'stroyed with the flood,
Then wellaway, for she undone was clean.

                                                                    (ll.1–15)

To Chaucer's courtliness, Wyatt, here, adds a racy anecdotal tone. The form begins to sit easy in the language. Wyatt's chief employment of *terza rima*, however, was in his *Penitential Psalms* (Psalms 6, 32, 38, 51, 102, 130 and 143), complete with Prologues. He doesn't hesitate there to employ rhymes such as *bountiful, wonderful,* and *plentiful,* as in Psalm 51, or *impediment, government* and *intent* in Psalm 102. The threefold rhyme is a pressure, and this is a way of solving it. But then Wyatt is a truly substantial poet with a flexible line and a humane intensity of purpose.

Surrey employs *terza rima* in his *A Satire against the Citizens of London*, where Surrey answers a charge of dissolute behavior and breaking windows. He, however, unlike Wyatt, deploys tetrameter, and his invective fairly bounces along:

Indured hearts no warning feel.
O! Shameless whore! is dread then gone?
Be such thy foes, as meant thy weal?
O! member of false Babylon!
The shop of craft! The den of ire!
Thy dreadful doom draws fast upon.
Thy martyrs' blood by sword and fire,
In heaven and earth for justice call.
The Lord shall hear their just desire.

                                                                    (ll.51–59)

Its level attack invites the possibility of tedium but the poem is, mercifully, not long enough for that. It is, in some ways, a lark, much like the breaking of the windows.[2]

Sir Philip Sidney's *Arcadia* contains passages of verse in *terza rima*, for example on Book II, where Plangus and Basilius engage in dialogue, as here:

Ah, where was first that cruel cunning found,
To frame of earth, a vessel of the mind,
Where it should be to self-destruction bound?

What needed so high spirits, such mansions blind?
Or wrapped in flesh what do they here obtain.
But glorious name of wretched human kind?
Balls to the stars, and thralls to fortunes reign"
Turn'd from themselves, infected with their rage,
Where death is fear'd and life is held with pain.

(Sidney, "Plangus and Basilius" ll.7–16)

Samuel Daniel employs *terza rima* and the form crops up here and there, but is next importantly addressed by Milton, who in his paraphrases of *Psalms i–viii*, employs a range of different stanza, metrical, and rhyming forms, *terza rima* being the form for *Psalm ii*:

Why do the Gentiles tumult, and the Nations
Muse a vain thing, the Kings of th' earth upstand
With power, and Princes in their Congregations
Lay deep their plots together through each Land,
Against the Lord and his Messiah dear?
Let us break off, say they, by strength of hand
Their bonds, and cast from us, no more to wear,
Their twisted cords: he who in Heaven doth dwell
Shall laugh, the Lord shall scoff them, then severe
Speak to them in his wrath, and in his fell
And fierce ire trouble them; but I, saith hee,
Anointed have my King (though ye rebel)
On Sion my holy hill.

(Milton, "Psalm ii" ll.1–15)

The lines are characteristically fluid and powerful, the syntax running over from line to line, the caesura supple, the stresses shifting from iambic to trochaic, in a series of contractions and explosions, the energy of thought and feeling engaged in a wrestling match with the demands of form, the wrestle itself producing the energy that Blake so admired in Milton. It shows what is possible beyond the systematic and the elegant.

The *terza rima* sonnet's most famous appearance is in Shelley's five-sonnet sequence "Ode to the West Wind" where the tercets are succeeded by a rhyming couplet:

O wild West Wind, thou breath of Autumn's being,
Thou, from whose unseen presence the leaves dead
Are driven, like ghosts from an enchanter fleeing,
Yellow, and black, and pale, and hectic red,
Pestilence-stricken multitudes: O thou,
Who chariotest to their dark wintery bed
The winged seeds, where they lie cold and low,
Each like a corpse within its grave, until

> Thine azure sister of the Spring shall blow
> Her clarion o'er the dreaming earth, and fill
> (Driving sweet buds like flocks to feed in air)
> With living hues and odours plain and hill:
> Wild Spirit, which art moving everywhere;
> Destroyer and preserver; hear, oh, hear!
>
> (ll.1–14)

Here the blowing and listing vowels, the rushing consonants of the tercets, and the entire onward drive of the *terza rima* is given great momentum, but halted by the second line of the couplet at the end of the sonnet, so every time the wind blows it stops, then starts up again, like a series of gusts hitting an obstacle before sweeping past them.

Other landmarks of *terza rima* in English verse include Byron's "Prophecy of Dante"; Robert Browning's "The Statue and the Bust," and Elizabeth Barrett Browning's "Casa Guini Windows," her two-part poem about the Risorgimento; and Thomas Hardy's "Friends Beyond," which has longer and shorter lines, and moves between yarn, dialogue, and dance.

It is Shelley's form that Robert Frost uses in *Acquainted with the Night*:

> I have been one acquainted with the night.
> I have walked out in rain - and back in rain.
> I have outwalked the furthest city light.
> I have looked down the saddest city lane.
> I have passed by the watchman on his beat
> And dropped my eyes, unwilling to explain . . .

Down to:

> . . . Proclaimed the time was neither wrong nor right.
> I have been one acquainted with the night.
>
> (ll.1–6, 13–14)

In the twentieth century those poets whom we would expect to try such forms, do try it. John Crowe Ransom, in that wonderful, ironic, arch high-tone of his, begins his poem "Vaunting Oak" like this:

> He is a tower unleaning. But how he"ll break
> If Heaven assault him with full wind and sleet,
> And what uproar tall trees concumbent make!
>
> More than a hundred years and a hundred feet
> Naked he rears against cold skies eruptive,
> Only his temporal twigs unsure of seat,

And the frail leaves of a season, who are susceptive
To the mad humors of wind, and turn and flee
In panic round the stem on which they are captive.

(ll. 1–9)

W.H. Auden employs it for Antonio's poem in "The Sea and the Mirror":

As all the pigs have turned back into men
And the sky is auspicious and the sea
Calm as a clock, we can all go home again.

Yes, it undoubtedly looks as if we
Could take life as easily now as tales
Write ever-after: not only are the

Two heads silhouetted against the sails
—And kissing of course—well-built, but the lean
Fool is quite a person . . .

(ll. 1–9)

It is a bold poet who rhymes on "the" and breaks not only a line but a stanza on it. The calm authority of Auden's voice enables him to make free with convention and set new ones. "The Sea and the Mirror," like Milton's versions of the Psalms, are the five-finger exercises of a man who seemed to have six, and could impose himself on, and reinvent, any form he chose, as though he ran it.

Archibald MacLeish ("Conquistador," 1932), Richard Wilbur ("First Snow in Alsace," 1947; Allen Tate ("The Swimmers," 1953), Thom Gunn ("The Annihilation of Nothing" from "My Sad Captains," 1961), James Merrill (in "The Book of Ephraim," 1976, that became part of "The Changing Light at Sandover," 1982) among others have written beautiful, important poems in *terza rima* of various kinds. Wilbur's seven-line *terza rima*, titled *Terza Rima*, was published in December, 2008 in *The New Yorker*. It is a microscopic tour de force, switching from light verse to horror in the blink of an eye.

Two Ghosts of *Terza Rima*

There are more solid and more shadowy ghosts. They continue to haunt poets. Appropriately enough, in T.S. Eliot's "Little Gidding," the passage in Part II begins:

In the uncertain hour before the morning
Near the ending of interminable night
At the recurrent end of the unending
After the dark dove with the flickering tongue

> Had passed below the horizon of his homing
> While the dead leaves still rattled on like tin
> Over the asphalt where no other sound was
> Between three districts whence the smoke arose
> I met one walking, loitering and hurried
> As if blown towards me like the metal leaves
> Before the urban dawn wind unresisting.
> And as I fixed upon the down-turned face
> That pointed scrutiny with which we challenge
> The first-met stranger in the waning dusk
> I caught the sudden look of some dead master
> Whom I had known, forgotten, half recalled
> Both one and many; in the brown baked features
> The eyes of a familiar compound ghost
> Both intimate and unidentifiable . . .

(II.25–44)

The seventy-two-line passage, though without rhyme, is fully and consciously Dantean, and is in fact a meeting with the ghost of Dante: potent, stately, unhurried, ominous, laden with ideas and symbols.

> Let me disclose the gifts reserved for age
> To set a crown upon your lifetime's effort.
> First, the cold friction of expiring sense
> Without enchantment, offering no promise
> But bitter tastelessness of shadow fruit
> As body and soul begin to fall asunder.
> Second, the conscious impotence of rage
> At human folly, and the laceration
> Of laughter at what ceases to amuse.
> And last, the rending pain of re-enactment
> Of all that you have done, and been; the shame
> Of motives late revealed, and the awareness
> Of things ill done and done to others' harm
> Which once you took for exercise of virtue.
> Then fools' approval stings, and honour stains.
> From wrong to wrong the exasperated spirit
> Proceeds, unless restored by that refining fire
> Where you must move in measure, like a dancer.
> The day was breaking. In the disfigured street
> He left me, with a kind of valediction,
> And faded on the blowing of the horn.

(II.76–96)

And Derek Walcott's book-length epic poem, *Omeros* (1990), clearly has *terza rima* in mind, often beginning with a firmly rhymed tercet or two, then retaining the tercet but moving the rhyme about, so the reader is invited into the chain dance of the concept but retains the freedom to range between shifts and echoes, even while the poem continues to rhyme across stanzas. In an online interview with Luigi Sampietro, Walcott is asked why he chose *terza rima* and answers:

> I think I began the sections without knowing what I was doing. I think it began in blank verse—or unrhymed, rough pentameter. And, then, I remember that there were other sections that were like couplets: some sections dealing with some figures like Philoctete or Timon of Athens. And, then, when it began to take shape—then it began to fall into a kind of rough-textured *terza rima*. Although it's syllabically—in twelve syllables—nearly every section, apart from one or a few chapters.
>
> I thought that the—and this is very technical, but it may be of interest—the usual meter for heroic or narrative verse in English is pentametrical. But the echo of the pentameter, it seems to me, it's felt to be a little conventional and a little pre-deter-mined. And, of course—I think—even if you add rhyme to that, you have a risk of either quatrains or couplets.
>
> So, I preferred to use a longer line—a hexametrical line. Because I felt that the prose—the narrative experience in the poem—would"ve had less of a sort of an epic echo if it were in hexameter as opposed to if it were in pentameter —in which it would already begin to certainly have echoes of Milton, or Tennyson—something Victorian—in terms of the measure of it. And I don't think that the pentameter would've allowed me the kind of prosaic space that I wanted for the action of the narration—the prose element in it. I think that in the pentametrical measure ordinary things tend to get over-emphasized by the beat—I think. Whereas *here* there is more flexibility, more caesuras. You can relax, you can pick up—accelerate as you wish.
>
> And then the rhyme design, the *terza-rima* design. It's almost a combination or a Homeric meter with . . . Although I don't know Greek. But I'm not sure that it's fair to Homer to do him in pentameter . . . Because—I don't know—it becomes, really, Victorian,—and heroic, in the wrong sense. So, it was like a sort or combination of a Homeric kind or measure—although I didn't think of Homeric, necessarily. I thought hexametrical. And of course, a Dantesque thing of the *terza-rima* design.
>
> (Sampietro, online)

Here is that "Dantesque thing" in action:

> Plunkett's ances-tree (his pun) fountained I blossoms
> and pods from a genealogical willow
> above he blotter's green field. One pod was the Somme's.
>
> It burst with his father's lungs. Then a pale yellow
> asterisk or a great-uncle marked Bloemfontein.
> At the War Office he'd paid some waxworks fellow
>
> to draw flowers for battles, buds for a campaign.
> The cold-handed bugger'd done it for a fortune.
> Undertaker's collar, bald as a snooker-ball,

as hunched as a raven, he plucked tiles in a turn
from their cliffs of gilt ledgers, picking with his bill
from Agincourt to Zouave, returning to where

he found blue blood in the Plunketts.

(Walcott, *Omeros*, Chapter XVI, ll.1–13)

It is broad in the beam, moving along wide seas, making room for itself, as it goes, driving, as Walcott says, the "prose" of the narrative along with its sheer flexibility, retaining its twelve-syllable space, one of the grand works of our time.

Beyond and With Ghosts

And so we return to Dante, that "Dantesque thing," as a particular form of locomotion in verse, striding or lurching or blasting or genuflecting in courtly fashion as it goes; sometimes heavily muscular, sometimes a touch military, at other times almost drifting, as the object of rhyme floats ever further, always somewhere in front with the ghost of Dante never far off, generally a little behind or ahead, but sometimes, as in Eliot, moving with the poem, side by side in conversation, as all verse is in conversation with what preceded it or is to come, much like the *terza rima* itself, each element of time attached to the other.

Speaking for myself as a frequent deployer of *terza rima*, I began experimenting with form as architecture and engine in the mid-1970s, but the need for architecture and engine only became evident once I returned to the country of my birth, Hungary, in 1984, after twenty-eight years' absence, and having already published three generously received books. The mass of impressions, half-submerged memories, potential obligations and emotions seemed to demand longer poems, fuller explorations. Four long poems emerged out of the experience, which was genuinely life-changing. All four looked to form, specifically to stanza and rhyme, as architecture—which was peculiarly appropriate as it was chiefly the buildings of Budapest that moved me and seemed to require an answer. The three first fruits of the reconnection to Hungary were *The Photographer in Winter* (also the title of the book that appeared in 1986), that was composed of eight sections of four verses each, the verses consisting of six lines, rhyming *abbcca*, like a series of enclosed capsules (I now think of them as rows of windows in a tenement block). *The Swimmers*, in the same book, was comprised of four sections of five rhyming quatrains each, and *The Courtyards* of six three-verse sections, rhymed like *The Photographer in Winter*, but with a seventh hanging section of one full verse with a repeated line. It is clear now that these six-line verses and the idea of the coda verse, or the single coda line, led naturally enough to *terza rima*.

What followed these attempts at longer work was the title poem of the next book, *Metro*. The poem consists of ten sections of six thirteen-line sonnet echoes and it wants to tell a story, essentially the removal of my mother from Budapest to Ravensbruck concentration camp in 1944. None of the three earlier sequences were stories as such: they were collections of moments, tiny film-clips at the longest. The difficulty with *Metro* was that the story required information. There are as a result passages of concentrated poetry and others of background. The former—and some of it is the most vivid poetry I had written to that time - was impossible without the latter, but the latter was still not satisfying as poetry.

Terza rima proper first occurs in my work in a later sequence, *Transylvana*, based on a visit to my mother's Transylvanian home town, Cluj, in Romania. The experience was disturbing. Cluj, and Romania generally, seemed to be a hellish place, so it was natural to turn to *terza rima*, and having turned to it, it felt supple and mobile. The poem could do its tour of the pockets or *bolgia* of hell—its *malebolge* as Dante described them, much as Dante did his, and the guide to this hell, my elderly, long-lost uncle Ferenc, could be regarded as a kind of Virgil. Virgil is what he is named in the poem, and it is his itinerary the poem follows.

From that time on all the bigger themes involving a ghostly passage seemed to demand *terza rima*. So the episodes of *An English Apocalypse*, a tour of the *bolgia* of England, and the attempt at an episodic memoir of *Flesh: An Early Family History*, those holed *bolgia* of memory. I have not attempted a long single narrative in *terza rima*, partly because I have no confidence that I am a story-teller, and partly because, as I suggested earlier, *terza rima* might become wearisome at great length.

Art, said Emily Dickinson, is a house that tries to be haunted. It is therefore not impossible that I, or anyone else whose imagination is driven by the engine of form, and requires some kind of architecture to accommodate a variety of ghosts, should not find *terza rima* an appropriate engine to build, and then inhabit that house.

NOTES

1 Cary's translation was, in fact, preceded by Henry Boyd's. Boyd's *Inferno* appeared in 1785 (Dublin and London), the complete *Comedy* being published in 1802. Boyd uses a six-line *aabccb* unit, composed of firmly end-stopped pentameters.

2 In his notes to the poem, the editor of the 1854 *Poetical Works of Henry Howard, Earl of Surrey*, Robert Bell, remarks on Dr Nott (a previous editor, of the 1815 *Works*) who had tried to defend Surrey's roistering by attributing the window-breaking to an excess of religious zeal in wanting to convert people from Romanism that, according to Nott, "grew out of that romantic turn of thought and enthusiastic mode of contemplating common objects, which was peculiar to him," Bell remarks: "It must, undoubtedly, be admitted, that his mode of contemplating common objects was remarkably peculiar, if it induced him to hit upon this method of reforming the Londoners."

REFERENCES AND FURTHER READING

Alighieri, Dante. *The Divine Comedy*, tr. Melville B. Anderson. Oxford: Oxford University Press, 1932.

Alighieri, Dante. *Dante's Divine Comedy, The First Part: Hell*, tr. Thomas Brooksbank. London: John W. Parker & Son, 1854.

Alighieri, Dante. *The Divine Comedy of Dante*, tr. Henry F. Cary. London: J.M. Dent & Sons, 1910.

Alighieri, Dante. *Dante's Divine Comedy: The Vision of Hell*, tr. Charles Bagot Cayley. London: Longman, Brown, Green, and Longmans, 1851.

Alighieri, Dante. *The Inferno*, tr. John Ciardi. New York: Mentor, 1954.

Alighieri, Dante. *The Inferno of Dante: A New Verse Translation, Bilingual Edition*, tr. Robert Pinsky. New York: Farrar, Straus and Giroux, 1994.

Alighieri, Dante. *The Divine Comedy: Hell*, tr. Dorothy L. Sayers. London: Penguin Classics, 1971.

Alighieri, Dante. *Cantos from Dante's Inferno*, tr. Armand Schwerner. Jersey City: Talisman House, 2000.

Alighieri, Dante. *The Inferno*, ed. and trans. Philip H. Wicksteed. London: J. M. Dent & Sons, Ltd., 1941.

Auden, W.H. "The Sea and The Mirrow." *Collected Poems*, ed. Edward Mendelson. London: Faber and Faber, 1976.

Balmer, Josephine "The lost in translation: 'Hell'—Dante Alighieri, tr. Steve Ellis," The Independent, March 13, 1994.

Bergvall, Caroline, *Fig*. Cambridge: Salt, 2005.

Browning, Elizabeth Barrett. *The Works of Elizabeth Barrett Browning*. London: Wordsworth, 1994.

Browning, Robert. *Poems of Robert Browning*. London: Oxford University Press, 1923.

Byron, George Gordon, Lord. *The Poetical Works of Lord Byron* London: Oxford University Press, 1912.

Chaucer, Geoffrey. "A Compleynte to His Lady," *The Works of Geoffrey Chaucer*, ed. Alfred W. Pollard. London: Macmillan, 1903. 334.

Daniel, Samuel. In *A Complete Edition of the Poets of Britain, Volume the Fourth*. London: John & Arthur Arch, 1793. 117.

Eliot, T.S. *The Complete Poems and Plays of T.S. Eliot* London: Faber & Faber, 1969.

Frost, Robert. *"Acquainted with the Night,"* *Complete Poems*. London: Jonathan Cape, 1959. 281.

Grierson, Herbert J.C. and Smith, J.C. *A Critical History of English Poetry*. London: Chatto & Windus, 1970.

Gunn, Thom. *Collected Poems*. London: Faber & Faber, 1994.

Hardy, Thomas. *The Complete Poems of Thomas Hardy*. London: Macmillan, 1976.

Howard, Henry, Earl of Surrey. "A Satire against the Citizens of London," *Poetical Works*, ed. Robert Bell. London: John W. Parker & Sons, 1854.

Milton, John. "The Verse," Paradise Lost, *The Poems of Milton*, ed. John Carey and Alistair Fowler . London: Longmans 1968.

Ransom, John Crowe. "Vaunting Oak," *Selected Poems* London: Eyre & Spottiswode, 1970.

Sampietro, Luigi. Derek Walcott on Omeros, http://users.unimi.it/caribana/OnOmeros.html.

Shelley, Percy Bysshe. "Ode to the West Wind," *Poetical Works*. London: Oxford University Press, 1914. 573.

Sidney, Sir Philip. "Plangus and Basilius," *The Countess of Pembroke's Arcadia*. London: Routledge, 1907. 187.

Szirtes, George. *New and Collected Poems*. Tarset: Bloodaxe, 2008.

Walcott, Derek. *Omeros* London: Faber & Faber, 1990.

Wilbur, Richard. "Terza Rima," The New Yorker, December 8, 2008. www.newyorker.com/fiction/poetry/2008/12/08/081208po_poem_wilbur.

Wyatt, Sir Thomas. *Collected Poems*, ed. Joost Daalder. London: Oxford University Press, 1975.

14
Ottava Rima

Quietly Facetious upon Everything

Michael Hinds

The typical story of *ottava rima* details how it began as a stanza in Italian narrative verse popularized by Boccaccio in *Teseide* (1340), and then prospered through its adaptation into English by Byron into the remarkable experiment in language and genre that is his *Don Juan* (1819–1824). In Italian, *ottava* is an apparently natural demonstration of the innate harmoniousness of the Italian language, an aura that is only enhanced by the obscurity of its origins; in English, however, the form proves the sheer durability and maneuverability of that hybrid tongue, projecting a music of its own that is obviously "unnatural" but simultaneously indicative of the sheer resourcefulness, determination, and *chutzpah* of the poet daring enough to attempt its stanza. Whether in the Italianate version's eight hendecasyllabic lines, rhyming *ababa-bcc*, or the English version's adoption of iambic pentameter, *ottava* has doubled up as an effective form of straightforward yarn-spinning, both heroic and mock heroic, yet it has also proven capable of subtlety and nuance throughout its (admittedly patchy) history.

In Italian, *ottava* exemplifies continuity with the classical tradition, notably in how Ariosto's *Orlando Furioso* (1516), which in turn had been inspired by Boiardo's *Orlando Innamorato* (1486), combines the encyclopedic proliferations of Ovid with the linear romance of Virgil. Ariosto followed Boccaccio in using *ottava* as a mode of romance, but he also expanded his poetic geography beyond a narrowly defined courtly space:

> Le donne, i cavallier, l'arme, gli amori,
> le cortesie, l'audaci imprese io canto,
> che furo al tempo che passaro i Mori
> d'Africa il mare, e in Francia nocquer tanto,
> seguendo l'ire e i giovenil furori

A Companion to Poetic Genre, First Edition. Edited by Erik Martiny.
© 2012 John Wiley & Sons, Ltd. Published 2012 by John Wiley & Sons, Ltd.

d'Agramante lor re, che si diè vantop
di vendicar la morte di Troiano
sopra re Carlo imperator romano.

(I.1–8)

Of Dames, of Knights, of armes, of love's delight,
Of courtesies, of high attempts I speake,
Then when the Moores transported all their might
On Africke seas, the force of France to breake;
Incited by the youthfull heate and spight
Of Agramant their king, that vowed to wreake
The death of King Trayano (lately slaine)
Upon the Romane Emperor Charlemaine.

(I.1–8)

This is how *ottava* enters into the English language with Sir John Harington's translation of Ariosto from 1591; this is poetry of imperial ambition, making a claim on both the known and unknown world, affording itself as much room as the poet can imagine. From its very beginnings then, *ottava* is an exemplarily orientalist mode, in that it both indulges in exoticism and far-flung luxuriance, but also insists upon its formal discipline for a moralistic channeling and licensing of that apparent decadence. Ariosto's poem is grounded in—perhaps afflicted by—its sense of moral purpose. Tasso's version of *ottava* in *Gerusalemme Liberata* (1581) is even sterner again (rendered below in Thomas Fairfax's translation from 1600):

Canto l'arme pietose e 'l capitano
che 'l gran sepolcro liberò di Cristo.
Molto egli oprò co 'l senno e con la mano,
molto soffrí nel glorioso acquisto;
e in van l'Inferno vi s'oppose, e in vano
s'armò d'Asia e di Libia il popol misto.
Il Ciel gli diè favore, e sotto a i santi
segni ridusse i suoi compagni erranti.

(I.1–8)

The sacred armies, and the godly knight,
That the great sepulchre of Christ did free,
I sing; much wrought his valor and foresight,
And in that glorious war much suffered he;
In vain 'gainst him did Hell oppose her might,
In vain the Turks and Morians armed be:
His soldiers wild, to brawls and mutinies prest,
Reduced he to peace, so Heaven him blest.

(I.1–8)

For all of its sense of a high calling, this version of *ottava* is much less influential in English (registering only perhaps with Milton) than Boccaccio's version that comes down via Chaucer and Pulci to Byron and Keats.

Ottava is intermittently detectable in other traditions, such as the Spanish (Ercilla, Boscan, and Lope de Vega), Yiddish and Russian (notably "The Little House in Kolomna" by Byron's greatest imitator, Pushkin). It can also be clearly argued that Pushkin's sonnet-novel *Eugene Onegin* (and its 1995 offspring, Vikram Seth's *The Golden Gate*) are as much inspired by the novelistic aspects of *Don Juan* as they are by the tradition of the sonnet sequence. Its closest relative in French, not least in terms of its atmospherics, is the octave deployed by Villon in his ballads (*ababbcbc*).

Between Ariosto and the romantics, *ottava* appears very infrequently in English (Sidney, Spenser, Daniel, and Drayton are among those who dabble); significantly, however, rather than as an abiding narrative form, it is deployed most memorably in English poetry of the Renaissance as a terminator, a mode of punctuate intervention. So in *Lycidas*, *ottava* is summoned by Milton for the poem's final stanza to provide closure with the couplet but simultaneously to connect to the form's potential as a mode of renewal and regeneration, as it is in Ariosto. Significantly, it is not Milton's uncouth swain who adopts the new form, but rather it is indicative of a new voice at the poem's end, that of a fully realized and confident poet. In this sense, *ottava* is a mode of maturity, exemplifying experiential, and existential wisdom:

> Thus sang the uncouth Swain to th'Okes and rills,
> While the still morn went out with Sandals gray,
> He touch'd the tender stops of various Quills,
> With eager thought warbling his Doric lay:
> And now the Sun had stretch'd out all the hills,
> And now was dropt into the Western bay;
> At last he rose, and twitch'd his Mantle blew:
> To morrow to fresh words, and Pastures new.

(ll.186–93)

In a similarly decisive manner, Lorenzo Da Ponte makes *ottava* the mode of choice for Don Alfonso's definitively cynical verdict on femininity in scene xiii of the libretto for Mozart's *Cosi Fan Tutte* (1789):

> Tutti accusan le donne, ed io le scuso
> Se mile volte al di cangiano amore;
> Altri un vizio lo chiama ed altri un uso,
> Ed a me par necessità del core.
> L'amante che si trova alfin deluso
> Non condanni l'altrui, ma il proprio errore;
> Già che Giovanni, vecchie, e belle e brutte,
> Ripetetel con me: 'Così fan tutte!'

(II.xiii.50–57)

> Everyone blames ladies, but I forgive that
> They change lovers a thousand times a day;
> Others call it inevitable, others pure bad,
> To me it is just what the heart will say.
> A lover who discovers he's been had
> Cannot blame others, the error is his property.
> Whether young or old, beautiful or plain,
> Say with me, "Women are all the same!"

Don Alfonso's aria confirms that *ottava* had never disappeared from use in Italian, even if it was not exactly epidemic. Forteguerri's *Ricciardetto* (1738) and Casti's *Animali Parlanti* (1802), however, *were* popular long poems, effectively verse novels, both worthy of attention alone for being decisive in influencing Byron to attempt works in the form. Five years after William Tennant's 1812 piece of carnivalesque in *ottava*, *Anster Fair*, John Hookham-Frere's mock-heroic account of Arthurian legend *Prospectus and Specimen of an Intended National Work* or *The Monks and the Giants* represented the full comeback of *ottava* in English. This was reinforced by Byron's appreciative reading of Frere, which duly inspired him to perform his translation of Pulci's *Morgante* (1487), a poem in *ottava* that in itself was a mock-heroic sequel to Ariosto. Byron quickly moved onto his own *Beppo* (1817), the work that prepared the ground for *Don Juan* (1821), the epic that proves the greatness of *ottava* in terms of its potential for both sustained narrative and radical experimentation, but which consequently also provides too powerful a model for any subsequent writer to match.

Just before its first publication, Byron wrote to Thomas Moore in September 1818 that the poem was "meant to be a little quietly facetious upon every thing"(180). This sounds like a timid enough ambition, and it is reflected in Byron's assertions to his publisher John Murray (August 12, 1819) that he had no grandiose plans for the poem:

> You ask me for the plan of Donny Johnny; I *have* no plan—I *had* no plan; but I had or have materials . . . If it don't take, I will leave it off where it is, with all due respect, to the Public . . . Why, man, the soul of such writing is its license; at least the *liberty* of that license, if one likes. You are too earnest and eager about a work never intended to be serious. Do you suppose that I could have any intention but to giggle and make giggle?
>
> (213)

This apparent carelessness about the poem's destiny in fact disguises that what Byron was evolving in *Don Juan* was a life-text, a poem that could—and would—only end with the death of the author. The poem's lack of predetermination finds immediate expression in the opening to Canto I, where Byron notoriously declares that his poem is founded in a fundamental lack:

> I want a hero: an uncommon want,
> When every year and month sends forth a new one,

Till, after cloying the gazettes with cant,
The age discovers he is not the true one;
Of such as these I should not care to vaunt,
I'll therefore take our ancient friend Don Juan—
We all have seen him, in the pantomime,
Sent to the devil somewhat ere his time.

(I.1–8)

Don Juan's octaves continually attempt to satisfy that want, its repeated stanza a form of mechanism for the maintenance of eternal *jouissance* until death; the choice of *ottava* as this mechanism is in fact even more significant than Byron's choice of hero. An apparently ideal marriage of two sex-machines; the erotomaniac Sevillan and the deracinated Anglo-Scots aristocrat, does not generate wantonness but rather abstinence. From its beginning, *Don Juan* deploys *ottava* to create tantalization rather than gratification. The poem deals in delay, sometimes putting off his punchline couplet for several stanzas, as here in Canto I:

Young Juan wander'd by the glassy brooks,
Thinking unutterable things; he threw
Himself at length within the leafy nooks
Where the wild branch of the cork forest grew;
There poets find materials for their books,
And every now and then we read them through,
So that their plan and prosody are eligible,
Unless, like Wordsworth, they prove unintelligible.

He, Juan (and not Wordsworth), so pursued
His self -communion with his own high soul,
Until his mighty heart, in its great mood,
Had mitigated part, though not the whole
Of its disease; he did the best he could
With things not very subject to control,
And turn'd, without perceiving his condition,
Like Coleridge, into a metaphysician.

He thought about himself, and the whole earth
Of man the wonderful, and of the stars,
And how the deuce they ever could have birth;
And then he thought of earthquakes, and of wars,
How many miles the moon might have in girth,
Of air-balloons, and of the many bars
To perfect knowledge of the boundless skies;-
And then he thought of Donna Julia's eyes.

In thoughts like these true wisdom may discern
Longings sublime, and aspirations high,

> Which some are born with, but the most part learn
> To plague themselves withal, they know not why:
> 'T was strange that one so young should thus concern
> His brain about the action of the sky;
> If you think 't was philosophy that this did,
> I can't help thinking puberty assisted.

(I.713–44)

At once parodistic and rhapsodic, from the jocose to the bellicose, Byron gives us both pathos and bathos; throughout its cantos, *Don Juan* dramatizes a tension between exuberantly abundant content and its channeling in form, suggesting plenitude even as *ottava*'s couplet brings things to an ending. *Ottava* allows him continually to digress rhymingly, even though digression is not necessarily what we might understand rhyming to encourage; so some octaves read like exercises in mere daring, such as this stanza in prescriptionese, which implies that one can say anything in *ottava* and no-one will mind:

> But here is one prescription out of many:
> "*Sodæ-Sulphat. 3vj.3fs. Mannæ optim.*
> *Aq. fervent. f. /3ifs. 3ij. tinct. Sennae*
> *Haustus*" (And here the surgeon came and cupp'd him)
> "*Rx Pulv. Com. gr. iij. Ipecacuanhæ*"
> (With more beside if Juan had not stopp'd 'em).
> "*Bolus Potassæ Sulphuret. sumendus,*
> *Et haustus ter in die capiendus.*"

(X.321–28)

Such exercises in license aside, the usual tendency of *ottava* towards argument means that it is often most effective as a satirical instrument, as is clearly demonstrated in *Don Juan* but also in perhaps the outstanding parts of Keats's "Isabella, Or the Pot of Basil," a poem which comes to life when Keats forgets the strangulated erotics of his main plot to inveigh against the grotesque proto-industrialists that are Isabella's Florentine brothers:

> With her two brothers this fair lady dwelt,
> Enriched from ancestral merchandise,
> And for them many a weary hand did swelt
> In torch mines and noisy factories,
> And many once proud-quiver'd loins did melt
> In blood from stinging whip—with hollow eyes
> Many all day in dazzling river stood,
> To take the rich-ored driftings of the flood.
>
> For them the Ceylon diver held his breath,
> And went all naked to the hungry shark;

> For them his ears gush'd blood; for them in death
> The seal on the cold ice with piteous bark
> Lay full of darts; for them alone did seethe
> A thousand men in troubles wide and dark:
> Half-ignorant, they turn'd an easy wheel,
> That set sharp racks at work, to pinch and peel.
>
> Why were they proud? Because their marble founts
> Gush'd with more pride than do a wretch's tears?
> Why were they proud? Because fair orange-mounts
> Were of more soft ascent than lazar stairs?
> Why were they proud? Because red-lin'd accounts
> Were richer than the songs of Grecian years?
> Why were they proud? Again we ask aloud,
> Why in the name of Glory were they proud?
>
> > (ll.105–28)

Why indeed? *Ottava* here has contorted Keats into a poet as rhetorician, and further directs him into anti-semitism in the subsequent octave as his ardor mounts, all of which shows the power of this form as a medium, but also its propensity for cant and bombast; it makes Keats very unKeatsian indeed:

> Yet were these Florentines as self-retired
> In hungry pride and gainful cowardice,
> As two close Hebrews in that land inspired,
> Paled in and vineyarded from beggar spies.
>
> > (ll.129–33)

Although these stanzas show us *ottava*'s innate potential for thuggery, they do nevertheless counter any argument that the problem with *ottava* is that it reduces thought to stanza-length; Keats may just be getting progressively outraged, but he *is* progressing.

Nevertheless, *ottava* can sometimes be merely cheap and nasty rather than self-righteously outraged. In *Don Juan*, Byron's genius is matched by his willful *animus*, and the form's laconicism proved a perfect medium for his malice. In this, Byron is connecting through *ottava* to the Latinate tradition, in particular Juvenal and Catullus, whose poetry is often a vehicle for expressing noble outrage in scabrous language, as in the Dedication's assault on Southey, whose poetic career is compared to a noisy orgasm without any ejaculate to substantiate it:

> You, Bob, are rather insolent, you know,
> At being disappointed in your wish
> To supersede all warblers here below,
> And be the only blackbird in the dish.

And then you overstrain yourself, or so,
And tumble downward like the flying fish
Gasping on deck, because you soar too high, Bob,
And fall for lack of moisture quite a dry Bob.

(ll.17–24)

With rhyming that comes close to tabloidese, *ottava* becomes a mode of the anti-sublime, a way of wittily removing the terror and the beauty from everything, and maybe the poetry too. As Byron wrote of *Don Juan* "a playful satire, with as little poetry as could be helped, was what I meant"; but then we have Yeats, surely the most poetic of poets, who turns increasingly in his later poetry to *ottava* as a mode of decisive self-reflexivity. So *ottava* for Yeats is a mode ideally suited for public occasions, as in "Among School Children," where the great senator requires an aptly oratorical mode of address, or in "The Circus Animal's Desertion," where he writes his spectacular song of valediction to both his public and his own inspiration, becoming not altogether quietly facetious about himself.

Ottava's final couplet particularly suits Yeats, with his gift for lines that resound apothegmatically. It also allows for a certain violence of contrast that the bullying tendency in Yeats finds congenial. In *The Tower*, *ottava* is a recurring major mode, a form of intervention in "Meditations in a Time of Civil War," and adopted for the entirety of "Sailing to Byzantium" and "Nineteen Hundred and Nineteen," the fourth stanza of which counts as one of Yeats's most extraordinary (and therefore, most representative) achievements. Unlike his other exercises in *ottava*, "Sailing to Byzantium" is a rich mythical weave, yet it is also personal to its core, and perhaps Yeats's most metonymic of all poems, in that it chants so loudly back to much of his other work. Yeats's greatest feat, however, is in how he knows that the gravitational pull of bathos is palpable at times in *ottava*, as the couplet always has to have its say. In this way, it is the least sublime of forms, always demystifying and seeking to get on with business. Peculiarly, however, what Yeats does is to reverse the traditional movement of the octave, beginning his poem with what sounds like an admonitory last line: "That is no country for old men" (1). Beginning the poem with what would normally be an octave's vanishing point, reversing gravity, Yeats generates sublime potential from what might conventionally have been a terminal prohibition.

Arguably, literary history suggests that *ottava* has proved too intractable for English in hands other than Byron's; Chaucer adopted the raw story, the *fabula*, of Boccaccio's *Teseide* for *The Knight's Tale*, but he did not want anything to do with its form (although perhaps he wanted to suggest that his Knight had read Boccaccio). Of Shelley's many versions of the Homeric Hymns, only that to Mercury is rendered in *ottava*. The most surprising omission of all is that of Auden, a poet seemingly tuned perfectly towards the writing of *ottava*, but who is limited to a couple of near misses, with excursions in rhymed and unrhymed octaves throughout the *Collected Shorter Poems*, notably "Through the Looking Glass" and "In Sickness and in Health." In the poem that seems to demand the use of *ottava* as a fundamental requirement, "Letter to Lord

Byron," he instead makes a gag (if not a virtue) out of *not* deploying it, using rhyme royal as Chaucer did before him:

> Ottava Rima would, I know, be proper,
> The proper instrument on which to pay
> My compliments, but I should come a cropper;
> Rhyme-royal's difficult enough to play.
> But if no classics as in Chaucer's day,
> At least my modern pieces shall be cheery
> Like English bishops on the Quantum Theory.
>
> (I.141–47)

Mostly, the twentieth century shows *ottava* in a state of disrepair, a form only barely amidst a scatter of other forms. Having said that, a significant number of modern poets feeling the pressure of Yeats's shadow have attempted variations on the form without adopting it entirely; and so James Wright worked very effectively using the rhyming octave without ever using *ottava*'s classic *abababcc,* particularly in his relatively early poems "Old Man Drunk" and "Evening." Indeed, there is a considerable list of twentieth-century poets who use variants on *ottava* to a remarkable range of effects: Thom Gunn's biker hymn, "On the Move" adopts *abaccddb*, his *chiaroscuro* Caravaggio piece, "In Santa Maria del Popolo" uses *ababcdcd*; Elizabeth Bishop's unusually intimate (consequently unpublished in her lifetime) "It Is Wonderful to Wake up Together" is a rare instance of the form being used for pillow talk. This poem also helps to query any assumption that an *ottaviste* has to be male, opinionated, and craving of attention. Randall Jarrell's prisoner-of-war camp poem "Stalag Luft" is nearly a perfect *ottava*, with its half-rhyme final couplet. The noisily post-Yeatsian James Merrill, has "Yannina" a poem in near-*ottava*, and "Santorini: Stopping the Leaks."

Of all these other modern and postmoderns, Kenneth Koch is unique, in that he writes *ottava* in a manner that is directly emulatory of Byron , not only in his adoption of the classic *abababcc* stanza, but also in his persistence with the form almost until death through three linked major poems: *Ko* (1959), *The Duplications* (1977), and *Seasons on Earth* (1987). *Ko* is a lunatic epic, a tale of a Japanese student who comes to the US for a baseball career. It takes Koch considerable time to acquire confidence in his use of *ottava*; he works incredibly hard with *Ko* to maintain his cluttered and frenetic narrative, and the strain shows in the effortful rhyming that takes place in the poem; *The Duplications*, a sequel of sorts to *Ko*, is much less forced, if no less screwball, with a cast including Minnie and Mickey Mouse, shape-shifting nymphs and some survivors from the earlier poem. *Seasons on Earth*, however, is a brief and wholly achieved poetic essay, fundamentally disinterested in any story other than that of the *ottava* itself:

> My life was in the poem and just outside it.
> Nothing was written as it "really happened"

But all took place as rhyme and chance decided.
My typewriter was there, my pencils sharpened.
Ko pitched and made the team and was delighted
And threw so hard the grandstand beams were opened;
Exit the old catcher. I spent hours
Walking around in the all-kinds-of-flowers.

(ll.169–76)

The influence of *ottava* can be felt powerfully even in long poems that do not rhyme; in his *Fredy Neptune: A Novel in Verse* (1999), Les Murray generates narrative octaves in blank verse, where rhyme occasionally occurs, but not systematically:

I was sent across to the warship. Up on deck
The band was sweating, pumping Oompa and heirassa
To us below, to encourage our mad shovelling.
A man dropped dead beside me. His face hit the bulkhead bong
as he fell. So when the ship'd only clean man
came and nodded Enough, with his Higher Matters expression,
a lot of us sprawled asleep, right on the coal.
When I woke up, we were steaming full ahead, at sea.

(I.33–40)

This is *ottavo blanco*, the inveterately macho Anglo-Saxon descendant of *ottava*, generating rough music rhythmically rather than rhymingly. It is unmistakably a variation on the Byronic stanza, yet there is almost too much room for variation in the octave once rhyme is done away with, and as such, the poem fails. Given how hard it is to achieve, it is no surprise that *ottava* should be relatively rarely adopted, and when it is, only by poets with a peculiarly exceptional self-confidence in their ability to find that rhyme when necessary.

Anthony Burgess's *Byrne: A Novel* (1996), its author's last book, was composed mainly in a Byronic combination of *ottava* and the Spenserian stanza from *Child Harolde*. As such, *ottava* has come back home to its roots in romance. Burgess managed to get away with his manifestly tin ear by making his inadequacy as a rhymester into part of the poem's performative fabric:

Why choose this agony of versifying
Instead of tapping journalistic prose?
Call it a tribute to a craft that's dying,
Call it a harmless hobby. Art, God knows,
Doesn't come into it. Poets, high flying,
Don't need these plodding feet with blistered toes,
Old-fashioned rhymes, prosodic artifice
Essential to an effect such as this.

(I.1137–44)

Excusing himself thus, Burgess can then perform offences against poetic decorum such as the following:

> 'An ithyphallic thrust is not a key,'
> Tom said, and pumped his mild voice to a shout,
> With perfect phonemes in a cantrip. He
> Knew the damned inventory inside out.
> TE YESU LL'Ã HA TAE KATA HA TSISI
> TSIU HA KABE SITA . . . Had perhaps that tout
> Of Brian's called an agent, stood him lunch? 'I kn-
> Ow one thing. Always do your homework, sunshine.'
>
> (V.330–37)

Burgess constantly reminds the reader that *Byrne* is not really a poem but a novel, despite being written entirely in verse, and mostly in *ottava*; what is being written here is decorated prose, as Barthes in *Writing Degree Zero* described poetry in the era of classicism. *Ottava* is very much a form that belongs thoroughly to that era: in many ways as a consequence of it being so unrepentantly latinate, it appears ante-Mallarméan and anti-symbolic, where sense prevails over sensibility. In this way, Byron's *apologia* for the temper of *Don Juan* is founded here on his forceful sense that he is working out of a sense of authoritative continuity that is moral rather than formal; this also conforms to our sense of *ottava*'s archaism in that the writers he cites are mostly classics of our prose:

> They accuse me—Me—the present writer of
> The present poem—of—I know not what—
> A tendency to under -rate and scoff
> At human power and virtue, and all that;
> And this they say in language rather rough.
> Good God! I wonder what they would be at!
> I say no more than hath been said in Dante's
> Verse, and by Solomon and by Cervantes;
>
> By Swift, by Machiavel, by Rochefoucault,
> By Fenelon, by Luther, and by Plato;
> By Tillotson, and Wesley, and Rousseau,
> Who knew this life was not worth a potato.
> 'T is not their fault, nor mine, if this be so—
> For my part, I pretend not to be Cato,
> Nor even Diogenes. —We live and die,
> But which is best, you know no more than I.
>
> (VII.17–32)

Classicism worn so overtly becomes a matter of camp, if not quite kitsch; yet here is where we can locate the Bakhtinian potential of *ottava*. This apparently most monologic of forms appears to bear its author's mastering voice very heavily, yet simultaneously *ottava* discovers diversity, digression, and perverseness despite its formal regularity. The expansive scope of *ottava* allows for a chaotic naturalism to emerge, an appetite for all matter of material; as such, this peculiarly immodest form possesses nevertheless the dignified mission of recording what Wallace Stevens called "our bawdiness" (9).

In a poststructuralist atmosphere, a modern poet deploying *ottava* might be constructed as indulging archaism, making a radically reactionary insistence of rhyming for rhyme's sake, keeping troubling experiment at bay. If *ottava* is the least sublime and least conjectural of all forms of poetry, the opposite of poetry as conceptualized by Blanchot (331–36), it is at the same time a mode that relies to a great degree on the poem as the overt performance of the poet (even if that poet, like Burgess, is not really a poet). Language in *ottava* does not speak to itself, rather it insistently demands the attention of another. It asks that readers record its functioning. Every rhyme in every stanza, but particularly the last couplet, becomes a form of saying *whaddya think?* This vaudevillian aspect has found very apt expression with American *ottavistes*, notably Kenneth Koch, as mentioned above, but even more vividly with Wayne Koestenbaum, whose *Model Homes* (2004) is an orgiastic effort of self-reflexivity, creating a state of poetic play that morphs into panicky *jouissance*. Koestenbaum's running gag, that he will not and cannot quite start his poem, becomes the only gag. Of course, you cannot finish what you cannot start, and the *ottava* machine grinds on. Unlike Burgess's self-denying poem, whose first-person speaker emerges in the text very seldom, and only then to perform a clearly novelistic role of ironic commentator on his main plot, Koestenbaum's first-person speaker adamantly refuses to embark on any narrative whatsoever; his self-reflexivity creates a psychological deadlock just as *ottava* presents a formal one. Koestenbaum spends most of his time in the poem talking about whether his poem is progressing or not, pre-emptively accusing his mother of being responsible for its failure should it fail:

> I'll sponge this subject till its drops are dry:
> My mother is a poet. So am I,
> Thus when I write these words, I stare her "I"
> Straight in the eye, and her eye matches my
> Jammed incapacity.
>
> (III.17–21)

Otherwise he relates a life of pleasurable idling, whether he is browsing the web for male escorts and masseurs (and rating their services subsequently), or indulging in the anticipation of lunch:

> I ate lasagne, vegetarian—
> The béchamel too salty—then killed time
> Surfing for bodyworkers, and found Brian.
>
> (V.33–36)

He also allows himself a meticulous chronicling of every meal's digestive aftermath:

> Adult, I work at home—that way, I solve
> The bathroom question—keep my own, unique,
> Unshared ceramic vessel to absolve
> Digestive system sins. To take a leak
> Is metaphysically to dissolve
> First matters in a bowl, where solids speak.
> I'll change the subject now: this is unpleasant.
> I have a nickname for my waste: *a present.*

                                                    (VI.31–38)

Whatever routinely erotic or quotidian material (wearing his simultaneous debts to Byron and Frank O'Hara pretty heavily) Koestenbaum talks about, he nevertheless ends by referring back to the business of his poem; this is because of the *ottaviste*'s inveterate fetishization of the process of making *ottava*, as if a DVD of a Hollywood blockbuster had spliced its "making-of" documentary into the main feature:

> Form's vascular: its limits keep me hard.
> I shouldn't use such metacritical
> Vocabulary while I'm playing bard.
> Meter's a tongue depressor: medical.
> Dr. Watson, dead now, was our lifeguard:
> In dreams he cuts my cord umbilical
> Again and again, and gives the shots that knock
> The bearer out (forgive me) like livestock.

                                                    (XIII.97–104)

Form is a means to an end for Burgess, an interesting way of telling a story, but for Koestenbaum it is just the end; *ottava* is simply the form that stops and starts and stops again, stanza by stanza. Just keeping it ticking over is work enough, and so he will not get to tell his tale, whatever it might be. If the dominant theme of *ottava* is always *ottava* itself, it seems amazing that these poems can endure for so long, what with the form's innate paralysis, a sense that you are reading on the spot. The infinitesimally finite effect of the *ottava* stanza is continually to terminate the poem with each resounding couplet, only to have it resurrected with every new stanza. This is the most Beckettian of poetries, therefore, in its constant inscription of an ending, yet again and yet again; for Koestenbaum, however, *ottava* is also a mode of queering, of drawing the reader into the rhythms of his libidinous economy. For every *ottaviste*, being quietly (or rowdily) facetious about everything, via the production of endless octaves, can be a life's work.

REFERENCES AND FURTHER READING

Ariosto, Ludovico. Orlando Furioso (1516). www. liberliber.it/biblioteca/a/ariosto/orlando_ furioso/html/index.htm.

Auden, W.H. *Collected Poems*. London: Faber, 2007.

Barthes, Roland. "Is There Any Poetic Writing?" from *Writing Degree Zero* (1953), in *Poetry in Theory*, ed. John Cook. Oxford: Blackwell Publishing, 2004: 301–06.

Blanchot, Maurice. "Mallarmé's Experience," in *Poetry in Theory*, ed. John Cook. Oxford: Blackwell Publishing, 2004: 331–36.

Burgess, Anthony. *Byrne: A Novel* (1995). London: Verso, 1996.

Byron, George Gordon, Lord. *Don Juan* (1819–1824). Harmondsworth: Penguin Classics, 2005.

Byron, George Gordon, Lord. *Lord Byron: Selected Letters and Journals*. Ed. Leslie A. Marchand. John Murray: London, 1982.

Fairfax, Edward, trans. Jerusalem Delivered (1600). http://omacl.org/Tasso.

Harington, Sir John, trans. *Sir John Harington's Translation of Orlando Furioso*. Edwardsville: Southern Illinois University Press, 1962.

Keats, John. *Lamia, Isabella, the Eve of St. Agnes and Other Poems* (1820). Harmondsworth: Penguin Classics Poetry First Editions, 1999.

Koch, Kenneth. *On the Edge: Collected Longer Poems*. New York: Knopf, 2009.

Koestenbaum, Wayne. *Model Homes*. Rochester, NY: BOA Editions, 2004.

Milton, John. *Complete Poems*. Harmondsworth: Penguin, 1999.

Murray, Les. *Fredy Neptune*. New York: FSG, 1999.

Stevens, Wallace, "A High-Toned Old Christian Woman," *The Collected Poems*. New York: Vintage, 1982.

Tasso, Torquato. *Gerusalemme Liberata* (1581). www. liberliber.it/biblioteca/t/tasso/gerusalemme_ liberata/html/testo.htm.

Tucker, Herbert F. *Epic: Britain's Heroic Muse*. Oxford: Oxford University Press, 2008.

Vassallo, Peter. *Byron and the Italian Literary Influence*. New York: St. Martin's Press, 1984.

Yeats, W.B. *The Tower* (1928). Harmondsworth: Penguin Classics Poetry First Editions, 1999.

15

"Named Airs"
American Sonnets (Stevens to Bidart)

Meg Tyler

We ascribe beauty to that which is simple; which has no superfluous parts; which exactly answers its end.

Ralph Waldo Emerson, "Beauty," in *The Conduct of Life*, 1860

Each sonnet bears forward its history, as when rain moves in, bringing with it the broken sound of all rainy days. See how Wallace Stevens makes music and sense of repetition in "Autumn Refrain," autumn a season which endlessly repeats itself and is endlessly varied:

> The skreak and skritter of evening gone
> And grackles gone and sorrows of the sun,
> The sorrows of sun, too, gone . . . the moon and moon,
> The yellow moon of words about the nightingale
> In measureless measures, not a bird for me
> But the name of a bird and the name of a nameless air
> I have never—shall never hear. And yet beneath
> The stillness of everything gone, and being still,
> Being and sitting still, something resides,
> Some skreaking and skrittering residuum,
> And grates these evasions of the nightingale
> Though I have never—shall never hear that bird.
> And the stillness is in the key, all of it is,
> The stillness is all in the key of that desolate sound.

(ll.1–14)

The sounds, however desolate, are what lure at us at poem's beginning and keep us hooked at poem's end. The sonnet form provides the perfect environment for the study

---

A Companion to Poetic Genre, First Edition. Edited by Erik Martiny.
© 2012 John Wiley & Sons, Ltd. Published 2012 by John Wiley & Sons, Ltd.

of sound patterns and Stevens plays on this notion; when evening goes, and night sets in, we become more aware of noises, the motions and sounds of the things we cannot see. The onomatopoeic "skreak" and "skritter" suggest the screeching and skittering of creatures unseen. Note how the made-up word "skreak" gains authority with repetition, becomes comprehensible and even begins to collect a history, as the sonnet travels forward and Stevens places the term in different contexts, allows other words to form a semantic network around it.

If we repeat things often enough, they take on a reality or presence of their own. "The repetition of words and refrains and the creation of a certain rhythm of lament have the effect of controlling the expression of grief," Peter Sacks writes, "while also keeping that expression in motion" (Sacks 23).[1] And this three-sentence long sonnet never pauses for long. Stevens relies on the power of incantation, repeating and reshaping words to cast a spell on the listener, as he clearly takes joy in the sounds and structures of language. The poem moves from the onomatopoeic "skreak," "skritter," and "grackles" to a concern with the recognizable "sorrow," "sun," and "moon," symbols of the eternal.[2] By the final couplet of "Autumn Refrain" we arrive at a suggested conclusion, "And the stillness is in the key" (1.13). The "stillness" itself is key, the stillness and solidity of the sonnet form, which after centuries of tampering and re-tuning is something "that resides."

Composed for eight hundred years, sonnets have gone from being little songs (*sonetti*) to little stages for acting out irreconcilable oppositions and making sense of them. The parallelism at play in "Autumn Refrain" sings to the parallelism of earlier sonnets; all sonnets require a careful act of balancing. Part of this balance depends upon the layering of words and their sounds, ones that often transmute before our eyes: in Stevens, "measureless" shifts towards "measures," "resides" at the end of line nine becomes "residuum" in the next, and "still" ventures into "stillness." In each case the word shifts from an adjective, adverb or verb to a noun, a thing. If a poem is an act of becoming, by poem's end the thing has been made.

End rhyme needn't be exact, or pronounced, trumpeting the past strategies of Renaissance poets. We still recognize "Autumn Refrain" as a sonnet. End rhyme is quieter now. Contemporary poets resist engaging this tradition. Hence, the lines of modern sonnets often find adhesive in occult rhyme, a "nameless air" that croons from an at-first-unseen corner, or a hinge that appears at one of the poem's crossings: the chiasmic gone/sun/sun/gone. As with the sonnet, an 800-year-old monument, "Being and sitting still, something resides." In stasis, an object gathers residue of the once-living, like furniture collecting dust in a house full of people. Modern poets have gone prospecting in the new territory Eliot glimpses at the end of *Reflections on Vers Libre* (1917). Eliot anticipated that the "rejection of rhyme" would impose

a much severer strain upon the language. When the comforting echo of rhyme is removed, success or failure in the choice of words, in the sentence structure, in the order, is at once more apparent. Rhyme removed, the poet is at once held up to the standards

of prose. Rhyme removed, much ethereal music leaps up from the word, music which
has hitherto chirped unnoticed in the expanse of prose.

(Eliot, 188–89)

Eliot suspected that the sonnet—unlike the heroic couplet in the hands of a good
satirist—might have lost its edge in the twentieth century. He mentions "the decay
of intricate formal patterns." But since that time, the sonnet has staged a comeback;
it is now being pursued again with a breaking of conventions.

In Stevens's sonnet (he wrote few), whatever resides—memory? the memory
of certain sounds and sights?—"grates these evasions of the nightingale." If the
nightingale is the bird of poetry (which the American knows only in a poem),
then her song is evasive; she may sing an autumn-is-here song but the real sounds
of autumn seem more like "skreak" and "skritter," intimating something
unknown, scary, what time-passing will bring, what facing the return of winter might
mean. The allusions to Keats's "To Autumn" and "Ode to a Nightingale" return
us for a brief moment to poems of bright intensity, whose sounds are both cheering
and desolate. And desolation is what brings forward both these poems. As Adorno
writes, "art is the sedimented history of human misery." Stevens's sonnet closes
with "that desolate sound" which returns us to its beginning, "the skreak and skritter
of evening gone," of time past swiftly, of the break in the flow as the moment is
recorded.

The sonnet daunted and taunted Robert Lowell. In an after word to *Notebook 1967–68*,
he wrote: "My meter, fourteen-line unrhymed blank verse sections, is fairly strict at
first and elsewhere, but often corrupts in single lines to the freedom of prose. Even
with this license, I fear I have failed to avoid the themes and gigantism of the sonnet"
(Lowell 160). Although the sonnet could be seen as a form for miniaturists, Lowell
was clearly mesmerized by its call, the towering shadow of the sonnet in English
tradition, or its "gigantism" as he calls it. Yet in the same breath he expresses his
reaction against it—his metered lines "corrupt" to the freedom of prose.

Of writing *Life Studies*, in a 1961 interview with Frederick Seidel, Lowell said:

> I began to have a certain disrespect for the tight forms. If you could make it easier by
> adding syllables, why not? And then when I was writing *Life Studies*, a good number
> of the poems were started in very strict meter, and I found that, more than the rhymes,
> the regular beat was what I didn't want.

(Lowell, *Collected Prose*, 243)

Regular beat was what Lowell began to work against—even though the violence in
his own life, of illness, was cyclical, a frequent if unwelcome visitor, he resisted the
regular intrusion of certain patterns in poetry. Yet at the same time he continued to
be drawn to traditional poetic forms that called for the use of repetition. The sonnet
form, perhaps the most conventional of poetic apparatuses, drew him into its force-

field for many years and throughout the composition (and revisions) of several different books. Lowell composed over 400 sonnets.

Note how Lowell opens each of the first two lines of "History" (1973) with a strongly stressed syllable, insisting upon the breaking of previous order, iambic cadences, a strategy he learned from Milton who often substituted a trochee in the first foot of a line. He keeps to a ten-syllable per line length but the opening accented syllable disturbs our idea of a pentameter's movement:

> *His*tory *has* to *live* with *what* was *here*,
> *Clut*ching and *close* to *fumb*ling *all* we *had*—
> It *is* so *dull* and *grue*some *how* we *die*
>
> (ll.1–3; emphasis mine)

The loosening of the meter is an intentional weakening.[3] The present participles— "clutching" and "fumbling"—accentuate the suggestion of weakness; these are not strong, simple present verbs after all, but verbs transformed into lesser "-ing" ending participles. The third line opens with vague, exhausted phrasing ("It is so . . .") which adds to the impact of "dull." Christopher Ricks pointed out that "there is not a kind of violence, a time and a place for it, that [Lowell] did not imagine on our behalf" (Ricks, "The War of Words" 256). The fumbling for regularity, the dull and gruesome manner of dying, do a mild violence to the grace of the pentameter.

Instead of turning the gaze on the beloved Lowell looks at his own features in the mirror; in this, he pays allegiance to Petrarchan sonnets which busily regard and dismantle the structures of self: "O there's a terrifying innocence in my face / drenched with the silver salvage of the mornfrost" (ll.13–14). Lowell has borrowed from the natural world to describe his features; the "mornfrost" could be the glimmer of sweat (from fear, horror) against the silver of stubble. Again, he begins these lines with strongly stressed syllables, as if in gazing at the mirror he thinks of the mirror-like sound created when a trochee and an iamb are paired. The way the features of a familiar face are reversed in the mirror, Lowell is interested in seeing or hearing a difference. Lowell repeats sounds that assert their difference from the expected or predictable.

American poets following in the wake of Lowell have strained similarly against and toward the sonnet—even those who eschew metrical regularity. For example, the American poet Frank Bidart has written only a handful of fourteen-line poems; the sonnet is the ground against which the figure of each of these poems should be seen. Like his predecessor Lowell, Bidart is consciously reckoning with the sonnet tradition. In *Watching the Spring Festival* (2008), two poems carry on a conversation with the tradition, "You Cannot Rest" and "Coat." "You Cannot Rest" is a fourteen-line poem with a white space in between each couplet; this poem turns in part on its relationship to Elizabeth Bishop's "North Haven," the elegy for Robert Lowell (which ends, "Sad friend, you cannot change"). While "You Cannot Rest" flamboyantly defies the traditional shape of the sonnet, it adheres to its emotional proportions, offering shifts in thinking and a concluding couplet, which reflects upon the whole. Reading this poem as a sonnet which resists certain conventional strains and conforms to others reveals Bidart's engagement in and management of the tradition.

In a perspicacious essay, "Frank Bidart and the Tone of Contemporary Poetry," Langdon Hammer writes that

> In place of meter, in order to bring the voice to life, Bidart chose to write in what he calls "lines." These lines differ from Frost's in several ways. They are non-metrical, and they do not substitute for meter a normative pattern of line-breaks (as many modes of free verse do). They therefore have no uniform shape or duration: their form is never determined in advance.
>
> (Rector and Swenson 16)

What happens, however, when the form is determined in advance, for example, when Bidart writes sonnets? I will look closely at a few of Bidart's sonnets (or approximate sonnets)—he has composed only six fourteen-line poems as far as I know—and share my thoughts about his "non-metrical lines" and structures.[4]

Of getting his voice onto the page, Bidart has said, "The voice only embodies itself in words as the words break themselves into lines" (Bidart, *In The Western Night* 236). If, as Hammer has it, "to make language "come alive," [Bidart] feels he must break it," does Bidart do the same with conventional structures like the sonnet? (Rector and Swenson 17) To make such a structure "come alive," must it be broken? And what does that mean anyway, to break something?

Let's start with a definition of terms. "Break" (OE, *brecan*), according to the *OED*, means, "to sever into distinct parts by sudden application of force, to part by violence" (1); "to part or lay open the surface of anything, as of land (by ploughing)" (5a); "to make a rupture of union or continuity" (V); and "to alter abruptly the direction of a line" (31) (*OED*, 507–09). All of these definitions could apply to what Bidart is doing on a variety of levels in his work. And he does it with consciousness of *what* he is breaking away from. Not all contemporary poets are as knowledgeable of past traditions, the study of meter no longer a required part of a poet's institutional education. As Lloyd Schwartz has astutely observed,

> Frank's verse is never far removed from traditional prosody, and that part of the literary richness of his writing has to do with his consciousness of formal traditions . . . His underlying pentameters create another system of counterpoint. Some of his more recent poems employ his own form of couplets that are still real couplets, making the kinds of parallelisms couplets are meant to make. I remember looking at a draft of the title poem of *Golden State* and noticing some shorter lines could be combined to form perfect iambic pentameter. Frank tried resetting the lines more conventionally, just to see what they looked like, and the energy drained out of them.
>
> (Rector and Swenson 36)

So breaking—through enjambment and the placing of lines jaggedly across the page—is something Bidart does by necessity, to keep the "energy" from draining out of lines. He wakes the reader up by demanding that we look for ordering devices and guiding poetic principles elsewhere.

But what of the sonnet? In English, poets have redefined its potential since its inception. Spenser, Shakespeare, Milton, Wordsworth, Hopkins, etc.—all have had a say, whether in prose or within the sonnet's frame, about what a sonnet is and can do (I think of Hopkins's insistence that by running rhymes of octave into sestet a prolapsis or hernia occurs and the sonnet is "crippled for life"). Minimal scholarly consensus actually exists on exactly what features distinguish a poem as a sonnet. The standard definition comes from *The Princeton Encyclopedia of Poetics* (1993) which regards it as "a fourteen-line poem in iambic pentameter (in Eng.)" with some kind of pattern of rhyme. In *Poetic Meter and Poetic Form* (1965), Paul Fussell claimed that the sonnet's "rhyme scheme and the mode of logical organization implied by it determine its type" (Fussell 114). What happens to the classification of poems that look like sonnets but have no rhyme scheme and whose lines do not conform to the ten-syllable pattern? John Hollander, in *Rhyme's Reason* (1981), has offered that there are "two general sorts" of sonnet, the Elizabethan and the "Italian kind" (Hollander 19). (As for the Italian kind, early Sicilian court poets wrote sonnets that did not rely upon rhyme but upon repeated words.)

Which sort is Frank Bidart's recent "Song," a fourteen-line, unrhymed poem, arranged in uneven lines (and has elements of the villanelle)? "Song," incantatory, mimicking the willed drift into creative activity, begins:

> You know that it is there, lair
> where the bear ceases
> for a time even to exist.

The same command ("Crawl in") is repeated at the beginning of the next three stanzas:

> Crawl in. You have at last killed
> enough and eaten enough to be fat
> enough to cease for a time to exist.

> Crawl in. It takes talent to live at night, and scorning
> others you had that talent, but now you sniff
> the season when you must cease to exist.

Notice that each of these middle three stanzas ends with the infinitive "to exist."

> Crawl in. Whatever for good or ill
> grows within you needs
> you for a time to cease to exist.

The poem concludes with this couplet: "It is not raining inside / tonight. You know that it is there. Crawl in" (ll.1–14). Published in 2005 in *Star Dust*, "Song" is a broken sonnet about the anxiety that arises over making things, an anxiety which (like the sonnet) recurs and yet is varied. The title places it self-consciously in poetic tradition. John Donne's 1633 collection, called "Songs and Sonnets" linked his lyrics with popular sonnet sequences and love poems in the Petrarchan tradition, but the poems themselves actually resisted the traditions. Bidart engages in a similar act of revision in "Song." (Bidart inherited from Bishop an idiosyncratic use of form; here I think of her 1979 "Sonnet," the lines of which are three to six syllables in length). We cannot read a sonnet without keeping in mind the contours and preoccupations of other sonnets.

As in other sonnets, there is symmetry and asymmetry in "Song." Bidart uses four tercets (rather than quatrains) and stages the poem's close with a traditional couplet shape. The lines carry anywhere from, arguably, two or three to six strong beats; some of the other lines seem (as Schwartz suggested about "Golden State") as if they could be half a pentameter each. Why sever the lines like this—to demonstrate a self aware of its own fracture? To show that using a sonnet as a vehicle for introspection is inadequate or false? Less beholden to the five-foot line than to the sinews of speech, Bidart in "Song" relies on one charged metaphor, lots of repeated sounds and circular phrasing (each refrain subtly different from the last)—all of which are hallmarks of many sonnets.

Sonnets traditionally promise an emotional or logical shift. What kind of turn takes place in "Song"? The speaker commands himself to crawl into the

> lair
> where the bear ceases
> for a time even to exist.
>
> (ll.1–3)

This "lair" can be read as either a hibernatory corner, a place that will afford the speaker sleep, or it can be seen as a frame of mind (so very different from the normal waking mind) where he is able to write.[5] Even though the speaker "knows" that the "lair" of (sleep or) poetry-writing can offer escape if not respite, he resists it. The repeated command, "Crawl in" tells us that this is not easy to do, to give in to immersion. In between the utterances are instances of Hamlet-like rationalization, the slippery reasoning that is less effective than action. He tries to talk himself into the transition. Self-recrimination marks the lines:

> Crawl in. You have at last killed
> enough and eaten enough to be fat
> enough to cease for a time to exist.
>
> (ll.4–6)

The poem simultaneously longs for and expresses a fear of this change. Bidart is, after all, also musing on endlessness, what it is to cease "to exist." The second stanza could also refer to the form the poem has assumed. As was the case when Eliot wrote "Reflections on Vers Libre" in 1917, perhaps the sonnet has now done enough work to cease for a while to exist. Some of this anxiety seems worked through by poem's end. We see this in a structural adjustment. The first line begins with the acknowledgment, "You know that it is there" (l.1). This reappears in the final line, but is set off by full stops and falls in between the phrases "tonight." and "Crawl in": "tonight. You know that it is there. Crawl in" (14). It is worth noting that the final line begins with iambs and closes with what could be read as a trochee or spondee. Notice also the position of the phrase "Crawl in;" in its first three instances, it appears at the beginnings of lines. Now it has managed to crawl across the page to the fifth foot of the final line. By relying on repeated phrasing rather than rhyme scheme for sound-patterning, Bidart not only pays tribute to the strategies of the earliest sonnet writers, the thirteenth-century Sicilian court poets, he also awakens the sonnet from its slumber in a transformed state.

There are many instances of sound congruence in this sonnet. The close linkage of "lair," "where," "bear," and "there" at the outset lures us aurally into the world of the poem. This hypnotic effect complements the attempted act of willed hypnosis on the part of the speaker, who urges himself toward dreamless sleep. The act of reading or writing a lyric poem, if it is good, and does its work at spellbinding, mimics dreaming, as it leads to a momentary loss, and in turn, a heightening of consciousness. The mundane qualities of existence (sitting in an uncomfortable chair) fade for a short duration.

The personal pronoun "you," which we recognize as the addressee of most sonnets, accumulates to excess here (reminiscent of Shakespeare's Sonnet 15 where "you" recurs seven times in the sestet). The eight references to "you"—which is tantamount to pointing a finger—emphasizes the poem's interest in the dangers of what Iris Murdoch calls "the fat relentless ego" (Murdoch 51). As Hammer points out, "Bidart imagines the repetitions of ordinary life as a 'relatively unexceptional surface,' . . . The aim of works of art is to 'make life *show* itself.' And the life Bidart wants to reveal is deep beneath the surface" (Rector and Swenson 16). Beneath the surface here is an acknowledgment of our greed, our endless hunger, and our guilt. Is there ever any pure space of respite away from these things? The repetition of "enough" three times signals such a wish.

The first four stanzas close with the word "exist" (and our existence vacillates between sleep and waking), a pattern broken in the final couplet, where the two end words are respectively, "inside" and "in." The poem gestures at movement, from the starting position of being without, or outside—"there"—to something closer, if not quite within, then at least the language has moved from out "there" to "in." The poem successfully accomplishes a muddying of the distinction between sleep (wherein we find dream) and waking; are they two distinct realms? And which one is more real? (If a lyric poem is a dream-space, a charmed moment, is it less real than a dream?)

Apart from Bidart's insistence upon the addressed "you," Bishop's 1979 "Sonnet" has much in common with "Song." If a title reveals something about a poem, what does generic terminology offer? It might suggest that the structure is even more self-consciously a structure than usual. Bidart and Bishop engage in an act of revision. Neither "Song" nor "Sonnet" has the expected reach of a sonnet—the lines fall short of ten syllables. And yet the emotional impact of both poems is great. The broken lines reveal a self aware of its (compositional) fracture. Bishop reveals to us "a creature divided"; most of her lines are essentially half a pentameter. Note the rhyme pairs, and that these rhymes are inexact:

Caught—the bubble	[a]
in the spirit-level,	[a? then we discover it is in fact **b**]
a creature divided;	[c]
and the compass needle	[a]
wobbling and wavering,	[d]
undecided.	[c]
Freed—the broken	
thermometer's mercury	
running away;	[d]
and the rainbow-bird	
from the narrow bevel	[b]
of the empty mirror,	
flying wherever	
it feels like, gay!	[d]

(ll.1–14)

This sonnet offers a "wavering" rhyme scheme. Bishop partners the end words: "bubble" (l.1) and "needle" (l.4); "level" (l.2) and, nine lines later, "bevel;" "divided" (l.3) and "undecided" (l.6); "wavering" (l.5) "away" (l.9) and "gay" (l.14). In Bishop's truncated sonnet, we see, as Christopher Ricks suggests, that "every rhyme is an act of finding and reminding" (*Dylan's Visions* 45).[6] A late rhyming pair, "mirror" and "wherever" could suggest that to use the sonnet as a path towards insight or intro-spection is misleading, the frame an "empty mirror."

"Sonnet" is like a "spirit-level," as it struggles with proportion, as symmetry and asymmetry fight it out within its taut frame. What pleasure there is in the breaking, allowing the mercury to run away, releasing the volatile element (associated with the divinity Hermes) which forced the poem into being. Just as a thermometer holds mercury, a sonnet's meter is the measure that tries to contain or register the livelier spirit, the poem's human breath. The *meter* in thermo*meter* recalls Stevens's "measure-less measures"; even in dismemberment the member remains visible.

What Bidart inherited from Bishop was an idiosyncratic use of form. In the 1990s, however, Bidart engaged the sonnet form directly in "Love Incarnate," from the 1997 volume, *Desire*. This poem is a version of the first sonnet in Dante's thirteenth-century *Vita Nuova* (the first-ever sonnet sequence, in which Dante describes his terrifying love for Beatrice). As Sir Thomas Browne wrote in the seventeenth century, "hee that should order his affayres by dreames, or make the night a rule unto the day, might bee ridiculously deluded" (Keenes 185). And yet the power of dreams over our lives is very real. "Love Incarnate" reads:

> To all those driven berserk or humanized by love
> this is offered, for I need help
> deciphering my dream.
> When we love our lord is LOVE.
>
> When I recall that at the fourth hour
> of the night, watched by shining stars,
> LOVE at last became incarnate,
> the memory is horror.
>
> In his hands smiling LOVE held my burning
> heart, and in his arms, the body whose greeting
> pierces my soul, now wrapped in bloodred, sleeping.
>
> He made him wake. He ordered him to eat
> my heart. He ate my burning heart. He ate it
> submissively, as if afraid, as LOVE wept.
>
> (ll.1–14)

In the original version, the poem appears in between prose paragraphs that describe the same dream as the sonnet, which as Dante claims in Mark Musa's translation "is divided into two parts. In the first part I extend greetings and ask for an answer, while in the second I signify what requires an answer" (Musa 7). What Dante asks for is an interpretation of his dream followed by an account of the dream itself.

How does Bidart take this suggested structure and amplify it in his version? Immediately recognizable as a sonnet, Bidart's version has an octave split into two quatrains followed by a sestet divided into tercets. The stanza shapes have symmetry, a 4–4–3–3 pattern. And this movement—a slight decreasing in size—feels right here. It suggests not necessarily a diminishing but a heightening (reminiscent of Hardy's "The Voice," as the stakes rise, the lines and stanzas contain less). The punctuation follows a similar pattern to the stanza shape. The first three stanzas contain three sentences, all end-stopped at line's end. The last tercet, however, disturbs the pattern of punctuation; a full stop appears mid-line in line twelve; two full stops (when the horror of eating the heart occurs) appear in line thirteen; and the final line is divided into phrases separated by two commas.

In his version, Bidart resists the tyranny of Italian rhyme scheme and in its place offers a semblance of corresponding sounds. In the first stanza the word "love" closes lines one and four (in the original it is "core" and "Amore"); it is both rhyme and repetition. Lines two and three are unrhymed. The second stanza is similar, lines five and eight offer sound congruence, in "hour" and "horror" (similar to the original, "l'ore" and "orrore"). Lines six and seven, ending in "stars" and "incarnate," share an internal rhyme. So there is an increasing movement toward sound linkage which reflects, however imperfectly, an Italian *rima baciata* (kissing rhyme) scheme; here it appears as *abca* (as in the above first four lines of the Bishop "Sonnet"), *deed*, etc. In the third stanza, an approximation of a consistent scheme continues; all the lines end in "-ing" words: burning, greeting, sleeping. In the last stanza, all three end words share the final phoneme "t," as in "eat," "it," "wept."

When the word "love" first appears in the body of the poem, in lines one and four, it is in lower-case letters. Only a few words later, love expands into capital letters, an aspect it retains for the rest of the poem. How does Bidart change its meaning through capitalization? Love starts off as an abstract noun, a generalized experience—who hasn't been "driven berserk or humanized by love"? In the fourth line it appears as a verb ("When we love"), and is then transformed into a noun, again, but this time it is a specific and urgent figure in a dream. Although the word "love" is mirrored in successive lines, what we see (in our mind's eye), connected to the word, is different.

This mirroring effect brings me to the final sonnet I should like to mention, "Self-Portrait, 1969" from the 1973 volume *Golden State*. In this poem, which recalls Lowell's "History," Bidart describes looking at himself at age 30 in the mirror. This is what a sonnet has traditionally been, a vehicle for introspection, for looking within. If "the history of the sonnet is partly," as Phillis Levin argues, "a history of increasing realism to the beloved," then as we see in "Self Portrait," it also tells a story of increasingly realistic portraits of the self, away from the surreal qualities of Dante's sonnet (Levin xlvi). The poem questions what the speaker sees:

> He's still young—; thirty, but looks younger—
> or does he? . . . In the eyes and cheeks, tonight,
> turning in the mirror, he saw his mother,—
> puffy; angry; bewildered . . . Many nights
> now, when he stares there, he gets angry;—
> something unfulfilled there, something dead
> to what he once thought he surely could be—
> Now, just the glamour of habits . . .
> Once, instead,
> He thought insight would remake him, he'd reach
> —what? The thrill, the exhilaration
> unravelling disaster, that seemed to teach
> necessary knowledge . . . became just jargon.

> Sick of being decent, he craves another
> Crash. What reaches him except disaster?

(ll.1–14)

Bidart's "Self Portrait" looks and sounds like a sonnet with its octave, followed by a quatrain and a rhyming couplet (another/disaster). The lines are pentameters (although not iambic—Bidart: "When I tried to "translate" the phrases in my head into formal metrical or rhymed structures, they went dead. It seemed that my own speech just wasn't, as so much English always has been, basically iambic" (*In The Western Night* 224) and there is a Shakespearean rhyme scheme in place: *abab cdcd efef gg*. The nature of the insight offered here is startling and yet at the same time perfect for the sonnet container, that what one craves is a catastrophe, to help the self "move forward" as it were. What makes it markedly different from other sonnets is the excessive ("exaggerated and expressive") punctuation. In the first line alone we encounter two Dickinson-like dashes, a semi-colon and a comma, followed by more of the same and ellipses.[7]

We also hear an echo of Bishop again, but this time not from her sonnet but rather her villanelle, "One Art." Bishop ends four of her villanelle's stanzas with the word "disaster." The poem—markedly repetitive—concludes:

> —Even losing you (the joking voice, a gesture
> I love) I shan't have lied. It's evident
> the art of losing's not too hard to master
> though it may look like (Write it!) like disaster.

Bidart's poem pivots around loss, too. The second to last line mimics the feeling of loss articulated in "One Art": "he craves another" (l.13), but the line enjambs and we see what the self is craving is a "Crash. What reaches him except disaster?" (l.14). The sonnet is always an allusive form, and in this particular instance, it is also carrying on a conversation with another form's tradition. Bidart both disturbs what we expect to be the direction of a line (in the concluding couplet) but also refuses to clarify a direction his sonnets might be moving in at the end of the twentieth century.

In his 2005 "Song," Bidart uses less traditional and less explicit ordering devices than in "Love Incarnate" and "Self Portrait, 1969." Perhaps the occasion of the Dante translation in the mid-90s gave him license (freedom) to return to conventional structures without fear of the language going "dead." Translation can act as a kind of protective barrier between the poet and the material. And when he composed "Self Portrait, 1969" he was about to become deeply engaged in sonnet-transcription with Robert Lowell.

That Bidart's few sonnets are pronouncedly concerned with nighttime and dreaming is also worth noting—as Adam Phillips writes, "One of the things we are implicitly seeking reassurance about is that there are two distinct realms: night and day, sleeping and waking, dreaming and… what?" (Phillips 108). Bidart's work often conflates what seem to be distinct realms—the experimental and the conventional, the emotional and the intellectual, for instance. However "broken" his recent sonnet looks or sounds, because continuity or uniformity has been interrupted (and lines abruptly alter in direction or appear to turn off at an angle), it is my contention that his attempt, conforming to the familiar and broaching newness, extends the early claims of the tradition. What T.S. Eliot said in defense of how few poems he wrote each year is relevant when thinking about Bidart's few but capacious sonnets: "They should be perfect in their kind and each should be an event" (Eliot, *Letters* 185, April 21, 1919).

Checked by Modernism, sonnets waned as a genre in the first half of the twentieth century, with a few exceptions. However, as the century progressed, the sonnet staged a comeback. Its popularity among poets grew. Traditionalists tried to abide by rhyme schemes established by their Renaissance predecessors. Poets like Paul Muldoon have created a new rhyme scheme which at once mocks and pays tribute to older forms. Alice Oswald borrows from the sonnet forms used by both John Clare (rhyming couplets) and John Milton. Other practitioners have done away with end rhyme but have tried to keep in place the sonnet's change in direction, the shift in thinking that takes place after the volta. After all, a sonnet is less a song than a space for meditation. Contemporary sonnets bear a close resemblance to syllogism and reflect on the status of poetry as argument. We see this in John Ashbery's 2009 "Last Sonnet." But without some kind of sound-patterning, however wavering, in place, a sonnet's acoustic power would seem to go to waste. John Clare writes in his sonnet "Trespass:" "I dreaded walking where there was no path." A sonnet is a kind of path, a way beaten or trodden by (metrical) feet. A good poet takes this piece of cleared ground and strategically embeds it with the sonnet's particular texture of sounds, and most specifically, rhyme, to create paths the reader can follow.

NOTES

1   Cf. Freud.
2   This could be an allusion to the disruption in the natural order of Theocritus *Idyll I*. At the end of this elegy, a curse sounds out, "Let all things be changed, and let the pine tree bear pears, since Daphnis dies, and let the stag drag down the dogs, and let the *screech* owl from the mountains contend with *nightingales* . . . " (my italics).
3   Of the free-verse poems in *Day by Day* that followed the writing of his sonnet books, Lowell remarked in a letter to Bishop that "I use iambics often loosened into anapests."
4   In addition to the four mentioned in this essay, "Coat" (in *Watching the Spring Festival*) and "Music like Dirt" (in *Star Dust*) are the only

fourteen-line poems in his published work. "Music like Dirt" includes a refrain ("music like dirt) repeated in four of the lines. Also, the third section of Elegy, "Lover," (from *The Book of the Body*, 1977) is a seven-couplet-long "dialogue."

5   Hibernation—or rather, estivation, "summer sleep" (from the Latin *aestas*, summer) may be closer to Bidart's language, the letters e-s-t-i appear in cease to exist.
6   Rhyme is, as Ricks suggests, "intrinsically, a form of again (a gain, too), and a form of ending" (*Dylan's Visions*, 32).
7   Lloyd Schwartz has written a beautiful essay (see Rector and Swenson's *On Frank Bidart* in bibliography) about Bidart's punctuation so I won't add more here.

References and Further Reading

Bidart, Frank. *In The Western Night: Collected Poems: 1965–1990*. New York: Farrar, Straus & Giroux, 1990.

Bidart, Frank. *Desire*. New York: Farrar, Straus & Giroux, 1997.

Bidart, Frank. *Star Dust*. New York: Farrar, Straus & Giroux, 2005.

Bidart, Frank. *Watching the Spring Festival*. New York: Farrar, Straus & Giroux, 2008.

Eliot, T.S. *The Letters of T.S. Eliot*. Ed. Valerie Eliot. San Diego: Harcourt Brace Jovanovich, 1988.

Eliot, T.S. *To Criticize the Critic and Other Writings*. Lincoln and London: University of Nebraska Press, 1965.

Freud, Sigmund. "Remembering, Repeating, and Working Through," *Penguin Freud Reader*, ed. Adam Phillips. London: Penguin Classics, 2006.

Fussell, Paul. *Poetic Meter and Form*. New York: Random House, 1974.

Hollander, John. *Rhyme's Reason*. New Haven: Yale University Press, 1981.

Keenes, Geoffrey (ed.). *The Miscellaneous Writings of Sir Thomas Browne: Including Miscellany Tracts and Repertorium*. Chicago: University of Chicago Press, 2008.

Levin, Phillis (ed.). *The Penguin Book of the Sonnet: 500 Years of a Classic Tradition in English*. New York: Penguin Books, 2001.

Lowell, Robert. *Collected Prose*. Ed. Robert Giroux. New York: Noonday Press, Farrar, Straus and Giroux, 1987.

Lowell, Robert. *Notebook 1967–68*. New York: Farrar, Straus and Giroux, 1969.

Murdoch, Iris. "On 'God' and 'Good,'" in *The Sovereignty of Good*. London and New York: Routledge Classics, 1970. 51.

Musa, Mark, tr. *Dante's Vita Nova*. Oxford: Oxford University Classics, 1992.

Oxford English Dictionary, 2nd edn., Vol. 2. Oxford: Clarendon Press, 1989.

Phillips, Adam. "The Dream Horizon." *Raritan* 26:1, 2006: 108.

Rector, Liam and Tree Swenson (eds.). *On Frank Bidart*. Ann Arbor: University of Michigan Press, 2007.

Ricks, Christopher. *Dylan's Visions of Sin*. London: Penguin, 2003.

Ricks, Christopher. "The War of Words: The Poetry of Robert Lowell," in *The Force of Poetry*, Oxford: Oxford University Press, 2001. 256–73.

Sacks, Peter. *The English Elegy: Studies in the Genre from Spencer to Yeats*. Baltimore: Johns Hopkins University Press, 1987.

16

African American Sonnets

Voicing Justice and Personal Dignity

Jeff Westover

There is no monolithic blackness nor a single tradition of sonnet writing among black writers. Elizabeth Alexander sums up this idea in the second stanza of her 24-line poem "Today's News": "I didn't want to write a poem that said 'blackness / is,' because we know better than anyone / that we are not one or ten or ten thousand things" (ll.14–16). To keep Alexander's point in mind, in what follows I focus primarily on political protest and personal dignity in sonnets by twentieth-century African American poets. While my approach turns from the tradition of the love sonnet to the subsidiary tradition of the political sonnet, one could just as easily address the way black poets since the Harlem Renaissance have adapted the sonnet to write about love. My choice is simply a pragmatic one, based on the central fact of racism and the historic response of black writers to it.

Echoing important political sonnets by Milton, Wordsworth, and Shelley while addressing racism and the rich resources of black culture to counteract it, Henrietta Cordelia Ray, Paul Laurence Dunbar, Claude McKay, Countee Cullen, Margaret Walker, Robert Hayden, and others make their contributions to the political sonnet tradition by celebrating such luminaries as Toussaint L'Ouverture (Ray), Frederick Douglass (Dunbar and Hayden), Booker T. Washington, Marcus Garvey (McKay), Mary McLeod Bethune and Malcolm X (Walker). In other sonnets, Gwendolyn Brooks and Melvin Tolson address political issues more broadly. More recently, Marilyn Nelson has published a sonnet sequence commemorating Emmet Till, while Natasha Trethewey published another about black Civil War soldiers. Still other sonnets by African Americans are less public and formal, focusing more on personal experience and a wide range of issues, including, of course, love. For example, Helene Johnson praises the individuality of a young man in "Sonnet to a Negro in Harlem," while Gwendolyn Brooks celebrates a woman full of life and vigor in "The Rites for Cousin Vit" and provides a series of character profiles of black veterans during World War II

A Companion to Poetic Genre, First Edition. Edited by Erik Martiny.
© 2012 John Wiley & Sons, Ltd. Published 2012 by John Wiley & Sons, Ltd.

in "Gay Chaps at the Bar." Rita Dove offers many sonnets in the context of the Persephone myth in *Mother Love*, Jay Wright reflects on his spiritual experience, Lucille Clifton dreams about the Virgin Mary, God, and the poet, June Jordan cele-brates shadows or addresses a lover, Michael Harper pays tribute to Sterling Brown and Paul Laurence Dunbar, Sonia Sanchez reflects on love, Cornelius Eady honors Muddy Waters, Yusef Komunyakaa meditates about racism, his father, and Charlie Parker, while Carl Phillips muses about desire and spirituality, and Elizabeth Alexander reflects on Paul Robeson or is visited by Pablo Neruda in a dream.

Like Shelley in "Ozymandias" or Wordsworth in his sonnets to Milton and Toussaint L'Ouverture, African American poets criticize injustice or celebrate the achievements of important forebears. For example, in "Douglass" (1903) Paul Laurence Dunbar echoes Wordsworth's apostrophe to Milton in "London, 1802." Both sonnets call upon famous predecessors to help mitigate a contemporary crisis. Like Wordsworth's Milton, Dunbar's Frederick Douglass represents an inspiring moral ideal. In both poems, the power of this ideal manifests itself in the form of a commanding voice. While Wordsworth links Milton to natural elements ("Thy soul was like a star, and dwelt apart / Thou hadst a voice whose sound was like the sea" [ll.9–10]), Dunbar figures Douglass as an authoritative captain: "Oh, for thy voice high-sounding o'er the storm / For thy strong arm to guide the shivering bark" (ll.11–12). Like Wordsworth's Milton, Douglass offers hope through the inspiring power of his speech. Both poets also use sea and storm imagery to condemn the injustice of the present and underscore the heroic stature of their addressees. For Dunbar, America is at sea, for her colored citizens suffer from a racist "tempest of dispraise" (l.8) in the Jim Crow aftermath of the Civil War, a conflict whose causes have "Not ended" (l.6). Dunbar pleads with Douglass "To give us comfort through the lonely dark" (l.14).

While Dunbar stresses Douglass's imposing physical presence and charismatic language in the sestet of his tribute, he emphasizes Douglass's role as an effective witness to the crimes of slavery and racial injustice when he calls Douglass "the eyes of that harsh long ago" in the octave of the poem. Dunbar highlights the central-ity of Douglass's vision through alliteration (Saw, salient, cross) and enjambment that suspends and spotlights the verb (l.4). In his own 1962 sonnet in honor of Douglass, Robert Hayden shares Dunbar's emphasis on the great man's vision. "When it is finally ours, this freedom" (l.1) Hayden writes,

> this man, this Douglass, this former slave, this Negro
> beaten to his knees, exiled, *visioning* a world
> . . . shall be remembered.
>
> (ll.7–8 and 11; emphasis added)

With the same brisk energy of Hayden's "visioning," Dunbar makes Douglass's pro-phetic testimony vivid by associating the comparatively passive act of perception ("Saw") with the emphatic modifier that follows it ("salient"). Although "salient" modifies "such days" (l.2), its proximity to "saw" (l.4) makes the reader associate the term with Douglass himself, enhancing the characterization of him as a prominent moral witness.

Voice is as fundamental to another important sonnet of 1903 by Dunbar, "Robert Gould Shaw."[1] In this poem, the voice is that of Fate, but the soldier Shaw responds to it with the same determination and integrity of purpose that define Douglass. Dunbar frames his octave as a question in which he asks Shaw, who led a company of black soldiers during the Civil War, why he sacrificed his advantages "To lead th' unlettered and despised droves / To manhood's home and thunder at the gate?" Unlike the ringing sestets of "Douglass" and "Harriet Beecher Stowe" (1895), "Robert Gould Shaw" ends on a distinctly pessimistic note by stressing the futility of Shaw's sacrifice: "thou and those who with thee died for right / Have died, the Present teaches, but in vain" (ll.13–14). While the poet calls on Douglass to help confront the troubles of a present crisis, here he reproaches his era's failure to live up to Shaw's example.

The centrality of voice in these poems reminds readers how important oratory has been to the African American quest for freedom. Voice also figures individuality and verbal dexterity, two key values for African American poets. Helene Johnson's 1927 "Sonnet to a Negro in Harlem" focuses on the distinctively personal quality of voice in her celebration of the beauty and charisma of the young man she addresses:

> You are disdainful and magnificent—
> Your perfect body and your pompous gait,
> Your dark eyes flashing solemnly with hate.
>
> (ll.1–3)

She relishes his majesty:

> Your shoulders towering high above the throng,
> Your head thrown back in rich, barbaric song,
> Palm trees and mangoes stretched before your eyes.
>
> (ll.6–8)

Like Dunbar's Douglass, whose voice can be heard above the storm of social conflict, Johnson's young man stands above the crowd. Her focus on a moment of pleased abandon echoes Whitman's "barbaric yawp" and distinguishes her poem from the oratorical formality of Dunbar's tributes. Johnson's portrait also echoes those tributes, however, for it celebrates the young man's personality by focusing on the singularity of his voice. She uses the primitivism in vogue during the Harlem Renaissance to enhance her portrait of the young man's individuality and his connection to his African ancestry. (While Johnson's Negro is far more flamboyant, perhaps he shares something of the "subtle poise" Countee Cullen admires in "Atlantic City Waiter.") The imaginative brilliance of his song creates a vivid picture. The landscape of his music is lush, fertile, and free, in contrast with the urban environment in which he lives. Johnson contrasts the African pastoral of his song with the drab atmosphere of "this city street" (l.14) in order to praise the young man's captivating beauty and denounce the racial oppression that constrains him.

In the paradox of lines four and five, Johnson characterizes her protagonist as his own man: "Small wonder that you are incompetent / To imitate those whom you despise" (ll.4–5) Johnson's sound effects and line break ("incompetent" versus "imitate") transfigure a racially prejudiced view of the black man into a compelling picture of nonconformist self-respect. Johnson's artfully quick shift from the stereotypical to the self-reliant shows the same flair that she admires in the young man. Johnson doubles the contrast between the pastoral and the urban with another contrast between a pair of rhyming lines from the sestet: "Let others toil and sweat for labor's sake / . . . Scorn will efface each footprint that you make" (ll.9, 12). By exposing the futility of effort in a Jim Crow world, Johnson dismisses stock notions of black laziness in order to let her readers appreciate the man's allure. The final lines of the sonnet ally themselves with the young man by sharing his disdain and pleasure: "I love your laughter arrogant and bold. / You are too splendid for this city street" (ll.13–14).

In the elocutionary voice of "Yet Do I Marvel," Countee Cullen zeroes in on a different conflict, the one between racial injustice and the poetic vocation, by characterizing that injustice on a cosmic scale. Like "From the Dark Tower," and like Shakespearean sonnets that contrast a host of negations with an assertive closing couplet, "Yet Do I Marvel" makes its readers feel the oppressive weight of a world in which the poet is not at home. It does so, however, to underscore the paradox of a God who simultaneously handicaps the black poet and demands from him an inspiring performance. Evoking the tradition of theodicy, Cullen implies that, in a context of racial inequity, the Miltonic effort to "justify the ways of God to men" goes ironically awry (*Paradise Lost* I.25). Starting off with a conventional stance ("I doubt not God is good, well-meaning, kind"), Cullen inaugurates a series of tragic quatrains, focusing by turns on the fact of mortality, classical myths of futility, and God's inscrutability in order to drive home the depth of the conflict that defines him as a poet (l.1). (Thylias Moss focuses on similar issues in a more audacious and expansive way in "Passover Poem," but without concluding that her identity as a poet is put in jeopardy by them.) While Cullen's sonnet sums up the dilemma of being a black poet in a white man's world, he nevertheless succeeds in singing, alerting readers to the divine imperative behind his poetic voice and to the specificity of his condition. The sonnet pulls off its performance with skillful panache.

The same might be said of "From the Dark Tower" (1927), a poem which recounts its racial wrongs in a series of elegant sentences that express both restraint and stubborn hope. If the quatrain makes the word "mute" a key end-rhyme, the poem as a whole exemplifies Cullen's eloquent expressiveness, which gives the speaker gravity and dignity. While the octave depicts "The golden increment of bursting fruit" with glamorous abandon, it firmly shows that this harvest will not be enjoyed by those who produced it. The humiliations of subjugation come to a head near the end of the octave when the speaker insists that his fellow blacks will "Not always bend to some more subtle brute" (l.7). To offset this catalogue of wrongs and express the idea that black is beautiful Cullen draws on the star imagery of Petrarchan tradition.[2] In the opening lines of his sestet, Cullen invests his picture of darkness with subtle allure: "The night whose sable breast relieves the stark, / White stars is no less lovely being dark" (ll.9–10). By punning on "relieves" to mean both "provide comfort in the face of white oppression" and "artfully contrast lesser white light with an encompassing black background," Cullen figures blackness as warmly protective and richly exotic. In this scenario, the inspiring darkness rivals the alluring starlight. Cullen has reversed the usual treatment of stars in sonnets as guiding lights (as in Shakespeare's "star to every wand'ring barque" [l.7] or Keats' "Bright star! would I were as steadfast as thou art" [l.1]). Cullen's praise of black beauty may not be as triumphant as Jean Toomer's at the end of "November Cotton Flower" in *Cane* (1923):

> Superstition saw
> Something it had never seen before:
> Brown eyes that loved without a trace of fear,
> Beauty so sudden for that time of year.
>
> (ll.11–14).

But the power of Cullen's imagery is no less compelling.

Like the communal speaker of Dunbar's "We Wear the Mask," moreover, Cullen's speaker knows how to "hide the heart that bleeds" (l.13). His darkness, however, is a fecund one, for in it, "agonizing seeds" offer a potentially more promising harvest than the one at the beginning of the sonnet. Cullen uses the same themes of farming and theft as Arna Bontemps and Sterling Brown do in "A Black Man Talks of Reaping" (1926) and "Salutamus" (1927). Although the outcome of "From the Dark Tower" may differ from Bontemps' poem in only a minor way, the splendor of Cullen's night does offer a note of hope that is missing in Bontemps' quatrains but present in the sestet of Brown's "Salutamus" ("lads as brave again / Will plant and find a fairer crop than ours") (ll.10–11). While the last phrase of Bontemps' poem is "bitter fruit" (l.12), Cullen ends instead with "agonizing seeds" (l.14) that strain to grow new shoots and that "will, in time, produce for the speaker and not for others" (Weil 227).

Claude McKay wrote many stirring political sonnets. Not all of them appear in *Harlem Shadows* (1922), but many of his most familiar ones *are* featured there, from the thrilling contradictions of "America" and the bitter sense of placelessness in "Outcast" and "Enslaved," to the sympathetic portrait of "The Harlem Dancer" and the blistering depiction of racial terrorism in "The Lynching," and finally to the famous ringing tones of "If We Must Die." A slightly earlier sonnet that is just as good, "Samson" (1920), recounts the story of the biblical figure in the first two quatrains of the sonnet and then applies it in the last six lines to the contemporary scene in a way that parallels Dunbar's appeal to Frederick Douglass for inspiration and guidance in the midst of contemporary conflict. McKay is more emphatic and head-on, however. For he rounds out his sonnet with a direct address to his contemporaries instead of evoking a predecessor: "O sable Samsons, in white prisons bound," he commands,

> Put forth your swarthy hands: the pillars found,
> Strain mightily at them until at length
> The accursed walls, reared of your blood and tears,
> Come crashing, sounding freedom in your ears.
>
> (ll.9, 10–14)

This part of the poem shares some of the militancy of "If We Must Die," but it also infuses the call to action with a historical resonance that enriches and deepens the poem's perspective. In particular, McKay's treatment of the walls as products of unfree black labor and as a collective symbol of psychological repression transfers the story of Samson's revenge to the plight of his black contemporaries in a dramatically exciting way.

"Samson" recalls an 1842 poem by Longfellow, "The Warning," which adapts the same story to antebellum America to criticize the moral scandal of slavery. The final stanza of "The Warning" explains its title:

> There is a poor, blind Samson in this land,
> . . .
> Who may, in some grim revel, raise his hand,
> And shake the pillars of this Commonweal,
> Till the vast Temple of our liberties
> A shapeless mass of wreck and rubbish lies.
>
> (ll.13, 15–18)

McKay echoes the idea of black Samson's blindness, but he also enriches Longfellow's use of the story with his reference to "your hidden strength," which not only appeals to the psychological resources of blacks, but also extends the blindness to racist whites who fail to recognize the worth of their fellow black citizens. Like Longfellow, McKay pays out his sentence over several lines. In "The Warning," this creates suspense, while in "Samson," the lines build to a stirring rhetorical climax through parallel imperatives ("Put forth"; "Strain mightily"), dramatic caesurae which enhance the rhythm of succeeding phrases, and the culminating hard-c sounds in "accursed walls" and "Come crashing." McKay updates the story, but his poem also points to the fact that not enough had changed between Longfellow's day and his own.

In "America," McKay both opposes American racism and revels in the "vigor" (l.5) of the country's "cultured hell" (l.4). He is simultaneously enthralled by her "bigness" (l.7) and ready to be "a rebel . . . / . . . within her walls" (ll.8–9). The last four lines correspond to the crashing walls at the end of "Samson," but they also bring to mind Shelley's "Ozymandias":

> Darkly I gaze into the days ahead,
> And see her might and granite wonders there,
> Beneath the touch of Time's unerring hand,
> Like priceless treasures sinking in the sand.
>
> (ll.11–14)

While McKay admires America's "might and granite wonders," he also puts them into perspective by adopting Shelley's long-term view of the "Mighty" (l.11), where "a shattered visage lies" (l.4) in the sinking sands of time. McKay further enriches the historical resonance of his dark vision by echoing Wordsworth's "unimaginable touch of Time" (the last line of "Mutability").

In the ebullient "The Rites for Cousin Vit" (1945), Gwendolyn Brooks celebrates the distinctive personality of Cousin Vit in a way that recalls Helene Johnson's "Sonnet to a Negro in Harlem." Ostensibly about a funeral, Brooks' sonnet moves quickly to the living energy of the deceased woman, first through the claim that the casket "can't hold her / That stuff and satin aiming to enfold her" (ll.2–3). By lines 5 and 6, in fact, Vit "rises in the sunshine," alive in the mind of the speaker, who savors the memory of Vit's vivacious quirky spunk. As Stacy Carson Hubbard argues, "The poem's project is the creation, or recreation, of the woman, her resurrection, like that of some parodic Christ more snakily subversive than holy" (60). The sonnet is strewn with excess: "Too much. Too much" (l.5); "Too vital and too squeaking" (l.9). It ends on an emphatic "Is," a stative verb charged with exciting energy and celebrating the essence of the woman it honors. The slant rhyme on her flamboyant "hiss" emphasizes all the more her off-kilter and irrepressible joie de vivre. "Exuberance is beauty," as Blake puts it in *The Marriage of Heaven and Hell* (64). Like Johnson, Brooks uses the highly rhetorical form of the sonnet to celebrate the distinctive being of an individual. According to Hubbard, in fact, Brooks sees "the boxing of vitality essential to the achievement of form . . . as both a sacrifice and a process of self-creation and self-definition" (61). In a society that denigrated blackness as a matter of course, this cultural work is both a moral achievement and an admirable artistic feat. More personal than the formal poems about public figures by Dunbar, McKay, and Hayden, these character profiles occupy an equally important role in African American sonnets.

Hayden himself offers one of these profiles in "The Performers," which celebrates the extraordinary qualities of ordinary people. Grouped into an octave and sestet, but without strict end-rhymes, the charming speaker of this poem admires the work of window-cleaners with grace and gentle humor by contrasting his own imagination with their daily exploits. The first sentence, which is gingerly distributed over five lines, aptly imitates the workmen's assured and artful movements:

> Easily, almost matter-of-factly, they step,
> two minor Wallendas, with pail and squeegee along
> the wintry ledge . . .
> and leaning back into a seven-story angle of space
> begin washing the office windows.
>
> (ll.1–5)

The first four commas subtly break up the action, which helps readers feel what it is like to be up on the "wintry ledge" with the men, but also to notice how routine this work is for them, and how efficient and nonchalant they are in performing it. The speaker reveals his admiration for them when he briefly imagines himself among them, but by the sestet, he's "safely back at [his] desk"—presumably performing his own work as a writer (1.9). The lines of Hayden's sonnet perform their own graceful balancing act to praise the work of these men. Recognizing their labor as "a risky business," he offers thanks to the men in the penultimate line of the poem. "The Performers" ends with a surprising final flourish when "one of the men" thanks the speaker in return (14). Hayden winks with amusement at the reader by indicating the importance of his work as a poet, which pays homage to the ordinary labors of the men the poem describes, thereby affirming their worth and dignity. The workman's responsive "Thank *you*" also reminds readers that the poet himself is one of the performers identified in the title. Poetry honors the artful in the ordinary, bringing into view parallel forms of work that would otherwise go unnoticed.

In the 1949 sonnet sequence "Gay Chaps at the Bar," Brooks weds the personal and the public in a significant way, so that her sequence builds on both the sonnet heritages I have briefly outlined above. By calling attention to the color bar in the military during World War II, the sequence reminds readers of fundamental social injustice. As Ann Folwell Stanford puts it, "in these poems, Brooks reconstructs 'The Enemy' not as foreigners holding howitzers, but as fellow Americans with white skin" (197). However, by imagining her way into the thought-world of black soldiers in several sonnets of the sequence, Brooks also gives her readers access to the private life of men experiencing not only combat but also racism and segregation within the ranks. The second sonnet of the sequence ("Still Do I Keep My Look, My Identity"), for instance, expresses a clear concern with the dignity of the individual black soldier. Focusing on the body as an expression of selfhood, the poem stakes a claim for the unique worth of each individual by insisting that "Each body has its art, its precious prescribed / pose" (ll.1–2).

Just as earlier African American sonneteers offered tributes to important public figures, Rita Dove pays homage to the painter Frida Kahlo in "Sonnet in Primary Colors" (1995). Dove writes that Kahlo "painted herself a present," which can mean (a) that she gave herself a self-portrait, (b) painted herself as a gift to her viewers, and (c) depicted a meaningful present moment through a powerful act of will and imagination. Like the simple, self-reflexive "This" that opens Dove's sonnet, these meanings offer an aesthetics that Dove celebrates in the painter but also claims for her own work. "Sonnet in Primary Colors" therefore shares the aesthetic concerns of Hayden's "The Performers."

Dove portrays Kahlo as a winged woman with a heavy single eyebrow ("the woman with one black wing / perched over her eyes" [ll.1–2]), a prominent feature of Kahlo's many self-portraits. Dove's description corresponds to the butterflies in the last stanza, so that the resurrection symbolism in Kahlo's bedstead-altar to the heroes of communism is also embodied in her own being. In the sestet, Kahlo's sometime-husband Diego Rivera's love-skull contrasts with the butterfly image. It is a memento mori "in the circular window / of the thumbprint" of Kahlo's own skull, the thumbprint "searing her immutable brow" (ll.13–14). A thumbprint is an identifying personal mark, though in this case it seems to bear the stamp of Rivera's imagination, perhaps both as an inspiration and a dark mark of mortality, like the ashes smeared on the foreheads of believers on Ash Wednesday. The circular window may be a kind of third eye, representing the imaginative vision which Kahlo's stark and moving self-portraits embody. This interpretation corresponds to the fact that Frida is heroically "erect," proudly upright. The sestet's repetition of *rose* shows how she woke from sleep and from a thousand daily deaths ("rose to the celluloid butterflies of her Beloved Dead / . . . And rose to her easel"; ll.8, 11). The artist manages to stand tall despite her injured spine, which Dove characterizes as a "flaming pillar" and which Kahlo depicted as a Greek column in a 1944 self-portrait, *La columna rota* (*The Broken Column*).

This sonnet celebrates Kahlo's heroic individualism in the face of crippling pain and the enormous power of her art. In a way that corresponds to Brooks' death and resurrection symbolism in "The Rites for Cousin Vit," the butterfly metaphor and the repetition of the act of rising, along with the word "immutable" in the last line, underscore Kahlo's vitality through a rebirth motif and an emphasis on the lasting power of her art. Dove only uses the personal names of the artists in her poem, suggesting not only that Kahlo's fame is great enough that her first name suffices to identify her, but also that the stamp of the personal is foremost in her life and painting. Because the sonnet clearly refers to the many self-portraits Kahlo produced, the poem also pays homage to her distinctive personal identity as it defines and expresses itself in the richly vivid details of her paintings. Like the singular personalities of Helene Johnson's "Sonnet to a Negro in Harlem" and Brooks' "Rites for Cousin Vit," Kahlo's specificity is at the heart of Dove's "Sonnet in Primary Colors." The primacy of Kahlo's imagination strongly registers in the prism of Dove's sonnet, whose form bears the inimitable contours of the personal.

As in Brooks' "Gay Chaps at the Bar," moreover, in "History" Dove focuses on the interaction between the personal and the public. This poem offers a context for imagining the interaction between personal experience and the public arena so that both can be valued equally: "Everything's a metaphor, some wise / guy said, and his woman nodded, wisely" (ll.1–2). Although the opening lines of the poem make a claim that the rest of the sonnet takes seriously, they are marked by a tongue-in-cheek tone. The wise-mouth speaker wonders,

> Why was this such a discovery
> to him? Why did history
> happen only on the outside?
>
> (ll.3–5)

The wit lingers in the disbelief of the speaker's subsequent questions: the *wise* at the end of the first line turns into a succession of *why*s, splintering off into challenging questions that reframe the meaning of metaphor, language, and history. The female speaker is more wise than the man she thinks about because her insight about metaphor is a home truth that she feels in her bones. The more abstract, "outside" view of history is presumptuous because it tends to see this view as the "only" one. This official and abstracting view of history, the speaker shows, precludes experiential ones, remaining blind to the value of the immediate, the perceptual, the instinctive, the imagined, and the maternal. Everyday "inside" history, on the other hand, is the stuff of lived experience, the domain of dream and desire. And it is vitally real for the individual who experiences it.

Marilyn Nelson and Natasha Trethewey address history in more recent sonnet sequences. In the case of Nelson, I examine a poem about an ancestor, "Chosen," and her crown of sonnets called *A Wreath for Emmett Till* (2005). In the case of Trethewey, I discuss "Native Guard" (2006), her sequence of ten sonnets in the Pulitzer Prize-winning collection of the same name. The interwoven sonnets by Nelson and Trethewey, moreover, recall the interwoven sequence ("Her Island") that closes Dove's *Mother Love* (1995).

In "Chosen" and *A Wreath for Emmett Till*, Nelson shows how history is interior as well as "outside," private as well as public. In "Chosen," Nelson tells a story of personal terror and joy that has the power of a fable because it represents the experience of many enslaved women. While it may be inaccurate to claim that the sonnet portrays the violence at its heart as a *felix culpa*, it is nonetheless true that the poem insists upon the surprisingly joyful outcome of a horrifying experience:

> Diverne wanted to die, that August night
> his face hung over hers, a sweating moon.
> . . .
> If she had died, her one begotten son,
> her life's one light, would never have been born.
>
> (ll.1–2 and 4–5)

Nelson welds the terror and pain caused by a slaveholder's rape of her ancestor Diverne to the tender joy Diverne feels at the birth of her son. And since the son, Pomp Atwood, is Nelson's forebear, the poet shows how intimately intertwined her family is with that of a menacing whiteness. Referring to Diverne and her rapist Master Tyler, Nelson ends her sonnet with these lines:

> Pomp was their
>
> share of the future. And it wasn't rape.
> In spite of her raw terror. And his whip.
>
> (ll.12–14)

Nelson equally stresses the felicity of Diverne's love for her newborn son and the culpability of Master Tyler. In fact, while "Chosen" and "one begotten son" are messianic terms applied to mother and child, the last fierce words of the poem ("her raw terror" and "his whip") focus on Diverne's violation (l.14). The slant rhyme of "whip" and "rape" in the closing couplet belies the denial in the penultimate line ("it wasn't rape").

Nelson published *A Wreath for Emmett Till* in 2005, the fiftieth anniversary of Till's murder. In a brief preface, Nelson describes the form of her poem:

> A crown of sonnets is a sequence of interlinked sonnets in which the last line of one becomes the first line, sometimes slightly altered, of the next. A heroic crown of sonnets is a sequence of fifteen interlinked sonnets, in which the last one is made of the first lines of the preceding fourteen.
>
> (*Wreath*, n.p.)

Although she does not refer to John Donne, Nelson's use of the crown-form and of Christian religious imagery recalls Donne's sequence of seven Holy Sonnets, which he entitled *La Corona*.

In the preface, Nelson also identifies herself in a personal way with the tragedy of Till's murder: "I was nine years old when Emmett Till was lynched in 1955. His name and history have been a part of most of my life." In the second sonnet of the sequence, she plays upon the theme of memory by comparing herself to a tree: ". . . I remember, like a haunted tree / set off from other trees in the wildwood" (ll.3–4). In a note, Nelson explains that her simile echoes Paul Laurence Dunbar's poem "The Haunted Oak," which is also a poem about lynching. The idea of painful but responsive remembering is a central one in the sequence, and Nelson expands and strengthens the impact of that idea through the allusions which connect this sonnet and the entire sequence with a wider cultural history, including not just Dunbar's poem but also "Strange Fruit," the song about lynching Billie Holiday made famous:

> If trees could speak, it could
> describe . . .
> the strange fruit that still ghosts its reverie.
>
> (ll.5–7)

Nelson revisits and enriches her allusion to Dunbar's poem by situating it in a long-range and organic view of history embodied by the tree metaphor in the eleventh sonnet of her wreath:

> Thousands of oak trees around this country
> groaned with the weight of men slain for their race,
> their murderers acquitted in almost every case.
>
> (ll.2–4)

Through the language of flowers in the first line of this sonnet (trillium, Queen Anne's Lace) and in many others in the sequence, Nelson commemorates Till's youth. Through the oak tree metaphor, she situates his murder within the wider context of other lynchings. Till is portrayed as a Christ figure in the sequence (an idea the illustrator Philippe Lardy reinforces near the center of the book with a tondo of Till's face framed by a bird's nest made of thorns and chains), and Nelson imagines an alternate history of his life that aims to redeem his tragic death. Her most compelling effort to honor him comes in a call to remember his murder in the penultimate sonnet of the sequence:

> People may disappear, leaving no trace,
> unless we stand before the populace,
> orators denouncing the slavery
> to fear.
>
> (ll.4–7)

Nelson challenges her readers to respond to Till's murder by recognizing its relationship to other tragedies in other places (like the "disappeared" peoples of Latin America) and by perpetuating the tradition of great African American oratory that sought to defeat slavery and other forms of racial injustice. Nelson's reference to oratory functions as a metaphor for her poem and for African American culture in general, particularly by reminding her readers of such great black speakers as Malcolm X, Martin Luther King, Sojourner Truth, and Frederick Douglass. Without explicitly naming these individuals, she aligns herself with them and with their verbal artistry. Like Dunbar and Hayden in their tributes to Douglass, she evokes the charismatic authority of such speakers. Like the sonnets celebrating individuality by Johnson, Hayden, Brooks, and Dove, Nelson's sequence pays homage to the dignity of an individual.

In a brief sequence of his own, Yusef Komunyakaa also focuses on the connection between "outside" public history and the inner history of the self. In "History Lessons," from *Magic City* (1992), he shows how history is learned through the lived experience of stories and angry incidents. All three of the sonnets in the sequence are about lynchings. The last sonnet refers to Emmett Till, which connects the speaker's personal world to the public history of lynching. The reference to Till also connects Nelson's sequence to Komunyakaa's. Komunyakaa frames his accounts as direct personal experience: the "I" of each sonnet hears the story of a lynching or, in the case of the last sonnet, personally reacts to the racist baiting of a "pick-up man from Bogalusa Dry Cleaners" (l.30). When the man tells the woman whose fresh dresses he is delivering, "Emmett Till had begged for it / With his damn wolf whistle," the speaker says,

> The hot words
> Swarmed out of my mouth like African bees
> & my fists were cocked,
> Hammers in the air.
>
> (ll.32–39)

After the deliveryman hastily departs, the speaker tells us that the woman "pulled me into her arms / & whispered, *Son, you ain't gonna live long*" (41–42). This protective maternal warning dramatizes the personal impact of history in a way that unites the personal and the public viscerally, by showing the "inside of history" as it plays itself out in the speaker's development. Whether lover ("cocked") or mother-figure ("*Son*"), the woman's action in the closing lines protect the speaker in a way that reverses Emmett Till's situation, who was far from his mother and home when he was murdered. The reversal doesn't undo or erase the bitterness of Till's murder, but it does resist the violence of its legacy, even as the irony of the poem reminds readers that the violent potential of racism continues to be a threat.

Natasha Trethewey shows herself to be equally concerned with the personal and communal in "Native Guard," her sequence commemorating black Civil War soldiers in Louisiana. Since the sequence imitates a journal, each sonnet is subtitled with a date. Trethewey foregrounds the role of writing and observation as a metaphor for the special work of the black poet in a way that corresponds to Nelson's focus on oratory near the end of *A Wreath for Emmett Till*. More broadly, her speaker also echoes the artist-figures in Dove's "Sonnet in Primary Colors" and Hayden's "The Performers." Trethewey makes her readers aware of the special importance of writing through the palimpsest image of her speaker's cross-hatched journal and through her emphasis on his work as a writer of letters on behalf of others ("February 1863" and "March 1863"). Trethewey makes her speaker even more of a poet-figure when he emphasizes his role as a reporter ("I now use ink / to keep record" ["November 1862," ll.11–12]), observer ("I studied natural things . . . / Now I tend Ship Island graves" ["August 1864," ll.4, 9]), and especially as a witness:

> I'm told
> it's best to spare most detail, but I know
> there are things which must be accounted for.
>
> ("August 1824," ll.12–14)

In the second sonnet, "December 1862," Trethewey's soldier refers to the journal he appropriates, which is

> near full
> with someone else's words, overlapped now,
> crosshatched beneath mine. On every page,
> his story intersecting with my own.
>
> (ll.11–14)

The soldier's "intersecting" journal entries symbolize the intertwining of racial history in American culture. It is a historical symbol in the sequence, but it corresponds to the personal fact of Trethewey's mixed ancestry, which she addresses more directly in other poems in the volume. (The cover of the book, moreover, reproduces an actual diary page by Colonel Nathan W. Daniels, the historical basis for the journal in Trethewey's poem.)

Trethewey compounds the significance of the crosshatched journal in "January 1863," the fourth sonnet in the sequence, when her speaker makes this entry in his journal:

> Later , as we worked,
> I joined in the low singing someone raised
> . . .
> It was then a dark man
> removed his shirt, revealed the scars, crosshatched
> like the lines in this journal, on his back.
>
> (ll.4–5 and 7–9)

By figuring the slave's scars as a bodily text (a trope already signaled in the first sonnet when the speaker contrasts his own whip-scars with the words he writes in his journal), Trethewey invites her readers to view her poetry as a form of testimony, a testimony that both commemorates the brutalization of black bodies throughout American history and triumphs in the power of words to express and remember personal and historical experience.

Wanda Coleman does something similar in "American Sonnet (10)" from *Hand Dance* (1993). Like Nelson's "Chosen," her poem pays homage to ancestral motherhood, but it includes the Middle Passage and masses of women in the epic sweep of its vision:

> our mothers wrung hell and hardtack
> from row and boll. fenced others'
> gardens with the bones of lovers.
>
> (ll.1–3)

The rhythm and sound effects of the first two lines convey the hard physical labor of the mothers Coleman commemorates, while the imagery of "bones" (l.3) and "Moloch's mansions" (l.9) figure slavery as a form of systematic murder. Coleman's "seeds of blight" (l.8) also echo the metaphor in Cullen's "From the Dark Tower" and Brown's "Salutamus," reminding her readers of the central but devastating role that slaves played in the creation of national wealth. Her poem ends with a testimonial vision that corresponds to Hayden's visionary Douglass and Nelson's plea to remember Emmett Till: "our hungered eyes do see/refuse the dark" (l.9).

As I suggested in the introduction, this essay addresses only a sample of the many sonnets published by African American writers. By identifying such key concerns as the dignity of the individual, the analogy between black oratory and poetry, and the political and more personal traditions of the sonnet in black culture, I have tried to show some of the inspired and innovative ways in which African American poets have adapted the sonnet form. Interested readers may explore sonnets by writers I have not discussed, such as Alice Dunbar Nelson, Anne Spencer, Melvin Tolson, Gwendolyn

Bennett, Margaret Walker, James A. Emanuel, Gerald Barrax, Jay Wright, Lucille Clifton, June Jordan, Michael Harper, Sonia Sanchez, Ed Roberson, Afaa M. Weaver, Cornelius Eady, Carl Phillips, Elizabeth Alexander, Camille T. Dungy, and Wendy S. Walters in such anthologies as *Caroling Dusk* (Cullen), *Every Shut Eye Ain't Asleep* (Harper and Walton), *The Oxford Anthology of African-American Poetry* (Rampersad and Herbold), and *Black Nature* (Dungy), as well as in many individual volumes, some of which are listed in the bibliography.

NOTES

1 Henrietta Cordelia Ray also published a sonnet on Shaw. According to Joan R. Sherman, Ray's collection, *Sonnets*, was published in 1893 (Sherman xxix).

2 While the slogan "black is beautiful" is associated with the 1960s and 1970s, its application to the 1920s is not an anachronism. In "The New Negro" (1925), Alain Locke writes about a new racial consciousness and pride in the 1920s, and to show this, he quotes the work of several contemporary poets, including Langston Hughes, Claude McKay, and James Weldon Johnson. Locke published his essay together with the work of many contemporary black writers, including Countee Cullen, in the March 1925 special issue of *Survey Graphic*. "Beautiful" is a key word in Langston Hughes's 1923 poem "My People": "The night is beautiful / So the faces of my people" (ll.1–2). The word appears in all three of the poem's stanzas.

REFERENCES AND FURTHER READING

Alexander, Elizabeth. "Today's News." *The Oxford Anthology of African-American Poetry*. Ed. Arnold Rampersad and Hilary Herbold. New York: Oxford, 2006. 1.

Brooks, Gwendolyn. *Blacks*. Chicago: Third World Press, 1987.

Brown, Sterling. *The Collected Poems of Sterling A. Brown*. Ed. Michael S. Harper. Evanston: Triquarterly Books–Northwestern University Press, 1996.

Clifton, Lucille. *Blessing the Boats: New and Selected Poems, 1988–2000*. Rochester, NY: BOA Editions, 2000.

Coleman, Wanda. *Hand Dance*. Santa Rosa, CA: Black Sparrow Press, 1993.

Cullen, Countee. *My Soul's High Song: The Collected Writing of Countee Cullen, Voice of the Harlem Renaissance*. Ed. Gerald Early. New York: Anchor–Doubleday, 1991.

Dove, Rita. *Mother Love*. New York: W.W. Norton, 1995.

Dunbar, Paul Laurence. *The Collected Poetry of Paul Laurence Dunbar*. Ed. Joanne M. Braxton. Charlottesville: University of Virginia Press, 1993.

Dungy, Camille T. *Black Nature: Four Centuries of African American Nature Poetry*. Athens: University of Georgia Press, 2009.

Harper, Michael S. *Images of Kin: New and Selected Poems*. Urbana: University of Illinois Press, 1977.

Harper, Michael S. and Anthony Walton, eds. *Every Shut Eye Ain't Asleep: An Anthology of Poetry by African Americans since 1945*. Boston, MA: Little, Brown, and Co., 1994.

Hayden, Robert. *Collected Poems*. Ed. Frederick Glaysher. New York: Liveright, 1985.

Hubbard, Stacy Carson. "'A Splintery Box': Race and Gender in the Sonnets of Gwendolyn Brooks." *Genre* 25 (1992): 47–64.

Johnson, Helene. *This Waiting for Love*. Ed. Verner D. Mitchell. Amherst: University of Massachusetts Press, 2000.

Jordan, June. *Directed by Desire: The Collected Poems of June Jordan*. Ed. Jan Heller Levi and Sara Miles. Copper Canyon Press, 2005.

Komunyakaa, Yusef. *Pleasure Dome*. Middletown: Wesleyan University Press, 2001.

McKay, Claude. *Complete Poems*. Ed. William J. Maxwell. Urbana: University of Illinois Press, 2004.

Nelson, Marilyn. *The Fields of Praise: New and Selected Poems*. Baton Rouge: Louisiana State University Press, 1997.

Nelson, Marilyn. *A Wreath for Emmett Till*. Boston, MA: Houghton Mifflin, 2005.

Phillips, Carl. *From the Devotions*. St. Paul, MO: Graywolf Press, 1998.

Sanchez, Sonia. *Shake Loose My Skin: New and Selected Poems*. Boston, MA: Beacon Press, 1999.

Sherman, Joan R. *Collected Black Women's Poetry*. Vol. 3. Oxford: Oxford University Press, 1988.

Stanford, Ann Folwell. "Dialectics of Desire: War and the Restive Voice in Gwendolyn Brooks's 'Negro Hero' and 'Gay Chaps at the Bar.'" *African American Review* 26.2 (1992): 197–211.

Tolson, Melvin. *"Harlem Gallery" and Other Poems of Melvin B. Tolson*. Ed. Raymond Nelson. Charlottesville: University of Virginia Press, 1999.

Trethewey, Natasha. *Native Guard*. Boston, MA: Houghton Mifflin, 2006.

Weil, Eric A. "Personal and Public: Three First-Person Voices in African American Poetry." In *The Furious Flowering of African American Poetry*, ed. Joanne V. Gabbin. Charlottesville: University of Virginia Press, 1999. 223–38.

Wright, Jay. *Transformations*. Baton Rouge: Louisiana University Press, 2000.

17

The Liberties of Blank Verse

Patrick Jackson

Unrhymed iambic pentameter, or blank verse, was first written by the Earl of Surrey in the early sixteenth century when he used it to translate two books of Virgil's *Aeneid*. Since then, every major poetic genre has been produced with it (epics, narratives, dramatic monologues, lyrical poetry, and verse plays) and many, perhaps most, major Anglophone poets have used it (from Shakespeare and Milton to Seamus Heaney and Robert Lowell). This range and variety is due in part to blank verse's tremendous versatility. The fact that it does not demand rhymes, of course, is one reason for its suppleness, but another is that blank verse does not require a fixed number of stanzas or lines. With its regular rhythm of stressed and unstressed beats, blank verse has also been called the meter that most resembles common English speech, making it appealing to writers who want a balance between crafted and natural language. It has even been suggested that blank verse, because it is defined by its pattern of stresses, is a more suitable form for English poetry than those forms that emphasize rhyme, such as sonnets and quatrains, which work better in languages like French and Italian where stresses are less important and rhymes are significantly easier to find. Because of its versatility and its compatibility with the English language, blank verse has played a central role in the development of English poetry, allowing a great amount of freedom to poets interested in experimentation and with creating their own distinctive voices. For these same reasons, it is a precursor and a counterpart to modern free verse in English.

The origins of blank verse can be traced to both French and Italian poetry. *Vers de dix* is a rhymed, ten-syllable French verse and was used for long poems in the eleventh and twelfth centuries (Duffell 45). It is the predecessor of the *alexandrine*, which contains twelve syllables (or six iambic feet) and is the standard heroic line in France, just as pentameter has become the standard heroic line in England. The *endecasillabo*,

A Companion to Poetic Genre, First Edition. Edited by Erik Martiny.
© 2012 John Wiley & Sons, Ltd. Published 2012 by John Wiley & Sons, Ltd.

which may have developed out of *vers de dix* in the thirteenth century, became one of the dominant forms of the Italian Renaissance (Duffell 46). *Endecasillabo* lines place their last stress on the tenth syllable, which, in its strictest of uses, iambic pentameter also does. One particular version of *endecasillabo*, *endecasillabo sciolti*, was unrhymed, and therefore would have served as a model for Surrey's blank verse.

Surrey used his new form in part because it emulated the style of classical Greek and Latin epics, which were written in unrhymed hexameters. The decasyllables in Dante's *Inferno* and Chaucer's *Canterbury Tales* had already worked to achieve a similar effect, though not without giving up rhyme. Blank verse also recalls the past of England. English poetry, which has its roots in the accentual, alliterative verse written before the Norman Conquest, might be said to center itself around its thuds and swishes more than its pitch and resonance. Surrey's new style took advantage of his language's tradition and its inherent strengths. As O.B. Hardison argues, Surrey was "seeking an equivalent rather than a duplicate verse form" of Virgil ("Tudor" 243). By doing so, he sought not only an appropriate mode of expression for Virgil's great work but a way to elevate English poetry to the level of that great work.

Surrey's translations of the *Aeneid* show how difficult it is to apply strict rules to blank verse. For instance, like his French and Italian predecessors, he places a caesura after the fourth syllable of most lines (lines marking caesuras are added):

> With thretning chere | thus slided through our town
> The subtil tree, | to Pallas temple ward.
> O natiue land, | Ilion, and of the Goddes
> The mansion place! | O warrlik walles of Troy!
> Fowr times it stopt in thentrie of our gate[.]
>
> (Book II, l. 303–07)

The break between each hemistich can be made with punctuation (the first four lines) or without (the last line), though, as is demonstrated here, Surrey often chooses to emphasize it. Besides using punctuation, he occasionally achieves this emphasis with rhyme:

> And first of all | eche serpent doth enwrap
> The bodies small | of his two tender sonnes:
> Whose wretched limmes | they byt, and fed theron.
> Then raught they hym, | who had his wepon caught[.]
>
> (Book II, l. 269–72)

The rhymes "all" and "small" and "limmes" and "hym" suggest Surrey also hears rhymes at other caesuras, such as in the words "chere" and "tree" in the first passage quoted. There are examples not only of internal rhyme in Surrey's translation but of end-rhyme, demonstrating that, even at its inception, blank verse was not a pure form. Instead, it has always been prone to change and unconformity.

Blank verse's transition to the stage initiated a variety of key changes. In 1561, about fifteen years after Surrey published his translations, Thomas Norton and Thomas Sackville wrote and produced *Gorboduc*, English literature's first blank-verse play, and it was not long before blank verse became the preferred form for drama. In subsequent years, Elizabethan playwrights reshaped blank verse in a great number of ways, making it a place for experimentation in poetics and style. Besides eliminating the fourth-syllable caesura, more or less for good, Elizabethan playwrights experimented with enjambment, with inverting the stress of the five feet (especially the first foot), with feminine endings, with substituting anapests for iambs, with "promoting" typically unstressed words into stressed positions, and with mixing in prose passages between versed ones. (Of course, many of these things might be found intermittingly in Surrey or in Norton and Sackville but only rarely and with the sense that they are irregularities rather than modes of expression.)

Nowhere is this development in Elizabethan blank verse clearer than with Shakespeare's plays, where from early to late, his style matures considerably. Even Shakespeare's earlier dramas show his interest in innovating blank verse, especially his feminine endings (lines that end on unstressed syllables). Most of Shakespeare's contemporaries, as Surrey had done, wrote only masculine endings (lines that end on stressed syllables). Perfect iambic pentameter, in the strictest sense, demands masculine endings, for feminine endings must either change the length of the line, adding or subtracting a syllable, or they must disturb the iambic rhythm of the line to accommodate the inversion of the fifth foot. Shakespeare almost invariably chooses to create room for his feminine endings by doing the former, as he has Hippolyta do in this passage from *A Midsummer's Night Dream*:

> But all the story of the night told over,
> And all their minds transfig'rd so together,
> More witnessesth than fancy's images.
> And grows to something of great constancy.
>
>   (V.i.23–26)

The first pair of these lines end unstressed and contain an eleventh syllable while the following two, which also end in polysyllabic words but with masculine stresses, maintain the expected ten syllables. Shakespeare might add a syllable (for eleven total) or drop one (for nine total) to make room for his feminine endings, but he very rarely forced a feminine ending into ten syllables. This might suggest that Shakespeare, like many English poets, was more concerned with the beats of his lines than with syllables or feet. Or perhaps Shakespeare was drawing on the Italian tradition of the *endecasillabo piano*, used by Dante, which is an eleven-syllable line that places its final stress on the tenth syllable and does not count the unstressed syllable after it.

The other two salient features of Shakespeare's blank verse did not develop until his later plays: a liberal practice of enjambment and an increased propensity for non-iambic feet. This passage from *The Tempest*, when compared to the passage from the earlier play quoted above, demonstrates how much Shakespeare's style evolved by the end of his career:

> *Miranda.* If by your art, my dearest father, you have
> Put the wild waters in this roar, allay them.
> The sky it seems would pour down stinking pitch,
> But that the sea, mounting to th' welkin's cheek,
> Dashes the fire out. O! I have suffered
> With those that I saw suffer. A brave vessel
> (Who had, no doubt, some noble creature in her)
> Dash'd all to pieces! O, the cry did knock
> Against my very heart! Poor souls, they perish'd.
> Had I been any God of power, I would
> Have sunk the sea within the earth or ere
> It should the good ship so have swallow'd and
> The fraughting souls within her.
> *Prospero.*   Be collected.
>
> (I.ii.1–13)

Of these thirteen lines, six of them (nearly half) are enjambed: lines 1, 6, 8, 10, 11, and 12. Combined with the internal full stops in lines 5, 6, 8, 9, and 13 and the feminine endings in lines 5, 6, 9, and 13, such enjambment gives very few hints to a listening audience where the line breaks are at all. The conjunctions "ere" and "and" with the enjambment are also noteworthy. A conjunction blurs the end of the line more than the other examples here because it is the very opposite of a natural stop. Even when Shakespeare did enjamb his lines in his earlier work, he did not use conjunctions, so this practice in his later plays shows the full degree of his willingness to open up the end of his verses.

The passage above also has four lines that depart from the expected iambic meter: lines 2, 4, 5, 6. Some of these are difficult to scan with any final authority. Line 5, for instance, might be said to stress the first, fourth, fifth, sixth, and tenth syllables. Or perhaps the first, fourth, fifth, seventh, and tenth syllables could be stressed. Line 2 is even more curious, since it can be read iambically, but it feels unnatural to stress "the": "Put *the* wild *wa*ters *in* this *roar*, all*ay* them." It is very possible a speaker or actor would instead stress the third syllable, making the first foot into an anapest ("Put the *wild*") or stress the first syllable and invert the first foot ("*Put* the wild *wa*ters"). The matter is subjective, but however one reads these lines, there remains a tension between the expected (what repeats) and the novel (what varies).

It is blank verse's capacity for this tension between the expected and the novel that is one of its greatest strengths, and Shakespeare took full advantage of it. The basic model of blank verse—five iambic beats in ten syllables, no rhyme, no set stanza length—is not nearly as prescriptive as other forms such as quatrains, couplets, and sonnets. Still, it is regular enough that deviations in its pattern are recognizable to both the eye and the ear. Shakespeare's feminine endings, enjambment, and non-iambic meters are all ways of playing against the expected patterns, but without ever threatening to dissolve those patterns. So, too, is his practice of interweaving prose passages into his blank-verse plays so that some characters and some scenes, written in prose, offer themselves as counterpoints to the rhythms of the verse.

Shakespeare tends to dominate any discussion of the Elizabethan and Jacobean theater, but many other playwrights of the time used blank verse effectively, including Christopher Marlow, Thomas Kyd, Thomas Middleton, and Ben Jonson. Most took a conservative approach, falling somewhere between *Gorboduc*'s strict meter and Shakespeare's earlier style. But some went considerably farther than even late Shakespeare did with their attempts to reshape blank verse. Among these playwrights, John Webster is probably the best example. Writing his first plays just as Shakespeare was writing his last ones, Webster pushed the limits of dramatic blank verse, stretching and squeezing it so much that many lines are not immediately recognizable as iambic pentameter. In this line from *The Duchess of Malfi*, for instance, Webster uses fifteen syllables: "Oh, but you must remember, my curse hath a great way to goe" (IV.i.121). Martin Duffell scans this line convincingly as five anapests ("Oh, but *you* must re*mem*ber, my *curse* hath a *great* way to *goe*") (145). As such, a line like this is not technically iambic pentameter and therefore, by itself, not blank verse. However, taken within the context of a blank-verse play, this line must be read as a variety of blank verse. Webster, like Shakespeare, understood that the overall pattern of unrhymed iambic pentameter lends itself to unorthodox lines, allowing the poet not only to write with the pattern but to write against it. Thus, his verse can shrink as well as expand, twisting its meter however it wants as long as the play never lets the audience forget the master form. He might bend blank verse—sometimes uncomfortably—but he does not break it.

Although blank verse went through many changes in the early seventeenth century, John Milton's *Paradise Lost* added even more. Milton did not make the same attempts at pushing the limits of the blank-verse meter as Shakespeare and Webster did. In some respects, Milton's prosody is more restrained than the dramatists. Unlike Shakespeare, for example, he has a strong tendency to avoid feminine endings and, in comparison to writers such as Webster, he keeps his meter very even, avoiding anapests and other trisyllabic feet. But despite all of this, his blank verse feels wholly new, and his impact on its development was just as great, perhaps greater than his predecessors.

There are many elements of Milton's blank verse that demonstrate its distinctiveness, including Milton's complex syntax, his elision, and his own patterns of foot inversion. But the three major characteristics that mark Milton's blank verse as innovative, even revolutionary, are his dizzying stacks of enjambed lines, his development of the verse paragraph, and his reapplication of the form to epic poetry (though, as many have noted, Milton himself seems to have believed he was the first to do this, forgetting Surrey). Here is Milton's description of Satan as he first finds himself in hell:

At once as far as Angels' ken he views
The dismal Situation waste and wild,
A Dungeon horrible, on all sides round
As one great Furnace flam'd, yet from those flames
No light, but rather darkness visible
Serv'd only to discover sights of woe,
Regions of sorrow, doleful shades, where peace
And rest can never dwell, hope never comes
That comes to all; but torture without end
Still urges, and a fiery Deluge, fed
With ever-burning Sulphur unconsum'd[.]

(Book I, ll.59–69)

One of the striking characteristics of this passage is that its eleven lines are all one sentence. Another striking characteristic, which is very much related to the first, is that a great majority of its lines are enjambed. The exact definition of enjambment, which, in general terms, refers to one line of verse running into the next without pausing, is not always agreed upon. Some scholars have found more than half of Milton's blank verse to be enjambed, while others have found a little less than half. But every reader recognizes that Milton exceeds the practices of any of his predecessors. The words come flowing, letting the current of iambs pull them along, and unencumbered by any rule that necessitates a pause or stop after the fifth foot. Milton does not, in fact, seem to pause after any of the fifth feet much more than he pauses after any of the first four.

Milton shows that the traditional relationship between end-stopped lines and enjambment can be switched and still be effective. In passages such as the one above, he reverses the expectation of regular end-stopped lines, something that even late Shakespeare does not do. Readers who absorb Milton's pattern come to see the end of the line as a place not to rest but to tumble past. Enjambment, in short, becomes the predicted pattern and not a variation from it. This creates a constant forward momentum, stretching out long, complicated sentences over many lines of pentameter (sentences that are all the more complicated by Milton's Latinate vocabulary and elaborate syntax). In an epic poem about supernatural events and beings, all of which lie beyond the pale of human comprehension, Milton's style is as appropriate as it is mesmerizing. He works on a grand scale, and his blank verse helps convey a sense of this immensity.

One reason Milton is able to draw out such long, rhythmic verses is simply his choice of genre. Because it is written for private readings rather than for public performances, Milton's blank verse exists on a wholly different "stage" than the dramatists. Thus, his verse naturally exploits different facets of blank verse than a playwright can. Shakespeare's audience cannot hear the line breaks in the actor's voices, making sustained enjambment tricky, but Milton's readers can see the line breaks and so can visually fix the lines into a stable form even if they cannot do so aurally. Writing narrative rather than dramatic blank verse also let Milton develop the verse paragraph. The verse paragraph was always available to a blank-verse poet (Surrey used it), but it would have been virtually meaningless to a dramatist, and so it was not seriously experimented with until Milton. Verse paragraphs offer another form of structure to the poem, another place, alongside full stops and line breaks to divide and allot the verse. Milton can, for example, begin a new verse paragraph to shift *Paradise Lost* suddenly to a dramatic monologue, as he often does with characters such as Satan and God. Verse paragraphs also help Milton alter the tone or mood of the verse and organize complex ideas.

As is evident from his short apologia "The Verse," which he added to the second edition of *Paradise Lost*, Milton understands the freedoms of his brand of blank verse. Responding to criticism leveled at his epic poem, Milton argues that it resists the oppression of "custom." Chief among these oppressive customs is rhyme, which he calls "the Invention of a barbarous Age" that does more to inhibit than facilitate expression. Without the interference of rhyme, he argues, the sense of his poem can be "variously drawn out from one Verse into another" (210). That is, the length of the expression, whether in a few words or in a long verse paragraph, can match the intended meaning.

Milton's poetry demonstrates the close relationship that blank verse has with free verse, and looking back, we can now detect ways in which Milton laid some of the groundwork for modern poetics. While Milton's iambic pentameter, the backbone of any blank verse, remains more or less conventional, other elements, particularly the frequent enjambments and the verse paragraphs, let Milton's poetry, much like free verse, open up wider rhythms that can carry over several lines at a time rather than within a single line or two. Ironically, Milton sees his choice of blank verse as drawing on tradition—particularly from the classical tradition—rather than as a progressive step forward. *Paradise Lost*, he argues in "The Verse," should "be esteem'd an example set, the first in English, of ancient liberty recover'd to Heroic Poem from the troublesome and modern bondage of Riming" (210). But, as Hardison argues, the approach Milton outlines here "permits a flexibility close to that of free verse" (*Prosody* 275). Indeed, three centuries later, the free-verse poet Robert Creeley would make a very similar claim when he suggested to Charles Olson that form should only be an "extension of content."

Ultimately, Milton's verse still depends more on convention than on revolution, more on what is expected than on originality. Only the free verse of modern poetry could claim to cross the threshold in between and become more varied than fixed. However, with Milton, we can see a dramatic shift in English poetry, one that gives a nod toward the future. T.S. Eliot, who was himself instrumental in the ascendency of free verse in the twentieth century, argued that *Paradise Lost* is "a perpetual sequence of original acts of lawlessness" (268), and he explicitly links Milton's blank verse with free verse. Not without some mischief, but not wholly unserious either, Eliot adds that he is tempted "to declare Milton to be the greatest master of free verse in our language" (271). What Eliot recognizes here is that "liberty" of form, though it was not yet outweighing "custom," started to inhabit a larger role with Milton, and, significantly, he sought that liberty (or, for Eliot, "lawlessness") through blank verse.

Though the century after Milton produced many blank-verse poems, it was dominated by heroic couplets, and, just as importantly, it was dominated by the artistic sensibilities behind those heroic couplets. This is not to say that the eighteenth century ignored Milton; in fact, it offered him no shortage of admirers. George Saintsbury writes, without overstating the matter too much, that "all non-dramatic blank verse that follows after the death of the author of *Paradise Lost* is 'after him' in the two senses—posterior to him, and imitated, as best the imitator might, from him" (2.473). At the same time, however, the leading poets of the day, such as Dryden, and later Pope, preferred rhymed iambic pentameter rather than unrhymed, and so necessarily placed an emphasis on the end of each of their lines that is distinctly unMiltonic. The rhymes not only shape the meter of the verse but the sense as well, creating an epigrammatic effect—closed and poignant witticisms rather than the heavenly flights or hellish plunges of Milton's enjambment.

Such a sensibility carries over to much of eighteenth-century verse, including blank verse. Here is a passage from James Thomson's *The Seasons*, the most celebrated blank-verse work of the time:

> Now, flaming up the heavens, the potent sun
> Melts into limpid air the high-raised clouds
> And morning fogs, that hovered round the hills
> In parti-coloured bands; till wide unveiled
> The face of nature shines, from where earth seems,
> Far-stretched around, to meet the bending sphere.
>
>   ("Summer" ll.199–204).

This writing can be said to be "after Milton." *Paradise Lost*'s influence is evident in Thomson's rearranged syntax, his extended sentence, and his enjambment. But all of this is done with a lighter touch. In a study of the heroic couplet's influence on blank verse in the eighteenth century, Richard Bradford sees a "cautious fettering of techniques" in poems like *The Seasons*, especially when this verse is compared Milton's (350). For instance, though the syntax is conspicuously "poetic," it hardly offers the labyrinth-like turns of Milton. The enjambment is even more telling. Thomson enjambs his lines significantly less than Milton, and when he does, he tends to be less inventive. The descriptions, for instance, that follow the lines ending with "sun" and "unveiled" are fairly predictable. What does the sun do? It melts the clouds. What is being unveiled on this summer day? The shining face of nature. In comparison, Milton's enjambments are often much less predictive. In the passage from Milton quoted earlier, the "flames" that come at the end of the fourth line give "no light," and the "fiery Deluge" in the tenth line, though it is "fed" at the end of that line, leaves the sulfur it feeds on "unconsum'd" in the next. Milton's enjambments lead to surprise; Thomson's often tell us where they are headed. Like the heroic couplet, eighteenth-century blank verse tends to form itself around the end of the line and avoid meaning that might spill out of it.

The nineteenth century saw more successful blank verse. Though these poems are often not as spectacular and pyrotechnical as *Paradise Lost*, they instead carry out experiments in expression that Milton's epic did not attempt. William Wordsworth, for instance, is less interested in formal dynamics than with questions about genre and diction. He shows that blank verse can be used successfully for shorter poems and that it can be an effective vehicle for a plainer, more common speech. Here is a passage from the narrative poem "Michael" that demonstrates this:

> With daylight Isabel resumed her work;
> And all the ensuing week the house appeared
> As cheerful as a grove in Spring: at length
> The expected letter from their kinsman came,
> With kind assurances that he would do
> His utmost for the welfare of the Boy[.]
>
> (ll.304–09)

On the one hand, this is clearly poetry and not prose. Wordsworth's simile about the house reminds the reader of this, and the lines do not take great liberties with the iambic meter, only adding an unstressed syllable in the second and fourth lines. On the other hand, the poem, which is told in a framed narrative, has the cadence of someone telling a story to an audience, and the syntax, compared with Milton, is remarkably straightforward. Wordsworth has learned from Milton's enjambment, letting the lines spill into each other without a great concern for pausing after the fifth foot. But whereas Milton uses enjambment explosively, Wordsworth uses it to produce a more natural, speech-like rhythm. Of course, other Romantics did not follow Wordsworth's example. Percy Bysshe Shelley and John Keats, most notably, favored a loftier style, one closer to Milton's. But even their verse is generally much more restrained than Satan's monologues in *Paradise Lost*.

Throughout the second half of the nineteenth century, blank verse only ascended higher in prestige, and many more poets came to use it. In England, these poets included Alfred Lord Tennyson, Robert Browning, Elizabeth Barrett Browning, Matthew Arnold, and, in America, William Cullen Bryant and John Greenleaf Whittier. The most important of these poets—that is, the poets who had the most influence on later blank verse—were Tennyson and Robert Browning, each of whom wrote both epics (Tennyson's *The Idylls of the King* and Browning's *The Ring and the Book*) and dramatic monologues in blank verse. The style of these poems often reflects their subject matter: Tennyson, who usually writes about noble or mythological characters (King Arthur, Ulysses), produces elevated, euphonious lines, while Browning, who is more interested in amoral and even criminal characters (such as the speaker of "Fra Lippo Lippi"), prefers colloquial diction. As with the Romantics, who showed that lyrical poems could be written in unrhymed iambic pentameter, Tennyson and

Browning expanded the form in terms of genre, in particular by perfecting the blank-verse dramatic monologue.

But perhaps the most important change to happen to blank verse in the nineteenth century had nothing to do with the verse itself but with the way it was perceived. Because of its pervasiveness and apparent naturalness, blank verse became emblematic of English poetry. By the turn of the century, it was considered a platform on which poets could demonstrate their skills, writing in the same manner as Shakespeare and Milton. Inevitably, this led many twentieth-century poets to view blank verse as an institution to be resisted. Such resistance is most famously characterized by Ezra Pound's edict in Canto 81 to "break the pentameter," which means for him a rejection of all conventional, fixed verse, not just pentameter. Blank verse, in other words, represents the tradition for many modernists; any new verse, in Pound's mind, necessarily revolts against it.

It is ironic that blank verse, which had shown itself to be so flexible, both in form and genre, had come to represent for some poets a rigid, outdated practice, one that needed to be "broken" by free verse. But though blank verse has been strongly associated with tradition and, thus, often thought of as the antithesis of open form, it has also been a model and a reference point for many practitioners of open form. T.S. Eliot recognizes this when he says that free verse should have the "ghost" of meter working behind it (34). For him, free verse needs to suggest (without fully establishing) a stable rhythm, even in its variations. Such a poetic ideal reverses the ideal of many blank-verse poets who feel that their regular iambic pentameter should be textured with variations.

Blank verse and free verse work from many of the same fundamental principles, but with different emphases. In both cases, three central formal elements are at work: rhythm, line and stanza breaks, and caesuras. Other elements exist in both blank verse and free verse, such as alliteration or assonance, but rhythm, lines, and caesuras always work in blank verse and nearly always apply in free verse. In short, the open form revolution of twentieth- and twenty-first-century English poetry, though clearly different from blank verse in some ways, can be said to rely on the same model. Indeed, in the family tree of poetics, blank verse may be more closely related to free verse, at least in matters of form, than to traditional fixed verse. The difference comes down to what the poet most values. Though poets such as Shakespeare and Milton seem at odds with poets such as Pound and John Ashbery, they nevertheless are working with many of the same assumptions about the play between repetition and variation—but the former poets value repetition more and the latter value variation more.

Consequently, though free verse has been more widely practiced than conventional forms in the last century, blank verse has never ceased being a vital form. Even as Pound and Eliot were steering the canon toward unmetered verses, blank verse was successfully practiced by other modernists such as W.B. Yeats, Robert Frost, and Wallace Stevens, each with his own distinctive style. Yeats, for instance, uses it not only in his verse plays but in some of his lyrical poems, the effect of which, as in "The Second Coming," frequently carries a prophetic, stately tone, a quality enhanced by blank verse's elevated status: "The blood-dimmed tide is loosed, and everywhere / The ceremony of innocence is drowned" (5–6). Frost, in contrast, writes in colloquial blank verse, showing that it can mimic rural New England accents as well as it can loftier ones. Many of his poems (such as "Home Burial," "The Code," "Snow," and "The Death of the Hired Man") contain dialogue between different speakers, emphasizing the conversational rhythms and the elasticity of blank verse.

Stevens's blank verse, which takes up a great deal of his oeuvre, is his preferred vehicle for his philosophical poetry, mirroring the starts, pauses, and turns of his restless mind. The ability to imitate the minutiae of the human consciousness is often thought to be a strength of free verse, but Stevens shows that blank verse is just as capable. Here, for example, are the first lines of "Man Carrying Thing":

> The poem must resist the intelligence
> Almost successfully. Illustration:
>
> A brune figure in winter evening resists
> Identity. The thing he carries resists
>
> The most necessitous sense.
>
> (ll.1–5)

The break at the end of the first line suggests the speaker is making a categorical statement, that poetry should simply be set against "intelligence." However, since this itself is a rational, intelligent statement, and thus contradictory to its own meaning, the poem must immediately weaken its assertion in the second line with the qualification "almost successfully." The subsequent lines perform in a similarly mimetic and ironic fashion. The colon at the end of the second line, for instance, is placed just before the blank space of the stanza break, momentarily disrupting the lucidity of the poem with white emptiness just at the point that it promises to give a concrete "illustration." Even when this illustration is given in the next stanza, it refuses any facile interpretation. This is partially due to Stevens's language, which is both obscure ("brune," which means burning) and nebulous ("the thing"). But the ambiguity is also due to his mastery of the blank-verse line. The word "resists," which comes at the end of line 3 and again at line 4, suggests itself each time as an intransitive verb, but each time it becomes a transitive verb when the object of the sentence is revealed in the next line. The momentary interruption of white space created as our eyes scan for the object of the sentence mimics the strain of the mind as it reaches out for the "identity" of the brune figure and the thing he carries. Theme and form fuse. Like the human consciousness it imitates, Stevens's poem passes back and forth between certainty and uncertainty, knowing and not knowing, and his blank verse enacts this elusiveness, playing with enjambment and stanza breaks in a way of which both Milton and Pound might approve.

The tradition of exploring the capabilities of blank verse continues to this day, and, over the last half-century, a wider array of blank verse has been written than ever before. A short list of modern blank-verse poets includes James Merrill, Gwendolyn Brooks, Roy Fuller, Howard Nemerov, Mona Van Duyn, Edwin Muir, Robert Lowell, Seamus Heaney, Derek Walcott, Richard Wilbur, Andrew Hudgins, Rachel Hadas, Christian Wiman, and Joshua Mehigan. Some of these poets, such as Fuller and Wilbur, compose carefully measured lines that vary only to register important changes in mood or subtle inflections of thought. Other poets, such Lowell and Walcott, write poems that test the defining properties of blank verse. Lowell writes unrhymed sonnets, for instance, in blank verse, but their iambic pentameter is often very loose, spreading out their iambs into anapests or (less often) squeezing them together into spondees. Walcott's blank verse, meanwhile, often mixes in unpatterned rhymes, a practice sometimes seen as at odds with the fundamental concept of blank verse. Robert Shaw, in his excellent and comprehensive book *Blank Verse: A Guide to Its History and Use*, believes that poetry like Walcott's "raises difficult questions of definition. When does 'occasional rhyme' become more than occasional?" (215). When is blank verse no longer blank verse? The distinction is not always easy to make, especially as a myriad of contemporary poets apply their styles to the form.

The question of what counts as blank verse, which goes back at least as far as Webster's *The White Devil*, is important. But it should never lead to the misperception that blank verse is static or rigid. To think of blank verse as firmly fixed ignores its history of experimentation and variation as well as the innate liberties that Milton recognized in it. The opposite mistake is made when free-verse poems are thought of as being completely "free," as though the poets who write them do not impose restraints upon them, such as rhythm or the common decision to use line breaks. Certainly, closed forms and open forms are different, but the divide between them might not be as deep as we frequently assume. Some would even argue that, just as free verse once offered an alternative to the dominant practice of traditional forms like blank verse, blank verse now offers an alternative to the dominant practice of free verse, and that, despite conventional thinking, their relationship is more complementary than adversarial. However we define its present-day role, blank verse continues to appeal to poets. From Surrey to Lowell, and from Milton to Walcott, it has remained both dynamic and vitally unpredictable.

REFERENCES AND FURTHER READING

Attridge, Derek. *The Rhythms of English Poetry*. London: Longman, 1982.

Bradford, Richard. "Rhyming Couplets and Blank Verse." Ed. Christine Gerrard. *A Companion to Eighteenth-Century Poetry*. Oxford: Blackwell, 2006. 341–55.

Brooke, Tucker. *The Tudor Drama: A History of English National Drama to the Retirement of Shakespeare*. Hamden: Archon, 1964.

Duffell, Martin J. *A New History of English Metre*. London: Legenda, 2008.

Eliot, T.S. *The Selected Prose of T.S. Eliot*. Ed. Frank Kermode. New York: Harcourt, 1975.

Hardison, O.B. *Prosody and Purpose in the English Renaissance*. Baltimore: Johns Hopkins University Press, 1989.

Hardison, O.B. "Tudor Humanism and Surrey's Translation of the 'Aeneid.'" *Studies in Philology* 83.3 (1986): 237–60.

Milton, John. *Complete Poems and Major Prose*. Ed. Merritt Y. Hughes. New York: Odyssey, 1957.

Saintsbury, George. *A History of English Prosody.* New York: Russell, 1961.

Shakespeare, William. *The Riverside Shakespeare.* Boston, MA: Houghton, 1997.

Shaw, Robert. *Blank Verse: A Guide to Its History and Use.* Athens: Ohio University Press, 2007.

Stevens, Wallace. *The Collected Poems.* New York: Vintage, 1982.

Surrey (Henry Howard). "Translation of the Aeneid, Book II." *Specimens of English Literature.* Ed. Walter William Skeat. Oxford: Clarendon Press, 1892. 205–14.

Thomson, James. *Poetical Works.* Ed. J. Logie Robertson. London: Oxford University Press, 1965.

Webster, John. *The Complete Works of John Webster.* Ed. F. L. Lucas. New York: Gordian, 1966.

Wordsworth, William. *William Wordsworth: Selected Poems.* Ed. Walford Davies. London: Dent, 1975.

Wright, George T. *Shakespeare's Metrical Art.* Berkeley: University of California Press, 1988.

Yeats, W.B. *The Collected Poems.* Ed. Richard J. Finneran. New York: Simon & Schuster, 1989.

18

Arcs of Movement

The Heroic Couplet

David Wheatley

Some literary forms unmistakably bear the imprint of their age. Arriving in England courtesy of Sir Philip Sidney, the sestina trails the glamour of a foreign luxury item, embodying the European influences that trumpet the arrival of the Renaissance; in their whimsy and mock-solemnity the limerick and triolet are recognizably the products of Victorian self-assurance in its more leisurely *quarts d'heure*; and E.E. Cummings' typographical innovations and Charles Olson's Projective Verse are as much tributes to the invention of the typewriter as to the ripeness of those poets' imaginations. The heroic couplet is unusual, however, in providing the vehicle for a historic shift in English poetry not once but at least twice in its history: first, with the replacement of accentual verse by accentual-syllabic verse in the later middle ages, and later again with its establishment as the standard verse form of the Augustan period and the epitome of Augustan sensibility, with its preference for a poetry of correctness, statement, and formal decorum. It lost its centrality but by no means perished under the Romantics (Byron's *The Corsair* and Keats's *Endymion* and *Lamia* are in heroic couplets), and occupies an important place in the work of several noted formal poets of the twentieth century (Yvor Winters, J.V. Cunningham, Thom Gunn).

In classical poetry the commonest form of couplet was the elegiac distich, in which a dactylic hexameter was followed by a dactylic pentameter; but as the couplet form was naturalized in later vernaculars it shifted towards isometric (and rhymed) regularity. In English, Chaucer pioneered the heroic couplet in *The Legend of Good Women*:

> A thousand tymes have I herd men telle
> That ther ys joy in hevene and peyne in helle,
> And I acorde wel that it ys so;
> But natheles, yet wot I wel also

A Companion to Poetic Genre, First Edition. Edited by Erik Martiny.
© 2012 John Wiley & Sons, Ltd. Published 2012 by John Wiley & Sons, Ltd.

> That ther nis noon dwellyng in this contree
> That eyther hath in hevene or helle ybe,
> Ne may of hit non other weyes witen
> But as he hath herd seyd, or founde it writen;
> For by assay ther may no man hit preve.
>
>   (ll.1–9)

The poem's form contributes to its modernity in more ways than one: its satirical humor is often directed at the contemporary fashion for retelling stories from classical myth with a moralizing twist, a style that anticipates Pope's mock-heroic epics by more than three centuries. The couplet form sets a conversational tone, acknowledging and contesting convention ("But natheles . . .") with a light touch and self-conscious literary wit that, coming after *Beowulf* and Anglo-Saxon poetry, allows English literature to speak a whole new language, in more ways than one.

Different line-lengths all have their own distinctive valencies and associations for writers. On one side of the pentameter, the tetrameter or octosyllabic line was much favored by Jonathan Swift, and has remained in favor among satirists ever since, while sustained use of a shorter line, such as the trimeter and dimeter, is much more rarely encountered. With longer lines, the six-stress hexameter or alexandrine offered the Augustans relief from strict adherence to the pentameter, as in this self-reflexive couplet from Pope's "Essay on Criticism"—"A needless alexandrine ends the song / that like a wounded snake, drags its slow length along" (ll.356–57)—stretching from pentameter to alexandrine in its second line. (The practice of following a pentameter with an alexandrine can also be found in the occasional Augustan substitution of a triplet for the couplet, all on the same rhyme, with the alexandrine, if used, at the end.) Beyond the alexandrine lies the heptameter ("fourteener") line employed by Arthur Golding in his Elizabethan translation of the *Metamorphoses*, beyond which it becomes a matter of debate whether the listener continues to hear the line as a composite metrical unit.

Between these poles, then, sits the pentameter, which by Elizabethan times had established itself as the single most commonly used line in English. Its naturalization, in the form of the heroic couplet, did not take place without dissent: in *The Arte of English Poesie* (1589) George Puttenham disdains the rhyming couplet, ruling it vulgar. One difference between Chaucer and Pope is Chaucer's less developed sense of the caesura, whose evolution marks the real transition from a decasyllabic line to the modern pentameter proper. The caesura marks a pause in the line, which may or may not correspond to a syntactical pause, but whose breathing point introduces an essential unit of variety or countercurrent against the metrical flow. In the heroic couplet this will usually be found after the second or third foot, breaking the unit of verse down into asymmetrical sub-units and allowing for a complex back-and-forth between one line and the next, as the semantic unit coincides with the line-break or is broken-backed across it.

A fundamental distinction among couplets is that between the "closed" and the "open," with the former turning in on itself and self-contained, while the latter flows freely between preceding and following couplets. The Augustan heroic couplet tends towards the closed, but contrasting examples can be found within the work of Christopher Marlowe, who did much to advance the form in the Elizabethan period. His translations from *Ovid's Elegies* are in the closed style, as emphasized by the question-and-answer exchanges of these lines:

> What makes my bed seem hard seeing it is soft?
> Or why slips down the coverlet so oft?
> Although the nights be long, I sleep not tho,
> My sides are sore with tumbling to and fro.
> Were Love the cause, it's like I should descry him.
> Or lies he close, and shoots where none can spy him?
>
> (ll.1–6)

Marlowe's later translations of *Hero and Leander* are written in a different register entirely. Marlowe is a master rhetorician whose writing often has a tactile, even pummeling quality, and he describes the lovers' final tryst in writing of remarkable muscularity, overspilling the boundaries of the "closed" couplet with unruly sexual energy:

> Even as a bird which in our hands we wring,
> Forth plungeth, and oft flutters with her wing,
> She trembling strove; this strife or hers (like that
> Which made the world) another world begat
> Of unknown joy. Treason was in her thought,
> And cunningly to yield herself she sought.
> Seeming not won, yet won she was at length,
> In such wars women use but half their strength.
>
> (ll.289–96)

Leander manfully overcomes Hero's resistance but it is a piece of "cunning" on her part when she yields, an act of controlled strength. The lovers' coupling has an air of combat about it, with control alternating from one partner to the other, just as the couplet shifts balance and emphasis from line to line, arguing with itself and thinking aloud as it goes.

If the couplet is an inherently dialogic form, it is unsurprising that it should have lent itself so well to collaborative authorship: *Hero and Leander* was finished by Chapman on Marlowe's death, the second half of Dryden's *Absalom and Achitophel* was written by Nahum Tate, and Pope's translation of the *Odyssey* was completed with the help of a pair of uncredited assistants. The subset of the couplet represented by the epigram (and its associated form, the epitaph) is also distinctive in straddling the divide between the authored and the anonymous, with no sense that examples by the latter need be more naïve or artless than the former. Elizabethan writing is littered with epigrams that seem to condense the period's courtly wit tradition into two short lines. Sir John Harrington plays on contemporary religious and political anxieties in "Of Treason": "Treason doth never prosper, and what's the reason? / For if it prosper, none dare call it treason."

Elizabethan poets who fell out of courtly favor had more to fear than bad reviews, and one such, Sir Walter Raleigh, wrote his poetic epitaph on the eve of his execution, but also found time to wax metaphysical on the same subject in "On the Snuff of a Candle the Night before He Died": "Cowards fear to die, but Courage stout, / Rather than live in snuff, will be put out."

The anonymous rhymer of "On Meeting a Gentlewoman in the Dark" tapped into the vibrant link between the couplet and the bawdy, which, as our twentieth-century examples will confirm, has continued to the present day: "To see such dainty ghost as you appear / Will make my flesh stand sooner than my hair."

Geoffrey Grigson's *Faber Book of Epigrams and Epitaphs*, from which I take these examples, offers further evidence of continuity in Rudyard Kipling's tetrameter version of a couplet of Simonides, titled "Common Form," written after the death of his son in the First World War: "If any question why we died, / Tell them, because our fathers lied." Grigson follows this with an anonymous and undated version of the same Greek text, "On the Army of Spartans Who Died at Thermopylae," that could be Elizabethan or twentieth-century: "Tell them in Lakedaimon, passer-by, / We kept the Spartan code, and here we lie."

Between major Elizabethan figures such as Marlowe and anonymous epigrammatists, however, stands the great mass of minor (or "silver") poets in which the sixteenth and seventeenth centuries are so rich, and many of whom handled the couplet with consummate skill. One of these, William Chamberlayne, has even been judged by a previous writer on the heroic couplet to be "perhaps the most neglected poet of any importance in English" (Hobsbaum 28). More deserving perhaps is Anne Finch, Countess of Winchilsea, whose "Glass" allows for finely polished reflections:

> O Man! What Inspiration was thy Guide,
> Who taught thee Light and Air thus to divide;
> To let in all the useful Beams of Day,
> Yet force, as Subtil Winds, without thy Sash to stay.

(ll.1–4)

The violent upheavals of the mid-seventeenth century, combined with the aversion to rhyme of its greatest poet, Milton ("the jingling sound of like endings"), put paid to this golden age of the couplet. Yet before the end of the seventeenth century, in the new cultural and political climate that accompanied the "Glorious Revolution" and the reign of Queen Anne, Dryden, and Pope after him, had reinvigorated the heroic couplet and placed it once more at the centre of English poetry.

Dryden, Pope, Johnson

It is hardly an exaggeration to call Dryden the most kickable of canonical English authors. As David Hopkins writes in a study of the poet, "Dryden's work is now hardly ever studied in schools, and is increasingly marginalized or bypassed on university courses"; an anthologist of seventeenth- and eighteenth-century literature, he reports, expresses "pleasure" at stripping Dryden of space in order to allocate it to Aphra Behn instead (Hopkins 4). In the face of such rejection, Dryden's defense may seem a duty, but to read his version of the *Aeneid* (he is arguably the greatest of English translators), the mock-epics *MacFlecknoe* and *Absalom and Achitophel* and the elegy "To the Memory of Mr. Oldham," all of them written in heroic couplets, is to be reminded that it can be a pleasure too. This last shows to perfection the tone of suavity and decorum that give its meaning to the epithet "Drydenesque." Oldham has died young, leaving much promise but little real achievement. Dryden does not gloss this over, but nor do we feel his praise is therefore compromised or self-serving, even as his own style signals its difference from the "harsh cadence" and "rugged line" with which he credits the younger man. Anticipating Shelley's "Adonais" and Yeats's "In Memory of Major Robert Gregory," he combines grief over the young man's death and claims that his achievements had already rendered any future span of life superfluous. Mourning and celebration intertwine as closely as the two halves of the poem's couplets:

> O early ripe! to thy abundant store
> What could advancing Age have added more?
> It might (what Nature never gives the young)
> Have taught the numbers of thy native Tongue.
> But Satyr needs not those, and Wit will shine
> Through the harsh cadence of a rugged line.
>
> (ll.11–16)

Comparisons of Alexander Pope to Allen Ginsberg are surely rare, but to read the opening of Pope's "Epistle to Dr. Arbuthnot" after the generic decadence of later Caroline poetry is to be reminded of the remarkable freshness and colloquialism of Ginsberg's "Howl" after the staleness of American poetry in the immediate post-war years. Whatever their form, there is no mistaking the remarkable freshness and vigor of Pope's opening:

> "Shut, shut the door, good John!" fatigued I said,
> "Tie up the knocker, say I'm sick, I'm dead,"
> The dog-star rages! nay 'tis past a doubt,
> All Bedlam, or Parnassus, is let out:
> Fire in each eye, and papers in each hand,
> They rave, recite, and madden round the land.
>
> (ll.1–6)

If the caricature against which Augustan poetry struggles today is of empty formalism over inspiration, it is an aspect of eighteenth-century literary life with which Pope was all too familiar. The maddening throng outside the poet's door in the "Epistle to Dr. Arbuthnot" is full of importunate poetasters, and in *The Dunciad* Pope devoted a whole mock-epic to this troublesome breed. Great genius is to madness close allied, as this most quotable of poets declared, and part of the genius of Pope's war on dullness (if not madness, though the categories overlap) is his use of the same couplet form in which his enemies would have written. Only the most insensible reader, however, could see in his visions of dullness anything but sparkling wit:

> Lo! thy dread Empire, Chaos! is restor'd;
> Light dies before thy uncreating word:
> Thy hand, great Anarch! lets the curtain fall;
> And Universal Darkness buries all.
>
> (ll.653–56)

Yet such insensible readers have not been wanting, down the centuries. In one of the great misreadings of literary history, Matthew Arnold would denigrate Dryden and Pope: they were "not classics of our poetry, they are classics of our prose" (Arnold 1452), offering strong evidence on his part of the "dissociation of sensibility" between feeling and intellect diagnosed shortly afterwards by T.S. Eliot.

It is not merely Pope and Dryden that such a judgment banishes from the canon. Publishing his great poem "The Vanity of Human Wishes" five years after Pope's death, Samuel Johnson forms a crucial link between the Augustan period and the modern age. This long poem ranks alongside his friend Oliver Goldsmith's "The Deserted Village" as a high watermark of the Augustan closed couplet: "See Nations slowly wise, and meanly just, / To buried Merit raise the tardy Bust" (ll.161–62). The caesura falls after the third foot in the first line but after the second foot in the second foot, giving a neatly chiastic structure of 3 + 2 / 2 + 3. The carefully weighed Augustan moralizing of "slowly wise" and "meanly just" is ideally suited to the economy of the couplet form, with its inbuilt tension and release, visible here in the "tardy" arrival at the end of the second line of the bust raised to belatedly recognized achievement.

"The Vanity of Human Wishes" is a version of Juvenal's tenth satire. While scourging folly and vice, the poem holds a pessimistic view of the likelihood that good will triumph, as in the famous passage on the scholar's life:

> Deign on the passing world to turn thine eyes,
> And pause awhile from Letters, to be wise;
> There mark what ills the Scholar's life assail,
> Toil, Envy, Want, the Patron and the Jail.
>
> (ll.157–60)

Johnson offers a stirring portrait of ambition and folly in his description of the downfall of Charles XII of Sweden:

> The vanquish'd Hero leaves his broken Bands,
> And shews his Miseries in distant Lands;
> Condemn'd a needy Supplicant to wait,
> While Ladies interpose, and Slaves debate.
> . . .
> His Fall was destin'd to a barren Strand,
> A petty Fortress, and a dubious Hand;
> He left the Name, at which the World grew pale,
> To point a Moral, or adorn a Tale.
>
> (ll.211–14, 219–22)

"The Vanity of Human Wishes" is one such admonitory "tale," offering the disgraced king the hospitality of its moralizing even as it strips him of his worldly pomp and pretension. The succession of three epithets across the couplet beginning "His Fall . . ." is withering, condemning the king to an ignoble and obscure end ("a dubious Hand"), while the dyadic structure of "point a Moral, or adorn a Tale" closes the poem on a note of almost sarcastic self-delight at the use it has made of this miserable specimen of self-delusion.

Alongside the canonical greats, a trawl through the *New Oxford Book of Eighteenth-Century Verse* reveals poet after poet whose names even scholars of English literature would struggle to recognize, but whose flawlessly competent heroic couplets are, much more so than that phrase might suggest, things of delight and wonder. Anna Seward provides a fitting companion piece to Christopher Smart's salute to his cat Jeoffry in "An Old Cat's Dying Soliloquy" and the short-lived Mary Leapor (1722–1746) writes stirring proto-feminist verse in "An Essay on Woman":

> Woman, a pleasing but a short-lived flow'r,
> Too soft for business and too weak for pow'r;
> A wife in bondage, or neglected maid
> Despised, if ugly; if she's fair, betrayed.
>
> (ll.1–4)

In *Oppian's Halieuticks* William Diaper chronicles the sex life of the tortoise, writing in Johnsonian style of the "resistless doom" of the male's advance (cf. "Resistless burns the fever of renown" and "And pour on misty doubt resistless day" in "The Vanity of Human Wishes"):

> The tortoise-courtship is a state of war.
> Eager they fight, but with unlike design,
> Males to obtain, and females to decline.
> The conflict lasts, till these by strength o'ercome

All sorrowing yield to the resistless doom.
Not like a bride, but pensive captive, led
To the loathed duties of an hated bed.

(ll.26–32)

Augustan poetry, for too many contemporary readers, is a solemn old tortoise, lumbering along uneventfully on its heroic couplets to nowhere in particular. But tortoises have their dignity and passion too, as Diaper's poem reminds us, and a view of English-language poetry which overlooked the Augustans, or relegated them to "classics of our prose" would be a radically defective response to a vital and exhilarating era, qualities it owes in large part to the adaptability of its favorite form, the heroic couplet.

Modern and Contemporary

In traditional Irish music, the uilleann pipes, or Irish bagpipes, can be played in either a closed or open style. In the closed style, the player covers the finger holes between notes, producing a staccato effect; in the open style, the notes are allowed to flow uninterrupted. The effects produced by the two styles are strikingly different, but by no means incompatible if, for instance, two or more pipers play together. Where matters of poetic form are concerned, by contrast, there is a widespread sense that the closed and the open do not mix. William Carlos Williams and Lyn Hejinian do not write heroic couplets or double sestinas, and John Crowe Ransom and Anthony Hecht do not write Projective verse. Ron Silliman has coined the term "school of Quietude" for American poets who shirk their national destiny by failing to throw off the European baggage of rhyme and meter: if Anne Bradstreet's skilful handling of heroic couplets in "To My Dear and Loving Husband" suggests that this is one of the finest early American poems in English, to Silliman it would be evidence instead that it remains a *British* and not an American poem.

The opposition is reductive to the point of caricature, but highlights the rarity of writers today who range over the entire formal spectrum, or at least more than one side of this presumed binary opposition. To most readers of twentieth-century poetry, Yvor Winters (1900–1968) is a quintessentially "closed" poet, a dogmatic formalist with only contempt for the filthy modern tide, but a closer look at his work reveals a more nuanced picture. His first two books, *The Immobile Wind* (1921) and *The Magpie's Shadow* (1922), are written in a style of Imagist evanescence, the latter comprising a sequence of six-syllable, mainly single-line poems, one of which, "still Morning," reads: "snow air—my fingers curl" (Winters 4). An essential feature of the heroic couplet is the element of dialogue, contrast or balance between its two lines, whereas this ultra-short poem hangs suspended: even within its six syllables we are aware of a disjunction, or a connection which it falls to us to supply in the absence of any "thus" or "therefore," between the "snow air" and the speaker's curling fingers.

Later Winters supplies these connections in densely compact formal verse. His poem "The Marriage" ends:

> Still I shall meet you on the verge of dust
> And know you as a faithful vestige must.
> And in commemoration of our lust,
> May our heirs seal us in a single urn,
> A single spirit never to return.
>
> (ll.21–25)

The usual charges against Winters are archaism and emotional poverty, against each of which the above lines deserve a defense. If Winters' vocabulary seems indistinguishable from that of George Herbert, it should be remembered that archaism has always been part of modern and modernist poetry, from Pound and Bunting to Geoffrey Hill and Edgar Bowers. The important question is what dramatic use the poet has made of this language, ancient or modern. Though stiff-seeming, it quickens into life in unexpected wordplay: "When flesh shall fall away, and, falling, stand / Wrinkling with shadow over face and hand" (ll.19–20). We are failing, mortal beings, but even as we fall we "stand." Young love or love beyond death are familiar themes, but love in age is a more challenging affair, and one from which Winters wrings dignified pathos.

Nevertheless, it must be conceded that not just the poem's formal template but its implied world-view too is fiercely conservative. Are the two related? The realm of the flesh is that of transient "lust," inferior to the spirit-realm in which the couple is reunited. The appeal to the speaker's "heirs" places married "lust" in an ennobling context of lineage and succession; and Winters' use elsewhere in the poem of "yea" positively creaks with solemnity. Yet the edition of Winters from which I quote these lines was edited by Thom Gunn, a fellow maker of formal verse, lifelong celebrant of cheap kicks, and no kind of social conservative whatever.

Reappraising Winters' legacy in an updated edition of the 1979 anthology *Five American Poets*, Clive Wilmers writes:

> The emotion, Winters argued, should be appropriate to the experience, and, for it to be so, the poet needs a rational discipline to order and control the means of expression. It is not the poet's business to submit to feeling, but to seek to appraise and understand the experiences that give rise to it.
>
> (Wilmer xx)

Any suspicion that this is a charter for emotional anemia can be allayed by appealing, again, to Thom Gunn. Gunn's hymn to leather-clad bikers, "On the Move," hails their uniform for the "donned impersonality" it confers, so that the young men "strap in doubt—by hiding it, robust" (Gunn 39). But emotional camouflage is not the same as the absence of emotion, and what unites Winters and Gunn is a refusal to sanction emotion on the basis of "personality" alone: Winters' poem is much more intimate in its occasion than Gunn's, but it too disperses the individual into the larger narrative of death and generational succession, just as both poets use the formal correctness of their couplet forms to filter and mediate the strength of personal feeling.

Winters is often grouped with J.V. Cunningham (1911–85), to whom he acted as a mentor, but who is in many ways a very different writer; to Cunningham's editor, Timothy Steele, Winters was "more a romantic and Cunningham more a classicist" (Cunningham xvi). One sign of this was his identification with the epigram, which he practiced with lapidary wit, notably in the sequence "Epigrams: A Journal" from his 1947 collection *The Judge Is Fury*. He excels at civilized disillusionment in the face of love and death, and if he seems more able than most writers to meet the challenge of mortality, it may be because, as he boasts, he has internalized it in his style: "Death in this music dwells. I cease to be / In this attentive, taut passivity" (Cunningham 48). In his own of "donned impersonality," the "taut passivity" is that of the poet and the couplet form alike.

Thom Gunn (1929–2004) comes a generation after Cunningham. Touted as a member of the formally conservative Movement in Britain in the 1950s, he escaped to San Francisco, where he would live for fifty years. Gunn studied with Winters and, despite the many temptations for a hedonistic Englishman surrounded by nascent Beat culture to reinvent himself in American free verse, remained stubbornly true to a tradition of formal verse whose exemplars included Fulke Greville and Samuel Johnson. "Barren Leaves" is a typically witty example of Thom Gunn's handling of the couplet: "*Spontaneous overflows of powerful feeling.* / Wet dreams, wet dreams, in libraries congealing."

"Barren Leaves" would seem to operate on a far less exalted level than the burnished rhetoric of Johnson or Pope, but even for a squib it is not without its serious side, to which the couplet form makes an important contribution. The poem epitomizes what Pound categorized as "logopoeia," "the dance of the intellect among words" (Pound, *Cantos* 25), and makes a serious critique of the Romantic theory of emotion recollected in tranquility. The bathetic fall from the high Romantic register of the first line to the belly laugh of the second is also a critique of Wordsworthian propriety, which found considerably less room for the bawdy side of experience than Pope or Swift had done just a hundred years before.

A number of poems in Gunn's *The Man With Night Sweats* (1992) are in heroic couplets, and in a short poem such as "Terminal," with its attention to the "arc of movement," Gunn uses the form as the vehicle for a meditation on freedom and constraint. Describing two men eight years apart in age, the older of whom is dying of AIDS, the poem begins:

> The eight years difference in age seems now
> Disparity so wide between the two
> That when I see the man who armoured stood
> Resistant to all help however good
> Now helped through day itself, eased into chairs.
>
> (ll.1–5)

The deictic "now" of lines 1 and 5 suggests immediacy but, in each case, opens a dual perspective onto past and present, as, similarly, does the progression from "help" to "helped" in lines 4 and 5, laying bare the sick man's physical decline. Physical strength has departed, but the old man's gestures retain the signature of the vigorous man he was, and contemplating an "arc of movement . . . / As if with that spare strength he used to enjoy," Gunn concludes: "I think of Oedipus, old, led by a boy" (ll.10–12).

A sign of the wider currency of the heroic couplet in modern times is its use in one of the strangest appropriations of poetry by twentieth-century fiction, Nabokov's *Pale Fire*. This novel begins with a 999-line poem in couplets by "John Shade," followed by the prose commentary of the poem's "editor" Charles Kinbote. The demented ingeniousness of Kinbote's readings may spring from his fertile imaginings (he is plainly mad), but remind us how much more there is to the heroic couplet than a parade of dry rationality. The poem itself, one ought to add, is not at all bad for a piece of self-conscious comic frippery:

> I was the shadow of the waxwing slain
> By the false azure in the windowpane;
> I was the smudge of ashen fluff—and I
> Lived on, flew on, in the reflected sky.
>
> (ll.1–4)

Nabokov's hyper-cultivated sensibility draws naturally on literary forms such as the heroic couplet, but contemporary understanding of literary form is not always so sophisticated, and often features an element of forcing or artificiality. A prime symptom of this is New Formalism, a movement of the 1980s that preached a *rappel à l'ordre*, rejecting the excesses of the 1960s, condemning the ignorance among younger poets of traditional form, and numbering among its ranks Dana Gioia, Brad Leithauser, and R.S. Gwynn. Despite the complex and unpredictable nature of the overlap between poetic form and politics (Ezra Pound was a poetic radical and a political reactionary, Yvor Winters, stoniest of formalists, was a political liberal), an unmistakable whiff of social conservatism attaches to much New Formalist writing. It is unsurprising therefore to find that Gunn was less than impressed by its promise of form stiffened into dogma. Dryden or Pope may have written to a theory of what was and was not poetry, but the test of their worth remains the work and not the theory.

Contemporary poetry abounds in warring schools, the best answer to which is the formal variousness and invention of a writer such as Gunn, as much at home in free verse or syllabics as heroic couplets, and refusing to elevate his aesthetic choices into a controlling style-sheet. The following example by Tony Harrison (b. 1937), a poet often touted for his formal skills (though not affiliated with New Formalism), serves as a warning of how badly the mishandling of the couplet, or the instrumentalization of form for its own sake, can derail a poem. It is part of "Two Poems for My Son in His Sickness" and engages in speculation on the efficacy of art in the face of human frailty:

> The question is: Do you think poetry,
> specifically *this* poem, was worth a try?
> If not, and you found no comfort, not one phrase
> to brave *memento mori* and *olés*,
> or redeem doomed spermatozoa, drive
> a stake through this undead art and you'll survive.
>
> (section xiv, ll.7–12)

Natural speech rhythms foreshorten the first line to four stresses; line three is more naturally an alexandrine; line 5 is a pentameter only if its first and fourth feet are scanned as trochees, its third as a dactyl and its fifth as a pyrrhic foot (one heavy stress); and line 6 is, unarguably, an alexandrine. These are not the subtle variations against the ground bass of the pentameter we find in Pope or Dryden; it is slithering bagginess. Formal poetry as poorly executed as this is much worse than any amount of unexceptionable free verse.

Thankfully, there are contemporary writers who can be trusted to differentiate between formal poetry and doggerel. Derek Mahon (b. 1941) has been among the most devoutly formal of his generation of Irish poets. His use of the heroic couplet derives more from Marlowe than the sterner example of the Augustans (and like Marlowe, he has translated Ovid); how unAugustan he is can be judged from his version of the Juvenal satire which forms the basis for "The Vanity of Human Wishes." Where Johnson enforces the "closed" couplet with clinical precision, Mahon's rhyme scheme wanders, apparently at random, and his syntactic units break the banks of the couplet form in the "openest" way possible.

Another skilled use of the open couplet can be found in Marilyn Hacker (b. 1942), in her "Crepuscule with Muriel," whose opening sentence ambles winningly through much wordplay and playful repetition:

> Instead of a cup of tea, instead of a milk-
> silk whelk of a cup, of a cup of nearly six
> o'clock teatime, cup of a stumbling block,
> cup of an afternoon unredeemed by talk.
>
> (ll.1–4)

The reversed second and third feet in the third line, giving trochees on "teatime" and "cup of," followed by a similar reversal on the first foot of the following line ("cup of"), are exemplary instances of the countercurrents that make for fresh and varied metrical writing.

Justin Quinn (b. 1968), the most formally gifted of Irish writers now in their thirties and forties, uses heroic couplets in self-consciously neo-classical vein in "Laurel." The poem identifies the Greco-Roman gods with the warmer climes of the Mediterranean, and opens by defrosting itself from the more northerly extremes of the Czech Republic, where Quinn lives:

> We sit in the apartment, evening light
> still blue and red though it's now getting late.
> Summer weather is suddenly upon us,
> a sort of strange, extraordinary bonus.
> This whole long winter's ice is edged and shoved
> away and off and down some twisting shaft—
> the awful cold, those months and days and hours,
> two heads locked into darkness, mine and yours.
>
> (ll.1–8)

Formal poetry too is a climate in which the contemporary writer will either feel at home, or not, and to the reader of major poets such as John Ashbery or Jorie Graham it may seem as though the world of heroic couplets has becomes a quaint anachronism (Ashbery has written fine formal verse in his time, including his couplet translations from Baudelaire and Arthur Cravan, but this is not the side of his work one sees in his imitators). Stephen Burt has identified a strand in contemporary writing he terms "elliptical poetry," much influenced by these writers (Burt 345–55), and whose signature style throws off the formal scruples we find in Gunn, Mahon, and Hacker. In the oneiric, paratactic world of an Ashbery poem the reader feels as though adjectives could be replaced by their diametric opposites without much violence to the overall effect; whereas the Augustan use of the heroic couplet is a consummately hypotactic art, insisting on the rightness of these words, in this order, in (or against) this meter. Can the couplet hold its own against the all-conquering regime of free verse? "To break the pentameter, that was the first heave," that prophet of literary modernist Ezra Pound wrote in Canto LXXXI (Pound, *Cantos* 532), but against this we might balance the adage of that prophet of musical modernity, Arnold Schoenberg, who counseled that there were still a lot of good tunes to be written in the key of C major. Poetry should be at least as well written as prose, Pound also recommended, and the sinewy art of the heroic couplet is one of the principal forms in which it gets to exercise this right, the logopoeic dance of the intellect among words we find in Dryden, Pope, Johnson, Winters, Cunningham, Gunn, and others. There are many good and great poems still to be written in formal verse in general and, for the writer who cares to meet their exacting but invigorating challenge, heroic couplets in particular.

References and Further Reading

Arnold, Matthew. "The Study of Poetry," in M.H. Abrams (ed.), *The Norton Anthology of English Literature* (5th edn., vol. 2). New York: Norton, 1986. 1441–53.

Burt, Stephen. "The Elliptical Poets," in *Close Calls with Nonsense: Reading New Poetry*. St. Paul, MO: Graywolf, 2009. 345–55.

Chaucer, Geoffrey. *The Riverside Chaucer*, ed. Larry D. Benson. Oxford: Oxford University Press, 1987.

Cunningham, J.V. *The Poems of J.V. Cunningham*, ed. Timothy Steele. Athens: Swallow/Ohio University Press, 1997.

Dryden, John. *Selected Poems*, eds. Steven N. Zwicker and David Bywater. London: Penguin, 2001.

Grigson, Geoffrey (ed.). *The Faber Book of Epigrams and Epitaphs*. London: Faber & Faber, 1977.

Gunn, Thom. *Collected Poems*. London: Faber & Faber, 1993.

Hacker, Marilyn. *Desesperanto: Poems 1999–2002*. New York: Norton, 2003.

Harrison, Tony. *Laureate's Block*. London: Penguin, 2000.

Hobsbaum, Philip. *Metre, Rhythm and Verse Form*. London: Routledge, 1996.

Hopkins, David. *John Dryden*. Tavistock: Northcote, House, 2004.

Johnson, Samuel. *Samuel Johnson: The Complete English Poems*, ed. J.D. Fleeman. London: Penguin, 1971.

Lonsdale, Roger. *The New Oxford Book of Eighteenth-Century Verse*. Oxford: Oxford University Press, 1984.

Marlowe, Christopher. *The Complete Poems and Translations*, ed. Stephen Orgel. London: Penguin, 1971.

Nabokov, Vladimir. *Pale Fire*. London: Penguin, 1991.

Pope, Alexander. *Selected Poetry*, ed. Pat Rogers. Oxford: Oxford University Press, 1994.

Pound, Ezra. *The Cantos*. London: Faber & Faber, 1986.

Pound, Ezra. *Literary Essays of Ezra Pound*, ed. T. S. Eliot. London: Faber & Faber, 1954.

Quinn, Justin. *Fuselage*. Loughcrew: Gallery Press, 2002.

Ricks, Christopher (ed.). *The Oxford Book of English Verse*. Oxford: Oxford University Press, 1999.

Wilmer, Clive. "Introduction" to *Five American Poets*, ed. Michael Schmidt. Manchester: Carcanet Press, 2010. xv–xxiv.

Winters, Yvor. *Selected Poems*, ed. Thom Gunn. New York: Library of America, 2003.

19

In a Sea of Indeterminacy

Fourteen Ways of Looking at Haiku

Peter Harris

Haiku as Koan

Gettan Osho said, "Keichu, the first wheelmaker, made a cart whose wheels had a hundred spokes. Now, suppose you took a cart and removed both the wheels and the axle. What would you have?

(Sekida 46)

One of the first koans that many Zen students encounter, "Keichu the Wheelmaker," broaches the question of when, during its disassembly, a cart stops being a cart. The question is a red herring; the koan's true purpose is to frustrate rational thinking until a student lets go and enters a pre-definitional state of awareness, prior to such mind-created distinctions as "essence." In Zen parlance, one must *be* the cart. But what if the question is "What is a haiku today?" The search for answers leads into a tangle of contradictory and discontinuous practices. Apart from brevity, there are no characteristics that hold true for all haiku. In mapping contemporary practice of what has become a global form, it makes sense to narrow the search for haiku-ness to certain overlapping family resemblances, none of which are held by all.

Haiku as Global Phenomenon

Because it is brief and apparently user-friendly, haiku has, since the end of World War II, become a global phenomenon that has proved helpful for students of poetry at all

---

A Companion to Poetic Genre, First Edition. Edited by Erik Martiny.
© 2012 John Wiley & Sons, Ltd. Published 2012 by John Wiley & Sons, Ltd.

levels, spurring them to practice economy of language and the use of image. To Gary Snyder, teaching haiku to children is liberating because the form provides an occasion for students "to look around, see what they see, have a thought, make an image, and write their own brief poem" (Wenzel). Not everyone would agree that haiku have proved liberating, but there is something undeniably democratic about the current uses of the form, if not its origins as a coterie activity in Japan. At its very best, haiku implies great discernment and spiritual development; nonetheless, after reading a number of haiku in a row, one can easily get a basic feel for the form's most common delivery system: two or three bits of data, preferably in image form, that are juxta-posed, often surprisingly. Because they can be completed quickly and pleasingly, "haiku" crop up by the millions in English-speaking countries, in Europe, as well as in Africa, and, of course, Japan.

Many European and South American poets have held the form in high esteem: Yves Bonnefoy, Jorge Luis Borges, Czeslaw Milosz, Paul Muldoon, Pablo Neruda, and Tomas Tranströmer, to name but a few. The list of prominent mainstream American poets who have published haiku runs into the dozens—most of the High Modernists, all the Beats, several Poet Laureates (Robert Hass, Billy Collins, and Ted Kooser), avant garde experimentalists (John Cage, Jorie Graham, and Leslie Scalapino).[1]

Haiku as Tip of a Pyramid

At the same time, at least in the United States, haiku are the object of some conde-scension among mainstream poets, many of whom work in the academy. Haiku are considered too common, too slight, and too easy for undiscerning amateurs to churn out by the dozen. Indeed, there are hoards of cutesy, pious, or light verse haiku out there—about pets, sports, corporate work, unemployment, computers, religion, and sex. Almost every form of human activity and condition of being has spawned haiku. To let one example stand for many, there is an online archive of 19,000 haiku about Spam, the meat product (Spam-ku). In that archive reside seventy-five often-funny Spam-ku exclusively devoted to cannibalism. Partly in response to this proliferation, a leading haiku poet and commentator, Lee Gurga, in "Toward an Aesthetic for English-Language Haiku," has proposed employing a pyramid based on three Japanese categories, with *zappai*, or comic entertainment haiku, at the bottom. Above that are *senryu*, which can be humorous, often are satirical, but which transcend junk verse in their aim for truth about the human realm. Much of what is commonly labeled haiku is actually *senryu*. The highest form, haiku, sits atop the pyramid and relates "the human condition to the larger issue of our place in the universe" (Gurga). While some would disagree with Gurga's categorizing, the pyramid does have the advantage of helping to bring a modicum of order to the over-elastic term *haiku*, a word that in mid 2011 garners over 50 million hits in an internet search.

The undifferentiated deluge of haiku has caused some literary journals to refuse to consider haiku for publication. Most haiku are published in specialist journals—

Modern Haiku and *Frog Pond* to take two prominent examples—that serve a population almost hermetically sealed off from mainstream poetry. Arguably, the specialists publish the most accomplished haiku. This paradox of haiku's ubiquity and marginalization provides an interesting window on the ideology of poetic fashion. The postmodern, ironic experimentalist sensibility that is increasingly influential in graduate schools is no more friendly to haiku poets than to sonneteers. Un-ironic poems focused on nature are suspect as escapist pastoralism, though with the rise of ecocriticism the traditional nature haiku may be rehabilitated. Yet even prominent poets who are also ecological activists—for example, Pulitzer Prize-winners W.S. Merwin and Gary Snyder—tend to deemphasize haiku in their selected poems. In an interesting twist, Snyder is a recipient of the prestigious Masaoka Shiki International Haiku Grand Prize, and his latest collection, *Danger on Peaks*, contains more than a dozen haiku-like poems; yet he is on record as saying we really should not be referring to American adaptations as haiku proper (Wenzel). Recently, he has referred to a group of his haiku-like work as "frags" (Snyder, "Nine Frags" 3).

Haiku as an Adapted Japanese Form

Many poets may not be as familiar as Snyder is with the untranslatable syntactic subtleties of classical haiku or with the influence of Zen. Haiku evolved in the seventeenth century, as an abbreviated variant of renga, a much older, longer form, composed collaboratively, by members of the court and by literati. By the time of Bashō (1644–94), those first three metrical/syntactic units had detached themselves and become the individual, stand-alone activity we now know as haiku, which, as Koji Kawamoto explains, meant "comic" or unrefined verse (711). Thus early haiku were transgressive, closer to what we might call *zappai* or *senryu*. Bashō, though not the originator, brought legitimacy and prominence to the form, and he remains, for many, the unsurpassed master.

In terms of form and content, the four classical characteristics that are probably the most familiar today are the use of natural image, the 5–7–5 syllabic grouping, the seasonal reference, and the caesura. Many contemporary theorists and practitioners—the Canadian George Swede, for example—feel deeply about the primacy of natural image, particularly as it is conducive to awe (Swede 22–28). In an increasingly urban world, however, haiku tend to give way to human-focused, often ironic *senryu*. The 5–7–5 pattern is now widely ignored because syllables in Japanese are shorter than in English, roughly in a ratio of 17 to 12, respectively. The classical reference to a season (*kigo*)—as in plum blossoms for spring—was not a feature of *senryu* to begin with and, for a complex of reasons elucidated by the cross-cultural haiku theorist Richard Gilbert, is often omitted or distorted in current haiku (Gilbert 197–216). Still in wide currency, however, is the caesura, in Japanese *kireji* or "cutting word"; it is often expressed in English in combination with an ellipses or a dash, signaling a leap from one context to another.

Beyond these basics, a host of other qualities come into play in most classical Japanese haiku, many of them conditioned, albeit indirectly, by the aesthetic and spiritual influence of Zen, wherein an austere, disciplined absorption in the natural world has primacy as a source of insight and renewal. Such haiku court mystery or what we might variously call semantic openness, indeterminacy, and reliance on implication. Most classical, and many contemporary, haiku are meant to be expressed in a single breath (Swede 15–17). Many at least seem to efface the ego of the observer; many assume the absolute identity of subject or observer and the object. Simplicity, economy of means, avoidance of generalization, reliance on image, lightness of being, compassion, and gentle wit all permeate most classic, and many contemporary, haiku. Just as competing definitions of haiku abound, so do misconceptions about the "requirements" of classical haiku. In "Beyond the Haiku Moment: Bashō, Buson and Modern Haiku Myths," the noted Bashō scholar Haruo Shirane finds exceptions in classical texts to the supposed strictures that haiku be based on direct observation as opposed to memory, and that it eschew metaphor and allusion. He also points out that early haiku translators and commentators, particularly R.H. Blyth, overemphasized the influence of Zen thought (Shirane).

Haiku as a Paradigm for Modernism

In a well-rehearsed chapter of literary history, haiku and Japanese aesthetics entered into English-speaking literary culture largely though the efforts of the Imagists, particularly Ezra Pound. Pound found both Chinese and Japanese poetry deeply congenial. Haiku overlaps with many of the essential principles of what would come to be known as High Modernist poetics: economy, intensity, reliance on the image, clarity, the use of juxtaposition, and a minimum of discursive commentary. Though the appeal of haiku per se soon faded, its effects remained arresting, particularly its use of unadorned image, juxtaposition, and openness or reliance on implication. Three of the most discussed American poems of the twentieth century all owe an obvious debt to the form: Pound's "In a Station of the Metro" (1916), Wallace Stevens' "13 Ways of Looking at a Blackbird" (1923), and William Carlos Williams' "The Red Wheelbarrow" (1923). Pound's is the closest to a classical haiku; Stevens' is characteristically oblique; Williams' is as direct as can be, emphasizing the self-sufficient suchness of being, particularly the mutually arising matrix of ordinary being—chickens, rainwater, a wheelbarrow. The opening line "So much depends upon" might be the invisible superscript of many outstanding haiku poems, and not haiku poems alone, in English.

Haiku as Beat Phenomenon

After the High Modernists' forays into the form, a hiatus ensued until after World War II, when one of the first Westerners to study Zen, the British writer, R.H. Blyth, published his four volume *Haiku*, an anthology of classic Japanese work (*Haiku*). He provided the models that inspired the Beats in the 1950s. Kenneth Rexroth, the convener of the famous inaugural Beat poetry reading at *Six Gallery* in San Francisco in 1955, also played a role in introducing the Beats to Japanese poetry. Although Jack Kerouac is noted for his novels, he was deeply involved in haiku as a way of focusing, composing over a thousand of them (Kerouac). In terms of enlarging haiku awareness, it was Kerouac's fictional character, Japhy Rider, modeled after Gary Snyder, in *The Dharma Bums*, who did as much as anyone. Though Kerouac largely ignores the 5–7–5 syllabic requirement, his haiku followed the lead of Blyth in sticking to three lines, a practice that has the virtue of indicating pauses and syntactic relations.

Though an important progenitor of American haiku, Gary Snyder prefers not to call his haiku "haiku." He has, however, occasionally broken his own rule, as in the sequence "Hitch Haiku" from *Back Country* (New York: New Direction, 1968), but the Zen aesthetic permeates much if not all his work, as in his colloquially American "Hiking in the Totsugawa Gorge":

> pissing
> watching
> a waterfall
>
> (*Regarding Wave* 74)

Though humorous, it is something more than witty, at least if one reads it in the context of Snyder's Zen studies. Beyond the obvious, hyperbolic parallelism of the two streams, this poem embodies the intersection of the relative and the absolute. In Zen, the universe is all "one body," and in that body there is only one stream, and yet there are two—both containing one another and the poet. This non-dual ideation works for Snyder's poem in the same way it does in Bashō's most famous and endlessly referenced haiku about frog–water–sound, "An old pond: a frog jumps in—the sound of water" (Sato 118). At the instant of the frog's contact with the water, everything—the frog, the speaker, the pond and the water's sound—disappears into an indissoluble unity, while also remaining distinct.

Pioneering Specialist: Cor van den Heuvel

By choosing to include haiku in a collection of essays that examines genres and forms with longer traditions in English, the editor of this volume has seen fit to shed light on a practice often segregated from high prestige, mainstream, and avant garde poetics. Thus, a chance arises to encounter writers who might otherwise go virtually unnoticed. There are many, many poets worthy to be mentioned here, and to choose only three—one prominent and senior, one obscure and in the middle of her career, and one obscure and still near the beginning—is foolhardy and patently unjust.[2]

Cor van den Heuvel is both a prominent haiku specialist and editor of *The Haiku Anthology*, which was the first major collection of North American haiku. A transitional figure, he began his career before haiku-writing had become a highly distinct subculture. The following brief account is taken from the helpful website *Terebess Asia Online*, whose project "Modern American Haiku Poets" provides biographies, divided into ethnicities and audiences that mirror sub-cultures within the haiku movement (Modern). Van den Heuvel first heard haiku in San Francisco in 1958, in the early stages of the Beat poetry scene. The reader was Gary Snyder. By the early 1960s, van den Heuvel had become part of the poetry scene in New York City, reading along with Robert Kelly, Jackson Mac Low, and Diane Wakoski. By the 1970s, however, he had leagued in with the group of specialists who had formed the American Haiku Society. By 1978 he was president of that society, had compiled the first of three editions of *The Haiku Anthology* (van den Heuvel), and was in a position to help influence the tone and the guidelines for those interested exclusively in haiku (Modern). He, for example, is one to insist on haiku's affirmation of the absolute unity of the speaker with the natural world.

Most, not all, of his verse takes place in three lines, generally preserving the seasonal reference, while eschewing the 5–7–5 format. His subject matter ranges across a spectrum from baseball *senryu* to the surreal:

> empty wheelchair
> rolls
> in from the waves
>
> (Modern)

His best poems flash with precise appreciation, as in the following music-themed pieces:

> neon puddles
> in front of the waterfront bar
> sound of a blues piano
>
> (Modern)
>
> behind the curtain
> the opera star carries her roses
> through a dark forest
>
> (Modern)

The first of these invites the reader to consider the relation between the splash of neon light in the puddles and the sound of the blues. Perhaps there is a parallel between the ephemeral colored puddle and soon-to-be-forgotten urban blues. Perhaps there is the implication that the blues bring color to the water the way blues brings color to grief. Perhaps. The second of these haiku is less an aperçu and more an act of imaginative projection. One presumes the speaker cannot see the opera star but rather imagines her after the final curtain call, walking to her dressing room. Though the phrase is not fresh, the "dark forest" is the stroke that makes the poem. It leaves the reader to wonder if the magic of the opera has or has not faded. Is she still buoyed up or has she plunged from celebrity to a lonely world of threatening darkness? Or both? The staying power of the haiku is proportional to its resistance to univocal closure.

Though length and depth have no necessary connection, anyone surveying a large swatch of contemporary haiku will appreciate how difficult it is to generate much resonance (in Japanese, *yūgen*) in three lines. Van den Heuvel achieves his fair measure in the following two poems about shadows:

> From behind me
> the shadow of the ticket-taker
> comes down the aisle
>
> > (Modern)
>
> the shadow in the folded napkin
>
> > (Modern)

The first poem roots its effect in a clear setting: the speaker, one presumes, is on a train when he experiences the often uncanny feeling of being approached from behind, presaged by a shadow. One might wonder if the ticket-taker is also The Ticket-Taker. But if the poem were in any overt way to hint at such allegory, it would zoom from modest and authentic to presumptuous and false. The second poem, about the napkin, transpires in a single line, its brevity in keeping with its focus on the unobtrusive. Here "so much depends upon" on a mere shadow in a cloth used to wipe one's mouth. The poem would be ruined if it generalized that everything contains a secret, a shadow, a mystery.

Roberta Beary

By focusing on the discrete moment of perception, as in the noticing of the shadow in the napkin, haiku specialists, even in their collections, tend to stress mutability and to avoid narrative. But in reading a book of some seventy haiku, often couched in an explicit or implied first person, the reader, as co-creator, can hardly help connecting the dots, even if the author has taken care to scatter the narrative element. Such is the case with, Roberta Beary's *The Unworn Necklace*. Though synchronized with changing seasons, it returns several times to the subject of father–daughter relations and even more often to the demise of the speaker's marriage. Though Beary resists a single focus for her collection, it contains a broken, but chronological, sequence tracing the end of the speaker's marriage. She eases in and out of subject. In the eighth of seventy haiku and *senryu*, Beary sets up the theme of truth and lies; in the ninth, her speaker veers memorably into autobiography:

> white lie
> the mirror doubles
> the white chrysanthemum
>
> (16)
>
> rainy season
> again he tells me
> she means nothing
>
> (17)

Though these are discrete poems, they work together by virtue of an implied contrast between a white and a pernicious lie. Even when the marriage narrative is dropped in favor of a poem about tending a garden, the tone of pained mindfulness is the same as the outlook on the marriage:

> hands stained
> with tiger lilies
> all day this heat
>
> (31)

Only after considerable divagation, does the collection return to the marriage inching towards its end:

> talking divorce
> he pours his coffee
> then mine
>
> (35)
>
> custody hearing
> seeing his arms cross
> I uncross mine
>
> (40)

In the first of these, little is said but much is implied about the husband's presumptuousness. In the second, the attitudes are more indeterminate. When the speaker sees the husband cross his arms, does she uncross hers to induce him to keep open to negotiation? Or is she conceding something in the custody arrangements? Turning on such Jamesian moments, and courting no sentimentality, Beary's poems deserve the unusual recognition they received outside the haiku community. Beary's book was named, by the avant garde poet Ron Silliman, as runner-up for the William Carlos Williams Award, sponsored by the Poetry Society of America (Silliman).

The Generalist and the Specialist: Billy Collins and Scott Metz

The most discerning critics of junk or amateurish haiku tend to be the serious haiku specialists and critics. Phillip Rowland, for example, confronts the easy temptations of the form: "How often is our poetry—haiku being particularly vulnerable, on account of its brevity—a poetry of the quick fix, or short cut: a neat preemption of failure to think further and really explore what the language can do?" (Rowland). Serious haiku-writers find themselves sandwiched between hobbyists who write sentimental verse and mainstream poets who either ignore or only dabble in the form. Among the most highly visible contemporary poets in America, Paul Muldoon (from Ireland) and Billy Collins are also distinct in having published haiku collections (Muldoon, Collins). Though Collins' selected poems, *Sailing Alone around the Room*, has sold an unprecedented quarter of a million copies, he has made a point of publishing his haiku collection with a small specialist press. In that one egalitarian gesture, he crossed a boundary not often transgressed. And yet, if not a dabbler, Collins is still a visitor, not yet a master of haiku. For example, in his cleverly named *She Was Just Seventeen*, one of the better poems is this skillful but less-than-deeply-resonant effort:

> Full moon on new snow,
> and in the corner
> an open can of white paint.

To invoke the moon in a haiku or any poem is not to break new ground. But here the moon provides a foil for a humorous comment on how humans mimic nature's whiteness: a paint can weighed in balance with new snow and the moon.

An exclusive denizen of the haiku world, the young poet Scott Metz might well be considered an avant gardist, both for his sometimes outré subject matter and for the generous measure of indeterminacy in his verse. In the following example, among other ambiguities, it is not possible to clearly distinguish between literal and metaphorical:

> More rain the sisters slip into their mother tongue
>
> *(Modern Haiku* 37:3)

Metz employs an unbroken line here in a way that generates velocity and a sense of simultaneity that is in tension with its subtlety. But if it were broken into three lines—

> More rain
> the sisters slip
> into their mother tongue

—the pun on *slip* would have dominated and diminished the poem. As it stands, the single line puts the focus on the elusive implications raised by the poem as a whole. What has the rain to do with the sisters returning to their mother tongue? Does its liquidity induce a fresh access of native fluency? Is the rain metaphorical, some fluid quality of language that increasingly permeates their intimate conversation? Is the "mother tongue" metaphorical, implying the sisters are like drops of water dissolving in their origins? Are the sisters slipping rain into the mother tongue as one "slips" a drug into a cocktail? Though there is no way of proving it, one is tempted to say that this degree of semantic openness becomes more likely if, as Metz does, one focuses exclusively on the haiku form.

Robert Hass

Of America's most eminent mainstream poets, the two who have most thoroughly internalized the haiku aesthetic are Gary Snyder and W.S. Merwin. Merwin's achievement will only be suggested here by this brilliant expression of longing:

> Your absence has gone through me
> Like thread through a needle.
> Everything I do is stitched with its color

(Merwin 84)

In the generation after Merwin, Robert Hass, former Poet Laureate, has done as much as anyone to bring focus to the form through his translations of Bashō, Issa, and Buson (Essential). In his own poetry, he is faithful to whatever skillful means come to hand. Among those means, haiku habits recur, if only occasionally, in all his collections, often in hybridized forms that may be part of the future of haiku by mainstream poets.

Haiku serves Hass's penchant for combining narrative with apparently discontinuous juxtaposition. Even in haiku-like sequences, he does the un-haiku-like thing of enjambing stanzas, making them interdependent and reliant on prior syntax, ideas, and detail. In *Time and Materials* the poems tend to be long-lined and philosophical. But there are exceptions, for example, "Breach and Orison." The opening tercet of Section I is perhaps too aphoristic to accord with the traditional spirit of haiku; yet the aphorism is anchored to an image that works in ways that suggest haiku's influence:

> What are the habits of paradise?
> It likes the light. It likes a few pines
> on a mass of eroded rock in summer.

(14)

The pines and eroded rock, in subsequent stanzas, provide a metaphorical context for an exchange, not in haiku form, between a woman who asks a man what he would do if he were her. He responds, "If I were you-you . . . I'd do exactly / what you are doing." It is unclear if he is supporting her, or mocking her impossible proposition, or doing both at once. Almost everything is left unsaid about the nature of this relationship, and yet, in the final, haiku-like stanza, Hass gives us three contexts in which to savor the mystery of the woman's uncertainty—the natural, the human, and religious worlds:

> Wind in the pines like the faint rocking
> of a crucifix dangling
> from a rearview mirror at a stopsign.

(14)

These three lines may be taken as one kind of an epitome of how haiku and *senryu* have interpenetrated mainstream American poetics. The natural world persists as it might in any traditional haiku: pines, wind. But nature is woven with culture, while imagery or metaphor steeps in ironic reflection—in this case, the lingering promise of Christianity: a cross dangling from the rearview mirror of an absolutely secular car—rocking on in California. One imagines that Hass resorts to haiku or haiku-like structures to begin and end this poem because the form is intrinsically amenable to the challenge of implying a great deal memorably, through image, in a short compass.

Chase Twichell

Chase Twichell has been for some years a formal student of Zen. Especially in *The Snow Watcher* she writes in astringently self-questioning ways about the tension between a yearning for calm and a churning mind. While there are virtually no obvious haiku in her work, they nonetheless make incognito appearances when she works in linked tercets. In "Secrets," Twichell, the speaker, marries elliptical reticence with a wrenching disclosure of sexual abuse:

> SECRETS
> All my childhood was spent
> in a clubhouse for one.
> Who knows the password?
>
> I'm still afraid of the subway.
> What does it mean,
> the sudden telling of a secret?
>
> There was a pure light in childhood.
> It was a laser. The girl stayed in the dark,
> but the pure thing burned everything.
>
> The light again. The word *pure.*
> She lay on a dish-towel. Then with the same
> fingers he played the piano.

> Fold up the little towel
> and put it away. Fold up
> the little towel, put it away.

                                                                                    (32)

The tercet form, whether or not we call it haiku or senryu, suits this subject in much the same way that Dickinson's elliptical condensations suit her vision; here, each utterance seems just barely to cross the threshold from shamed silence to speech—yet to resonant effect. The five-stanza sequence condenses the classic form of the short story. The first stanza is expository; the second foreshadows the lasting effects of an unnamed affliction; the third builds suspense. In the fourth stanza, the poem comes to a climax, underscored by the devastating observation that the abuser's fingers are those of a pianist. The fifth stanza, the denouement, veers farthest from a recognizable haiku, repeating, with a minor variation, the imperative sentence, "Fold up the little towel / and put it away." Despite its distance from the way haiku generally deploy sense data, the fifth stanza resembles a haiku in the way it invites the reader to co-create a set of possible implications. The imperative form suggests that the speaker might be coaching herself to let go of an intrusive memory or, in a more sinister twist, she might be ventriloquizing the abuser's command to hide the evidence of the crime. Or both, but in what order?

Ted Kooser and Jim Harrison

Collaborative poetry, particularly among men, is relatively rare in contemporary poetry. *Braided Creek: A Conversation in Verse* is a notable exception. It features the unsigned poems of Jim Harrison, a poet, novelist, and Zen practitioner, and Ted Kooser, a former Poet Laureate. In the haiku spirit of deemphasizing the ego, each specific poem is unsigned. Moreover, no one here claims to be writing haiku, or epigrams, or anything more than "verse." Yet some of the poems—one suspects they are mostly Kooser's—are indeed aphoristic and epigrammatic: "the wit of the corpse / is lost on the lip of the coffin" (5). Others are closer to haiku and clearly steeped in Zen: "Only today / I heard / the river / within / the river" (9). Some are plus-size *senryu*, as in this bitter reflection by a posthumous speaker:

> DNA shows that I'm the Unknown Soldier.
> I can't hear the birds down here,
> only politicians shitting out of their mouths.

                                                                                    (65)

They often are earthy, as in this *senryu* on defecating:

> Straining on the toilet,
> we learn how
> the lightning bug feels

                                                                                    (56)

Harrison and Kooser shift from mood to mood, from moments of sexual desire to the much more prominent reflections on bereftness and old age:

> Winter knows
> when a man's pockets
> are empty
>
> (24)

> Like an old dog
> I slowly lower myself
> in a heap of sighs
>
> (78)

The first, winter haiku, lives in the ambiguity between winter as a predator and winter as kinsman in emptiness. The second, like many others in the volume, emphasizes the speaker as a dying animal. The natural world of the Midwestern landscape permeates these meditations in a way not common in American poetry.

Ian Marshall

In a striking experiment, the essayist and eco-critic, Ian Marshall, has transformed Thoreau's *Walden* into 293 haiku (Marshall). Thoreau's austere appreciation of nature has long been linked to Asian thought in general and to Zen in particular. Marshall's claim, which the haiku seem to substantiate, is that peak moments at Walden Pond tend to be charged with classic haiku spirit, often with strong natural images (xvi).

Thoreau's ability to fuse apparently disparate contexts comes through again and again in these haiku, as in the "deep ecology" poems:

> the oxen
> their vegetable-made bones
> the lumbering plough
>
> (3)

> drinking deeper from the stream
> fish in the sky
> bottom pebbly with stars
>
> (9)

Marshall's search for proto-haiku by Thoreau, though often successful, raises, as he acknowledges, questions about appropriation, about arbitrary rearrangement, and presumptuous redaction (xxv). And yet, in the best of them, we get Thoreau's unmistakable tang liberated from Thoreau's sometimes tendentious moral explainery:

> wind on my cheek
> heathen as I am
> I turn the other to it
>
> (63)

the West
our own interior
white on the chart

(84)

The first of these beautifully captures Thoreau's contrarian views on Christianity, and his preference for unmediated immersion in nature. The second, so evocative, brings us round to a linkage between continental conquest and self-ignorance. In the West, one suspects there will always be too much white on the interior chart of its inhabitants.

Haiku's Current Future

It is probable that the two streams of haiku in American poetry, outside of primary and secondary education, will remain divided. Specialists, like makers of racecars, will continue to explore the possibilities of the form, largely unnoticed by the makers who dominate the literary magazines. Of this obscurity, this traveling beneath the radar of official literary history, Gary Hotham's haiku might be seen as making a comment:

this day in history—
the air
the leaves fall through

In the long view, haiku and mainstream poetry are falling leaves—one not better than the other, both on the way to disappearance and recycling.

Haiku, when practiced by mainstream poets, will continue to hybridize, to emphasize linked sequences that will often allow for narrative. Abstract thinking may seep into these adaptations until the family resemblance to haiku becomes so remote as to be meaningless. And yet in a broader sense, Seamus Heaney is probably right in his discussion of the "Japanese effect." In an essay accompanying the Irish anthology, *Our Shared Japan*, which brings together work of almost every major Irish poet on the subject of the encounter with Japan, he traces the aesthetic gist of this effect back to Pound's "In a Station in the Metro":

The apparition of these faces in a crowd;
Petals on a wet, black bough.

About this, Pound had written that it might seem meaningless to those unused to its aesthetic, to which Heaney responds:

The poem is far from meaningless, and it is largely thanks to its existence that readers (and writers) in English have drifted 'into a certain vein of thought.' Thanks to these fourteen words, we are now well attuned to the Japanese effect, the evocation of that precise instant of perception, and are ready to grant such evocation of the instant a self-sufficiency of its own.

(214–15)

To allow a perception its self-sufficiency, and not use it to gloss something abstract, might seem interesting but relatively trivial when held in balance with the great conditioning forces of gender, race, economics, and class. But the "Japanese effect" might not be so trivial in the long run, if there is to be a long run. Because of the way that great haiku arrest the moment of our distraction, cultivate contemplation, prefer image and implication to explanation, and do more with less, they might just be too fundamental to do without. Who knows but that haiku poets are the unacknowledged antennae of the race?

NOTES

1 This list could be extended indefinitely: W.H. Auden, Amiri Baraka, Stephen Berg, Olga Broumas, Hayden Carruth, Diane di Prima, Sam Hamill, Jim Harrison, William Heyen, Jane Hirshfield, Lawson Fusao Inada, Robert Kelly, Joanne Kyger, Jackson Mac Low, Michael McClure, Kenneth Rexroth, Sonia Sanchez, William Stafford, Ruth Stone, Lucian Stryk, Nathaniel Tarn, Chase Twichell, Ann Waldman, Philip Whalen, and Richard Wilbur. It cannot be a coincidence that all but a few of these poets have been deeply influenced by Buddhism.

2 A partial list of noteworthy, mostly senior, haiku poets, with nationalities appended, would include Ai Li (UK), Bob Boldman (US), LeRoy Gorman (CAN), Lee Gurga (US), Gary Hotham (US/UK), Jim Kacian (US), Peggy Lyles (US), Marlene Mountain (US), Raymond Roseliep (US), Alexis Rotella (US), Robert Spiess (US), George Swede (CAN), Anita Virgil (US), Nicolas Virgilio (US), and Ruth Yarrow (US).

REFERENCES AND FURTHER READING

Beary, Roberta. *The Unworn Necklace*. Liverpool: Snapshot Press, 2007.

Blyth, Reginald H., trans. *Haiku*. 4 vols. Tokyo: Hokuseido, 1949–1952.

Collins, Billy. *She Was Just Seventeen*. Lincoln, IL: Modern Haiku Press, 2006.

Harrison, Jim and Ted Kooser. *Braided Creek: A Conversation in Poetry*. Port Townsend, WA: Copper Canyon Press, 2003.

Hass, Robert, ed. *The Essential Haiku: Versions of Bashō, Issa and Buson*. Hopewell, NJ: Ecco Press, 1994.

Hass, Robert. *Time and Materials: Poems 1997–2005*. New York: HarperCollins, 2005.

Heaney, Seamus. Afterword. "Petals on a Bough." *Our Shared Japan: An Anthology of Contemporary Irish Verse*. Eds. Irene de Angelus and Joseph Woods. Dublin: Dedalus, 2007. 211–18.

Gilbert, Richard, "Kigo and the Seasonal Reference." *Poems of Consciousness: Contemporary Japanese and English-Language Haiku in Cross-Cultural Perspective*. Winchester, VA: Red Moon Press, 2008. 197–216.

Gurga, Lee. "Toward an Aesthetic for English-Language Haiku." *Modern Haiku* 31:3 (2000). *Baymoon* (2003): n.p.

Kawamoto, Kaji. "The Use and Disuse of Tradition in Bashō's Haiku And Imagist Poetry." *Poetics Today* 20.4 (1999). 709–21.

Kerouac, Jack. *Book of Haikus*. Ed. Regina Weinreich. New York: Penguin, 2003.

Marshall, Ian. *Walden: By Haiku*. Athens, GA: University of Georgia Press, 2009.

Merwin, William S. *Winged Migration: New and Selected Poems*. Port Townsend, WA: Copper Canyon Press, 2005.

"Modern American Haiku Poets: Cor ven den Heuvel." *Terebess Asia Online (TAO)* n.d.

Muldoon, Paul. *Hopewell Haiku*. Easthampton, MA: Warwick Press, 1997.

Rowland, Phillip, "*From Haiku to the Short Poem: Bridging the Divid. Modern Haiku* 39:3 (2008): n.p.

Sato, Hiroaki. *One Hundred Frogs: From Renga to Haiku to English*. New York; Weatherhill, 1983.

Sekida, Katsuki. "Case 2: Keichu the Wheelmaker." *Two Zen Classics: The Gateless Gate and the Blue Cliff Record*. Boston, MA: Shambhala, 2005. 46–47.

Shirane, Haruo. "Beyond the Haiku Moment: Bashō, Buson and Modern Haiku Myths." *Modern Haiku* 31:1 (2000). *Haikupoet*, n.d.

Silliman, Ron. Silliman's Blog. April 2, 2008.

Snyder, Gary. *Danger on Peaks*. Washington DC: Shoemaker Hoard, 2004.

Snyder, Gary. "Hiking in the Totsugawa Gorge." *Regarding Wave*. New York: New Directions, 1970.

Snyder, Gary. "Nine Frags." *American Poetry Review* 38.4 (2009).

Swede, George. "Towards a Definition of the English Haiku." *Global Haiku: Twenty-Five Poets World-Wide*. Ed. George Swede and Randy Brooks. Oakville, Ontario: Mosaic Press, 2000. 14–34.

van den Heuvel, Cor. *The Haiku Anthology*. New York, Doubleday, 1974.

Wenzel, Udo. "Gary Snyder Talks with Udo Wenzel." News of the Day, News of the Moment. 2007. Terebess Asia Online. n.d.

20

On the Pantoum, and the Pantunite Element in Poetry

Geoff Ward

The pantoum, to use its French and English spelling, derives historically from the *pantun*. One of the three principal genres of Malay folk poetry, it emerged during the fifteenth century. As distinct from the more proverb-based *peribahasa*, and the unrhymed but rhythmical *bahasa berirama*, the *pantun* is, at least according to *The New Princeton Encyclopedia of Poetry and Poetics*, "constructed of two couplets, rhyming *abab*, the first . . . more or less general and the second in some way a narrowing or application of the first" (Preminger and Brogan 731). Such an arrangement of shapes, mirrorings and "narrowing" does admittedly recur in world poetry of all sorts. For example, this encyclopedia description of the *pantun* fits William Wordsworth's "A Slumber Did My Spirit Seal," or its well-known Victorian successor by Ernest Dowson beginning "They are not long, the weeping and the laughter . . ." (2) very neatly; so neatly, in fact, as to at least raise the question as to whether the European "pantoum" is essentially a variant on the short-to-medium length lyric poem, and only in its superficial armature a distinct form. Nevertheless, in the discussion of pantoums by nineteenth- and twentieth-century writers that follows, it will be useful to keep in mind such basic verse shapes as the encyclopedia's definition describes, involving mirroring and the recursive tenure on a first line or phrase in a poem in order to power the second, which narrows or intensifies it. Also relevant, in however transmuted a form, is the reported chanting of Malay folk poetry by a "reciter of spells," and the supposed umbilical connection of folk poetics to "a magical origin and utility" (Preminger and Brogan 731). Even when these alleged organic–social–magical links are put under scrutiny, and even when stripped of its mystique by the ironies of postmodernity, the pantoum, more than other verse forms, retains the audible resonance of incantation, and a sense of the spell.

A Companion to Poetic Genre, First Edition. Edited by Erik Martiny.
© 2012 John Wiley & Sons, Ltd. Published 2012 by John Wiley & Sons, Ltd.

The pantoum enters French poetry of the nineteenth century as part of the cultural expropriation and importation of Asian exotica. The intrinsically delicate and ornate features of the short poem can be understood in this historical context as having been co-opted in one of the classic feints of Orientalism—to contain what is other, and therefore threatening, by miniaturizing it beautifully. After its introduction into European writing by the French Orientalist Ernest Fouinet, and its exploration by Victor Hugo in the notes to *Les Orientales*, the pantoum was essayed by Théodore de Banville, Louisa Siefert, and Leconte de Lisle, and, joining the wave of interest in the revival of fixed verse forms, spread its influence, via the pivotal figure of Charles Baudelaire, across European Symbolism and its offshoots such as "decadent" literature of the British 1890s. (Its further revival by John Ashbery in the post-1945 American context will be discussed later.) It is no accident that, in its adoption by Symbolist poetry in general and Baudelaire in particular, the form grows in intricacy. The pantoum therefore became (or at least, could in some cases become)

a poem of indeterminate length composed of quatrains in which the second and fourth lines of each stanza serve as the first and third lines of the next, through [to] the last stanza, where the first line of the poem reappears as the last and, in some Eng. pantoums, the third line of the poem as the second. Thus the pantoum begins and ends with the same line and, throughout, the cross rhymes scissor the couplets, different themes being developed concurrently.

(Preminger and Brogan 876)

To a greater extent, therefore, than any other fixed verse form still in use, the pantoum evidences the fact that the meanings of words and lines are altered instantly by their immediate context, even where that context is one of intense compression, and predetermined structure, and where the same verbal formulae are repeated word for word. What looks like sameness turns out to spell difference. This duality of statements which clearly do and yet, just as clearly do not repeat themselves, is a source of the uncanny sensation picked up by the reader—and perhaps the writer.

In this context, the closest analogue to the pantoum from a formal viewpoint may not be another high-art form such as the sonnet or sestina, or even other forms of French origin such as the rondeau or villanelle—but rather the blues. In the classic twelve-bar blues, each verse has three lines ending on a rhyme or half-rhyme, the first two lines being identical, the sense of the second altered retrospectively by the final line, and the meaning of the whole striated by repetition, variation, and, as with the pantoum, exact repetition that nevertheless generates variation. Here, for example, is the final verse of Rabbit Brown's "James Alley Blues," recorded in the late 1920s and possibly dating as a composition from the 1890s:

Sometime I think, you too sweet to die.
Sometime I think, you too sweet to die.
And another time I think, you ought to be buried alive.

There is insufficient space to trace the curve of tonal changes throughout this early twelve-bar from New Orleans, which is by turns vicious, comic, and tender. A certain psychological acuity over the tensions to be negotiated in any domestic relationship is formalized in the repetitions and abrupt variations of Brown's blues. This leaves the phrasing of line 2 of the verse quoted in an utterly ironic and undermined relationship to the third line, where the first line (though its wording is identical) rests in an uneasy balance with the third, like the sugar and salt traded grudgingly across the kitchen table in an earlier verse. A comparable blend of conscious primitivism and artful repetition-with-variation is characteristic of Bob Dylan's more recent use of the blues, as in this verse from "She Belongs to Me" (1965):

> She wears an Egyptian ring, it sparkles before she speaks.
> She wears an Egyptian ring, it sparkles before she speaks.
> She is a hypnotist collector, you are a walking antique.

The impossible is made possible through the magical image of a ring that sparkles on the hand just before the voice of its owner speaks. The third line, typical of the mid-1960s in its scornful demarcation of those who are hip, from those who are terminally square (cf. "Ballad of a Thin Man," among many other examples), implies that the speaker is no different from the ring, save in his ability to walk, an ability that the power of the "hypnotist collector" might very soon take from him, and which in any case, as in the everyday phrases "walking wounded" or "dead man walking," suggests zombie-like automatism more than independent perambulation. The ironic insinuation is that the unconscious and real title of his song might more properly be "I Belong to Her." The word-for-word repetition of line 1 in line 2 is clearly building a tension that will be released in the faintly surreal phrasing of the third line quoted. Curiously, however, the very exactness of the repetition emphasizes "her" magical and hypnotic power only to commodify her as an icon. The ring that sparkles to announce the voice that speaks is as automated as the text message icon on a smartphone. The magician, therefore, in the miniature world of the pantoum, the blues or any miniature verse form, may also be a marionette—a deployed verbal artifact like any other, made up and then paraded for certain distinct purposes. In turning shortly to the micro-effects of a poem by Baudelaire, in which entrapment, magic, and miniaturization render theme and formal device inseparable, it may be useful to recall this poet's interest in dolls and marionettes, explored in the 1853 essay "The Philosophy of Toys," but relevant to a host of images in the poetry, and to a tradition stretching across the nineteenth and twentieth centuries, from Kleist through Rilke to Surrealism, Joseph Cornell and beyond. This tradition is prepared to construct or interpret the work of art, be it visual or verbal, as a box filled with enigmatic curiosities, or a doll's house.

Before moving on to Baudelaire, it may be worth pausing to state the obvious. There will be readers of poetry (and listeners to music) for whom the blues is simple stuff, not so much a box of enigmas as an, at best, primitive folk form, kept alive only by the commercially successful adaptations by its rock-and-roll descendants. But then

there are many for whom poems are jingles, simply, the whole apparatus of rhyme
and meter a sequence of clockwork chimes and echoes. Poets from the time of
Baudelaire onwards have had to deal with this, either strategically, tacitly—or by
breaking away completely into the many variants and ongoing mutations of free verse
that originate essentially with Whitman and the later Mallarmé. Austin Dobson, who
is credited with writing the first pantoum in English, resorted to a strategy of complicity that allowed him to align his own limitations as a writer of light verse with
a (marginally) more sophisticated understanding of the pantoum's box as a trap that
will infuriate the reader with its buzzing repetitions, requiring a collusive smashing
of the box to pieces while still keeping faith with its fixed-form strictures:

> In Town
> "The blue fly sung in the pane."
> *Tennyson*
>
> Toiling in Town now is "horrid,"
> (There is that woman again!)
> June in the zenith is torrid,
> Thought gets dry in the brain.
>
> There is that woman again:
> "Strawberries! fourpence a pottle!"
> Thought gets dry in the brain;
> Ink gets dry in the bottle.
>
> "Strawberries! fourpence a pottle!"
> Oh for the green of a lane!
> Ink gets dry in the bottle;
> "Buzz" goes a fly in the pane!
>
> Oh for the green of a lane,
> Where one might lie and be lazy!
> "Buzz" goes a fly in the pane;
> Bluebottles drive me crazy!
>
> Where one might lie and be lazy,
> Careless of Town and all in it! One
> Bluebottle drives me crazy:
> I shall go mad in a minute!
>
> Careless of Town and all in it,
> With some one to soothe and to still you;
> I shall go mad in a minute;
> Bluebottle, then I shall kill you!

With some one to soothe and to still you,
As only one's feminine kin do,
Bluebottle, then I shall kill you:
There now! I've broken the window!

As only one's feminine kin do,
Some muslin-clad Mabel or May!
There now! I've broken the window!
Bluebottle's off and away!

Some muslin-clad Mabel or May,
To dash one with eau de Cologne;
Bluebottle's off and away;
And why should I stay here alone!

To dash one with eau de Cologne,
All over one's eminent forehead;
And why should I stay here alone!
Toiling in town now is "horrid."

Dobson's use of the pantoum form assumes that the reader's growing irritation at its repetitions will match the irritability of its narrator at the trapped bluebottle. His farcical breaking of his window in an effort to kill the noisy insect announces that the poem's own noise is about to end. The poem, collected in 1895, satirizes the image of the vain aesthete, much as the cartoonists of *Punch* did, as fevered but indolent. The narrator longs for a lane, where "one might lie and be lazy," but here in London he is already conspicuously without employment, his inkwell dry. At the namby-pamby rather than the Dorian Gray end of the aesthete's spectrum, his idea of liquid release from aridity entails being sprayed with perfume by a lightly clad female member of his own family, an image-train that becomes stranger the more one thinks about it, and quite beyond the scope of this essay to untangle. Dobson, like Andrew Lang, W.E. Henley and others, was responding to Edmund Gosse's "A Plea for Certain Exotic Forms in Verse" of 1877. Dobson was the first writer to essay a *ballade* in English, and his parallel exercises in the triolet and rondeau forms are not all light-verse, but rather tend towards an equally Victorian note of melancholy pathos. This of course would be picked up, along with other facets of aestheticism, by the Modernist generation of T.S. Eliot, whose "Thoughts of a dry brain in a dry season" (78) from "Gerontion," along with other images of aridity (though ones, in Eliot's case, not to be slaked by lightly clad females spraying eau de Cologne) may have drawn obliquely on Dobson's work, alongside other *fin de siècle* sources.

"In Town" is the only pantoum considered in this essay to conform to the stricture that the final line of a pantoum should repeat word for word the first, though Dobson neglects to observe the rule that the unrepeated first and third lines in the first verse should find a delayed repetition in the last. The point is not so much that such departures should be read as impurities or dilutions, as that the pantoum as it plays out in Anglophone poetry is adapted as it goes, here gaining in length and intricacy, there shedding end-rhymes or other aspects. The tradition is more one of the pantunite poem than of a timeless pantoum. But then, much the same could be said of the addition or subtraction of rhyme or the *envoi* from the sestina; or of the changes in the sonnet form, on its journey from Petrarch to Ted Berrigan via the modifications introduced by Wyatt and Shakespeare. Carolyn Kizer, in a wryly amusing poem of 1996 entitled "Parents' Pantoum," makes use of the repetitions that the form makes possible in order to address the mirroring and echoes across the two generations of parents and children which both are perfectly capable of missing. The back-and-forth movement across the generations, sometimes comic, at times affecting, leads to a final, lone line which has no echo anywhere else in the poem—"We offspring of our enormous children"—but which encapsulates its meaning. But then, in the thirty-seven lines of Kizer's "pantoum" there is no meter, no end-rhymes, and the repetition—strictly speaking—of only a single line, plus half a dozen further half-lines. It could be argued that this loosening of the form contributes to, rather than diminishing the weaving-effect of the pantoum, the fainter echo making it something one has to pinpoint for one's self as reader, rather than being struck full on by word-for-word repetition. Alternatively, it could be argued that Kizer's pantoum is not a true pantoum, but a poem characteristic of a time of truce among the warring tribes of poetic practice, one where formalist poetry has become comfortable with elements of freedom, and "experimental" verse, meanwhile, having no political avant-garde to which to attach itself, is comfortable with its regained right to parade the traditional verse accoutrements. Thirdly, it could be argued that it is mystery, rhetoric and a form of perfumed darkness that make a pantoum a pantoum. (A poem such as Kizer's that neatly sums up and highlights its intended meanings in a lone final line is no mystery.) By these lights, Tennyson's gorgeously, romantically gothic poem "Mariana," from which Austin Dobson drew his epigraph "The blue fly sung in the pane," is more of a pantoum, atmospherically speaking, than Dobson's essentially comic adaptation from the French, or Kizer's classroom exercise.

   And so it is time to turn to the pantoum of pantoums, Baudelaire's "Harmonie du Soir," one of *Les Fleurs du Mal* published first in the *Revue française* in 1857.

> Voici venir les temps où vibrant sur sa tige
> Chaque fleur s'évapore ainsi qu'un encensoir:
> Les sons et les parfums tournent dans l'air du soir;
> Valse mélancolique et langoureux vertige!
>
> Chaque fleur s'évapore ainsi qu'un encensoir;
> Le violon frémit comme un cœur qu'on afflige;
> Valse mélancolique et langoureux vertige!
> Le ciel est triste et beau comme un grand reposoir.

Le violon frémit comme un cœur qu'on afflige,
Un cœur tendre, qui hait le néant vaste et noir!
Le ciel est triste et beau comme un grand reposoir;
Le soleil s'est noyé dans son sang qui se fige.

Un cœur tendre, qui hait le néant vaste et noir,
Du passé lumineux recueille tout vestige!
Le soleil s'est noyé dans son sang qui se fige . . .
Ton souvenir en moi luit comme un ostensoir!

It may be helpful to readers if a translation of "Harmonie du Soir" into English is included at this point to set alongside the original, and of course there are a myriad available. First, here is a *fin de siècle* translation by Alfred Douglas, remembered now chiefly as the lover of Oscar Wilde, but a proficient versifier of his time:

Now is the hour when, swinging in the breeze,
Each flower, like a censer, sheds its sweet.
The air is full of scents and melodies,
O languorous waltz! O swoon of dancing feet!

Each flower, like a censer, sheds its sweet,
The violins are like sad souls that cry;
O languorous waltz! O swoon of dancing feet!
A shrine of Death and Beauty is the sky.

The violins are like sad souls that cry,
Poor souls, that hate the vast, black night of Death;
A shrine of Death and Beauty is the sky.
Drowned in red blood, the Sun gives up his breath.

This soul that hates the vast black night of Death
Takes all the luminous past back tenderly,
Drowned in red blood, the Sun gives up his breath.
Thine image like a monstrance shines in me.

Douglas's rendering is fit for purpose, enabling an interested Anglophone reader to catch the general drift. His straightforward, Anglo-Saxon planting of feet comes nowhere near the virtuoso tensions in the French original between metrical exigency and voluptuous delay around syllables; Baudelaire's pantoum is a small box, imagistically, but also a "langoureux vertige" of time-based, sighing sounds. However, assuming for the moment that Douglas grants two and not three syllables to the word "languorous," which the relatively clipped tone and tempo of his version make plausible, there is an appealing modesty in his choice, as translator rather than originator, to keep the Anglophone iambic pentameters at ten rather than eleven syllables. (The one deliberate exception, "Takes all the luminous past back tenderly," is the best line in the translation, and manages to equate to the French original while importing a touch of Tennyson, which works.) This translation is clean and clear, intended to assist. Naturally a good deal is lost, not least the French poet's mastery of tenebrous and opalescent images couched in a sonic near-swoon. Douglas' translation also gains from an easy confidence in deploying the rhetoric of Thee-ing and Thou-ing, essentially an advantage born of translating a work from (just about) the same half-century.

A version by Roy Campbell, published in 1952, merits brief attention, if only for purposes of historical contrast. As translation, it is mediocre. It has been selected not in order to denigrate a once-celebrated poet, but because the particular ways in which it precisely *fails* to work can tell us something useful about the original, about pan-toums, and about the later, highly significant revival of the form by John Ashbery.

> A heart that hates oblivion, ruthless censor,
> The whole of the bright past resuscitates.
> The sun in its own blood coagulates . . .
> And, monstrance-like, your memory flames intenser!

"The fiddle," which occurs elsewhere in Campbell's translation, is not the same instru-ment as Baudelaire's sonorous "violon." The echoing of "censer" in "censor," above, while it departs from the original, could be held to be in keeping, by extrapolation, with the drive to repetition intrinsic to the pantoum, but grates because it is the only instance of such a potentially rewarding re-doubling. Far more grating is the use of "immenser" in lines eight and eleven, capped catastrophically by the concluding clanger ". . . your memory flames intenser!" Here, however, something significant is at work, in the sense that the clumsiness of "immenser" is audibly a stumble by a poet writing in an age when the consensus around strict verse form has shifted. The metrical skills of W.H. Auden reigned paramount in Anglophone poetry without surprising anyone, by 1952, spawning imitations that were academic exercises in the worst sense. Meanwhile American experimentation in free verse was about to explode but had not yet done so, in the form of Allen Ginsberg's *Howl* (1955) and the work of Charles Olson, Frank O'Hara, John Ashbery, and the other poets, generally born in the 1920s and sampled in Donald Allen's anthology *The New American Poetry* (1960). Campbell, like many of his generation, is caught in transition between an inability to either excel in the old fixed forms, or ditch them and light out for new territory as confidently as Robert Creeley or Frank O'Hara were beginning to do. These small, these micro-effects of echo, image, and syllable in a pantoum and its translations can be read against a wider political history of Orientalism which should not be allowed to drown their specificity as realized works. Equally they cannot be understood outside a history of verse form in which Baudelaire, little read or vilified in his lifetime, turned out retrospectively to have played a key architectural role, even, as here, in his inspired borrowings and adapted forms.

His poem is characteristically rich, full of scents, textures, sensory interminglings. Just as perfumes and sounds "tournent" synaesthetically in the evening air, so the "tige," the stem at the end of line 1, secretes itself only to reappear inside the "vertige," the dizziness of line 4, part of an incessant, "triste et beau" kaleidoscope of openings and closings. Later the "soir" of the poem's title will reappear in "reposoir," by way of "encensoir." And so on. These repetitions-with-variations are expressed simultaneously by the imagery of the content, and the shapes, mirroring, and narrowings of the pantoum's form. The effect is auditory but also phenomenological, as inner and outer become deliberately confused, or reversed. While the poor heart, the "cœur tendre," is exposed to the void, the whole of the sky shrinks into the form of a "reposoir," though whether this altar is for an outdoor Mass or for the indoor administration of the last rites is left deliberately unclear. Baudelaire's habitual drift is always downwards to the grave, corpses, vaults, worms; everything in his world is a *memento mori*; and so many of his titles, as with "Harmonie du Soir," undermine with a Poesque glee the blandness of their conventional, initial associations. It is also characteristic of Baudelaire that, while the poem is in thrall to the death-drive and a neurasthenically alienated subjectivity, the forms and scents and weather of the world are not banished, but contained and made vivid by the incantatory power of the verse. The pantoum is inherently Baudelairean. It is surprising that, as far as we can tell, he only wrote the one.

Moving to larger and more conjectural issues to do with verse and signification, the pantoum, perhaps more than any other verse form, exposes the basic failure of language as the bearer or sign of reality, failure from which poetic expression wrests, if not victory, then consolation. Words haunt or describe or signal the things that they cannot in themselves be. Yet as words, so to speak, fall away from things, their own quiddity as language is reasserted, an assertion compounded in the armature, or perhaps more accurately the exoskeleton, of fixed verse forms. Perversely, this redoubling of distance between word and object creates, in the rich layering and interweaving of a form such as the pantoum, a phantom reappearance of the object, not this time as the intended, always failing target of words propelled through time, but something born inside the poem as a miniature entity.

John Ashbery has made more productive use of the form than any other poet since 1945, beginning with "Pantoum" in his first collection, *Some Trees* (1956), and returning to the form as recently as 2007, in *A Worldly Country*. Ashbery is also the American poet most attuned to the history and resources of French poetry from Baudelaire to Rimbaud and Surrealism, as is made obvious by his entitling one collection of poems, *Hotel Lautréamont* (1992). The poem that gives the book its title is a long pantoum. (Moreover, the illustration chosen for the cover reproduces a tiny collage by Joseph Cornell from the 1930s, thereby pointing up the tradition of the art-box mentioned earlier.) One intriguing aspect of this particular pantoum is that it breaches the etiquette whereby a poem self-refers by articulating a particular form, but does not confuse itself or the reader by alluding to other poetic forms which are not to be articulated. Ashbery's poem breaks this rule by being a pantoum ostensibly, in part, about the ballad form. It begins "Research has shown that ballads were produced by all of society / working as a team," and instances "Windsor Forest," "The Wife of

Usher's Well," and, even less plausibly, a violin concerto by Sibelius. By intoning a
set of assertions all of which could immediately be contested as ludicrous (while
deploying expertly the vestiges of a possible rational connection), Ashbery's poem
foregrounds one form of the disjunction between word and object proposed above as
an underlying model for poetry of all kinds. The focus on the ballad may in part be
read as a feint which ultimately spells an inward commentary on the pantunite form,
as the poem works to turn a negative manifestation of entrapment, which is social
and psychological, into the positive formal and aesthetic entrapment of objects in a
verbal box, which is the achieved pantoum. A loose dialectic of vocabularies moves
the poem forward. The first vocabulary is distinctively twentieth-century and
Modernist, as instanced by society allegedly working as a team, and continuing
through phrases such as "The people . . . knew what they wanted," "a more modern
note," "collective euphoria," "our commonalty," "history," "error," all echoing the
discourses of Marxism and social engineering that by 1992 were regarded as having
failed completely. The second vocabulary is that of a rediscovered past vitality beneath
modernity, exemplified by the old verse form of the ballad, and by such observations
as "In troubled times one looked to the shaman or priest for comfort and counsel"
(26). This harking back to "older, lighter concerns" collides however with a third
vocabulary of superficially purposeful momentum, striated by a surrealistic absurdism
that undermines any idea of a stable political credo while reasserting the powers of
poetry itself, a characteristic move in Ashbery's work:

> But it is shrouded, veiled: we must have made some ghastly error.
> You mop your forehead with a rose, recommending its thorns.
> Must we thrust ever onward, into perversity?
> Only night knows for sure; the secret is safe with her.
>
> (ll. 57–60)

The implication is a quiet manifesto for the pantoum as exemplar of poetry in its
politically impotent but aesthetically creative distance from customary language and
social practice. The handkerchief of thorns is a dream-object, the kind of impossible
thing made possible first by Symbolism, as in Baudelaire's synaesthesia and Isidore
Ducasse, Comte de Lautréamont's own wild conjunction of the umbrella and the
sewing-table, and rediscovered as a resource beneath the paradoxically more outworn
credo of a later period, that of Modernism. Here "Hotel Lautréamont" shows a consonance with what Ashbery has termed the "other traditions" of semi-neglected
writers such as Thomas Lovell Beddoes, Raymond Roussel, Nicholas Moore, and
others whose rhetorical skills are inseparable from dream, willful eccentricity and
perversity. In the end, not that there is such a thing, Ashbery is a Romantic modern.
  John Ashbery's poem can profitably be contrasted with a pantoum by his near
contemporary, fellow-American poet, Donald Justice. Justice is interested in pessimism as intrinsic to lyric poetry, and the pantoum, with its chant-like repetitions and
faintly eerie form, lends itself to this interest. (The best pantoums, such as Baudelaire's

and Ashbery's, are poems of unease. To Austin Dobson, it had been a caprice.) Justice's "Pantoum of the Great Depression" contains mild ironies that are very close to Ashbery's in tone: "There were the usual celebrations, the usual sorrows. / I don't remember all the particulars" (ll.10–11). However, in this pantoum the massive pressures of history, more specifically the Depression of the 1930s, come to subjugate these neo-Prufrockian ironies and dominate the poem:

> We did not ourselves know what the end was.
> The Great Depression had entered our souls like fog.
> We had our flaws, perhaps a few private virtues.
>
> But we did not ourselves know what the end was.
> People like us simply go on.
> We have our flaws, perhaps a few private virtues.
> But it is by blind chance only that we escape tragedy.
>
> (ll.30–36)

The overt repetitions of the pantoum constrain by their nature the operations of "chance," implying that the escape will not happen.

In conclusion, pantoums are still written, but the influence of Baudelaire's remains inescapable. In "Contre-Baudelaire," a section of his most recent collection *Starlight* (2010), the Australian poet John Tranter offers fifty-six versions of poems from Baudelaire's *Les Fleurs du Mal* which in some ways "echo" and in some respects "respond and sometimes argue with" the original (135). Tranter takes apparently outrageous, though often carefully judged and in consequence outrageous, liberties with the original. "Les Chats," for example, translated as "Goats and Monkeys," begins

> Top executives and poets alike, when they
> grow old, keep pets: marmosets, little horses
> with ribbons around their necks, capybaras.
>
> (ll.1–3)

The Noah's Ark of pigs, monkeys, dogs, and other creatures that follow, excreting as they go, fouls the attic of the poem so as to both exemplify and parody my picturing of a poem as a box of imagistic tricks in the way that the Baudelaire–Joseph Cornell doll's house tradition supports. Equally canny is Tranter's take on Baudelaire's "La Géante," retitled in translation "Big Girl's Blouse," (163) in which the giantess's body

> would grow a foot a day, her legs
> swell like tree trunks, and her childish play would
> lay waste to housing estates.
>
> (ll.5–7)

This deliberate travesty of the original, not that the original lacked for outlandishness and strategic bad taste, does no injustice to Baudelaire in part because its chosen forms of humor are those initiated by the New York School of John Ashbery, Frank O'Hara, and their contemporaries. John Tranter's *Starlight* is dedicated to Ashbery and includes a reworking of the latter's long poem "Clepsydra." This circularity takes nothing away from Tranter's own vitality and originality as a poet (his novel in verse *The Floor of Heaven* is an absolute masterpiece among poems in English from the last few decades), but indicates simply that individual poems and poets of substance are in constant, knowing engagement with the shifting history of the forms they use and inhabit. Tranter interprets the pantoum as a form initiated by Baudelaire and mediated by Ashbery. Indeed, his choice of goats, monkeys, and so on as substitutes for Baudelaire's cats may be consciously or otherwise influenced by a pantoum of Ashbery's, "Phantoum" (2007) which features goats, emus, auks, and—Baudelairean choice—an albatross. To revert to the relatively clunky translation by Roy Campbell sampled earlier, it is clear that the clumsiness was a function of the piece being written at a moment of transition in poetic practice. It is possible that John Ashbery's frequent and deliberate clumsiness-that-isn't, his penchant for bathos, comic *bouleversements* and so on, are, in part, pre-emptive strikes against his writing being changed in its effects by historical factors external to it. John Tranter is another poet with a fine-tuned receptiveness to such transitions, as is shown in his reworking of Baudelaire's "Harmonie du Soir" (191):

> Flowers reek like perfume in a bowl.
>   Country and western, steel guitars, and worse,
> songs that moan and echo like a curse.
>   The sky is blue, like fifties rock and roll.

(ll.5–8)

It hardly needs me to point out that this departs from both the original French, and from Baudelaire's classic left-margin lineation. However Tranter instates something like Baudelaire's own fascination with clanging dissonance, mechanical reproduction, bad taste, and rotten-hearted sentiment from a context of contemporary retro-reassurance. It is arguably more true to the original by these lights than a dictionary-perfect retrieval of monstrances, censers, and so forth might have been.

The pantoum, therefore, merits rescue from its relegation to unread manuals on verse practice and the more obscure corners of literary importation. This is partly because it is still a live option to poets in a tradition from Symbolism to the New York School and its inheritors. Moreover, as it has been the intention of this essay to show, the very distance of the form from supposedly more naturalistic poetic shapes and ways of address, the pantoum's very eccentricity, highlights issues to do with the connection between linguistic expression and material reality in a uniquely intense way. The potential of the form has not been exhausted, and as the editor of one *Poet's Manual* writes, there remains, latent, "a mood of obsessive and threatening horror in a pantoum that has not yet been written" (Stillman 70). But, at the end of the day, the pantoum is unique among verse forms, in that its claim to lasting interest rests on its having been a form chosen by one of the greatest poets of the last two centuries for the purposes of a single exercise. All subsequent pantoums of note are "phantoums," in fact the best most of all, reminding us in the very exoticism and weirdness of their imagery, their ghost-train vertigo and chanted repetitions, their claustrophobic vaults and enigmatic boxes, of Baudelaire, the originator of the "other" tradition they revivify.

REFERENCES AND FURTHER READING

Ashbery, John. *Hotel Lautréamont*. Manchester, UK: Carcanet, 1992.

Ashbery, John. *Other Traditions*. Cambridge, MA: Harvard University Press, 2001.

Ashbery, John. *A Wordly Country*. Manchester, UK: Carcanet, 2007.

Baudelaire, Charles. *Œuvres complètes*. Paris: Seuil, 1968.

Brown, Richard. "Rabbit." *James Alley Blues*. Recorded 1927. Lyrics transcribed from *Anthology of American Folk Music*, ed. Harry Smith. Washington DC: Smithsonian Folkways Recordings, 1997.

Campbell, Roy. http.fleursdumal.org/poem/142. See also Campbell, *Poems of Baudelaire*. New York: Pantheon, 1952.

Dobson, Austin. "In Town." As given in *The Making of a Poem: A Norton Anthology of Poetic Forms*, ed. Mark Strand and Eavan Boland. New York: Norton, 2000. 45–47.

Douglas, Alfred. www.poemhunter.com/poem/harmonie-du-soir.

Dowson, Ernest. *The Poems of Ernest Dowson*. London: John Lane, The Bodley Head, 1911.

Dylan, Bob. www.bobdylan.com/#/songs. (Lineation adjusted to match what is heard in recordings, rather than given on the page.)

Eliot, T.S. *Poems 1909–1925*. London: Faber and Gwyer, 1925.

Justice, Donald. "Pantoum of the Great Depression." As given in *The Making of a Poem: A Norton Anthology of Poetic Forms*, ed. Mark Strand and Eavan Boland. New York: Norton, 2000. 47–48.

Kizer, Carolyn. "Parents' Pantoum." As given in *The Making of a Poem: A Norton Anthology of Poetic Forms*, ed. Mark Strand and Eavan Boland. New York: Norton, 2000. 48–49.

Preminger, Alex and Brogan, T.V.F., eds. *New Princeton Encyclopedia of Poetry and Poetics*. Princeton: Princeton University Press, 1993.

Stillman, Frances. *The Poet's Manual and Rhyming Dictionary*. London: Thames and Hudson, 1966.

Tranter, John. *Starlight: 150 Poems*. Brisbane: University of Queensland Press, 2010.

21
"Gists and Piths"[1]
The Free-Verse Revolution in Contemporary American Poetry

Marie-Christine Lemardeley

Free verse is poetry devoid of any apparent constraint in its prosody (from the Greek *prosodia*: "tune," verse theory, the study of sound-patterning in verse), thus reducing the importance of meter, rhyme, and stanza. It breaks from the numerical models and scansion techniques of Latin and Greek poetry. Free verse contains the *turn* inherent in the etymology of the word verse (Latin, *versus*), while prose is a contraction of the Latin *proversus*, literally forward, as in "prosa oratio," a speech going straight ahead without turn. Different types of free verse highlight the diversity of its interpretations in twentieth-century American poetry, which have given rise to paradoxical notions of freedom and rhythmic organization, orality, and textuality. The most recent experiments in free verse include non-linear poetries questioning the distinction between verse and prose.

Oracular Verse

Free verse differs from blank verse, a type of unrhymed verse in iambic pentameter, and may be seen as heir to the tradition of oral poetry. "Sumerian, Akkadian, Egyptian, Sanskrit, and Hebrew poetries, all share one characteristic: in their texts, repetition and parallelism create prosodic regularity, while meter in any of its types does not yet regulate the verse" (Preminger and Brogan 425). Likewise, the long lines of the *Song of Solomon* as translated in the King James Bible (1611) are ancestors of modern free verse.

They certainly inspired Walt Whitman in "Song of Myself"; indeed Whitman's *Leaves of Grass* (1855) can be considered as a watershed in the practice of free verse.

A Companion to Poetic Genre, First Edition. Edited by Erik Martiny.
© 2012 John Wiley & Sons, Ltd. Published 2012 by John Wiley & Sons, Ltd.

His verses echoing the cadences of the King James Bible and relying on anaphora and catalog exemplify a distance taken with the rigidity of meter. In "Proud Music of the Storm," Walt Whitman ponders the musical intertwining of sound and sense:

> Then I woke softly,
> And pausing, questioning awhile the music of my dream,
> And questioning all those reminiscences, the tempest in its fury,
> And all the songs of sopranos and tenors,
> And those rapt oriental dances and religious fervor,
> And the sweet varied instruments, and the diapason of organs,
> And all the artless plaints of love and grief and death,
> I said to my silent curious soul out of the bed of the slumber-chamber,
> Come, for I have found the clew I sought so long;
> Let us go forth refresh'd amid the day,
> Cheerfully tallying life, walking the world, the real,
> Nourish'd henceforth by our celestial dream.
>
> (ll.143–54)

The "clew" to his new-found form is what he calls "rhythmus," another name for the affective cadence giving shape to the subtle and unpredictable movements of the singular soul:

> And I said, moreover,
> Haply what thou hast heard O soul was not the sound of winds,
> Nor dream of raging storm, nor sea-hawk's flapping wings nor harsh scream,
> Nor vocalism of sun-bright Italy,
> Nor German organ majestic, nor vast concourse of voices, nor layers of harmonies,
> Nor strophes of husbands and wives, nor sound of marching soldiers,
> Nor flute, nor harps, nor the bugle-calls of camps,
> But to a new rhythmus fitted for thee,
> Poems bridging the way from Life to Death, vaguely wafted in night air, uncaught, unwritten,
> Which let us go forth in the bold day and write.
>
> (ll.155–64)

While discarding the worn reservoir of Romantic metaphors he heralds a new type of prosody that does not rely on known melodies but invents its own pace as it moves forward in as yet unwritten verse.

The long lines aim to stir the reader into identification with a freedom of speech typical of Nonconformity in the wake of Emerson and Thoreau. Whitman shares Emerson's ambitious project characterized by optimism, a certain innocence and a spiritual connection with nature. Emerson ascribes to the poet an eminent place in society and considers the poem an aspect of nature's presence: "For it is not meters, but a meter-making argument that makes a poem—a thought so passionate and alive that like the spirit of a plant or an animal it has an architecture of its own, and adorns nature with a new thing" (Emerson 450).

The irregular cadences of Whitman's "barbaric yawp" in *Leaves of Grass* contribute to the creation of a new American diction, in which soul and flesh are one:

> I celebrate myself, and sing myself,
> And what I assume you shall assume,
> For every atom belonging to me as good belongs to you.

(ll.1–3)

In Whitman's practice, free verse entails a notion of revolt and a spectacular liberation from tradition, in particular a tradition of reverence for European, especially British elders, quite in keeping with Emerson's cultural declaration of independence in "The American Scholar": "We have listened too long to the courtly muses of Europe" (70). The example of Walt Whitman inspired many modern poets to cast off the rigidities of a genteel tradition and give sanction to openness both in form and emotion.

Crisis in Poetry

The phrase "free verse" itself is ambiguous since "verse" designates both poetry and the lines that constitute a poem. As verse has long meant "metrical composition," free verse appears as a contradiction in terms. Free verse seems at first an approximate translation of the French symbolists' *vers libre*. In 1886 Gustave Kahn published two poems by Arthur Rimbaud, "Marine" and "Mouvement," in his Paris magazine *La Vogue*, as well as Jules Laforgue's translation of some of Whitman's *Leaves of Grass* and experiments by other French poets including Kahn himself.

Free verse was soon taken over by the American avant-garde. In the March 1913 issue of *Poetry*, published by Harriet Monroe in Chicago, F.S. Flint, quoting an unknown "Imagiste" (Pound), listed these characteristics of the movement:

(1)   direct treatment of the 'thing' whether subjective or objective;

(2)   use of absolutely no word that does not contribute to the presentation;

(3)   as regarding rhythm, to compose in the sequence of the musical phrase, not in the sequence of the metronome.

(in Preminger and Brogan 574)

This last precept focuses on the need to follow the natural cadences of language instead of trying to artificially fill the gaps imposed by pre-ordained metrical constraints. Pound points to the liberating aspect of free verse whose conspicuous goal is to undo the shackles of conventional metrical form, while disturbing the Victorian complacency associated with meter. The main object of his harsh and unfair criticism is Milton, as in chapter 5 of *ABC of Reading* in which he finds exception to one line:

When Milton writes
'Him who disobeys me disobeys'
he is quite simply, doing wrong to his mother tongue. He meant

Who disobeys him, disobeys me.

It is perfectly easy to understand WHY he did it, but his reasons prove that Shakespeare and several dozen other men were better poets. Milton did it because he was chock a block with Latin. He had studied his English not as a living language, but as something subject to theories.

(Pound, *ABC* 51)

Thus not only does Pound reject the regular meters of accentual-syllabic verse but he also dismisses stilted rhetoric, in favor of the condensation of the haiku-like image, as in his memorable poem:

In a Station of the Metro

The apparition   of these faces   in the crowd   :
Petals   on a wet, black   bough   .

Blanks and punctuation are actively involved in the poetic process, as is indicated by the clear orders he gives the printer in his letter to Harriet Monroe of March 30, 1913: "In the 'Metro' hokku, I was careful, I think, to indicate spaces between the rhythmic units, and I want them observed" (Pound, *Letters* 53).

Pound's appeal to a radically critical attitude to meter in the sense of Mallarmé's "Crisis in Poetry" (*Crise de vers*, 1896), was qualified by T.S. Eliot's remark in his "Reflections on *Vers Libre*" (1917) that free verse gains its power from a more or less hidden tension with the templates of metered poetry:

The most interesting verse which has yet been written in our language has been done either by taking a very simple form, like the iambic pentameter, and constantly withdrawing from it, or taking no form at all, and constantly approximating to a very simple one. It is this contrast between fixity and flux, this unperceived evasion of monotony, which is the life of free verse . . . the ghost of some simple meter should lurk behind the arras in even the 'freest verse'; to advance menacingly as we doze, and withdraw as we rouse. Or, freedom is only true freedom when it appears against the background of an artificial limitation.

(Eliot 187)

Such an interpretation of free verse has long been the norm, yet in *The Ghost of Meter. Culture and Prosody in American Free Verse*, 1993, Annie Finch recognizes the limits of such a constant reference to regular metrics:

The efforts of Whitman and Crane to establish a free-verse alternative to the norm of iambic pentameter fully achieved their goal in the mid-twentieth century. Sexton,

Ginsberg and the other poets of midcentury wrote free verse more or less on their own terms, referring back to meter much less, and less urgently, than any poets before them.

(132)

The question is not so much to distinguish free verse from metered verse, as to analyze how free verse creates rhythm by other means than the feet inherited from Latin and Greek versification: "the prosody of free verse is rhythmic organisation by other than numerical modes" (Hartman 24–25). As Pound declares in *Canto* LXXXI: "(To break the pentameter, that was the first heave)" (*Cantos* 532).

The accusation of formlessness was entered by Robert Frost who famously quipped that writing free verse is like playing tennis with the net down. In "The Figure a Poem Makes," an essay introducing his *Collected Poems* of 1939, Frost recognizes only one type of verse written in iambic meter: "All that can be done with words is soon told. So also with meters—particularly in our language where there are virtually but two, strict iambic and loose iambic" (17).

Frost felt his desire for order threatened by free verse's attempt to approximate natural speech, when to him poetry's aim should be to create a subtle interplay between "the sounds of sense" and the regularity of meter:

If one is to be a poet he must learn to get cadences by skilfully breaking the sounds of sense with all their irregularity of accent across the regular beat of the meter. Verse in which there is nothing but the beat of the meter furnished by the accents . . . we call doggerel. Verse is not that. Neither is it the sound of sense alone.

(Thompson 80)

Pound himself came to condemn free verse: "*vers libre* has become as prolix and verbose as any of the flaccid varieties that preceded it . . . The actual language and phrasing is often as bad as that of our elders without even the excuse that the words are shovelled in to fill metric pattern or to complete the noise of a rhyme-sound" (Pound quoted by Perloff in Bernstein, *Close Listening* 86). As Eliot had already observed in his 1917 "Reflections," "there is only good verse, bad verse and chaos.." Finally, despite their divergent points of view Pound, Eliot, and Frost agreed on the rejection not of forms but of "dead form."

Poems for the Eye and for the Ear

The attempt to capture the naturalness of everyday speech, and claim it as the American idiom, incited William Carlos Williams to resist abstraction: "When Williams calls *Paterson* "a reply to Greek and Latin with the bare hands" he is identifying his poem as an attempt to end the split between American writing, speech, and landscape by getting rid of the English and European lamination" (Quartermain 14–15). In the article on "free verse" that he wrote for the first edition of the *Princeton*

Encyclopedia of Poetry and Poets in 1965, Williams argued that irregularity was the distinctive feature of free verse:

> The irregularity involves both the eye and the ear. Whether the measure be written down with a view to the appearance of the poem on the printed page or to the sound of the words as spoken or sung is of no consequence so long as the established irregularity is maintained.
>
> (in Preminger and Brogan 78)

Nevertheless the realization that no art form can really be "free" prompted him to invent the "variable foot," "as a means of bringing the warring elements of freedom and discipline together . . . Thus as in speech, the prosodic pattern is evaluated by criteria of effectiveness and expressiveness rather than mechanical syllable counts" (in Preminger and Brogan 289). But the "variable foot" failed to account for his own work and was not pursued. In order for the American vernacular to materialize, Williams devised short poems whose simplicity of diction evokes the core of American experience and stems from his objectivist credo of "no ideas but in things," which does not mean that ideas do not exist but that they must be embodied as is intimated in the title of his philosophical essay *The Embodiment of Knowledge*. Yet in such an emblematic poem as "The Red Wheelbarrow," it is not the naturalness that is striking but the careful framing of the object that turns it into a fresh object of vision, in the manner of Marcel Duchamp's Ready-mades.

Combining Whitman's long prophetic verse with imagistic surrealistic sparks, Allen Ginsberg's "Hebraic-Melvillian bardic breath" in *Howl* (1959) provides a daring alternative to the implicit norm of iambic pentameter. His famous motto "First thought best thought" does not do justice to the careful composition of his verse but insists on the effect of spontaneity that he aims to convey thus establishing a sort of parallel between free verse and free jazz: "Spontaneous insight—the sequence of thought-forms passing naturally through ordinary mind—was always motif and method of these compositions" (Ginsberg, *Collected Poems* XX). Relying heavily on juxtaposition, Ginsberg's poetry revives Pound's ideogrammic method. The syntactical condensation imparts, in Pound's phrase, a sense of "direct presentation." Long rhapsodic lines, combined with condensed imagistic detail, imitate the rhythms of speech: "I saw the best minds of my generation destroyed by madness, starving hysterical naked" (*Collected Poems* 1). Regarding his poem "Wichita Vortex Sutra," Ginsberg equates his declamation with the random moves of a road-trip: "Page arrangement notates the thought-stops, breath-stops, runs of inspiration, changes of mind, startings and stoppings of the car." Free verse becomes a seismograph of emotions, creating gaps between words by unusual juxtapositions. In 1988 American composer Philip Glass brilliantly set "Wichita Vortex Sutra" to music before including it in an opera entitled *Hydrogen Jukebox* which features Allen Ginsberg reading. In what he calls his "improvised poetics," Allen Ginsberg constantly wonders "where to break the line . . . Actually it is a natural speech rhythm that comes when you are speaking slowly, interestedly to a friend. With the kind of breaks that are hesitancies waiting for the next thought to articulate itself" (*Composed on the Tongue* 18–20). The act of reading, especially when it does not erase the "hesitancies" (a Melvillian term reminiscent of Billy Budd's stammer), mimics the composition itself and becomes part of the poetic process.

Removing the Masks

After hearing Ginsberg at a public reading in San Francisco, Robert Lowell, already an acclaimed New England poet, chose to address his *taedium vitae* explicitly and somewhat shockingly at the time in *Life Studies* (1959). The openness of his "confessional poetry" was mirrored in his choice of free verse, as a means to emulate the candor he admired both in Ginsberg's *beat* rantings and Elizabeth Bishop's reticent poems. Although a close study of his verse shows it is highly structured, the tone of casualness prevails due to "light stresses, falling rhythms and internal rhymes" (Perloff, *Poetic Art* 172–74). The last poem of *Life Studies* "Skunk Hour" is highly condensed and at the same time memorably provocative:

> A car radio bleats,
> "Love, O careless Love . . ."
> I hear
> my ill-spirit sob in each blood cell,
> as if my hand were at its throat . . .
> I myself am hell; nobody's here—
>
> (ll.31–36)

Interestingly enough, Lowell, like Pound, considered Flaubert, with his search for "le mot juste," as an absolute model: "I felt that the best style for poetry was none of the many poetic styles in English, but something like the prose of Chekhov or Flaubert" (Lowell, *Collected Prose* 227).

Most of Anne Sexton's poems in *To Bedlam and Part Way Back* (1960) are written in a similar vein. Sylvia Plath who, like Sexton, attended Lowell's creative-writing classes at Boston University, also used free verse relying on the power of vivid metaphor. Free verse is then romanticized into a figure of revolt against the homogenized 1950s. The "free" of free verse has come to be identified with sexual freedom, revolt against the Vietnam War, and women's liberation.

Adrienne Rich's experiments with free verse, and the expressive value she gave to pauses and silences, demonstrate the vitality of free verse in American poetry in the second half of the twentieth century. Rich's feminist awakening chose the channel of free verse to assert itself. At a poetry reading in 1964, she concluded a speech entitled "Poetry and Experience" as follows:

Instead of poems *about* experiences I am getting poems that *are* experiences, that contribute to my knowledge and my emotional life even while they reflect and assimilate it. In my earlier poems I told you, as precisely and eloquently as I knew how, about something; in the more recent poems something is happening, something has happened to me and, if I have been a good parent to the poem, something will happen to you who read it.

(Rich, *Adrienne Rich's Poetry and Prose* 165)

Poetry as experience means the contract with the reader has changed. Instead of recognizing predetermined patterns, the reader of free verse experiences new configurations of emotion and meaning. Tentativeness and imperfection are preferred to eloquence. "The Mirror in Which Two Are Seen as One" from *Diving into the Wreck* (1973) consists of sixty-six lines of irregular length and rhythm, with few traditional signs of punctuation except in the first end-stopped line. The absence of signs to bring the stanzas to a close reinforces the impression that the poem is not a product but a process, as if experience were recorded with the urgency of life itself, the reader being left with the task of choosing when to introduce stops for breath. In "Cartographies of Silence" from *The Dream of a Common Language* (1978), Rich asserts the power of "silence not absence" (28), and the need for words out of which a truth can be born in all its incompleteness:

> what in fact I keep choosing
> are these words, these whispers, conversations
> from which time after time the truth breaks moist and green.
>
> (ll.94–96)

Free verse allows for the conjunction of apparent spontaneity and a resolute search for truth, that follows the groping and erratic paths of human uncertainties.

The fact that several contemporary poets turned to free verse after composing regular meter seems to indicate a desire to break loose from tradition, thus reproducing the American *epos* of emancipation from the English masters. Since it is not guided by meter and rhyme nor contained by stanzas, free verse relies on the reader's participation; the performance of the poem whether it be read aloud or in silence depends on the reader's/listener's involvement for its realization. For the irregularity to exist it has to be sustained by the reader's attention.

Writing Is Text not Lines

Free verse is very demanding of the reader's participation and finally the question remains what distinguishes free verse from prose:

Free verse is the introduction into the continuous flow of prose language, which has breaks determined entirely by syntax and sense, of another kind of break, shown on the page by the start of a new line, and often indicated in a reading of the poem by a slight pause. When we read prose, we ignore the fact that every now and then the line ends, and we have to shift our eyes to the beginning of the next line. We know that if the same text were printed in a different typeface, the sentence would be broken up differently with no alteration in the meaning. But in free verse, the line on the page has an integrity and function of its own. This has important consequences for the movement and hence the meaning of the words.

(Attridge 172)

Such an emphasis on the importance of the line in free verse paves the way for a minimalist definition of poetry, which leaves the question open-ended.

In free as in metered verse, enjambment is used to draw attention to syntactical units, often by forceful disjunction. Line division substitutes for punctuation and creates meaningful equivocations: "when lineation goes against rather than with the syntax—a phenomenon for the eye rather than for the ear—a semantic shift takes place" (Perloff, *Dance of the Intellect* 95). This is often the case in poems written by Objectivists (Cid Corman, Robert Creeley, George Oppen, Lorine Niedecker), in which the syntax goes against the line, thus questioning its integrity.

However diverse its forms in twentieth-century American poetry, the common feature of free verse is lineation. Doing away with the orderly stanzas of fixed forms, free verse underscores the line. But the multiple types of free verse tend to make this emphasis on the line somewhat fragile. The Objectivist conviction put forward in Charles Olson's "Projective Verse" (1950), that "form is never more than an extension of content" and the notion of the page as a field of forces ("composition by field") results in focusing on words and even syllables as the essential energy of the poem. As well as being indebted to Pound's emphasis on clarity and precision, the Objectivists also abide by Williams's conception of the poem as "a small (or large) machine made of words." Experiments in concrete poetry and poems for the eye such as E. E. Cummings's question the validity of the line as a minimal constituent of free verse.

Indeed the Language poets (Charles Bernstein, Ron Silliman, Bruce Andrews, Susan Howe, Lyn Hejinian, and others) adopt a more radical stance towards free verse and stretch it to the limits, blurring the boundaries between poetry and prose. The importance of lineation as well as the notion of presence are forcefully questioned by the *Language Poets* writing in a renewed Poundian vein and in light of Gertrude Stein's experiments with grammar.

In *Content's Dream*, Charles Bernstein emphasizes the music of the poem "the music being hearing the sound *come into* meaning rather than a play with already existing meanings by way of meter" (391). But music does not mean harmony or regularized stresses; the prosody of nonmetrical verse relies heavily on what Bernstein calls "distress and asymmetry . . . dissonance and irregularity, rupture and silence constitute a rhythmic force (or aversion of force)" (Bernstein, *Close Listening* 14).

Bernstein rejects the notion of a poetry of presence in favor of a radical search for meaning that includes artifice: "In Stein's modernist composition, the meaning is not something seated *behind* the words, but something revealing itself *in* the words, to formulate this in a way that echoes both Otto Weininger and Ludwig Wittgenstein" (Bernstein, *Poetics* 145). Steeped in Michael Fried's *Artifice of Absorption*, or Claude Lévi-Strauss's *Tristes Tropiques* Bernstein blends theoretical pronouncements and random notes without trying to hide the discontinuities. No unique self or voice holds his verse together; language becomes opaque again, by being rid of the unifying power of habit. The fake transparencies of everyday speech are held up to close scrutiny and the verse is free also to question the univocity of meaning: "I care most about poetry that disrupts business as usual, including literary business: I care most for poetry as dissent." In other words, as Peter Nicholls aptly underlines, the Language poets value what Eliot rejected, the very "uprooting" of language, the failure to "digest and express new objects, new groups, of objects, new feelings, new aspects" (Eliot quoted by Nicholls 24). They value a form of immersion into a milieu bared of distinctive, personal qualities.

A convincing example of such play at the borders of the political and the personal, poetry and prose, is Hejinian's *My Life* written under arbitrary formal constraints. *My Life* was first published in 1978 when Lyn Hejinian was thirty-seven: it then comprised thirty-seven sections composed of thirty-seven sentences. Eight years later, the author added eight sections and eight sentences in each section. The count however is never put forward as in the OULIPO (*Ouvroir de Littérature Potentielle*) designs whose architecture is kept secret. *My Life* presents a textual surface whose genre is difficult to define. The text opens with: "*A pause, a rose, something on paper* A moment yellow, just as four years later, when my father returned home from the war, the moment of greeting him, as he stood at the bottom of the stairs, younger, thinner than when he had left, was purple—" (Hejinian, *My Life* 7). Conflating a personal memory and the elusiveness of remembrance in an association of colors, the texture relies on insistent repetition: "*A pause, a rose, something on paper*" plays the part of a title beside the text and that of a leitmotiv inside it. Only defined by the duration of its author's life since the number of chapters and sentences grows with the years, the text, if not interminable, eschews closure. The revolt against the rigidity of meter has turned into a rejection of closure posited as a means to resist the claustrophobia of sensations: "The experience of feeling overwhelmed by undifferentiated material is like claustrophobia. One feels panicky, closed in. The open text is one which both acknowledges the vastness of the world and is formally differentiating. It is the form that opens it, in that case" (Hejinian in Hoover 653). The publication in 2003 of *My Life in the Nineties*, testifies to the possibility of considering this autobiography as an ongoing process: "The lack of plot and love of detail should organize my life not according to years or hours but according to spots and stops" (14). The continuity of story and plot is challenged by an emphasis on contiguity.

Thus, by definition, free verse fosters multiplicity. The openness emblematized by Walt Whitman's obtrusive presence of the "Me, myself" has given way to a deliberate exposure of language as a field of dispassionate phrases not devoid of strangeness and irony. Such powerful poetic constructs defy the separation between free verse and prose, poem, and text, and show that free verse after revolutionizing poetry by introducing the rhythms of American speech is now re-empowering prose with the density of verse.

NOTE

1 "A Japanese student in America, on being asked the difference between prose and poetry, said: Poetry consists of gists and piths." Ezra Pound, *"Dichten = Condensare,"* ABC of Reading 92.

REFERENCES AND FURTHER READING

Attridge, Derek, *Poetic Rhythm: An Introduction.* Cambridge: Cambridge University Press, 1995.

Bernstein, Charles, ed., *Close Listening: Poetry and the Performed Word.* New York: Oxford University Press, 1998.

Bernstein, Charles, *Content's Dream. Essays 1975–1984.* Evanston: Northwestern University Press, 1986.

Bernstein, Charles, *A Poetics.* Cambridge, MA: Harvard University Press, 1992.

Easthope, Anthony and John O. Thompson, eds., *Contemporary Poetry Meets Modern Theory.* New York: Harvester, 1991.

Eliot, T.S., *To Criticize the Critic and Other Writings.* New York: Farrar, Straus & Giroux, 1965.

Emerson, Ralph Waldo, *Essays and Lectures.* New York: Library of America, 1983.

Finch, Annie, *The Ghost of Meter. Culture and Prosody in American Free Verse.* Ann Arbor: University of Michigan Press, 1993.

Frank, Robert and Henry Sayre, *The Line in Postmodern Poetry.* Urbana: University of Illinois Press, 1988.

Frost, Robert, *The Complete Poems.* New York: Holt, 1949; Cape, 1951.

Ginsberg, Allen, *Collected Poems, 1947–1980.* Penguin, 1987.

Ginsberg, Allen, *Composed on the Tongue.* Ed. Donald Allen, San Francisco: Grey Fox Press, 1983.

Ginsberg, Allen, *Howl, Original Draft Facsimile.* Ed. Barry Miles, New York: Harper, Row, 1986.

Hartman, Charles O., *Free Verse. An Essay on Prosody.* Princeton: Princeton University Press, 1980.

Hejinian, Lyn, *My Life.* Los Angeles: Green Integer, 2002.

Hejinian, Lyn, *My Life in the Nineties.* New York: Shark Books, 2003.

Hejinian, Lyn, "The Rejection of Closure," *The Language of Inquiry.* Berkeley: University of California Press, 2000. 40–58.

Hoover, Paul, ed., *Postmodern American Poetry. An Anthology.* New York: Norton, 1994.

Lowell, Robert, *Collected Poems.* Ed. Frank Bidart and David Gewanter. New York: Farrar, Straus and Giroux, 2003.

Lowell, Robert, *Collected Prose.* Ed. Robert Giroux. London: Faber 1987.

Nicholls, Peter, "Difference Spreading: From Gertrude Stein to $L=A=N=G=U=A=G=E$ Poetry," in *Contemporary Poetry Meets Modern Theory,* ed. Anthony Easthope and John O. Thompson. New York: Harvester, 1991. 116–27.

Perloff, Marjorie, *The Dance of the Intellect. Studies in the Poetry of the Pound Tradition.* Cambridge, MA: Cambridge University, 1985.

Perloff, Marjorie, *The Poetic Art of Robert Lowell.* Ithaca, NY: Cornell University Press, 1973.

Perloff, Marjorie, "After Free Verse. The New Nonlinear Poetries," in *Close Listening: Poetry and the Performed Word,* ed. Charles Bernstein. New York: Oxford University Press, 1998.

Pound, Ezra, *ABC of Reading* (1934). New York: New Directions, 1960.

Pound, Ezra, *The Cantos of Ezra Pound.* London: Faber, 1986.

Pound, Ezra, *The Letters of Ezra Pound, 1907–1941,* ed. D.D. Paige. London: Faber, 1951.

Pound, Ezra, *Literary Essays*, ed. T.S. Eliot (1935); rpt. New York: New Directions, 1968.

Preminger, Alex, *Princeton Encyclopedia of Poetry and Poetics*. Princeton: Princeton University Press, 1965.

Preminger, Alex and T.V.F. Brogan, *The New Princeton Encyclopedia of Poetry and Poetics*. Princeton: Princeton University Press, 1993.

Quartermain, Peter, *Disjunctive Poetics: From Gertrude Stein and Louis Zukofsky to Susan Howe*. Cambridge: Cambridge University Press, 1992.

Rich, Adrienne, *Adrienne Rich's Poetry and Prose*. Ed. Barbara Charlesworth Gelpi and Albert Gelpi. New York: Norton, 1993.

Rich, Adrienne, *Diving into the Wreck. Poems 1971–1972*. New York: Norton, 1973.

Rich, Adrienne, *The Dream of a Common Language. Poems 1974–1977*. New York: Norton, 1978.

Thompson, Lawrence, ed. *Selected Letters of Robert Frost*. New York: Holt, Rinehart and Winston, 1964.

Whitman, Walt. *Leaves of Grass*. Ed. Sculley Bradley and Harold Blodgett. New York: Norton, 1973.

22

The Emergent Prose Poem

Andy Brown

Defining the term, and locating the origins of the "prose poem" is a problematic business. There are but a few main critical texts on contemporary prose poetry—"there is not, currently, a full-length critical study of the British prose poem" (Santilli, *Citings* 20)—and only a handful of serviceable anthologies of the contemporary possibilities of the form. In his essay "Stepping into the Unknown," David Miller comments, on the possibilities of prose poetry, noting that: "The prose poem has a long history marked by important contributions from a large number of major poets, especially in France, where poets from Baudelaire and Rimbaud onwards have worked in the genre" (in Loydell and Miller 179). If Miller's origination of the prose poem in mid-nineteenth-century France is predictable—most scholars seem keen to place it here, after Aloysius Bertrand's *Gaspard de la Nuit* (1842) and Baudelaire's *Petits Poèmes en prose* (1869)—he does, at least, remind us that "the genre has been very much alive in Germany, Scandinavia, Latin America, Russia, Japan and the United States" (179).

Nikki Santilli's excellent study, *Such Rare Citings*, also links the prose poem to the German Romantic critical fragment and the French post-Symbolist tradition, although in her feature article "The Prose Poem in Great Britain," she confesses to being surprised from the selected writers' responses that their professed influence "was over-whelmingly French" (60). In *Poets' Prose: The Crisis in American Verse*, Stephen Fredman does not use the term "prose poem" at all, preferring the term "poets' prose." Whilst Miller finds Fredman's term "far too ambiguous and unspecific" (181), Fredman himself argues that the term "prose poem" is itself "unsatisfactory for two reasons: it is an oxymoron aimed at defamiliarizing lyric poetry, and it remains redolent of the atmospheric sentiment of French symbolism" (Fredman, vii). Other commentators (see Godbert, as well as Clements and Dunham) are at pains to assess definitions of the term "prose poem." Attempting such a definition is not my concern here: writers

A Companion to Poetic Genre, First Edition. Edited by Erik Martiny.
© 2012 John Wiley & Sons, Ltd. Published 2012 by John Wiley & Sons, Ltd.

ancient and modern have used poetic prose devices to write works that defy categorization—poetic prose, prose poem, set pieces, miscellanea, or even "writings" as Seamus Heaney has called his own prose poems.

French writers had experimented with such techniques in the 1700s, well before Aloysius Bertrand. Maurice de Guérin was writing prose poetry in the 1830s, prior to Bertrand, although de Guérin's works were only published posthumously in 1860 in *Journal, Lettres et Poèmes*. The consensual critical fixation on Bertrand as the originator of the form, and on the French Symbolist tradition as its epitome, is strange, because texts that share features in common with the prose poem date back much further. In the Bible, the Book of Job for instance consists of a prose prologue and epilogue, framing the main poetic body. In other Books, biblical history is broadly related in two main styles: the "Priestly" and the "Prophetic." The "Priestly" style is precise and official, detailing religious and legal rites, without imaginative narration or description; the "Prophetic" style, on the other hand, is narrative, dynamic, imaginative, and aesthetically heightened. Prophetic lessons, legends, and fictions are placed alongside facts.[1] Prose poetry also occurs in the early sacred texts of other cultures. The Hindu *Upanishads*, for example, have their own unique style. Their exposition takes four main forms: 1) dialogue with catechism, 2) narrative scenes, 3) similes, metaphors, illustrations, and 4) symbolism. Hymns, mantras, verses, and prose verses, are all to be found within.

Ancient prose poetry also occurs in secular books. The tenth-century *Pillow Book* of Sei Shonagan, is a list-like book akin to many present-day variations on the prose poem. Sei Shonagan's journal, describing life in a tenth-century Japanese court, records personal, everyday thoughts alongside official matters. Loosely structured, the *Pillow Book* utilizes listing, in ways that present day prose poets would acknowledge as antecedent: Elegant Things ("a white coat worn over a violet waistcoat"); Things that Cannot be Compared ("laughter and anger, the little indigo plant and the great philodendron"); Embarrassing Things ("a man proudly reciting his poor poetry"); and Pleasing Things ("Someone has torn up a letter and thrown it away. Picking up the pieces, one finds that many of them can be fitted together"). Such collections of jottings were part of a recognized genre of prose at the time: the Japanese literary form called *zuihitsu*, a style of free-associations, literally meaning "following the brush," but also meaning "miscellaneous writings" and "essay" (both terms that one finds in discussion of the contemporary prose poem).

The genre of *zuihitsu* evolved, from the classical Japanese texts to the Modernist era, supported by the emergence of literary journalism and a growing readership, into the "age of the *zuihitsu*" in the early twentieth century. Then it merged with Modernist, autobiographical, and popular literary styles, in the works of writers such as Uchida Hyakken (1889–1971), whose works play with autobiographical truth and modernist self-referentiality. There is also a Chinese tradition of such writings, and one might usefully read the work of the Korean-American writer Theresa Cha, whose autobiography *DICTEE* mixes ideograms, photographs, verse, prose, and prose poetry in a similarly miscellaneous fashion.

Much older, non-European prose poetry also appears in the form of Japanese *haibun*, originated by the Japanese monk and poet Matsuo Bashō (1644–94). Haibun is a combination of prose poem and haiku, traditionally written in the form of a travelogue. With its block of prose either topped, tailed, or interspersed with an ideogrammatic haiku, the *haibun* is a form of visual prose poetry that predates the European "origin" of the form by 200 years. Present tense, brevity, Zen "detachment," and pictorialization are all foregrounded, whilst the contrast between the density of the prose and the lightness of the haiku provides a harmonic intensity: the haiku amplifies the prose in a tangential fashion. American postmodernist poets, notably John Ashbery and Sheila E. Murphy, have since appropriated the form in the U.S. where it has emerged as the idiosyncratic "American Haibun," bearing only residual similarities to the traditional travelogue form.

There are other, non-western traditions of the prose poem, to be found in the Fabulistic style of the Russian Turgenyev, and his twentieth-century counterpart Solzenhytsen. One might also identify prose poetry in the euphoric, highly rhythmic, and image-heavy prose of earlier English literature, such as that of Thomas de Quincey (1785–1859), or the Protectorate clergyman Jeremy Taylor (1613–67). Whilst it might be anachronistic to attribute the term "prose poem" to all of these works, particularly as they predate the first usage of that term, they nonetheless are clear antecedents of the present-day prose poem.

It is to this "set piece" or "miscellaneous" definition of the prose poem that we might most usefully turn when faced with a piece of writing that is neither poetry nor prose, yet paradoxically contains elements of both fused with some other literary strategy. Prose poetry, like poetry, heightens rhythms, figuration, and the musical devices of language. As we shall discuss later, it also often heightens rhetorical strategies to enable the logic of the prose to emerge in the processes of the moment. The length of prose poems varies, but usually ranges from half of a page to three or four pages (those longer are often considered experimental prose or poetic prose, although John Ashbery's *Three Poems* are notably longer). In their comprehensive work, *An Introduction to the Prose Poem*, Clements and Dunham usefully summarize (with examples) these various miscellaneous approaches to the prose poem, including approaches such as: the Abecedary; Anecdote; Aphorism; Epistolary form; Essays; Extended Metaphors; Fables; Flash poems; List poems; Meditations; Monologue and Dialogue; Object poems; Rants; Sequences; Self-Referential poems; Surreal poems, and Variations on Themes. To these we might also usefully add the following set-pieces and brief examples:

Autobiographical	(Seamus Heaney, Lyn Hejinian)
Cubist	(Gertrude Stein)
Daybook and Diaristic	(David Lehman, Robert Lax)
Diagrammatic	(Robert Crawford, W.H. Auden)
Documentary	(Alice Oswald)
Flâneur	(Baudelaire)

Footnotes	(Stephen Berg)
Formal variations	(prose sonnets, prose sestinas etc.)
American Haibun	(John Ashbery, Sheila E. Murphy)
Historical	(David Jones)
Knots/Dialogue	(R.D. Laing, Maxine Chernoff)
Love Prose Poem	(J.L. Borges)
Palimpsests	(Tom Philips, Andy Brown)
Parable	(Russel Edson, J.L. Borges)
Shaggy Dog Tale	(John Ash)
Symbolist	(Rimbaud, Mallarmé)
Travelogues	(Raoul Schrott, Italo Calvino)

and any number of pre-existing textual devices such as dream diaries, recipes and instructions, and jokes, all of which appear in examples of the contemporary prose poem.

Some Defining Features

In *Such Rare Citings*, Nikki Santilli identifies the importance of "the frame" or "border" for the prose poem: "The frame is fore-grounded because it is the area common to both sides of the dialectic" (186). In John Burnside's prose poems, the frame or border negotiates the all-important movement between inner and outer worlds. In "Suburbs" (in *Common Knowledge*), for example, the border is present in the very locale itself—suburbs themselves being those borderlands "on the already mythical rim of the countryside." The liminality goes deep in "Suburbs," manifested in images of private, enclosed spaces and public exterior spaces; driveways, garden borders, walls, and fences ("a cat walking on fence rims"); windows, doors, drawn blinds and parted curtains; skins and pond edges. The narrator of "Suburbs" is forever "spying into" the domestic interior. They stand "At the edge of the wood" or listening to "conversations at gates and hedges," or thinking about "the Janus-Christ of thresholds and crossings."

Nikki Santilli also discusses some of the common rhetorical effects that characterize prose poetry, from the "Biblical Style," through to the contemporary, in particular the techniques of "furtherance," "leaping," "trailing," and "regression." "Furtherance" is a rhetorical inching forward to the "absent context" (154). A is paralleled by B. B reflects back to A whilst on to C etc. "The fractional advance suggests that the ground is being comprehensively covered" (154). Furtherance is "extension in any direction" (159), and leads to poetic patterning.

Both of the prose poem sequences in Burnside's *Common Knowledge*—"Annunciations" and "Suburbs"—use these devices. "Suburbs" begins, "Wet Sunday afternoon; after the rain a bible wind ripples the sheet puddles on Station Road; along the hedges by the girls' school an elaborate birdsong streams through the wet scent of roses, like a new form of music evolving out of water" (39). Furtherance is employed here, from one instance of wetness to the next; from "wet" to "rain," to "puddles" on the road, to birdsong "streaming" and the "wet scent." The paragraph mimetically achieves that which its last phrase says; it creates "a new form of music evolving out of water." The meaning of the prose poem literally emerges as each phrase listens to the previous and responds accordingly, in a developmental way, so that the prose poem tests its own way like a walker stepping out onto ice. The effect is described in different terms by Fredman as "the generative sentence" in his detailed exegesis of a single line from William Carlos Williams' *Kora in Hell*: "Beautiful white corpse of night actually!" (20). In Fredman's "generative sentence" the prose poem's grammar "leads the writing through a succession of ideas, resisting the gravitational pull of the complete thought" (Fredman 55).[2]

In the second sequence of prose poems, "Annunciations," John Burnside's archangel first appears as "almost invisible" (17), from "some near-liquid state" (19) and materializes further to become "possessed of an absolute beauty," until, "The scent of grass. The taste of seed, the tight feel of his own body, every sensation that convinced him of his own reality has begun to fade. His flight has become a memory, which he already knows is a form of self-deception" (23). The angel's evanescence; the annunciation; his gender; the physical and psychological state of the Virgin; each is furthered in Burnside's poem in the manner described by Santilli. There is no narrative moment of closure on the annunciation; there is no definable moment of conception. The Virgin simply "looks up. This is her moment. She is no longer a vessel; she has been filled and emptied again" before she "thinks of a dawn, happening somewhere else, before she disappears."

Furtherance in the prose poem is closely linked to the rhetorical device of "trailing," in which the last linguistic element, rather than the main subject of the sentence, generates the next sentence. This is clearly visible in Carolyn Forché's well-known prose poem "The Colonel." An unknown narrator visits a dictatorial colonel in Central America. This short prose poem begins:

> What you have heard is true. I was in his house. His wife carried a tray of coffee and sugar. His daughter filed her nails, his son went out for the night. There were daily papers, pet dogs, a pistol on the cushion beside him. The moon swung bare on its black cord over the house. On the television was a cop show. It was in English. Broken bottles were embedded in the walls around the house to scoop the kneecaps from a man's legs or cut his hands to lace. On the windows there were gratings like those in liquor stores.
>
> (20)

Here we have an important military man in a house which, perhaps, suggests a wife, who appears in the next sentence. We probably expect them to have children, and they do. A daughter and a son. Who presumably have a pet? Yes, a dog. And, anyway, don't shady dictatorial types always characteristically have an animal at their side? They also necessitate guns, and one is therefore made to appear. The strong image of the moon as a light-bulb, swinging bare on its black cord, introduces the idea of electricity. Hence an electric appliance, a television, in the next sentence. The same fulfillment of expectations occurs after the gruesome image of a man's hands "cut to lace." Lace conjures curtains, and curtains mean windows. And suddenly they are there: "cut his hands to lace. On the windows there were gratings," contrasting metal gratings with lace (as we shall see, also known as "regression"). More overt trailing, or *anadiplosis* (the end of one sentence continuing the next) is seen with the maid: "a gold bell was on the table for calling the maid. The maid brought green mangoes." So the prose poem emerges until the Colonel shockingly throws down some severed human ears; a final image which, of course, trails us right back to the start of the poem, and to *hearing*.

Santilli also describes "regression" as a defining rhetorical technique for the prose poet. Regression is "furtherance through perceived difference" (158), as in the "lace/gratings" example above. A good example comes at the start of Samuel Beckett's prose work *The Unnamable*:

> Where now? Who now? When now? Unquestioning. I, say I. Unbelieving. Questions, hypotheses, call them that. Keep going, going on, call that going, call that on. Can it be that one day, off it goes on, that one day I simply stayed in, in where, instead of going out, in the old way, out to spend day and night as far away as possible, it wasn't far.
>
> (267)

The differences and contradictions are self-evident: questions are followed by the word "unquestioning"; "going on" (that most Beckettian of endurance activities) contrasts with "going off" ("off it goes on," paradoxically); day contrasts with night; "staying in" with "going out," and getting "as far away as possible" contrasts yet again paradoxically with "far away" not being far at all. The effect is, of course, existentially unsettling, mimicking the constant movement of the Modernist mind that is doubtful of its own memories and processes. A more contemporary example of regression, and one which uses the "perceived difference" and contrast as a more positive way into memory, can be found in Jess Lee Kercheval's prose poem "Italy, October," which begins:

> To be here is to be where fruit you have never seen before grows on equally strange trees. The fruit is not, as you first thought, oranges, though it is orange in colour. Nor is it a tangerine or some strangely coloured apple. Then you see it in the market, each soft fruit cradled in its own nest of woven plastic.
>
> (in Clements and Dunham 29)

The poet throws us immediately into a territory of perceived difference: we have never seen the fruit before, or so we are told, let alone the "equally strange trees" on which they grow, which we also can't see. We know the poet is writing about themselves in the second person, but the "you" inevitably invokes "us" as readers, highlighting the differences of perception and memory. The poet continues this by contrasting the fruit we can't see with fruits that we know, and goes on to give the local name for the fruit "Kaki," after which "you think to look up kaki in your pocket Italian dictionary, which says it means persimmon." And now, through contrast of color, perceived texture and, crucially, through the differences that are signaled by language, we come to know what this strange poem fruit is: a persimmon. At this point, the writer's and reader's memories become conflated in yet a further dialogue of perceived difference: have I ever seen, held, smelled, eaten a persimmon? Are they like the writer says? How different are they to these other fruits? How strange are the trees? Is this prose poem a sort of persimmon itself? Linguistic "regression" here literally regresses us through our own memories and, through sensory expression, enables us to interrogate both our memories and the language we use to invoke them.

The effects of both furtherance and trailing share close similarities with Robert Bly's prose poem technique of "leaping." Fredman describes Bly's leaping as, "the considerable distance between associations, the distance the spark has to leap," noting how the technique "gives the lines their bottomless feeling, their space, and the speed of association increases the excitement of the poetry" (9). Examples of leaping in Bly's *Selected Poems* include the leap from images such as: waves on rocks, to ducks flying over the waves, to vultures "coasting" over the desert ("November Day at McClure's Beach," 90); an old, hollow, cottonwood stump, to "Its Siamese temple walls" ("A Hollow Tree," 91); a starfish, to dinosaurs, to a glacier "going sixty miles a year" ("The Starfish," 92); rolling waves on a beach, to lions "coming in steady," to an airplane sweeping "low over the African field at night, lost, no tin cans burning; the old woman stomps around her house on a cane, no lamp lit yet" ("Calm Day at Drakes' Bay," 93), and many others. The surprising nature of Bly's leaps develop his imagery through rapid association: waves can clearly be associated with lions (powerfully attacking the beach, their manes blowing) and lions naturally link us to the African plains, but it takes controlled sound patterning and a leap, to connect American waves to the African plains.

Bly is also well known for writing "object poems." In his essay, "The Prose Poem as an Evolving Form," included in his *Selected Poems*, Bly describes the object poem in prose as one that "centres itself not on story or image but on the object, and it holds onto its fur, so to speak" (199). He cites Francis Ponge as his predecessor in this form, but one could include others, such as Gertrude Stein in *Tender Buttons*. Ponge himself strikes an ardent ecologic pose in writing about object poems: "We have only to lower our standard of dominating nature, and to raise our standard of participating in it" (qtd. in Bly 200). Bly also distrusts this mind/world binary, arguing that the good object poem overcomes "the category-making mentality that sees everything in polarities: human and animal, inner and outer, spiritual and material, large and small" (201), a position in accord with Santilli's acknowledgment of the border as a defining feature of the prose poem. Bly sees his own object poems as partly focusing on "the changes the mind goes through as it observes" (201). Bly also posits some emergent properties in the prose poem for readers: "if three 'oh' sounds appear in the first sentence, intelligences below rational consciousness register these 'oh' sounds, even counts them, and will expect the following syllable to continue embodying the sound, or to modulate it" (203). The poet is, of course, alive to these expectations of sound, as well as to rhythms, tones, registers, and other musical effects in language. "The poem awakens expectations for each of these separate elements" (204) and the good poet controls the development of the patterns: the words almost take on a life of their own, and listen to their neighbors for consonances, assonance, echoes, and dissonances, looking for patterns within and from themselves.

This fact that all poets look for patterns in the signs of their poem is obvious, but its functions are foregrounded in the prose poem when the prose poet lacks recourse to other formal concerns (stanzaic shape, verse form, meter, and other prosodic effects) most commonly associated with lineated verse. It is also most clearly seen in the rhetorical function of metonymy in the prose poem. Metonymy is an essential device for the prose poet, as it deals with synecdochal details standing in for the absent whole. The conjuring of the absent context is a necessary feature of words and of prose poems, as Santilli has argued:

> the Romantic fragment provides the ideological basis for the prose poem form. Its concern with the nature of truth; a device to represent totality as the only possible approximation to this idea and the fragmentary way in which this is achieved; the principles guiding the parameters of the form and the absence of the work itself are all common properties of both type of composition.
>
> (*Citings* 39)

The metonymic development of an object in prose is a parallel for the prose poem as a fragment to its whole. For John Burnside, for example, metonyms of the "domestic commonplace" characterize much of his early work. In the prose poem sequence "Annunciations," the Virgin is "preoccupied with some domestic chore. Behind her is a household of things: objects she has used but never seen: earthenware, knives, linen" (19). Similar illuminations of the everyday recur in another lineated verse poem in this collection, as in:

> Late afternoon in October:
> light feathers the kitchen walls,
> finds long-lost cousins
> in saucepans and colanders
>
> (62)

where "feathers" and "light" recall the presence of the angel of "Annunciations" and the "saucepans and colanders" echo its "household things." This trope also finds echoes in "Suburbs," in which we read of the "kinship of everyday objects . . . surfacing, now and always, into the moment" (47); "surfacing" implying a rise from the depths of their own *othered* (and perhaps only fleetingly knowable) being, as well as a rise from the depths ("The deep house") of language. These commonplace objects, suddenly made apparent and mysterious are also present in the spied-on interiors of suburban houses "of people we imagined were rich: interiors of perfect stillness, unbearably tidy; Imari bowls and baby grand pianos, gloves on hall tables; mirrors; paintings of boats and landscapes" (42). Here they possess space ("even the space in the room seemed nothing other than an additional item"), if only to be possessed themselves; to become possessions, "capable of being polished and insured" (42).

The prose poem—like the suburbs in-between city and countryside—is a liminal zone between reality and imagination. The suburbs and the poem are almost one, "this space, with its locked doors and drawn blinds, belongs to my simple idea of order, which is nothing more than a notion of worthwhile and calculable risk" (48). If the things of "Suburbs" seem perhaps domestically "safe" rather than "risky"— growing plants, enjoying the morning kitchen, waiting for the postman and the milkman—Burnside also shows how that simplicity might be "a deception" (45), taking us through a rapidly shifting, leaping set of metonymic images: "those Japanese paper flowers which unfold in water," "empty back roads," "the tug of silence," "a lamp in a window beyond, where someone has sat up all night, drinking tea, remembering something like this" (45). This someone, this other, to whose consciousness Burnside is attuned and who informs his own consciousness, comes into the poem as consciousness "emerging between two curtains in a waft of perfume"—consciousness of the world passes across the boundary of dwelling; across the boundary of world and mind.

This two-way boundary between the self and the social (individual psychology and "the forest") forms the central concern of Burnside's whole collection *Common Knowledge*: the self is not something contained within ourselves; it is constantly transgressing boundaries and borders; slipping through the gaps between them, even if it needs linguistic communication to become communally relevant. Individual rituals and the meanings that accrue to them through repetition (including language use), take on symbolic social functions. There is even some kind of non-religious spirituality here; one that finds transcendence through the transformation of quotidian things. This is what the prose poem is so good at; discovering and uncovering its own patterns ("The suburb has its own patterns" [42]) and these are ultimately emergent social patterns, "arrangements of bottles on front steps and scraped ice on driveways, enactments of chores and duties, conversations at gates and hedges, sweeping and binding movements" (42).

Radical?

This brief discussion has put forward the manifold roots of the prose poem and challenged the critical fixation on the French origin of the form. It has also discussed prominent rhetorical and stylistic features of prose poetry, and posited a "miscellaneous" or "set piece" approach to the form, as well as examining the breakdown of "borders." Its final intention is also to challenge common notions of the prose poem as "radical": Santilli states that the British prose poem is "more likely to be written by avant garde, experimentalist, and counter-cultural writers" ("Prose Poem" 59). Whilst this may have been true in the 1960s and 1970s, I believe this is no longer simply the case, as we shall see from subsequent mainstream examples. Stephen Fredman also argues for the prose poem's radical status: in discussing John Ashbery's prose poems *Three Poems*, Fredman argues that we will be disappointed if we try to read his work "conventionally, seeking to extract meaning from a profound idea captured in a striking image" (114). Quite why a reader cannot have profound ideas, striking images, *and* a fascination with the workings of language is unclear, but such binary oppositions seem ideologically entrenched in discussions of "radical" and "mainstream" poetry, particularly where the prose poem is concerned (see Brown). Why focusing on language might prevent an author from writing more "conventional" poems that reveal meanings through the revelations of things, is also unclear. Why should a "conventional" lyric prose poem by John Burnside, for example "Suburbs," not also be "about" language (for surely it is) just as much as it might be about the suburbs? What is it about the "conventionality" of the lyric that stops it also being "about" the words? The binary is unhelpful.

When one considers that many of the techniques employed by "radical" language-centered poets are techniques that have been used for a very long time—collage, assemblage, cut-up, found material, mathematical formulas, and other processes—it becomes nonsensical to think of these any longer as "radical." As Albert Sonnenfeld writes (in *Citings*):

> The prose poem . . . is formally a profoundly conservative and traditional structure in its ceremonials of entrance and exit; that no matter how radical its content, how relentless its striving for apparent or real incoherence, the prose poem undergoes the secondary elaboration of syntactical coherence and its boundaries most often are clearly defined and marked.
>
> (187)

Others have also begun work on the widespread appearance of the prose poem in mainstream British poetry.[3] Just as with the critical fixation on Aloysius Bertrand as the "originator" of the form, I believe we need to move on from the avant-garde appropriation of the prose poem as a vehicle of "radical" expression—the appearance of prose poetry in mainstream British writing is a welcome development of its traditions.

In 1971 Geoffrey Hill published *Mercian Hymns*, a book that has become, perhaps, the most celebrated example of the British prose poem. Shortly afterward Seamus Heaney published *Stations*, a series of autobiographical prose poems some of which are still included in his *Selected* and *Collected Poems*. In fact Heaney continues to write prose poetry, with several examples appearing in his recent collection *District and Circle*. Faber & Faber continue to champion the prose poem—from its early appearance in T.S. Eliot's oeuvre ("Hysteria" in *Prufrock*) through to the work of Maurice Riordan (*The Holy Land* is comprised of over half prose poetry) and Alice Oswald, whose acclaimed bookwork *Dart* blends prose, poetry, documentary, and interview into one of the most radical reworkings of poetry of place. We can clearly see that the "radical" boundary is simply no longer helpful.

Nor does it stop there. Mainstream British publishers Jonathan Cape champion the work of John Burnside; the editor at Cape, Robin Robertson, also writes and publishes prose poetry in his acclaimed books for Picador. Robertson's sequence, "Camera Obscura" (in *A Painted Field*), blends verse, prose, and epistolary and diaristic form in a miscellaneous way that is as clearly prose poetry as it is verse. Other examples exist in his work. Cape also publishes the work of Canadian poet, prose poet, and essayist Anne Carson, recipient herself of the T.S. Eliot Prize. Carson's "mock essay" prose poems are exemplars of the form; just as other international voices published in Britain, such as Raoul Schrott's *The Desert of Lop* (Picador) exemplify the prose poem as travelogue.

Two final recent examples: in 2007 Luke Kennard was the youngest poet ever to be honored with short-listing for the Forward Prize, for *The Harbour beyond the Movie*. Abounding with prose poems, *The Harbour*, alongside his second book *The Migraine Hotel*, prove that what matters is the quality of the writing itself, rather than the radical positioning of the voice, and that there is a healthy readership for prose poetry in Britain. Another writer who was also once feted as the voice of a new generation of poets is Simon Armitage. In his recent book of sequences, *Out of the Blue*, Armitage includes a remarkable prose poem in his sequence on the 9/11 attacks:

> Go up go down. Sit tight for now. Or move. Don't move. It's all in hand. Make a call on the phone. Stay calm. Then shout. Stay calm, then SHOUT. Come back. I think we should leave but not in the lift. This staircase closed. This stairwell black. Keep cool. Keep your head . . . Call home. It's daddy, ask mummy to come to the phone. Get mummy, tell mummy to come to the phone. Just DO AS YOU'RE TOLD. This glass, like metal. If we step out there . . . if we stay in here. This glass, like metal. Just DO AS YOU'RE TOLD. Get mummy, tell mummy to come to the phone.
>
> (19)

As this excerpt shows, Armitage's prose poetry is rhythmically tight, claustrophobic, panicked, and yet strangely calm. It is packed with rhetorical strategies of furtherance, leaping, repetitions with variation, and metonymy. As a set-piece in and of itself, it makes for a hard-hitting moment in the sequence, and yet it is filled with little set-pieces itself (telephone calls; the language of emergency routines; news broadcasts, and so on). This prose poem creates a monolithic block of intensity and emotion that is as radical and politically challenging as any prose poem that wears its radical linguistic innovation on its sleeve.

NOTES

1 Nikki Santilli writes in depth on this "Biblical Style" in both *Such Rare Citings* and her edited feature, "The Prose Poem in Great Britain."

2 A notion of "incompleteness" that echoes Santilli's argument that the prose poem stands in relation as a (Romantic) fragment to the absent whole and that furtherance is a rhetorical inching forward towards the "absent context" (*Such Rare Citings* 154).

3 See Luke Kennard, PhD thesis, "The Expanse: The Transatlantic Tendencies of the Prose Poem," University of Exeter, 2008.

REFERENCES AND FURTHER READING

Armitage, Simon. *Out of the Blue*. London, Enitharmon, 2008.

Beckett, Samuel. *Trilogy: Molloy. Malone Dies. The Unnamable*. London: Picador, 1979.

Benedikt, Michael. *The Prose Poem: An International Anthology*. New York: Dell, 1970.

Bly, Robert. *Selected Poems*. New York: Harper & Row, 1986.

Brown, Andy (ed.). *Binary Myths 1 & 2*. Exeter: Stride Books, 2002.

Burnside, John. *Common Knowledge*. London: Secker & Warburg, 1991.

Clements, Brian and Dunham, Jamey (eds.). *An Introduction to the Prose Poem*. Connecticut: Firewheel Editions, 2009.

Delville, Michel. *The American Prose Poem: Poetic Form and the Boundaries of Genre*. Gainesville: University of Florida Press, 1998.

Forché, Carolyn. *The Country between Us*. London: Jonathan Cape, 1983.

Fredman, Stephen. *Poet's Prose: The Crisis in American Verse*. Cambridge, New York: Cambridge University Press, 1983.

Godbert, Geoffrey (ed.). *Freedom to Breathe: Modern Prose Poems from Baudelaire to Pinter*. Exeter: Stride, 2002.

Lehman, David. *Great American Prose Poems from Poe to the Present*. London: Scribner, 2003.

Loydell, Rupert and David Miller (eds.). *A Curious Architecture*. Exeter: Stride, 1996.

Miller, David. "Stepping into the Unknown: Stride and the Possibilities of Prose." In *Ladder to the Next Floor*, ed. Rupert. M. Loydell. Salzburg: University of Salzburg, 1993. 170–85.

Santilli, Nikki. "The Prose Poem in Great Britain." In *Sentence: A Journal of Prose Poetics* 3, 2005: 57–114.

Santilli, Nikki. *Such Rare Citings: The Prose Poem in English Literature*. Cranbury, London, Ontario: Associated University Press, 2002.

23
Concrete/Visual Poetry

Fiona McMahon

We need a form or, it is more likely, forms organic to the nature of our own world which, rather than being walled in, extends itself outward into space.

Mary Ellen Solt, "A World Look at Concrete Poetry" (1968)

We do not usually see *words, we* read *them, which is to say we look through them at their significance, their contents. Concrete poetry is first of all a revolt against this transparency of the word—as is all poetry.*

Rosmarie Waldrop, "A Basis of Concrete Poetry" (1976)

Introduction: A Lineage of Visual Poetics and the Print Experience

And I set you down an ocular example, because ye may the better conceive it. Likewise, it so falleth out most times, your ocular proportion doth declare the nature of the audible, for if it please the ear well, the same represented by delineation to the view pleaseth the eye well, and *e converso*. And this is by a natural sympathy between the ear and the eye, and between tunes and colours, even as there is the like between the other senses and their objects, of which it appertaineth not here to speak.

George Puttenham, *The Arte of English Poesie*, 1589 (174–75)

Concrete poetry, an experiment with word, image, and sound, came to light during the second half of the twentieth century at opposite ends of the globe. An international movement, its theoretical foundations were formed by the Brazilian Noigandres group in 1952, only to be echoed shortly after in the work of the Swiss poet Eugen

A Companion to Poetic Genre, First Edition. Edited by Erik Martiny.
© 2012 John Wiley & Sons, Ltd. Published 2012 by John Wiley & Sons, Ltd.

Gomringer. From the very start, concrete poetry has enjoyed the sensory "sympathy" ("between the ear and the eye, and between tunes and colours") that is historically associated with poetry. As such, it stands only at a slight remove from George Puttenham's vision of a multimodal synaesthetic art, drawing upon not only the languages of literature, music, and the visual arts but non-literary discourse. While proving a productive model in the literary arts, the transgression of such boundaries has inevitably led to some confusion over how to classify bodies of work in visual poetics. They have been called picture poems, shaped poems, graphic musical notation or scores, poetic labyrinths, and poetic grids, amongst other terms. Insofar as a critical consensus exists on this point, the term "visual poetry" is generally used as a broad category encompassing a long history of word and image experiment; as for "concrete poetry," methodological revisions postulate the legitimacy of a separate generic status (Clüver 278; Reis 287).

Since its inception in the early 1950s and its "post-concrete" offshoots in the 1960s through to the present day, concrete poetry has been characterized by its removal from conventional literary categories. At the same time, it has fostered a wealth of contributions to the field of experimental poetics, with historical roots in Switzerland, Brazil, and Germany and a line of international development ever since. As a multilingual phenomenon, concrete poetry spans different cultural traditions and languages, major experiments having been undertaken in English, French, German, Italian, Portuguese, and Spanish. What all these manifestations have in common is a concern for the very substance of language itself rather than the mimetic ends to which it can be put. As such, the disconnection in concrete poetry from the narrative possibilities of language is counterbalanced by an adherence of equal strength to formal conceits that explore the material possibilities of language. The activity of representation becomes a marginal phenomenon within the concrete text because its focus lies in scrutinizing the relations presiding over linguistic meaning.

For Dick Higgins, the Fluxus artist who was a practitioner from the early 1950s and publisher of concrete poetry through his work at Something Else Press, concrete poetry is to be understood first and foremost in its historical context. Thus it is defined chronologically, in his analysis, as a "new guise" of visual poetry (Higgins, *George Herbert's Pattern Poems* 18). In keeping with the historical approach Higgins develops in his comprehensive account of the word–image relation—*Pattern Poetry: Guide to an Unknown Literature* (1987)—the very complexity and longevity of the lineage of visual poetry is most effectively viewed from the perspective of a narrative. This is described as "the story of an ongoing human wish to combine the visual and literary impulses, to tie together the experience of these two areas into an aesthetic whole" (Higgins, *Pattern Poetry* 1).

Documenting more than 2,000 works in European, American, and Oriental literatures, Higgins's classification offers a useful distinction between modern visual poetics and its oldest antecedents. Unlike concrete poetry, what is referred to as "pattern poetry" designates poems whose content bears a direct relationship to their shape. The origins of this tradition, Higgins explains, is located in a spiral-shaped text of ancient

Crete—the "Phiastos Disk" of 1700 BC. This is identified as a precusor to Hellenistic pattern poems beginning in the fourth century BC and to the later Latin shaped-poem, termed "carmen figuratum," for which a renewed interest would appear during the Renaissance. From the perspective of English-language pattern poems, the taxonomy for hieroglyphic poetry developed by George Puttenham in his 1589 study, *The Arte of English Poesie* was particularly influential. Furthermore, the recovery of a mimetic figurative tradition was facilitated by Renaissance re-editions of the *The Greek Anthology*, a medieval collection that included a small number of surviving Hellenistic patterns poems. Among the better-known examples, those shaped as altars and as a pair of wings would come to be associated with an imitative strain in English-language pattern poetry—the example of George Herbert's "Easter Wings" (Figure 23.1) from his 1633 collection *The Temple* (38) being the most frequently cited example of this (Higgins, *Pattern Poetry* 4–5; Higgins, *George Herbert's Pattern Poems* 3–12):

Lord, who createdst man in wealth and store,
Though foolishly he lost the same,
Decaying more and more,
Till he became
Most poor:
With thee
O let me rise
As larks, harmoniously,
And sing this day thy victories:
Then shall the fall further the flight in me.

My tender age in sorrow did begin:
And still with sicknesses and shame
Thou didst so punish sin,
That I became
Most thin.
With thee
Let me combine,
And feel this day thy victory:
For, if I imp my wing on thine,
Affliction shall advance the flight in me.

Figure 23.1 George Herbert, "Easter Wings."

```
     pulpit              tulips
    pul    pit        tul    ips
   pu   l   p i t   tu   l   i  ps
  p  u   l   p i t t u   l   i  p  s
  p  u   l   p t i u t l   i  p   s
  p  u   l   t u p l  i t   i  p   s
  p  u  t  u  l  l i  p  i   t  p   s
  p  t  u   l  i  u p  l  p   i  t  s
   t  u  l   i  p  p s u   l   p i  t
   t  u  l   i  p  s p u   l   p i  t
    tu   l   i  ps   pu   l   p  i t
     tul    ips       pul   pit
      tulips             pulpit
```

Figure 23.2 bpNichol, "Easter Pome." Reprinted by permission of the estate of bpNichol.

The dynamics of this long lineage of figurative poems continues to be played out in a more contemporary context. Its narrative may take an explicitly derivative turn for instance, as in the case of the Canadian poet bpNichol, who carries the example of the Hellenistic wings and those of George Herbert into the twentieth century with his 1977 "Easter pome" (Figure 23.2; Nichol 122):

The metaphor of flight borrowed from Herbert's meditation on religious faith is organized as a reductive revision of its themes—Christ's resurrection and man's salvation reduced to the nominal reality of a "pulpit" and "tulips." Furthermore it reads as a homage to the dramatic visual construction of "Easter Wings" and to the overall inventiveness of visual poetry. Appearing well after the end of what is generally considered as the period of orthodox concretism (1952–58), "Easter pome" demonstrates how the abiding influence of the mimetic, shaped-poem has continued to find expression in the contemporary literary imagination. Though far from neglecting the minimalism of early concrete and the critical vision of language with which it is associated, the poem suggests a long chronology of post-concrete writing that evolves within a more fluid aesthetical framework. For instance, amongst North American poets, the body of work produced by the poet John Hollander brings into focus a strong lineage with pattern poetry by celebrating the thematic relevance of the figure.[1] In the case of bpNichol, the retrieval of the figure is a means of testing the range of craft available to the poet and his visual sensibility. In fact, before turning to the typewriter, bpNichol drew the initial conceit of the wings freehand, marking out the vertical and horizontal axes of a grid on paper and only then filling the cells of the grid with the letters of his punning tribute.

However, even before such late twentieth-century reappropriations, there are key periods in the history of modernity where "patterns" of poetry have become more closely concerned with graphic notation and the plasticity of the page than with the ancient precept of resemblance. It is instructive for instance to consider the contribution of Guillaume Apollinaire's *calligrammes*, whose legacy presents examples of both realistic and abstract figures. Indeed, though in some instances imitative, as in the falling drops of rain in his 1918 poem, "Il pleut," Apollinaire's pictorial lyric frequently draws attention to the scripts of the individual letters, whether handwritten or printed, and to the spatial relations of the figures on the page (Bohn 53). In this, it is a notable example, along with Stéphane Mallarmé's groundbreaking poem, "Un Coup de dés jamais n'abolira le hasard" ("A Roll of the Dice Will Never Abolish Chance") (1897), of how the investigation of iconicity in poetry becomes fused with the kind of typographical arrangement later to inform the concretist project. Other explicitly typographical innovations would stem from the experiment, initiated by Mallarmé, according to which the page is transformed into an abstract plane of enigmatic linguistic and graphic signs. Amongst the early twentieth-century literary avant garde, there are a range of artistic and ideological sensibilities at work that make formal generalizations problematic. However, the typographic innovations of Russian *zaum* poets, Italian Futurists, Dadaists, and English Vorticists all bear some relation to the singularity of Mallarmé's project, combining as it does an examination of the material properties of language, those of the book and of the referential value of poetry (Drucker, "Experimental" 40–42).

If we look to the founding practitioners and theorists of concrete poetry, the heritage of Mallarmé's formalism extends much further into the twentieth century. In the case of the Swiss-Bolivian, Eugen Gomringer, his 1953 publication, *konstellationen*, is a direct homage to the formal purity of the Mallarméan concept of the poem as a material "constellation" (Solt 10). In his 1954 manifesto, "From Line to Constellation," Gomringer explains:

> The constellation is the simplest possible kind of configuration in poetry which has for its basic unit the word, it encloses a group of words as if it were drawing stars together to form clusters . . .
>   In the constellation something is brought into the world. It is a reality in itself and not a poem about something or other.
>
>   (Solt 67)

In the contemporaneous work of the Brazilian founders, Augusto de Campos, Decio Pignatari, and Haroldo de Campos, the emphasis falls less on aggregates of formal elements, as in "clusters," than on juxtapositional relations. These are defined according to the terms of Ezra Pound's "ideogrammic method," a structural model that eschews description and relies instead upon paratactic relations to elicit meaning. In the "Pilot Plan for Poetry," the main Brazilian manifesto published in 1958, there is a clear rejection of the sequential intelligence underlying linear-temporal verse and a simultaneous espousal of the notion of a spatial or visual syntax: "Concrete poetry: product of a critical evolution of forms. Assuming that the historical cycle of verse . . . is closed, concrete poetry begins by being aware of graphic space as structural agent. Qualified space: space-time structure instead of mere linear-temporistical development" (Solt 71). There are other continuities to be seen between the concretist approach to the modern print experience as a "tension of things-words in space-time" (Solt 72) and a modernist legacy attributed to Ezra Pound and the earlier Mallarméan experiment. For the Brazilian concrete poets, the ideogram is only one aesthetic tool with which to revitalize poetic expression. For the aims of their project, as outlined in the "Pilot Plan for Poetry," are aligned with a host of attempts in the modernist lineage to oppose discursive normativity: the typographical invention in "Un Coup de dés," the synaesthetic, "verbivocovisual" organization of James Joyce's *Ulysses* and *Finnegan's Wake* and Apollinaire's calligrammatic poems (Solt 72). The very name they chose for themselves in 1952—the *Noigandres* group—was a homage to this critical framework (Solt 12). As a reference to a line from Ezra Pound's *Canto* XX— "Noigandres, eh, *noi*gandres / Now what the DEFFIL can that mean!" (90), this allusion invoked poetry as a field of innovation. It was a reminder that Pound's call to "MAKE IT NEW" (265), while signaling the importance of continued advances in speculative writing, nonetheless designated a specific line of poetic tradition. This was true in 1952 for Haroldo de Campos, Augusto de Campos, and Décio Pignatari, just as it was, to quote William Carlos Williams, in a more general sense the aim of the modernist poet, namely "to make of his words a new form: to invent that is, an object consonant with his day" (265).

The extent to which the early concretists envisioned their work in the oxymoronic context of a tradition of invention is clearly demonstrable. It was apparent in the concern expressed both for the materials of innovation and for their reception. They had learned from the example of their avant-garde forerunners that one effective path to aesthetic inquiry was to be found through the visual and sound technologies available to the artist. From the outset the speculative advances of concrete poetry were implemented through the appropriation of interartistic media and the technologies with which they were associated. The innovations associated with recent digital, post-concrete experiments demonstrate the longevity of this approach.

A Tradition of Intermedial Poetry

If we concern ourselves first with what is recorded as "pure" or "classical" concrete poetry (Solt 59), it would be difficult not to recognize its interartistic premise. This feature was comprehensively demonstrated by Mary Ellen Solt in her 1968 anthology, *Concrete Poetry: A World View* and amply illustrated by other leading anthologies, such as Emmett Williams's *An Anthology of Concrete Poetry* (1967) and Stephen Bann's *concrete poetry: an international anthology* (1967). In counterpoint to the foundational affinity between poetry and music, the reader was invited to experience poetry as a visual expression as opposed to a primarily aural one—an invitation made all the more compelling by the foregrounding of the medium of print in which the poems were cast. However, insofar as concrete poetry has always been engaged in the metapoetic reappraisal of literary antecedents, the aural tradition of poetry handed down from bards, minstrels, troubadours, and balladeers was never entirely cast aside and managed to play its part in this expanded conception of poetry. Indeed, the faculty of concrete poetry for synthesizing the codes of different sign systems is apparent in the direction it took alongside other experiments in the arts throughout the latter half of the twentieth century. The range of these interconnections includes, as the English critic Mike Weaver was to explain in 1964: "visual (or optic), phonetic (or sound) and kinetic (moving in a visual succession)" (Solt 7). As early as 1953, the "Manifesto for Concrete Poetry" produced by the Swiss artist Öyvind Fahlström insisted that sound performance be placed at the heart of the concrete experience (Solt 78). At the same time in Brazil, newly published poems were devised as hybrid structures of line and color, in reference to the Austrian composer Anton Weber's system of alternating tones, colors, and melodies, defined as "Klangfarbenmelodie."[2] On a wider, international scale, the work of performance and sound poetry in the Happenings of the 1960s similarly allowed for the simultaneous interplay of orality and space. During the same period, the interrelational qualities of concrete poetry were at the forefront of Italy's *poesia visiva* and Spain's *poesía visual*.

In recent years, theoretical positions pointing to a process of "polygenesis" reveal a broad heuristic approach to the plurality of modes and contexts to which concretist experiments may be associated (Pineda 379). Today, in any appraisal of its many crosscurrents, the term "intermedia" introduced by Dick Higgins in 1965 for works that "lie conceptually between two or more established media or traditional art forms" presents a useful critical perspective through which the resistance to categorization displayed by concrete poetry may continue to be examined (*Some Poetry Intermedia* 414). This intermedial feature is accounted for as a hallmark in what is defined as "the creation of verbal artefacts which exploit the possibilities, not only of sound, sense and rhythm—the traditional fields of poetry—but also of space" (Draper 329).

The interrelationship of poetic composition with the techniques and representational aims more readily associated with the visual arts invokes, as though a modern variant, the Horatian classical analogy, *ut pictura poesis* ("as a painting, so also a poem"). This is a parallel that has seeped into the vocabulary of literary criticism, linking both art forms in the pursuit of mimesis. Indeed historically, as a model for the unity of the arts, the notion of the "picture-poem" has helped define the vocation of poetry from the dual vantage point of verbal and visual representation and ultimately establish pictorialism as an aesthetic and rhetorical mainstay of literature. Though concretism is similarly concerned with appropriating the expressive register available to the painter, its aims are closest on the whole to those of non-representational painting. Instead of the referential dimension of pictorial poetry, what it proposes to display is the material architecture of poetic composition as expressed through the arrangement of graphic signs. As Rosmarie Waldrop explains: "concrete poetry makes the sound and shape of words its explicit field of investigation. Concrete poetry is *about* words" (Waldrop 315). Paired with this shift in emphasis from the semantic to the material resonance of linguistic materials, the concrete poet works to create "a new relationship to space (the page or its equivalent) and/or to time (abandoning the old linear measure)" (Solt 7).

In the words of Eugen Gomringer, the spatial dimension of concrete poetry boasts an iconic vocabulary that underlines not only the interconnectedness of the arts but its formalist models. In an approach indebted to the modernist aesthetic of the formally autonomous object, the poem becomes "memorable and imprints itself upon the mind as a picture"; "[it] becomes an object to be both seen and used" (Solt 67). As this definition appears to suggest, concrete poems are associated with a literary avant garde whose concerns lie with poetic expression as a sphere of linguistic inquiry that brings to the fore the material conditions of textmaking. Under the terms of Gomringer's 1954 statement—"From Line to Constellation"—the joint assessment of the semantic and aesthetic functions of language is articulated in the poem's design. As such, the reader's attention is drawn more closely to features of the printed page often overlooked amongst the tools of the poet's craft, such as typeface, font, and the use of margins and blanks. In keeping with the concretist intention of "making an object to be perceived rather than read" (Solt 7), a concerted effort is thus made to devise new patterns of reader reception.

A visual "constellation" is what embodies the relationship between poetic composition, the print experience, and the entry of the reader into that equation. The emphasis placed upon the spatial dimension of poetry is no less important, according to Gomringer's visual "constellation," than the "bare linguistic structure" upon which it is built (Solt 67). Indeed when retracing the stages in the development of concrete poetry as a historical genre, the common denominator, as Mary Ellen Solt observed in her 1968 anthology is *reduced language* (7; original emphasis). The goal of reduction is apparent collectively in the manifestos that were produced in the 1950s by a variety of practitioners around the world. In the case of Gomringer, the example of constructivist and formalist schools of visual art learned from the Swiss artist Max Bill were transposed to the field of poetry: "Restriction in the best sense—concentration and simplification—is the very essence of poetry" (Solt 67).[3] In the Brazilian "Pilot Plan for Poetry," the concrete poem is defined as "an object in and by itself" (Solt 72), the intention being, as Claus Clüver remarks, for the poem to "minimalize its verbal material to maximize its effect" (270). This tendency is exemplifed in Gomringer's 1954 poem, "Silencio" (Figure 23.3; Solt 91), a "constellation" that appears to query the reach of the Mallarméan typographical experience:

The rhetorical repositioning called for by the manifestos of the 1950s is apparent in this case. In a highly self-referential display of the functional range of concrete poetry, the anaphoric pattern of the word "silence" is used to build a rectangular block of letters around a central gap. The visual effect of the layout is twofold. First, the

silencio silencio silencio

silencio silencio silencio

silencio silencio

silencio silencio silencio

silencio silencio silencio

Figure 23.3 Eugen Gomringer, "Silencio." (Solt 91/Williams n.p.)

dualistic relationship of the phonic and linguistic characteristics of poetry is put into play through the iteration of the absence of sound, in itself a noiseless proposition. This is achieved against the background of the white space of the page, a feature of this poem's design that aspires to carry rhetorical effectiveness. It suggests an exacerbated expression of Gomringer's ideal of a poetry of "concentration and simplification" that entails a stripping away of semantic complexity and nuance (Solt 67). Through the interplay of sound and sight, the block of print appears to reaffirm the primacy of the word while the blank provides an image of silence, as if to lay claim to a meaningfulness in its own right. In the end, what is illustrated through this experiment in reduction is a paradoxical engagement with the senses. For if the poem affects transitions from one sense register to the next, the poem remains as though inert. As a result, the intelligible and imaginary world that may be revealed through the senses is limited by the closure of the poem's rhetorical and semantic context. In substance, though the metaphor may call for the reader to look inward, what is reflected back is confined to an image of one's own contemplative silence.

Given the absence of context and linear syntax, as in the latter example, the criticism most frequently leveled against concrete poetry concerns the hermeticism that is perceived in its visual arrangements. There is no denying that the propensity of the ideographic dimension to supercede the discursive function of the poem clearly sets concrete poetry apart from traditional verse; it also suggests how the advent of a visually inflected poetry has changed the very experience of poetry, for readers and writers alike. In light of this, it is relevant that the concretist project is introduced in part as a response to the rise of new mass media. For example, in Gomringer's view, one of the singular functions of poetry is to display an attentiveness to codes prevalent in contemporary culture, including those generated by advertising and other commercial media. To some degree, Gomringer's precept is indicative of the kind of productive relationship between print technology, sensory experience and human consciousness as a whole that Marshall McLuhan would later describe in his 1962 study, *The Gutenberg Galaxy: The Making of Typographic Man* (1962).[4] Significantly for Gomringer however, this is an essentially desirable evolution that will help redefine the cultural relevancy of poetry. As he explains in 1954: "Headlines, slogans, groups of sounds and letters give rise to forms which could be models for a new poetry just waiting to be taken up for meaningful use" (Solt 67). According to this formulation, the permeability of concrete poetry to modes of syntactic and discursive simplification popular in advertising for instance proceeds from a "reorganization of imaginative life" (McLuhan 3). In turn, if successful, this serves to ultimately widen the field of poetic experiment. However, as time has shown, such a change in the experience of poetry only furthers its marginalization within the literary sphere. Indeed, as Pedro Reis observes with respect to the historical reception of concrete poetry in canonical circles: "[it] was often refused the category of literary genre," suggesting that "it was something non-poetic or even anti-poetic—or that it meant the end of poetry altogether" (290).

The Performance of Concrete and Post-Concrete Poetries

The extension of the experience of poetry outside the confines of any specific literary genre and into the social world falls in step with the emphasis upon the role, in Gomringer's words, of "the new reader." As Gomringer states in 1954: "[The poet] determines the play-area, the field of force and suggests its possibilities. The reader, the new reader, grasps the idea of play, and joins in" (Solt 67). The reader is called upon to play an increasingly important role as the conventional uses of allusion, rhyme, meter, and lineation are abandoned. In other words he becomes part of the creative process that is conceived both as a "system" and as a "playground" (Gomringer).

In the absence of linear syntactical relations, the performative faculty of the concrete poem replaces grammatical patterns of understanding with visual ones. As a consequence, there arises a degree of semantic ambiguity. This is understood by some as a "loss of semantic control" on the part of the poet and the subsequent transferral of rhetorical prerogative to the reader (Draper 330). This is not to suggest that such a model lends itself to the negative dynamics inferred by some twentieth-century experiments in the arts. For instance, the concrete reader is at some remove from the breakdown in structural relations idealized in the Italian Futurist conception of *Parole in libertà* (1912). Instead, the involvement of the reader is akin to a form of ekphrastic participation wherein reader reception rests upon a heightened awareness of craft and of the aesthetic properties of the poem as an object. It may be inferred from this configuration that the root association of poetry with *poeisis* or "making" be extended to include reader-participation. If so, the reader acquires the position of both viewer and co-creator of a complex hieroglyphic.

Indeed, for Claus Clüver, the manner in which the reader is invited to "operate" the text may have either a physical or a conceptual relevance for the poem (370). First, this concept of the reader as an active participant is reminiscent of the presentational emphasis of the Hellenistic pattern poem and to the modes of viewing encouraged by one of its variants known as *technopaegnia*. These poems function as votive poems, embodying the specific shapes of objects (Axe, Wings, Egg, Altar). Their particularity however is twofold: given that the allusions, metrical organization and line length that form the *technopaegneon* are designed to perform a riddle, another distinguishing feature of this poetic form is its epigrammatic playfulness (Trypanis 341).

To some degree, the performative aspect of the Hellenistic model is revealed in the ingenuity displayed in subsequent examples of visuality. The word games that are celebrated so widely for instance in Lewis Carroll's tale, *Alice in Wonderland* (1865)—acrostic, lipogram, palindrome—are taken up again enthusiastically in the twentieth century. Among the plentiful experiments with paronomasia (a play on words, including assonance and consonance) in concrete and post-concrete poetries, take, for example, the two following poems by the Scottish poet, Ian Hamilton Finlay:

In the first case, a single word, "Acrobats" (Figure 23.4; Williams n.p.) is set off along the horizontal, vertical, and diagonal axes of the page. This is achieved so that the semantic content of the poem be repeated in the layout of the individual letters as they perfom different stunts across a grid-like canvas. In doing so, the poem under-

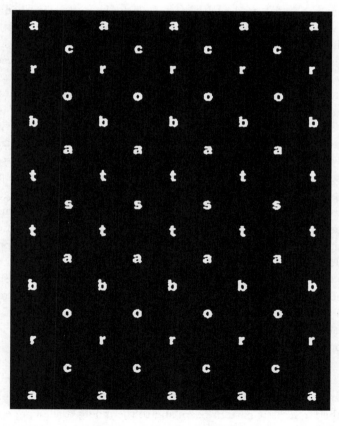

Figure 23.4 Ian Hamilton Finlay, "Acrobats." Reprinted by permission of the Estate of Ian Hamilton Finlay.

lines the dual relevance of language as a set structure and as a stage for the witticisms of invention. For concrete poetry, the conceit that displaces language from a set paradigm of print to an array of semiotic configurations is foundational. The artifice and the structural dynamic of such an endeavor is illustrated further in Finlay's second poem bearing the enigmatic title, "XM" (Figure 23.5; Williams n.p.):

In a manner reminiscent of Alice's rendition of "The Mouse's Tale" in Lewis Carroll's 1865 story, the serpentine layout of this poem has the reader puzzle over the words as they unfold on the page. Here, the key to a riddle is unraveled as the poem unfolds sequentially on the page, from top to bottom. The ambiguous succession of letters that run in a twisting line at the top of the poem is met midway along by a phrase that denotes a context of a pastoral character, referring as it does to a small stream or brook (*burn*) and a "mill." Thanks to the determiner "this," a narrative direction appears to take hold—"this is the little burn that plays its"—but then the poem quickly breaks up into nouns and phonetic clusters formed to imitate music: "mm / mMm / m / mmouth- / organ / by / the / m / mm / mmm / mMm / mill / x / mm / Mmm." Thus the individual letters, "m" and "x," function as phonetic symbols and as metaphors for two different landscapes: the first, a semantic landscape depicting a bucolic scene of a rippling brook by a mill whose music blends with that of a mouth organ; in the second instance, there is a sensory landscape that is playfully contrived to be seen and heard.

The derisive activity of concrete poetry is equally apparent in the manipulation of the tools of print technology, exploited in some instances to a point of near exhaustion. This has been a pivotal feature of the different forms of *scription* entertained by the poet Steve McCaffery and other poets associated with the typewriter art of the 1970s (Bob Cobbing, bpNichol, Henri Chopin, Pierre Garnier). As in the case of visual experiment involving rubber-stamps, tissue texts, hand-lettering, and stencil, typewriter technology upholds the concretist emphasis upon the unique quality of each poem. The technology that Steve McCaffery extends to his *xerography* poems, however, exemplified in his *Carnival* series (1967–75) ritualizes techniques of overlay in a new fashion.[5] In what is labeled "xerox disintegrations" (400), poetry's adherence to technology is taken to parodic heights as the creative process is posited as a means to manufacturing illegibility.

Conceptually, practitioners of typewriter poetry have been resourceful when it comes to carrying over a tradition of openendedness. For most, this entails more than being mindful of creative design. This may take the form of a tribute to past traditions uniting typographical play and iconicity, as in the following celebration by Steve McCaffery of the painterly shapes of the American twentieth-century poet E.E. Cummings (Figure 23.6):

Here, through this example of amorphous typescript, the association of occasional verse with the early tradition of pattern poetry is extended into the modern-day context. In a parodic gesture reminiscent of the verbal and visual play in Cummings's poetics, the principal object of this mechanized portrait comes close to linguistic disintegration. Nevertheless the poet's initials, "e" and "c" are rehearsed as part of an elaborate game of ink overlay. Thus though thoroughly abstract, the shape that is

```
                    m Mm
                      x
                      m
                   m Mm
                      x
                      m
                    mm
                  m
                mm
                 x
           MmM
         mm
           m
         mm
       m
         x
       mmm
       m
         m
       mm
         x
         m
            mmMm
              m
                x
                  m
                mm
              m
                this
                  is
                 the
               little
            burn
            that
            plays
              its
              mm
         mMm
         m
         mmouth-
         organ
              by
              the
              m
            mm
              mmm
            mMm
            mill
              x
            mm
         Mmm
```

Figure 23.5 Ian Hamilton Finlay, "XMPoem." Reprinted by permission of the Estate of Ian Hamilton Finlay.

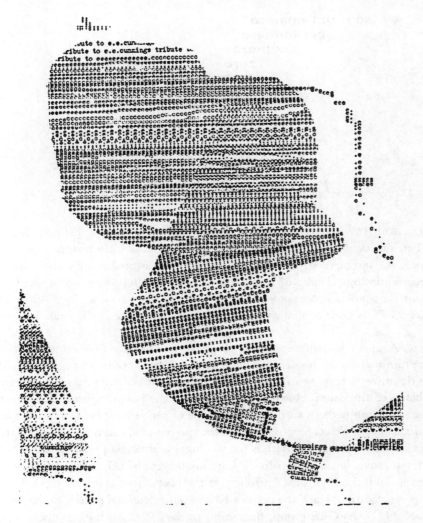

Figure 23.6 Steve McCaffery, "Unpublished Outtake," from *Carnival*. Reprinted by permission of Steve McCaffery.

employed upholds the commemorative basis of some visual poetries (Higgins, *Pattern Poetry* 6). It is a reminder that at its beginnings, the performative character of concrete writing is also tied to its social underpinnings.

Conclusion: Expanding the "Scriptural Imagination"

An equal awareness of the rituals of language and those of society is a quality with which Augusto de Campos, one of the founding members of the Brazilian *Noigandres* group wished to associate concrete poetry. If poetry was approached as a medium

```
        sem um numero
           um numero
              numero
                 zero
                   um
                    o
                   nu
                 mero
               numero
             um numero
           um sem numero
```

Figure 23.7 Augusto de Campos, "Sem um numero."

through which to subvert conventional linguistic meaning, it became tied in the Brazilian practice with other expressions of revolt of a socio-historical nature. For instance, the intent to strike a parallel between the formalist concretist aims and a critique of ideological subordination is apparent in the following poem, published in 1962 in the *Antología Noigandres*. As Mary Ellen Solt explains, "Sem um numero" (Figure 23.7)[6] is documented as a "Social protest poem about the Brazilian peasant" (254):

Here, Augusto de Campos uses the concretist rule of reduction to metaphoric ends. As the minimalism of this semantic and spatial frame appears to suggest—with one semantic universe turning in upon itself—nominalist isolation may be equated with the theme of alienation. However the success of the poem's critical design remains unclear, pointing perhaps to the limited scope of such experiment once the play and formalism of orthodox concretism spills over into political comment. In contrast, what it does successfully communicate is the willingness amongst practitioners of concrete poetries to envision, as Augusto de Campos has explained, its exploratory formal tendencies in unison with the "ideology of the poet-critic" (Greene n. p.).

This is a vocation which the politicized and self-referential poetics of the American L=A=N=G=U=A=G=E group, beginning in the 1970s, elaborates upon. The very activity of this group rests upon the scrutiny of normative patterns of meaning and writing. The group's affinities for the materializing aims of concrete poetry have been made clear on more than one occasion. In recent years this lineage formed the basis of an extensive retrospective exhibition, entitled "Poetry Plastique," to which contributions were made by some of the group's leading poets and theorists.[7] The goal of this retrospective was to examine the proximity of visuality in poetry with currents of contemporary art. In doing so, it highlighted the proclivity of visual poetics to direct attention to the material conditions of writing and to the reciprocal relations that are established with other modes of discourse. In the context of contemporary assessments, it follows that the multiple operations of concrete poetry have a greater critical currency than any single generic label or systematic theory.

The polysemous character of visual poetry in the digital environment—the most recent expression of a concrete lineage—is perhaps one example of this enduring feature. It calls to mind the plea Eugen Gomringer made in 1956 for a transnational language for poetry, described as "International-Supranational": "I am . . . convinced that concrete poetry is in the process of realizing the idea of a universal poetry" (Solt 68). Today, the increasingly plural character of media, beginning with the polymorphous, multirelational space of the World Wide Web, suggests in some respects the realization of this ideal.

Another abiding connection with a lineage of visuality is to be found in the renewal of the relationship between technology and a tradition of speculative writing. Once a process of transformation affecting the page, shifting the focus from text face to pictural plane or musical score, the interaction between technology and literary culture supposes new inscriptions of aesthetic experiment. Indeed, as part of the continuing innovations associated with visual poetry, it follows that the "electronic space" of the Web is now posited as "a space of poesis" (Glazier 5). After the materiality of hand-presses, offset printing, the chapbook, mimeography, and xerox, poets are exploring the materiality of writing thanks to digital vocabularies. Indeed, with the integration of online hypertext and URL paths in poetic practice, the e-poet is learning to expand the "scriptural imagination" to new media (McGann 137). As creator and director of the Electronic Poetry Center—one of the principal sites for the development and dissemination of digital poetry[8]—Loss Pequeno Glazier has defined the web as an "instance of writing" (4) that both accomodates and generates such an expansion. If concreteness is taken to mean the material essence of language, there is no end to the scriptural dynamic that this evolution entails in such a fluid, provisional environment. The conversion by Augusto de Campos of his poems to video and digital media is one demonstration of this. Some of these are reproduced as videotexts and computer holograms on UbuWeb, a comprehensive internet resource for historical and ongoing experiment in visual and sound poetries that was inspired by the utopian transnational orientation of concrete poetry and its "universally accessible content."[9] Though the environment of writing may change, on and off the page, in and out of the book, poetry will continue to search for intelligible paths that are alive to the senses. How relentlessly modern poetry has charted this search and the stumbling blocks that inevitably appear. We might read as much in the words of the American poet, George Oppen, writing in 1968:

> And the pure joy
> of the mineral fact
>
> Tho it is impenetrable
>
> As the world, if it is matter,
> Is impenetrable.

(148)

NOTES

1 For a sampling of current and historical examples of visuality in poetry, see the Sackner Archive of Visual and Concrete Poetry: http://ww2.rediscov.com/sacknerarchives.

2 For a study of *Poetamenos* (1953) by Augusto de Campos in relation to the Vienna School and the "Klangfarbenmelodie" of Anton Webern, see Drucker, "Experimental, Visual" 45.

3 See Drucker, "Experimental, Visual" 42–43.

4 "When technology extends one of the senses," Marshall McLuhan concludes that "a new translation of culture occurs as swiftly as the new technology is interiorized" (McLuhan 40).

5 For a discussion of an American lineage of visual poetics with respect to typewriter art, see McMahon 133–52.

6 The poem translates as follows: "without a number, numberless / a number / number / zero / a/one / the/zero / naked / mere, genuine / number / a number / without a number, numberless." See Solt 95; 254.

7 The L=A=N=G=U=A=G=E poets Charles Bernstein, Steve McCaffery, Lyn Hejinian, Robert Grenier, Clark Coolidge were among those writers and visual artists participating in the 2001 Poetry Plastique exhibition at the Marianne Boesky Gallery.

8 http://epc.buffalo.edu.

9 www.ubu.com/resources/index.html.

REFERENCES AND FURTHER READING

Bann, Stephen, ed. *concrete poetry: an international anthology*. London: London Magazine Editions, 1967.

Bernstein, Charles and Jay Sanders, eds. Poetry Plastique. New York: Marianne Boesky Gallery and Granary Books, 2001.

Bohn, Willard. *The Aesthetics of Visual Poetry: 1914–1928*. Cambridge: Cambridge University Press, 1986.

Clüver, Claus. "Concrete Poetry: Crtitical Perspectives from the 90s." *Experimental—Visual—Concrete. Avant-Garde Poetry since the 1960s*, eds. David K. Jackson, Eric Vos and Johanna Drucker. Amsterdam and Atlanta: Rodopi, 1996. 265–85.

Draper, R.P. "Concrete Poetry." *New Literary History* 2.2 (1971): 329–40.

Drucker, Johanna. "Experimental, Visual, and Concrete Poetry: A Note on Historical Context and Basic Concepts." *Experimental—Visual—Concrete. Avant-Garde Poetry since the 1960s*, eds. David K. Jackson, Eric Vos and Johanna Drucker. Amsterdam and Atlanta: Rodopi, 1996. 39–61.

Drucker, Johanna. *The Visible Word: Experimental Typography and Modern Art: 1909–1923*. Chicago: University of Chicago Press, 1994.

Glazier, Loss Pequeno. *Digital Poetics. The Makings of E-Poetries*. Tuscaloosa and London: University of Alabama Press, 2002.

Gomringer, Eugen. *The Book of Hours and Constellations*, trans. by Jerome Rothenberg. New York: Something Else Press, 1968. "Gomringer's Pre-Face" n.p.

Greene, Richard. "From Dante to the Post-Concrete: An Interview with Augusto de Campos." *The Harvard Library Bulletin* 3.2 (1992): n.p. *Ubu Web*.

Herbert, George. *The Complete English Poems*. Ed. John Tobin. London: Penguin Books, 1991.

Higgins, Dick. *George Herbert's Pattern Poems: In Their Traditions*. West Glover and New York: Unpublished Editions, 1977.

Higgins, Dick. *Pattern Poetry: Guide to an Unknown Literature*. Albany: State University of New York Press, 1987.

Higgins, Dick. *Some Poetry Intermedia*. New York: Unpublished Editions, 1976. Rpt. *The Avant-Garde Tradition in Literature*, ed. and intro. Richard Kostelanetz. Buffalo: Prometheus Books, 1982. 414–15.

McCaffery, Steve. *Carnival. The First Panel 1967–70. The Second Panel 1971–75*. Toronto: Coach House Press, 1973; 1977. *Unpublished Outtakes*.

McCaffery, Steve. "The Yale *Symphosymposium* on Comtemporary Poetics and Concretism: a World View from the 1990s." *Experimental—Visual—Concrete. Avant-Garde Poetry since the 1960s*, eds. David K. Jackson, Eric Vos and Johanna Drucker. Amsterdam and Atlanta: Rodopi, 1996. 400.

McGann, Jerome. *The Textual Condition*. Princeton: Princeton University Press, 1991.

McLuhan, Marshall. *The Gutenberg Galaxy: The Making of Typographic Man*. London: Routledge & Kegan Paul, 1962.

McMahon, Fiona. "Iconicity and Typography in Steve McCaffery's Panel-Poems." *La revue Lisa* 5.2, 2007: 133–52.

Nichol, bp. *An H in the Heart. bpNichol: A Reader*. Toronto: McClelland & Stewart, 1994.

Oppen, George. *Collected Poems*. New York: New Directions, 1975.

Pineda, Victoria. "Speaking about Genre: The Case of Concrete Poetry." *New Literary History* 26. 2, 1995: 379–93.

Pound, Ezra. *The Cantos of Ezra Pound*. New York: New Directions, 1989.

Puttenham, George. *The Arte of English Poesy. A Critical Edition*, ed. Frank Whigham and Wayne A. Rebhorn. Ithaca, NY and London: Cornell University Press, 2007.

Reis, Pedro. "Concrete Poetry: A Generic Perspective." *Experimental—Visual—Concrete. Avant-Garde Poetry since the 1960s*, eds. David K. Jackson, Eric Vos and Johanna Drucker. Amsterdam and Atlanta: Rodopi, 1996. 287–302.

Solt, Mary Ellen, ed. *Concrete Poetry: A World View*. 1968. Bloomington and London: Indiana University Press, 1970.

Trypanis, C.A. *Greek Poetry. From Homer to Seferis*. London and Boston, MA: Faber & Faber, 1981.

Waldrop, Rosmarie. "A Basis of Concrete Poetry." *Bucknell Review* (1976). Rpt. in *The Avant-Garde Tradition in Literature*, ed. and intro. Richard Kostelanetz. Buffalo: Prometheus Books, 1982. 315–23.

Williams, Emmett, ed. *An Anthology of Concrete Poetry*. New York: Something Else Press, 1967.

Williams, William Carlos. *The Autobiography of William Carlos Williams*. New York: New Directions, 1967.

24

Poems that Count

Procedural Poetry

Hélène Aji

Oulipo or Not Oulipo?

In 1960, the foundation of Oulipo by François Le Lionnais, author of the group's Premier (First Manifesto), around French poet Raymond Queneau's tutelary figure, marks the formalization of a different aesthetics. Against inspiration and the sublime in its often vague and bombastic definitions, Oulipian poets elaborate what Hervé Le Tellier calls a poetics of "intelligence" (Le Tellier 9). It would be insufficient to understand this notion of "intelligence" as yet another signal of the increasing hermeticism, and elitism, of poetry as the twentieth century unfolded: by forming a group, which came to include Georges Perec, Jacques Roubaud, then Harry Matthews, to name but a few, Oulipians paradoxically face the necessity of responding to the difficulties of postwar poetry, the very poetry deemed impossible by such theorists as Theodor Adorno, and the need to re-found the poem after the formal crisis induced by free verse, and the increasingly blurred limit between poetry and prose.

This "crisis" has been studied by Stephen Fredman in his landmark *Poet's Prose: The Crisis in American Verse* under the sign of a tragic undoing of American poetry, when free verse, failing to find its aesthetic criteria, dissolves into either the "linear fallacy" defined by Marjorie Perloff (the fallacy of "chopped up *prose*" ["Linear Fallacy," 858] using lineation as the sole formal determination for poetry in a diluted conception of free verse), or becomes indistinguishable from the essay or the memoir in prose. And indeed in the 1980s, when Fredman writes, the poem can be seen as lost in the vastness of the many discourses linguistics grapples with and seems to reduce to artifacts of language. Yet the poem can also be considered as reaching its full "freedom" and expansion when every language act is *potentially* a poetic gesture, and poetry is the "language art" (Antin 130). Now one may argue that it mostly started in the 1920s,

A Companion to Poetic Genre, First Edition. Edited by Erik Martiny.
© 2012 John Wiley & Sons, Ltd. Published 2012 by John Wiley & Sons, Ltd.

with two poets both American, one based in the U.S. and determined to find out an "American poetics" (Aji), the other exiled to Europe and fascinated with the plurality of meanings made possible by micro-variations in "composition": William Carlos Williams, in his push to free the poem in English from the fetters of metrics, and still regulate it through a type of measure, an inductive form emerging from the crystallization of meaning in language; and Gertrude Stein in her focus on the constraints imposed by language on perception and the subsequent grammar of infinite repetitiveness and minute variation that informs her poetic texts.

Both adumbrate poetic stances that have manifold expressions in later poetry which is not akin to the methods of Oulipian poetics. However they also inform the developments of procedural poetry in English, when the theorizations of Oulipo return to systematize practices that had emerged from the chaos of post-Depression times, and then from the repressions of the postwar era. Oulipo brings in the notion of a subject permanently and irredeemably caught in the very "structure" of his expressive modes, thus opening up a multiplicity of debates centered on the attempts at assessing and gaining control over these restrictions. Procedural poets push forward and investigate the issues central to postmodernism. It is vain to try and make a complete list, but let it be evident that procedural poetry in English is pervasive well outside the Oulipian circle, since it is contemporaneous to its development and not just an import from France in the wake of French theory. There are thus British poets, such as Tony Lopez, Canadian poets in the line of Steve McCaffery or Christian Bök, and Americans out of Black Mountain College in the 1960s, around John Cage, Jackson Mac Low, and Merce Cunningham, among the Language Poets in the 1980s and 1990s, and in the circles of the Conceptual Poets of the 1990s and early twenty-first century.

Despite a rather impressive development, procedural poetries have often been considered with condescension for various reasons, which all have to do with poetics and the poetic agenda of those who look at them. At worst, they are dismissed as obscure, pointlessly complex modes of composition which produce even more obscure and hermetic texts, failing to trigger off the reader's empathetic projection and vicarious expression of self. At best, they are deemed interesting in a philosophical reflection on the author's authority which they imply and more often than not thematize in the hypotactic discourse they unfold. More disturbing perhaps than these contradictory appraisals is the fact that procedure as a text-generating method is almost unavoidably reduced to "play," as in Marjorie Perloff's formulation of the modernist shift "from free verse to procedural play" (*Radical Artifice* 134–70). Such an expression, even as it justifiably chronicles and emphasizes a key moment in the evolution of poetic *praxis* and theory, also unwittingly downgrades the very texts it aims to describe as serious and valuable.

And indeed, because procedural poetry is often based on game-related methods (manipulating cards, dice, etc.) and because it imposes compositional constraints that jeopardize meaningfulness, one is tempted to dismiss it as purely experimental and in no way a viable option for poetry. Moreover one is also tempted to contrast it with free verse, forgetting that there might never have been such a thing as "free verse."

One should rather talk of changes in the nature of compositional constraints and their problematic role in the definition of authorship, of the field of poetry, and ultimately of the conception of the poet's part in the world, and in the writing of this world's histories.

The Three Rs

In what Michael Davidson calls the "crisis of expressivity," the emphasis is laid on the "productive nature of language in forming the subject" and in the development of a "process- or action-oriented aesthetics" (205). The focus moves away from the poem as monolithic product to the modes of its production, and the streamlining of these modes according to procedures or rules turns the poem into what John Ashbery calls "an all-purpose model" (251). This is far-removed from the "graph of consciousness," which Perloff used to define the form of Pound's *Cantos*, and indeed this type of formalism revolves around the issues of projection both in the context of a poetics and of a theory of reading. The problematic node can be summarized by an articulation of the basic "three Rs": reading, writing, reckoning. Poets revise their conception of poetry and its issues in terms of reader response (their own, as readers of former writers, informed by irrepressible processes of influence; and their readers'), in terms of intertextuality (existing in language is perceived as existing in intertextuality, since no work can be deemed to be new, made of exclusively new material, the very use of words is quotation), and in terms of evaluation and recognition (procedure intervenes as the means to evidence, quantify, and manipulate the conditions of reading and writing).

One particularly emblematic example of this reflection on the poet's position in literature and in the world would be the chance-generated text that Jackson Mac Low elaborates sometimes in collaboration with John Cage. The approach to such texts has too often been narrowly ectoskeletal (external and structural)—exclusively descriptive of the procedure involved—a consequence of the near impossibility to narrativize stable meanings for the consequent poems. Far from being "anti-content," or "non-referential" (Davidson 214) though, these texts do not solely explore the range of syntactic and/or semantic possibilities for the sake of themselves. Commenting on Mac Low's work, Charles Bernstein underlines the reverberations of the procedural decisions generating the texts:

> The Mac Lowian systematic poem refuses the normal process of identification of a 'self' (voice, persona, sensibility) in the text as expressed or revealed—of writing as confessional or personally expressive. Faced with the Mac Lowian structurally generated poem, one is hard put to "read into" it to recognize the mapping of the author's consciousness or a narrative or pictorial image.
>
> (*Content's Dream* 252–53)

> Mac Low . . . has generally been more interested in his written texts in building struc-
> tures than in inhabiting them . . . His work is a great testament to the possibility for
> structures in and of themselves, and for the sufficiency of possibility. That it is archi-
> tectures that shape the world, but *we* who must fill them up.
>
> > *(Content's Dream* 257)

But such a reading also has to come to terms with the persistence of authorship even
when meaning has become problematic: as Bernstein suggests but does not account
for, "the circuit of intentionality is not so easily broken. Words get in the way"
(*Content's Dream* 253).

In fact the very exhibition of procedure also gets in the way, as it allows for commentary and provokes a reading into the procedure of meanings that the poem seems
to preclude. Asserting, as Bernstein has done, that in procedural texts "language
speaks for itself" (*Content's Dream* 253) presupposes a radical dissolution of agency.
What procedure is trying to do is at least partially relinquish the arbitrariness of
psychological decision and selection, as well as the fixity of "inherited form" to establish a "programmatic" (Perelman 167 n.1) formalism in which, to take up Lyn
Hejinian's parallel with Adamic scenarios, "what naming provides is structure, not
individual words" (*Language of Inquiry* 53). What the procedural poem is supposed to
do is work out the consequences of such a structure-oriented poetics: the authoritarian
posture of one magisterial self telling another is ideally to be replaced by the distribution of the subject-function to all the individuals involved with the poem.

But, of course, this never happens. Procedure simply suggests a more anarchic, to
take up Jackson Mac Low's term, production of poetry, which does not mean the sup-
pression of any order, but the emergence of a different type of order than expected,
one less dogmatically and arbitrarily regulated by the authorial figure. The following
are examples by a panel of poets of possible procedures, their actualizations, and suggested interpretations.

Jackson Mac Low: Re-Citing/Re-Siting

As Mac Low evokes the writing of *Barnesbook: Four Poems Derived from Sentences by Djuna
Barnes*, he underlines the distinction between the "nonintentionality" that procedure
allows for and an absence of determinism. The use of his computer program Diastext—
"an automation of the 'diastic reading-through text-selection methods' that [he] first
developed in January 1963" (*Barnesbook* 47)—makes him unable to "predict what will
be drawn from a source text," but it does not suppress the fact that he has chosen the
seed word and the source text—the seed being "used to select words (or other linguistic units) that *spell it through* repeatedly throughout a poem" (48) in a manner
akin to the acrostic. Nor does it suppress the fact that he maintains the possibility of
editing the resulting text. As a consequence, Mac Low's procedural poems are not, as

is too easily formulated, chance-generated, but, as he puts it, devised according to compositional methods that include *"rule-guided interaction with nonintentionally-generated materials"* (51; original emphasis). In a final twist, one is made to realize the possibility of formalizing the generative activity of self in language, to the extent of replacing it with a subject producing and inhabiting structures that others can in turn inhabit. The poetic text becomes an architecture with Diastext-based composition as one possible architectural organization:

> Such the *is* in them.
> "Then the ones,
> Robin their extremity
> of extremity—
> with years,
> ledge?"
> Extremity,
> extremity,
> extremity,
> extremity
> were responsible for other and painful ran building,
> apart."
>
> ("Barnes 2," *Barnesbook* ll.84–95)

However, since the poems of the *Barnesbook*, Mac Low eventually acknowledges, are also "acts of homage," this product of his procedure becomes a form of elegy. Procedural poetry, thus, does not preclude the persistence of expressive intention, but because it asserts the status of ectoskeletal form not as "a fixture but an activity" (Hejinian, *Language of Inquiry* 275), it displaces the locus of meaning from content to form, text, and context. Simultaneously and paradoxically, it opens the text to the proliferation of compositions and readings, as it formats the range of activity of the individual. In a 1990 unpublished admonition to younger poets, Mac Low exclaims "Make Your Own System!":

> Through inventing their own methods for making poems, they may become conscious of what they have absorbed from their cultural environment and of their freedom to choose other assumptions and other ways of working and making than those they've received without fully realizing it and introjected—unconsciously made part of themselves. I regard this and similar exercises as ways through which writers may empower themselves.
>
> (Mac Low Papers MS 180, Box 67, Folder 28 "Make Your Own System!" 3)

What Mac Low's successive methods entail, as a series of forays into the unchartered territory of poem-making, is not the erasure of the author, suppressed as it were by mathematics, combinatory, or aleatory formulae. Rather they give systematic insight into the very processes of reading and writing—the degrees of intervention of an author, the alternative modelizations of one's action in the world. In "Call Me Ishmael," reading and writing become one single movement outlining the trajectory of composition and foregrounding the sharing of words and structures between two texts. Melville's *Moby Dick* is turned into the matrix for the new poem, through a procedure that can be replicated with any other text:

Circulation. And long long	(*call*)
Mind every	(*me*)
Interest. Some how mind and every long	(*Ishmael*)[1]

(Mac Low, Representative Works ll.1–3)

Using a complex variation on acrostics, the first stanza of the poem is made of the first words starting with the same letters as the words in the novel's first sentence, while the second one is made of the second words starting with the same letters as the first sentence of the novel, and so on. The resulting poem stands on the border of agrammaticality but retains sufficient syntactic coherence to call forth interpretations. In a surprising manner, it produces the allusive portrait of a neo-Romantic I, repressed as well as expressed by the poetic rules of composition. Conceiving of intertextuality as the inescapable condition of writing, Jackson Mac Low's decompositions and re-compositions of Melville, Barnes, but also Gertrude Stein convey a vision of writing as the witnessing of reading. In this perspective, re-citing might amount to re-siting—repositing the text in a different context, evidencing its alteration, in a gesture that is at the heart of the epistemological questionings of the late twentieth century.

Ron Silliman's Exponentials

"Willie's Clatter" by Jackson Mac Low uses the beginning of Lucas's series (2, 1, 3, 4, 7, 11, 18, 11, 7, 4, 3, 1, 2) to regulate the number of lines in a poem, stopping at 18 and forming a circular numerical pattern. This series is derived from the Fibonacci series ($u_{n+1}=u_n+u_{n-1}$; i.e., 1, 1, 2, 3, 5, 8, 13, 21 . . .) which is exponential and has been used by Ron Silliman to count sentences in the paragraphs of his book-long poem *Tjanting*. In both cases, the poems function according to exponential-based formulae, and thematically emphasize the issue of growth (in time and/or in space) and limitation. As the poems unfold, Mac Low's is constantly returning to its beginning, failing to break through the eighteen-line ceiling for a stanza, whereas Silliman's ends abruptly on the poet's arbitrary decision or obligation to stop. Silliman's last paragraph begins on page 52 of the book to end on page 204, presenting an enormous baggage of accumulated statements and interrogations akin to the overgrown memory of a fully grown, aging individual. Recurring statements, ruled by internal structures of repetition, underline the rumination that memory implies. It also reminds the reader of the repetitiveness of writing—and of the fact that in reading one also repeats and re-encounters what is already known and experienced, at least in fragments.

Not this.

What then?

I started over & over. Not this.

Last week I wrote "the muscles in my palm so sore from halving the rump roast I cld barely grip the pen." What then? This morning my lip is blisterd.

Of about to within which. Again & again I began. The gray light of day fills the yellow room in a way wch is somber. Not this. Hot grease had spilld on the stove top.

Nor that either. Last week I wrote "the muscle at thumb's root so taut from carving that beef I though it wld cramp." Not so. What then? Wld I begin? This morning my lip is tender, disfigurd. I sat in an old chair out behind the anise. I cld have gone about this some other way.

                                                              (Silliman, *Tjanting* 16)

The poem is based on the very suspension of narrativization and identification through the break of logical links between sentences. It however possesses a regularity which, if one cannot call it metrical, remains a type of prosody, as one can see in the recurrence of three phrases and their variations ("not this"; "what then?"; "I started over & over"). It is no chance that these very phrases compose the nodal questioning of the poem, raising the poet's issues on writing, its modalities, its consequences, its difficulties. Over and over again, the poem returns to the micro-drama of a morning's history without ever fixing it into a stable depiction. As the text grows, and overgrows, in keeping perhaps with the poet's distress when unable to start his work, the physical and mental pains become at the same time very real and almost unspeakable.

Bob Perelman calls this text "paratactic" (69), but the paratactic effect is never fully achieved because the mathematical constraints contract a syntax that imitates the blurring of the real induced by the iterated attempts at trapping it into words. As the poem unfolds, both writer and reader are forced to move forward along towards the end of the poem. "What then?" (204) is the question that remains when, conforming to the very beginning, the poet chooses the "form of [his] execution" (16) by replacing the monstrous last paragraph by silence. Existence emerges from the ordeal as disjointed, without logic, cumulative as well as irredeemably limited. "Executed," the work dies inexorably in the concreteness of a book's last page. Similarly, one is tempted to say, lives end, leaving nothing but the paper trails of their histories.

An Autobiography of Lacunae: Lyn Hejinian's *My Life*

As is in fact the case with many procedural poems, the central issue of Lyn Hejinian's *My Life* is writing, when fiction, in the same way as "non-fiction," is understood as yet another form of witnessing, a textual artifact accounting for a set of facts or events. What is a poem; what is prose; what is a novel? These apparently hackneyed questions boil down to a radical research on the forms of discourse and their ideological implications. As memory is at work to reform the past, language is also at work to conform it to social expectations. Finding the poetic form that will allow for the unveiling for this underlying functioning of textuality is what preoccupies her—more than the autobiographical impulse of self-representation. The "I" of *My Life* is a structure, a system (to take up Mac Low's term) that processes facts of the past into events of the present. As one seems to know about the past, one writes through it and over it:

> I am always conscious of the disquieting runs of life slipping by, that the message remains undelivered, opposed to me. Memory cannot, though the future return, and proffer raw confusions. Knowledge is part of the whole, as hope is, from which love seeks to contrast knowledge with separation, and certainty with the temporal. Abridgement is foolish, like a lopping off among miracles; yet times is not enough. Necessity is the limit with forgetfulness, but it remains undefined. Memory is the girth, or again.
>
> (Hejinian, *Writing Is an Aid to Memory* n.p.)

In the same way as life slips by, Hejinian's grammar slips in this quotation but always in a significant manner: memory's powerlessness remains suspended; the plural is turned into a singular as it is petrified into monolithic memory; remembering might mean knowing, but this knowledge is as tenuous and fragile as love, or hope. Memory is global, it is a "girth," that sums up, lumps details together, tames, and fuses together the diversities of experience. In the manuscript for a lecture on *My Life*, Hejinian recognizes these interrogations about memory as "obsessions" ("Notes for a talk on *My Life*," MS 74, Box 40, Folder 12). Arithmetic and repetitions rule over the composition of the autobiographical poem, providing possible models for the functioning of memory. As the empty spaces of partial remembrance become obvious through sentences that fail to fully cohere into a narrative, the logic of the autobiography comes into question: what the poem fails to provide is the conventional causal reorganization of one's life that the reader expects. Re-vised, Hejinian's life remains as partial and arbitrary as it actually might have been, a life full of disruptions and incidents, in which the unforeseeable cannot be seen again in its entirety or as a natural development.

There are thus three versions of *My Life*, each one insisting on the idea that the past cannot be recovered but as its crystallizations in the present. The first version, published in 1980, contains 37 chapters made of 37 sentences for a 37-year-old poet. The second version, published in 1987, contains 45 chapters made of 45 sentences for a 45-year-old poet. The added sentences are never placed simply at the end of a chapter: the additions of memory to each age of the poet are spliced into the text, underlining the idea that the memories of all ages are transformed—increased—by the poet's very aging and attempts at recollecting. The more one remembers, it seems, the more there is to remember. Memories do not return untouched: the present has congealed on them to turn them into things of today. The text of the past cannot be written (or read) but in the present. Hejinian's autobiography is necessarily a procedural poem because it aims at accounting for the limits of memory, its functionings and the "reason" (in the mathematical sense of the term) for its lapses. From being "an aid to memory," writing becomes what enacts the failures and delusions of historiography, when the example of the self's history undermines the certainties of collective discourse: "Caesar's battles are but Caesar's prose" (*My Life* 64).

Kenneth Goldsmith's Mediations

Each of Kenneth Goldsmith's texts is based on the transfer of a given discourse, whose content is not under the poet's control, into a different media. Thus he draws from the quotidian in its most minute details to produce text that is either borrowed and collaged or simply transcribed. In *Day* (2003), he types down the September 1, 2000 issue of the *New York Times* from the top left of the front page to the bottom right of the last page, thus producing an impressive volume of highly tedious thus hardly legible text of 836 pages. In *The Weather* (2005), as David Antin defines it on the back cover, four seasons of daytime all-news radio broadcasts for the city of New York make up the texture of a year which happened, after the project was started in December 2002, to be the year the war in Iraq began. David Antin thus presents the text as a transcript which turns into an epic of survival in New York:

> Starting at the winter solstice, Kenneth Goldsmith by subtle framing has turned a literal transcript of a year's worth of radio weather reports into a classical narrative of New York's four Seasons . . . Spring includes two weeks of weather from the battlefields of Iraq as the vernal equinox follows two days after the invasion . . . The year] concludes with a descent into the promise of a milder Winter. New York has survived once more.
> (Antin, in Goldsmith, *The Weather* back cover)

Before that, in *Fidget* (2000) and in *Soliloquy* (2001), Goldsmith had respectively put down all the movements his body had performed in one day, and all the words he had uttered in one week, in a diptych of self-centered triviality. Following *The Weather*, we have *Traffic* (2007) and *Sports* (2008), which complete a trilogy of the most common, and most repetitive, announcements in radio broadcasting.

In *Day*, "really reading" the newspaper by retyping it implies a rule that runs against the conventional modes of its reading: strangely enough, despite its discontinuous organization, and stories cut up into a few columns on different pages, the newspaper appears to the common reader as coherent, and not as the collage that it is, a collage through which reading is channeled, and ideologically sorted. Once retyped, and turned first into a digital text, then into a book, however, the newspaper begins to crack at the seams, so that the method of this collage can be questioned, and the cracks can be seen for the voluntary cuts that they are.

The strategy folds back on the photographic, and the optical, awakening the reader to what lies both around and under the language artifact. About *Fidget*, Ruben Gallo follows Walter Benjamin's definition of the "optical unconscious" to argue that the text "deploys a number of innovative techniques to reveal aspects of everyday reality that are unusually accessible to the naked eye" (Gallo 54). But beside the revelation of usually unheeded everyday details in close-up, the method of *Day* and *The Weather* overexpose them as textual events, that can be recast, remodeled, retranscribed, *re-mediated* so as to inflect their content. Thus Kenneth Goldsmith's work entails a sudden, ironic focus on the mass media, not as pseudo-original matter for poetry, but as one surface of discourse, most often unprobed as texts matter-of-factly circulate, are categorized, integrated, and discarded. The change of medium for the media triggers an interrogation on what could be deemed the textual unconscious surrounding and underpinning any text. With the eruption of war—and in the current work an outlook on 9/11—both the discourse of the media and the discourse of the poem emerge as sometimes unaware matrixes of history.

Then it'll start to rain tomorrow, probably late in the day, we'll have rain tomorrow night on into Saturday, with a high Saturday into the fifties. No, uh, genuine prospects of sunshine until Sunday, but even then it'll be chilly, a high around fifty. Uh, battlefield weather is sunny and hot in, uh, Baghdad, the temperature into the low nineties at this moment, and it'll be middle-to-upper nineties tomorrow, and over the weekend with one hundred degrees plus, in the southern and eastern deserts. Some gusty winds over the weekend could cause isolated pockets of, uh, blowing sand and reduced visibilities, but nothing near as widespread as last week. Right now it's forty-four and mostly cloudy in Central Park, temperature today going up to about fifty.

(Goldsmith, The Weather 43)

Obsessed with Forgetting: Jerome Rothenberg's *Gematria*

To compose is to remember, so that procedural poetry adds in fact to the well-known three Rs, a fourth one, which accounts for the very choice of its rules and asserts their significance well beyond the playful and the anecdotal. This is decisively sealed by Jerome Rothenberg's use in some of his poems of gematria (the Hebrew word *gematria* is derived from the Greek, meaning geometry) to associate words and make up lines and stanzas. Imported from the Jewish Kabbalah's practice of combining words (and generating meanings for the texts) by using the numerical value of each letter of the Hebrew alphabet, it is at the origins of what Rothenberg calls "a poetry of numbers" (*Pre-Faces* 156). Words are linked through the sum of their letters' values, which creates multiple modes of reading, in a network encompassing all the words used in the Ancient Bible. In Rothenberg's gematria poems, numbers allow for a revival of the essential poetic practice of "naming":

For myself the numbers have been a presence beneath speech, but I have known them also, being Jewish, in the letters of the alphabet I work with. My father drew them with his finger on the kitchen table. And I have lain awake like him & counted numbers in sequences that play on mind & body until the rhythm of numbers, letters, shapes, & forms is inescapable—as still another source of naming.

(Pre-Faces 157)

Gematria poems might be seen only as resurgences of ancient tradition, a personal return to individual sources of inspiration, but they in fact function as memorials, witnessing the potential webs of meaning constantly at work in language, not through psychological processes of association but according to a method that transcends the individual and his mental capabilities. Memory is what we inhabit as we inhabit language. To write and to read is to reckon in the double sense of recognizing and counting. And the poetic "voice" is to be doubly re-envisioned as evidenced in these two examples of the word's numerical equivalents: an answer; and humbly one among many voice(s) . . .

THE VOICE (1)   THE VOICE (2)
will answer   A voice.

(Gematria Complete)

With "14 Stations" (*Gematria Complete* 145–58), a series of gematrias based on the names of fourteen concentration camps, Rothenberg re-members the Holocaust according to a method that paradoxically inscribes the disaster into language itself at the same time as it pushes it outside the confines of memory. The Yiddish transcriptions of the names of the camps yields numerical values that allow to find word equivalents in the text of Torah. Translated into English these words form poems strangely evocative of the unspeakable horrors of extermination. But as the poems unfold, the names of the camps cannot be retrieved through a reverse process: they are irredeemably outside the network of biblical words that compose the vocabulary of gematria. As forgetting is forbidden by the import of the camps' numerical values into language, they are expelled from the domain of usable and retrievable words, in a process that follows the destinies of the deported. In these poems, the process of "transvaluation" (Meilicke 26) stops at Dachau and Buchenwald:

The Third Station: Buchenwald
deliver me
from them
your cattle
rising
your assembly
lords of fat
deliver me
from color

(Gematria Complete ll.1–8)

Through the gematria procedure, Rothenberg actualizes the fundamental issue of the post-Holocaust poem: that words are not alone, but work in paradigms, whose diversity conventional syntax and modes of composition only allow to begin to explore. He also reminds the reader of the poem's inscription in the ethical necessity to account for history on a collective as well as individual level.

Towards an Ethical Imperative: "Optimistic Disenchantment"

Procedural poetry, in the case of many other poets we have not been able to examine here, intervenes as a (last?) resort to action in a context of overall skepticism and pessimism: what if art did not/could not exist anymore? How to write when all writing is rewriting? How to inhabit the intertextual condition since it cannot be overcome? How to acknowledge that the intertext is not exclusively literary but posits us in history? Raymond Queneau was weary of systems that would disregard "the plural and historical condition of mankind" (Le Tellier 285). Jacques Reda called him "disenchanted," in the way that disenchantment tempers utopian impulses and keeps in mind the "terrifying possibilities of regression, discontinuity, tragic barbarianism inherent to History, the science of men's unhappiness" (Le Tellier 285–86). And in "Happily," Lyn Hejinian reminds us of the word's etymology, as what is "happily" returns to what happens by chance and takes on a disquieting dimension.

In *Moi, Pierre Rivière, ayant égorgé ma mère, ma sœur et mon frère . . . Un cas de parricide au XIXe siècle*, Michel Foucault asserts that the interest of the documents surrounding a crime that was not so exceptional in nineteenth-century France lies in the memoir written by the accused in his own defense. The memoir is "beautiful" (16) and it is *a* history, among a multiplicity of histories of the crime. "All seem to be dealing with the same thing," but in such a heterogeneous manner that all discourses play against and with one another weaving complex "relations of power and knowledge" (16–17). Rivière's text is a memoir in the strongest sense of the term: not only a remembrance of the crime, it is made to be "deposited in memory" (324). Rivière's text is at the same time retrospective and programmatic.

Intersecting with these theoretical issues, the poetic preoccupations of procedural poets engulf this double movement of retrospection and prospection, with the impulse to recognize, accept, work with the limitations brought about by language and history. Bearing with the disenchanted assumption that all discourses are ideological and shouldering the most ancient ethical burden of the poet as psychopomp, they optimistically, if provisionally, produce a variety of compositional rules bearing witness to the possible—its "happy" beauties and disasters in "poems that count."

NOTE

1   My marginal notes.

REFERENCES AND FURTHER READING

Aji, Hélène. *Ezra Pound et William Carlos Williams: pour une poétique américaine*. Paris: L'Harmattan, 2001.

Antin, David. "Is There a Postmodernism?" *Bucknell Review* 25:2 (1980): 127–35.

Ashbery, John. "The Impossible." *Poetry* 90 (July 1957).

Benjamin, Walter. "The Work of Art in the Age of Mechanical Reproduction" (1935). *The Work of Art in the Age of Its Technological Reproducibility and Other Writings on Media*, ed. Michael W. Jennings, Brigid Doherty, and Thomas Y. Levin. Cambridge, MA: Harvard University Press, 2008.

Bernstein, Charles. *Content's Dream: Essays 1975– 1984*. Los Angeles: Sun & Moon Press, 1986.

Davidson, Michael. *The San Francisco Renaissance: Poetics and Community at Mid-century*. Cambridge: Cambridge University Press, 1989.

Foucault, Michel. *Moi, Pierre Rivière, ayant égorgé ma mère, ma sœur et mon frère . . . Un cas de parricide au XIXᵉ siècle*. Paris: Gallimard, Folio Histoire, 1973. American edition: *I, Pierre Rivière, Having Slaughtered My Mother, My Sister, and My Brother: A Case of Parricide in the 19th Century*, trans. Frank Jellinek. Lincoln, NE: University of Nebraska Press, 1982.

Fredman, Stephen. *Poet's Prose: The Crisis in American Verse*. New York: Cambridge University Press, 1990.

Gallo, Ruben. "*Fidget*'s Body." *Open Letter* 12:7 (2005): 50–57.

Goldsmith, Kenneth. *Day*. Great Barrington: The Figures, 2003.

Goldsmith, Kenneth. *Fidget*. Toronto: Coach House Books, 2000.

Goldsmith, Kenneth. *Soliloquy*. New York: Granary Books, 2001.

Goldsmith, Kenneth. *Sports*. Los Angeles: Make Now Press, 2008.

Goldsmith, Kenneth. *Traffic*. Los Angeles: Make Now Press, 2007.

Goldsmith, Kenneth. *The Weather*. Los Angeles: Make Now Press, 2005.

Hejinian, Lyn. *Happily*. Sausalito: Post-Apollo Press, 2000.

Hejinian, Lyn. *Lyn Hejinian Papers (MSS 74)*. Mandeville Special Collections, Geisel Library, University of California San Diego.

Hejinian, Lyn. *The Language of Inquiry*. Berkeley: University of California Press, 2000.

Hejinian, Lyn. *My Life*. Los Angeles: Green Integer, 2002.

Hejinian, Lyn, *Writing Is an Aid to Memory* (1978). Los Angeles: Sun & Moon, 1996.

Le Tellier, Hervé. *Esthétique de l'Oulipo*. Bordeaux: Le Castor Astral, 2006.

Mac Low, Jackson. *Barnesbook: Four Poems Derived from Sentences by Djuna Barnes*. Los Angeles: Sun & Moon Press, 1996.

Mac Low, Jackson. *Jackson Mac Low Papers (MSS 180)*. Mandeville Special Collections, Geisel Library, University of California, San Diego.

Mac Low, Jackson. "Willie's Clatter." *Mantis* 3 (2002): 76–78.

Meilicke, Christine A. *Jerome Rothenberg's Experimental Poetry and Jewish Tradition*. Bethlehem, PA: Lehigh University Press, 2005.

Perelman, Bob. *The Marginalization of Poetry: Language Writing and Literary History*. Princeton: Princeton University Press, 1996.

Perloff, Marjorie. "The Linear Fallacy in the Place of Poetry: A Symposium." *The Georgia Review* 35:4 (1981): 855–69.

Perloff, Marjorie. *Radical Artifice: Writing Poetry in the Age of Media*. Chicago: University of Chicago Press, 1991.

Rothenberg, Jerome. *Gematria Complete*. Grosse Pointe Farms: Marick Press, 2009.

Rothenberg, Jerome. *Pre-Faces and Other Writings*. New York: New Directions, 1981.

Silliman, Ron, *Tjanting* (1981), Cambridge: Salt, 2002.

25
Modes of Found Poetry

Lacy Rumsey

*I have great respect for the way I find things. Every time something falls I look. I cannot believe
the relationships. The intricacy. The object. You hear a noise and you say "What is that?"*

Frederick Sommer

Take an object.
Do something to it.
Do something else to it.

Jasper Johns

Found poetry poses a challenge to genre analysis. In the first place, it seems to have
the simplest of all generic bases: the presentation as poetry of "found language"—
language which within a previously occurring text or utterance has not been considered as poetry, nor as literature more broadly. Once that is stated, what is there left
to say? In the second—for there *must be* something left to say—the term has a complicated history, giving rise to categorial confusions between *found poetry*, *found poem*,
and *found text*. In the third, the term "found poetry," and perhaps the found poem
itself, have in recent years somewhat fallen from favor—a recent essay by Keith Tuma,
unambiguously entitled "Beyond Found Poetry," sets out grounds for its violent rejection. This neglect or hostility occurs despite the fact that the use of found language
is arguably more prevalent in poetry than ever before. Little extended critical, historical, or theoretical analysis of found poetry exists: this account seeks to cover, in a
preliminary fashion, some of the ground.

It has more than once been suggested that the earliest of all found poems are to
be found among the *Dix-neuf poèmes élastiques* (1919, *Nineteen Elastic Poems*) published
by the Swiss (and subsequently French) modernist Blaise Cendrars: Marjorie Perloff

A Companion to Poetic Genre, First Edition. Edited by Erik Martiny.
© 2012 John Wiley & Sons, Ltd. Published 2012 by John Wiley & Sons, Ltd.

cites "Mee too buggi," taken from a travel journal of the nineteenth century and first published in journal form in 1914, while John Robert Colombo points to "Dernière heure" (a title which the American poet Ron Padgett translates as "News Flash"), whose opening and closing lines are as follows:

> Oklahoma, 20 janvier 1914
> Trois forçats se procurent des revolvers
> Ils tuent leur geôlier et s'emparent des clefs de la prison
> Ils se précipitent hors de leurs cellules et tuent quatre gardiens dans la cour
> Puis ils s'emparent de la jeune sténo-dactylographe de la prison
> Et montent dans une voiture qui les attendait à la porte
> . . .
>
> Mr. Thomas, ancien membre du Congrès qui visitait la prison
> Félicite la jeune fille
>
> Télégramme-poème copié dans *Paris-Midi*
> *Janvier 1914*[1]

(ll.1–6, 15–17)

"Dernière heure"—which was written in the context of a poetic reaction against the rejection of everyday language seen as characteristic of Symbolist poets such as Mallarmé—displays a range of those characteristics that typify what is widely thought of as a found poem: it presents as a poem a text that is originally written by someone other than the poet; it gives the source of that text, such that the poet's status as finder rather than author is not in doubt (this is not the case for "Mee too buggi," whose discretion on this point may cause the poem to cross somewhat the frontier between found poetry and plagiarism); the source is non-literary, specifically a newspaper; the poem relineates the source text such that it has the unjustified right-hand margin of verse, and does so on syntactic grounds.

These latter characteristics—source (non-literary) and relineation—have often been taken as defining found poetry. Yet lineation is no more indispensable to found poetry than it is to other forms of poetry—indeed, it is precisely because it *is* no longer indispensable to other forms of poetry that found poetry such as Kenneth Goldsmith's *Day*, discussed below (and, from a slightly different perspective, in the preceding chapter by Hélène Aji, "Poems that Count: Procedural Poetry"), can do without it. This is not to say that line-breaks in found poems, where they exist, are of no importance; on the contrary, they can, as in any other poem, play a crucial part in the creation of a complex perceptual and cognitive experience, by virtue of their contribution to the poem's shape on the page, their parsing of and interference with the poem's syntax, their foregrounding of individual textual units, their guidance to rhythmic and intonational phrasing. Yet the operation of most importance to the creation of the larger category *poem*—*poem* being used descriptively rather than evaluatively—precedes such formal operations; it is carried out by the conventions that, in a given historical context, give the reader to understand that a given text is to be read with the particular attention and expectations reserved for poetry. These conventions—which Genette calls the "disposition poétique" (150), and which Culler relates to what he calls "the convention of significance" (175; see also Holden)—are activated by any broadly accepted means; a century after Modernism, it is sufficient for a text to be labeled "poetry" on publication, whatever its formal characteristics, for the possibility of its being read attentively to be created.

Its non-literary nature is what most clearly distinguishes found language, the basis of found poetry, from other forms of quotation, and thus enables us to draw distinctions between found poetry and those other forms of quotational poetry that have flourished since the Modernist period. A poem such as T.S. Eliot's *The Waste Land* (1922) quotes very widely, but predominantly from sources already recognized as literary; it was those of Eliot's fellow Modernists who were less influenced by Symbolism, notably William Carlos Williams and Marianne Moore, who expanded the domain of the quotable to overtly non-canonical, non-literary material—the "business documents and school-books" against which Moore's poem "Poetry" (1924) asserted a refusal to discriminate. If reliable definitions of the literary are no more available than uncontroversial definitions of poetry—both may best be treated as conventional or pragmatically defined categories—it is safest to say that found poetry is distinctive in that its quotations are from sources which are *susceptible* to being considered as non-literary—and that, at the time and in the context of its composition, probably were. The wide variety of non-literary sources that have been used in found poetry demonstrate the breadth of poets' adherence to Williams's contention in an interview from the *New York Post*—an interview itself extracted as found text in Williams's long poem *Paterson* (1946–58)—that "anything is good material for poetry" (222).

If found poetry refers to any poem or passage of a poem that relies on found language, the *found poem* is more narrowly defined. For the found poem has a single ostensible source: the poem *is* what has been found and redistributed under a new designation, perhaps—as will be discussed below—in a slightly modified form. Every line of Cendrars's "Dernière heure" is presented as having appeared in the newspaper article from which it was taken—although, as discussed below, this is not in fact quite the case. Every line of William Carlos Williams's "The Fight" (1941) will be assumed by most readers to have been heard by the poet on a single occasion (presumably a medical consultation)—with the exception of its final two lines, which report that occasion:

> That looks like teeth
> don't you think so?
>
> All I want to know is
> is it dangerous? That's
> all I care about it.
>   overheard by:
>   William Carlos Williams

(ll.23–29)

Non-found material in a found poem is, as here, typically limited to elements, such as a title or footnotes, that identify the text as a poem and give its source.

Texts that include passages of found material from various sources, or that combine found and non-found text, are not normally referred to as found poems, even if the former may be labeled found poetry. Instead, the terminology employed in describing such texts frequently draws on the vocabulary of the visual arts—appropriately enough, since the links between visual artists' and poets' use of found material have been significant ones throughout the genre's history. Texts that include both found language, or indeed literary quotation, and original material are frequently said to constitute an example of *collage*; where poems are made up exclusively of found material from different sources they are sometimes called *assemblages*, by analogy with similar practice in the visual arts. John Giorno's political texts of the 1960s are of this kind; a sequence such as "Constitution of the United States" (1966) combines extracts from the U.S. Constitution with contemporary mass-media and other found material, including newspaper court reports and advertisements:

> "Don't bother.
> I don't want to be tried.
> I killed her.
> I did it.
> I did it."

> Color television stocks
> leaped as much as $8 higher
> and featured in a strong and active
> stock market today.
>   ("Article IV, Section 2," ll.27–35)

Poems of collage and assemblage can be understood as varieties of a generalized Modernist practice of juxtaposition; in consequence, this study will focus more particularly on the found poem.

For some readers, the principal question that found poems raise is that of the degree of intervention that has been made by the poet who has taken it upon himself or herself to transcribe and recategorize the found material. All found poetry, clearly, involves a degree of transformation of the quoted material, if only because the simple fact of the change in the context of a text's reception that found poetry effects is a radical one. On the one hand, the generic associations of poetry cause readers to bring expectations of significance to bear on the found poem. On the other, found poetry is presented without those textual and contextual elements—the rest of the book/newspaper/conversation in which the material first occurred, and the pragmatic and cultural environment of that first occurrence—that will have guided the material's original readers or listeners in their inference of the text's underlying premises and assumptions. Lacking such support in its new context, found material will be interpreted in the light of readers' pre-existing assumptions, which are potentially entirely different to those which characterized the text's reception in its original context of publication or utterance. Moreover, the fact of quotation may enable readers better to attend to the formal qualities of the quoted language, as William Flesch has suggested: "In quotation, the word sloughs off the transparent content it has in context and takes on some of the opacity or refractoriness of form . . . [I]n quotation, prosody may come to the fore" (45). Apart from the necessary processes of selection and recategorization, the modification of the source text that is most widely accepted within found poetry is, as suggested above, its relineation. Also conventionally accepted is a certain amount of paring away—avowed or not—of material judged extraneous. That these transformations of the found text are both so widespread and so acceptable reminds us that, except in certain cases, the implicit claim of found poetry is that of a *relationship* to a prior verbal event, textual or uttered, and not its straightforward bodying-forth onto the page.

The constraints on that relationship are defined by readers' expectation and tolerances, and, no doubt, by the availability of the original source; as a result, they vary from poem to poem, and period to period. It is usually the case that significant rewriting of the source material will cause a poem to be considered as something different from a found poem. Charles Reznikoff's magnum opuses *Testimony* (1965), based on law reports, and *Holocaust* (1975), based in part on documents from the Nuremburg trials, do not repeat their sources verbatim or in a mildly edited form (and indeed do not claim to); the texts contain considerable rewriting, some of it with a clear rhetorical goal. Although Reznikoff's texts are still sometimes considered found poems, the degree of the poet's intervention—as well as the poems' relative length—has tended to work against that categorization, and the term *source-based poetry* has been used instead. Readers have not always been so rigorous, however, and other poems widely considered as found poems can be seen to include some fairly substantial modification. This is the case, notably, for Cendrars's "Dernière heure." Research has shown (see for example Goldenstein) that Cendrars not only condenses and otherwise modifies the style of the article on which his poem is based; he also transforms rather radically the fate of Mr. Thomas, who, far from congratulating the typist, had been reported by *Paris-Midi* to have been killed in the jailbreak. The historical importance of "Dernière heure," and its relative lightness of tone, as well as the more down-to-earth consideration that knowledge of these modifications is not available to most readers, may help to explain the text's having maintained the status of found poem. Readers thus appear to treat found poems somewhat as translations, with a varying tolerance for authorial license; in judging Cendrars, as, for example, in judging Pound's versions of the poetry of Propertius, they are either unaware of the creative looseness of the relationship between source and poem, or consider it unproblematic.

Poems in which source texts have been subjected to extensive or varied modification, and in which that modification is clearly apparent to readers, are sometimes referred to as *treated found poetry*. The most widely influential form of such treatment is that which consists in the omission or erasure of significant passages of the source text—omissions that are usually readily deducible as such by readers, and that transform it in profound ways. The practice has its roots in other genres, and in the visual arts; the founding object is Tom Philips's ongoing *A Humument: A Treated Victorian Novel* (1970-), which, inspired by the cut-up prose developed in the late 1950s by William Burroughs and Brion Gysin, scored through, and then painted over, almost all of the words on every page of *A Human Document*, a Victorian novel published in 1892. Among erasure-based treated quotational poetry, that for which the largest claims have been made is Ronald Johnson's *Radi Os* (1977), although this, like subsequent imitations, uses a highly literary source, "etch[ing]" into pages from books 1 to 4 of *Paradise Lost*. Such a practice constitutes a variety of the subjective attention which underlies many more traditional approaches to the writing of poetry. Treatments of found material that are more radical in their apparent circumvention of subjectivity will tend to be considered as falling into the neighboring genre of procedural poetry, discussed elsewhere in this volume; these include the chance- or rule-based alterations of found material that characterize work by Jackson Mac Low and John Cage. Similarly, the graphic redistribution of found text in ways more dramatic than simple lineation will usually result in a poem's being considered as concrete or visual poetry. As in all such cases, of course, judgments at the points of intersection of these genres are provisional.

In its desire to understand "foundness" as a distinctive feature, theorization of found poetry has tended to assign a single significance to its unusual pragmatic status. For Ronald Gross, for example, writing in 1967, the purpose of found material is to offer a "shock of recognition," as mass-cultural material intrudes into the domain of the poetic (quoted Holden 22). Much current criticism, on the other hand, assumes that the particular importance of found poetry's pragmatic status is metapoetic—Jena Osman, for example, writes that "[Tom] Philips's procedure is incredibly valuable because it usefully *redefines* what 'being a poet' means" (241, emphasis in original). Approaches such as these may prove useful within a particular set of interpretative preferences, or in response to particular found poems or styles. However, it would be mistake to treat found poetry as having a single nature or activity. Although found poetry is arguably a *kind* in the sense that Alastair Fowler uses the term—a historically defined genre with strong family resemblances between texts—it is a particularly open one, being equally aptly defined as a species of *publication*. Since found poetry is a means of circulation or distribution of pre-existing texts and utterances, the poetries which it can support are of extremely various nature.

What seems to be necessary, therefore is a preliminary description of some of the differing *modes* of found poetry: *mode* here being defined along the lines suggested by Fowler, who, having noted that it constitutes "the easiest of all terminological recourses" (106), nonetheless makes extensive use of it as a way of distinguishing between different varieties or extensions of the kinds that form the highest level of his theory of genre. In order not to multiply categories uselessly, this study will content itself with suggesting four modes of found poetry that between them correspond to much of the most-discussed found poetry that has so far been written; they are proposed in the spirit of John Swale's remark that the value of genre analysis is clarificatory, rather than classificatory (37):

- *anthologizing*: circulates material which readers infer to have been deemed by the poet to be of particular intrinsic value, this value being sufficiently anchored in the attributes of the text itself that it is not destroyed by the loss of that text's original context;
- *documentary*: circulates material which readers infer to have been deemed valuable in its capacity to bring to their attention a particular detail or circumstance in the world;
- *critical*: exploits the change of context between original and found-poem publication in order to facilitate a re-interpretative, often ironic response to the quoted material;
- *conceptual*: has as principal effect on readers the perception of an incitement to connect the found poem with ideas and debates in poetics or related theoretical fields—for example, by reconsidering their assumptions about the definition or nature of poetry or the poet.

These descriptions are not exhaustive, and are by no means mutually exclusive; nor are they fully discrete, since some of these modes overlap.

The anthologizing mode is reflected in one of the most important early discussions in English of the use of found material, included in the American poet Louis Zukofsky's 1931 essay "Sincerity and Objectification." Noting his fellow Objectivist poet Charles Reznikoff's repeated use of quoted material in his poetry, Zukofsky argues that: "It is more important for the communal good that individual authors should spend their time *recording and objectifying good writing wherever it is* . . . than that a plenum of authors should found their fame on all sorts of personal vagueness—often called 'sophistication'" (201, emphasis added). Zukofsky's own critical practice followed this approach; his essay on Henry Adams (1924–29), for example, to say nothing of *Bottom* (1965), his study of Shakespeare, is unusually rich in lengthy quotations. Zukofsky's great long poem, *"A"* (1959–75), also anthologizes found material; *"A"* (section 12) includes a long disquisition from a letter by Schoenberg on the roles of emotion and intelligence in art, a joke about self-exculpation in Italian recollections of Mussolini, *dicta* from the poet's father and son, and several letters to the poet and his wife from a young Army private with awkward written English. The value to be gained from these different found texts and utterances is not equivalent, not always of the same kind; nor it is necessarily equivalent to, nor of the same kind as the more canonically literary text that *"A"*-12 quotes in its entirety, the sonnet-epitaph for the Princess of Espinoye attributed to Elizabeth I. Yet the poem makes it evident that all are worth preserving, distributing, reading.

The American Objectivist tradition achieved particularly notable results with its carrying of the anthologizing mode into the realm of speech, in particular via the quotation of individuals and groups not typically associated with eloquent or formally sophisticated language. The intrinsic interest of the particular quotations brings into play the anthologizing activity of the found poem; such texts may also be challenging to received notions of class or geographical origin, as to those of the generic specificity of poetry itself. If Williams's "The Fight" may seem relatively unamenable to a reading of it in an anthologizing light—though to the poet himself, fascinated by the characteristics of American speech, it almost certainly had such status—others in the series of short poems that he published in the 1930s and 1940s are much more so. "No Good Too" (1948) is one such; unlike "The Fight," it is not explicitly marked as being made of overheard speech, but the reader is nonetheless likely to interpret it as such, and thus as a found poem:

> No Good Too
>
> She's the girl
> had her picture
> in the papers: just
> 14 years old and
>
> ran off with
> the guy her mother
> brought home
> from a gin mill

There are certainly multiple uses to be made of a poem such as this; what should not, however, be overlooked is its status as a craftily succinct piece of language—reliant, as gossip often is, on an implicit appeal to shared knowledge and assumptions, but also making very subtle use of rhythm. As so often in Williams, line-break in this poem appears to be of minimal consequence for vocal performance. When read aloud, the poem's first stanza is likely to be organized around a series of short, punchy intonation-groups as the gossip is transmitted detail by detail; its second, on the other hand, stretches into a burst of five-beat meter as the climax of the story is reached:

```
| she's the girl |

had her picture in the papers |

just fourteen years old |

and ran off with the guy her mother brought home from a gin mill |
  -o-   B     -o-    B  o  B  -o-      .B    -o-  B  o
```

This final sequence is relatively regular in its distribution of double offbeats (-o-) between the beats; its cumulative rhythmic effect exercises considerable rhetorical power.[2]

One of William Carlos Williams's successors in the investigation of the aesthetic potential of found language, Jonathan Williams (no relation), practiced the anthologizing mode extensively. His best-known volume, *Blues & Roots / Rue & Bluets* (1971), contains a variety of spoken and written language from the inhabitants of the Appalachian Mountains, a region often stereotyped as backward and unsophisticated. Describing his method in writing the poems which he bases on this language, Williams notes that they consist of "conversations quoted exactly but cast into line to reveal their native intention" (Williams, *Ear* n.p.), thus ascribing the principal artistry to the other speakers, rather than to himself. Such a grounding of poetic achievement in the citizen, rather than in the poet, has potentially broad implications. Of an epitaph of which he elsewhere makes a found poem (reading "LIVED ALONE / SUFFERED ALONE / DIED ALONE"), written for the grave of a hermit by the keeper of the local general store, the poet notes that: "What gets me, of course, being the sanguine democrat I occasionally am, is that a shopkeeper, who probably never heard of the word *poet* or read a line of what they call 'poetry' in his whole life, could get these words to work like that" (*Blackbird Dust*, 10–11). Williams's found poetry is thus characterized by a triple focus: metapoetic, civic, but above all aesthetic.

A different set of responses is invited by the variety of anthologizing found poetry that collects work which departs radically, and often comically, from expected norms of communication or expression. The best-known repository of such work—which consists in posters, flyers, unusual advertisements—is Ubuweb (ubu.com) a website run by poet and conceptual artist Kenneth Goldsmith. A notorious example is reproduced in Figure 25.1.

The potentially comic unexpectedness of this is multiple: the faulty grammar, the perhaps unnecessarily precise drama of the narrative, the idea that a dog's head—rather than the customary whole dog—should be missing, and should be the sole subject of the photograph, the idea that the remains of a dog's head might be sufficiently valuable to merit a reward. At date of writing, Ubuweb collects this and many other curiosities in a section of the site entitled "Outsider," thus connecting it to traditions of outsider art and *art brut* (that is, art created by individuals operating outside traditional artistic culture, and generally marginal in other ways); an earlier, more direct name for the section was "Found + Insane." Although the use of the word "insane" has a certain history in aesthetics, it may be rather hastily reached for here; the filling of such a category with comic pieces such as this risks serving at least in part to reassure readers of their own sanity and reasonableness (and perhaps their difference from immigrants who use English in ways they do not) as they point, tourist-like, at The Strange. Found material such as "Ling Ling" has many routes to distribution, the most successful of which—compilations such as Davy Rothbart's *Found*, or even *National Lampoon's Totally True Facts*, in which "Ling Ling" has also appeared—make no claim of poetic status for their contents.

As well as their aesthetic or comic potential, all of the pieces quoted so far also, of course, have a referential function, serving as a pointer to particular circumstances and experiences. In *documentary* uses of found material, this referential function dominates: what is at stake is, above all, the transmission to the reader of information about

MISSING
DOG HEAD

You finding Ling-Ling's head?
Someone come into yard, kill dog,
cut off head of dog.
Ling-Ling very good dog.
Very much want head return.
REWARD   Call 871-7421

Figure 25.1 "Ling Ling" (poster).

the world. The information can be anecdotal; the reader of Annie Dillard's sequence "Emergencies" (1995), whose source text is a volume entitled *Prehospital Emergency Care and Crisis Intervention*, gains some knowledge of the working experiences of paramedics, and of the final moments of some of their patients:

> If a patient asks, "I'm dying,
> Aren't I?" respond
> With something like, "You
> Have some very serious injuries,
> But I'm not giving up on you."
>
> ("Answer," ll.5–9)

More frequently, however, documentary uses of found material have pointed to contexts of interpretation that are overtly political. The documentary impulse was strong in various cultural forms in the 1930s, a period associated in America with Objectivism, and in both America and Britain with a close imbrication of poetry with Marxist and socialist ideas. Charles Reznikoff's poetry draws on both influences; this passage, from *Testimony*, is extracted from an account of a deaf old man accustomed to being taunted by boys:

> Now there were only two boys
> and they, too, were shouting at him
> and pulling at his coat;
> for a locomotive was coming down the track he was about to cross.
> The old man thought that they were just having the usual fun
> and turned, lifting his stick as if to strike them,
> and pulling himself free
> stepped upon the track just in front of the speeding train.
>
> (vol. 1, p. 248)

As with Dillard's poem, the language is far from being devoid of interest; Reznikoff's rendering of the case summaries in clear, simple language seems to connote a certain faith in institutions and in the speech they can encompass. For most readers, nonetheless, what will dominate the experience of reading *Testimony* is the sense of gaining access to a particular set of human experiences, and to the implication that these experiences may be representative of many other lives than those described in each case.

As noted above, Reznikoff's poetry is often considered source-based poetry rather than found poetry, given the extent of his editorial interventions, and indeed, documentary found poetry—as opposed, for example, to the documentary use of found material within assemblage or collage-based structures—is relatively rare. Much more common is the *critical* mode, whereby the found material functions not simply as a conduit to the experiences or circumstances to which it refers, but is itself subjected to linguistic and ideological critique. Such critiques are typically focused on material that is invested with a certain prestige or status within dominant ideologies: news reports, advertisements, official documents. The change of context—and of readership—effected by the redistribution of the poem in found-poem form opens the material up to a set of assumptions unanticipated by its original authors, and thus to the possibility of an ironic reading.

Found poetry which engages with other discourses in this way rarely relies solely on the removal of the original context to bring about substantial re-interpretation. Instead, poems engage in a certain amount of recontextualizing activity, encouraging the reading of the text in the light of particular kinds of assumptions. A simple example is Bern Porter's assignment of the title *The Waste Maker* to his 1972 compilation of extracts from newspapers and magazines, most of them advertisements. More complex encouragements to a critical stance may be constituted by poetic form, as in David Antin's "code of flag behavior" (1968). The poem consists of material taken from the "Respect for Flag" sections of the United States Code, a document which brings together "the general and permanent laws of the United States." It was published in 1968, at a time when the Vietnam War—among other phenomena—was leading to great contestation of American national policy. This context alone would encourage an ironic response to official instructions concerning the national flag; such a response is made even more likely by the poem's formatting and lineation.

"code of flag behavior" begins with fairly lengthy lines; the absence of punctuation and unusual formatting, apparently a mid-line tab stop, suggest the distancing of the quoted material from its habitual functions, and its opening-up to ironic or oblique responses:

> the flag should never be displayed with the union down   except
>   as a sign of distress

> (l.1)

More dramatic is the sudden restriction in line length as the poem ends:

> when the flag is in such condition that it is no longer fit
>   for use
>   as an emblem of display
> it should be destroyed
> in a dignified way
> preferably by burning

> (ll.15–19)

The poem's progress slows considerably in these lines, as the lineation breaks the sentence down into its component phrases. The loss of speed encourages a sense of dwelling on the possibility it describes, and allows the reader to imagine the act of flag-burning—and the symbolic rejection it makes available of a flag or polity that is "not fit for use"—in ways very different to those imagined by the authors of the U.S. Code.

Among more contemporary works, Juliana Spahr's *Power Sonnets* use the conventions and expectations of the fourteen-line form—notably the reader's knowledge that the structure of the English sonnet permits the final two lines to carry particular epigrammatic punch—to guide readers' judgments of the relative importance of aspects of the text; this is the final "couplet" of "After Kendra Mayfield, 'Why Girls Don't Compute', *Wired* Website, 3:00 a.m. Apr. 20, 2000 PDT":

> interests. "Software is primarily aimed at boys. To counteract that, we desperately
>   need software out there for girls"; "It's not really violence that turns girls
> off," repetitious, boring games are more likely to turn girls off than violence.
>   Researchers also stressed educating girls.

> (ll.13–14)

No single response is legislated for by these lines; one—depending, of course, on the reader's own assumptions—is that *of course* the education of girls, in its fullest sense, is more important than tweaking computer-game design, and that if researchers only "also stress" this they—and the society they report back to—may be asking the wrong questions. The effectiveness of the poem derives from the overlaying of the poet's implicit judgment as to the fundamental importance of the education of girls—a judgment expressed structurally—onto one which makes it seem a mere afterthought.

Found poetry's metapoetic implications are activated each time a reader considers a found poem's status as poetry, or its connection to one or another of the legitimating discourses of poetics or art theory. This activation can occur whatever the reader's other responses to the poem; in the anthologizing mode, as in the work of William Carlos Williams and Jonathan Williams, for example, it is possible to respond with pleasure to the rhythms of found speech while assessing how that pleasure might alter one's conception of poetic rhythm. The distinctive characteristic of found poetry in the *conceptual* mode—the mode in which the genre most fully connects with the Duchampian strain in twentieth- and twenty-first-century art—is that, within that mode, a poem's implications for poetics are central to the experience of it, potentially to the exclusion of most other interest.[3]

Conceptual found poetry, like many versions of the genre, developed most rapidly in the 1960s; it is implicit in the early poetry of David Antin, as in the text-based work of artists like Carl Andre and Vito Acconci, and draws on the conceptual work done by much procedural poetry. Its best-known contemporary practitioner is Kenneth Goldsmith, among whose works is *Day* (2003), which consists of a transcription of a single day's issue of the *New York Times*. At well over 800 pages long, *Day* is probably the largest single found poem in existence; extracts from it look like this:

> In the last couple of years, however, the taboo has lifted somewhat and fur has quietly crept back into the American fashion world, first by showing up in the lines of many top fashion designers on collar trims and accessories. Now, however, it has asserted itself in full-page fashion layouts.
>
> (*Day* 230)

> 27.06 10.00 IngrmM 10 5557 15.69 15.00 15.00–0.50 10.88 7.63 Innkeepr 1.12
> 10.8 69 351 10.38 10.25 10.38 - 10.00 4.25 InputOut dd 981 9.19 8.56 9.00–0.19
>
> (*Day* 264)

Although the second of these extracts—from a list of New York stock prices—has a certain mesmeric charm, aided by the relineation away from stock prices' usual columnar format, what complex and engaging experiences the text offers are very probably those that can be got from any day's edition of the *New York Times*. Yet the text is clearly not an example of the documentary mode. The central difference—the added value, in comparison to the experience of the *Times*—lies, of course, in the contextual assumptions that readers bring to bear on a text like *Day*, as on classics of minimalist and Pop Art such as the Brillo boxes of Andy Warhol. As is often the case, the poet—or his publisher—helps readers to locate them:

With this simple act of transcription, Goldsmith critiques the culturally cherished values of creativity and originality in writing. Following the traditions of Andy Warhol's work in the visual arts, or the ubiquitous practices of sampling and plunderphonics in contemporary music, Goldsmith asks, "Nearly one hundred years after Duchamp, why hasn't appropriation become a valid, sustained, or even tested literary practice?" . . .

"Even John Cage, whose mission it was to accept all sound as music, ultimately failed; his filter was on too high," says Goldsmith. "However, if Cage claimed that any sound can be music, then by extension we can conclude that, properly framed, any language can be poetry."

(back cover)

Leaving aside the claim of the untested nature of appropriation in writing—a claim which the various poems quoted in this article might suggest is unfounded—it is clear that the back cover is in many ways the most important page of Goldsmith's book; it encourages the reader to connect the text to its supporting context, and to participate in conversation about the debates to which it alludes. Yet all found poetry permits that, and much of that discussed so far, especially that which combines the activities of different modes, does much more.

For all the variety of its achievement—its circulation of texts whose recategorized and modified forms provide or incite readers to pleasure, information, critique, theoretical reflection—found poetry, particularly of the untreated variety, appears to have a slightly uncertain status at the present time. It can be seen in non-poetic, and particularly journalistic contexts, as in the humorist Hart Seely's excerpting of the words of U.S. Defense Secretary Donald Rumsfeld for *Slate* magazine:[4] a development which, of course, adds another layer to the generic recategorizations with which the genre began. In more specifically poetic contexts, on the other hand, found poetry appears relatively out of favor, with procedural or collage-based approaches to found material much more prevalent. Its adoption by other kinds of writer may be one of the factors behind found poetry's decline in appeal to poets and their audiences, as may the related fact of the genre's dependence on the power of a conventional response that is likely to have weakened over time. One may also cite the greater contemporary availability of other means of circulating found text, a reduced interest in groups of language users perceived as culturally underrepresented, and the diffidence within contemporary experimental poetics towards poetry that invites reading as the product of particular intentions; since found poems are dependent on a single and identifiable communicative decision on the part of the poet—that to present a chunk of previously existing text as a poem—found poetry is a genre in which the inference of authorial intention plays a particularly large part in readers' experiences of individual poems. Found poetry's current loss of strength as a vehicle for serious work may represent the gradual exhaustion of a genre, or a mere hiatus. Whichever proves to be the case, the genre has contributed poetry of much greater diversity than is sometimes thought.

NOTES

1 Ron Padgett translates these lines as follows: "OKLAHOMA, *January 20, 1914* / Three convicts get hold of revolvers / They kill their guard and grab the prison keys / They come running out of their cells and kill four guards in the yard / Then they grab the young prison secretary / And get into a carriage waiting for them at the gate / . . . / Mr. Thomas, former member of Congress who was visiting the prison, / Congratulates the girl / / Copied telegram-poem in *Paris-Midi* / January 1914." Blaise Cendrars, *Complete Poems*, trans. Ron Padgett (Berkeley: University of California Press, 1992), p. 68.

2 The rhythmic notations are taken from the beat–offbeat metrics developed by Derek Attridge. See, for example, Carper and Attridge.

3 Of D.H. Lawrence's "The Rocking Horse Winner," which he includes in his work *No. 111*, Kenneth Goldsmith states: "To this day I have never 'read' that story! . . . I trust you when you say it's a great story, but for me to treat it as such would be to undermine the structural and appropriative concept that I am trying to get across." Marjorie Perloff, "An Interview with Kenneth Goldsmith," *Jacket* 21, n.p., http://jacketmagazine.com/21/perl-gold-iv.html.

4 The interesting and rather unsettling ambiguity of Seely's volume should be noted; it can be read as anthology as well as as critique.

REFERENCES AND FURTHER READING

Antin, David. *Selected Poems: 1963–1973*. Los Angeles: Sun & Moon, 1991.

Carper, Thomas and Derek Attridge. *Meter and Meaning: An Introduction to Rhythm in Poetry*. London: Routledge, 2003.

Cendrars, Blaise. *Poésies complètes, avec 41 poèmes inédits*, ed. Claude Leroy. Paris: Denoël/Le Grand Livre du Mois, 2001.

Colombo, John Robert. "A found introduction." In *Open Poetry: Four Anthologies of Expanded Poems*, ed. Ronald Gross and George Quasha. New York: Simon and Schuster, 1973. www.ubu.com/papers/found_poetry.html.

Culler, Jonathan. *Structuralist Poetics*. London: Routledge, 1975.

Dillard, Annie. *Mornings like This: Found Poems*. New York: Harper Perennial, 1995.

Flesch, William. "Quoting poetry." *Critical Inquiry* 18 (1991): 42–63.

Fowler, Alastair. *Kinds of Literature: An Introduction to the Theory of Genres and Modes*. Cambridge, MA: Harvard University Press, 1982.

Genette, Gérard. *Figures II*. Paris: Seuil, 1969.

Giorno, John. *Subduing Demons in America: Selected Poems 1962–2007*, ed. Marcus Boon. Berkeley: Soft Skull, 2008.

Goldenstein, Jean-Pierre. "Vers une systématique du poème élastique." *Europe* 566 (1976): 115–30.

Goldsmith, Kenneth. *Day*. Great Barrington: The Figures, 2003.

Holden, Jonathan. "The 'Found' in Contemporary Poetry." In *The Rhetoric of the Contemporary Lyric*. Bloomington: Indiana University Press, 1980. 22–37.

Johnson, Ronald. *Radi Os* (1977). Chicago: Flood, 2005.

Osman, Jena. "Gumshoe Poetry." In *Poetry and Pedagogy: The Challenge of the Contemporary*, ed. Joan Retallack and Juliana Spahr. New York: Palgrave Macmillan, 2006. 239–50.

Perloff, Marjorie. "Found Poem." In *The New Princeton Encyclopedia of Poetry and Poetics*, ed. Alex Preminger and T.V.F. Brogan. Princeton: Princeton University Press, 1993. 423–24.

Philips, Tom. *A Humument: A Treated Victorian Novel*. 4th edn. London: Thames & Hudson, 2005.

Porter, Bern. *The Waste Maker*. Somerville, MA: Abyss, 1972.

Reznikoff, Charles. *Testimony: The United States (1885–1915): Recitative*. 2 vols. Santa Barbara: Black Sparrow, 1978–79.

Rothbart, Davy (ed.). *Found: The Best Lost, Tossed, and Forgotten Items from Around the World*. New York: Simon & Schuster, 2004.

Seely, Hart. *Pieces of Intelligence: The Existential Poetry of Donald H. Rumsfeld*. New York: Free, 2003.

Spahr, Juliana. From *Power Sonnets*. In *The Reality Street Book of Sonnets*, ed. Jeff Hilson. London: Reality Street, 2008. 305–10.

Swale, John M. *Genre Analysis: English in Academic and Research Settings*. Cambridge: Cambridge University Press, 1990.

Tuma, Keith. "Beyond Found Poetry." In *An Exaltation of Forms: Contemporary Poets Celebrate the Diversity of Their Art*, ed. Annie Finch and Kathrine Varnes. Ann Arbor: University of Michigan Press, 2002. 352–57

Ubuweb. www.ubu.com.

Williams, Jonathan. *Blackbird Dust: Essays, Poems, and Photographs*. New York: Turtle Point, 2000.

Williams, Jonathan. *Blues & Roots / Rue & Bluets: A Garland for the Southern Appalachians*. New York: Grossman, 1971, with photos by Nicholas Dean. 2nd edn Durham, NC: Duke University Press, 1985.

Williams, Jonathan. *An Ear in Bartram's Tree: Selected Poems 1957–67*. New York: New Directions, 1969.

Williams, William Carlos. *Collected Poems, Volume II: 1939–1962*. Ed. Christopher MacGowan. London: Paladin, 1991.

Williams, William Carlos. *Paterson*. Rev. edn. ed. Christopher MacGowan. New York: New Directions, 1992.

Zukofsky, Louis. *"A."* Berkeley: University of California Press, 1978.

Zukofsky, Louis. "Sincerity and Objectification: With Special Reference to the Work of Charles Reznikoff" (1931). In *Prepositions +: The Collected Critical Essays*. Hanover, NH: Wesleyan University Press / University Press of New England, 2000. 193–202.

Part II

26

"Horny Morning Mood"
The Aubade and Alba

Kit Fryatt

Defined primarily by content rather than form, the aubade presents certain difficulties of generic classification, and modern poets' use of the term has tended to exacerbate these. The category of the dawn song or poem is vast: they are found in almost all cultures and have been composed since the earliest times. Perhaps originally religious, dawn poems are also associated in most of these cultures with secular eroticism, as demonstrated by Arthur T. Hatto's voluminous study in comparative literary anthropology, *Eos: An Inquiry into the Theme of Lovers' Meetings and Partings at Dawn in Poetry* (1965). Western European readers readily identify dawn poetry with courtly love and troubadour culture. The Old Occitan form known as the *alba*, in which adulterous lovers receive a warning to part from a sympathetic observer, and which takes repetition of the word "alba" (dawn) as a structuring principle—though technically distinct—is often considered synonymous with the aubade. Aubades more closely defined are meeting rather than parting poems, songs sung by lovers to wake their beloveds and gain admittance to their chambers. Since modern poets have tended to confuse and conflate the alba and the aubade, in this chapter I consider both, and restrict potentially huge scope by choosing to focus on twentieth-century poems in English to which their authors have given the title "Aubade" or "Alba."

Even a poet as immersed in the culture of medieval Occitania as Ezra Pound might use the term "alba" very loosely—his poem of the title, collected in *Lustra* (1916) is spoken by a lover, not by the third party traditional to the Provençal form. It is, moreover, linked by the motif of wet leaves or petals to such imagist and Orientalizing lyrics as "Liu Ch'e," "Ts'ai Chi'h," and "In a Station of the Metro" rather than, for example, the contemporaneous versions of Bertran de Born. The motif is extraordinarily polyvalent: it might suggest transience, anonymity, regret, abandonment, or, as here, where the beloved is as "cool" as the "pale wet leaves of lily-in-the-valley,"

A Companion to Poetic Genre, First Edition. Edited by Erik Martiny.
© 2012 John Wiley & Sons, Ltd. Published 2012 by John Wiley & Sons, Ltd.

post-coital exhaustion nonetheless retaining poise. Judeo-Christian tradition, which associates lily-of-the-valley with both the Sulamite and the Virgin Mary, reinforces the sense of tension between desire and restraint.

To the reader familiar with Pound's sexy coolth, Amy Lowell's "Aubade," collected in *Sword Blades and Poppy Seeds* (1914), seems an exemplar of what he, during one of their disputes over the control of the Imagiste movement, dubbed "Amygism." Lover addresses beloved, comparing her body to a "white almond" peeled from the "green husk" (l.2), finding in the "smooth and polished kernel" (l.4) a "gem beyond count-ing" (l.5). Lowell's perfervid metaphors find few imitators in the twentieth-century aubade, but her poem does share some features with its successors. Dawn is implied in the poem's color-play of white and green and its figures of a fresh nut and sparkling jewel, but without the title the reader may not intuit an early-morning setting. Similarly, many of the poems explored in this chapter de-emphasize dawn itself while claiming the venerable tradition and familiar set of associations represented by the term "aubade." Lowell's conditional mood suggests the uncertainty becoming a lover—trepidation links virtually all of the poems discussed here; William Empson's "Aubade" even finds literal expression for the theme. However, the resemblance is limited: Lowell's syntax may be tentative, but her metaphors and lineation anticipate the *ioi entier* that Pound's speaker has enjoyed (in this sense, the two poets maintain titular and terminological distinction—Lowell's speaker awaits a meeting; Pound's has nothing to do but depart). Imagining the beloved stripped naked contracts the whole body to a sensitive "kernel," a movement anticipated by setting the word "Beloved" as a line on its own. The intense focus of clitoral orgasm dissipates in the concluding fifteen-syllable "hexameter" ("beyond counting" self-reflexively comments on the hypermetrics) as the figure too, becomes inexact, from "fingering . . . the kernel" to a "gem" shining in "hands" (ll.4–5). There are dangers attendant on using imprecise language to convey relaxation, and Lowell cannot be said to avoid them. Pound's dialectic between sweaty consummation and cool dewiness, chastity and sexu-ality maintains tension despite the mood of completion—Lowell slackens while her lover is still speaking of the encounter as a possibility. However, the two poems have more in common with one another than they do with the century of aubades that succeed them: they are, as most of those are not, primarily, centrally, and sincerely concerned with sex.

Pound's slightly later dawn lyrics, collected as part of the short sequence "Langue d'Oc" in *Quia Pauper Amavi* (1919), impress us with a sense of return to origin. Pound translates troubadour texts which established the dawn lyric as a distinct form in Western European tradition, and which for many readers remain definitive. The first in the sequence, after an epigraphic "Alba," "Compleynt of a gentleman who has been waiting outside for some time," is a version of Giraut de Bornelh's "Reis glorios," among the best known of troubadour songs and the most famous surviving alba. Giraut's poem is spoken by a friend of a lover, set outside the chamber to watch for potential intruders while the latter spends a night with his lady. He turns to the rising sun with an address to all intents indistinguishable from Christian prayer, "Reis glorios, verais lums e clartatz" ("Glorious King, true, clear light"). The next five stanzas are addressed to the lover, urging him to wake and be gone for the sake of his reputation and his lady's. Each stanza concludes with the refrain "E ades sera l'alba" ("And it will soon be dawn"). Some versions include a final stanza, with a variant refrain, in the voice of the lover, in which he says he cares nothing for the dawn and refuses to leave his beloved for the sake of "lo fol gilos," that jealous fool her husband.

Giraut's reputation in his own time was of a versatile master who eschewed arcane allegory and defended accessible expression (to say that he was a twelfth-century Philip Larkin is probably to stretch a point, but in addition to technical virtuosity they share the distinction of having composed the best-known dawn poems of their respective times and languages). Beginning with the wry title, Pound persistently turns Giraut's direct clarity to self-conscious, ironic fustian. "Reis glorios" is grecianized to "plasmatour" (l.1) (the apparent pun on astrophysical plasma is fortuitous—the idea that space may be composed of charged particles was proposed in 1913, but the term *plasma* was not used in this sense until a decade after the publication of Pound's translation); the watcher uses archaisms and neologisms: "swenkin" (l.11), "welkin" (l.12), "venust" (l.21), which have no parallel in Giraut's song, introducing a farcical note which, while scarcely alien to some aspects of troubadour culture, is not characteristic of this particularly elegant song. Pound's idiom suggests a sort of mastery very different from Giraut's—that of the waggish don, deflecting the implied homoeroticism of the relationship between watcher and lover in a way which would probably not have seemed necessary to the nineteenth century, let alone the twelfth. Pound uses the same idiom and vocabulary in "Langue d'Oc"'s other alba, where it sits, if anything, more awkwardly upon its source, an anonymous pastoral with a female speaker which approaches folk tropes at the respectable distance required by courtly convention. The six-stanza original frames the lady's regret at the approach of dawn with two stanzas in the anonymous voice of the *chanson d'aventure* (a medieval form in which the speaker meets by chance a young woman and engages in—often amorous—dialogue with her). The translation in "Langue d'Oc" reduces her speech to two stanzas, using the second to effect a transition between the Poundian voice which translates "Dieu" as "Plasmatour" and faux-rustic simplicity: "Fore God how swift the night!" (l.8), and reassigning the fourth to the woman's lover, who does not speak in the original.

Pound's versions refer their readers to sources only via an estrangement which is inevitable, since twentieth-century readers do not inhabit the culture of medieval Occitania, but which he magnifies with mock-scholarly diction and jokey, blokey anxieties. It is notable that the alba in particular attracts such treatment—the three other versions in the sequence, even "Canzon," an attempt to mimic the formal complexity of Arnaut Daniel's songs—are by comparison unselfconscious, less heavily inflected by nervous masculine postures. In giving anxiety priority over eroticized gracefulness, Pound breaks with his own earlier "Alba" as much as with troubadour song; moreover, he sets the dominant tone for very nearly the next century's worth of dawn-lyric in Anglophone art poetry. Vocabulary close to that of everyday speech is recovered quickly—plasmatours and venusings cede to consciousness of conflict global and total in ways unimaginable even in 1919—but sensuality is slow to return.

Mid-twentieth-century aubades dispense with lovers and sexual situations to the extent that ironic use of the term becomes standard. The facetiousness of Pound's "Compleynt" is also dismissed, as the dawn poem becomes a medium for the expression of disappointment and fear. Edith Sitwell's "Aubade" is rustic in subject matter but urbane in approach, describing the early morning routine of Jane, "a country servant, a girl on a farm, plain and neglected and unhappy" in the synaesthetic terms of modernist painting. The poem's speaker sees (and "hears") effects of dawn light which are invisible to Jane in her world delimited by "Eternities of kitchen garden":

> the creaking empty light
> will never harden into sight
>
> Will never penetrate your brain.
>
> (ll.14, 10–12)

Rhymes and rhythms, insistent and off-kilter, suggest Jane's awkwardness, and form a contrast with the speaker's Cubist sensibility: "in a very early dawn," Sitwell notes, "the light has a curious uncertain quality . . . it falls in hard cubes, squares and triangles, which, again, give one the impression of a creaking sound" (19). The simultaneous condescension to and compassion for Jane's "sad bucolic stupidity" (19) has a parallel in the *chanson d'aventure*, in which the speaker's role is often implicitly to offer rebuke as well as dispassionately report on the predicament of an unfortunate lass. But where such misadventure in the folk tradition usually has a cause in sexual misconduct, Jane's is the result of sexual neglect. Her "cockscomb flowers" and "cockscomb hair," as well as furnishing a phallic pun, may ultimately be derived from a ballad trope—the insult offered in Child #112, "The Baffled Knight," to a frustrated suitor by a resourceful young woman, but by Sitwell transferred to a sterile female:

> We have a tree in our garden,
> Some call it of rosemary, sir;
> There's crowing-cocks in our town
> That will make a capon of you, sir.
>
> We have a flower in our garden
> We call it the marygold, sir

Sitwell's high modernist attention to light, texture, and music is the kind evoked, to be dismissed with contempt, by Samuel Beckett's "Alba." Like many of Beckett's earlier poems (it was collected as part of *Echo's Bones* in 1935) "Alba" joins allusions and generic characteristics with skill, without ever quite achieving the status of an independent work of art. Yet because of its synthetic nature it preserves features of

the medieval dawn lyric which are progressively effaced in twentieth-century iterations of the mode. "Alba" successively acknowledges the arcane aspect of troubadour
tradition, "Dante and the Logos and all strata and mysteries" (l.2), its sensuousness,
"grave suave singing silk" (l.6), and its politics of gender and power,

> who though you stoop with fingers of compassion
> to endorse the dust
> shall not add to your bounty.
>
> (ll.10–12)

before reaching a conclusion of scoured, solipsistic emptiness:

> there is no sun and no unveiling
> and no host
> only I and then the sheet
> and bulk dead
>
> (ll.14–17)

For all that "Alba" might be read seriously, even solemnly, in isolation, however, an
awareness of the character so named in Beckett's fiction returns the reader to a mood
of more than Poundian facetiousness—gravity and suavity cannot abide long in the
modern dawn poem.

For the poets of the interwar years, dawn often symbolizes uncertainty, a sense that
a new day can bring only more turmoil and suffering. A change from private and
domestic settings to public and civic ones, characteristic of the poetry of the 1930s
in general, is pronounced in the decade's aubades. It is rather as if the aubade itself,
rather than one of its personnel, has departed, left the enclosed world of lovers for, in
Louis MacNeice's words, "a precise dawn / Of sallow and grey bricks, and newsboys
crying war." The confidential first-person plural segues into the editorial: "What have
we after that to look forward to?" asks MacNeice's speaker (l.4). These effects obtain
even when, as in William Empson's "Aubade," the situation is a post-coital one.

Usually a copious annotator, Empson provides only one brief note to this poem,
though significantly, it relates to political context: its composition in the early stages
of the second Sino-Japanese war. John Haffenden's edition of the *Complete Poems* supplies much fascinating biographical detail about the poem's origin in Empson's
relationship with a woman named Haru during his time in Japan, including a clari-
fication of lines which to many readers might seem to link this aubade to the traditions of courtly love: "The thing was being woken he would bawl / And finding her
not in earshot he would know" (ll.18–19). Not *lo fol gilos*—Haru was single, worked
as a nanny for a diplomat, and "he" is her infant charge. One of Empson's structuring
principles is apparently to resist the aubade's identifying markers at every turn:
the poem begins not at dawn but "Hours before" it; it is not light which wakes the
lovers, but the motion of an earthquake; little of longing or lingering; instead the

brisk words derived (presumably, since the male speaker stays put) from something said by the departing woman: "It seemed the best thing to be up and go," which forms a refrain. Neither this nor the other refrain, "The heart of standing is you cannot fly," mentions the dawn; in fact, it seems that the speaker, having been woken long before daybreak and parted from his lover shortly afterwards, sleeps through the dawn itself: "I slept, and blank as that I would yet lie" (l.22). The latter is one of two plays on the verb "to lie"—the other, when the speaker makes a rather perfunctory gesture towards asking his lover to stay, "Some solid ground for lying could she show?" (l.15) elicits her response giving paid work priority over pleasure, subordinating adult diversion to the care of a child. These puns resist sexual connotation: they pertain to the mood of deceit or self-deceit, and to the poem's interest in physical posture in a shaken world, but even filthy-minded readers will struggle to co-opt Empson's "lie" and "lying" to "lying with" or "get laid." Conversely, the *non sequitur* "None of those deaths were her point at all" (l.17), seems to invite a sexual reading, in which "death" indicates orgasm and "point" is at once a deflection of "prick," a euphemism for the female genitals, the goal of climax, and perhaps, given the Renaissance mood of orgasmic "death," the "points" of a man's breeches, the undoing of which signifies undress, only to say that none of these are the "point" of this encounter, and this poem.

The speaker's cynicism is emphasized by the rhetorical questions and hard-bitten resignation of the final stanzas, in which he turns to contemplate global warfare, inescapable by mere expatriation: "the same war on a stronger toe" (l.31). Despite the Donnian cadence of "Tell me more quickly what I lost by this" (l.37)—sexual innuendo emerges in a mood of hostility to the erotic: "tell me with less drama what they miss / Who call a die a god for a good throw" (ll.38–39),

> But as to risings I can tell you why.
> It is on contradiction that they grow.
> It seemed the best thing to be up and go.
> Up was the heartening and the strong reply.
> The heart of standing is we cannot fly.
>
> (ll.42–46)

"Risings," "grow," "Up," and "heartening" all might imply male erection, (though their political connotations—specifically, with reference to the Sino-Japanese conflict—are still the more obvious) and in that company "the heart of standing" might, as it has not before, suggest the same. But this pithy series of epigrams, each sentence its own line, militates strongly against sensuality; while the structure (a kind of extended villanelle) which places both refrains in the final stanza, means that utilitarian good sense, "the best thing to be up and go" halts a reflection on erotic irrationality "risings . . . on contradiction . . . grow" and a statement of human capacity-in-limitation (we can stand upright because our bones are too heavy to permit flight) rebukes too much ecstatic "heartening."

Empson's "Aubade" replaces the stock figure of the jealous husband with a child with, it seems, the specific intent of desexualizing a post-coital situation. MacNeice's postwar dawn lyric announces its refusal of the erotic in its title: "Aubade for Infants." The personified sun of this poem, "hooting, hot of foot" who "Ignites the dumps of sodden cloud / Loud and laughing, a fiery face. . ." (l.5, 9–10) is reminiscent of the trolls who, in poems written during the Blitz, are MacNeice's metaphor for aerial bombardment. The sun speaks in a "bass" voice (the timbre may be a fling at the facetious though still sexualized mood of Pound's "Compleynt," in which the lover's voice is so described) and in archetypal terms which recall, in particular, "Troll's Courtship" (*Collected Poems* 219–20):

> Maybe you think that I am young?
> I who flung before my birth
> To mother earth the dawn-song too?

(ll.13–15)

MacNeice glances here, albeit in very general fashion, at the possible origins of dawn poetry in ancient religious ritual. Literary allusions, meanwhile, color MacNeice's poem with apocalypse: his sun might derive from both the "fiend hid in a cloud" of William Blake's "Infant Sorrow"; Galahad's glimpse of the Grail in Alfred Tennyson's *Idylls of the King*: "I saw the fiery face as of a child / That smote itself into the bread." "Aubade for Infants" predates by a couple of weeks the atomic bombing of Hiroshima and Nagasaki, bearing on publication in *Holes in the Sky* (1948) and in E. R. Dodds' *Collected Poems* (1965) the date "July 1945." MacNeice only occasionally dated his poems in print, and this ascription seems to acknowledge that while nursery rhyme may be a form in which it is possible to approach conventional bombing, it cannot contain the horror of nuclear warfare. Aubades (if not infantile ones) prove a genre accommodating to public anxieties as to private griefs and fears.

The more liberal sexual mores of the latter part of the twentieth century prompt something of a revival of the sensuous aubade, as the increasing popularity of the term as a title renders a full survey beyond the scope of a brief essay. Richard Wilbur's "A Late Aubade" wittily registers the loosening and expansion of the sub-genre: taking place at "almost noon," it is late in more than literary-historical terms; first published in the summer of 1968, it notes playfully the redundancy of *carpe diem* tropes in an era of free love:

> If you *must* go,
>
> Wait for a while, then slip downstairs
> And bring us up some chilled white wine,
> And some blue cheese, and crackers, and some fine
> Ruddy-skinned pears.

(ll.24–28)

Nuala Ní Dhomhnaill's "Aubade," consumed by the vast majority of its readership in English translation by Michael Longley, enacts both the erotics of collaboration between a man and a woman and parting theme: the poem departs from its Irish original to currency in a global language. But the speaker of Ní Dhomhnaill's poem is not among "the young couples yawning in unison / Before they do it again" (10–11), but a participant in a struggle to

> glue together
> the silly little shards of our lives
> So that our children can drink water from broken bowls.
>
> (ll.15–17).

The most substantial achievements in the twentieth-century dawn lyric, however, are more possessed by death than sex, and the tenor of the sub-genre grows, if anything more specifically elegiac as the century progresses. One of Elizabeth Bishop's earliest drafts for an elegy commemorating her lover Lota de Macedo Soares (a project which the poet eventually came to envisage at book-length, but never completed) is headed "Aubade and Elegy." A page of notes in typescript, it nonetheless has the force of incantation, suggesting the powerful synthesis of pleasure and death drives which might have propelled a finished poem:

> No coffee can wake you no coffee can wake you no coffee
> . . .
> For perhaps the tenth time the tenth time the tenth time today
> and still early morning I go under the crashing wave
> of ~~your~~ death
>   I go under the black wave of ~~your~~ death
>
> (ll.1, 4–7)

Alice Quinn notes the rhetorical similarity to the draft of an earlier poem, "St John's Day": "no, no prayer / can wake him" (ll.20–21), which might prompt the reader to reflect on the availability of the aubade to theological and philosophical speculation.

W.H. Auden's late and little-read "Aubade," collected in his posthumous "last poems," *Thank You Fog* (1974) is also an elegy, for the philosopher and historian Eugen Rosenstock-Huessy. It draws extensively on Rosenstock-Huessy's ideas about the relationship between speech, time, and self-consciousness. Apart from the speaker's waking in the third and fourth lines of the poem, there is nothing to indicate a morning setting; no sex here, no lover addressed or referred to: "Love is no help" (l.26) in managing interconnections between self and world. Its four fourteen-line trimeter stanzas bristle with capitalized nouns and pronouns, giving priority to abstraction and social relations over the selfish particularity that characterizes love-lyric. "Verses" (l.41) have a place, albeit circumscribed, "on fit occasion . . . *sotto voce*" (ll.39–41), in the formation of a heavenly Jerusalem which is constituted by speech and listening. John Fuller notes: "Auden's conclusion is . . . a reworking of the troublesome line 'We must love one another or die' from 'September 1, 1939' that triumphantly reasserts human immortality as the condition of being listened to by future generations" (Fuller 545).

It is mortality and an absence of hope which characterize the most listened-to of twentieth-century aubades, perhaps the only example of the genre which most general readers would be able unhesitatingly to name: Philip Larkin's. This thanatotic masterwork has been the subject of extended discussion (for example, at chapter length by M.W. Rowe) and a survey of poetic genre could not hope to add detail to that formidable corpus of close reading. Rowe's comprehensive study asks a question, however, on which an overview of the modern aubade might reasonably begin to draw to some kind of conclusion: "When Larkin used the term 'Aubade' was he making reference to the *alba* tradition or was he using the term to mean a morning serenade?" (187). Rowe stresses Larkin's relative conformity to the former, commenting "the only major irony in Larkin's title [is that] the narrator has no lover to part from . . . other features of the alba—the dread and pain of dawn, for example—would just be straightforwardly true" (188), while insisting he meant the latter, for its stock of spurious connotation:

> the warm south and Provençal mirth . . . courtly love and the celebration of an exalted woman . . . a life of wandering and artistic freedom . . . a young, richly costumed, amorous performer; a life set amongst castles, winding staircases, woods, the glint of dark wine in goblets.
>
> (Rowe 188)

which might readily be undermined by figuring religion as "a vast moth-eaten musical brocade" or setting the urban quotidian against a kind of nuclear winter: "The sky is white as clay, with no sun" (ll.23, 48). But Rowe's interpretation involves Larkin in a certain patronage of his readership—the title's irony is more readily available to those with a vulgar notion of the aubade as the business of a jongleur in tights than to anyone who might have skimmed a translation of Giraut de Bornelh. It feels quite wrong, since above all, Larkin's "Aubade" is concerned to eschew patronage: it refuses consolation with an argument which the speaker believes is so robustly irrefutable that he is prepared to risk sounding simplistic: "nothing to think with / Nothing to love or link with" (ll.28–29) "Being brave / Lets no-one off the grave" (ll.38–39). The reader soon notices that these savage expressions, intensified by deliberately crude rhyme and the penultimate trimeter of each stanza are structurally integral. This readiness to appear foolish or barbarous in the service of profound conviction, while working to modulate foolishness and barbarity out of the composition, is the absolute reverse of condescension.

Larkin's virtuosity allows the reader to pose a slightly different question—what does a poem gain in employing a generic title such as "Aubade" or "Alba," evocative of a particular tradition but with no formal and very scant thematic rationale? The answer would seem to be less and less, the better the poem is, and for a poem of the quality of Larkin's, none at all. *Pace* Rowe, it would lose nothing by being called "Dawn" or "Morning Song," since the conception of the aubade on which it relies for irony (if indeed it does so rely) is so much cruder than poem itself as to render the putative irony null.

The popularity of "Aubade" as a title is something of an affront to genre studies, which assumes that literary categories have structural and aesthetic value, and are not frivolously chosen and decoratively deployed. A formal standard for the dawn poem—never strongly maintained, even in the genre's medieval heyday—does not seem now recoverable. We should not, though, despair of thematic rigor. It is retained in the one field of lyric endeavor where the words "alba" and "aubade" are almost never used: that of popular song. A vivid sense of the erotic possibilities of dawn links, for example, Blind Willie McTell's exquisite blues "Mama Taint Long Fo Day," in which the singer is released from the clutches of midnight depression by his lover's "sunshine," Rod Stewart's "Maggie May," which imposes faux-Americana on a cautionary Liverpudlian ballad, and temporal play (it is autumn; the youthful singer must leave his older lover) upon the matitutinal situation, and Ian Dury's "Wake up and Make Love with Me," a virtuoso display of vowel music, internal rhyme, and domestic naughtiness from which I take the title of this essay. Art poetry's rage to name seems to have produced in the case of the aubade a certain critical effeteness, a category so loosely understood as to undermine its own necessity for existence—but independent of the gelid grasp of nomenclature, the thing itself—the erotic dawn song—is as perennial as the morning glory.

References and Further Reading

Auden, Wystan Hugh. *Thank You, Fog*. London: Faber & Faber, 1974.

Beckett, Samuel. *Collected Poems 1930–1978*. London: John Calder, 1984.

Bishop, Elizabeth. *Edgar Allan Poe and the Jukebox: Uncollected Poems, Drafts and Fragments*, ed. Alice Quinn. Manchester: Carcanet, 2006.

Bonner, Anthony. *Songs of the Troubadours*. New York: Schocken Books, 1972.

Child, Francis James, *The English and Scottish Popular Ballads*, 5 vols 1884–1892, repr. New York: Dover, 1965.

Dury, Ian. *New Boots and Panties*. London: Stiff Records, 1977.

Empson, William. *The Complete Poems*, ed. John Haffenden. London: Penguin, 2000.

Fuller, John. *W.H. Auden: A Commentary* Princeton: Princeton University Press, 1998.

Kehew, Robert (ed.). *Lark in the Morning: The Verses of the Troubadours*. Chicago: University of Chicago Press, 2005.

Larkin, Philip. *Collected Poems*, ed. Anthony Thwaite. London: Faber & Faber, 1988.

Lowell, Amy. *Sword Blades and Poppy Seed* (1914), repr. Whitefish, MT: Kessinger, 2009.

MacNeice, Louis. *Collected Poems*, ed. Peter McDonald. London: Faber & Faber, 2007.

Martiny, Erik. "Aurora's Avatars: A Generic Approach to Modern Dawn Poetry." *Etudes Anglaises* 4 (2010): 437–50.

McTier, William Samuel (Blind Willie McTell). *Mama Taint Long Fo Day*. Atlanta: Victor, 1927.

Ní Dhomhnaill, Nuala. *Pharaoh's Daughter*. Oldcastle, Co. Meath: Gallery, 1990.

Pound, Ezra. *Lustra of Ezra Pound*. London: Elkin Matthews, 1916.

Pound, Ezra. *Quia Pauper Amavi*. London: The Egoist, 1919.

Rowe, Mark. W. "Larkin's 'Aubade.'" *Philosophy and Literature: A Book of Essays*. Aldershot and Burlington: Ashgate, 2004, 182–219.

Sitwell, Edith. *Selected Poems with an Essay on Her Own Poetry*. Boston, MA: Houghton Mifflin, 1937.

Stewart, Rod. *Every Picture Tells a Story*. London: Mercury, 1971.

Wilbur, Richard. *Collected Poems 1943–2004*. Orlando: Harvest, 2005.

27

Nox Consilium and the Dark Night of the Soul

The Nocturne

Erik Martiny

This chapter stands as a pendant to Chris Fitter's study "The Poetic Nocturne: From Ancient Motif to Renaissance Genre" in that it offers an extension of its field of inquiry beyond the Renaissance, charting the nocturne's development through its various heydays in the eighteenth and nineteenth centuries to its most recent manifestations. After examining nocturnal poetry composed by the Graveyard poets, and Romantic texts such as Samuel Coleridge's "Frost at Midnight" and John Keats's "Ode to a Nightingale," I draw attention to the darkly pessimistic turn the genre took in the Victorian period in poems such as James Thomson's *The City of Dreadful Night*, Matthew Arnold's "Dover Beach" and Gerald Manley Hopkins's "I Wake to Feel the Fell of Dark, Not Day." I also briefly look across the Atlantic, for contrasting skies, towards Walt Whitman's numerous nocturnes.

The second half of the chapter centers mainly on Thomas Kinsella's political poem "Nightwalker." In this Irish context, I also examine the use of the nocturne as a vehicle for elegy in Paul Durcan's "Night Elegy for Thérèse Cronin," to conclude with a consideration of poems such as Peter Redgrove's neo-Gothic night piece "Frankenstein in the Forest" and Anne Frydman's "Overnight Travelers without Berths."

In his extended essay devoted to the nocturne, Chris Fitter observes that although literary historians have tended to situate the birthplace of the nocturne in the eighteenth century, it actually predates Graveyard poetry, taking its roots in the Renaissance, a period during which the genre grew to achieve cult status. As Fitter points out, seventeenth-century nocturnes overturn the classical, medieval and biblical tradition of representing night as oppressive or evil. The Renaissance development of the genre is "intent on refiguring those cold, dead and sunless hours feared by most of mankind over millennia into an order of exquisite and numinous experience" thus "revaluing night as a time of beauty and profundity" (3).

A Companion to Poetic Genre, First Edition. Edited by Erik Martiny.
© 2012 John Wiley & Sons, Ltd. Published 2012 by John Wiley & Sons, Ltd.

Fitter amusingly points out that prior to this, in fourteenth-century England, a royal charter allowed for nightwalkers to be imprisoned, as their motivations could only be criminal. By contrast, the Renaissance saw the emergence of the recreative stroll of the urban scholar. Fitter observes how the nocturne also rose to prominence under the influence of Italian and Dutch pictorial breakthroughs in the depiction of night scenery and the fashionable cult of the solitary melancholic. This lead to a rethinking of the poetic significance of darkness which began to be portrayed in two ways: devotional poets employed the nocturne as a mystical genre while Cavalier poets used it to create (sometimes parodic) amorous fairylands.

I would like to add a third category which is closer in spirit to many modern nocturnes. While it is no doubt excessive to suggest that Anne Finch's "A Nocturnal Reverie" (a poem written in the immediate wake of the seventeenth century) had a direct influence on the contemporary nocturne, it does contain the seeds of the modern approach to the poetry of night. Despite the fact that Finch did also write devotional verse on other occasions, "A Nocturnal Reverie" works towards an eschewal of both religious weighting and fairyland or mythological decorativeness. Although the poem begins by evoking Zephyr and calling the nightingale "Philomel" (a common designation which can also be found later in Coleridge, Swinburne, and Arnold's nightingale-centered poetry), Finch soon turns away from these perfunctory mythological gestures to consider the more secular sounds, sights, and smells of the night. The poem possesses a modern relish for the ordinary, for the natural wonders, what Finch calls "Joys in the inferior world" (l.46) ("inferior" meaning terrestrial, non-spiritual) thus establishing the night scene as a *tempus amoenus*, a solacing temporal refuge from the anxieties and confusion of the diurnal world.

By comparison, the eighteenth-century Graveyard poets tend to be more archaic in their ornate mythological references and supernatural evocations. Some graveyard nocturnes make the hidden world of phantoms cry out, often obliterating the ordinary sounds of night. Robert Blair's "The Grave" recounts how

> Wild shrieks have issued from the hollow tombs;
> Dead men have come again, and walked about;
> And the great bell has tolled, unrung and untouched
>
> (ll.51–53)

Similarly, in Edward Young's "Night Thoughts," the night becomes a "land of apparitions, empty shades" (ll.117–18). The allegorical apparatus of Thomas Parnell's early seminal poem "A Night-Piece on Death" (which appeared posthumously in 1721, eight years after Finch's nocturne) affiliates it with the medieval tradition, upon which the Gothic mode is founded.

Contrasting with the *ars moriendi* aesthetics of the Graveyard poets, Coleridge's "Frost at Midnight" (1798) offers itself as a eutopian nocturne which reworks and expands the Renaissance tradition of representing the night as a positive moment of comfort and regeneration. In the second stanza, Coleridge expresses the pleasures of recalling his own birthplace; the speaker's night thoughts lead him to explore the connective virtues of fatherhood as he imagines the perfect place that awaits his newborn son, a location entirely given over to the sublimity of nature, a world whose rigors will merely serve to sweeten his son's soul: "Therefore all seasons shall be sweet to thee" (l.65). One of the major motifs of nocturnal poetry, the moon, stands in here for God's presence as a kind of solacing nocturnal sun. The poem ends with an image of perfectly symmetrical lunar illuminism: "quietly shining to the quiet Moon" (l.74).

Despite the fact that Coleridge wrote some very fine nightingale-centered poems, the most feted nocturne of the Romantic period is John Keats's "Ode to a Nightingale." On one level, Keats's ode is very much in keeping with the Renaissance formulation of the nocturne as a rhapsody exalting the wonders of the night. If Coleridge's "Frost at Midnight" is closer to Renaissance devotional nocturnes, Keats's pagan references to "the Queen-Moon" (l.36) who is "Clustered around by all her starry Fays" (l.37) at least initially affiliate it to Cavalier nocturnals. It goes beyond this kind of fairy-centered verse, however, to include a more numinous, albeit still decidedly pagan, desire to be absorbed entropically by the spirit of the night whose densest, most enchanting incarnation is the nightingale.

Although this nocturne was apparently written in the morning, after breakfast, according to Keats's friend Charles Armitage Brown (Bate 501), the central stanzas focus on the invisibility that the darkness affords the speaker: the nightingale itself is never seen, only heard, thus adding to the spiritual value of this nocturnal epiphany. Likewise, the speaker "cannot see what flowers are at [his] feet" (l.42) and imagines the experience of disappearing, either through death by leaving "the world unseen" (l.19), or on the "viewless wings of Poesy" (l.33).[1] The speaker's emphasis on "embalmed darkness" (l.43) anticipates D.H. Lawrence, and later Peter Redgrove, in their desire to marginalize the tyranny of the eye. Although Keats's ode does initially pay homage to the sense of sight, particularly with its memorable "beaded bubbles winking at the brim, / And purple-stainèd mouth" (ll.17–18), the main aim of the following stanzas is to extol the virtues of the non-visual senses.

Keats's nocturne offers a Romantic version of the monastic doctrine of *fuga mundi*, in that its woodland setting offers an escape from the industrial world. Its nocturnal imagery also expresses an explicit longing for entropic dissolution, and a concomitant need to flee even the rural realm, this world and its almost cannibalistic "hungry generations" (l.62). Nature, darkness, death are thus the three deepening levels of solace in which the speaker seeks to hide.

Late nineteenth-century English nocturnes tend to leave aside the unbridled optimism of Coleridge's "Frost at Midnight," preferring to expand the dark imagery that paradoxically both embodies and alleviates pessimism. In France, Decadent *fin-de-siècle* writers often represented night as a moment of freedom from convention, a time in which the dandy writer could live *à rebours* (to echo the title of Joris-Karl Huysmans's novel), against the grain of the rest of humanity to express his singularity and escape from diurnal vulgarity. By contrast, late Victorian poets often tended to use the genre of night poetry to express soul-destroying negativity, a tendency which might be said to have been most forcefully formulated in Coleridge's own pessimistic nocturne "Dejection: An Ode."

Written during his tormented stay in Ireland as university lecturer, Hopkins's "terrible" sonnets, "I Wake and Feel the Fell of Dark, Not Day" and "Carrion Comfort" both hark back to a pre-Renaissance vision of night as hellish, making it into a symbol of God's absence from the speaker's side. In "I Wake and Feel the Fell of Dark, Not Day," the torments of the night make us no more than "our sweating selves" (1.14), close to the condition of the damned.

I would like to point out here that eighteenth- and nineteenth-century night pieces often tend to bear close resemblance to a representation of night that is found in a sixteenth-century notion conveyed to Christianity by the Spanish mystical poet St. John of the Cross. His seminal poem, "La Noche Oscura del Alma" ("The Dark Night of the Soul"), recounts the journey of the soul from its bodily home to union with God. With its ecstatic tone and positive rendering of night imagery ("O guiding dark of night! / O dark of night more darling than the dawn!" 21–22), the poem seems to be in keeping with, and possibly also to have had an impact on, the seventeenth-century vision of night as it is represented in such poems as Henry Vaughan's "The Night" with its memorable "deep but dazzling darkness" (1.50) as a theophanic moment.

Written after his poem, St. John of the Cross's treatise places his rather euphoric poem in a more somber perspective as a dark and terrible purgation: it is ultimately this image of the Dark Night of the Soul which has been handed down to Christianity in current reference to the phrase. The expression is now often used to relate not to the state of perfection reached after the purgatory steps taken through the night but to the desolate hours in which the believer experiences a sense of being abandoned by God and left in a state of torment as in Hopkins's sonnet. This afflicting and purgative view of the night is also one which informs such poems as John Donne's "A Nocturnall upon S. Lucies Day": the poem ends with the conclusion that "He ruin'd mee, and I am re-begot / Of absence, darknesse, death; things which are not" (ll.17–18).

Like Hopkins, James Thomson was a Victorian insomnia-sufferer racked by acute bouts of depression. His lengthy poem *The City of Dreadful Night* is a kind of requiem for the universe, so dark is its negation. Thomson's paroxysm of nocturnal despondency offers a series of ruminations upon loneliness, the meaninglessness of existence, and a sense of spiritual death. The poem takes Bunyan's City of Destruction and Dante's City of Dis to even darker extremes, without hope of progress towards any kind of Celestial City. The only glimmer of hope, embodied by an Angel, is turned to stone by a Medusa-like Sphinx in section XX. Although the poem uses the same kinds of allegorical figures favored by the Graveyard poets writing a century before Thomson, they do not weigh the poem down: "The City of Dreadful Night" achieves some original descriptions of the hellbound starless night, combining the nocturne with its diurnal counterpoint, the aubade, to absorb that optimistic and generally celebratory genre within this nihilistic nocturne's darkest wings: "But as if blacker night could dawn on night / With tenfold gloom on moonless night unstarred" (XXI, ll.57–58).

Although it envisions London as the "City of tremendous night" (l.30), Thomson's nihilism was also mostly acquired during his stay in Ireland where he was influenced by the rationalist and atheist philosopher Charles Bradlaugh who later published Thomson's poem in his magazine *The National Reformer*. It is interesting to note how British writers often seem to have acquired their pessimism after having been sent abroad to Ireland, no doubt in part as a reaction to surroundings which they felt were hostile to their presence. There are a number of cases in which this holds true, along-side Thomson and Hopkins: the pessimism of the second half of Spenser's *The Faerie Queene* has for instance also been read as a reaction to the state of the British Empire in Ireland, especially after his country house was sacked in 1598 during the rebellion of the O'Neills.[2]

Matthew Arnold's "Dover Beach" raises the black flag of Victorian pessimism almost as high as Thomson. In this night piece, darkness is not initially used nega-tively. Indeed images of nocturnal calmness and atmospheric beauty predominate:

> The sea is calm tonight.
> The tide is full, the moon lies fair
> Upon the straits; on the French coast the light
> Gleams and is gone; the cliffs of England stand,
> Glimmering and vast, out in the tranquil bay.
> Come to the window, sweet is the night-air!
>
> (ll.1–6)

The remainder of the poem, however, inflects this apparently eutopian description towards dystopianism. In retrospect, even light imagery serves to underpin the transi-ence, inconstancy and instability of everything: "Gleams and is gone" (l.4) offers an early sign that darkness is going to be employed in its most ancient, pre-Renaissance sense as a manifestation of negativity. The poem ends on a series of images that have been used as titles for a spate of darkly pessimistic twentieth-century dystopian novels, as well as a film noir (the equivalent of the nocturne in the history of film) by Fritz Lang:

> And we are here as on a darkling plain
> Swept with confused alarms of struggle and flight,
> Where ignorant armies clash by night.
>
> (ll.35–37)

Written in 1851 (published in 1867), in the bloody aftermath of the 1848 wave of European revolutions and not that long after Charles Lyell's geological debunking of Creationism, "Dover Beach" employs the night setting as a metaphor for political and existential chaos. Later twentieth-century poems such as W.H. Auden's "Nocturne" in the early 1950s and Thomas Kinsella's "Nightwalker" in the late 1960s use darkness as an objective correlative for social and political benightedness too.

Arnold's use of form in "Dover Beach" can be interpreted in two divergent ways. It has been called "the first major 'free-verse' poem in the language" (Collini 41): although it uses irregular verse paragraphs rather than stanzas, and has lines of varying length and meter, it does nevertheless use rhyme in a sustained though somewhat irregular manner. This technical choice can be read as a non-traditional organic looseness corresponding to the poet's sea-borne desire for escape; alternatively, the poem's typographical and metrical irregularity could be viewed as a mimetic reflection of the existential disorder and confusion that Arnold expresses.

On the other side of the Atlantic, Walt Whitman returned with great frequency to the genre of the night poem throughout his career, most notably in "Vigil Strange I Kept on the Field One Night," "Look Down Fair Moon," "Night on the Prairies," and "A Clear Midnight," to name but a few. Written only a few years after "Dover Beach," Whitman's "On the Beach at Night," and its sequel "On the Beach at Night Alone," both seem to be in conversation with Arnold's nihilistic nocturne. "On the Beach at Night" is similar to Coleridge's "Frost at Midnight" in as far as it dramatizes the interaction of a father and child in a nocturnal setting. Whitman transforms Arnold's images of transience into immortal permanence, stating clearly that despair is only produced by lack of experience and flawed perception. Without wishing to claim that the child figure in Whitman's poem is a belittling image of Matthew Arnold, one might nevertheless argue that, in simplified form, the child's impressions do recapitulate Arnold's vision of loss. Adopting the fatherly persona of some of his early poems, Whitman brushes aside both transience and loss:

> With these kisses let me remove your tears,
> The ravening clouds shall not long be victorious,
> They shall not long possess the sky, they devour the stars only in apparition.
>
> (ll.16–18)

While Whitman often adopts the sense of wonder, the intensity of feeling and the linguistic ebullience of the child, he inverts Wordsworth's premise that the child is father of the man in this poem, showing up the limitations of the infant's point of view through the images of darkness and clouded skies, which he also calls "the doubts of night-time" (l.28) in "There Was a Child Went Forth."

Whitman's sequel nocturne, "On the Beach at Night Alone," reinforces this sweepingly optimistic vision of the nocturnal universe: darkness paradoxically offers greater vision than daylight since it allows us to see the much more distant details of the firmament. This being said, while Whitman's lyrically discursive nocturnes argue nihilism out of existence, they are also in intratextual tension with another of his own poems in *Sea-Drift*: the second poem in the collection, "As I Ebb'd with the Ocean of Life," employs the same tidal imagery as Arnold to evoke an acute sense of self-loss and loss of faith in general.

Like their predecessors, twentieth-century night poems often fall into two categories that allow for some overlap. The first of these extends the troping of night as hell; the second is sometimes laced with negative night thoughts but is globally soothing. Generally speaking, those that depict the night in appeasing and beautifying terms tend to possess titles such as "Nocturne," thus forging a link with the mellifluous musical composition, and the visually atmospheric pictorial depiction of the genre which adheres to the tradition of *nox consilium*, the notion according to which the night brings wise counsel and a sense of harmony.

T.S. Eliot's tortured early night pieces, "Preludes" and "Rhapsody on a Windy Night," in a sense project Arnold's nature-centered nocturne into an even less comforting seedily urban locale. As the speaker of "Preludes" puts it, night merely serves to reveal, rather than cover up, a "thousand sordid images" (l.27). In "Rhapsody on a Windy Night," the usually comforting moon is personified as a mentally impaired and physically diseased crone figure: "The moon has lost her memory. / A washed-out smallpox cracks her face" (ll.55–56). Like the Decadent French writers who so inspired Eliot, the night is pictured here as the preserve of the man who has decided to experience the underside of life and press against the limits of the human condition, simultaneously expressing the difficulty of coping with modern life and its expectations. Diurnal existence is viewed as worse than darkness as it requires preparation that is perceived as a chore, a soul-defeating rigmarole: "The last twist of the knife" (l.78).

In Eliot's early verse, dawn-inspired poems offer no reprieve from nocturnal suffering. If anything, the prospect of the dawn is even more forbidding. Despite the torments of the night, Eliot's nihilistic nocturne does provide a certain escape from the obligations and forced promiscuity of the day. In "Morning at the Window," the poem that follows "Rhapsody on a Windy Night" in *Prufrock and Other Observations*, the euphonic sounds that traditionally permeate albas and aubades are replaced by the discordant, jarring noises of "rattling breakfast plates in basement kitchens" (l.1) accompanied by a series of visual images implying universal dejection.

Like the aubade, the nocturne harbors a rather limited set of expectations. When faced with a poem entitled "Nocturne," the only expectations most readers have will be that the poem is going to deal with a generally soothing or comforting contemplation of the beauties of a night scene. The more anxiety-ridden poetry of insomnia of the eighteenth and nineteenth centuries tends not to employ the "Nocturne" title. Let us nevertheless consider two recent examples of poems bearing the title "Nocturne" that do, in some degree, entertain the idea of negativity: one by W.H. Auden and another by Frank O'Hara. Although Frank O'Hara's "Nocturne" does voice some negative feelings of loneliness, ill-being ("Everything sees through me, / in the daytime I'm too hot / and at night I freeze" ll.14–16) and pessimism about the future, nocturnal beauty is still present as a solace. The scene is presented with O'Hara's characteristically gorgeous streaks of color that mimetically evoke the effects of drip-painting on an already Impressionistic canvas:

> The sky is grey
> and clear, with pink and
> blue shadows under each cloud.
> A tiny airliner drops its
> Specks over the UN Building.
>
> (ll.7–11)

The nocturne that Auden wrote in 1951 interestingly balances two perceptions of the moon, one in a mythologized, romanticized manner ("And sweeps into the open sky / Like one who knows where she belongs" ll.3–4); the other in a "tougher mind" (l.15) which presents the moon in disillusioned, clinical terms. The night is finally posited as an aesthetic and spiritual refuge from the falsities and shallowness of the day:

> A counter-image, anyway,
> To balance with its lack of weight
> My world, the private motor-car
> And all the engines of the state.
>
> (ll.37–40)

Auden's "Nocturne" is a more discursive version of O'Hara's more exclusively atmospheric poem. Auden reworks the ancient trappings of personification in a rather less colorfully imaginative way than Frank Marshall Davis's "Four Glimpses of Night," but in a more intellectually strenuous manner. After having evoked the Moon Goddess in a deliberately stereotypical way as a hybrid Pagan-Christian "Mother, Virgin, Muse" (l.6), Auden demythologizes the night as a totally lifeless and indifferent "bunch of barren craters" (l.11). The poem dialectically opposes the poet's two radically different responses to the night, arguing for the rightness of the rational, slightly cynical, and pessimistic "tougher mind" (l.15), but ultimately reluctant to relinquish the nighttime as a *tempus amoenus*, a poetic, sacred, and primeval rampart against the diurnal *tempus terribilis* associated with the hell of modernity, noise, and "all the engines of the State" (l.40).

This tendency to retreat from anthropomorphism only to give in to it by poem's end is also a feature of such poems as Coleridge's "The Nightingale." The impulse towards connection with the outside world and a concomitant resistance to pathetic fallacy is a feature that appears in many nocturnes. Attendant upon this is the recurrent, indeed almost invariable, presence of a salvational image (most typically the moon or a songbird) even within some of the darkest night pieces.

Like Auden's "Nocturne," Philip Larkin's "Sad Steps" (1968) pits traditionally elated lunar poetry ("Lozenge of love! Medallion of art!," l.11) against a more skeptical, disenchanted vision of the moon as a symbol of plenitude that only serves to mock the speaker's sense of emptiness, his loss of youth and mirth, as he takes a few "sad steps" (echoing Philip Sidney's "With How Sad Steps, Oh Moon"), almost shedding his "few, sad, last grey hairs" (to echo Keats) on his way to the lavatory. As often with Larkin, gloom is tempered by bathos.

One recent striking attempt to recover the exalted atmosphere of sacred nocturnes is Billy Collins's "Moon." Like Larkin's "Sad Steps," it is one of the few modern nocturnes that overtly points to a previous canonic poem of the genre. Larkin takes the focus away from Sidney's lovelorn melancholy transforming it into a feeling of dejection caused by loss of self and youth; Collins erases almost every trace of Arnold's pessimism in "Dover Beach." Although the first and last lines of Collins's "Moon" begin and end with the words "tonight" and "night," just as in "Dover Beach," the rest of the poem departs almost entirely from Arnold's hypotext, within the confines of this minimalistic framing device. He also briefly evokes Arnold's touchstone text, and makes a parallel with a poem by Coleridge which can be easily identified as "The Nightingale":

> It's as full as it was
> in that poem by Coleridge
> where he carries his year-old son
> into the orchard behind the cottage
> and turns the baby's face to the sky.
>
> (ll.7–11)

The "eternal note of sadness" that Arnold is at pains to make us hear is replaced in Collins's poem by a characteristically American neo-Transcendentalist's desire to regenerate and recharge the reader with a sense of wonder at the beauty of the firmament. As in all of Collins's poems, there is a great warmth and intimacy created between the speaker and his addressee:

> And if your house has no child,
> you can always gather into your arms
> the sleeping infant of yourself,
> as I have done tonight.
>
> (ll.19–22)

If the moon can sometimes be used as a symbol of cratered nullity, more often than not it symbolizes wholesome plenitude.

Although it borrows its title from W.B. Yeats's "Byzantium" with its "night-walkers' song" (1.3) (which in turn is an echo of Coleridge's "night-wandering man" [1.16] in "The Nightingale"), Thomas Kinsella's "Nightwalker" has arguably more in common with T.S. Eliot's tormented insomniac. The poem's first words are reminiscent of the "burnt-out ends of smoky days" (4) that open Eliot's "Preludes." Kinsella's preoccupation with blood and structure belong more overtly to Yeats's vocabulary:

> Mindful of the shambles of the day,
>   But mindful, under the blood's drowsy humming,
> Of will that gropes for structure; nonetheless
>   Not unmindful of the madness without,

> The madness within—the book of reason
> Slammed open, slammed shut:
>
> (ll.1–6)

As a Condition-of-Ireland poem of the late 1960s, Kinsella's "Nightwalker" is one of the most ambitious nocturnes of the twentieth century. Its strongly oneiric and allegoric overtones capture the poet's fears of Ireland's Faustian pact with scheming one-eyed, moneyed politicians, Mammon and multinationals. Arnold's nihilistic nocturne is the blueprint for Kinsella's poem to the extent that it deploys the temporal setting of night both as the last refuge of beauty, self-possession, and interiority, and simultaneously as a visual sign of moral benightedness. Arnold's turbid and ebbing "Sea of Faith" is revisited in Kinsella's poem when the speaker realizes that "I have heard of this place. I think / This is the Sea of Disappointment" (ll.240–41).

Typically, the negative nocturne blurs the boundary between night and day by having recourse to the Darkness at Noon motif that is found in other genres such as heroic fantasy, science fiction, film noir, and Tech noir: "The Wakeful Twins / *Bruder und Schwester* . . . " (ll.60–61) who come to invest in Ireland towards the end of the first part of the poem nightmarishly evoke the specter of Nazi Germany in a particularly dark moment that nevertheless occurs during the day, adding a metaphoric layer of darkness to the darkness in which the speaker currently finds himself:

> A red glare
> Plays on their faces, livid with little splashes
> Of blazing fat. The oven door closes.
>
> (ll.68–70)

Kinsella's reminders of Christian-Pagan sacred verse are ambivalent:

> Moon of my dismay, Virgin most pure,
> Reflected enormous in her shaggy pool,
> Quiet as oil. My brain swims in her light
> And gathers into a book beneath her stare.
>
> (ll.199–202)

As in Sidney's "With How Sad Steps, Oh Moon, Thou Climb'st the Skies," Kinsella's moon is made to both reflect and allay the speaker's sorrow, in a way that is characteristic of the workings of pathetic fallacy. The moon in "Nightwalker" is portrayed as both pure and polluted as the speaker hesitates between despair and religious hope. By the end of the fourth section, the moon's bipolar symbolism intensifies, being characterized as both oppressor and progenitor. As such, the poem offers a striking example of the ambivalent response to darkness in most negative nocturnes.

In this last part, I would like to turn briefly to three night pieces by Peter Redgrove, Paul Durcan and Anne Frydman to dwell on some of the nocturne's most recent manifestations. The first poem, by the late Peter Redgrove explores the night piece in a neo-Gothic mode. Like Redgrove's previous "Renfield before His Master" (*The Apple-Broadcast*), "Frankenstein in the Forest" (*Dr Faust's Sea-Spiral Spirit*) re-enters the Gothic novel in an unabashedly pleasure-driven spirit, without any of Mary Shelley's fear of the dark arts or immorality. Redgrove's poem is in the continuity of George Meredith's "Satan by Starlight" and D.H. Lawrence's Lucifer poems in its apparent glorification of the satanically gleaming darkness: these poets take the imagery of seventeenth-century sacred nocturnes in a decidedly unexpected direction. Redgrove's Frankenstein poem is in keeping with his usual all-encompassing celebration of existence (which regularly led him to write seemingly amoral poems embracing everything from the sensations caused by his own car accident, to death and even nuclear holocaust). Nocturnal obscurity in "Frankenstein in the Forest" is used primarily as a dramatic backdrop to create a chiaroscuro effect that highlights the working of electricity, but also to represent the murderous drive and the mystified forces of the unknown: "The darkness has eaten everything except his face" (l.20).

Loss of sight and darkness is everything but emptiness in Redgrove's work; on the contrary, in this poem as in many others, darkness is posited as pure potential, it is a highly fertile force, a place that harbors as much magic as an alchemist's alembic. Redgrove has also written a number of striking poems on the advantages of both blindness and closed eyes: in these poems darkness becomes the medium through which other "deeper" senses such as olfaction can be experienced in their purest form. The non-visual senses are generally perceived as more metaphysical and participatory.

Paul Durcan and Anne Frydman offer two examples of the nocturne used for elegiac purposes. Since his ample elegizing of the Irish poet Patrick Kavanagh in *Greetings to Our Friends in Brazil*, Durcan has recently paid passing homage to his ideal literary forefather: in *Cries of an Irish Caveman*, Kavanagh reappears in "Night-Elegy for Thérèse Cronin," a poem that expands the fertile category of the Nightwalker poem. This night-elegy is actually set in the daytime: Durcan appropriately refers to Arthur Koestler's apocalyptic image of "Darkness at noon" (l.4), incidentally anticipated by Baudelaire's darkness at dawn in "Le Crépuscule du Matin," as a fitting image for mourning. As in Kinsella's poem, the poet-speaker embarks on a walk around Dublin (a kind of darker version of Leopold Bloom's diurnal journey across the city), offering a series of apocalyptic images of darkness. The doom-laden imagery is then gradually lifted from Thérèse Cronin's eyes as the darkness begins to lighten, and Thérèse (as well as the reader) is offered Durcan's most consolatory vision of the custodian of Dublin's ink and water: the Ultimate Forefather Himself, a bronze sculpture of Patrick Kavanagh. Durcan alludes to the unforgettable swan that swims swiftly through Kavanagh's poem, "Lines Written on a Seat on the Grand Canal, Dublin": "head low with many apologies" (l.9), providing this Nightwalker poem with its final salvational epiphany:

> I pass P.K. on his seat
> Stopping out in the rain,

> Bareheaded, with the hat beside him
> For company, a pair of swans
> Crossing the bar of his gaze.
>
> (ll. 23–27)

As in Kinsella's "Nightwalker" in which reprieve comes through the speaker's return to his wife after his odyssey through the city of night, the element of saving grace comes not from a personified moon or star figure as it often does in traditional nocturnal poetry but from a more human figure. Kinsella's epiphanic vision of his wife at the poem's close is both strong and fragile at once; Durcan's cast bronze forefather on the bench possesses the permanence, steadfastness, and majesty attributed to the stellar realm with none of the negative cold and distant unattainability and solitude of the star. While the moon is often used as a comforting analogue for the unrequited lover or the isolated romantic, its very distance from the Earth enforces its ambivalence as a symbol of appeasement.

I turn, finally, as a concluding elegiac homage to Anne Frydman's "Overnight Travelers without Berths," a poem which appeared recently in *The Yale Review* a few months after Frydman's untimely death in 2009. The poem creates a brooding image of the night as Underworld during a nocturnal Scandinavian sea crossing in mid-Winter. It goes on to consider what the captain of the ship tells the speaker concerning the suicides of those lovelorn ones who jump overboard in the dead of Winter. Frydman registers her own sense of loss very gently in a single word as her speaker finishes listening to the captain recounting these stories of loss:

> And I thought,
> that's unhappy love. And went below
> to wake my then husband.
>
> (ll. 21–23)

The understated, and therefore all the more moving, "then," coupled to the titular first line that suggests exclusion from warmth, registers what Henry David Thoreau memorably called "quiet desperation." As many other nocturnal poems show, modern night verse juxtaposes beastliness and beauty, serenity and tormented disillusion, the nuministic and the nihilistic.

Without succumbing to Harold Bloom's over-generalization of the anxiety of influence, one might wonder in what degree poets writing contemporary nocturnes suffer from comparison with previous poems in the genre. While the most obvious models are probably Keats's "Ode to a Nightingale" and Arnold's "Dover Beach," there is little hard evidence to suggest that these act as blueprints or even touchstones for later poets writing nocturnes.

What modern writers of the night piece show is that they use the word 'nocturne' as a title usually if they wish to eulogize the night and express expansive feelings. Poets with a satirical, condemnatory, nettlesome, or nihilistic agenda often tend to avoid generic contact with the lyrical and lenitive associations provided by the link with the genre of the musical or pictorial nocturne. Seventeenth-century nocturnes present the night itself as either a theophanic setting or at the very least as a symbol of purgation through visual deprivation; if the night is not always sufficient consolation in itself in recent nocturnes, these generally contain at least one of the major salvational images (moon, star, nightingale, kindred spirit). In poems that seek to express or even darken the notion of the Dark Night of the Soul, Shelley's famous image of the poet in *A Defence of Poetry* still holds true: "A poet is a nightingale who sits in darkness and sings to cheer its own solitude with sweet sounds." Although many writers tend to write in the morning, getting up to literary composition like any other job, some do make a point of composing late at night. Eavan Boland calls this the "witching hour" ("Witching" l.31). Gertrude Stein also preferred to write all night until the break of dawn: living linguistically isolated in a French village was for her only the first degree in a sense of privacy which needed to be supplemented by the seclusion afforded by the night.

NOTES

1 Keats "borrowed" this last image from Milton's "Passion": "Or should I thence hurried on viewless wing" (l.50). Milton's crucifixion poem is also something of a nocturne which uses the dark setting as a sign of elegiac sorrow that Christ's Nativity is followed by his Passion: "But headlong joy is ever on the wing, / In Wintry solstice like the shortend light / Soon swallowed up in dark and long out-living night" (ll.5–7).

2 Other more recent poets such as Philip Larkin and George MacBeth have felt more at home in Ireland: MacBeth lived there until his death happily writing poetry and pornographic novels; Larkin felt very much at home in Belfast enjoying a hermit's love of remoteness and separation from the local population.

REFERENCES AND FURTHER READING

Arnold, Matthew. *Poems: New and Complete*. London: BiblioBazaar, 2010.

Auden, W.H. *Collected Poems*. New York: Modern Library, 2007.

Bate, Walter Jackson. *John Keats*, Cambridge, MA: Belknap Press of Harvard University Press, 1963.

Baudelaire, Charles. *Les Fleurs du Mal*. Gallimard: Paris, 1972.

Blair, Robert. *The Poetic Works*. London: Kessinger, 2007.

Bloom, Harold. *The Anxiety of Influence: A Theory of Poetry*. New York: Oxford University Press, 1973.

Boland, Eavan. *Collected Poems*. London: Carcanet, 1995.

Coleridge, Samuel. *The Complete Poems of Samuel T. Coleridge*. London: Kessinger Publishing, 2005.

Collini, Stefan. *Arnold*. Oxford: Oxford University Press, 1988.

Collins, Billy. *Taking off Emily Dickinson's Clothes: Selected Poems*. London: Picador, 2000.

Davis, Frank Marshall. *Black Moods: Collected Poems*. Chicago: University of Illinois Press, 2002.

Donne, John. *Complete English Poems*. London: Everyman, 1994.

Durcan, Paul. *Cries of an Irish Caveman*. London: Harvill, 2001.

Durcan, Paul. *Greetings to Our Friends in Brazil*. London: Harvill, 1999.

Edgecombe, Rodney Stenning. "Larkin's 'Sad Steps' and the Augustan Night Piece." *Twentieth-Century Literature*. 54.4. 2008: 493–513.

Eliot, T.S. *Collected Poems*. London: Faber & Faber, 1974.

Finch, Anne. *Selected Poems*. London: Fyfield, 2003.

Fitter, Chris. "The Poetic Nocturne: from Ancient Motif to Renaissance Genre." *Early Modern Literary Studies*. 3.2. 1997: 1–61.

Frydman, Anne. "Overnight Travelers without Berths." *The Yale Review*. 94.4. 2009: 32.

Hopkins, Gerald Manley. *The Poems of Gerald Manley Hopkins*. Oxford: Oxford University Press, 1970.

Huysmans, Joris-Karl. *Against the Grain*. London: BiblioBazaar, 2007.

Keats, John. *The Selected Letters and Poems*. Ed. J.H. Walsh. London: Chatto and Windus, repr. 1962.

Kinsella, Thomas. *Collected Poems*. Manchester: Carcanet, 2001.

Larkin, Philip. *Collected Poems*. London: Faber & Faber, 1990.

Milton, John. *The Complete Poems*. London: Dent and Sons, 1980.

O'Hara, Frank. *The Collected Poems*. Berkeley: University of California Press, 1995.

Parnell, Thomas. *The Poetical Works*. London: BiblioBazaar, 2008.

Redgrove, Peter. *The Apple-Broadcast and Other Poems*. Routledge and Kegan Paul, 1981.

Redgrove, Peter. *Dr. Faust's Sea-Spiral Spirit*. London: Routledge and Kegan Paul, 1972.

St. John of the Cross. *The Poems of Saint John of the Cross*. Chicago: University of Chicago Press, 1995.

Shelley, Percy Bysshe. *In Defence of Poetry and Other Essays*. London: Dodo Press, 2008.

Sidney, Philip. *The Complete Poems*. London: BiblioBazaar, 2009.

Thomson, James. *The Poetical Works of James Thomson*. London: Reprint Services Corporation, 1992.

Whitman, Walt. *The Complete Poems*. London: Penguin, 1986.

Yeats, William Butler. *The Poems*. Ed. Richard J. Finneran. London: Macmillan, 1991.

Young, Edward. *Night Thoughts*. Cambridge: Cambridge University Press, 2008.

28
Heaney, Virgil, and Contemporary *Katabasis*

Rachel Falconer

In *The Periodic Table*, Primo Levi describes chemical distillation as a process which enacts "a metamorphosis from liquid to vapor (invisible), and from this once again to liquid; . . . in this double journey, up and down, purity is attained, an ambiguous and fascinating condition" (58). *Katabasis*, the descent and return of a living being into the underworld, could well be understood in these terms: as a chemical morphosis from weight to lightness and back again to the weight of being. To be sure, the double journey occurs in the inverse direction—uncannily, one *sinks* into lightness—but what is attained by the end is equally ambiguous, equally fascinating. I contend here that *katabasis* is a literary genre which contemporary poets have used in order to reflect on their relation to literary ancestors, to discover continuities and coherences in otherwise fragmented or grief-struck lives, to defamiliarize and critique present-day politics, or to affirm certain values in the face of destabilizing global events. Amongst the late twentieth- and early twenty-first-century individual poems or collections which have revived the *katabatic* journey are, to name but a few, Seamus Heaney's *Station Island* and *Spirit Level*, Derek Walcott's *Omeros*, Alice Notley's *The Descent of Alette* and *Disobedience*, James Merrill's *Divine Comedies*, Peter Reading's *Perduta Gente*, Eavan Boland's *The Journey*, Tony Harrison's V, Geoffrey Hill's *The Triumph of Love*, Carol Ann Duffy's *Rapture* and *The World's Wife*, Ted Hughes's "For the Duration" and *Birthday Letters*, Paul Durcan's "Daddy, Daddy," parts of Peter Redgrove's *Assembling a Ghost*, Eilean Ni Chuillenain's *The Second Voyage*, John Montague's "The Cage," Adrienne Rich's *Diving into the Wreck*, and Paul Muldoon's *Hay*.[1] But rather than attempting a survey of this rich field, or a blazon of its *katabatic* parts, I would like to focus on a recent collection which, while no less acclaimed, has not been considered in depth as a *katabasis*. Seamus Heaney's *District and Circle* (2006) exemplifies, with brilliant and beautiful economy, how this ancient genre still serves to frame and make

A Companion to Poetic Genre, First Edition. Edited by Erik Martiny.
© 2012 John Wiley & Sons, Ltd. Published 2012 by John Wiley & Sons, Ltd.

sense of individual experience, whilst providing a ballast against new turbulences of the twenty-first century: terrorism, globalization, and erosion of the natural world.[2]

Katabatic poetry is essentially a narrative rather than a lyric form, because it relates a journey through which a character or persona undergoes an education or a trial of the self to achieve a certain wisdom (see Clark, and Falconer, *Hell in Contemporary Literature* 42–52). That said, the journey is uniquely one of compression and distillation, so that the narration of one particular stage retains the genre memory of the others. Thus, *katabasis* may be described as having a four-part structure: threshold crossing, series of trials, "ground zero" confrontation with the other, return. But this diffuse process is often distilled into a three-part structure (where "trial" and "confrontation" are elided), or a two-part structure (descent and return, where trial and confrontation are implicit in "descent"). Or, finally, all these stages can be compressed into one gesture, the descent, since in every descent narrative there is an implicit return because without it, the narration would not be possible. The journey towards wisdom can be structured as a conversion, often religious, in which the old self must die at the nadir of the journey in order for a new self to find grace. Yet even this process can be compressed into a single episode since, as David Pike argues, "conversion conflates the two moments so that God himself is encountered at the nadir of the descent" (*Passage through Hell* 29). A *katabasis* can, then, comprise a full-length epic poem, as in the case of Notley's *The Descent of Alette* or Reading's *Perduta Gente.* Or it can be compressed into a brief narrative, as in Eavan Boland's title poem, "The Journey." Or it can achieve the temporal concentration of lyric, as in Hughes's "The Prism" (*Birthday Letters*), or of discursive argument, as in U.A. Fanthorpe's "The Guide" (*Standing To*). In Virgil's *Aeneid,* the descent to the underworld, occurring midway through the epic, transforms Aeneas from Trojan refugee into the ambiguously pure founder of Rome. As well as providing the linchpin between Odyssean and Iliadic halves of the poem, the *katabasis* also serves as a summation and distillation of the entire arc of Aeneas's adventures, from the fall of Troy to the death of his antagonist, Turnus. In other words, the *katabasis* (or *descensus ad inferos,* as the Romans termed it) radiates outward from its central point, to circle and frame the entire journey as a descent from an earthly paradise to a morally complex, mortal history (cf. Frye 97). Likewise the *nekyia,* occurring at the near-midpoint of Homer's *Odyssey,* illuminates the *katabatic* shape of Odysseus's entire journey from Troy to Ithaca. At its most radically distilled, an entire *katabasis* may be implied in two lines or one. Think of Dante's "midway in the journey of our life / I found myself in a dark wood" (*Inf.* 1.1–2) or Ezra Pound's "And then went down to the ship" (*Three Cantos* 3). Such distillation is only possible because *katabasis* is such a memorious genre.[3] Pound's line resonates with the memory of Homer's *Odyssey,* and Dante's opening line conjures the whole of the *Inferno* (and arguably, the entire *Commedia*). The telescoping structure of *katabasis* is thus dependent on memory, just as memory is its principal subject.

In Seamus Heaney's *District and Circle,* only the title poem describes a palpably mythic underworld journey, but here too the *descensus* radiates outward to include the entire collection in a unitary *katabatic* shape. There are, on the one hand, a series of poems which represent the start of the new millennium as a cataclysmic fall or upheaval of underearth. Some of these refer to violence on the global scale, most notably "Anything Can Happen" which we shall discuss in detail below, and "Höfn," which alludes to climate change. Others depict violence on the local scale, with hammers struck ("Midnight Anvil"), and walls disintegrating under blows ("A Shiver"). Sometimes the violence is something we bring on ourselves ("To have known it in your bones, directable," "A Shiver" l.10). Other times it seems vast and amoral, as when a slicing machine dices turnip heads, drops "its raw sliced mess" into buckets, and is heard to comment, "This is the way that God sees life" ("The Turnip-Snedder" ll.19, 13). These poems register the turbulences of what Heaney, quoting Auden, has described as "the new age of anxiety."[4] In *katabatic* terms, they form the ground or context in which the descent will take place. There has to be a massive upheaval to produce the disorientation which would *require* such an extraordinary journey. Disorientation etymologically means "turned towards Dis" (or Hades). Dante descends to Hell, "che la diritta via era smarrita" ("for the straight way was lost," *Inf.* 1.3).

In *District and Circle*, set against the poems of turbulence and disorientation are those which depict various figures willingly setting forth on descent journeys, or merely riding the waves, demonstrating an endurance that defies spiritual shipwreck. Amongst these is the unmistakably *katabatic* "District and Circle," the second poem we shall consider in detail below, but this descent trajectory also structures other poems, such as "Poet to Blacksmith," "The Lagands Road," and "The Tollund Man in Springtime." If my argument that the collection comprises a sustained *katabasis* holds true, then the many poems devoted to Heaney's literary mentors and friends may be read as conversations with underworld *umbrae*, whose traditional function is to bestow on the descent hero their knowledge of the past and future. By conversing with ghosts, the descent hero acquires understanding of his own addressivity in time, the way his acts flow from the legacy of the dead, and will extend that legacy into the future (see R. Harrison 90–105). *Katabasis* is also about faith found in friendship, the shared values discovered and exchanged in conversation. The performative act of *katabatic* poems is to assert that this process of exchange can extend beyond death. Finally, *District and Circle* concludes *katabatically* with "The Blackbird of Glanmore," in which the emergent poet allies himself to the ambivalent figure of the blackbird, at once an omen of death and bringer of song. In this poem, the blackbird presides over the untimely death of Heaney's young brother, "A little stillness dancer— / Haunter-son, lost brother" (ll.14–15), which calls to mind Virgil's elegiac lines for young Marcellus, nephew of Augustus, whose death was mourned by all Rome at the time Virgil was composing the *Aeneid* (*Ae.* 6.868–86).

In *District and Circle* as a whole, Heaney circles backward in time to recover memories of previous poems and the districts of his rural Irish childhood: Mossbawn, Anahorish, and Moyulla. Like the District and Circle lines of the London Tube, the descent journey here is both linear and circular—a downward spiral in the manner of Dante's pilgrim. In Heaney's millennial collection, the desire to renew one's attachment to a district, or as Bakhtin would say, one's addressivity, arises in part as a response to the scale of dislocation caused by 9/11 and global terrorism. In Bakhtin's coinage, "addressivity" (*obrashchennost*, also translated as answerability or responsibility) means the sense of having a physical address in time and space (which we lack, for example, in Internet exchanges), and by extension a sense of both addressing oneself to a particular context, and feeling addressed by, or answerable to, that context (*Art and Answerability* 39). But it seems we cannot fully address ourselves in, and to, the present, without first affirming our anachronic ties. Robert Harrison argues, I think rightly, that only by choosing one's ancestors does one become fully conscious of one's own mortality, of being-toward-the-dead. Counter-intuitively, it is by choosing our ancestors that we acquire the freedom to explore possible futurities, for as Harrison writes, "it is from *them* (my personal, cultural, or freely chosen traditions) that I receive the sum of those repeatable possibilities that I am thrown back upon in anticipatory resoluteness" (R. Harrison 97). This is surely one of the principal drives of *katabatic* poetry, for as Harrison points out, "in Hades Aeneas learns that past and future in fact copenetrate and codetermine each other" (95). The Polish poet Czeslaw Milosz is one of Heaney's chosen ancestors, and is overheard saying, "The soul exceeds its circumstances." Heaney's Tollund Man agrees,

> Yes.
> History not to be granted the last word
> Or the first claim.
>
> (4.1–3)

The underworld is the achronic space where the descent hero chooses a fellowship from amongst the dead, a group of interlocutors who together will exceed their individual circumstances, although this is not the same as the modernist claim that through art they might transcend history altogether.

Originally, the *nekyia*, or conversation with the dead, comprised a separate literary tradition from *katabasis*, as only the latter depicted an actual journey through the underworld (Clark 32). But from Homer onwards, the two genres have freely overlapped; indeed one might argue that the aim of the *katabatic* journey is to arrive at the *nekyia*, for conversation with the dead is nearly always what we crave the most. This is why the most chilling moments in *katabatic* narratives are when the dead fail or refuse to speak: when Dido turns away from Aeneas, or when Dante's Lucifer proves incapable of speech. In *District and Circle*, Heaney chooses an extraordinary number of ancestors, testament to the collection's emphasis on friendship and the need for a heterochronic, multi-layered historical perspective. Along with Czeslaw Milosz, the underworld shades with whom he stops to converse include fellow writers George Seferis, Pablo Neruda, Dorothy Wordsworth, W.H. Auden, C.P. Cavafy, Rainer Maria Rilke, and Ted Hughes. As Hawkins and Jacoff remind us, the model for this kind of dialogue is Dante's *Commedia*, which is largely comprised of conversations with the dead (xxiv). Dante famously enlists himself amongst the six greatest poets in *Inferno* 4, along with Homer, Virgil, Horace, Ovid, and Lucan. T.S. Eliot's "familiar compound ghost" is based on Dante's later encounter, deeper in Hell, with his old school-teacher Brunetto Latini, and together, according to Hawkins and Jacoff, they "made the meeting with a dead poetic mentor one of the most enduring "scenes" in modern poetry" (xxiv).

As we shall see, Virgil is pre-eminent amongst the ancestral *umbrae* of Heaney's underworld. The sixth book of the *Aeneid* recounts the hero's descent into Hades, but that episode is already memorious of other descents—not only that of Homer's Odysseus, and Virgil's Orpheus (narrated in *Georgics* 4), but also of an earlier trauma in Aeneas's own life. In *Aeneid* 2, Virgil recounts the razing of Troy, the epic's first scene of infernal destruction, a night which Aeneas experiences in a blind confusion. This book begins with Aeneas, now safely arrived at Dido's court in Carthage, attempting to render an account of that unspeakable trauma: "Infandum, regina, iubes renouare dolorem" ("it is an unspeakable pain you ask me to revive, o queen," *Ae.* 2.3). His hesitation at the threshold of speech reminds us that *katabatic* narrative is nearly always already doubled in the sense that the poet has to descend in memory to recollect the underworld journey. So the first *katabatic* episode in the *Aeneid*, the fall of Troy, is quite consciously doubled from the start. The *katabatic* trajectory of *District and Circle* also begins with a doubled account of a cataclysmic fall, in this case, an account of a contemporary disaster glimpsed palimpsestically through the translation of a classical text. Originally published as "Horace and the Thunder," "Anything Can Happen" is a free adaptation of Horace's *Odes* 1.34, in which the poet is jolted out of his lax, free-wheeling attitude to the gods by a sharp reminder of their infinite powers. Jupiter can strike thunder down from a clear sky (which the Epicureans held to be impossible), and Fortune can uncrown and recrown a dictator in an instant. Composed at the invitation of Amnesty International, Heaney's adaptation of the ode conceals and reveals a poetic response to 9/11. Here Jupiter's lightning strikes "the Atlantic shore," a clever transposition of Horace's Atlantean mountain (which, in Roman times, was considered the western-most edge of the world). And this show of force reminds the poet that "the tallest towers" can "Be overturned," a clear reference to the destruction of the World Trade Centre twin towers (ll.8–9). By retrospectively placing "Anything Can Happen" at the start of *District and Circle,* Heaney figures post-9/11 New York as a newly fallen Troy.

Some readers have objected that "Anything Can Happen" buries the particular horrors of 9/11 under an unnecessary layer of classical allusion.[5] Urbane Horace is not even translated to an urban setting. Besides the reference to "towers" (which in the earlier version was "things" ["One Poet"]), Heaney's catastrophes appear to occur in a natural rather than man-made environment. Still more objectionable, potentially, is the implication that 9/11 could be read as an act of god, or even (as some religious extremists held it) as divine vengeance against an infidel nation (see Carey). In Horace's text it *is* Jupiter who authors the violence:

> valet ima summis
> mutare et insignem attenuat dues
> obscura promens

God has the strength to exchange lowest with highest, destroy the famous and bring the hidden to light

But this expression of what was already a Roman truism need not be aimed at strengthening the reader's religious faith. Horace's Jupiter is neither likeable, nor particularly just. Heaney's adaptation is still further from justifying divine vengeance. It is not even clear in his poem that the violence stems from a sentient and rational god. Over four stanzas, the action shifts from that of a personified god in the first two stanzas to that of an inhuman force in the third and final stanzas. Jupiter manfully hurls the lightning, but it is raptor-like Fortune which rends and tears, causing its victims to gasp and bleed. Moreover the final two stanzas are thickly studded with abstract nouns for subjects: "Ground gives," "Anything can happen," and "nothing settles." At least syntactically, none of these acts occurs as a result of a god's conscious moral will. Again, one could object that Heaney's poem obscures the conscious *human* intent behind the September 11 attacks. But for the victim or witness, terrorist violence is experienced as random and inexplicable, which is one reason why it is so horrifying.

Moreover, read as the initiatory episode in a *katabatic* narrative, the poem's mythological frame is both generically appropriate and effective. *Katabasis* has claims to being classed as a literary genre, rather than just a topos or thematic motif, because it embodies a generic world-view which is encoded in a particular organization of time and space (Bakhtin, *The Dialogic Imagination* 86). In *katabatic* texts, time and space are always drastically verticalized. The dominant trajectory of the *katabatic* hero is downwards but true to Newtonian law, this motion collects into a knot of tension that eventually catapults the hero upwards again. In "Anything Can Happen," Jupiter's blow is, quite literally, kata-strophic; it drives downward through a verticalized landscape, shaking first sky, then earth, then "clogged underearth." At the end of the poem, we witness the upward recoil as "The heaven's weight / Lifts up off Atlas like a kettle-lid" (ll.13–14). *Katabatic* texts also represent time as cut off from historical development, and compressed into repeatable patterns, paradigms, and mythic forms. These contrasting senses of time are represented through spatial metaphors, historical time figured as movement along a horizontal axis, and mythic time, movement up and down a vertical one. In the *katabatic* "image of the world structured according to a pure verticality," as Bakhtin writes of Dante's *Commedia*, "all temporal and historical divisions and linkages [are replaced] with purely interpretative, extratemporal and hierarchicized ones" (*The Dialogic Imagination* 157) The fact that, in "Anything Can Happen," 9/11 can only be represented indirectly, through mythic accounts of Jupiter and Fortuna, registers the depth of its traumatic impact.

For this reader, the moments of recognition are all the more powerful for being distanced and defamiliarized through Horace. But it should be emphasized that Heaney's mythic method differs from high modernist ones, in that it does not impose the same hierarchy of value of mythic past over present history (cf. Pike, *Passage through Hell* 2). Indeed Heaney has objected to the way that Eliot's later poetry strove to create an image of Dante as orthodox and "classically ratified"; this image excluded all the "untamed and thoroughly parochial elements of Dante's use of the vernacular" ("Envies and Identifications" 247–48, 255). Far from being "classically ratified" or orthodox-sounding, by contrast, Heaney's imitation of Horace sounds vigorously Anglo-Saxon; Fortune has a "stropped beak" (calling to mind Heaney's friend Ted Hughes's crow) and Atlas has a "kettle-lid." Amid "capstones" and "fire-spores," we are in little danger of elevating a mythically orthodox Latin over a present-day, degraded vernacular. Heaney uses myth not to devalue the present, but to defamiliarize and hence re-evaluate it. In "Anything Can Happen," for example, there is a sense in which the "burial" of 9/11 under a layer of classical myth is an act which preserves the catastrophe intact, protecting it from linguistic over-exposure. Only glimpses of the historical reality are exhumed here, but elsewhere in the collection, other buried figures rise up from the earth (notably, "The Tollund Man in Springtime"), all of whom have been preserved by lying hidden and dormant in the earth. Heaney's poem is thus "telluric," of the earth, in several senses ("Anything Can Happen" 16): it represents the earth receiving a shattering blow, it buries a contemporary catastrophe under a protective layer of classical myth, and it disorients the reader, setting up the need for a willed descent to counter-balance the catastrophic fall.[6]

While there are metaphorical descents in several poems in *District and Circle*, only the title poem narrates a recognizably generic *katabatic* journey. "District and Circle" is structured into five sonnets, with varying near-rhyme schemes. Each has a strong thematic and grammatical *volta* at the sixth or eighth line; so each enacts, in a sense, its own mini-descent and return.[7] As Heaney explains, the first and final stanzas were originally composed as part of a sonnet sequence on the Tollund Man, familiar from Heaney's earlier work, but transplanted here to a contemporary urban context:

> this Iron Age revenant was, as they used to say in stage directions, "discovered" in a new setting, keeping step with me in the world of surveillance cameras and closed-circuit TV, of greenhouse gases and acid rain. He functioned as a kind of guardian other, risen out of the Jutland bog.
>
> ("One Poet")

Not physically present in "District and Circle," he remains, nevertheless, an invisible guide, an internalized alter-ego surveying the London scene with the eyes of a foreigner. When the poet asks, "Had I betrayed or not, myself or him?" (3.8), the "him" may refer to the busker previously encountered at the station entrance, or to the poet's father who appears later in the poem. But it may also refer to the displaced figure of the Tollund Man, since to abandon one's guide to the underworld is to risk getting lost, betraying oneself and the purpose of the journey.

And how might one characterize the purpose of this *katabatic* journey? At the most practical level (but not to be dismissed in a collection that celebrates dailiness), it concerns the daily task of getting to and from work. Heaney writes from memories of traveling between Earls Court and St. James's Park, as an employee of the London Passport Office in 1962 (Parker 8). Originally a diptych of two sonnets, "District and Circle" is named after the two Tube lines that serve those stations (Heaney, "One Poet"). Metaphorically, the poem conveys the poet's unease that in this London setting, he may be losing touch with Irish places, and hence his own addressivity. The descent he undergoes is, then, in part to exhume the language of the farmer father's son, so that the urban commute can be recast in the language of his rural childhood. In the middle section of the poem, as he anchors himself in the train ready to depart, he effects a metamorphosis of language and self, declaring his readiness to

> take my stand
> From planted ball of heel to heel of hand
> As sweet traction and heavy down-slump stayed me
>
> (4.4–5)

The beautiful symmetries of rhyme and chiastic repetition ("ball of heel to heel of hand") underline the achievement of a connection and a balance between past and present selves. In the humic language of "planted heel," the poet conveys his intention to keep faith with the past.[8]

But if this is a poem about rooting one's present self in a personal, individual past, events occurred during the genesis of "District and Circle" which added a public and political dimension to this gesture. The London Underground was bombed on July 7, 2005, shortly after Heaney had decided to make this the title poem of his collection. "My first impulse was to change again," he comments, "but the more I thought about it, the more it seemed right to keep faith with the London lines" ("One Poet"). Although no direct mention is made of the attacks in the three sonnets added subsequently to the middle of the poem, the poet now faces two tasks: to maintain his childhood alliances with Derry and Antrim, and to "keep faith with" the crowd of Londoners underground—both those with whom he surged to work each day in 1962, and those who lost their lives in the 2005 bombings. The mythic descent to the underworld becomes a means of confirming fellowship with those dead in particular. Since the poem is set in a period forty years prior to the attacks, no mention is made of the commuters who will later die in the underground trains. But in the underworld, the past is recovered in its connection with latent futurity. This *katabatic* foresight is starkly illustrated in the closing lines of the poem, when the poet feels himself "hurtled forward" on the departing train, his face reflected "in a window mirror-backed / By blasted weeping rock-walls" (5.13).

Once again Heaney might be accused of excessive indirection if "District and Circle" were to be read as a representation of 7/7, an event which, incidentally, was commonly described in news reportage at the time as a descent into or an eruption of Hell, complete with epic heroes and devils (see Falconer, "Hell in Our Time"). But Heaney eschews the more obvious Satanic metaphors and, rather than attempting to *represent* the terrorist attacks, he writes to *resist* their intended effects of escalating violence or fear. For as Leon Wieseltier wrote in his obituary of Czeslaw Milosz, there are "two ways of resisting evil: . . . action against it and contemplation despite it." Heaney "contemplates despite evil" by insisting on the ongoingness of culture. Since their construction at the start of the twentieth century, the London and Paris undergrounds have been mythologized as infernal spaces in visual art, literature, film, and popular culture (see Pike, *Metropolis on the Styx*). Heaney thus writes in a recognizably modern tradition when he likens his daily commute on the District and Circle lines to a *katabatic* journey. For poets writing after 7/7, that analogy has obviously taken on a new layer of signification. But Heaney will not allow the terrorist context to overwhelm the genre memory of the *descensus* as a journey towards self-knowledge and wisdom. His Miloszian resistance lies in composing a *katabatic* poem that is at once unmistakably contemporary and deeply classical.

Or to be more precise, deeply Virgilian. If the literary climate in the 1990s proved conducive to Ovidian "shape-shifting, performance, and disguise," then, as Rowena Fowler argues, that preference may be shifting in the new millennium to Virgil. Twenty-first century poems "After Virgil," she writes, tend toward unitary forms, a more conciliatory mood, and "a kind of alert integration" (Fowler 240). "District and Circle" provides an exemplary model of "alert integration" in the Virgilian mode. As we have seen, Heaney engages with other *katabatic* texts such as Dante's *Inferno* and Eliot's *The Waste Land*. But his most prolonged conversation is with Virgil and *Aeneid* 6. I say "conversation" because no allusion to Virgil in the poem is inertly repetitive. Virgil is called upon to take part in a dialogue amongst equals, as Heaney finds ways to extend the Roman poet's ability to speak to our present and future. This intertextual dialogue could not be further from Harold Bloom's theory of poetic influence as an Oedipal struggle between strong and weak poets. If choosing one's ancestors in the underworld entails "the renewal and determination of legacy, rather than merely its pious reproduction" (R. Harrison 95), then metatextually, Heaney carries out that task of authentic repetition with respect to his chosen ghost, Virgil.

Virgil is a poet of shadows and pathos and loss. But he is also a poet of integration and unitary forms, as Rowena Fowler argues. What seem particularly important to Heaney, especially in "District and Circle," are the balances and symmetries in Virgil's way of thinking, his imagery, and his structuring of the verse line and paragraph. The passage which describes Aeneas stepping into Charon's boat to cross the Styx into the underworld is one which richly illustrates Virgil's instinct for symmetry, and its echoes can be heard throughout Heaney's "District and Circle." Charon draws the boat close to shore,

> inde alias animas, quae per iuga longa sedebant,
> deturbat laxatque foros; simul accipit alueo
> ingentem Aenean. gemuit sub pondere cumba
> sutilis et multam accepit rimosa paludem.
> tandem trans fluuium incolumis uatemque uirumque
> informi limo glaucaque exponit in ulua.

> Then he hurls out the other souls, who were sitting along the long benches, and he
> clears the gangways, and at the same time, he takes on board the mighty Aeneas. The
> leaky boat groaned under the hero's weight, and took in quantities of marsh water
> through its slats. At last he transports them across the flood, both prophet and man
> unharmed, and deposits them in the shapeless mud and gleaming swamp-grass.
>
> (*Ae.* 6.411–16, my trans.)

The first thing to point out here is the regular pairing of verbs ("deturbat," "laxat";
"accipit," "accepit"), nouns ("vatemque virumque"; "limo," "ulva") and adjectives
("informi," "glauca"). These alert us to deeper symmetries binding together the
various actants in this scene: the other souls ("alias animas") clear a space which is
then filled by the outsized hero ("ingentem Aeneam"); and the weight of Aeneas
causes a fresh weight of marsh-water to enter the boat. Most importantly for the
parallel with Heaney, a *katabatic* movement (the boat sinking down under the unusual
weight of a flesh-and-blood passenger) is balanced against a smooth transverse one
(despite its burden, the boat moves fluidly, "tandem trans fluvium," across the surface
to the muddy shore beyond). All these pairings convey a scene which is tense with
opposing energies and desires. Charon violently imposes his will on the dead souls;
Aeneas outranks and (literally) outweighs them; the infernal river would no doubt
like to drown both man and seer, but it accords them passage. These oppositions
pave the way for the heavier demands the underworld will impose on Aeneas, a
balance needing to be struck between memory and forgetfulness, violence and peace,
love and empire. Aeneas stays on course by adhering to a narrative of himself articulated by the sibyl, his guide: "Troius Aeneas, pietate insignis et armis, /ad genitorem
imas Erebi descendit ad umbras" ("Trojan Aeneas, famous for goodness and strength,
descends to seek his father in the lowest shades of Erebus" *Ae.* 6.403–04). Even self-
knowledge, then, is a process of give-and-take; it requires the acceptance of a conversation and a burden and a relationship. Virgilian symmetry doesn't imply stasis;
it implies control.

This concern with symmetry and balance is, if anything, more pronounced in
Heaney's "District and Circle."[9] Again the verbs are paired: larked, capered (1.9),
trigger, untrigger (1.10), nod, nod (1.13–14), and a double pair filling an entire line,
"Rumbled, quickened, evened, quieted." (2.6). As in the Charon episode in the *Aeneid*,
so here the verbal symmetries reflect the poem's preoccupation with balancing opposing temporalities, energies and desires. Like Aeneas stepping out onto the boat, the
poet here has to test his weight against the crowd, "half straggle-ravelled and half
strung / like a human chain" (3.3–4). Is he part of the "all" (3.14) or is he separate,
and are they linked or each separate, "Blindsided to themselves and other bodies"?
(4.14) How one relates to the other is in part a question of one's chronotopic address,
as Bakhtin has convincingly argued. Space and time in "District and Circle" are
verticalized, as is characteristic of *katabatic* poems. Not only does the poet's journey
consist of a physical descent into the station, but he is descending from the present
context to memories of his childhood past, as well as memories of the literary
past, especially Aeneas's threshold crossing into Hades. On the other hand, the

underground also has its own diachronicity. As Bakhtin writes of *Inferno*, "the images and ideas that fill this vertical world are in their turn filled with a powerful desire . . . to set out along the historically productive horizontal, to be distributed not upward but forward" (*The Dialogic Imagination* 157). Inside Earls Court and St. James's Park stations, escalators move the crowds up and down but also "*along* the dreamy ramparts" (2.1, 4, my emphasis). In *katabasis*, the souls of the dead desire conversation with the living so that they can become more historical, more alive. The living protagonist, on the other hand, becomes a little ghostly when conversing with the dead. Entering Hades, Aeneas passes a vast elm tree with dreams clinging to its every leaf; and leaving it, he passes through the ivory gate of false dreams (*Ae.* 6.282–84, 893–901). There is a distinct possibility, then, that the foreknowledge he acquires about the future glory of Rome may be nothing but a subjective dream. In "District and Circle" the poet enters the station with the dreamer's uncanny sense of foreknowledge: "I knew I was always going to find" (1.4). In contrast to the Roman hero, whose weight displaces the souls of the dead in Charon's boat, Heaney's poet is greeted as a fellow underworlder by the busker at the threshold, "his two eyes eying me / In an unaccusing look I'd not avoid" (1.5–6). The poet pockets the coin that traditionally accords passage into Hades, because he shares some kinship with this figure (perhaps a fellow Irishman): "For was our traffic not in recognition?" (1.12). And as he descends, he feels cut off from the overworld which in his backward gaze becomes an earthly paradise, where sunbathers in the park are "habitués / Of their garden of delights" (2.13–14). So to a greater extent than Aeneas, he is open to the underworld's various wants and demands. This is all metaphorically implicit in the way he carefully takes his position inside the train, grabbing a strap to secure himself along a vertical axis, and bracing himself warily for the lurch of forward movement (4.4).

We have suggested that *katabasis* stages a dialogue with the dead as a means of enabling the protagonist to choose his or her own "repeatable possibilities" in the future (Harrison's paraphrase of Heidegger). In Heaney's "District and Circle," though, no one speaks. There are cheerful tunes from the busker's tin whistle, and threatening sounds of an engine rumbling and doors growling, but no exchange of human word. The commuters at first "street-loud" succumb to "herd-quiet" underground, as if they'd been bewitched by Homer's Circe (3.7). Elsewhere in the collection, Heaney gives speech to a wide array of absent mentors and friends. But here the poet is silently absorbed in his own thoughts amid the mute and anonymous crowd. Does this descent journey, then, lack a *nekyia*, a conversation with the dead? What it appears to do is reignite a debate within the poet himself, in which an other or others lay claim to his allegiance:

> Had I betrayed or not, myself or him?
> Always new to me, always familiar,
> This unrepentant, now repentant turn

(3.7–9)

The question of betrayal arises specifically from the uncanny dream-space, where things are always new and familiar, and where the poet can both resist and acquiesce to a neglected faith. It is also specifically in the time of the conversionary turning point, the now-or-neverness at the nadir of descent, that the self splits and doubles to become "myself or him."

In the fourth and fifth stanzas, we hear only the poet's thoughts but he occupies two chronotopes, urban and rural, present and past. As argued above, this is where the poet balances the two selves that occupy these different chronotopes, and here we might add a few words more about that process. Stepping onto the train, like Aeneas onto the boat, he finds his balance by taking his stand, as it were, in the roots of the English language. In this transformative space, each word signifies right down to its etymological meaning so that we see the root exposed, like a tooth under X-ray. The strap which the poet grabs to plant himself, hand to heel, is a "stubby black roof-wort," where "wort" comes from Old English *wyrt* meaning "root," and "roof" from Old English *hróf*, one of whose early meanings, interestingly, was "coffin-lid." The poet himself stands "spot-rooted, buoyed, aloof" (4.7), and one thinks now not merely of the image of Aeneas afloat, but more radically, of "buoyed" from Old French *boye*, meaning "a fetter or chain," and "aloof" from the preposition *a* plus Dutch *loef*, in connection with Middle English *lof*, *loof*, meaning some kind of rudder, with (as the *OED* puts it) "the idea of keeping a ship's head to the wind." The effect on the reader is not to lose us in a Borgesian labyrinth of endless signifying, but rather to make us aware of how much this simple gesture of balancing oneself on a Tube train can mean. Against the dreaminess of the mythic underworld Heaney sets the tactility and concreteness of language.

"So deeper into it": one descends into the underworld not to recover the ancient history of language, however fascinating that may be, but to find the person one has loved and lost (5.1). Aeneas finds Dido but she turns away; he finds his father and tries to embrace him but there is no substance to embrace. Insofar as Anchises is permitted to address his son and pass on knowledge of the past and future, Hades yields much but it doesn't yield all. Heaney's underworld yields even less in that he only catches a glimpse of his lost beloved, and that turns out to be a mere reflection of himself in the window: "My father's glazed face in my own waning/ And craning . . ." (5.3–4). Some have argued that the underworld is always patriarchally structured, that women can function as guides, but only male ghosts can impart prophecy of the future. According to Bernard Dick "the displacement of the female" is "one of the essentials of the *descensus*" (45). Whether or not that was ever true (which is doubtful; recall that it is Creusa's ghost who tells Aeneas about his imperial legacy, *Ae.* 2.783), it is certainly not an "essential" of contemporary *katabasis*. The poet's glimpse of his father here elides two episodes in the *Aeneid*, the hero's two encounters with Anchises and Dido. It is Dido whom Virgil compares to an uncertain moon, and it is she who refrains from speech (*Ae.* 6.450–76). Here both absent father and poet wane uncertainly. The poet's father here imparts no knowledge of the past or future to his son. Instead what follows the ellipsis are two empty half-lines, cutting a gulf between quatrains. So, no prophecy; just silence. But there is the shock of recognition (and we know from earlier that the poet's "traffic" here is in recognition) of his father's face in his own. Like so many of the structural features of this poem, identity is presented as a diptych, a pair of reflecting portraits. That might be read as a displacement of the maternal, or the female, in male identity-construction if it were not for the fact that the encounter recalls fleeting glimpses not only of Dido, but also of Creusa, Eurydice, and others, indeed "a human chain" of underworld ghosts. But it's the loss of his father that matters to the poet here, and it is the sight of his own face "waning" into his father's as it ages, which gives him the only certain knowledge of the future to be gained from this underworld journey. That includes knowledge of his own mortality but also, conversely, of how his father is still alive through him. The strengthened sense of a generational link is also implicit in the description of the poet's arm aloft "like a flail," clearly a farmer father's son as well as a poet.

At the end of a *katabatic* journey, the protagonist emerges from the underworld radically changed: whether converted from a state of sin to one of grace, or from sickness to health, or ignorance to wisdom. No one escapes such an experience entirely unscathed, and sometimes the loss is much greater than the gain. All the same, implicit in most *katabases* is the view that value can be derived from the *via negativa*, however extreme the *via* is. If *katabasis* aims towards a unitary, integrated view of life, however, this is not to say that its conclusions are simplistic. There is always an unresolved ambivalence about the return: Aeneas departing via the ivory gates, Dante gaining a mysterious twelve hours at the centre of Hell, and so on (see Falconer, *Hell in Contemporary Literature* 43–44). "District and Circle" ends in a ragged, rhythmically irregular rush, as the poet is "hurtled forward" through the tunnel. On a literal level, there is no reascent from this underworld journey, as the final image is of the poet being transported into the tunnels, not out (5.10). The final sestet is set off by a strong paragraph break, the last two lines are metrically incomplete, and the final line is a sentence fragment consisting of one word, a hyphenated neologism: "Flicker-lit." One presumes it is the poet, not the rock-walls, who is "flicker-lit," but the grammar of the sestet is frayed enough to support both readings.

Indeed there is something persistently humic about the image of the poet in the final lines: "the only relict / Of all that I belonged to" (5.10–11). "Relict" is a rare word, trailing paragraphs of obsolete meanings in the *OED*. Its secondary and tertiary meanings pertain to inanimate objects which retain some memory of the past: a receptacle for holding a relic (*OED* 2a); or a thing (3d), species (3e), part of a language system (3f), or rock (3g), surviving from a previous age. Burial protects and preserves these objects but often as anachronisms, lumpishly resistant to assimilation and interchange in the living present (cf. Parker 10). The primary meaning of relict, however, is "widow" (1a); though rare, one still finds the word on gravestones, i.e., in a context where a living person is mentioned specifically in her connection with the dead.[10] As Steven Matthews suggests, the poet seems to be aligning himself with the survivors of massacre, such as those depicted in Heaney's earlier collection, *North* (93). But I think there is also a more specific identification with Virgil's "widow Dido," who is famously both faithful and unfaithful, and hence herself an ambiguous, "flicker-lit" figure. While other classical sources portray her as faithful to the memory of her husband Sychaeus, in the *Aeneid* Dido betrays his memory and succumbs to her passion for Aeneas (for other sources, see MacDonald 73). When Aeneas meets her in the underworld, Dido is with Sychaeus and is once again the faithful widow. But this renewal of faith requires a betrayal (the rejection of her past with Aeneas), just as the earlier betrayal of her husband's memory demonstrated a trust in Aeneas. In "District and Circle" the underworld is the dialogic dream-space in which identities double and combine; the voice of the other is heard in the self, the other's face seen in the reflection of one's own. Questioning himself ("Had I betrayed or not, myself or him?"), the poet internalizes the other that he seeks, in this case Dido, for whom the question of faith was ultimately so destructive. So even as he reclaims old allegiances with the people and places of his past, he acknowledges the difficult tensions involved in this renewal of faith.

If the poet is allowed to return from the underworld with a newly forged sense of connection to his father, whose face bears the sign of both his past and his future, then the price for this connection may well be a sense of estrangement from the present. If that is the private cost, still the sestet as a whole stresses the integration and continuity of his experience: "And so by night and day to be transported . . . with them" (5.9–10). He is not alienated but traveling with "them," where "them" may refer equally to his fellow commuters and to his Irish past ("all that I belonged to"). Despite the terrorist attack that will blast through and disrupt this process, claiming more than fifty lives, the daily shuttling of souls will continue, connecting the underground present to the underworld past and future. This is because, as *katabasis* shows, we belong equally to the dead as to the living.

NOTES

1   For overviews, see Martiny and Thurston.

2   It takes courage to write about Seamus Heaney because one realizes how much better he could do it himself. I owe my present audacity to conversations with Adam Piette and Neil Roberts.

3   J.L. Borges's story "Funes el memorioso," about a man who dies from an excessively good memory, used to be translated as "Funes the Memorious" (it has since become "Funes, His Memory" in Andrew Hurley's recent translation). So for me the English adjective "memorious" has a Borgesian ring, and denotes possession of, or dispossession by, a vertiginously prodigious memory. Cf. also "The Maker," Borges's story about Homer going blind and drawing up images from a well of memory.

4   "The blow struck on the local anvil and the strike against the twin towers are the tuning forks for poems that appear in the early pages of the book that I would eventually call *District and Circle*. To begin with, I even thought that 'Midnight Anvil' might be a good overall title, in so far as its suggestions of hammering force and ominous dark matched the mood of the new age of anxiety" (Heaney, "One Poet") He borrows this phrase from Auden's long poem, *The Age of Anxiety: A Baroque Eclogue* (1947).

5   For example, Michael Schneider writes, "as a 21st-century poet of the pastoral, he verges

perilously toward a nostalgia out of place in a post-9/11, global-capitalist world." *Pittsburgh Post-Gazette*, October 8, 2006. www.post-gazette.com/pg/06281/727732–148.stm. Thanks to Annabel Mills for reading through a first draft of this chapter, and in particular for an insightful question about this paragraph.

6 "By employing this extremely rare adjective . . . from the Latin '*tellur-*, *tellus* . . . Of or belonging to the earth', Heaney acknowledges the language of the original, and so reminds contemporary readers of their simul-taneous separation from and closeness to Rome, its culture and worldview" (Parker 3).

7 'The poet frequently has recourse to this highly governed, strongly traditional form when political and personal concerns are at their most intense.' (Parker 3)

8 On "humic language," see R. Harrison 1–16. On "District and Circle" as a poem about faith, see Motion.

9 On balance in Heaney's poetry, see also Wheatley 2.

10 I am grateful to Neil Roberts for this observation.

REFERENCES AND FURTHER READING

Bakhtin, Mikhail. *Art and Answerability: Early Philosophical Essays*, ed. M. Holquist and V. Liapunov, trans. V. Liapunov. Austin: University of Texas Press, 1986.

Bakhtin, Mikhail. *The Dialogic Imagination: Four Essays*, ed. Michael Holquist, trans. Caryl Emerson and Michael Holquist. Austin: University of Texas Press, 1981: 84–258.

Carey, John. "Resurrection Man." Sunday Times, April 2, 2006. http://entertainment.timesonline.co.uk/tol/arts_and_entertainment/books/poetry/article699309.ece.

Clark, Raymond. *Catabasis: Vergil and the Wisdom Tradition*. Amsterdam: Gruner, 1979.

Dante, Alighieri, *The Divine Comedy. Inferno 1: Text*, trans. Charles Singleton. Princeton: Princeton University Press, 1989.

Dick, Bernard F. "*The Waste Land* and the *Descensus ad Inferos*." *Canadian Review of Comparative Literature* 2:1. 1975: 35–46. http://ejournals.library.ualberta.ca/index.php/crcl/article/viewFile/2258/1664.

Falconer, Rachel. *Hell in Contemporary Literature: Western Descent Narratives since 1945*. Edinburgh: Edinburgh University Press, 2005.

Falconer, Rachel. "Hell in Our Time: Reading 9/11 and Its Aftermath as a Dantean Descent into Hell." In *Hell and Its Afterlife: Historical and Contemporary Perspectives*, ed. M. Toscano and I. Moreira. Farnham: Ashgate Publishing, 2010. 217–36.

Fowler, Rowena. "'Purple Shining Lilies': Imagining the *Aeneid* in Contemporary Poetry." In *Living Classics: Greece and Rome in Contemporary Poetry in English*, ed. S.J. Harrison. Oxford: Oxford University Press, 2009. 238–54.

Frye, Northrop. *The Secular Scripture: A Study of Romance*. Harvard, MA: Harvard University Press, 1976.

Harrison, Robert Pogue. *The Dominion of the Dead*. Chicago: University of Chicago Press, 2003.

Harrison, S.J. *Living Classics: Greece and Rome in Contemporary Poetry in English*. Oxford: Oxford University Press, 2009.

Hawkins, Peter S. and Rachel Jacoff (eds.). *The Poets' Dante: Twentieth-Century Responses*. New York: Farrar, Straus and Giroux, 2002.

Heaney, Seamus. *District and Circle*. London: Faber & Faber, 2006.

Heaney, Seamus. "Envies and Identifications." In *The Poets' Dante: Twentieth-Century Responses*, ed. Peter S. Hawkins and Rachel Jacoff. New York: Farrar, Straus and Giroux, 2002. 239–58.

Heaney, Seamus. "One Poet in Search of a Title." *The Times*, March 25, 2006. http://entertainment.timesonline.co.uk/tol/arts_and_entertainment/books/article1082510.ece.

Horace [Q. Horati Flacci]. *Opera*, ed. Edvardvs C. Wickham. Oxford: Oxford University Press: 1975.

Levi, Primo. *The Periodic Table*, trans. Raymond Rosenthal. New York: Schocken Books, 1984.

MacDonald, Joyce Green. *Women and Race in Early Modern Texts*. Cambridge: Cambridge University Press, 2010.

Martindale, Charles (ed.). *The Cambridge Companion to Virgil*. Cambridge: Cambridge University Press 1997.

Martiny, Erik. "Modern Versions of Nostos and Katabasis: A Survey of Homeric Hypertexts in Recent Anglophone Poetry." *Anglia* 127.3. 2009: 469–79.

Matthews, Steven. "Bucketful by Glistering Bucketful." *Poetry Review*: 91–93. www.poetrysociety.org.uk/lib/tmp/cmsfiles/File/review/962matthews.pdf.

Motion, Andrew. "Digging Deep." *The Guardian*, April 1, 2006. www.guardian.co.uk/books/2006/apr/01/poetry.seamusheaney1.

Parker, Michael. "Fallout from the Thunder: Poetry and Politics in Seamus Heaney's *District and Circle*." *Irish Studies Review* 16:4. 2008: 369–84.

Pike, David L. *Metropolis on the Styx: The Underworlds of Modern Urban Culture, 1800–2001*. Ithaca, NY: Cornell University Press, 2007.

Pike, David L. *Passage through Hell: Modernist Descents, Medieval Underworlds*. London: Cornell University Press, 1997.

Pound, Ezra. *Three Cantos* 3. In *Poetry* 10.5. 1917: 250–51.

Thurston, Michael. *The Underworld in Twentieth-Century Poetry: From Pound and Eliot to Heaney and Walcott*. Basingstoke: Palgrave Macmillan, 2009.

Virgil [P. Vergili Maronis]. *Opera*. ed. R.A.B. *Mynors*. Oxford: Oxford University Press, 1980.

Wheatley, David. "Orpheus Risen from the London Underground." *Contemporary Poetry Review* 2006. www.cprw.com/Wheatley/heaney.htm.

Wieseltier, Leon. "Czeslaw Milosz, 1911–2004." *New York Times*, September 12, 2004. www.nytimes.com/2004/09/12/books/review/12WIESELTIER.html.

29

The Aisling

Bernard O'Donoghue

All readers of Irish poetry have some sense of what the aisling is: a vision poem in which a woman representing Ireland appears to the dreaming narrator and offers some insight or prophecy, usually about the fate of Ireland. As a literary form it is largely associated with poetry in Irish in the eighteenth century; sometimes it is revived or alluded to—sometimes to satirical purpose—in twentieth-century English poetry in Ireland by writers from Yeats to Austin Clarke to Paul Muldoon. But its origins date from long before the eighteenth century, deep in the mainstream of the European tradition of dream-vision. This dream-vision poetry from which it derives is arguably the principal medieval literary form: it is the genre of the *Romance of the Rose* in the thirteenth century. The greatest work of the Middle Ages, Dante's *Divine Comedy*, is related to it. But there are Irish vision-poems which are earlier than that, poems of a genre from which some scholars have wished to derive inspiration for Dante's *Comedy*—the *Aisling Oengus* (the inspiration for Yeats's "The Song of Wandering Aengus") and *Aisling MeicConglinne* (drawn on by Clarke in his play *The Son of Learning* which contains his best-known translation, "The Scholar's Life"), so the Irish claim to a major contribution to the medieval form has some foundation. In the two medieval *Aislings* just named, the protagonist undergoes a journey to the afterlife (like Virgil's Aeneas of course, long before) just as Dante's narrator does.

In all these medieval cases one or more venerable personages appears to the narrator and reveals some important insight. In that way the form is directly linked to the categorization of late Latin dream-poetry by Macrobius[1] as explicated by Chaucer in the early part of his *Parliament of Fowls* (1380s). Macrobius identified three kinds of reliable dream which he called "somnium," "visio," and "oraculum." Of these terms, between which he makes somewhat arcane distinctions with reference to the authoritative figures which appear in them, *visio*—"vision"—is the one which had the most

A Companion to Poetic Genre, First Edition. Edited by Erik Martiny.
© 2012 John Wiley & Sons, Ltd. Published 2012 by John Wiley & Sons, Ltd.

general application, for example to the fourteenth-century English poems *Piers Plowman* and *Pearl*. Those two poems also exemplify another feature of the dream-vision which we will see is important for the aisling: they are both allegorical consolations, in which the misery or uncertainty of the sleeping narrator is resolved by the appearance of a personified figure. "Visio" is also the Latin term which was applied to the pre-Dantesque "Vision of Tnugdal" in Ireland (edited by Rodney Mearns: Heidelberg: Carl Winter, 1995). In medieval Irish "aisling" was a fairly general term for a dream or vision, on the rather inconclusive evidence of the dictionaries of Ó Duinnín and Ó Dónaill. In the otherworldly, visionary sense, it seems interchangeable with *fís*, which is cognate with "visio(n)." The origin of the term itself is obscure.[2]

But the main history of the aisling as a distinct literary term begins with the late seventeenth century. The justification for the foregoing brief pre-history is as a reminder that the apparent emergence of the poetic form fully fledged in that period is misleading. The magisterial account by Breandán Ó Buachalla of the great Munster aisling poets of the late seventeenth and eighteenth centuries goes back no earlier than the accession of James I in 1601, when the presence of a Stuart king—for good or ill—first becomes an issue for Ireland.[3] This is also the starting-point of the most important anthology of poetry in Irish in the post-medieval era, *An Duanaire* ("The Poetry-Anthology," Ó Tuama and Kinsella). In the introduction to that anthology, Seán Ó Tuama describes how the decline of "the noble Irish families, of whom there were many hundreds" (xix) after the defeat at Kinsale in 1601 marked the end of a cultural environment in which the highly sophisticated and elaborate syllabic Bardic poetry could thrive, leading to the emergence of a less formally brilliant form of accentual verse.

This was the new world out of which the aisling as we know it re-emerged, although—as we will see in looking at the poems of Aodhagán Ó Rathaille—bitterness at the perceived loss of a nobler past remained a major theme of the aisling-poets. The elements of the form are remarkably consistent from the first. They are usefully set out in one of the classic discussions of Irish poetry in English, Daniel Corkery's *The Hidden Ireland*.[4] The given situation in these political poems (which Corkery says are the invention of Ó Rathaille) is unvarying. Like his medieval predecessors, the narrator of the poem falls asleep, usually in a gloomy frame of mind prompted by poverty or political circumstances, and is visited by a visionary woman of great beauty (though sometimes old, weary, and withered: hence the brilliance of the reversal of the theme at the end of Yeats/Gregory's *Cathleen Ni Houlihan*):

> *Peter:* Did you see an old woman going down the path?
> *Patrick:* I did not, but I saw a young girl, and she had the walk of a queen.[5]

The dreamer typically asks this *spéirbhean* (literally "sky-woman") if she is one of the classical figures of female beauty: Helen or Athene or Flora. She replies that she is none of these, but Ireland personified. She predicts the return of a Stuart king to end Irish hardships (exacerbated under the Penal Laws of the period after the accession of

William and Mary in 1688). The narrator awakens in happier spirits, consoled by the vision and with renewed hope.

Before going into the celebrated poems of the Munster writers in detail, a second prehistory should be mentioned, in keeping with Ó Buachalla's starting-date. After the accession of William and Mary, and the Battle of the Boyne in 1690, the restoration of the Stuarts became the focus of the aspiration towards political liberation in Ireland, as in Scotland. But that situation at the end of the seventeenth century in Ireland mirrored what happened at the beginning of the century: the 1607 "Flight of the Earls." After defeat at Kinsale and bitter Irish disappointment in James I, the son of the Catholic Mary Queen of Scots, who might have been expected to be better disposed to Ireland than Elizabeth, the Irish leaders of the "Nine Years War," O'Neill and O'Donnell, left Ireland for Europe, prompting a yearning for a returning leader which lasted throughout the century. The stories and dreams of these "Wild Geese" echo through seventeenth-century Irish poetry and songs. So, though the wish amongst the great and authoritative Munster poets in the eighteenth century was for a Stuart restoration, that wish fitted into an established pattern of yearning for a lost monarch.[6] In Ulster (where the aisling has generally been seen as having less prominence than in the south-west of Ireland), the Earls—the O'Neills—often remain the longed-for rulers into the following century amongst poets such as Art Mac Cumhaigh (1738–73) whose "Úr-Chill an Chreagáin" ("The Churchyard of Creggan") is one of the greatest of the aislings, as we will see.[7] And, in the same way that the longed-for reversal of the "Flight of the Earls" anticipates the fantasy of Stuart restoration in the aisling, so will the Napoleonic theme—"Boney" (from Bonaparte), "The Bonny Light Horseman"—carry the theme forward into the nineteenth century in Irish poetry and song, based on the hopes of French aid in the 1790s.

But why did this form of poetic wish-fulfillment become such a major part of the Irish tradition, staying in the mind of Irish writers in English too, right up to the present day?[8] After all, the European dream-vision declined rapidly into vapidity from the fifteenth century onwards. Furthermore, as Ó Tuama says, the form itself "becomes no more than a rigid formula" amongst its lesser practitioners (*An Duanaire* xxvii). Yet in Ireland it gained a new vigor by amalgamating "the ancestral notion of the sacred relationship of rightful ruler" with the traditional "divine female personification of territory—ultimately Ireland" (Ó Crualaoich 55). Two principal explanations for the possibility of this revitalization have been suggested. The first, paradoxically, is the decline of the virtuoso Bardic forms of poetry that prevailed in Old Irish, as part of the collapse of Gaelic culture with the Elizabethan land-settlements. Corkery's chapter 3, "The Bardic Schools," describes this impressive and demanding stylistic tradition along with its decline; but, more revealingly for the history of the aisling, his following chapter deals with "The Courts of Poetry," the local assembly of poets (called "Dámhscoil" in Irish after the Bardic school). Although these are characterized as producing verses in less intricate, accentual lines, rather than the more virtuoso syllabic forms of the Bardic schools, they offered an established local forum for the production of poetry, a forum on which the great vision-poets of the eighteenth century built. But it means that the principal motivation of the literary form was not really hope for political redemption through Stuart restoration (or French or Spanish invasion, or the return of the O'Neills), as much as the nostalgic expression of bitter regret for a past age of cultural strength.

The second explanation for the spectacular success of the aisling poets is more important—indeed it is, according to Corkery, the central distinction of the form: its stylistic brilliance. The first—and ultimately most impressive, though not always seen as the most attractive—of the poets is Aodhagán Ó Rathaille (c. 1670–1726), "that Dante of Munster" as Corkery calls him (156). Corkery tries desperately to capture the distinction of Ó Rathaille, invoking Shelley and Mozart as well as Dante. He does describe the distinction well in introducing Ó Rathaille's most spectacular aisling (though perhaps not his greatest poem, to the modern taste), "Gile na gile"; but in English its brilliance can only be suggested, because the original is stylistically untranslatable. Corkery insists again and again on stylistic brilliance as the greatest achievement of the aisling poets. Although the accentual forms of the post-1600 poets do not have the demanding rule-driven intricacy of the Bardic forms, the most spectacular of the aisling poems, above all Ó Rathaille's "Gile na gile," have a stylistic exuberance that cannot be recaptured. (Indeed the unevocative traditional translation of that opening phrase, which has come to be used as a title for the poem, "brightness of brightness," illustrates the problem.)

Such untranslatability means that it is very difficult to illustrate this extraordinary stylistic virtuosity. It has been said that Frank O'Connor established a voice for Ó Rathaille in English, and his translations often have style.[9] But in the heading to his translation of "Gile na gile," O'Connor says

> I have suppressed this early translation for close on thirty years, and reprint it merely to complete the picture of O'Rahilly's poetry. In Irish the poem is pure music, each line beginning with assonantal rhymes on the short vowel "i" (like "mistress" and "bitter"), which gives it the secretive, whispering quality of dresses rustling or of light feet scurrying in the distance.
>
> (104)

The only full volume of Ó Rathaille's poems was edited in parallel-text for the Irish Texts Society by the great dictionary-maker Ó Duinnín (a later neighbor of the poet from the district west of Rathmore in East Kerry).[10] It has been said that the introduction to the edition overstates the political significance of this great aisling at the expense of its style: "Ó Rathaille is more of a poet and less of a patriot than Dinneen imputes to him."[11] If this is true, it is understandable because the context of the poem around 1700 is so vital (the impoverishing repressions of the early Penal Laws), and the formalities of the poem are so hard to reproduce. The most functional translation is certainly Thomas Kinsella's plainstyle version in *An Duanaire* (151–53), but that makes no claim to reproducing anything like the baroque formalities of the original.

Unusually, "Gile na Gile" begins with the sight of the visionary *spéirbhean,* "the sky-woman,"[12] who mostly in the aisling is encountered some time after the *chanson d'aventure* opening, familiar from medieval visions, in which a narrator describes an experience (the *aventure*) that befell him, often starting with an encounter with a woman: "Gile na gile do chonnarc ar slí in uaigneas" ("Brightness of brightness, lonely I saw on the road"). Part of the distinction of the poem is that the *bruinneall* ("fair maiden": it is line 16 before she is described as anything more fully personal than the atmospheric "brightness" of the opening with its crystal, blue-green eyes, and dew-flecked hair) is identified—never by name—as representing a bride whose breasts are being pawed by "a pot-bellied clown's caresses" (O'Connor 105). The narrator tells her in dismay that she should not consort with such creatures "when a man the most fine, thrice over, of Scottish blood / was waiting to take her for his tender bride" (*An Duanaire* 153). The maiden weeps bitterly at this reproach, then finds a groom to convey the narrator out of the fairy dwelling in Luachair (Sliabh Luachra, Ó Rathaille's district), whereupon her identification is repeated from the first line: "she who was the brightness of brightness that lonely I saw on the road." Then follows the *ceangal*— the knot which is appended in a different metrical measure to the end of the poem, like the medieval *envoi* which survives as the Irish *amhrán* ("song") into the modern period. This concluding "knot"—the coda which ties up the poem's meaning (omitted in O'Connor's translation)—is a bitter, explicit declaration of the political moral: "my pain, my calamity, humbling, my sorrow and loss," that this luminous maiden is irretrievably attached to one of that foreign, horned crew, until "the lions" return across the sea.

Although it does not have the smooth—perhaps too smooth—narrative progression of later aislings, "Gile na gile" (probably the first of Ó Rathaille's three major aislings) has all the elements of the form: the visionary maiden, the Stuart "Pretender," absent saviors and vile enemies. Similarly inventive in its deployment of the elements of the form, and only slightly less brilliant in its baroque finish, is Ó Rathaille's poem headed "An Aisling" ("The Vision") in *An Duanaire*: "Maidin sul smaoin Titan a chosa do luaill" ("One morning before Titan had thought about stirring his feet"). The narrator meets a troop of cheerful maidens who lead him to a mountain-top in North Munster where he is addressed by the aisling queen Aoibhill (we will meet her in a more menacing guise in the aisling parody "The Midnight Court" in due course). She assures the narrator that candles are to be lit to welcome the faithful returning king. Delight at the prospect starts him from his dream, and (again like his medieval pre-decessors) he wakes "doilbhir, duairc" ("gloomy, joyless") with a reprise of the opening line: "That morning before Titan had thought about stirring his feet." The strangest of Ó Rathaille's great aislings—the one which perhaps most links with his other poems—is "Mac an Cheannaí," "The Redeemer's Son." Its opening words are the source of Ó Buachalla's title (see note 3 above): "Aisling ghéar do dhearcas féin": "I saw for myself a bitter vision." This poem is less baroque in form than the others we have looked at, but it has a greater and more cryptic narrative power. The poem uses the ambiguity of the term "ceannaí" ("buyer") exactly as it was used in Middle

English: Christ as the redeemer (buyer) of mankind out of damnation. (Another Yeatsian echo comes to mind: the redemptive activity of "The Countess Cathleen," on the verge of blasphemy in the same way.) But, as often in the medieval lyric, the religious parallel turns out to be irrelevant. This bitter vision begins with the apparition of a "slender girl whose name was Éire" (an unusually explicit identification), riding towards the narrator and declaring that her love *Mac an Cheannaí* was on his way. But since her previous Irish kings are fallen—Conn and Art and the others—she is reduced to looking South, South-East, and West day after day, for the coming of her redeemer. Her Friars have been driven overseas, so she will remain—a dry branch without a partner—until her real lover comes. The narrator tells her that the Redeemer's Son has "met his death above in Spain" (a reference, it is thought to the death of Carlos II of Spain which would date the poem around 1700); her body shakes, she screams and falls lifeless.

The strange thing about Ó Rathhaille's aislings is that they appear to be premonitions of a form that attains its definitive shape in the poems and songs of his successor Eoghan Rua Ó Súilleabháin (1748–84), born a few miles away from Ó Rathaille's birthplace. Even if his aislings do not have the ambitious formal virtuosity of Ó Rathaille's, Eoghan Rua is the greatest exponent of the aisling as a form. He is a poet of the people in a way that his predecessor, with his bitter laments for the passing of a cultural elite, was not. His songs and poems have survived in popular local tradition in a way only rivaled amongst named poets by the blind Mayo poet Anthony Raftery in the early nineteenth century, and Eoghan Rua is repeatedly invoked as a figure of the poet by twentieth-century writers, as Yeats's Red Hanrahan or in Thomas Flanagan's *Year of the French* for example. In this way he may be a more crucial figure than Ó Rathaille in the appeal of the form for the writers of the Celtic Revival and their successors from the late nineteenth century onwards. Yeats wanted to be Celtic, but he also wanted to be popular. Eoghan Rua is the exponent of an intricate form that is edging towards full-scale popularity before it reached the limitations of what was *only* popular (like Jem Casey in Flann O'Brien's *At Swim-Two-Birds*, it is tempting to say).[13] He is a figure of the popular poet of mythic standing: but he is also a brilliant poet and songwriter who has been called—not altogether inappropriately—the Irish Burns. And in conceding the greater intricacy in Ó Rathaille's style, we should remember that Eoghan Rua was known locally as "the poet of the sweet mouth."

Eoghan Rua, then, is much more than a popular poet. His oeuvre is well summarized by Seán Ó Tuama in *An Duanaire*: "A great many of his compositions . . . are of the *aisling* type; these are all extremely musical and of astonishing technical virtuosity, but some of his occasional non-political verse . . . has more insight and humanity" (183). The same thing has been said of Ó Rathaille whose greatest—and possibly last—poem is "Cabhair Ní Ghairfead" ("I'll call for no help") which ends with the line famously quoted by Yeats in his "The Curse of Cromwell": "His fathers served their fathers before Christ was crucified" (Yeats, *Poems* 580). As an example of Eoghan Rua's humane occasional verse Ó Tuama mentions the great "Chara Mo Chléibh" ("Friend of My Heart"), the poem addressed to the blacksmith Séamus MacGearailt, asking him to make him a spade for his work as a *spailpín*, a wandering farm-laborer. This poem has recently attained a new popularity with Seamus Heaney's brilliant translation of a section of it as "Poet to Blacksmith":

> The plate and the edge of it not to be wrinkly or crooked—
> I see it well shaped from the anvil and sharp from the file,
> The grain of the wood and the line of the shaft nicely fitted,
> And best thing of all, the ring of it, sweet as a bell.
>
> (Heaney, *District and Circle* 25)

But Eoghan Rua's great aislings are our concern here, the poems without which the form could not be defined so certainly. To be fair to Ó Rathaille, we can see his influence on Eoghan Rua: the shimmering, misty opening of "Gile na Gile" in "Ceo Draiochta" ("Magic Mist") for instance. The tunes of several of Eoghan Rua's songs are still in circulation; some have been used for songs in English and for Irish-English macaronic songs (the measure of "Ceo Draiochta," for instance, is the same as the popular modern song in English "Mo Bhuachaillín Donn"). More significantly, this magnificent seventy-two-line poem manifests all the elements of the aisling. It starts with the narrator in deep gloom, "like an idiot wandering the country," who lies down in tears, praying to the King of Glory for mercy. As the thrush sings over him, a fairy girl sits beside him (the *spéirbhean* here is a slightly more approachable "sí-bhruin-neall," "fairy-maiden"), uttering "fairy-harp notes" and he asks who she is, in the traditional way. Is she Helen of Troy, "The Fair-One caused hordes to be slaughtered / as they write in the Battle of Troy?" (Kinsella in *An Duanaire* 189). Or is she Gormlaith or Gráinne (the Irish mythical women are a more usual occurrence in Eoghan Rua and his contemporaries than in Ó Rathaille)? No, she is the queen who ruled over Ireland in the past, and she too prays to the "son of Glory" to send the lion back to the relief of his people. The narrator mourns (as in "Gile na Gile") the plight of this female paragon amongst goatish "boors" whom he would gladly flay if the "son of Glory" would send the rightful king to her aid. "If our Stuart would return over ocean, with a '*fleet*'[14] of Spaniards and the followers of King Louis," he would fight and stand guard to the end of his time. Characteristically, Eoghan Rua's poem ends on an upbeat, as Ó Rathaille's "bitter aislings" never do.

Eoghan Rua was born in 1748, so by the time of this poem—long after Culloden—the longing for a Stuart savior must have been no more than convention. It is notable too that the undeveloped religious ambiguity of "Mac an Cheannaí" is turned into a more routine form of popular piety ("King of Glory"): something which is also found with Raftery in the following century. As a second example of Eoghan Rua's aislings (and of course this limited representation greatly underrepresents his contribution to the form), I will mention briefly a poem which is an active local survival, as both text and music, "Im' Aonar Seal" ("Alone a while").[15] Its tune, called "An Binsín Luachra" ("The Bunch of Rushes"), is a very popular slow air in his locality. This poem too begins in mist, early in the night where the narrator sees a "fair queen" approaching him. At the end of a particularly elaborate description the narrator asks if she is Deirdre or Curoi's wife (who aided Cuchulainn). Her declaration is less explicit than usual, and the poem ends with a prophecy that the Gaels will live in riches and their boorish captors be impoverished, when the lettered clergy, undisguised, will proclaim anew the son of God. For all its charm and metrical expertise, this is a poem from a time when the tradition was losing its political urgency, replacing it with a rather more routine piety.

Aislings by other poets should be mentioned: for example "An Buachaill Bán" by Seán Ó Coileáin (1754–1816), a later contemporary of Eoghan Rua from West Cork. This poem is notable for making the *spéirbhean* list the male heroes of the heroic past in a strikingly learned way: Hector, Aeneas, and Pan, as well as the Irish mythological figures Naoise and the children of Lir. It is a highly accomplished poem (worthy of its author who wrote "Machnamh an Duine Dhoilíosaigh," an elegy centering on Timoleague Abbey which has been called the "Irish Gray's Elegy"), but it is a bravura showpiece for the form from which the political edge of Ó Rathaille has entirely gone. An even more significant poem, coming from Co. Armagh, is the beautiful "Úr-Chill an Chreagáin" ("The Churchyard of Creggan") by a short-lived contemporary of Eoghan Rua, Art Mac Cumhaigh (1738?–1773).[16] Of all the later aislings, this is arguably the poem which, despite its lucidity, is most fully in the spirit and style of Ó Rathaille, in its employment of the long line and in the edge it brings to the "aisling ghéar," the bitter poem, particularly by invoking the poet's rights. The sleeping poet is greeted with a kiss by a maiden at daybreak. She urges him to leave his sorrow and to travel West with her to a sweet land of honey where the foreigners are not yet in control, and where the halls are filled with poetic music. The narrator says he would dearly love to, but it would be disloyal to abandon his beleaguered friends and the wife he wooed when she was young. In a stanza of sudden bitterness, the maiden says his surviving relations are no friends; they leave him impoverished and mock his poetry. Now he asks if she who wants him to accompany her on her Westward journey is Helen or one of the Nine Muses.[17] She answers in a mysterious quatrain that she is a fairy child who inspires poetry on both sides of the Boyne, at night on Tara and in Tyrone (broadly where the poet is now) in the morning. She is in grief for the departed O'Neills and the leaders who valued poetry. But since the 1690s—after Aughrim and the Boyne—the poet would be better off living in a fantasy world of fairyland than in foreigner-riven Ireland. The poet concludes with an appeal to the maiden, if she is to be his love, that he must be buried with the Irish of Creggan, whether he dies by the Shannon, on the Isle of Man or in Egypt. Even from this brief synopsis, it will be clear that this poem is restoring an urgent note into the aisling which goes back to its origins a century before, as well as concern for the now neglected status of the poet.

In general though, after the poets of the later eighteenth century it was not common for the aisling to express any real political or personal feeling. So, by a wonderful irony, the greatest poem in the tradition—an anti-aisling—was written at the century's end, a text which perhaps established the form in the Irish tradition in

English more than any of the preceding poems in the form itself. This masterpiece, *Cúirt an Mheán Oíche,* "The Midnight Court," was written by a schoolmaster-poet from Ennistymon, Co. Clare with the improbable name of Bryan Merriman who died in Limerick in 1803. Its coherent survival is something of a miracle; *Cúirt An Mheán Oíche* was never written down by its author, and first published in 1850 in an edition by John O'Daly. In the twentieth century, a number of excellent translations have been produced, including versions by Frank O'Connor, David Marcus, Thomas Kinsella, Ciaran Carson, and (in part) by Seamus Heaney who intercuts it interestingly with Ovid (Heaney, *The Midnight Verdict*).

The poem begins with an extensive and misleadingly lyrical *chanson d'aventure* setting which attests Merriman's stylistic brilliance. On many a summer's morning, in heavy Eoghan Rua-like dew, the poet would raise his darker spirits by walking in an idyllic pastoral scene:

> To look for a while above the woods
> would brighten the heart worn out with pains,
> weary and senseless, and full of cares.

But "yesterday morning" (l.23) the sky was free of dew and the poet falls asleep, whereupon he

> suffered in dream a swirling torment
> that stripped and racked me and pierced my heart
> in a heavy swoon, as I lost my wits.
>
> (Kinsella's version, ll.38–40)

So we wait for the consolatory sky-woman to restore his "wits" or raise his spirits. Here is Carson's account of her arrival:

> A female approached from the side of the quay,
> Broad-arsed and big-bellied, built like a tank,
> And angry as thunder from shoulder to shank . . .
> Formidable, fearsome the leer of her grin,
> Purple-gummed, ulcered, with no teeth within . . .
>
> (Carson 20)

And so it goes on. The poem becomes a trial of the sexually inadequate males of Ireland in the presence of the fairy queen Aoibheall (encountered more decorously in Ó Rathaille's "An Aisling" above). Time and again through the poem, we find features of the traditional aisling pulled askew (like the mistless opening and the disfigured appearance of the *spéirbhean*). When a "seanduine suarach" ("a miserable old fellow") furiously takes issue with the unmarried young woman (one of the charms of the maiden in "Im' aonar seal" was that she was not associated "le chéile fós": not yet wedded), to insult her he uses the language traditionally applied to the hateful foreigner-usurpers of Irish rights: the "evil of her breeding": "nothing to boast of in your ugly forebears / but senseless slobs." He goes on to say,

> And everyone's saying—it's more than mere prattle—
> How brats with no income, no sheep and no cattle,
> Can wear buckled shoes, and a ludicrous hat,
> Handkerchief fluttering this way and that
>
> (Carson, 33–34)

Behind the social commentary here is a specific parody of the elegant *spéirbhean*; the more you read Merriman in detail, the more obvious it becomes that he is satirizing the details of the aisling situation specifically with extraordinary completeness.

I have dwelt on this poem, which is strictly a variant on the genre, to suggest at least one rationale for the popularity of the aisling past its own time: beyond its own linguistic and cultural base, indeed. The seed of the parody is there in the poets themselves: the later, more popular exponents, like Eoghan Rua Ó Súilleabháin and his successors, were writers too of the highly developed *aor*—satire—a form that goes back to the Middle Ages in the Irish tradition.[18] It is tempting to suggest that the Gaelic cultural tradition was less comfortable with the fine and bitter self-regard of Ó Rathaille—his defiant elitism—than with the mockery (often self-mockery) that prevails from Eoghan Rua (and indeed from Ó Rathaille's own "More power to you, Cromwell"[19]) to Flann O'Brien and Paul Muldoon. Without this development, it is hard to explain how a literary form that had served its time and gone into a kind of decline (the fate of the medieval vision-poems and the *meistergesang*, the successor of the great medieval poems of the *minnesänger*) should have remained such an active presence in the minds of the Irish writers after 1900: Yeats, Synge, James Stephens, Austin Clarke, and their followers.

I have mentioned already (note 5 above) Declan Kiberd's linking of Yeats's *A Vision*—mainly through the improbable indefinite article in its title—with the aisling's reliance on visionary informants. Further versions of the aisling in the modern period, and poems linked to it, are very easy to find. A famous example is Francis Ledwidge's "Lament for the Poets: 1916":

> I heard the poor old woman say:
> "At break of day the fowler came
> And took my blackbirds from their songs"[20]

Pádraig Pearse's most famous poem "Mise Éire" ("I am Ireland: I am older than the Old Woman of Beara") clearly refers to the tradition. Michael Hartnett's "sonnet" begins "I saw magic on a green country road— / That old woman, a bag of sticks her load" (Montague's *Faber Book* 368). Significantly there are three poems called "Aisling" by Austin Clarke, all of which manifest the full complement of formal features: the *chanson d'aventure* opening; the encounter with the sky-woman who is identified as

Ireland after the questioning of her classical identity, both Gaelic and Greek; the repetition of the first line as the last (Clarke 173, 299, and 445). Beyond the mainstream poetic canon, the revival of Irish music as a popular presence from the 1950s onwards, through ballads and traditional instrumental music, led to a more or less scholarly exploration of the music of the harpers of the aisling period, which in turn produced new songs based on the visions and the Wild Geese ("As I Roved Out," "Thousands Are Sailing," and so on).

But as a different, more allusive kind of suggestion of the aisling's tenacity in modern Irish writing in English we might recall a very celebrated passage from the early twentieth century. At the end of section four of Joyce's *Portrait*, a section in which Stephen Dedalus has been considering a change of his life towards traditional Christian morality, he walks by the sea at Howth and sees a girl standing in the water:

> she seemed like one whom magic had changed into the likeness of a strange and beautiful seabird. Her long slender bare legs were delicate as a crane's and pure save where an emerald trail of seaweed had fashioned itself as a sign upon the flesh . . . Her bosom was as a bird's soft and slight, slight and soft as the breast of some darkplumaged dove. But her long fair hair was girlish, and touched with the wonder of mortal beauty her face.

There is a strong air of the *spéirbhean* here, but, as with the later aisling poets, her function is inverted. "Heavenly God! cried Stephen's soul, in an outburst of profane joy" (144). The nature of the secular vision becomes even clearer: "A wild angel had appeared to him . . . an envoy from the fair courts of life" (145). This vision is an unmistakable reapplication of the sky-woman of the aisling, but one which reverses both her traditional functions: the political and the hieratic. She is a figure of the secular and the erotic.

This episode also exemplifies a major issue for the use of the aisling by modern writers, a problem shared with the whole medieval world of courtly love and its afterlife and one which has been discussed enlighteningly by Ó Crualaoich (67ff.). It is invariably a male-centered form in which the woman, even when she is accorded a kind of discursive power, is always the object of the poem. The problem is addressed powerfully by many of the leading Irish women poets of the modern era, especially Nuala Ní Dhomhnaill. Indeed the gender reversing of the situation in the poem is perhaps the most significant revision of the aisling genre in the modern era. In Ní Dhomhnaill the influence of the tradition, particularly as modified and parodied by *The Midnight Court*, is central, in her series of poems voiced for Gaelic goddesses and queens, Mór or "An Mhór-Rion" ("The Great Queen") or Medb: "War I declare from now / on all the men of Ireland" ("Medh Speaks," Ní Dhomhnaill 111); "The fairy woman came / with a Black and Decker" ("The Tree," Ní Dhomhnaill 93); "The fairy woman walked / into my poem" ("Abduction," Ní Dhomhnaill 61). The inclination towards the female mythopoeic in modern Irish women poets has often been observed, in Eiléan Ní Chuilleanáin, Eavan Boland (whose middle name is "Aisling"), Celia de Fréine, and many others. Even where the reference is not expressly to the *spéirbhean*, the world of the aisling, in which the location of the female object is a vexed matter for the modern reader, comes to mind repeatedly: for example, in Ní Chuilleanáin's "Pygmalion's Image" or parts of the sequence *The Rose-Geranium*: "When she opened the egg the wise woman had given her, / she found inside some of her own hair and a tooth, still / bloody, from her own mouth" (29).

This more questioning contemporary reflection of the aisling is not confined to female Irish poets either. A classic instance is Justin Quinn's "Ur-Aisling"; and I want to end with a contemporary Irish poet who has drawn on the aisling expressly for largely—but by no means wholly—satirical purposes: Paul Muldoon. Like Clarke, Muldoon has written a poem entitled "Aisling," a particularly haunting application of the political capacity of the form:

> Was she Aurora, or the goddess Flora,
> Artemidora, or Venus bright,
> or Anorexia, who left
> a lemon stain on my flannel sheet. . . .
> In Belfast's Royal Victoria Hospital
> a kidney machine
> supports the latest hunger-striker
> to have called off his fast.

(Muldoon, *Poems* 127)

Muldoon also forges links to the medieval Irish tradition in his poems "Immram" (94ff.) and "Immrama" (85), both lightly alluding to the medieval voyage-poem that features his name *Imram Curaig Maile Dúin*. But his most substantial contribution to the understanding of the aisling comes in his Oxford Clarendon Lectures in 1998, published in 2000 as *To Ireland, I,* a brilliantly untrammeled series of alphabetically linked reflections on Irish writing. He quotes Mangan's translation of "Gile ne Gile" in full (101), linking it to the end of Joyce's "The Dead." The first writer Muldoon considers in the book is Amergin, the shape-changing prototypical Irish poet, and he returns to him in approaching the esoteric in Irish poetry. At that point (73), Muldoon translates aisling as "vision-voyage" (rather than dream-vision). He returns at more length to the form in examining Mac Cubhaig's "Aisling," and linking it through Howth (Beann Éadair) with *Finnegans Wake* and "the *aisling* vision more gorgeous than the one before" there (*FW*, 179). Muldoon extends the analysis to consider "Úr-Chill an Chreagáin" before ending with the analysis of the English word "spalpeen" as linked to the Irish word "speal," a scythe (from which he could have branched out again to consider Eoghan Rua's "An Spealadóir," "The Scythesman").

Many further proofs of the presence of the aisling in modern Irish literature could be given. For whatever reason, the unlikely and imaginative survival of this medieval dream vision (or "vision-voyage") seems to exceed any other native motif in the modern

Irish literary mind. The function of the aisling in the time of the Penal Laws is clear enough; it served both as an expression of political hope in a time of disempowerment in Gaelic Ireland. It also served as a claim for a cultural distinction—the sophistication of Bardic poetry—at a time when Irish was failing as a written language. It translated into oral culture as popular song. The more remarkable fact though is the way it became a recurrent literary device, reflecting a distinctive facet of Irish history and culture, often expressed more through satire than through nostalgia. We might make a link too with the frequency of the revenants—usually linked to Dante's afterlife—in the poetry of Yeats and Heaney. But what remains most remarkable is the way that the contours of the form—above all visionary insight through observation of a woman—recur through the great documents of modern Irish writing.

I am including here, finally, a poem of mine entitled "Aisling," as an instance of the way that the idea of an encounter with an unfamiliar female figure survives into modern practice, as a version of the *spéirbhean* or hag or *cailleach*.

Aisling
My dreams now increasingly move along
the unmetalled roads of childhood: sometimes
I'm already on them before I fall fully asleep,
watching the camber edging round the corner.

But often too I dream of a wrecked room,
unreclaimed when the old house was done up.
There's mould on everything, and grass
invading from the broken chutes outside.

My clear duty is every time the same:
to clean it out, ready for the nextcomers.
But then something intervenes to mean
I don't need to prepare it after all.

And then I am back out on the roads again,
at the turn by Julia's well, or further down
by Dan Jims' boreen, by the primrose stream
that Dominic dammed to make pools for his cows:

where I once really met a tinker couple
trudging through the rain ahead of me.
No matter how slow I walked, I couldn't fail
to overtake them, when they stood and watched

a donkey grazing by the verge, a ravelled rope
around his neck. The woman drew her shawl aside,
showing her face, and questioned me directly:
"Do you know is anyone the own of him?"

NOTES

1 Ambrosius Theodosius Macrobius (fl. c. AD 430) wrote a commentary on "The Dream of Scipio," the last section of Cicero's *De Republica* (54–51 BC), in which he distinguished between dreams on the grounds of their reliability or otherwise. In two of his categories, "visio" and "oraculum" an authoritative figure appears and imparts crucial information or prophecy, in the manner of the aisling.

2 The term has no entry in the *OED*, and the lack of an authoritative etymological dictionary for Irish makes it hard even to surmise any kind of history. Professor Thomas Charles-Edwards notes that in *Cormac's Glossary* from c. 900 there is a kind of folk-etymology for it as "lingid as, vel. absque lingua": "without language: with no speech in it."

3 *Aisling Ghéar* (Dublin 1996). There is an excellent account of the "politico-literary discourse" of the genre, and how it brings together Jacobite politics and the woman of the dream-vision, in Ó Crualaoich 54–71.

4 Dublin 1924: much republished since. I am citing the Gill and Macmillan edition of 1967.

5 Yeats, *Plays* 231. For an intriguing view of Yeats's connection with the form, see Kiberd.

6 This trope is everywhere in Irish literature: a very distant instance is the heartbroken cry of Mr. Casey in Joyce's *Portrait of the Artist as a Young Man*: "Poor Parnell: he cried loudly. My dead king!"

7 For a view of the Ulster school of aisling song-writers, as a riposte to the dominance of the Munster-centered account of Corkery, see Ní Uallacháin.

8 The best discussion of *how* it happens, rather than why, is Ó Crualaoich 55ff.

9 Frank O'Connor, *Kings, Lords and Commons* (Macmillan, 1959). An impressive volume of translations of the major poems is Michael Hartnett, *Ó Rathaille* (Oldcastle: Gallery Press, 1998).

10 Ó Rathaille, *Dánta Aodhagáin Uí Rathaille*, ed. P.S. Dinneen and Tadhg O'Donoghue, 2nd edn., 1911.

11 Quoted from Dinneen's biographers by John Jordan in Mac Réamoinn 82. For a good account in Irish of Ó Rathaille, see Ó Tuama.

12 In fact "sky-woman" seems a strange term for the prophetic visionary woman. Heather O'Donoghue points out that the word "spá" in Old Norse means "prophecy," so "spá-koma" as a kind of calque-translation for "prophecy-woman" would be closer to the role of the "spéirbhean."

13 This may sound like an unseemly parallel in this context. But in *At Swim-Two-Birds* O'Brien illustrates a lively and informed awareness of the development of the Irish poetic tradition in both Irish and English, from the brilliant medieval syllabics of *Buile Suibhne* to the popular doggerel of "The Pint of plain is your only man"—and of course he exploits the comic potential of both.

14 The English word is used, perhaps because Eoghan Rua himself served in the British Navy: it is also used in another of his popular aislings, "An Spealadóir" ("The Scythesman").

15 For a translation, see McMahon and O'Donoghue 113–15. The book also has a good pen-picture of Eoghan Rua, 251–52.

16 Mac Cumhaigh is also the poet of a self-assigned aisling "Aisling Airt Mhic Cumhaigh," set surprisingly in the harbour of Howth and discussed ingeniously by Muldoon in *To Ireland, I*, 79–80. See below.

17 One of Paul Muldoon's running themes in *To Ireland, I* is connections with Joyce's story "The Dead" at the end of *Dubliners*. This maiden's invitation to the dreamer to accompany her Westward might recall Gabriel's sleepy conclusion that it is time for him to "set out on his journey westward" and, if so, whether the story's Miss Ivors is a modern *spéirbhean.*

18 In his authoritative study, *The Irish Comic Tradition*, Vivian Mercier argued that a central feature of that tradition was to turn to satire at every opportunity.

19 See John Montague's fine translation in his *Faber Book of Irish Verse*, 143.

20 Ledwidge 155, where it is entitled "The Blackbirds." See MacDonagh and Robinson

217. Of course Ledwidge's greatest and most familiar poem, "Thomas MacDonagh" has a marked aisling motif to it: "when the Dark Cow leaves the moor" (Ledwidge 153).

References and Further Reading

Carson, Ciaran, *The Midnight Court: A New Translation of "Cúirt an Mheán Oíche" by Brian Merriman*. Oldcastle: Gallery Press, 2005.

Clarke, Austin, *Collected Poems*, ed. Liam Miller. Dublin: Dolmen Press and London: Oxford University Press, 1974.

Corkery, Daniel, *The Hidden Ireland* (1924). Dublin: Gill and Macmillan, 1967.

Heaney, Seamus, *District and Circle*. London: Faber & Faber, 2006.

Heaney, Seamus, *The Midnight Verdict*. Oldcastle: Gallery Press, 2000.

Joyce, James, *A Portrait of the Artist as a Young Man*, ed. Jeri Johnson. Oxford: Oxford University Press, 2000.

Kiberd, Declan, "The Last *Aisling*—A Vision," in *Inventing Ireland*. London: Jonathan Cape, 1995. 316–26.

Ledwidge, Francis, *Complete Poems of Francis Ledwidge*, ed. Alice Curtayne. London: Martin Brian and O'Keeffe, 1974.

MacDonagh, Donagh and Lennox Robinson, eds., *The Oxford Book of Irish Verse XVIIth Century–XXth Century*. Oxford: Oxford University Press, 1958.

MacMahon, Sean and Jo O'Donoghue, eds., *Taisce Duan: A Treasury of Irish Poems with Translations in English*. Swords: Poolbeg, 1992.

Mac Réamoinn, Seán, ed., *The Pleasures of Gaelic Poetry*. London: Allen Lane, 1982.

Mercier, Vivian, *The Irish Comic Tradition*. Oxford: Clarendon Press, 1962.

Montague, John, *Faber Book of Irish Verse*. London: Faber & Faber, 1974.

Muldoon, Paul, *Poems 1968–1998*. London: Faber & Faber, 2001.

Muldoon, Paul, *To Ireland, I*. Oxford: Oxford University Press, 2000.

Ní Chuilleanáin, Eiléan, *The Rose-Geranium*. Dublin: The Gallery Press, 1981.

Ní Dhomhnaill, Nuala, *Selected Poems (Rogha Dánta)*, with facing translations by Michael Hartnett. Dublin: Raven Arts Press, 1988.

Ní Uallacháin, Pádraigín, *A Hidden Ulster*. Dublin: Four Courts Press, 2003.

Ó Buachalla, Breandán, *Aisling Ghéar*. Dublin: An Clóchomhar, 1996.

O'Connor, Frank, *Kings, Lords and Commons*. London: Macmillan, 1959.

Ó Crualaoich, Gearóid, *The Book of the Cailleach: Stories of the Wise-Woman Healer*. Cork: Cork University Press, 2003.

Ó Rathaille, Aodhagán, *Dánta Aodhagáin Uí Rathaille*, ed. P.S. Dinneen and Tadhg O'Donoghue. London: Irish Texts Society, 2nd edn., 1911.

Ó Tuama, Seán, *Filí faoi Sceimhle*. Dublin: An Gúm, 1979.

Ó Tuama, Seán and Thomas Kinsella, *An Duanaire. 1600–1900: Poems of the Dispossessed, curtha i láthair ag Seán Ó Tuama, with translations into English Verse by Thomas Kinsella*. Mountrath: The Dolmen Press, 1981.

Yeats, W.B., *The Variorum Edition of the Poems of W.B. Yeats*, ed. Peter Allt and Russell K. Alspach. New York: Macmillan, 1956.

Yeats, W.B., *The Variorum Edition of the Plays of W.B. Yeats*, ed. R.K. Alspach. London: Macmillan, 1966.

30
The Printed Voice

Yann Tholoniat

Broadly speaking, the dramatic monologue can be defined as a poem in which there is one (historical or fictional) speaker addressing an imaginary audience, and what makes it "dramatic" is that it is uttered in a critical moment for the speaker, not simply that the speaker cannot be equated with the poet, wearing a mask, as it were. The phrase "dramatic monologue" was coined by the poet George W. Thornbury in 1857, speaking about Robert Browning's art (Culler 366), and it has since served to characterize Browning's major poetical achievement as well as poems displaying similar generic features.

Around 2,300 years before, in Ancient Greece, actors wore masks on stage. One might argue that at a particular moment in ancient Greek drama, there appeared the first form of what could be called a dramatic monologue. Indeed, there was often a moment when the *persona* of the author came to introduce or to conclude the play and addressed the audience. This theatrical device, particularly used by Aristophanes, and other Greek and Roman playwrights after him, is called a *parabasis*, and describes the author coming to the front of the proscenium to engage in a dialogue with his audience. Another structural aspect of the dramatic monologue is *prosopopeia*, a figure of speech describing the personification of some non-human being or concept, or absent person, as capable of speech. This trope was favored by Quintilian who helped shape modern classical rhetoric, and by famous authors such as Ovid who in *Heroides* made use of it to make mythological heroes speak. As such, the dramatic monologue appears as a combination of parabasis and prosopopeia in variable proportions.

In the Renaissance, some of John Donne's best-known poems such as "The Flea" and "The Sun Rising" can be said to be dramatic monologues. In "The Sun Rising," an anonymous speaker addresses the sun in a vivid tone:

A Companion to Poetic Genre, First Edition. Edited by Erik Martiny.
© 2012 John Wiley & Sons, Ltd. Published 2012 by John Wiley & Sons, Ltd.

> Busy old fool, unruly Sun,
> Why dost thou thus,
> Through windows, and through curtains, call on us?

(ll.1–3)

The rise of the conversational poem in the eighteenth century gave birth to poems that were very close to dramatic monologues, but the presence of a (mostly silent) listener is not frankly asserted. William Blake, Robert Burns, or William Wordsworth paved the way for the genre before the term existed. Blake's "The Little Black Boy" (*Songs of Innocence*, 1789) gives voice to a black child who describes his social position to an English boy. Robert Burns's "Holy Willie's Prayer" (published posthumously in 1799) is a prayer addressed to God by a cantankerous reverend as he makes his confession. In doing so, he entreats the Almighty to dispose of his local enemies, a revenge Willy insists upon although it springs from petty matters. "To a Mouse, On Turning Her up with the Plouigh, November 1785" is addressed to frightened rodent:

Wee°, sleekit°, cow'rin, tim'rous *beastie*,	°small, sleek
O, what a panic's in thy breastie°!	°breast
Thou need na start awa° sae° hasty,	°away, so
Wi' bickering° brattle°!	°hasty, scurry
I wad° be laith° to rin° an' chase thee,	°would, loath, run
Wi' murd'ring *pattle*°!	°a plough-scraper

(ll.1–6)

"The Last of the Flock," by William Wordsworth (*Lyrical Ballads*, 1798), consists of the speech of a shepherd who has been forced, through poverty, to sell his lambs.

The heyday of the dramatic monologue is the nineteenth century. Critics generally believe that, as a reaction towards the lyrical stance of the Romantic poets, early Victorian poets tended to set a distance between their speakers and themselves by having obviously imaginary characters (remote in place and time) speak. Browning and Tennyson were very specific about distinguishing the speaker's *persona* or mask from the author's identity. The title of the poem very often provides clues as to the identity of the speaker, or the circumstances. It establishes the speaker's universe at the same time as it creates a temporal and cultural distance between speaker and reader, as in titles by Robert Browning: "Rudel to the Lady of Tripoli," "A Grammarian's Funeral, Shortly after the Revival of Learning in Europe." The gender of the poet and the speaker may differ: a man writes as a woman or a woman as a man, as in Browning's "Count Gismond," spoken by the count's wife. Browning is also famous for the abruptness of the beginnings of some of his poems. As one of his contemporaries wrote,

> Mr Browning rushes upon you with a sort of intellectual douche, half stuns you with the abruptness of the shock, repeats the application in a multitude of swift various jets

from unexpected points of the compass, and leaves you at last giddy and wondering where you are, but with a vague sense that, were you but properly prepared beforehand, you would discern a real unity and power.

(Davis 463)

This critic alludes to "Soliloquy of the Spanish Cloister," which begins thus:

> Gr-r-r — there go, my heart's abhorrence!
> Water your damned flower-pots, do!
> If hate killed men, Brother Lawrence,
> God's blood, would not mine kill you!

(ll.1–4)

The dramatic monologue is so strongly linked to the name of Robert Browning that an overview of his achievement is necessary to perceive the rules he delineated, as well as the flexibility of the genre. Browning was influenced by Walter Savage Landor. In *Imaginary Conversations of Literary Men and Statesmen* (four volumes published between 1823 and 1829), Landor wrote a number of dialogues ranging from classical times to his own day, covering a wide field of topics and tones, with action and incident. Robert Browning, after having written a closet drama (*Paracelsus*, 1835), then *Pippa Passes* (1841)—a work that evades generic definition, being half-lyrical, half-dramatic—and seven plays between 1836 and 1846—many of which were never actually performed—, resolutely devoted himself to the hybrid genre that he first called "dramatic lyrics," a phrase he used for his 1842 collection of poems (Tholoniat "De la voix au théâtre" and *"Tongue's Imperial Fiat"*). The term probably comes from Percy Shelley and his definition of *Prometheus Unbound* (1820) as a "lyrical drama." Browning expanded his range of experimental forms in the following collection entitled *Dramatic Romances and Lyrics*, published in 1845. His endeavor was to individualize each character (man or woman, young or old, painter or priest, Spaniard or German, etc.) by means of his or her voice. In these poems, Browning first organizes a constellation of preliminary elements (title, subtitle, epigraph, etc.) which are designed to allow the reader to perceive the speaker's voice from the start. As in "Fra Lippo Lippi" (published in *Men and Women* in 1855), the title provides the name of the speaker, the poet's mask. The table of contents of *Men and Women* looks very much like a list of *dramatis personae* at times. Indeed, Browning chose *Dramatis Personae* as the title for an 1864 volume which was very much in the same vein as *Men and Women*. Sometimes the subtitle and/or the beginning of the poem provide other elements, such as the time and place of speech, as is the case in "Fra Lippo Lippi":

> I am poor brother Lippo, by your leave!
> You need not clap your torches to my face.
> Zooks, what's to blame? you think you see a monk!
> What, 'tis past midnight, and you go the rounds,

>   And here you catch me at an alley's end
>   Where sportive ladies leave their doors ajar?
>
>   (ll. 1–6)

As we can see with this instance, Browning puts these peripheral indications to good use so as to play with the reader's expectations.

Moreover, he very deftly organizes a system of echoes in his titles: "The Italian in England," "The Englishman in Italy," "The Lost Leader," "The Lost Mistress," "Home-Thoughts, from Abroad," "Home-Thoughts, from the Sea," "Meeting at Night," "Parting at Morning," "Love in a Life," "Life in a Love," in *Dramatic Romances and Lyrics*, and "Before," "After," "In Three Days," "In a Year," "One Way of Love," "Another Way of Love," and, more subtly, "Fra Lippo Lippi," "Andrea del Sarto" in *Men and Women*. Browning also conceived poems composed of several complementary parts. "Cavalier Tunes" (*Dramatic Lyrics*) includes "I. Marching Along," "II. Give a Rouse," and "III. Boot and Saddle"; "I. The Flower's Name" and "II. Sibrandus Schafnaburgensis" make "Garden Fancies" (*Dramatic Romances and Lyrics*), whereas "James Lee's Wife" (*Dramatis Personae*) contains nine sections, each of which has its own title. Browning adds another layer of complexity to his dramatic monologues by putting them into a network of echoing allusions. In each particular volume (and one may also add, beyond each individual volume), temporal, geographical, subject-related elements contribute to strengthening the dialogical links between the poems. Antiquity is the background of such poems as "An Epistle Containing the Strange Epistle of Karshish, the Arab Physician," "Cleon," and "A Death on the Desert." The temperaments and aesthetic projects of Italian Renaissance painters are compared and contrasted in "Pictor Ignotus," "Fra Lippo Lippi," and "Andrea del Sarto." Deathbed utterances can be heard in "A Woman's Last Word," "The Bishop Orders his Tomb at Saint Praxed's Church" and "Confessions"; musicians speak in "Master Hughes of Saxe-Gotha," "A Toccata of Galuppi's," and "Abt Vogler."

Consequently, the juxtaposition of dramatic monologues turns them into a dialogue, and the constellation of echoing poems creates a polyphonic effect. *The Ring and the Book*, published in 1868–69, is in this respect a stylistic tour de force, Browning's *magnum opus*. Consisting of about 21,000 lines and divided into twelve books, this "novel in verse" is also one of the first detective stories in English literature. Moreover, the reader is expected to play the part of the detective. The plot is the following one: in seventeenth-century Rome, a young woman, Pompilia, has been stabbed to death by her jealous husband Guido, who stands trial for his murder. Each book is a dramatic monologue. The first and last books are spoken by the figure of the poet who addresses his readership about the characters and the development of the plot, with a desire to immortalize his characters vocally because, according to one of his statements, "The printed voice . . . lives now and then" (164). Books II, III, and IV are spoken by characters who embody rumors in Rome: "Half-Rome" supports Guido, while "Other Half-Rome" sides with Pompilia; "Tertium Quid" weighs the balance and refuses to take sides. Each of them has a "good" reason to have a biased judgment, something the reader discovers gradually and very often indirectly. Books V, VI, and VII are spoken by the protagonists. In Book V Guido finds justification for his murder by exposing his young wife's alleged affair with a priest, Caponsacchi, who answers his accusations in the following book. Pompilia, who is breathing her last, supports Caponsacchi's speech in Book VII. Books VIII and IX consist of the two lawyers' speeches for the trial. As no clear-cut decision emerges, the Pope, in Book X, after much hesitation, finally finds Guido guilty and sentences him to death. Book XI is Guido's last speech in jail, a few hours before the time of his execution. Full of malice and innuendoes, Guido's character tries to present himself as more sinned against than sinning. The reader has to make his or her own mind about him, as he or she is invited to do so in the last book, spoken by the poet. The architecture of *The Ring and the Book*, based on pairs and triads (rumors, protagonists, lawyers), a dense metaphorical network of echoes and allusions, with its alternation of pros and cons in relation to the protagonists and the relative importance of certain facts, is reminiscent of the structure of a polyphony.

As we have seen with the example of *The Ring and the Book*, the active participation of the reader is of course crucial in the apprehension of the subtleties of a dramatic monologue. "Andrea del Sarto," in *Men and Women*, is a case in point. As John Maynard has shown, the reader starts by siding with the henpecked eponymous painter, but as the latter tries to detain his wife from going out to meet her cousin (and more probably, her lover), he uses arguments which allow the reader to discern why his company is not as enjoyable as he might believe. The combination of this phenomenon with the echoing structure of the poems has a powerful consequence. Most of the dramatic monologues rely on the reader's perception of dramatic irony, the fact that he or she perceives more of what is at stake in the monologist's speech than he himself seems to understand. Indeed, Jean-Jacques Mayoux described dramatic irony in Browning's dramatic monologue as similar to the *lapsus linguae* on a large scale (Mayoux 200), although in general speakers wish to achieve some conscious purpose (to justify themselves or to argument a case, for instance).[1]

After *The Ring and the Book*, Browning went to experiment new ways of linking dramatic monologues so as to create what W.E. Harrold (1973) called "the overpoem" (Harrold 4). *Ferishtah's Fancies* (1884) consists of a series of twelve poems framed by a prologue and an epilogue, each poem falling into two parts: an allegorical fable followed by a moral lesson. *Parleyings with Certain People of Importance in their Day* (1887) contains seven dramatic monologues in which the figure of the poet imagines a conversation with artists of various fields.

Alfred Tennyson, succeeding William Wordsworth as poet laureate in 1850, wrote poems very similar to dramatic monologues ("Œnone," "The Lotos-Eaters," "Saint Simeon Stylites," "Ulysses," "Maud," for instance), but in most of these poems, the dramatic element does not urge the speaker into revealing himself or herself as is the case in Browning's poems. "Saint Simeon Stylites" for example is more of a monologue, a rumination of the speaker addressing God. That the poem has ironic overtones, and strikes one as echoing the situation of Burns's Holy Willie, does not make it particularly "dramatic." Indeed, Tennyson chose to call a poem of a similar form, "Maud," a monodrama, and he defines the genre as a poem in which "different phases of passion in one person take the place of different characters."[2] Tennyson's best instances of dramatic monologues are perhaps "Northern Farmer (Old Style)" and "Northern Farmer (New Style)," written in Lincolnshire dialect:

> Dosn't thou 'ear my 'ere°'s legs, as they canters awaäy?   °horse
> Proputty°, proputty, proputty—that's what I 'ears 'em saäy.   °property
> Proputty, proputty, proputty—Sam, thou's an ass for thy païns;
> Theer's moor sense i' one o' 'is legs, nor in all thy braïns.
>
>   ("Northern Farmer [New Style]," ll.1–4)

As we can see, a monologue may have different guises: it can be a soliloquy (an actor speaking alone on stage), a parabasis (an actor addressing the audience), a prosopopeia (the speech of an imaginary person or entity), a monodrama (where the driving force of the speech comes from emotions rather than from action), and finally, a dramatic monologue, in which one can distinguish another subgenre, the monopolylogue (a play with more than one character in which one actor plays every role), which literally designates a one-man show. Browning's "Fra Lippo Lippi" is a typical example: the speaker is a Renaissance painter and a monk, and in his speech he imitates, or rather impersonates in turn the voices of some of his relatives, fellow-monks, and even the voice of his auditor.

During the second half of the nineteenth century, other poets experimented forms inspired by the dramatic monologue. Robert Browning's wife, the poet Elizabeth Barrett Browning, wrote a moving and politically committed dramatic monologue: "The Runaway Slave at Pilgrim's Point," published in *Poems* (1850):

> I have run through the night, my skin is as dark,
> I bend my knee down on this mark . . .
> I look on the sky and the sea.
>
> O pilgrim-souls, I speak to you!
>
>   (ll.5–8)

Robert Buchanan, in *London Poems* (1866), and at the end of the century, John Davidson, allowed the marginalized voices of abandoned women, vagrants, and workers to be heard. Emily Pfeiffer, Constance Naden, May Kendall, and Augusta Webster also exploited the dramatic monologue as a powerful tool for social critique, especially from a woman's point of view. Some writers poked fun at what they considered to be Browning's stylistic whims (Tholoniat "Au miroir déformant du style"). C.S. Calverley, in "The Cock and the Bull" (1872), parodies the beginning of *The Ring and the Book*. J.K. Stephen, in "The Last Ride Together (From Her Point of View)" (1891), plays upon Browning's habit of paired poems, and provides an imaginary counterpart to Browning's "The Last Ride Together" (*Men and Women*, 1855).

Thomas Hardy and Rudyard Kipling sometimes followed Browning's influence and wrote fine dramatic monologues. Thomas Hardy took many notes concerning Browning's rhyme schemes in his notebooks, and put them to good use in "The Ruined Maid," for instance. Some of Kipling's *Barrack-Room Ballads* (1892) merge the dramatic monologue with music-hall ballads and marching songs; but the collection also contains more traditional monologues. "The Window at Windsor," for instance, consists in a colloquial speech addressed to a silent listener by a soldier whose patriotic concerns are undercut by his proletarian choice of vocabulary. "The 'Mary Gloster'" (1894) is a death-bed speech, reminiscent of Browning's "The Bishop Orders his Tomb at Saint Praxed's Church" and "Confessions":

> I've paid for your sickest fancies; I've humoured your crackedest whim—
> Dick, it's your daddy, dying; you've got to listen to him!
> Good for a fortnight, am I? The doctor told you? He lied.
> I shall go under by morning, and—Put that nurse outside.
>
> (ll.1–4).

Although most modernist poets tended to oppose what they considered to be the formal conventionality of Victorian poets, they appropriated their modes to suit their new purposes. Ezra Pound (1895–1972), as Ford Madox Ford noticed, owed a great deal to Browning. This is a debt Pound himself acknowledged, albeit indirectly, in the title of his 1909 *Personae* (a title he took up in 1926 for *Personae: The Collected Poems of Ezra Pound*), and directly in his essays about literature. Ezra Pound insists on the use of a persona, by which he means, writing of his early volume *Personae*, a "complete mask of the self"—he described himself as "casting off, as it were, complete masks of the self in each poem." In this sense, a persona is neither the "I" which equates to or is congruent with, without necessarily being identical to, the poet in Romantic, and other expressive, schools of poetics nor the autonomous fictional (in Northrop Frye's sense of the term) "I" of the Browningesque dramatic monologue. Rather, the persona articulates a series of shifts and displacements between the two; it may even be described as deconstructing the distinction, which goes back through Aristotle to Plato, between speaking in one's own voice (*in propria persona*) and assuming the voice of another. While Pound's concern with "masks" (and his experiments with "personae") can be traced to Wilde, and his choice of specific masks often takes him back to the Middle Ages or to Ancient Greece or China, it was central to his development of a modern poetic idiom and links his poetic practice, almost from the beginning, with modernist poetics of impersonality and with a wider modern questioning of received models of the self and of individual identity.

At the same time, T.S. Eliot turned back to Wordsworth's project (expounded in the 1800 preface of the *Lyrical Ballads*, which advocated reconciliation between poetry and everyday language): "the law that poetry must not stray too far from the ordinary everyday language which we use and hear. Whether poetry is accentual or syllabic, rhymed or rhymeless, formal or free, it cannot afford to lose its contact with the changing language of common intercourse" (Eliot 29). On his way back to literary history, he could not but meet Robert Browning's art of the printed voice. "The Love Song of J. Alfred Prufrock" (1915) bears an ironic title, since the middle-aged speaker of the poem is too shy to achieve a significant gesture that might change his dull, bourgeois life:

> Let us go then, you and I,
> When the evening is spread out against the sky
> Like a patient etherized upon a table;
> Let us go, through certain half-deserted streets,
> The muttering retreats
> Of restless nights in one-night cheap hotels
> And sawdust restaurants with oyster-shells.
>
> (ll.1–7)

In *The Waste Land* (1922), Eliot radicalizes the potentialities of Browning's dramatic monologue by going a step further. Like Browning and Pound, he saturates his work with literary and artistic allusions combined with the use of several languages both ancient and modern. The beginning of the twentieth century was also a moment when science's forays into the human psyche unveiled the hidden dimensions of the mind that have a bearing on the conscious level. Eliot's poetics sometimes appear as a process of collage and sudden juxtaposition of ideas and feelings giving birth to a stream of consciousness (as in James Joyce's novel, *Ulysses*, at the same period). The poem therefore appears as a mosaic of written quotations and soundbites, a vortex of cultural elements surfacing now and then in the polyphony of human history. Robert Frost wrote dramatic monologues in colloquial speech, housed in conventional meters. His favorite topics are the life of the New Englanders, their everyday activities, their experience of solitude and hardships.

In the second half of the twentieth century, Edwin Morgan chose to introduce unfamiliar perspectives on human experience, by having, not men and women, but the Loch Ness monster ("The Loch Ness Monster," 1968), a computer ("The Computer's First Christmas Card," 1968), or a dolphin ("The Dolphin's Song," 1970) speak. His most daring experiment is "Message Clear," a deconstruction of a single line drawn from the gospel of St. John ("I am the resurrection and the life"), reorganized over fifty-five lines including typographical gaps and a variety of missing letters. The various words and texts which emerge from the truncated line problematize questions of interpretation and communication, as there is no intention of creating the illusion of a "real" speaker. Richard Howard's "Nikolaus Mardruz to his Master Ferdinand, Count of Tyrol, 1565" (1995) is a tribute to Browning's "My Last Duchess" (*Dramatic Lyrics*, 1842) and a sequel to it at the same time. Like Browning, to whom he refers in the dedication page of *Untitled Subjects* (1969), Howard's interest in the dramatic monologue is to explore the historical dimension of texts as well as the textual dimension of history. But "Nikolaus Mardruz to his Master Ferdinand, Count of Tyrol, 1565" illustrates other features of the dramatic monologue. First, it makes use of archaisms, mannerisms, or words belonging to a specific jargon so as to identify the speaker:

> I see that the Duke,
> by his own lights or perhaps, more properly
>   said, by his own *tenebrosity*°,   °obscurity
>   could offer some excuse
>   for such cunctation° . . .   °tardiness
>
>   (ll.52–56)

Secondly, one notices the metalinguistic quality of the poem: the speaker comments upon the words selected by other persons or by himself. As a corollary, italics and capitalized words are used so as to lay the stress on important words or phrases in the poem—although of course they might mean more than the speaker himself expects. Finally, the poem displays a sophisticated typographical layout, so as to create effects of rhythm and suspense. Indeed, in its development over the twentieth century, the dramatic monologue increasingly insists on its condition as text.

More recently, Carol Ann Duffy's masterful use of the dramatic monologue enabled her, as one critic put it, "to popularise complex ideas about language and its political role and meaning" (Byron 130). Her poems deal with speakers who are abusers or abused individuals unaware of their own shortcomings. In "Standing Female Nude," a prostitute who sits for a painter provides oblique comments on the part played by women in art:

> Six hours like this for a few *francs*.
> Belly nipple arse in the window light,
> he drains the colour from me. Further to the right,
> Madame. And do try to be still.
> I shall be represented analytically and hung
> in great museums. The bourgeoisie will coo
> at such an image of a river-whore. They call it Art.
>
>   (ll.1–7)

A woman, as a sitter, a "muse" or a pictorial topic, tends to be considered only as a body, and finally as an object. Many modern dramatic monologues display a reflection on the dialectic of the self and the other, or more generally, on the self and otherness in a given society: between man and woman, old and young, past and present or future, morality and desire (or body and soul). Such poems explore the way our identity (the self or a collective identity) is constructed, according to the pressure of various socio-cultural contexts. As a consequence, a trend in recent dramatic monologues has been to have highly polemical or unreliable speakers. Problems in assessing the speaker's "moral" or social position contribute to the debunking of the idea of the autonomous subject. Developments of the monologue outside the field of poetry can be perceived in the work of contemporary songwriters, such as Bruce Springsteen and

Steve Earle. Springsteen, in the title song *Nebraska* (1982), assumes the voice of a serial killer minutes before his execution on the electric chair. From *Cruelty* (1973) onwards, the American poet Ai (Florence Anthony, 1947–2010) chooses well-known figures of stars (Marilyn Monroe, James Dean), politicians (Richard Nixon, Bill Clinton) or criminals as speakers for her poems. In "False Witness" (1999), a mother addresses her daughter, and the reader gradually understands that the speaker actually encourages her husband to abuse their child sexually. By exploring such topics, dramatic monologues can convey a very unnerving as well as unwilling sense of complicity. She once declared: "I feel that the dramatic monologue was the form in which I was born to write and I love it as passionately, or perhaps more passionately, than I have ever loved a man."[3] Other variations on the dramatic monologue conventions include the exploration of a specific female voice, the questioning of the cult of personality, various aspects of social critique, sequences of dramatic monologues (for example, Duncan Bush's "Are There Still Wolves in Pennsylvania," 1994). As in Richard Howard's "Nikolaus Mardruz to his Master Ferdinand, Count of Tyrol, 1565," late twentieth-century dramatic monologues tend to foreground the processes of representation.

Outside the English-speaking world, the dramatic monologue underwent similar developments. In the 1930s, the Spanish poet Luis Cernuda sought refuge in Great Britain, where he discovered the work of Robert Browning. In Greece, Constantine Cavafy, also influenced by Robert Browning, wrote historical and pseudo-historical dramatic monologues, some tinged with irony. The Argentinean poet Jorge Luis Borges, in a poem entitled "Browning resuelve ser poeta" ("Browning makes up his mind to be a poet," published in *La rosa profunda*, 1975), makes Browning speak for himself in a dramatic monologue. As a speaker, Browning describes some of the masks that he intends to put on, and he announces his poetic project: "En el dialecto de hoy / diré a mi vez las cosas eternas" ("In today's dialect I too shall utter eternal things"). In Italy, Eduardo Sanguineti (1930–2010) adapted the genre, and together with the figure of Pound, he influenced the poet Antonio Colinas (1946–), translator of both Pound and Sanguineti into Spanish, who wrote "Giacomo Casanova acepta el cargo de bibliotecario que le ofrece, en Bohemia, el conde de Waldstein" ("Giacomo Casanova accepts the charge of librarian offered to him by the count of Waldstein, in Bohemia," *Sepulcro en Tarquinia*, 1976).

If the dramatic monologue has recently been influenced by the invasive presence of various media (the computer, television), it has also managed to influence the media in return. Indeed, the innovative poetics of multiple voices embodying as many viewpoints was put to effective use in the field of cinema. The Japanese writer and translator of Browning in Japanese, Akutagawa Ryûnosuke (1892–1927), wrote his novel *Rashômon* using the stylistic device of multiple perspectives he had found in *The Ring and the Book*. The novel served as a screenplay to Akira Kurosawa's film, *Rashômon*, which won the Golden Palm at the Cannes Festival in 1950. In contemporary society, the dramatic monologue has undergone a popular resurgence in the form of ventriloquism and stand-up comedy, where the comedian engages in a dialogue with a puppet, an imaginary addressee, or the audience. Alan Bennett's *Talking Heads* (1988) and Eve Ensler's *The Vagina Monologues* (1996) share Browning's blending of poetic and theatrical monologues and dramatic irony. As one can see, the dramatic monologue opens up vistas that are surprisingly large: mixing memory and desire, irony and the grotesque, art and politics, and giving voices that attest the on-going flow of the human mind.

NOTES

1 Cornelia Pearsall argues that speakers always want to achieve a purpose.
2 According to Culler, the monodrama derives from works by Rousseau in France and Goethe in Germany. Introduced into England by Coleridge and Southey, the genre evolved from conversational poems to monodrama with Alfred Tennyson.
3 Quoted at www.english.illinois.edu/maps/poets/a_f/ai/about.htm.

REFERENCES AND FURTHER READING

Byron, G. *Dramatic Monologue*. London & New York: Routledge, 2003.

Culler, D.A. "Monodrama and the Dramatic Monologue." *PMLA* 90. 1975: 366–85.

Davis, P. *The Victorians (1830–1880)*. Oxford: Oxford University Press, 2002.

Eliot, T.S. *On Poetry and Poets*. London: Faber & Faber, 1957.

Harrold, W.E. *The Variance and the Unity: A Study of Browning's Complementary Poems*. Athens: Ohio University Press, 1973.

Jones, A.R. "*Robert Browning and the Dramatic Monologue: The Impersonal Act.*" Critical Quaterly 9.4. 1967: 301–28.

Langbaum, R. *The Poetry of Experience: The Dramatic Monologue in Modern Literary Tradition*. New York: Random House, 1957.

Martin, L.D. *Browning's Dramatic Monologues and the Post-Romantic Subject*. Baltimore: Johns Hopkins University Press, 1985.

Maynard, J. "Speaker, Listener, and Overhearer: The Reader in the Dramatic Poem." *Browning Institute Studies* 15. 1987: 105–12.

Mayoux, J.-J. "Robert Browning: une pensée victorienne." *Critique* 405–06. 1981: 199–220.

Pearsall, C. "The Dramatic Monologue." In *The Cambridge Companion to Victorian Poetry*, ed. J. Bristow. Cambridge: Cambridge University Press, 2000. 67–88.

Sessions, I.B. "The Dramatic Monologue." *PMLA* 62. 1947: 503–16.

Sinfeld, A. *Dramatic Monologue*. London: Methuen, 1977.

Tholoniat, Y. "Au miroir déformant du style: trois caricatures de Robert Browning (C. S. Calverley, 'The Cock and the Bull,' 1872 ; J. K. Stephen, 'The Last Ride Together (From Her Point of View),' 1891 ; Richard Howard, 'Nikolaus Mardruz to his Master Ferdinand, Count of Tyrol, 1565,' 1995)." *Cercles* 14. 2005: 1–14. www.cercles.com/n14/tholoniat.pdf.

Tholoniat, Y. "De la voix au théâtre au théâtre de la voix: l'envers du décor poétique de Robert Browning." *Cahiers Victoriens et Edouardiens* 67. 2008: 421–38.

Tholoniat, Y. "*Tongue's Imperial Fiat*": les polyphonies dans l'œuvre poétique de Robert Browning ("*Tongue's Imperial Fiat*": The Polyphonies in Robert Browning's Poetical Work). Strasbourg: Presses Universitaires de Strasbourg, 2009.

Tucker, H.F. "From Monomania to Monologue: 'Saint Simeon Stylites' and the Rise of the Victorian Dramatic Monologue." *Victorian Poetry* 22.2. 1984: 121–37.

31
Rewriting the People's Newspaper
Trinidadian Calypso after 1956

John Thieme

Keith Warner sub-titles his monograph *The Trinidad Calypso* (1983), "A Study of the Calypso as Oral Literature," and there has been widespread recognition that the genre is both the main narrative form of Trinidad and, in the hands of its leading practitioners, a form of folk poetry. However, as Gordon Rohlehr points out, its categorization as poetry has seldom been clearly defined and any account of calypso as poetry needs to take account of the fact that the calypsonian "combines the arts of musician, singer, raconteur, dramatist, showman and dancer" ("Sparrow as Poet" 84),[1] to which one might add the role of composer, since the majority of songs performed during the annual calypso season are written by the calypsonians who perform them.

There is no clear consensus as to when calypso first emerged as a distinct genre in its own right. Errol Hill locates the antecedents of modern calypso in the late nineteenth century (*The Trinidad Carnival* 57) and this is the view taken by the majority of commentators, though Keith Warner detects origins that go back to the late eighteenth century (9). In a chapter on "The Development of Creole Society, 1838–1938," Brigid Brereton suggests that "calypso emerged in its modern form about the turn of the [twentieth] century" (135). The Mighty Chalkdust emphasizes the emergence of calypso forms at the moment of Emancipation in 1838, while suggesting a longer genealogy (Liverpool 3) and Atilla the Hun [*sic*] goes so far as to suggest that "kaiso [calypso] may be traced back to the African slaves first brought to the West Indies during the 17th century" (Quevedo 9), while conceding that oral transmission has meant that "no historical evidence for this connection—kaiso and slavery" has yet been "unearthed" (4). Looking at all the evidence, it seems best to see its modern beginnings as dating from the late nineteenth century, while the first recordings of

A Companion to Poetic Genre, First Edition. Edited by Erik Martiny.

calypso, which were made by the New York Victor Gramophone Company in 1914 (Hill, *The Trinidad Carnival* 56), were a milestone in raising international awareness of the genre.

During the course of its evolution from its modern beginnings in the late nineteenth century, calypso has variously been a medium for storytelling, news reportage, social analysis, and an extensive range of comic commentary, which while uniquely Trinidadian shares traits with the practices of satirists from other cultures and periods. In his poem "The Spoiler's Return" (1982), Derek Walcott links the calypsonian the Mighty Spoiler (Theophilus Phillip) with Augustan satirists, both Roman and English, to suggest the underlying similarity of the impulses that drive their work. Thus the poem transfers the term the "Old Brigade" from the sense in which it would generally have been understood in Trinidad in the 1970s—to refer to a particular group of singer/composers in the calypso tents of the period—to Martial, Juvenal, and Pope. Spoiler asks for backing from these classical poets, who in Walcott's imagined version of him are his natural precursors:

> nothing ain't change but colour and attire,
> (so back me up, Old Brigade of Satire,
> Back me up Martial, Juvenal, and Pope
> (to hang theirself I giving plenty rope)

> (ll.33–6)

This chapter provides an overview of calypso's origins, history, and characteristics, before moving on to a brief consideration of the compositions and performance personae of the two most successful calypsonians to have appeared to date, the Mighty Sparrow (Slinger Francisco, b. 1935) and the Mighty Chalkdust (Hollis Liverpool, b. 1941). It discusses how both Sparrow and Chalkdust have refashioned traditional elements from the genre, mainly for the purpose of satirical social and political commentary. In so doing, it illustrates ways in which their calypsoes exhibit a self-conscious awareness of the evolution of the genre and respond to the changing social and political situation in Trinidad in the quarter of a century after 1956, a period during which the nation's politics were dominated by the figure of its prime minister, Dr. Eric Williams. Both Sparrow and Chalkdust have won the title of Calypso Monarch, awarded as part of Trinidad's annual Carnival celebrations, eight times: Sparrow began to compete in 1954, first won the Crown in 1956 and achieved his most recent success in 1992; Chalkdust, who began to compete in 1968, first won the title of Calypso Monarch in 1976 and was most recently successful in 2009. During the years they have been active, calypso has undergone major transformations and numerous calypsonians have debated the question of what the genre should be in metacalypsoes, with one school of thought advocating that it remain true to its "roots," while an opposing faction has argued for the admission of elements from African American and other New World black musical forms, to reflect the increasingly hybrid nature of Trinidadian culture and society. I particularly focus on the period after 1956, because in addition to coinciding with Williams's political pre-eminence, these were also years during which debates about calypso were at their most intense.

Provenance, History, and Contexts

In the Trinidad chapter of his travel book *The Middle Passage* (1962), V.S. Naipaul says of the Anglophone Caribbean, "The history of the islands can never be satisfactorily told . . . History is built around achievement and creation; and nothing was created in the West Indies" (29). It is the kind of anti-Caribbean comment for which Naipaul has become notorious and yet in one sense at least it is surprising, since Naipaul had himself, from boyhood, been a devotee of calypso, which his late brother Shiva refers to as one of Trinidad's "two indisputably original creations" (116);[2] and calypso is an integral component of both the social milieu and the narrative mode of the older Naipaul's linked short-story sequence *Miguel Street* (1959). Along with numerous other Trinidadian writers, most notably Sam Selvon and Earl Lovelace,[3] Naipaul adopts a storytelling mode that has much in common with calypso in *Miguel Street* and, again in the Trinidad chapter of *The Middle Passage*, he stresses the genre's hold on the Trinidadian imagination and its uniqueness as a local cultural form:

> It is only in the calypso that the Trinidadian touches reality. The calypso is a purely local form. No song composed outside Trinidad is a calypso. The calypso deals with local incidents, local attitudes, and it does so in a local language. The pure calypso, the best calypso, is incomprehensible to the outsider.
>
> (70)

Such notions of cultural "purity" are, of course, widely seen as suspect at the beginning of the twenty-first century, and they seem particularly inapposite when applied to a cultural form from a complex creolized society like Trinidad. By the time Naipaul was writing *The Middle Passage*, calypso was *very* clearly a cross-pollinated form (in fact it had been so from its beginnings) and one of its defining characteristics has been its capacity to import "foreign" strands into its ever mutating make-up. In the 1970s, its derivative soca (soul + calypso) introduced American soul music into its repertory, while David Rudder, Calypso Monarch in 1986, generated controversy by drawing on samba elements for one of his winning compositions, "Bahia Girl." Moreover, Naipaul's view that "[t]he pure calypso . . . is incomprehensible to the outsider" is challenged by the genre's having become popular throughout the Eastern Caribbean and also further afield, particularly as a consequence of Trinidadian migration to Britain, North America, and elsewhere.

Nevertheless, hybrid though it may be, calypso *is*, along with steelband, an "indisputably original" Trinidadian creation. Both are offshoots of the central event in the island's cultural calendar, its annual Carnival, a festival which lasts for just forty-eight hours, but which has a year-round importance in Trinidad's social life, both because of the lavish preparations that go into its making and its perceived role as a central expression of the Trinidadian psyche. Contemporary Carnival provides a livelihood for a significant segment of the island's inhabitants and offers a wellspring of possibilities for artistic creativity to the population at large, whether as performers, participants or simply onlookers. Calypso is umbilically linked to Carnival. Its season takes place in the two months leading up to the pre-Lenten festival and calypso awards in various categories, most notably for the year's Calypso Monarch and Road March (the people's choice of their favorite composition for "tramping" the streets), are tied to Carnival.

The etymology of the word "calypso" is uncertain, but it is widely believed to derive from the Hausa "kaito," a term used to convey praise or approbation (roughly equivalent to "bravo" or "hooray"),[4] and today the music is often referred to in Trinidad as "kaiso." However, another school of thought claims that "calypso" derives from the Spanish "cariso."[5] This suggests the influence of another aspect of the colonial history of Trinidad,[6] which also continued to be influential at the time when the music was emerging in the late nineteenth century, and more generally the influence of Hispanic culture from the South American mainland, arising from the island's proximity to Venezuela. In short, the origins of calypso are hybrid and, while a majority of commentators have very reasonably privileged its Afro-Creole elements over the other strands that have gone into its make-up, the debate over the origins of its name again points to the extent to which it is a popular art from that fashions something new from materials of mixed provenance.

Traditionally, calypsoes were improvised, humorous compositions, in which the calypsonian (the "chantuelle" or "shantwell," i.e. the male singer/composer) attempted to demonstrate his virtuosity against rivals, often by employing long words in a spirit of oratorical warfare. In the nineteenth century one particular form of the music, the "kalinda," evolved from the chants of stickfighters, whose martial endeavors were accompanied by combative rhetorical "speechification." As the years went by, verbal warfare superseded actual combat, but calypso remained dominated by macho attitudes and these can be seen at their most extreme in some of the Mighty Sparrow's most famous calypsoes, including "Ten to One is Murder" (1961), "The Village Ram" (1964), and "Congo Man" (1965). By and large, though, the martial dimension of calypso has been replaced by more playful treatments of male identity and the man–woman relationship.

As calypso developed in the first half of the twentieth century, it increasingly became a vehicle for conveying *any* and *every* kind of commentary on both local and international affairs. In an age before today's mass media became the main means of disseminating information, calypso was sometimes referred to as the people's newspaper; and the calypsonian has been seen as a descendant of the West African griot, who served as the oral repository of a tribe's history.[7] Famous calypsoes from the first half of the twentieth century include compositions about the first appearance of a zeppelin over Port-of-Spain (1933),[8] the fights between Joe Louis and Max Schmeling (1937–39)[9] and the abdication of Edward VIII from the throne of England in 1936 (1937).[10] Several memorable World War II calypsoes, including Lord Invader's (Rupert

Grant's) "Rum and Coca Cola" (1943) and "Yankee Dollar" (1946), focused on consequences of the friendly "invasion" brought about by the American military presence on the island, while the end of the war was celebrated in the Roaring Lion's (Hubert de Leon's) "All Day, All Night Miss Mary Ann" (1945). Postwar calypsoes particularly commented on the changing man–woman relationship and the nationalist politics of Eric Williams's PNM (People's National Movement), discussed below. Later calypsoes have continued to deal with virtually every aspect of the island's social life—from food prices[11] to Black Power[12]—while also continuing to comment on international affairs and, particularly in the period that provides my central focus: the state of the music itself.

In 1939, the first Calypso King, a title that would became a standard annual award, was proclaimed during the festivities of Carnival. This was followed in 1945 by the first people's choice of a winning Road March. Until the 1970s calypso remained an almost exclusively male preserve and the gender ethic implicit—and often very *explicit*—in most compositions was distinctly chauvinist. However, during that decade the emergence of female calypsonians such as Calypso Rose (Rose McCartha Sandy-Lewis), who won the calypso crown in 1977 and 1978, challenged the male monopoly of the genre and the title of King was changed to that of Monarch. Calypso continues to flourish, constantly transforming itself to incorporate new modes and reflecting the condition of Trinidad as it exists in a particular moment of time. Musically there have been changes, which have incorporated electronic and more recently digital technology. Thematically, the range of subjects, while constantly being updated, is as eclectic as ever. One of the most significant shifts has been occasioned by the ready availability of news in other media and this has resulted in an increased engagement with editorial commentary as opposed to straightforward reportage, though from its earliest days the people's newspaper never shied away from controversy.

Unlike reggae, there is no single formal defining feature that characterizes the meter and musical form of calypso. That said, it usually employs couplets, for example Lord Caresser's "Edward VIII":

> It's love, it's love alone
> That caused King Edward to leave the throne
> . . .

> On the tenth of December, we heard a talk
> That he gave the throne to the Duke of York.[13]

In *History of the Voice*, Kamau Brathwaite argues that calypso follows Caribbean speech patterns in employing dactyllic rather than iambic rhythms; Brathwaite contends that it "does not employ the iambic pentameter. It employs dactyls. It therefore mandates the use of the tongue in a certain way, the use of sound in a certain way, the use of sound in a certain way" (17). However, this is not always the case and Walcott takes a different view, for example in a comment on his assumption of the reincarnated Spoiler's voice in "The Spoiler's Return," a poem which he has said, depending on one's point of view, can either be seen as written in heroic couplets or in a popular form of calypso meter.[14]

In the early years of the twentieth century, the genre particularly favored extemporaneous composition. Raymond Quevedo (Atilla the Hun) comments that "[f]rom 1903 onwards till about 1921, the kaiso followed the oratorical pattern, that is to say the kaiso was in the nature of a rhetorical recitative in song, sung in the minor key with eight lines to the stanza" (20). Quevedo adds that the "ability to extemporise was the badge of excellence of the kaiso singer" (21), while bemoaning the fact that by 1956 this had become something of a lost art. It was, however, an art that was to be revived by Chalkdust, who particularly in his early career presented himself as a champion of "true" calypso, resisting the forces that were threatening to pervert the music. Sparrow's carefully orchestrated songs initially seem less obviously improvisational, but his highly developed sense of dramatic performance has ensured that no two renditions of his calypsoes are ever quite the same.

The Mighty Sparrow

Sparrow achieved instant fame when he won the title of Calypso King in 1956 for his composition "Jean and Dinah," a song which was a throwback to one of the most popular calypso topics of the previous decade, the aftermath of the impact of the American military presence in Trinidad in World War II. After the departure of the U.S. troops, a number of calypsonians playfully took their revenge on the good-time girls, who had deserted Trinidadian men for Americans during the war years: calypsoes on this theme included the Mighty Growler's (Errol Duke's) "Female Taxi-Driver" (1944), Lord Kitchener's (Aldwyn Roberts)'s "Ding Dong Dell" (1946), and the Mighty Spoiler's "Marabella Pork-Vendor" (1947).[15] Seen from one angle, the phenomenally popular "Jean and Dinah," in which Sparrow asserts he is taking over from the Americans, was anachronistic in 1956, but from another viewpoint its locating itself in relation to a group of songs dealing with a situation that had been current a decade before suggests a highly self-conscious use of intertextual reference; it seems to be informed by a confidence that calypso has become a dynamic folk form, which can feed off itself, independent of more contemporary social realities. As such it bears comparison with earlier poetic genres, such as eighteenth-century English satire, which confidently turns to Horace and Juvenal as models both for its practice and its themes, implicitly suggesting that satire is a self-renewing form and what was relevant for ancient Rome is equally so for contemporary Britain.

Sparrow's success in 1956 came at the same time as the rise of the PNM, which continued in government after Trinidad attained Independence in 1962, and, although his repertory moved between social commentary and more light-hearted songs, often heavily laced with sexual innuendo, the assertiveness of his early work can be seen as embodying a similar impulse to that of the new breed of nationalist politicians. In Gordon Rohlehr's words:

> The political calypsoes of the 1956 to 1962 era, dominated by the phenomenal output of the Mighty Sparrow . . . were a celebration of a predominantly African sector of the working and middle classes in the new political movement led by Dr. Eric Williams. They both legitimized the party and its leader, and defended it against incipient dissent by opposition forces.
>
> *(My Strangled City* 325–26)[16]

In "William the Conqueror" (1958), Sparrow depicts Williams as a "champion leader," whose "Big Brain" defeats "Big Belly," a figure representative of an earlier kind of Trinidadian politician, whose apparent macho strength is undermined when Big Brain impregnates him! In "Leave the Damn Doctor" (1960) Sparrow attacks Williams's detractors, enjoining them to leave him to get on with the business of government in peace. "P.A.Y.E." (1958) endorses the government's income-tax policy, while "Our Model Nation" (1962) is a patriotic celebration of Trinidad's attainment of Independence, which sees Williams as the natural successor of earlier nationalists such as Captain A.A. Cipriani and Uriah Butler, anti-colonial labor leaders in the interwar years. Sparrow's support for Williams and the PNM was not however unqualified and, a self-appointed champion of the underprivileged, he also composed calypsoes that gave voice to grass-roots disillusionment with the intellectual Dr. Williams. "No Doctor No" (1957) complains about the rising cost of food prices and taxi fares, admonishing "council men" for having scant regard for those who have voted for them and seemingly linking Williams with their activities. Later, in "Get to Hell Outa Here" (1965), Sparrow assumes the persona of Williams, satirizing him as an autocrat who had obstinately insisted on reinstating a controversial cabinet minister:

> This land is mine, I am the boss
> What I say goes and who vex lost
> I say that Solomon will be
> Minister of External Affairs
> If you ent like it
> Get to hell outs here.[17]

Ultimately, Sparrow's role as a political commentator, when not compromised by commercial considerations, as increasingly became the case in the 1970s and 1980s, is predicated on a particular conception of the function of the calypsonian. While his independent individualism can be seen as loosely analogous to the nationalist politics of the PNM, his actual political comments are thin on ideology and more interesting when seen as a particular way of performing a version of the calypsonian's identity. Sparrow takes the view that it is incumbent on the calypsonian to act as a community spokesperson, offering common-sense political advice to those who actually conduct the business of government. In "No Doctor No," he presents himself as a humble person ("only a calypsonian") whose duty it is to speak on behalf of the populace and throughout the years immediately before and after Trinidad's Independence, a period when his reputation was going from strength to strength, he continues to assume the role of spokesperson for the ordinary man and woman, frequently reasserting his own subaltern roots. Thus, in his 1964 calypso, "The Outcast," he engages in faux-naif self-deprecation as he pleads the case for respecting steelband men and calypsonians such as himself, who have traditionally been treated as pariahs by middle-class Trinidadian society. There is a degree of disingenuousness here, since by now he is highly successful, but his career has been built on a claim to being a man of the people and it is necessary to sustain this role in order to continue to have credibility. Earl Lovelace's novel *The Dragon Can't Dance* (1979), a work which debates the extent to which Carnival has been co-opted by the middle classes (whose influence is associated with the rise of the new nationalist politicians), includes the character of a calypsonian, Philo, who personifies the music's commercialization. Philo has been seen as a fictionalized portrait of Sparrow and Lovelace's text explores the extent to which he has moved away from traditional calypso values, finding success through the composition of suggestive salacious lyrics rather than social commentary.[18] This said, Philo remains a character whose dilemma is sympathetically explored from the inside and who is nostalgic for the deprived locality of Calvary Hill, the novel's main setting, where he feels his roots lie.

By the late 1970s Sparrow had drifted away from the PNM and supported an opposition party, the ONR (Organization for National Reconstruction). In a fanzine, celebrating his achievements, he justified this decision, saying that the country needed "a strong opposition," because in his view it was necessary "to keep even a good government on its toes" (Smith n.p.). However, by this point in his career serious political commentary on Trinidadian subjects is less evident in his music, while his skill in adapting to changing musical tastes is as marked as ever and hybrid, soca compositions such as "Don't Drop the Tempo" (1980), "Wanted Dead or Alive" (1980), and "Don't Back Back" (1984) are among his most memorable pieces from this period.

The Mighty Chalkdust

By this time the politics of a younger generation, influenced by the U.S. civil rights struggle of the 1960s and parallel Caribbean black consciousness movements, had come of age and Chalkdust had succeeded Sparrow as Trinidad's leading political calypsonian. In one important respect, however, Chalkdust's career followed a different trajectory to Sparrow's, since he resisted both the trend to incorporate elements from other musical forms into calypso and the move towards "spiciness" and "smut" that had increasingly been associated with the genre since Sparrow's advent on the scene. During the early years of his career, Chalkdust frequently composed and performed metacalypsoes that debated what forms and subjects were appropriate for the genre, seemingly fighting a rearguard action against the transformations that were taking place during the years of soca's growth in popularity, but his own contribution played a significant role in arresting this shift and the longevity of his success, confirmed by his regaining the calypso crown in 2009, has vindicated his adherence to a traditional view of calypso.

Chalkdust (his soubriquet was taken from his daytime job as a teacher), who has consistently critiqued political abuses in an oeuvre that now spans more than four decades, first performed in 1968. By 1976, feeling that the public's taste was completely given over to soca, he was contemplating retiring from the annual competition. He decided not to, choosing instead to make his doubts about the direction in which calypso was moving his subject; and he was rewarded by winning the 1976 Calypso Monarch title for his compositions, "Ah Put on Me Guns Again" and "Three Blind Mice." In the former, he dramatizes his situation as a calypsonian who has remained true to the time-honored conventions of the genre, adopting the persona of an involuntary satirist, a man compelled to speak out because he is unable to contain his indignation at the injustices and corruption he sees around him. The calypso begins with an account of how he had contemplated abandoning competing in favor of going abroad to further his studies in history and pursue his career as a teacher:

> So as man, I hang up me guns
> Goodbye band, my career is done
> Chalkie will teach the younger ones.[19]

His reason is that only "tempo," music sung at speed to a heavy beat, is finding favor with Carnival audiences. So, he says, he had thought he would retire from the fray, before the crowds rejected him, but he has been forced to "get sane" and rearm himself—to put on his guns again—because he is unable to stand idly by and watch injustices perpetuated. In one sense this is similar to Sparrow's adoption of the role of people's champion, but Chalkdust's stance is both more nuanced and more fully developed, and comparable to the persona adopted by a satirist such as Pope, who in the *Epistle to Dr Arbuthnot* represents himself as the involuntary victim of a society of madmen, compelled to write because he is assaulted on all sides and "can't be silent, and . . . will not lye" (l.34).

It is a familiar satirist's position. Pope's major classical model, Horace, presents himself as standing outside of Roman society, writing from his Sabine farm. Pope, isolated from certain sections of English society and denied a university education because of his Catholicism, depicts himself as writing from the margins, compelled to do so by his honesty and inability to hold his tongue. Chalkdust claims he has simply wanted to devote himself to educating children, but he has had to "get sane" and once more engage in calypso combat after witnessing the abuses surrounding him in the oil-rich society of 1970s Trinidad. Compounding the role of the classical satirist with a macho pose that would be more immediately familiar to the Trinidadian public, that of the avenging gunslinger of a Western movie,[20] he has had no choice but to comment on such issues as the disappearance of $10 million from the public coffers and the fact that the owners of big stores in Port-of-Spain have pushed poor apple vendors out into the rain. Given such abuses, he says, he has been forced to re-enter the calypso arena.

In "Three Blind Mice," Chalkdust refashions the traditional children's nursery rhyme for the purpose of mocking Eric Williams's response to three fellow-premiers from the Anglophone Caribbean: Jamaica's Michael Manley, Guyana's Forbes Burnham, and Barbados's Errol Barrow. The Williams of the calypso boasts that he can act in a cavalier manner towards his Anglophone Caribbean neighbors because of Trinidad's oil wealth. Sparrow had made a similar use of nursery rhyme in one of his most famous calypsoes, "Dan Is the Man in the Van" (1963), which incorporates lines from numerous nursery rhymes to mock the educational curriculum of the late colonial period. Chalkdust does something different: the Williams of "Three Blind Mice" mockingly applies the nursery rhyme title to his three prime ministerial peers, but the irony rebounds on him, since his adoption of a disdainful tone towards them is based on childish taunting, manifest in his repetition of both the rhyme's title and a catchphrase popularly attributed to him, "oil don't spoil."

The album on which these two winning songs appeared, "The Fourth Time Around," also includes a number of other compositions which, along with them, form an extended commentary on the nature of calypso. In "Too Much Tempo," Chalkdust argues against the incorporation of up-tempo elements into the genre; in "No Smut for Me," he inveighs against the infiltration of salacious material; in "Message to George Weekes," he informs a prominent trade-union leader that calypso is a more effective form of political action than a protest march; and in "Chalkie the Teacher," he tells a tourist that he can instruct her in Caribbean cuisine and various other local skills, but not calypso and steelband, because these are genetically inherited Trinidadian preserves!

Subsequently, in the years before Eric Williams's death in 1981, Chalkdust would continue to include the changing nature of calypso and the prime minister among his favored subjects. In "Calypso versus Soca" (1978), one of his most extended manifestoes against the admission of new elements, he sees calypso as a central repository of Trinidadian culture, arguing against those who have advised him to change his accent and sing soca, soul, reggae, or pop, so as to secure the "tourist dollar," saying that this would involve betraying one's roots and losing one's freedom. Eric Williams remains a central reference-point in "Letter to Eric" (1978), "Money Ain't No Problem" (1978), which again turns one of the prime minister's most famous aphorisms against him,[21] and "Eric Loves Me" (1979), where his satire reaches new heights with the suggestion, as Gordon Rohlehr puts it, "that Williams exist[s] only to provide material for Chalkdust's calypsoes" (*My Strangled City* 334).

Conclusion

The chameleon-like Sparrow, ever inventive but also ever willing to adapt to changes in taste, and the ostensibly more traditional Chalkdust, who resists the infiltration of new elements into calypso, may seem very different, but in addition to their talent for renewing calypso's capacity for satirical social commentary, they share an impulse to debate the nature of the medium, an impulse common to many, though not all, leading calypsonians. Chalkdust does this far more obviously than Sparrow, particularly through his taking on the persona of an upholder of the music's older conventions, but Sparrow very frequently reworks older kaiso forms (for example the kalinda in "Ten to One is Murder") and subjects (for example "Jean and Dinah") in a manner that demonstrates the extent to which calypso is a genre that feeds off itself. Complementary opposites though they may be, ultimately both Sparrow and Chalkdust exemplify calypso's highly self-conscious capacity for renewing itself, while adapting to changing times and mores.

NOTES

1 Rohlehr is particularly discussing the Mighty Sparrow and he comments on Sparrow's distinctive emphasis on movement and the body in performance, arguing that in his compositions "metre exists as a powerful force, which the singer cannot afford to ignore, but which he needs to conquer" and against which "he seems to be continually at war." He distinguishes this response to meter from the work of earlier calypsonians such as the Mighty Spoiler (Theophilus Philip), whom he describes as stretching words over "a frail skeleton" of meter ("Sparrow as Poet" 84).

2 The other is steelband.

3 See particularly, Selvon (*The Lonely Londoners* and *Ways of Sunlight*) and Lovelace.

4 Hill cites another definition from a Hausa–English dictionary: "An explanation expressing great feeling on hearing distressing news. *Alas! What a pity!*" (*The Trinidad Carnival* 61).

5 Along with the suggested Hausa and Spanish derivations of the term, Keith Warner cites three other possible etymologies, among them "the Carib word 'carieto', meaning a joyous song, which itself evolved into 'carieto'" (8).

6 Trinidad was a Spanish colony until 1797, when it passed into British hands.

7 See, e.g., Hill, "Calypso" 23.

8 Atilla the Hun includes the lyrics of his composition "Graf Zeppelin" in Quevedo 125–26.

9 A recording of "Louis-Schmeling Fight" by Atilla the Hun (Raymond Quevedo) and the Roaring Lion (Hubert de Leon), which deals with the first fight, is available on *The Real Calypso: 1927–1946*, Folkways Records RBF 13. Louis became a talismanic figure for black consciousness and his fights with Schmeling elicited a particularly engaged response on the part of calypsonians, who saw them in terms of black pride responding to Nazi racism. For an account of the numerous calypsoes about Joe Louis, see Rohlehr, *Calypso and Society* 196–200.

10 Lord Caresser's (Egbert Moore's), "Edward the VIII" is also included on *The Real Calypso: 1927–1946*, Folkways Records RBF 13. A story in Naipaul's *Miguel Street* takes its title, "Love Love Love Alone," from the calypso's refrain, using "Edward the VIII" for the purpose of ironic counterpoint. In the story a Portuguese woman, Mrs. Hereira, leaves the security her middle-class world to live with her lover, Toni, in Miguel Street, an act which parallels Edward VIII's abdication to marry Mrs. Simpson, but which predictably results in a very different outcome, when she leaves the street to escape Toni's beatings.

11 The subject of one of Lord Relator's (William Harris's) winning 1980 compositions, as well as Sparrow's "No Doctor No" (1957).

12 E.g. Chalkdust's "Answer to Black Power" (1971), Brother Valentino's (Anthony Emrold Phillip's) "No Revolution" (1971), and Lord

Pretender's (Aldric Farrell's) "Black Power" (1971).

13 Included on *The Real Calypso: 1927–1946.* Folkways Records RBF 13.

14 At a Welsh Arts Council conference on Walcott's work, held at Gregynog in October 1980 to mark the occasion of his being awarded the Council's International Writers Prize.

15 See Rohlehr, "Sparrow as Poet" 85; and Rohlehr, *Calypso and Society* 364–69.

16 Elsewhere Rohlehr extends the period slightly, saying that from 1956 to 1966 "Sparrow sang mainly to celebrate the faith of the predominantly African urban masses in the new political movement" ("Calypso and Politics" 7).

17 "Mighty Sparrow: King of the Caribbean" (DJB 26087). Williams repudiated requests for Patrick Solomon, Deputy Prime Minister of Trinidad from 1962 to 1966, to resign, after Solomon had allegedly requested the dropping of charges and the release from police custody of a boy, who was about to become his stepson. Solomon was Minister of Home Affairs from 1960 to 1964, when Williams, as Sparrow comments in "Get to Hell Outa Here" appointed him as Minister of External Affairs. www.nalis.gov.tt/Biography/Patrick_Solomon.html.

18 Philo's "Axe Man" calypso appears to be based on Sparrow's "Village Ram" and his calypso "Hooligans" evokes "Ten to One is Murder." Warner (135–36) likens Philo's "I Am the Ape Man not Tarzan" to Sparrow's "Congo Man."

19 "The Fourth Time Around" (Straker's Recordings GS 8886).

20 The cover for the album, "The Fourth Time Around," depicts him in this pose.

21 Cf. the use of "oil don't spoil" in "Three Blind Mice" and his use of another of Williams's often-quoted catchphrases for the title of his 1974 calypso "Massa Day Must Done." See Williams.

REFERENCES AND FURTHER READING

Brathwaite, Edward Kamau. *A History of the Voice: The Development of Nation Language in Anglophone Caribbean Poetry*. London and Port-of-Spain: New Beacon, 1984.

Brereton, Bridget. *A History of Modern Trinidad, 1783–1962.* Kingston, Port-of-Spain, and London: Heinemann, 1981.

Hill, Errol. "Calypso." *Jamaica Journal* 5.1. 1971: 23–27.

Hill, Errol. *The Trinidad Carnival: Mandate for a National Theatre*. Austin: University of Texas Press, 1972.

Liverpool, Hollis. *Rituals of Power and Rebellion: The Carnival Tradition in Trinidad and Tobago, 1763–1962.* Chicago: Research Associates School Times Publications and Frontline, 2001.

Lovelace, Earl. *The Dragon Can't Dance*. London: André Deutsch, 1979.

Naipaul, Shiva. "The Writer without a Society." In *Commonwealth*, ed. Anna Rutherford. Aarhus: Akademisk Boghandel, n.d. [1971?]. 114–23.

Naipaul, V.S. *Miguel Street*. London: André Deutsch, 1959.

Naipaul, V.S. *The Middle Passage: The Caribbean Revisited*. London: André Deutsch, 1962.

Quevedo, Raymond (Atilla the Hun). *Atilla's Kaiso: A Short History of Trinidad Calypso*. St. Augustine, Trinidad: University of the West Indies, 1983.

Pope, Alexander, *Poetical Works*. Oxford: Oxford University Press, 1978.

Rohlehr, Gordon. "Calypso and Politics." *Moko* 73. 1971: 7–8 and 14–18.

Rohlehr, Gordon. *Calypso and Society in Pre-Independence Trinidad*. Port-of-Spain: privately published, 1990.

Rohlehr, Gordon. *My Strangled City and Other Essays*. Port-of-Spain: Longman, 1992.

Rohlehr, Gordon. "Sparrow as Poet." In *David Frost Introduces Trinidad and Tobago*, ed. Michael Anthony and Andrew Carr. London: André Deutsch, 1975. 84–98.

Selvon, Samuel. *The Lonely Londoners*. London: Michael Joseph, 1956.

Selvon, Samuel. *Ways of Sunlight*. London: MacGibbon & Kee, 1957.

Smith, Keith (ed.), *Sparrow: The Legend*, Port-of-Spain: Inprint, n.d. [c. 1980].

Thieme, John. *Derek Walcott*. Manchester and New York: Manchester University Press, 1999.

Walcott, Derek. *The Fortunate Traveller*. London: Jonathan Cape, 1982.

Warner, Keith. *The Trinidad Calypso: A Study of Calypso as Oral Literature*. London: Heinemann, 1983.

Williams, Eric. *Massa Day Done*. Port-of-Spain: PNM Publishing, 1960.

32
Tragicomic Mode in Modern American Poetry

"Awful but Cheerful"

Bonnie Costello

Constance Rourke in 1931 declared humor an American characteristic, with language and character as the essential features of American humor. She noted the indigenous forms of comic voice that produced a "broad and experimental comic poetry" with a wide idiomatic source: the almanacs, the Crockett legends, the tall tales, Negro lore; and the immigrant traditions, especially Yiddish theater. Rourke heard this vital humor in the rhetorical tradition, exploited by Lincoln, that included fable, allegory, and tale grounded in metaphor. America's popular humor, she argued, constitutes a primitive poetry that keeps formal poetry free of a false gentility. She was the first to celebrate the comic spirit in Emily Dickinson's poetry—its sense of scale, its unstressed irony, its defiance of the crowd. She heard America's characteristic humor as well in the tragicomic vision of E.A. Robinson, in the Western exuberance of Vachel Lindsay ("a latter-day gamecock of the wilderness" [215]) and in the Yankee understatement of Robert Frost, with its unobtrusive, slow rhythms and self-consciousness.

Yet to a large extent our impression of modern poetry has been of something rather elegiac and earnest; certainly very little critical attention is given to humor. Modernism's imagination of catastrophe, the austere prohibitions of Imagism, the angst-ridden midcentury confessional poem, the protest poem of the 1970s, identity politics and the New Age eco-poem—all these have somewhat obscured a strong vein of humor still running through contemporary poetry in America. We tend to isolate "comic verse" as a minor genre—we think of epigrammatic wits such as Dorothy Parker and Ogden Nash, or congenial comics like Billy Collins, or language saboteurs like Charles Bernstein. But an audacious, risk-taking humor, as dark as it is "light,"

A Companion to Poetic Genre, First Edition. Edited by Erik Martiny.
© 2012 John Wiley & Sons, Ltd. Published 2012 by John Wiley & Sons, Ltd.

runs from Emily Dickinson to Charles Simic. It can be found in the greatest modern poets: Frost, Stevens, Williams, Moore, Hughes, Bishop, and Ashbery. It arises where we least expect it: in Louise Glück's complex web of human motives, in the dark metaphysics of Mark Strand. Humor remains an American "characteristic" and the comic a major poetic mode, if not a genre. We can identify its various forms and techniques, and its roots in popular traditions and American idiomatic speech.

What marks the comic element in contemporary poetry in its many forms is the way it arises, however exuberant and even joyful, within a predominantly anxious, troubled, or critical mood, especially since the Vietnam Era, which exposed so many ironies of American history. Humor often seems a last stand against hegemonic and impersonal power, or an antidote to despair. Irreverence often combines with an acknowledged impotence. Elements of the fantastic do not so much abandon the historically real as refuse to submit to official narratives. Rather than distract us, humor takes a turn with chaos and even madness, declaring its independence before the forces of repression and subjugation. More than a relief from grief and dread, it is a weapon against them. This is nothing new, of course. The tragicomic mode has a long history. The term *tragicomoedia* was originally coined by the Roman playwright Plautus (d. 184 BC), and is associated with dramatic tragedies that have comic scenes or characters, from Euripides to Shaw, Chekhov, and Beckett. Tragedy traditionally deals with human life pitted against inhuman powers, while comedy remains within a social context. But in the modern tradition, where social forces come to seem inhuman and absolute, where the sad clown supplants the tragic hero, and where a sense of tragic destiny is lost in the feeling of the absurd, these modes are often blended. In poetry the tragicomic mode can be seen in the burlesque antiheros of early modernism; it becomes central during and after World War I, especially in Surrealism and Dadaism.

Of course laughter has always existed in close proximity to anxiety, suffering, and anger, as a form of relief, defense, or subversion. In American culture, it finds a taproot in minstrelsy, blues, and jazz. But its prevalence and development in poetry since the mid-twentieth century suggests that the optimism and moral bearing we associate with earlier American comic imagination may be struggling with an increasing sense of uncertainty and vulnerability in other arenas, before impersonal, insurmountable evil, media spin, or just pervasive corruption and complacency. But "laughter is the best pesticide," as Vladimir Nabokov wrote, and American poets continue to help us clear the air. Poetry's special contribution to humor involves the foregrounding of language and form (as the revelation of character, or the tension of order and chaos, or collision of the elegant and the low). Optimism is resilient and finds energy from humor, and from the sheer inventiveness of the comic imagination, in parody, word play, madcap narrative, grotesque character portraits, arch understatement, or exuberant overstatement.

Elizabeth Bishop's hilarious "Filling Station" can be read as an argument for the value of this comic disposition within an "over-all / black translucency" (ll.4–5) where

> Some comic books provide
> the only note of color—
> of certain color.
>
> (ll.21–23)

Bishop's humor wins our allegiance through humility. She portrays a speaker whose sense of propriety and anxious distaste for anything animalistic or "dirty" (sex in particular) is reflected not only in the trimeter rhythm, but in her mixed idiomatic diction; she observes the filling station's "saucy / and greasy sons" (ll.10–11) and yet acknowledges that the "dirty dog" (l.20) is "quite comfy" in his "grease- / impregnated . . . wicker sofa" (ll.17–18). Bishop's humor has a redemptive thrust; as the speaker notices some crochet over a table on the porch of the filling station, she is hooked: the word "doily" is itself grease-impregnated. She sheds her class condescension to conclude, however sardonically: "Somebody loves us all" (l.41). Since the comic books "lie" on a "taboret" next to a "begonia" (ll.23, 25, 27), Bishop asks us to consider the similarities of comic and aesthetic form, and perhaps more specifically, jokes and poetry. That these are limited defenses is clear in the tragic "Sestina" from the same volume, where the "old grandmother" (l.2) is "reading the jokes from the almanac, / laughing and talking to hide her tears" (ll.5–6). But self-forgetful laughter is always important for Bishop, if not always salutary. It offers at least a respite from the magnetic darkness, often through an animal foil, as when the seal in "At the Fishhouses," emerges from the water "with a kind of shrug" (l.58; do seals have shoulders?). Even Robinson Crusoe's despair is tempered by the poet's distancing humor in a warped homily:

> I told myself
> 'Pity should begin at home.' So the more
> pity I felt, the more I felt at home.
>
> ("Crusoe in England," ll.62–64)

Bishop is by no means unique among midcentury poets in turning black moods into comedy. Robert Lowell, in his locked ward in "Waking the Blue," makes fun of his fellow inmates at the "house for the mentally ill" (l.10). But when he ultimately turns on himself, despair takes over: "What use is my sense of humor?" (l.11). John Berryman, in "Dream Song 76," considers, through self-directed laughter as much as through tears, "*If* life is a handkerchief sandwich" (l.6). Berryman was critical of Eliot's impersonality theory, but his humor is closest to Eliot's in its macabre, allusive burlesque, rendered through the Prufrockian persona of "huffy heavy-hearted Henry" ("Dreamsong 1," l.l), who sometimes appears in third person, and Henry's minstrel interlocutor "Mr. Bones" ("Dreamsong 4," l.18). Berryman's linguistic brilliance in *Dream Songs*, which turned dialect into poetry and syntactic delays into syncopated punchlines, intensifies more than mitigates the darkness of his vision. "Life, friends, is boring," admits Henry in "Dream Song 14" (l.1).

For Bishop, however, who, unlike Lowell, finds much use for her sense of humor, life's "untidy activity" appeared "awful but cheerful" ("The Bight," ll.35–36). Bishop is often compared, for good reason, to her mentor, Marianne Moore, but the nature of their humor is distinct. Moore knew how to convert idiomatic vitality, "plain American which cats and dogs can read," into poetry ("England" l.19). And her power of understatement and arch praise ("England / with its baby rivers and little towns… / the / criterion of suitability and convenience") is inimitable (ll.1–3). But Moore's satire, inspired by classical epigram, by the concise character portraits in La Rochefoucauld, and by the fables of La Fontaine, is less tolerant, and thereby perhaps more optimistic, as it separates itself from what it dislikes and sets up corrective mirrors, to arrogance and rapacity in particular. She makes a virtue of disdain in poems of bitingly polite retort such as "He Wrote the History Book." ("*The* book?" Moore's response to the remark is to rhyme "autograph" with "chaff" [l.5].) Bishop seems to have recognized this difference in their sensibilities in "Invitation to Miss Marianne Moore," an affectionately comic portrait of the older poet as a variety of good witch or New York bodhisattva "in a cloud of fiery pale chemicals" (3) flying "above the accidents, above the malignant movies, / the taxicabs and injustices at large" (ll.31–32). Such transcendence is rare in American poetry, and even Moore is wary of it. She is a fabulist, and man is a creature in her bestiary, an "armored animal" ("The Pangolin" l.1). But "among animals, *one* has a sense of humor" (l.81).

American modernist poets present a range of comic moods and manners. Unlike Moore, Wallace Stevens can be bawdy, designing to make "widows wince," or playful, indulging a taste for gorgeous nonsense (l.22). Yet here, too, humor is often the accompanist of darkness. Disturbing tragicomic elements stir within the apparently inane, insipid rhythms and rhymes of the limerick. In "The Pleasures of Merely Circulating" Stevens whistles in the gloom that there might be no meaning in the order of things, no "secret in skulls" (l.5). Poetic "nonsense" embraces formal order to highlight, as much as to resist, the chaos around it:

> Mrs. Anderson's Swedish baby
> Might have been German or Spanish,
> Yet that things go round and again go round
> Has rather a classical sound.

(ll.9–12)

William Carlos Williams is the most Whitmanian in his humorous celebration of the body. As he writes a sonnet to smell, or dances "naked, grotesquely / before the mirror" ("Danse Russe" ll.8–9) as the "happy genius" (l.18) of his household, or apologizes for some stolen plums, he affirms the power of the imagination to defy the forces of stagnation and withstand the black winds of the decreative process.

But contemporary comic sensibilities tend to be less confident of the strength or relevance of their audacities. This does not weaken the comic imagination, but redirects it. Humor becomes a light to help us navigate through that "over-all / black translucency" (Bishop, "Filling Station" ll.4–5). This is how Allen Ginsberg redirects the visionary optimism of Whitman within a darker, more surreal America, burdened by materialism, violence, and paranoia. Indeed, in "A Supermarket in California" Ginsberg invokes Whitman's spirit as Dante had invoked Virgil. But Whitman is now a tragicomic figure, a homeless man wandering among the produce ("what were you doing down by the watermelons? / . . . poking / among the meats in the refrigerator and eyeing the grocery boys" [ll.3–5), and later a Charon, disappearing into Lethe (ll.3–4). In Ginsberg's "America," Whitman's identification with the multitudinous nation builds to a comic mirror of madness, the explicit madness and deviance of the poet offering an inoculation against the unacknowledged, normative madness of Cold War America with its homophobia, racism, and political hysteria. Ginsberg disarms America by projecting his own zaniness, as well as his own spiritual silliness, or innocence, onto a world that is silly in its shallowness and violent bigotry, even if it is terrible in its effects. "America how can I write a holy litany in your silly mood?" (l.54). The poet's echoic voice absorbs mass-culture distortions of ethnicity—especially the Tonto-like Pidgin idiom of TV's so-called native America. As America's voice becomes madder, the alienated poet becomes the hero, offering his "strophes" for transport as an alternative to Henry Ford's automobiles, and putting his "queer shoulder to the wheel" (l.74).

Humor in Beat poetry depends on voice, and on a paratactic, maximalist style that builds in delirium. Ginsberg's fellow Beat poet Gregory Corso turns a mirror on American culture in his meditation "Marriage" ("Should I get married?" [l.1]). Pitting a celluloid image of modern courtship against his own rebellious energies, he belies the normative narratives of desire. Humor builds power through enumeration, which gradually transforms the congenial scenes of matrimony into a terrifying panopticon on private desires, provoking his rebellion:

> Niagara Falls! Hordes of us! Husbands! Wives! Flowers! Chocolates!
> All streaming into cozy hotels
> All going to do the same thing tonight
> The indifferent clerk he knowing what was going to happen
> The lobby zombies they knowing what
> The whistling elevator man he knowing
> Everybody knowing! I'd almost be inclined not to do anything!
> Stay up all night! Stare that hotel clerk in the eye!
> Screaming: I deny honeymoon! I deny honeymoon!
> running rampant into those almost climactic suites
> yelling Radio belly! Cat shovel!
> O I'd live in Niagara forever! in a dark cave beneath the Falls
> I'd sit there the Mad Honeymooner
> devising ways to break marriages, a scourge of bigamy
> a saint of divorce.

(ll.32–47)

The defiant, expansive energy and spoken-word immediacy of Beat poetry can be heard in recent jazz-inspired poets who remind us that new forms of political correctness are as restrictive of human feeling and connection as old ones. In "Woofer (When I Consider the African-American)" Terrance Hayes offers a long, unpunctuated riff on group identity in which the breathless, digressive form is itself an image of the boundless, unpredictable and resilient energy of the American melting pot. In this poem a comic but confident and potent voice displaces that of the angry black man. He operates within the painful paradoxes of American racial history, but he turns stereotyping into a vivid parade and gets the last laugh in the "great historical relay" (l.57), propelling us, with "blood filled baton" (l.57) toward a post-racial reality:

> I have been cursed, broken hearted, stunned, frightened
> and bewildered, but when I consider the African-American
> I think not of the tek nines of my generation deployed
> by madness or that we were assigned some lousy fate
> when God prescribed job titles at the beginning of Time
> or that we were too dumb to run the other way
> when we saw the wide white sails of the ships
> since given the absurd history of the world, everyone
> is a descendant of slaves (which makes me wonder
> if outrunning your captors is not the real meaning of Race?)
>
> (ll.42–51)

While one direction of modern humor is toward the maximalist, expansive free-verse rhythms developed by the Beats and executed so well by Hayes, another is toward powerful closure and compression, with the surprise and inevitability that rhyme and meter can produce. We tend to associate insistent meter and rhyme with light verse and light verse itself with trivial amusement. But the dark heart of modern American humor is audibly beating in these forms. Ogden Nash, the midcentury master of light verse, was also a latter-day fabulist, and often turned his cartoonlike imagination to the limits of human power and will, as in "The Termite":

> Some primal termite knocked on wood
> And tasted it, and found it good,
> And that is why your Cousin May
> Fell through the parlor floor today.
>
> (ll.1–4)

Robert Frost's late end-stopped, triple-rhyming "Provide, Provide" imitates aphoristic wisdom-turned-advertising-lingo, while twisting it to echo a sinister, self-deceiving materialism:

> Better to go down dignified
> With boughten friendship at your side
> Than none at all. Provide, provide!
>
> (ll.19–21)

The ancient epigram, with its swift and inescapable thrust, is a potent tool of satiric portraiture, and continues to serve modern poetry, not just to tickle the funny bone but to prod the stubborn ego or attack complacent or hypocritical values, as in J.V. Cunningham's "This Humanist whom no beliefs constrained / Grew so broad-minded he was scatter-brained" (1–2). The humor of the epigram thrives on the grotesque exaggeration and metaphoric depiction of traits; it retains its classical focus on salient attributes rather than local details. Theodore Roethke's "Academic" is a strong example and a kind of ante-epitaph:

> The stethoscope tells what everyone fears:
> You're likely to go on living for years,
> With a nurse-maid waddle and a shop-girl simper,
> And the style of your prose growing limper and limper.
>
> (ll.1–4)

Minimalist humor generally favors the epigram over the free-verse imagist poem, perhaps for the strong sense of closure and irrefutability that rhyme and meter provide.

In America the strongest tradition of formalist wit comes not from poets but from songwriters—Tin Pan Alley lyricists such as Cole Porter and Lorenz Hart. Porter drew on the new openness and jostling of high and low in the American cultural landscape, using rhyme to heighten incongruity: "You're an old Dutch master, / You're Mrs. Astor, / You're Pepsodent" (Porter, *"You're the Top"* refrain 5) or "You're a Bendell bonnet / You're a Shakespeare sonnet / You're Mickey Mouse" (refrain 1). Hart introduced grotesque elements into the romantic scene: "When love congeals / It soon reveals / The faint aroma of performing seals" (refrain 2).

American postmodern poets have often created comic effects by combining maximalist and paratactic impulses with elaborate, elegant fixed form. Bishop's "joking voice" (16) in the villanelle "One Art" adds a tragicomic element to a form best known in modern poetry for its elegiac turn. The sestina, another revived form, enhances humor's anticipation and timing, and gives an aesthetic shape to psychological obsessions and repetition compulsions. The extreme control of these forms can also suggest impersonal and obscure rules governing the vicissitudes of experience. John Ashbery's "Farm Implements and Rutabagas in a Landscape" is probably the most famous example of a comic sestina; it creates high/low incongruity by adapting the elaborate French form as a verbal analogy to the frames of a Popeye comic book sequence, with stanza breaks suggesting gaps in the frames. A more recent example of comic formal virtuosity comes from Albert Goldbarth, a recent recipient of the Mark Twain Poetry Award from the Poetry Foundation for his contribution to humor in American poetry. Goldbarth's sprawling style, full of anecdotal detours and elaborations, lends itself to free verse, but like Ashbery he also sometimes uses fixed forms as counterpoint to these maximalist gestures. In "Sestina: As There Are Support Groups, There Are Support Words" the rational, predictable structures of the scientist with his international vocabulary meet the word-bending energies of the poet, who is anxious about the direction science can sometimes take. Goldbarth mixes up the language of science, the language of poetry, and other "foreign" languages (the language of sex, somewhere in between) to produce a humor both linguistic and cultural. Alexander von Humboldt, the nineteenth-century scientist-explorer, provides the epigraph from which Goldbarth spins his web of words:

> The name of his native country pronounced on a distant shore could not please the ears of a traveller more than hearing the words "nitrogen," "oxidation of iron" and "hygrometer."

The poem begins: "When visiting a distant (and imponderable) shire,/one longs to hear the cry "Hygrometer!" As the poem continues, the recycled words ("shire," "hygrometer," "fair," "nitrogen," "translation," "siren") take in an increasingly disturbing history that includes Holocaust displacement, the atom bomb, and the wild assimilations of contemporary culture.

> Though she's for-
> tunate in having a lover who's CEO at Hygrometer,
>
> Potassium, Klein & Wong: it helps to pay the "hygrometer
> man" when he knocks at the door. I won't say that they fear
> this guy exactly, but he's a major badass nitrogen-
> sucking cyberwired ninja-kicking shitheel (or, translation:
> call him Sir). It makes one pine for a land where the birds all choir in
> sweetly trilling melodies on a flower-scented shore . . .
>
> (ll.29–36)

Humor here is not primarily situational, but wrung out of the tuneful palate that mixes high and low, science and art, black English and Yiddish, bureaucratic lingo and lyrical trill. In combination with the strictures of a traditional form such as the sestina, the unruly progress of language makes a powerful counterpoint.

The New York School—more a coterie than a school, really—made humor an essential element of its poetic project, reacting against what it perceived as a somber academicism in the mainstream. While combining Whitman's expansive parataxis with the irrational disjunctions of Dada and Surrealism, the New York School did not reject traditional forms. It embraced them in a mutinous mood, as equally valid, or arbitrary, as free verse. Like the Beats, New York School poets see humor as a defense against the authoritarian, rationalist, and bureaucratic aspects of culture, and draw on popular culture in an assault on elitism. Unlike the Beats, they approach art in a medium of play more than protest, or of play as protest. New York School poets employ parody as a major response to both literary and social convention, but without reference to any stable ideology of its own. While these poets, most of them intimately involved with the art world, revive modernism's value of art for art's sake, they embrace the anti-poetic and resist high/low distinctions, mixing the imagery, discourse, and experience of pop culture with high cultural references, forms, and tradition. In a traditional formalist poet such as James Merrill this indecorum carries a touch of irony and even condescension, but for the New York School poets it expresses the medium in which they move, its effect not so much democratic as irreverent, mysterious, and hyper-real. Narrative, which New Criticism resisted in favor of lyric pattern and tension, reemerges in their work, but with a digressive, improvisatory, paratactic thrust and media-drenched dream logic. A rhythm of abrupt entry and exit supplants the fictions of beginning, middle, and end. Voice is strong but severed from selfhood and interiority, in explicit rejection of confessional poetry's psychological probing. This is postmodern humor: without a center or mythos, open to chance, riding on a surface of heterogeneous discourse and imagery, not firmly positioned or directed but bemused and startled by its own adventures. Romantic lyric mood itself becomes an ambivalent object of self-conscious humor. Yet while avoiding ideology in favor of *jouissance* ("the sheer joy of it"), New York School poetry exposes and pitches itself against the repressive and violent forces of culture, and against the pastoral myths and icons that serve those forces. New York School humor stands not as the inverted mirror of American madness, protesting what it reflects, but as a voice within it, less angry and judgmental than perplexed, with a mixture of dread, exuberance, and amusement.

"Ah nuts!" (l.1) is the colloquial opening of Frank O'Hara's elegantly titled "Les Luths" (the lutes), immediately establishing a voice warmly irreverent toward the French vocative lyric. Dada-like incongruities abound; his poem "Today" begins: "Oh! Kangaroos, sequins, chocolate sodas!" O'Hara, the magnetic figure at the center of the New York School, often celebrates the pure pleasure of poetry. But he also produced a new kind of existential poetry in which the terror and anxiety underlying modern life are not so much evaded, addressed, or cured as incorporated into a tragicomic vision that refuses to moan or mourn. With death around every corner, the poet-Flâneur spins through the city like a top, veering off unpredictably. That unpredictability is itself part of the comedy, as in a Marx Brothers movie. O'Hara's world is full of icons—collapsible pop icons like Lana Turner and cardboard political icons like Washington—whose unreality plays comically against the poet's invented experiential voice.

O'Hara's humor depends on a variety of tactics in "Poem (Lana Turner Has Collapsed!), but central to the poem is the "collapsing" convergence of life and the movies in a campy evocation of a newspaper headline followed by the apparent non sequitur of the poet's personal life, which parodies a Lana Turner plot. The momentum of the gerunds ("trotting," "raining," "snowing," "hailing," "hailing," "snowing," "raining," "acting") collides with the past perfect of the newspaper headline, provoking the imperative "oh Lana Turner we love you get up" (l.16). The poem parodies the "what were you doing when" relationship to world-shaking events, as well as the public's appetite for celebrity news and vicarious living. Laughing through disaster is an ageless comic disposition. O'Hara makes fun of the Hollywood clichés of lovers seeking each other through natural disasters, which he turns to unnatural disaster in the image of traffic and later of the orgiastic excesses of his life. Timing and incontrovertible but unpredictable logic is an essential element of humor even within the random feel of his poems, as imperfect tenses bump up against finalities.

Death is less of a presence in the comic poetry of Kenneth Koch, O'Hara's most avowed disciple in the New York School. Though catastrophes abound, they tend to be more slapstick than tragic. Koch shares O'Hara's affability and irreverence and joins it with elements of Jewish parable, proverb, and wit. He is best known for his grotesque parodies, as in "Mending Sump" or "Variations on a Theme by William Carlos Williams," as much comic tributes as iconoclastic gestures, their humor built on the exaggeration of calamity, but also on the sense that our problems and conflicts are not as containable as the traditional pastoral lyric might suggest. Koch brings out the sadistic element in Williams's "This Is Just to Say":

> We laughed at the hollyhocks together
> and then I sprayed them with lye.
> Forgive me. I simply do not know what I am doing.
>
> (ll.4–6)

Self-mockery, and parody of artistic posturing more broadly, are favorite devices, though behind them lies a profound belief in the value of art:

> Athena gave Popeye a Butterfinger filled with stars
> Is the kind of poetry Z and I used to stuff in jars
>
> When we took a walk he was afraid
> of the dogs who came in parade
> To sniffle at the feet
> Of two of the greatest poets of the age.
>
> ("Days and Nights" ll.96–101)

Koch's voice is strongly colloquial and anti-academic, not at all elevated. But it often lifts into lyrical reverie, as in "One Train May Hide Another" where comic interludes leaven a somber meditation in the wisdom tradition. For all his chicanery, there is a practical, self-correcting side to Koch's humor: though he does celebrate an unconscious or irrational letting go as essential to the art of poetry, he does not like the absurd, which to his mind assumes an underlying order that has been disrupted. Koch instead sees the imagination as a fecund creator of orders even as it subjects them to constant change and imbalance. One finds more bawdy, surreal, demonic, and cockeye humor in Ron Padgett, a contemporary of Koch who is sometimes associated with the New York School.

Koch's legendary teaching nurtured an impressive second generation of serio-comic poets including David Lehman, Mitch Sisskind, David Shapiro, and Aaron Fogel. In

David Lehman's parody of Ezra Pound's "with usura" Canto XLV we find a direct link to Koch and his imitations of Williams and Frost.

> Picasso came not by tenure
> nor Charlie Parker. With tenure hath only the mediocre
> a sinecure unto death. Unto death I say!
> WITH TENURE
> Nature is constipated the sap doesn't flow
> With tenure the classroom is empty
> *et in academia ego*
> the ketchup is stuck in the bottle
> the letter goes unanswered the bell doesn't ring.
>
> (ll.20–28)

Aaron Fogel, while perhaps the least known, is the most versatile and inventive poet of this group, his straightforward, colloquial voice conveying both a rebellion against claims of class power and cultural authority, and a fascination with the mystical interventions of chance. In "The Man Who Never Heard of Frank Sinatra" he turns Koch's comic parable toward an O'Hara-style pop icon, but adds an outsider-artist's suspicion of fame. While convention might seize on a chance meeting with a celebrity, Fogel's view of chance takes the darker turn of missing what everyone else sees, and this itself becomes a piece of "luck":

> Once, just as he was about to hear the name Frank Sinatra
> A plane flew overhead—he was fifty-five years old—his hearing
>
> A little more impaired. He had heard of Humphrey Bogart,
> Of Elizabeth Taylor, of Walter Cronkite, and of perhaps a hundred
> Forty thousand other celebrities' names by the time he died,
>
> And yet he had never heard of Frank Sinatra. The Greeks had
> That famous saying, "The luckiest man is he who was never born."
> Which is kind of gloomy, but I think they were wrong.
>
> The luckiest man is he who never heard of Frank Sinatra.
>
> (ll.11–19)

That interest in the liberating aspect of negative chance and sabotage of intentional order can be heard in another Fogel poem, "Printer's Error," where the laboring printer, in a deathbed testimonial, pledges an oath to the sanctity of error:

> Therefore I,
> Frank Steinman,
> typographer
> for thirty-seven years,

and cooperative Master
of the Holliston Guild
eight years,
being of sound mind and body
though near death
urge the abolition
of all editorial work
whatsoever
and manumission
from all textual editing
to leave what was
as it was, and
as it became,
except insofar as editing
is itself an error, and

therefore also divine.

(ll.64–83)

Fogel's humor, whether he is tracking printers' errors or finding anagrams of the Torah in frog ponds, involves the sabotage of authority and its norms, and the collision of intension with chance.

John Ashbery, the most renowned figure to emerge from the New York School, is also the one whose humor is hardest to characterize. Ashbery's unruly, subversive spirit, and his mixture of high and low cultural references and idioms, links him to O'Hara and Koch. But in his derailed narratives and fantasy elements there is a sense of mystery and uncertainty, especially within the everyday, that unsettles the reader by its protean or ambiguous tone. The few who comment on Ashbery's humor have associated the serio-comic doubleness of Ashbery's work with low-key camp. This classification accounts for a great deal of the poet's style—his mix of avant-garde and kitsch, his deadpan wit, his "balancing act of daily quandary and epistemological crisis," his deranged clichés, mock certainties and uncertainties, his "half parodic self-reflective turns," his "drag performance" in such poems as "Variations Calypso and Fugue on a Theme by Ella Wheeler Wilcox" (in *Selected Poems*). But the camp designation gives too little emphasis to this sense of mystery in Ashbery, that goes well beyond the double mirror of cultural critique, and draws more directly from Romantic and post-Romantic sources such as Baudelaire, Kleist, and Hofmanstahl. In fact, many of Ashbery's poems begin in camp gestures and move out into deeper interrogations where not only social but also broader existential and epistemological challenges confront us. If these challenges are leavened by campy humor they are not so easily dismissed. Rather, the incongruities of his work produce an effect of the uncanny.

Ashbery's humor derives partly from the belatedness of visionary aims and his own unsettled place in lyric tradition: "The dentist moon hovered by the wire: *Sure / look in thy heart and write. But don't throw foreign articles*" ("Kamarinskaya" ll.14–15, in *Notes from the Air*) Indeed, tragi-comedy may come in part from the persistent activity of the disempowered imagination. The poems situate themselves in states of ennui that become thresholds for reverie; but these lead not to transcendence, only to alcoves within the flatness of modern experience. Ashbery's humor also reveals how habituated we are to extreme states. In "Elephant Visitors" (in *Notes from the Air*), the elephant in the room becomes part of the furniture: "Here, try the gloom in *this* room. / I think you'll find it more comfortable" (ll.8–9). "Laughing Gravy" (in *Notes from the Air*) begins:

> The crisis has just passed.
> Uh-oh, here it comes again,
> looking for someone to blame itself on, you, I.
>
> (ll.1–3)

But Ashbery's humor is not merely deflationary. These alcoves remind us that strangeness exists within the ordinary, and that one major role of humor is the discovery of the uncanny. Metaphor and simile serve this function throughout Ashbery's work, yoking the romantic to the quotidian, intertwining nature not only with art but with the plastic textures of the contemporary world, as in "Retablo" (in *Notes from the Air*):

> Probably the rain never got loose
> for all you know, but it did, it was like cellophane noodles escaping
> from a slashed envelope.
>
> (ll.38–41)

Here, as elsewhere, the disjunctions of scale, context, and substance both amuse us by the campy displacement of the real with the artificial, and transform two commonplace images by conjoining them.

If *Selected Poems* suggests Ashbery's gradual move away from early surrealist impulses, *Selected Later Poems* indicates some return to these methods. Indeed, *Hotel Lautréamont* (1992) alludes to both the surrealist writer named in the title and to the surrealist artist Joseph Cornell, whose collage boxes he often called hotels. Consider the opening of "Notes from the Air" with its false certainties and resonant uncertainties, its matter-of-fact treatment of exotic images and its dreamlike approach to household objects.

> A yak is a prehistoric cabbage: of that, at least, we may be sure.
> But tell us, sage of the solarium, why is that light
> Still hidden back there, among house-plants and rubber sponges?
>
> (ll.1–3)

While Ashbery curtails Romantic visionary power and reduces melodrama to soap-opera formulations, the sheer power of his comic invention offers an alternative to the sublimities it mocks. ". . . By an Earthquake" begins: "A hears by chance a familiar name, and the name involves a riddle of the past. / B, in love with A receives an unsigned letter in which the writer states that she is the mistress of A and begs B not to take him away from her. (ll.1–2). This could be a storyboard for daytime TV. But as the players proliferate, with A's and B's turning into A-8's and W's, the proverbial plot thickens and we enter a bizarre and comically disturbing course of events, where TV pastoral mixes with gothic fantasy: "Lassie and Rex tussle together politely; Lassie, wounded, is forced to limp home" (l.31). Finally, "Ildebrando constructs a concealed trap, and a person near to him, Gwen, falls into the trap and cannot escape" (l.62). We are reminded, at each turn, of the machine of narrative, which sometimes drops a stitch as it weaves a plot: "No one remembers old Everett, who is left to shrivel in a tower" (l.60). Within the system of narrative, as formulaic as a sestina or pantoum, the poet releases the uncanny; indeed, the system itself takes on a magical momentum.

That sense of uncanny laughter also pervades the work of Charles Simic, though in a compressed, minimalist style. The poets of the New York School tend to find their humor in paratactic excess of Whitmanian exuberance turned bizarre and mannerist. But Charles Simic develops comic brevity in a vein closer to that of Emily Dickinson, or Dickinson mixed with Dada, in his use of enigma and incongruity. While he joins New York School poets in making humor central to his art, he achieves a more terrifying voice, a "Voice at 3 a.m": "who put canned laughter / Into my crucifixion scene?" (ll.1–2). In Simic's black humor, metaphysics intersects with history, and the violence of history infiltrates the most ordinary objects. The catastrophes in Simic's world are all too real, the unseen, impersonal powers that threaten our existence indefatigable and, however enlarged and abstracted by the psyche, historical in their basis. Yet humor provides a psychic defense, a David of imagination against a mechanistic and sinister Goliath. His chief tool is the inversion of scale. Drawing on folklore and fable, Simic identifies with the small irritants—the bugs, the mice, those "teeny Dadaists" that wage a nonstop war against sublime power ("Non-Stop War with Bugs" l.7).

Simic approaches history not through narrative but through imagery; the everyday is infused with traumatic memory and anxiety, becoming totemic or demonic. But there is as much delight as terror in Simic's humorous inventions and discoveries of the extraordinary within the ordinary: "there are tasty little zeros / in the peanut dish tonight" ("Autumn Sky" ll.17–18). Like Joseph Cornell, Simic specializes in the marginal, shabby world of fantasy, a source of both humor and mystery: the world of broken dolls and back-alley sorcerers, of gag toys and carnivals, children's literature and folklore—where he finds the vestiges of the fantastic and reanimates them with the metaphysics of the ephemeral. The open artifice of these dream-worlds of shyster-shamans contrasts with the naturalized myths of official reality. "Country Fair" presents this inconsequential sideshow world as a mirror of our own freakish natures. Like Ashbery, Simic often works with stock plots and images, foregrounding rhetoric and generating strangeness within the familiar. A "cold dark night" gives the fair a stock *Twilight Zone* effect, but a freakish dog's extra legs, flapping behind him, which change nothing in the toss–and–return conditioned routine, suggest the excess of the imagination. Is the six-legged dog a figure then for the drunken couple and superfluous poet—the extra legs that have little use and just flap behind representing the observer's awareness? These are not the legs of narrative, which never gets off the ground at all—man kisses girl, dog fetches stick—but of imagination, which flaps in the air.

Charles Simic was U.S. Poet Laureate in 2007–2008, and it is perhaps a testament to the American character that most of our Poet Laureates have been humorists. Billy Collins, Laureate from 2001 to 2003, represents American humor in its popular, comic mode. Much of what he writes can be classified as contemporary "light verse," as in "The Golden Years":

> All I do these drawn-out days
> is sit in my kitchen at Pheasant Ridge
> where there are no pheasants to be seen
> and last time I looked, no ridge.

The persistent, sometimes same-word rhymes (ridge/ridge/bridge/midge/ledge) reinforce the sense of a locked destiny as the poem continues, but the comedy doesn't peer into the abyss, or rage against it. The speaker asks us to side with him in his bemused smirk at the irony of persistent American pastoral in a parking-lot landscape. Collins's wit frequently depends on drawn-out jokes. Here he enfolds all the place names into the narrative—"Quail Falls," "Fox Run," "Smokey Ledge," "Pheasant Ridge"— animating the images in order to show how dead they really are. But Collins is not really on any ridge at all—he's well entrenched in the middlebrow predicament he mocks.

The Laureate who followed Collins, Louise Glück, offers a more potent, and more searing, humor, in which the major motive is truth-telling. It is perhaps surprising that a poet like Glück, whose early work echoes Plath, should make humor a central part of her art. This is humor accomplished through the painful and difficult work of self-distancing, in which there are no victors. *Meadowlands*, which she published just before she became Laureate, uses Homer's *Odyssey* as the basis for a satire on marriage. Glück announces her tragicomic intent in her epigraph, which "chooses music" from two moods: "Figaro and Tannhauser." In *Meadowlands* we see Glück drawing on many of the classic devices of good joke-telling: the animal fable or animal foil, cross talk, parody, riddle, understatement, ironic juxtaposition, deflating incongruities of low and high motive and subject matter, logical swerves, suspension of the punchline. Again character-type is the core of this humor, with various contemporary portraits drawn as Homeric figures; the wife Penelope (her mixed motives); the sorceress Circe (who understands that men are pigs); the son Telemachus (who, in "Telemachus' Detachment" sees his parents' predicament as at once "heartbreaking," "insane," and "very funny" [ll.5–7]).

Glück's humor curtails the self-circulation of the lyric, creating distance and perspective against the narcissism and self-pity of the speaker. Humor puts lyric in a social dimension, pitting a single point of view against that of others with their various narratives and motives. In her recent work the distance is very great, even majestic in its stoicism, with an element of Yeats's tragic gaiety. In this perspective the suffering ego has long since been ejected in favor of a timeless, tragi-comic remembrance. When memory provides close-ups, then, they are offered in a dispassionate mood, by a voice dark in what it reveals, but beyond hurt, and stoically amused. As the title "Prism," from *Averno*, suggests, Glück is building multiple points of view into the lyric, but much of the humor comes from memory of a child being initiated into an adult world; the motive of accurate memory leads to ironic restatement:

> When I was a child, I suffered from insomnia.
> . . . Did I say "suffered"? . . .
> . . . better "suffered" than "preferred to live with the dog."
>
> (ll.5–8)

The art of juxtaposition allows Glück's humor of motives to assert itself in understatement:

> "You girls," my mother said, "should marry
> someone like your father."
>
> That was one remark. Another was,
> "There is no one like your father."
>
> (ll.1–4)

In Glück's recent poetry, a very austere, minimalist vision is tempered by humor, even as it belies romantic myths and false consolations. In *Averno*, the end of "A Myth of Devotion" is darkly funny. Hades

> wants to say *I love you, nothing can hurt you*
> but he thinks
> this is a lie, so he says in the end
> *you're dead, nothing can hurt you*
>
> (ll.42–45)

Glück makes a lyric music out of this stark humor of truth-telling and self-correction.

There is an element of detachment and resignation in Glück's late humor, but the audacity and optimism of American humor prevail in another Laureate, Robert Pinsky. He nudges the popular imagination away from its complacencies and toward its rebellions. Suspicious of his own dexterity, he praises in "Other Hand" (in *Gulf Music*) the awkward "lefty" (l.1), "the lesser twin" (l.9). "Comparison with his brother prevents him / From putting forth his best effort" (ll.12–13). Yet

possibly his trembling touch,
As less merely adept and confident,
Is subtly the more welcome of the two.

(ll.17–19)

The poet imagines an afterlife in which "the last shall be first" and "the yoke of dexterity finally laid to rest" (l.27). Pinsky applies humor, especially ethnic humor, where it is most needed, not only as shock treatment but as a healing power, creating a bond among men; for humor provides a lens through which all may look, without flinching, into the face of death. Pinsky's elegy to Elliott Gilbert, "Impossible to Tell" (in *The Figured Wheel*), is more than a eulogy to a great teller of jokes. It is a tribute to jokes and poetry at once, to their power to resist despair, and to their universality (however local and ethnic in detail). Jokes and poetry are inroads into a human condition otherwise "impossible to tell." The poem builds on the conventions of the elegy—evoking the muse (his name here is Basho), recalling memories of the deceased, bearing witness to the swirl and fall of leaves that mark the transience of all living things. Yet within this ancient frame Pinsky introduces—not once but several times—another ancient and universal practice, "the old form of the rude, full-scale joke" (l.5). The joke, Pinsky knows, requires the presence of a human voice—"impossible to tell in writing" (l.17). ("The joking voice, a gesture / I love," Bishop recalls in the elegiac "One Art" [ll.16–17]) Yet by calling up the memory of a great storyteller, Pinsky continues another tradition, the invocation to the deceased. "Arise and breathe!" (l.61). As Pinksy recalls the dead joke-teller's telling of a joke about the dead, about a tiny rabbi whose increasingly bizarre rituals fail to revive a corpse, they all live for us on the page, and death itself is suspended. The punchline: "'Hoo boy!' he says, 'Now that's what I call really dead'" (l.96). But the poem is not over. It is the poet's turn to tell a joke, told to him by a journalist, and this threaded telling becomes a form of afterlife. "It is the Belgian Army / Joke come to life" (ll.143–44) in a South African context. And the poem, which had been an elegy to a particular American Jew, now emerges as the story it had also been all along, of the power of humor and art to unite us in our common mortality, that "Allegiance to a state impossible to tell" (l.168).

My argument throughout this essay has been that contemporary poetry has increasingly tilted humor toward, rather than away from, the bleakest aspects of life. It has found a home in elegy, amidst violent history, within an "over-all / black translucency" (ll.4–5). It shines a dark light into bright complacency and radiates the darkness with the brilliance of its invention. Humor in contemporary poetry often expresses impotence in the midst of insane and boundless evil, but also refuses to sanctify the power that overwhelms it. Such desperate humor finds its apology in a poem by Heather McHugh, whose comic inventiveness serves not only the need for imaginative release from hostile orders in linguistic play, but also for an unflinching scrutiny and exposure of hypocrisy, evil and suffering. McHugh can write a very high level of light verse, as in the hilarious elegy "Half Border Half Lab" ("Customs and chemistry / made a name for themselves / and it was Spot" [ll.1–3]). But "The Woman Who Laughed on

Calvary" announces the high stakes of the humorists—when the overwhelming pressure from without provokes a pressure from within:

> Smilers, smirkers, chucklers, grinners,
> platitudinizers, euphemists: it wasn't you
>
> I emulated there, in that
> Godawful place. What kind
> of face
>
> to put on it? How simple
> is a simon's sign? To my mind
> laughter's not the mark of pleasure, not
> a pleasantry that spread; instead
>
> it's intimate with sheer
> delirium: spilt brain
> on split lip, uncontainable
> interiority—

(ll.1–13)

REFERENCES AND FURTHER READING

Ashbery, John. *Hotel Lautréamont*. New York: Alfred A. Knopf, 1992.

Ashbery, John. *Notes from the Air: Selected Later Poems*. New York: HarperCollins, 2007.

Ashbery, John. *Selected Poems*. New York: Viking Penguin, Inc. 1985.

Berryman, John. *77 Dream Songs*. New York: Farrar, Straus & Giroux, 1964.

Bishop, Elizabeth. *Poems, Prose, and Letters*. New York: Library of America, 2008.

Collins, Billy. *Ballistics: Poems*. Random House, 2008.

Corso, Gregory. "Marriage," in *Essential Pleasures*, ed. Robert Pinsky. New York: Norton, 2009. 442–45.

Cunningham, J.V. *Collected Poems and Epigrams*. London: Faber & Faber, 1971.

Fogel, Aaron. *The Printer's Error*. Oxford, OH: Miami University Press, 2001.

Frost, Robert. *Collected Poems, Prose, and Plays*. New York: Library of America, 1995.

Ginsberg, Allen. *Howl*. San Francisco: City Lights, 1956.

Glück, Louise. *Averno*. New York: Farrar, Straus & Giroux, 2006.

Glück, Louise. *Meadowlands*. New York: Ecco Press, 1996.

Goldbarth, Albert. *Saving Lives*. Columbus: Ohio State University Press, 2001.

Hart, Lorenz. "I Wish I Were in Love Again," in *Reading Lyrics*, ed. Robert Gottlieb and Robert Kimball. New York: Pantheon, 2000. 201–02.

Hayes, Terrence. "Woofer (When I Consider the African American)," in *Essential Pleasures*, ed. Robert Pinsky. New York: Norton, 2009. 272–73.

Koch, Kenneth. *The Collected Poems of Kenneth Koch*. New York: Knopf, 2005.

Lehman, David. *Operation Memory*. Princeton: Princeton University Press, 1990.

Lowell, Robert. *Collected Poems*. New York: Farrar, Straus & Giroux, 2007.

McHugh, Heather. *Hinge & Sign: Poems, 1968–1993*. Middletown: Wesleyan University Press, 1994.

Moore, Marianne. *Complete Poems.* New York: Viking, 1981.

Nash, Ogden. *Selected Verse of Ogden Nash.* New York: Modern Library, 1945.

O'Hara, Frank. *Selected Poems of Frank O'Hara.* New York: Knopf, 2008.

Pinsky, Robert. *The Figured Wheel: New and Collected Poems, 1966–1996.* New York: Farrar, Straus & Giroux, 1996.

Pinsky, Robert. *Gulf Music.* New York: Farrar, Straus & Giroux, 2007.

Porter, Cole. "You're the Top," in *Reading Lyrics*, ed. Robert Gottlieb and Robert Kimball. New York: Pantheon, 2000. 125–27.

Roethke, Theodore. *Collected Poems.* Garden City: Doubleday, 1966.

Rourke, Constance. *American Humor: A Study of the National Character* (1931). Garden City: Doubleday Anchor, 1953.

Simic, Charles. *The Voice at 3:00 A.M.: Selected Late and New Poems.* Orlando: Harcourt Brace, 2003.

Stevens, Wallace. *Collected Poetry & Prose.* New York: Library of America, 1997.

Williams, William Carlos. *Collected Poems of William Carlos Williams: Volume I, 1909–1939*, ed. Walton Litz and Christopher MacGowan. New York: New Directions, 1986.

33
Parnassus in Pillory

Satirical Verse

Todd Nathan Thompson

Though satirical verse is most often associated with classical Rome and neoclassical England, there is a longstanding and still-vibrant global tradition of satirical poetry. In fact, poetry from its earliest origins has been inextricably tied to satire, from Arabian satirical battle-chants to medieval Irish poets' satires (which were purported to raise welts on the faces of their victims) to Scotch *flyting* (a bantering exchange of satirical insults between two poets) to the *estrifs* produced by Provençal troubadours (Elliott, "Satire" 1114; Heath-Stubbs 1). According to satire theorist Robert C. Elliott, the roots of neoclassical and even modern satire draw on

> "primitive" beliefs which have had remarkable vitality throughout the entire history of satirical literature. The principal belief, of course, is that satire kills (or at least causes death), that magical power inheres in the denunciatory and derisive words of a poet whose function is to blame as well as to praise. In obscure ways these beliefs exert influence even today.
>
> (*Power of Satire* 47)

Indeed, one can trace the role that well-crafted poetic insults play in contemporary poetry slams and hip-hop songs to these ancient practices. In this sense, despite satirists' traditional denial of their own vitriolic intentions and capabilities, satirical poetry—whether articulated in Eskimo word-duels (Elliott, "Satire" 1114), neoclassical heroic couplets, or postmodern, Rabelaisian free verse—maintains a certain derisive power to denounce social ills, blast literary enemies, and question or repudiate political and aesthetic conventions.

A Companion to Poetic Genre, First Edition. Edited by Erik Martiny.

Satire's subversive energies make it notoriously resistant to precise generic definition. Critics have long argued over whether or not particular individual works should
be called satires, not to mention whether satire itself should be categorized as a separate genre or as a mode or sub-genre deployed within existing genres. One critic has
argued that a paradox of satire is that, "in apparently having no particular form, it
transforms such miscellany into a generic structure" (Guilhamet 17), in essence creating a new genre from the genres that it deforms through parody. Formal variation is
certainly inherent in satire, as a brief look at its etymology makes clear. The word
satire derives from the Latin *satura*, which means "'a medley' full of different things"
(*Oxford Classical Dictionary* 953); *satura lanx* was a ritual dish composed of first fruits
of various kinds and served during Roman harvest celebrations.

The Oxford Classical Dictionary defines satire (by its own admission "loosely") as "a
piece of verse, or prose mingled with verse, intended both to entertain, and to improve
society by exposing to derision and hatred the follies, vices, and crimes of men" (953).
For the purposes of this chapter, I will define satirical verse broadly, as a literature of
attack (however genial) composed in verse. Such attack is often but not always humorous or ironic in tone and directed against a specific target: a social, political, religious,
or literary transgression, or a personal or national enemy. I will delineate four separate
(but necessarily, at times, overlapping) modes of satirical poetry: 1) inter-textual literary satire, 2) satirical burlesque verse, 3) satirical epigrams, and 4) satirical poetry in
the genre-mixing Menippean tradition. For each mode I will briefly articulate the
classical tradition and its formal and thematic evolutions, then identify and analyze
some modern adaptations (or deformations) of that tradition.

Literary Satire

The origins of formal verse satire are generally ascribed to ancient Rome. Indeed, it
is recognized as "the only literary form created by the Romans" (*Oxford Classical
Dictionary* 953). Though Greek literature does feature some mocking abuse, Roman
authors—most famously Lucilius, Horace, Persius, and Juvenal—developed a satirical
verse tradition with first-person speakers who mocked contemporary moral and social
foibles in a fixed metrical form, usually dactylic hexameter. Subsequent generations
of poets all over the world have translated, updated, and otherwise refigured these
poets to fit their own societies. Several times and places have been particularly congenial to revivals of the Roman verse satire tradition. In Renaissance France, for
instance, a group of poets called the "Pléiade"—led by Joachim Du Bellay, whose
"Poète courtisan" (1559) satirizes a naïve courtier—rejected native medieval models
for Roman ones (Duval 81–82). In eighteenth-century France, Nicolas Boileau-
Despréaux wrote satires imitating Horace, Juvenal, and Persius. But it was in
Restoration England—sometimes known as the Age of Satire and which, like Augustan
Rome, featured relative political stability but a sense of moral decline—where the
classical tradition was most prominently reinvigorated. This revival began with John

Dryden, whose "Discourse Concerning the Original and Progress of Satire" (1693)—
which prefaces translations of Juvenal and Persius—analyzes Horace, Juvenal, and
Persius in order to formulate a definition of satire. Samuel Johnson adapted Juvenal's
third satire in *London* (1738) and his tenth satire in "The Vanity of Human Wishes"
(1749). Alexander Pope completed a free-from translation of Horace in *Imitations of
Horace* (1733–38), replacing Horace's allusions to contemporary Rome with references
to eighteenth-century London. Romantic poet Lord George Gordon Byron in turn
championed Pope and Augustan literary values, and composed *Hints from Horace*
(1811) in neoclassical heroic couplets.

In the twentieth century W.H. Auden wrote his "Letter to Lord Byron" (1937),
a long, conversational poem composed on a trip to Iceland. The poem, which parodies
the travel narrative and uses the trope of explaining twentieth-century culture "to
a long-dead poet" (l.133) as a means of satirizing current events, is also quite
self-conscious about its relation to the poetic tradition. For instance, in explaining his
use of *rhyme royal* (seven-line stanzas in iambic pentameter with an *ababbcc* rhyme
scheme) instead of the *ottava rima* (stanzas of eight iambic pentameter lines with three
alternate rhymes and one double rhyme, following the *abababcc* rhyme scheme), Auden
writes,

> Ottava Rima would, I know, be proper
> The proper instrument on which to pay
> My compliments, but I should come a cropper [that is, he would fail];
> Rhyme-royal's difficult enough to play.
> But if not classics as in Chaucer's day,
> At least my modern pieces shall be cheery
> Like English bishops on the Quantum Theory.
>
> (ll.148–54)

Here Auden connects to Byron (through the direct address as well as the reference to
ottava rima, which Byron had used in his satire *Don Juan* [1819–24]), to Chaucer (who
used *rhyme royal*), and to contemporary religious attitudes on science ("English bishops
on the Quantum Theory"). Additionally, the epistolary form connects Auden to
Horace, whose satires took the form of poetic letters to friends and patrons.

Later in the twentieth century, American poet Thomas Lux used free verse to
simultaneously mock and memorialize Pope in "Mr. Pope" (1990). He mentions
Pope's small stature and hunched back, and conjectures that for Pope there was

> most likely, never, *never*
> any sex. That he did not
> tolerate nincompoops,
> poetasters, or pompous fops
> one can understand.
>
> (ll.5–9)

Such intertextual articulations of praise and blame are common in literary satires and constitute a particularly self-conscious version of T.S. Eliot's conception in "Tradition and the Individual Talent" (1919) of a dynamic, constantly shifting literary tradition.

As Lux's poem demonstrates, modern writers tend to treat this tradition somewhat less respectfully than their predecessors. Several of Philip Larkin's poems, for example, begin with allusions to famous works and then undermine the loftiness of the association he has created through degraded tone and content. In his 1967 poem "Annus Miribilis" (which is also the title of a 1666 poem by Dryden and translates from Latin as "year of wonder"), Larkin subverts his titular allusion to Dryden with the first two lines: "Sexual intercourse began / In nineteen sixty-three" (ll.1–2). Similarly, Billy Collins scandalizes the virginal aura of Emily Dickinson as he imagines disrobing her while stealing some of her more famous lines. In "Taking off Emily Dickinson's Clothes" (1998) Collins visualizes undoing Dickinson's "clips, clasps, and moorings, / catches, straps, and whalebone stays" (ll.24–25). The poem ends,

> and I could hear her sigh when finally it was unloosed,
> the way some readers sigh when they realize
> that Hope has feathers,
> that reason is a plank,
> that Life is a loaded gun
> that looks right at you with a yellow eye.
>
> (ll.42–47)

Here Collins pushes to their extreme notions of "anxiety of influence," turning literary admiration into sexual conquest capped by serial plagiarism.

Collins performs a similar dialectic of respect and burlesque in his "Sonnet" (2001), which self-consciously mocks the form's conventions while performing them. The poem begins, "All we need is fourteen lines, well, thirteen now, / and after this one just a dozen" (ll.1–2), initiating a countdown to its own end. In line 8 the narrator announces the onset of the sestet, "where all will be resolved" (l.10) before making an allusion to Petrarch's "crazy medieval tights" (l.13). The informal, historically naïve feel of "crazy" and the poem's irregular meter and rhyme situate the speaker as a playfully colloquial commentator on the sonnet rather than a sneering, perfectionist practitioner.

For centuries, the satirical survey of the contemporary literary scene has been a popular choice for poets attempting literary satire. Miguel de Cervantes's *Viajeal Parnassus* (1614), for example, is a satirical epic whose plot revolves around defending Mount Parnassus from an invasion of poor poets. In "MacFlecknoe" (1682), Dryden depicts recently deceased (and generally unpopular) poet Richard Flecknoe as appointing Thomas Shadwell—Dryden's rival playwright—as heir and ruler over the realms of Nonsense. In doing so, he creates the bad-poet-filled realm of Dullness, a concept that Pope pushed even further in his mock-epic *The Dunciad* (1728–43), which lambastes individual authors in reaction to the commercialization of authorship and the subsequent rise of the Grub Street hacks (Heath-Stubbs 61–62). In the Romantic age, Byron wrote *English Bards and Scotch Reviewers* (1809) in heroic couplets reminiscent of his neoclassical forbearers. Victorian England saw Edward Bulwer Lytton skewer contemporary poets in *The New Timon* (1846), to which an offended Alfred Lord Tennyson retorted with *The New Timon and Poets*, which first appeared in London's satirical magazine *Punch* in 1846. In America, James Russell Lowell's *A Fable for Critics* (1848) and Augustine Duganne's *Parnassus in Pillory* (1851) surveyed the antebellum American literary scene.

Such satirical considerations of contemporary authors continued unabated into the twentieth century. For example, South African poet Roy Campbell, who also translated Horace, used heroic couplets to satirize the literary and artistic coteries of London in *The Georgiad* (1933) and of South Africa in *The Wayzgoose* (1928). Scottish poet Hugh MacDiarmid penned "Your Immortal Memory, Burns" (1926) to satirize the cult of Robert Burns in his country. In Ireland, Patrick Kavanagh wrote "The Paddiad" (1949), a Pope-inspired attack on inferior Irish poets. More recently, Richard Nason's *A Modern Dunciad* (1978), in an obvious nod to Pope, critiques modern American poetry and poets in neoclassical diction and meter. R.S. Gwynn's *Narcissiad* (1981, 2001) features a talentless contemporary poet—"This self-made-god, our latter-day Narcissus" ("The Education of Narcissus" 8)—as its protagonist amidst biting criticism of the poetry profession in the U.S. For, if Narcissus is a poor poet, he is an exemplary grant writer:

> With pen in hand he takes the poet's stance
> To write, instead of sonnets, sheaves of grants
> Which touch the bureaucrats and move their hearts
> To turn the spigot on and flood the arts
> With cold cash, carbon copies, calculators,
> And, for each poet, two administrators.
> In brief, his every effort at creation
> Is one more act of self-perpetuation
> To raise the towering babble of his Reputation.
>   ("The Education of Narcissus" ll.47–55)

In "The Triumph of Narcissus," the anti-hero is the "sole survivor" (l.10) of an internecine war between poets trying to destroy their competition. He ascends Mount Olympus in triumph, only to awaken Zeus with his horrible verse. Zeus, angered by the hubbub, transforms the vain Narcissus into a "monstrous thing" (l.109), a grotesque amalgam of poet-parts:

> See Auden's wrinkles coursing to its chin,
> Pound's leather neck and Delmore Schwartz's grin,
> Red, buggy eyes from Thomas, Cummings' hair,
> And aft Miss Amy Lowell's derrière,

> And, for a lasting insult, Sandburg's nose,
> And, finally, some of Edith Sitwell's clothes.

(ll.110–15)

Gwynn's satire thus connects the modern American poetry scene (and the latest phase of the professionalization of the craft) to earlier American poets (through bodily allusions), to neoclassical satirical verse (through its mocking use of heroic couplets), and to satirical verse's classical origins (through Zeus and Mount Olympus). Gwynn's literary satire, like Pope's, Dryden's, and Cervantes' before it, is mock-heroic: that is, it operates through the ironic employment of the tropes and formal devices of traditional heroic or epic poetry in order to display the triviality of its subject.

Satirical Burlesque

Burlesque and doggerel verse also function by incongruously juxtaposing the intellectual heft of verse form with degraded content. Northrop Frye, in *Anatomy of Criticism* (1957), panned doggerel as a "sub-poetic level of metrical talk" (5) that "has a prose initiative" (277) it tries but fails to express through poetic form. But poets and critics have long been aware of the satirical potential of intentional doggerel. David Rothman claims in his essay "Ars Doggerel" (1990) that doggerel, "at its best, is a delightful, powerful, cynical monster" (311). Authors such as Geoffrey Chaucer, especially in "The Tale of Sir Thopas," and John Skelton, in poems like *Speak, Parrot* (1521) and *Colin Clout* (1522), effectively used doggerel verse to attack literary, social, and religious targets.

But the most influential deployment of doggerel was undoubtedly by Samuel Butler, whose *Hudibras* (1662, 1663, 1677) fashioned an 11,000-line burlesque narrative on the narrative pattern of *Don Quixote* to house his bitter satire on Puritans. Butler's tetrameter couplets include frequent double rhymes for a comic, "deliberately grotesque" effect (Heath-Stubbs 35), debasing his protagonists as they attempt to comport themselves with particularly Puritan solemnity. The poem was wildly popular for over a hundred years, and the form—which came to be known as "Hudibrastics"—much imitated. In fact, during the American Revolution both British and American satirists levied their attacks in Hudibrastics; the most popular poem on the American side was John Trumbmull's *M'Fingal: A Modern Epic Poem in Four Cantos* (1776, 1782).

Dialect is another effective tool in the creation of satirical doggerel. Robert Burns, who owed his style as a satirist more to the medieval Scottish tradition of *flyting* than to the classical Roman verse satire (Heath-Stubbs 80), was a master of Scots dialect verse and often used it for satirical effect, as he did in "Holy Willie's Prayer" (1799), an attack on religious hypocrisy. In nineteenth-century America, James Russell Lowell, who admired Burns's common touch, attempted to capture the dialect of an anti-slavery New England farmer (as spoken through a fictional poet named Hosea Biglow) in his satires protesting the Mexican–American War in *The Biglow Papers* (1848). For example, in "No. 1: A Letter" he condemns war on religious and moral grounds. After announcing "Ez fer war, I call it murder" (l.33), Biglow wonders,

> Wut's the use o' meetin-goin'
> Every Sabbath, wet or dry,
> Ef it's right to go amowin'
> Feller-men like oats an' rye?
> I dunno but wut it's pooty
> Trainin' round in bobtail coats,—
> But it's curus Christian dooty
> This ere cuttin' folks's throats.

(ll.49–56)

Here Lowell's persona uses the discourses available to him—those of New England Congregationalism and farming—to articulate his moral outrage. In displacing his anti-war stridency into the dialect of a rural farmer, Lowell was continuing a tradition of homespun satirical narrators (e.g. Skelton's Colin Clout) whose hard-working humility contrasts with the hypocrisy and opulence they observe around them.

But, as some modern adaptations of satirical doggerel show, the irony implicit in the form also allows room for a certain level of detached urbanity. America's best-known modern political verse satirist, Calvin Trillin, is a polished wit, having served as "verse columnist" for *The Nation* and staff writer for *The New Yorker*. But he is also a self-avowed doggeralist (as the title of his 1994 collection *Deadline Poet or, My Life as a Doggeralist* shows). His most recent collection, *Deciding the Decider: The 2008 Presidential Race in Rhyme* (2008), operates by juxtaposing the sophomoric sing-songy-ness of his verse to the sophisticated topicality of its content. In "Obama, Rising," for example, the forced end-rhymes that lead us to classify the poem as doggerel actually serve as punchlines of Trillin's political jokes. In describing naysayers discouraging Obama from running for president, he writes,

> According to a long-established tenet
> He should mature for years yet in the Senate.
> (Producing legislation at a trickle,
> Some Senate members don't mature; they pickle.)

(ll.1–4)

Trillin also satirizes the very media coverage to which his poetic correspondence is a contribution. In "A Political Reporter Laments Being Assigned to Watch Al Gore's Waistline," the bored reporter-narrator explains that he has been given the assignment to observe Gore's diet in order to determine whether or not he will run for president in 2008:

> Last week, I told my desk that Gore might run,
> Though he appeared to be at least full-size:

> A waiter at a Georgetown place revealed
> Gore's order had included 'hold the fries.'
>
> (ll.9–12)

Poems like this mock the credence given to factual minutiae during electoral campaigns in the age of the twenty-four-hour news networks.

Though Trillin is not alone in leveraging the flaws of doggerel verse for effective political satire, most modern poets seem leery of intentionally writing bad verse. Rothman blames the relative paucity of modern doggerel on the ascendance of free verse as the dominant poetic structure. "Obviously," he writes in "Ars Doggerel," "it is hard to botch open forms in the way that doggerel botches meter and rhyme; open forms abjure the very kinds of prosodical structures that doggerel disfigures" (315). In other words, the twentieth-century move away from fixed form has, for the most part, engendered a commensurate departure from satirical riffs on such form.

Epigrammatic Satire

But a related mode of verse satire—the epigram—seems to have flourished in the twentieth and twenty-first centuries. The word "epigram" derives from a Greek word for inscription, and some early epigrams were printed on gravestones. These tiny, aphoristic poems have long done heavy satirical lifting. In ancient Rome, for example, Martial used epigrams as personal attacks. Satire critic Charles Knight describes Martial's epigrams as pushing

> Horatian *brevitas* to its ultimate limit. A poem as short as two lines must launch itself towards its victim . . . must identify the fault of which the victim is guilty, and must condemn it in a witty way . . . The metric and stylistic compression of the epigram intensifies its capacity to distort and insult.
>
> (19)

This description highlights the craft required to imbue epigrams in all literary cultures with appropriate satirical punch. In Japan, for instance, the *senryu* developed from the haiku and followed its metrical form but took a more cynical and satirical tone. Epigrams were also a natural fit for neoclassical satirists like Pope, who pushed his heroic couplets towards epigram with their closed, standalone feel.

But satirical epigrams may have reached their widest popular readerships in burlesque almanacs, a wildly popular genre in various incarnations, from François Rabelais's *Pantagrueline Prognostications* in medieval France to *Poor Robin's Almanac* in Restoration England to Benjamin Franklin's *Poor Richard's Almanac* in colonial America. In these almanacs, already stuffed with burlesque astrological predictions, calendars, and other useful and useless information, epigrams were a convenient way to cram entertainment and didactic messages into limited space. Franklin, for one, adopted existing aphorisms and epigrams from the English almanac tradition and refigured them in colloquial American language.

In the twentieth and twenty-first centuries, epigrams continue to have cultural currency. In fact, the very terseness of epigrams makes them accessible to modern readers in an era otherwise generally uncongenial to the demands of formal poetry. One critic writes, "It is natural that satirically inclined modern poets have often turned to the epigram. The epigram not only suits an age that favors shorter poems over longer ones, but also is historically associated with satire to a degree that no other short form is" (Steele 442). Somewhat ironically, this light form has been used to tackle very serious subject matter in war poetry, from Rudyard Kipling's World War I poems "Epitaphs of the War, 1914–1918" to Randall Jarrell's World War II poem "Death of the Ball Turret Gunner" to former Marine R.L. Barth's Vietnam epigrams in his 2003 collection *Deeply Dug In* (Steele 444–45). The epigram's brevity and the closure offered by its exact rhymes make it simultaneously comic and harrowing when dealing with the psychological complexities of combat. Barth, for instance, often emphasizes the gruesome poignancy of the wartime events he narrates by encapsulating them in heroic couplets. But epigrams are appropriate for pithy, ironic pronouncements on any subject; the brusqueness of the form gives epigrams a harsh, unapologetic edge.

Menippean Satirical Verse

The final mode of modern satirical verse that I will discuss draws its energies not from the Roman tradition of formal verse satire but rather from Menippean satire, which is generally defined broadly as satire combining prose and verse. This mode is named after third-century BC Greek Cynic philosopher Menippus, who wrote burlesque prose narratives with some poetic verses mixed in. (This method is alternatively known as Varronian satire, after first-century BC Roman author Terentius Varro, who also mixed prose and verse.) Despite this genre-mixing, Menippean satire has been largely associated with narrative forms: famous examples include Petronius's *Satyrica* and Seneca's *Apocolyntosis*, both dating to the first century AD; Erasmus's *The Praise of Folly* (1511); Sir Thomas More's *Utopia* (1516); François Rabelais's *Gargantua and Pantagruel* (1532–52); Jonathan Swift's *Gulliver's Travels* (1726); and Laurence Sterne's *The Life and Opinions of Tristram Shandy* (1760–67). All of these Menippean narratives import and parody discourses from other genres—including and especially scholarly diction—for satirical effect.

Narrative has, of course, long been a staple of both serious and comic poetry. But in the twentieth and twenty-first centuries—the age of free verse—poets, not limited to traditionally poetic diction or strict metrics, have begun to experiment with the importation of other types of language into their work. The result, often, is a stingingly ironic juxtaposition of the various "official" languages invoked and the poetic structure (announced by, if nothing else, line breaks) into which they have been transplanted. In many cases, technical, or legalistic discourse comes off as insensitive or malicious when juxtaposed to the humanizing energies of poetry.

Thomas Lux, for instance, often proceeds by putting into dialogue the factual tone of historical discourse and his own, humane poetic voice. In "Kalashnikov" (1994) Lux combines biographical details on Mikhail Kalashnikov, numerical statistics about the caliber and killing capabilities of the AK-47 assault rifle that he designed, and a poet's interest in the sound of words. The poem ends,

> Kalashnikov—it's not a dance,
> nor a troupe of funny jugglers,
> nor is it a vodka,
> and if you said a small city (pop. 49,000)
> in the southern Crimea,
> you'd be stone-dead wrong.
>
> (ll.23–28)

Here Lux interrupts his own playfulness with a sudden, deadpan recognition of the deadly power of the popular weapon he describes.

Similarly, Martín Espada's "The Community College Revises Its Curriculum in Response to Changing Demographics" (2000) parodies the cold language of a college course catalogue. Beginning as it does with a course title—*"SPA 100 Conversational Spanish / 2 credits"* (ll.1–2)—Espada's diction is decidedly non-poetic and has the feel of found poetry; it is only the line breaks that announce this as a poem. But the short lines into which this prose sentence is divided isolate and call attention the catalogue's language, highlighting the insidious way in which the educational system uses rhetoric to mask its perpetuation of racism.

Denise Duhamel's personifications of the Barbie doll in *Kinky* (1997) work in a slightly different way. In bringing Barbie to life in her Rabelaisian, narrative poems, Duhamel creates a grotesque being: alive but still plastic and missing vital body parts. For example, in *Kinky* Barbie and Ken—the latter of whom Duhamel describes in the poem as "part circus freak, / part thwarted hermaphrodite" (ll.15–16)—"decide to exchange heads" (l.1). But amidst all the fun of Barbie's adventures is a dark side— sexual abuse, drug use, infidelity, therapy, religious fanaticism—that allows Duhamel to use a personified toy to articulate a broad range of satire on rampant consumerism, traditional gender roles, and the excesses of modern popular culture. And, in "Manifest Destiny" (a jingoistic nineteenth-century American term used to justify zeal for territorial expansion), Duhamel shifts perspectives to consider a factory in the Philippines where Barbie dolls are manufactured. In the poem she compares the experience of women working in these factories to an episode of *I Love Lucy* in which Lucy and Ethel "try a day of work, boxing chocolates / on an assembly line" (ll.8–9), with comic results. The Philippine women, on the other hand, "ponder / big business" (ll.19–20). The poem ends:

> In dreams
> these women package Toys "R" Us uteruses
> while a sterile Barbie, her hair tucked up
> inside her Lucite helmet, plants
> a flag for Mattel on the cheesiest moon.
>
>   (ll.21–25)

The power of this poem derives from its position in *Kinky* alongside poems in which Barbie is a personified protagonist. As such, the Barbie about whom these factory workers dream is more real to the readers when she engages in the ultimate imperial expansion (colonizing the moon) under a corporate flag.

Conclusion

Satire theorists have often characterized satire as assuming a stable set of social standards. Frye, for instance, echoed Dryden in seeing satire as referencing "relatively clear," if unstated, moral norms, and in claiming that satire "assumes standards by which the grotesque and absurd are measured" (223). Given the persistence of such perceptions of satire as a conservative art, we might think that verse satire would suffer or even disappear in the postmodern age, when norms of any kind are more often questioned than assumed. But the modern poets examined above—though they proceed in different modes deriving from different traditions—all use satirical forms self-consciously and ironically in order to critique societal norms *themselves* instead of deviations from those norms. In this way modern verse satirists have innovated ancient forms to attack political, social, and aesthetic status quos.

REFERENCES AND FURTHER READING

Ammons, A.R. *The Really Short Poems of A.R. Ammons*. New York: Norton & Co., 1990.

Auden, W.H. and Louis MacNeice. *Letters from Iceland*. London: Faber & Faber, 1937.

Barth, R.L. *Deeply Dug In*. Albuquerque: University of New Mexico Press, 2003.

Collins, Billy. *Sailing Alone around the Room: New and Selected Poems*. New York: Random House, 2001.

Cope, Wendy. *Two Cures for Love: Selected Poems, 1979–2006*. London: Faber & Faber, 2008.

Duhamel, Denise. *Kinky*. Alexandria, VA: Orchises Press, 1997.

Duval, Edwin M. "Rabelais and French Renaissance Satire." In *A Companion to Satire: Ancient and Modern*, ed. Ruben Quintero. Malden, MA: Blackwell Publishing, 2007. 70–85.

Elliott, Robert C. *The Power of Satire: Magic, Ritual, and Art*. Princeton: Princeton University Press, 1960.

Elliott, Robert C. "Satire." In *The New Princeton Encyclopedia of Poetry and Poetics*, ed. Alex Preminger and T.V.F. Brogan. Princeton: Princeton University Press, 1993. 1114–17.

Espada, Martín. *Mayan Astronomer in Hell's Kitchen*. New York: Norton & Co., 2001.

Franklin, Benjamin. *The Papers of Benjamin Franklin*, ed. Leonard W. Larabee. 38 vols. New Haven: Yale University Press, 1969.

Frye, Northrop. *Anatomy of Criticism: Four Essays*. Princeton: Princeton University Press, 1957.

Guilhamet, Leon. *Satire and the Transformation of Genre*. Philadelphia: University of Pennsylvania Press, 1987.

Gwynn, R.S. *No Word of Farewell: Selected Poems, 1970–2000*. Ashland: Story Line Press, 2001.

Heath-Stubbs, John. *The Verse Satire*. London: Oxford University Press, 1969.

Knight, Charles. *The Literature of Satire*. New York: Cambridge University Press, 2004.

Larkin, Philip. *Collected Poems*, ed. Anthony Thwaite. London: Farrar, Straus and Giroux and the Marvell Press, 1988.

Lux, Thomas. *New and Selected Poems, 1975–1995*. Boston, MA: Houghton Mifflin Co., 1997.

Rothman, David. "Ars Doggerel." *Hellas* 1 (1990): 311–17.

"Satura." *The Oxford Classical Dictionary*. Oxford: Oxford University Press, 2nd edn. 1970. 953–54.

Steele, Timothy. "Verse Satire in the Twentieth Century." In *A Companion to Satire: Ancient and Modern*, ed. Ruben Quintero. Malden, MA: Blackwell Publishing, 2007. 434–59.

Swift, Jonathan. *The Basic Writings of Jonathan Swift*, ed. Claude Rawson. New York: The Modern Library, 2002.

Trillin, Calvin. *Deciding the Next Decider: The 2008 Presidential Race in Rhyme*. New York: Random House, 2008.

34

Poetry and Its Occasions

"Undoing the Folded Lie"

Stephen Wilson

Occasional poetry, or as *The New Princeton Encyclopedia of Poetry and Poetics* has it, occasional verse, can be relatively straightforwardly defined as poetry, or verse, written to celebrate or otherwise mark an event, or "occasion." Such poems may or may not be commissioned but the occasion will usually be public or official (a coronation or inauguration, the death of a national hero or leader, victory or defeat in battle, or the founding of a college or other institution) or social (a birthday or wedding or a sporting triumph) rather than private. Occasional poetry does not always enjoy a high level of critical esteem, the formulation "occasional verse" is sometimes used to suggest that it cannot truly be said to aspire to the condition of poetry. Andrew Motion, Poet Laureate from 1999 to 2009, complained that having to write occasional verse had been "very, very damaging to my work," also suggesting that occasional verse was not the real thing. I can see Motion's point and even, with some reservations, sympathize with it. It is undoubtedly the case that much occasional verse—for example, birthday-card rhymes or the doggerel of Alfred Austen (Poet Laureate from 1896 to 1913)—is conspicuously lacking in literary merit. However, the same could be said of a great deal of non-occasional verse and it must also be recognized that Horace's *Nunc est bibendum* (Odes i.37), Edmund Spenser's "Prothalamion," John Milton's sonnet "On the Late Massacre in Piemont," Andrew Marvell's "Horatian Ode upon Cromwell's Return from Ireland," Walt Whitman's "When Lilacs Last in the Dooryard Bloom'd," W.B. Yeats's "Easter 1916," and W.H. Auden's "September 1, 1939" are all occasional poems and also all highly distinguished poems.

Occasional poetry goes back a very long way and is to be found in the literature of many languages and cultures. Paul Merchant in his study of the epic speculates that the epic "may have originated in the need for an established history" (3–4) and, I believe, a similar point could be made in respect of occasional poetry. It seems prob-

A Companion to Poetic Genre, First Edition. Edited by Erik Martiny.

able that its origins lie in the urge of the tribe (or other social or political unit) to establish a record, to create a "history," and in a desire for communal celebration and commemoration. Occasional poetry survived its moment of origin with these functions in large measure intact. Sappho and Pindar and, later, Virgil and Horace wrote such poetry and the tradition was continued by the court poets of the Middle Ages and the Renaissance, and by the anonymous makers of ballads and folk songs. Poets were traditionally regarded as the bestowers and custodians of fame. It was the deeds of kings and heroes that made them worthy of fame but those deeds could not speak for themselves and so it was poets who conferred fame and the immortality that went with it. Horace's boast, in the final poem of his third book of odes, that he has constructed a "monumentum aere perennius" (a monument more lasting than bronze) that would resist the ravages of time and triumph over death is a sophisticated extension of this view. This claim reflects Horaces's justified pride in what he had achieved (a confidence that his work, and specifically the odes, would survive its author and its first audience) and a belief that, because a great poem outlasts a statue, poetry provides an effective mode of commemoration and tribute. A broadly similar view of poetry is memorably articulated in Ezra Pound's *Homage to Sextus Propertius*:

> And who would have known the towers
> pulled down by a deal-wood horse;
> Or of Achilles withstaying waters by Simois
> Or of Hector spattering wheel-rims,
> Or of Polydmantus, by Scamander, or Helenas and
> Deiphoibos?
> Their door-yards would scarcely know them, or Paris.
> Small talk O Ilion, and O Troad
> twice taken by Oetian gods,
> If Homer had not stated your case!
>
> (ll.27–36)

This is ironic in tone but Pound, as the *Cantos* testify, certainly believed that poetry has an important public role and would I think have subscribed to a modified form of this view of the poet and poetry. It should also be noted that "door-yards" here recalls Walt Whitman's poem on the death of Lincoln—"When Lilacs Last in the Dooryard Bloom'd."

The view that the poet is the arbiter of fame and that a poem can give form and meaning to an event, and fix it in the mind of the reader (poetry can be a highly effective mnemonic) is central to the concept of occasional poetry. This essentially didactic view of poetry may seem to be more appropriate to a pre-literate age but, as I have already suggested in respect to occasional poetry generally, such poetry continued to be written in later ages. Tennyson's "The Charge of the Light Brigade" and Yeats's "Easter 1916" (two poems discussed below) provide an illustration of this. Indeed, I would suggest that the survival of occasional poetry suggests that these ideas have a greater contemporary currency than is sometimes recognized.

These speculations raise a number of questions (including issues of orality and performance) that cannot be addressed here, but I think that I have established the existence of a long and continuous tradition of a poetry of record that is also a mode of communal celebration and commemoration. The communal, or public, dimension is of particular importance in any attempt to define occasional poetry: the occasional poet does not write simply or primarily for herself or himself but speaks to, and on behalf of, a collectivity of one sort or another (for example, a nation, a congregation or a generation). Recognizing this makes it possible to distinguish between the occasional and the topical, and on this basis I would suggest that, for instance, the lines from Byron's *Childe Harold's Pilgrimage*, Canto III, sometimes printed separately as "The Eve of Waterloo" (1816) and Louis MacNeice's *Autumn Journal* (1939) are topical while Wordsworth's "On the Extinction of the Venetian Republic, 1802" and Auden's "September 1, 1939" are occasional poems.

Occasional poetry continues to be written and read, one might even argue that there is more of it about today than ever before; the greeting-card industry supplies cards for a variety of occasions (births, birthdays, weddings and wedding anniversaries, divorces, bar mitzvahs, graduations, getting a job, retirement, and funerals) and, for a modest fee, anyone can commission a poem online. Official poetry in the form of the Poet Laureate of the United Kingdom and its equivalent elsewhere (particularly the Poet Laureate Consultant in Poetry to the Library of Congress in the United States) appears to be thriving. The Poet Laureate is appointed to write poems on royal and state occasions and on matters of national interest; this requirement is not absolute and he or she can choose what they write about although, clearly, some occasions are more difficult to ignore than others. The position can be traced back in something like its present form at least as far as Ben Jonson (appointed 1616) and it has been held by John Dryden, William Wordsworth, Tennyson, and, more recently, by Cecil Day-Lewis, John Betjeman and Ted Hughes. The present incumbent, Carol Ann Duffy, is the first woman to hold the post and since her appointment in 2009 she has published poems on, among other topics, climate change ("Virgil's Bees"), corruption in British politics ("Politics") and on the deaths of the last two veterans of World War I ("Last Post"); "Achilles (for David Beckham)," her offering on the foot injury sustained by England footballer David Beckham in the run-up to the 2010 World Cup ("his charmed foot on the ball . . . / but then his heel, his heel, his heel . . ."), has added a new and popularist dimension to the Laureate's role.

The office of Poet Laureate Consultant in Poetry to the Library of Congress, in which many distinguished poets (including Allen Tate, Robert Lowell, Elizabeth Bishop, Randall Jarrell, Robert Frost, Anthony Hecht, Rita Dove, Louise Glück, and Charles Simic) have served, was established in 1937 with the title "Consultant in Poetry to the Library of Congress," the words "poet laureate" were added by an act of Congress in 1985. William Carlos Williams was appointed in 1952 but did not serve because he was suspected of having socialist sympathies. The Poet Laureate Consultant in Poetry to the Library of Congress is described on the Library of Congress website as "the nation's official lightning rod for the poetic impulse of Americans," and is not strictly speaking an official occasional poet. The poems sometimes read at U.S. presidential inaugurations are closer to what is usually thought of as occasional poetry. This traditional began with John F. Kennedy who asked Robert Frost to read a poem at his inauguration in January 1961, adding that Frost did not have to write a new poem but could recite an old one and suggested "The Gift Outright" (first published in 1942). Frost did come up with a new poem—"Dedication," a conventional piece of occasional poetry that begins by praising Kennedy for being "the first to think of . . . summoning artists to participate / in the august occasions of the state" (ll.1–2) and having placed him in the tradition of "the great four, Washington, / John Adams, Jefferson, and Madison" (ll.25–26) ends by looking forward to the "glory of a next Augustan age" (l.71). However, on the day, Frost, who was 87 at the time, was unable to read "Dedication" and fell back on reciting "The Gift Outright." The tradition of inaugural poetry was revived by President Clinton: at his first inauguration in 1993 Maya Angelou read "The Rock Cries out to Us Today" (not entirely surprisingly, a paean to change, diversity, and equality) and at the second in 1997 Miller Williams read "Of History and Hope." In 2009, poet and academic Elizabeth Alexander recited her poem "Praise Song for the Day" at the inauguration of President Obama.

It could be argued that Woodie Guthrie's songs celebrating the achievements of President Franklin Delano Roosevelt's New Deal, and particularly those written about the Grand Coulee Dam project, constitute a distinctively American strain of occasional poetry. The dam, which is on the Columbia River in Washington State, was not originally a New Deal project but Roosevelt co-opted it for his program and work on it began in late 1933 (it officially opened in 1942). It was, by any measure, an epic undertaking: in its day it was the largest concrete structure in the world (it is still one of the largest) and the construction of it cost the lives of more than seventy men. In 1941 the Bonneville Power Authority commissioned Woody Guthrie to collaborate on the making of a documentary film about the building of the dam and the Columbia River Songs were the result of his brief period as a Federal employee. Guthrie's great achievement in songs such as "Roll on Columbia," "The Biggest Thing That Man Has Done," and particularly "Grand Coulee Dam" is to marry the conventions of occasional poetry, which are largely predicated on a great men and great deeds view of history, to the more popularist, democratic, and radical ethos of his work as whole.

Before moving on to a more detailed account of occasional poetry, and of individual occasional poems, I will briefly address some general or theoretical issues. The first of these concerns the question of genre. For Northrop Frye, "the study of genres is based on analogies in form" (95) that is to say on formal or objective features common to a group of texts (for example, the fourteen lines of the sonnet or sestina's stanza structure). Elsewhere, he describes "the basis of generic criticism [as] . . . rhetorical, in the sense that the genre is determined by the conditions established between the poet and his public" (247). Both of these statements are of considerable interest and are not, if I understand Frye correctly, necessarily contradictory but their value in the present context is limited or is primarily negative. Generically, occasional poetry is not defined formally or rhetorically but in terms of function, thus on January 20, 1961 Frost's

"The Gift Outright" became, in use, an occasional poem. A corollary of this is that occasional poetry can be found across a range of genres or, as I would prefer to put it, it is an omnibus genre containing a number of genres—elegy, epithalamium, panegyric and philippic, the ballad, the ode, and the encomium (the list is by no means complete).

It is sometimes objected that because, as Aristotle argued, poetry deals not with particulars but with universals, occasional poetry, which by definition deals with particulars, is a contradiction, indeed an impossibility, and therefore what is called occasional poetry is either not occasional or not poetry. On the other hand, it has been asserted that all poetry is occasional in the sense that all poetry has a *terminus a quo*, a point of origin, and that is often some event, incident or encounter (in other words, an occasion).

The first of these arguments can be met with a robust empiricism—the fact of the existence of a large body of occasional poetry means that it cannot be an impossibility; it could also be pointed out that it is precisely the business of occasional poetry to attach a wider, or universal, meaning to particular events. As to the second, it may be the case that all poetry is occasional but what defines occasional poetry is the nature of its occasion and its relation to the poem. As I have said, it is public, official, or social and the poet writes not as private individual but is a representative (in the case of court poets and modern laureates an official) voice addressing the reader as a social being, a fellow citizen—as a political animal in the widest sense. This is true even of those occasional poems that appear to address private themes; epithalamia and birthday poems are not celebrations of love or friendship as private or personal emotions but of weddings and birthday celebrations (the formal and social manifestations of those emotions). It should also be noted that the occasion of a successful occasional poem is not merely a peg on which to hang a poetic meditation nor is it erased or replaced by the poem; it remains as something autonomous but central to the poem.

In *Poetry, Narrative, History*, Frank Kermode describes "that type of history . . . that makes the past easier to deal with by punctuating the record with great crises and great persons" as "history as myth, or as poem." In these terms the study of occasional poetry can be described as the study of "the relation of such poems to the poems written about them, in celebration of the great events given historical centrality by communal acts of historical imagination" (50). He further observes: "poems [that] simply comply with their occasions . . . pass into oblivion with those occasions" (50). Kermode elaborates this argument in a brilliant reading of Horace's *Nunc est bibendum* (he calls it the "Actium Ode").

The Battle of Actium (31 BC) in which Octavian defeated Antony and Cleopatra was, in Kermode's words, a victory "worth celebrating." It put an end to the civil war between Antony and Octavian and to the danger posed to Rome by Egypt (and by Cleopatra in particular). This left Rome the hegemonic power in the Mediterranean world and Octavian the undisputed ruler of Rome thus creating the conditions that allowed the Roman Republic to become an empire and Octavian to become Augustus. In official Roman history (or myth-history) Actium was regarded as a literally epoch-making event and one might expect Horace's ode to be a celebration of that but, as Kermode argues, "anything like strict attention to the language of the poem at once leads the critic away from the simple historical record, and the simple historical myth" and reveals "an image not of public rejoicing but of something more private and more complex, resistant to communal simplicities" and it is that something "rather than some plain record of popular pleasure" that "we choose to preserve" (54–55).

Horace's treatment of the figure of Cleopatra is central to this argument (significantly Antony is not mentioned in the poem). Cleopatra was a "feared and despised . . . imperial rival . . . [who] threatened Rome with oriental barbarism," she is not named in the poem but is referred to as *regina*—a word that would have had no positive connotations in Roman ears (Kermode 52). Initially she is described as being deluded, or drunk, with ambition and hatred of Rome; then, in an account of the battle that exaggerates the extent of the Roman victory, Horace describes how Cleopatra is brought to her senses, sobered, by the pain of defeat and forced to flee from Octavian, like a dove or hare before a hunter. However, in the final lines of the ode, which describe how Cleopatra committed suicide rather than be taken prisoner and subjected to the ignominy of a Roman triumph, there is a significant change—she becomes a more dignified, almost an heroic figure, she was, Horace tells us, "non humilis mulier" (no common or ordinary woman). This shift in how Cleopatra is represented is indicative of that "something more private and more complex, resistant to communal simplicities" that has assured the poem's survival. No more adequate account of Kermode's compelling analysis of *Nunc est bibendum* is possible here but as, I hope, even this brief account makes clear that analysis provides a useful approach to occasional poetry generally.

Tennyson's "The Charge of the Light Brigade" (1854), which commemorates an incident in the Crimean War, is perhaps the most famous occasional poem in English. The charge was ill judged and although those who participated in it showed great courage they sustained heavy losses to no purpose; it was, in short, a military disaster. A frequently quoted stanza runs:

> "Forward, the Light Brigade!"
> Was there a man dismayed?
> Not tho' the soldiers knew
> Someone had blundered:
> Theirs was not to make reply,
> Theirs was not to reason why,
> Theirs was but to do and die:
> Into the valley of Death
> Rode the six hundred.
>
> (ll.9–17)

What Kermode calls the "historical myth" of this action sees the charge as an amalgam of folly and glory in which, finally, the glory redeems the folly. Tennyson and his first readers probably regarded the poem as complicit with this myth (and to a great extent it is) but the portrait of soldiers who follow orders unquestioningly but not blindly opens it to other readings—readings in which the glory does not redeem the folly but is negated by it. It is, I believe, largely because of such readings, or misreadings, that "The Charge of the Light Brigade" has survived (the lines "Theirs was not to reason why, / Theirs was but to do and die" are still widely remembered and quoted).

Rudyard Kipling's "Recessional" was written to mark Queen Victoria's Golden Jubilee in 1897. As the title suggests, the poem is a reflection on the Jubilee celebrations as they are drawing to a close (a recessional is a hymn that accompanies the withdrawal of the clergy after a service). Kipling begins by acknowledging the extent and power of the Empire, its "far-flung battle-line" and "dominion over palm and pine," but warns that even the greatest of empires decline and, eventually, fall:

> Far-called, our navies melt away;
> On dune and headland sinks the fire:
> Lo, all our pomp of yesterday
> Is one with Nineveh and Tyre!

(ll.13–16)

The British Empire can only avoid this fate by being different from other empires, not merely more powerful or bigger but dedicated to a higher purpose and so deserving of divine sanction:

> If, drunk with sight of power, we loose
> Wild tongues that have not Thee in awe,
> Such boastings as the Gentiles use,
> Or lesser breeds without the Law
> Lord God of Hosts, be with us yet,
> Lest we forget—lest we forget!
> For heathen heart that puts her trust
> In reeking tube and iron shard,
> All valiant dust that builds on dust,
> And guarding, calls not Thee to guard,
> For frantic boast and foolish word
> Thy mercy on Thy People, Lord.

(ll.19–30)

Essentially, "Recessional" is a quarrel between the popular imperialism of the Jubilee and Kipling's higher imperialism and it advances, by means of a trope derived and adapted from biblical exegesis (that of *figura*), an argument that runs (roughly) thus: the British (or perhaps the Anglo-Saxon race) are the modern counterparts of the Israelites, the chosen people of the Old Testament, a people of the "Law," and it is their obligation to bring the "Gentiles" to the Law and so redeem the world. However, it is not Kipling's contempt for popular imperialism or his exalted vision of the Empire that has ensured the survival of "Recessional," that can be found in many of his poems, but the sense of "something more private and more complex," some darker and more profound misgivings about the future of the British Empire or about the whole imperial project that are not articulated but which are suggested by the pervasive sense of something slipping away (receding) and the elegiac tone of the poem.

Yeats's "Easter 1916" offers a clear illustration of Kermode's view that the "great events" are "history as myth, or as poem" and that the poems about them are poems about poems. The Easter Rising was militarily unsuccessful, but largely because of a series of repressive retaliatory measures by the British (including the execution of the leaders of the insurrection) it came to be seen as an act of heroic sacrifice; and seen as such it galvanized a torpid nationalist movement into violent and effective life and is now regarded as a seminal event in the struggle for Irish independence (this is one sense of "the terrible beauty" of the poem's refrain). Yeats's attitude to the Rising was ambivalent, by 1916 he was moving away from his earlier nationalist positions (in any case he had never been precisely that sort of nationalist), and this is to an extent reflected in the poem. The Public Prosecutor in Auden's "The Public v. the late Mr. William Butler Yeats" who sneers that "to succeed at such a time in writing a poem which could offend neither the Irish Republican nor the British Army was indeed a masterly piece of work" (390) has a point, but that is by no means the whole story.

On one level, the central narrative trope of "Easter 1916" is the emergence of the future heroes of the Rising from the world "where motley is worn," the world of the "casual comedy," into the heroic sphere of public action, the world of the "terrible beauty." The often reluctant movement of the hero from private into public life is a common motif in public writing of all sorts, including occasional poetry, as is the contrast between the public and the private world, which celebrates the pleasures and seductions of the latter but finally acknowledges the higher, sterner, claims of the former. What is unusual about Yeats's poem is the weight it gives to the claims of the private. This is apparent in the following passage:

> Hearts with one purpose alone
> Through summer and winter seem
> Enchanted to a stone
> To trouble the living stream.
> The horse that comes from the road,
> The rider, the birds that range
> From cloud to tumbling cloud,
> Minute by minute they change;
> A shadow of cloud on the stream
> Changes minute by minute;
> A horse-hoof slides on the brim,
> And a horse plashes within it;
> The long-legged moor-hens dive,

> And hens to moor-cocks call;
> Minute by minute they live:
> The stone's in the midst of all.

(ll.41–56)

This statement of the claims of the private is not merely a generic convention, there is nothing perfunctory about it, rather it is an essential source of that deviance, that non-compliance with its occasion that characterizes the successful occasional poem. (If "Easter 1916" is compared to Canon Charles O'Neill's "The Foggy Dew," one of the most famous and popular of the songs about 1916 Rising, this point becomes clearer.) In "Easter 1916" the claims of the "private" are almost tantamount to the claims of life itself, and bring the poem's close to a point of radical breakdown:

> Was it needless death after all?
> For England may keep faith
> For all that is done and said.

(ll.67–69)

"Easter 1916" exhibits a high degree of self-consciousness, it is continuously and explicitly aware of its own status as a representation of the Rising and such speculations, however well founded, can take the poem and the poet nowhere. Yeats's response is to turn from them to the lapidary and unequivocal assertion of the achievement of the men of 1916 in the poem's final lines:

> I write it out in a verse—
> MacDonagh and MacBride
> And Connolly and Pearse
> Now and in time to be,
> Wherever green is worn,
> Are changed, changed utterly,
> A terrible beauty is born.

(ll.74–80)

What is presented in "Easter 1916" is a complex narrative of the evolution of a poet, and a poetry, of a particular type (the phrase "terrible beauty" here clearly also refers to the poem itself); Yeats could not write or re-write Easter 1916, he could only "write it out" as a lesson is, or used to be, written out in a copy book. On one level "Easter 1916" is precisely about Yeats's recognition of this. The legislative tone of these lapidary closing lines and the insertion of the poet alongside (Pádraig) Pearse, (James) Connolly, (Thomas) MacDonagh and (John) MacBride (four of the leaders of the Rising executed by the British) suggest an affinity between Yeats's poem and the bardic tradition of Irish poetry. Thus, although its self-consciousness and complex and problematic relationship to its occasion mark "Easter 1916" as very much a modern, or even a modernist, occasional poem, it also looks back to, and to an extent re-enacts, the origins of occasional poetry.

"September 1, 1939," W.H. Auden's poem marking the day on which Germany invaded Poland and so precipitated World War II, is also characterized by a high degree of self-consciousness and by complex and fraught negotiations between the public and private. Occasional poetry, as I have pointed out, often represents the realm of the private as a seductive alternative to the world of public actions and events but this is not the case here. Auden's poem opens, famously, with the poet sitting "in one of the dives / On Fifty-second Street" (ll.1–2) and the opening stanza presents an atomized world of displaced and alienated individuals, a world of uncertainty and fear that is permeated by the "unmentionable odour of death" (l.10). It is only a private world in so far as it has no larger communal or social dimension; the "low dishonest decade" that is drawing to a close and the "darkened lands of the earth" provide no context or alternative but only heighten the sense of anomie. The public world of "September 1, 1939" is not a world of social or communal relationships or one in which the individual can play any meaningful role but the world of "collective man" in which the citizen is a cipher. In such a world compliance is not an option for the citizen or the poet, and poetry, if it is to exist at all, must deviate from the dominant myth:

> All I have is a voice
> To undo the folded lie,
> The romantic lie in the brain
> Of the sensual man-in-the-street
> And the lie of Authority
> Whose buildings grope the sky:
> There is no such thing as the State
> And no one exists alone;
> Hunger allows no choice
> To the citizen or the police;
> We must love one another or die.

(ll.78–88)

This is hardly the business of an occasional poem but in the final stanzas that is precisely what Auden reveals "September 1, 1939" to be—an act of communal celebration and commemoration, an occasional poem that brilliantly affirms and transgresses the conventions of the genre:

> Defenceless under the night
> Our world in stupor lies;
> Yet, dotted everywhere,
> Ironic points of light
> Flash out wherever the Just
> Exchange their messages:

> May I, composed like them
> Of Eros and of dust,
> Beleaguered by the same
> Negation and despair,
> Show an affirming flame.

(ll.89–99)

On the basis of "Spain," "September 1, 1939," the two great elegies ("In Memory of W.B. Yeats" and "In Memory of Sigmund Freud") and the perhaps less well known birthday poem for Christopher Isherwood "August for the people and their favourite islands," sometimes referred to as "To a Writer on his Birthday," Auden can, I believe, justly be described as the greatest occasional poet in English since Andrew Marvell. He is also, as might be expected, a significant figure in the subsequent development of occasional poetry. Self-consciousness and non-compliance have, to a degree, always been a feature of successful occasional poetry but Auden takes them further and makes them part of the overt subject matter of the poem so that what previously emerged from a "strict attention to the language of the poem" (which is not quite the same thing as reading between the lines but for present purposes the two can be equated) is now more directly given. Auden has the occasional poem quarrel with its occasion and with itself, that is to say the poem contests its own status as an occasional poem and its capacity to fulfill the traditional functions of the genre. This is most obvious in "In Memory of W.B. Yeats" in which Auden states that "poetry makes nothing happen" thus denying the capacity of poetry to deal directly and indicatively with the world of deeds and actions and, as a corollary, the possibility of occasional poetry. After Auden, poets have continued to write occasional poetry but, to appropriate a phase from "In Memory of Sigmund Freud," they have "[found] it a little harder." I will move to a conclusion with a brief account of a distinguished example of a post-Auden occasional poem—Seamus Heaney's "Casualty."

"Casualty," published in *Field Work* (1979), is Heaney's response to the events of Bloody Sunday (January 30, 1972) when British soldiers shot dead thirteen men in Derry. The second section of the poem opens with a description of the funeral of the thirteen victims:

> It was a day of cold
> Raw silence, wind-blown
> Surplice and soutane:
> Rained-on, flower-laden
> Coffin after coffin
> Seemed to float from the door
> Of the packed cathedral
> Like blossoms on slow water.
> The common funeral
> Unrolled its swaddling band,
> Lapping, tightening

> Till we were braced and bound
> Like brothers in a ring.
>
> (ll.47–59)

This is a powerful piece of occasional writing and one which recognizes, and parallels, the power of the shared act of mourning and commemoration ("the common funeral") to unite the community ("we were braced and bound / Like brothers in a ring"). However, the casualty of the title is not one of the thirteen but an anonymous eel fishermen and friend of Heaney's (his name was Louis O'Neill). In a sense O'Neill was also a victim of Bloody Sunday:

> He was blown to bits
> Out drinking in a curfew
> Others obeyed, three nights
> After they shot dead
> The thirteen men in Derry
>
> (ll.38–42)

Immediately after the shooting the I.R.A. decreed that, as a mark of respect for the dead, all businesses including bars should close for a period of three days. It was an enforced act of communal mourning and businesses that did not comply risked being bombed. O'Neill, who "drank like a fish / Nightly" and "would not be held / At home by his own crowd," broke this curfew; he left the safety of his own community to find an open bar and died in the "bombed offending place." In a sense his death was an accident, he was not a specific target, he was simply in the wrong place and at the wrong time. In "Casualty," however, it is not that straightforward:

> How culpable was he
> That last night when he broke
> Our tribe's complicity?
> "Now, you're supposed to be
> An educated man,"
> I hear him say. "Puzzle me
> The right answer to that one."
>
> (ll.78–84)

Louis O'Neill, fairly obviously, is a version, a partial representation, of the poet, and his breaking of "our tribe's complicity" reflects Heaney's own problematic relationship with the "tribe"—a major theme of Heaney's work since *North* (1975). "Casualty" cannot provide the "right answer to that one" but the question is central to it and to Heaney's work as a whole (the final line of the poem reads "Question me again").

Positioning himself between the tribe, the community, and Louis O'Neill allows Heaney to achieve the balance of compliance and contestation that is essential to a successful occasional poem. It should also be noted that in "Casualty" Heaney employs both the first-person singular and the first-person plural, the shift from "I" to "we" in the last lines of his description of the "common funeral" ("Till we were braced and bound / Like brothers in a ring") signifies the integration of the individual into a collective act of mourning. Louis O'Neill is always "he" and "they" (After they shot dead / The thirteen men in Derry") denotes the British. Unlike the poet, O'Neill remains stubbornly distinct (the last image of him alive is of "his still knowable face" caught in the glare of the explosion that killed him); he never merges into the collective "we," nor does he become one of "them." Heaney did not attend Louis O'Neill's funeral ("I missed his funeral") but "Casualty," like the "the common funeral," laps him, and the thirteen "they shot dead," in "its swaddling band" in an act of communal mourning and commemoration. By doing so Heaney fulfilled the traditional functions of occasional poetry and extended the possibilities of the genre.

It should be pointed out that "Casualty" cannot be read as Heaney's definitive statement on what in "Whatever You Say Say Nothing" (*North*) he calls "the Irish thing." His more recent poetry is markedly less compliant with the tribe's myths and less amenable to its demands. This readily apparent in the fourth poem of "The Flight Path" sequence in *The Spirit Level* (1996) in which Heaney recalls an encounter, on a train travelling from Dublin to Belfast, with Danny Morrison, a leading member of Provisional Sinn Féin:

> So he enters and sits down
> Opposite and goes for me head on.
> "When, for fuck's sake, are you going to write
> Something for us?" "If I do write something,
> Whatever it is, I'll be writing for myself."
>
> (ll.23–27)

Commenting on this incident, and on the poem to which it gave rise, in an interview with Dennis O'Driscoll, he spoke of his resentment at his interlocutor's "presumption of entitlement" (257) and added:

> I simply rebelled at being commanded . . . This was in the pre-hunger-strike times, during "the dirty protest" by Republican prisoners in the H-Blocks. The whole business was weighing on me greatly already and I had toyed with the idea of dedicating the Ugolino translation to the prisoners. But our friend's intervention put paid to any such gesture. After that, I wouldn't give and wasn't so much free to refuse as unfree to accept.
>
> (258)

This clearly reflects the evolution of events in Northern Ireland and of Heaney's view of them: this section of "The Flight Path" opens with the words "The following for the record, in the light / Of everything before and since" (ll.1–2). To revert to the terms used earlier, Heaney has not become "one of them" but right and wrong are perhaps no longer as clear cut as was the case in the aftermath of "Bloody Sunday." Be that as it may, I would also argue that the difference between "Casualty" and the lines quoted above corresponds to the difference between Heaney as an occasional poet and Heaney as a non-occasional poet (the distinction between the occasional and the topical is also relevant here). In "The Flight Path" the poet's voice is individual and personal; for instance, he tells the reader that he was "just off the red-eye special from New York" and so, it may be assumed, was tired and perhaps even jet-lagged. In "Casualty" the personal and the individual are a significant and powerful presence but are subordinated and constrained by the demand of the occasional mode. As had been the case with Yeats sixty years earlier, it is precisely these generic constraints that leave Heaney "free . . . to accept" (although it is safe to say that "Casualty" was not what Morrison had in mind when he demanded "something for us").

"Casualty" demonstrates the continuing viability of occasional verse. The list of modern or contemporary poets who have written occasional poetry is a long and distinguished one and includes, besides Seamus Heaney, Dylan Thomas, Robert Lowell, Elizabeth Bishop, Philip Larkin, Ted Hughes, Allen Ginsberg, and John Ashbery. It is to be found in both "high" and popular culture—to the list above could be added the names of song writers such as Bob Dylan, Bruce Springsteen, and Shane MacGowan.

Occasional poetry returns us to the origins of poetry and so reminds us of the social and collective dimension of poetic production and makes available, or at least offers an insight into, pleasures of the poetic text that might otherwise be lost. The existence of occasional poetry is predicated on the belief that the poem is a product of history that can, in Auden's words, "re-enter history as an effective agent" (393), and so it also raises in a particularly interesting and urgent form the question of poetry and history. This instrumentalist view of poetry disconcerts the assumption shared by "structuralism, post-structuralism, and modern hermeneutics . . . that literary works exhaust their being in their linguistic structures" (Rainey 6). For me, such posing of questions to orthodoxy is salutary and supports the contention that occasional poetry is not an anachronism or a curiosity but something central and essential to the well-being of poetry as a whole.

REFERENCES AND FURTHER READING

Auden, W.H. *The English Auden: Poems, Essays and Dramatic Writing 1927–1939*, ed. Edward Mendelson. London and Boston: Faber & Faber, 1977.

Frost, Robert. "Dedication." Public Broadcasting Service (PBS). www.pbs.org/newshour/inauguration/frost_poem.html.

Frye, Northrop. *Anatomy of Criticism*. Princeton: Princeton University Press, 1957.

Heaney, Seamus. *Field Work*. London: Faber, 1979.

Heaney, Seamus. *North*. London: Faber, 1975.

Heaney, Seamus. *The Spirit Level*. London: Faber, 1996.

Horace. *The Odes (Bilingual Edition)*, trans. David Ferry. New York: Farrar, Straus and Giroux, 1997.

Kermode, Frank. *Poetry, Narrative, History*. Oxford. Blackwell, 1990.

Kipling, Rudyard. *Rudyard Kipling's Verse: Definitive Edition*. London: Hodder and Stoughton, 1940.

Library of Congress. "About the Position of Laureate." www.loc.gov/poetry/about_laureate.html.

Merchant, Paul. *The Epic*. London: Methuen, 1971.

O'Driscoll, Dennis. *Stepping Stones: Interviews with Seamus Heaney*. London: Faber, 2009.

Preminger, Alex, Brogan Terry V.F., Warnke, Frank J., eds. *The New Princeton Encyclopedia of Poetry and Poetics*. Princeton: Princeton University Press, 1993.

Rainey, Lawrence S. *Ezra Pound and the Monuments of Culture: Text, History, and the Malatesta Cantos*. Chicago: University of Chicago Press, 1991.

Tennyson, Alfred. *Poems and Plays*, eds. T. Herbert Warren and Frederick Page. Oxford: Oxford University Press, 1968.

Yeats, W.B. *The Poems*. Ed. Daniel Albright. London: Everyman, 1992.

35
On Verse Letters

Philip Coleman

> *A Configuration of the Incomplete*
>
> Octavio Paz, "Letter to León Felipe" (97)

I

According to the entry in the *New Princeton Encyclopedia of Poetry and Poetics* (1993), the "verse epistle" is a "poem addressed to a friend, lover, or patron, written in a familiar style and in hexameters or their modern equivalent" (Preminger and Brogan 1351). Two types of the poetic sub-genre are said to exist: "the one on moral and philosophical subjects, which stems from Horace's *Epistles*, and the other on romantic or sentimental subjects, which stems from Ovid's *Heroides*." The "verse letter" as such is not listed in the encyclopedia, but the editors' choice of the somewhat archaic phrase "verse epistle" is an interesting critical gesture in itself, suggesting that the form may be outdated or perhaps even obsolete in contemporary poetic practice. The term "letter" is in fact more appropriate when discussing modern and contemporary writing, as the entry for "epistle" in the *Oxford English Dictionary* makes clear in its claim that the word is "now used only rhetorically or with playful or sarcastic implication." In addition to its promotion of the term "epistle" over "letter," the *New Princeton Encyclopedia* entry also gives the impression that the verse letter has had very little currency in the twentieth century, citing only W.H. Auden's *New Year Letter* and Louis MacNeice's *Letters from Iceland* as modern examples. Before suggestions for further reading are given, the entry states that "[t]he romantics did not value" the verse letter either, "though Shelley, Keats, and Landor on occasion wrote them" (Preminger and Brogan 1351).

A Companion to Poetic Genre, First Edition. Edited by Erik Martiny.
© 2012 John Wiley & Sons, Ltd. Published 2012 by John Wiley & Sons, Ltd.

Given the fact that two scholars (R.A.H and T.V.F.B) collaborated on the writing of the *New Princeton Encyclopedia*'s entry it is odd that more twentieth-century examples are not cited. Even more curious, however, is the suggestion that Romantic poets "did not value" the verse letter. The problem is perhaps one of form: even if the verse letter may be said to have its origins in the metrically identifiable works of Horace and Ovid, later poets rarely stuck to this or, indeed, any particular formal template for very long. John Donne, perhaps the most important early modern writer of verse letters—the Oxford Donne includes a volume of his satires, epigrams, and verse letters in which the latter make up the bulk of the contents—remade the form in several different ways, from the rhymed iambic pentameter couplets of "The Storme" (addressed "To Mr Christopher Brooke") and "The Calme," to epistolary sonnets such as "To Mr T.W.," "To Mr C.B.," "To Mr S.B.," and "To Mr Rowland Woodward," a poem organized in twelve rhymed tercets. Donne's most famous verse letter, "To Sir Henry Wotton," which begins "Sir, more then kisses, letters mingle Soules; / For, thus friends absent speake" (*sic*; ll.1–2), speaks to the ultimately ineffable and therefore formless power of letters in poetic mediation. "But for these / I could ideate nothing," the speaker states in Donne's poem (ll.3–4), suggesting both the importance of the letter in allowing him to order his thoughts and, consequently, to express himself not just to Henry Wotton, the poem's primary addressee, but to his readers and, of course, himself. If the (modern) verse letter may not be defined or circumscribed with regard to a clear formal structure, then, neither is it the case that it serves only or exclusively to communicate a set of ideas or thoughts to a particular individual or reader. Moreover, it often serves to reflect an author's ongoing inner correspondence, as it were, with her/himself.

This self-reflexive aspect of the verse letter is also a major feature of the Romantic verse letter, which is almost written out of literary history in the *New Princeton Encyclopedia* entry. William Wordsworth's "Epistle to Sir George Howland Beaumont, Bart. From the South-West Coast of Cumberland" (1811) is a good example. The second verse paragraph begins by asking the question "What shall I treat of?" (l.59) suggesting that the poem was not written for a particular occasion—thereby challenging the claim that verse letters are often "occasional" in nature—but as a way for the poet to work through a range of possible subjects for poems, from the latest "[n]ews from Mona's isle" (which is found "unvaried in its style") to "more substantial themes" that, the poem suggests, are delivered and, indeed, *declared* by "our telegraph"—"the hovering clouds":

> Mona from our Abode is daily seen
> But with a wilderness of waves between;
> And by conjecture only can we speak
> Of aught transacted there in bay or creek;
> No tidings reach us thence from town or field,
> Only faint news her mountain sunbeams yield,
> And some we gather from the misty air,

And some the hovering clouds, our telegraph, declare.
But these poetic mysteries I withhold;
For Fancy hath her fits both hot and cold,
And should the colder fit with You be on
When You might read, my credit might be gone.

(ll.77–88)

Wordsworth's use of the word "telegraph" here is interesting, given that it first entered the English language in the 1790s and refers, in the first instance, to "[a]n apparatus for transmitting messages to a distance, usually by signs of some kind" (*OED* 1.a). In Wordsworth's poem the "hovering clouds" serve to transmit messages in a manner that augments the poet's sense of human being's organic connection to the natural environment, but the "telegraph" image also signals an awareness of an emerging modernity which may, in time, affect the poet's communication of the "poetic myster-ies" mentioned in the following line.

Wordsworth's poem posits an idea of poetic communication that includes and expands on the various meanings of epistolarity, and it is therefore highly appropriate that the poem is itself a verse epistle or letter. Contrary to the view expressed in the *New Princeton Encyclopedia*, the image of the poet as letter-writer and the practice of writing verse letters was very common among the Romantic poets, and in addition to this example by Wordsworth a full account of the its popularity among his con-temporaries might include a discussion of poems such as Samuel Taylor Coleridge's "Letter to Sara Hutchinson" (an important early version of "Dejection; an Ode"), Lord Byron's "Epistle to Augusta" and Robert Burns's "Epistle to J. L*****k, An Old Scotch Bard, 1 April 1785." In their studies of apostrophe and poetic address critics such as Jonathan Culler and Ann Keniston have explored the complexity of lyric projection in a wide range of poems, but many major Romantic poems "To" other poets, aspects of nature, or places, might also be considered as epistolary texts—poems such as John Keats's "To Autumn" or "To Melancholy" and Wordsworth's "To Toussaint L'Ouverture" and Anna Laetitia Barbauld's "To Mr Coleridge." (This idea, indeed, is suggested in the work of popular twentieth-century American poet Phyllis McGinley, whose *Love Letters* include "A Kind of Love Letter to New York" and "Love Letter to a Factory.") Moreover, and perhaps more importantly, these (and other) poems of the Romantics can be said to constitute an epistolary network by which the Romantic period in modern poetry's development can be mapped or apprehended. Such a mapping of poetry's histories and contexts in the Romantic period—by following routes of epistolary exchange through poems—can be extended into later or back into earlier periods, revealing the true pervasiveness of epistolarity as well as the formal variety of verse letters (and the problematic nature of periodicity) in the development of English and other, non-Anglophone, poetries, from Ovid to Charles Olson, Horace to K.A. Hays.

The kind of trans-historical and cross-cultural perspective on the "verse letter" afforded by this view is not dissimilar from the way that Jacques Derrida may be said to trace the history of Western philosophy in his book *The Postcard: From Socrates to Freud and Beyond*. Derrida, in fact, offers perhaps the most useful key to understanding the peculiar generic status of a text like the verse letter in the following passage from his essay "The Law of Genre":

> Genres are not to be mixed.
> I will not mix genres.
> I repeat: genres are not to be mixed. I will not mix them.
> Now suppose I let these utterances resonate all by themselves.
> Suppose: I abandon them to their fate, I set free their random virtualities and turn them over to my audience—or, rather, to your audience, to your auditory grasp, to whatever mobility they retain and you bestow upon them to engender effects of all kinds without my having to stand behind them.
> I merely said, and then repeated: genres are not to be mixed; I will not mix them. As long as I release these utterances (which others might call speech acts) in a form yet scarcely determined, given the open context out of which I have just let them be grasped from "my" language—as long as I do this, you may find it difficult to choose among several interpretative options. They are legion, as I could demonstrate. They form an open and essentially unpredictable series.
>
> (Derrida 55)

On the one hand—in the *New Princeton Encyclopedia of Poetry and Poetics*, for example— the verse letter has been circumscribed within certain formal frames of reference. On the other, however, it is a kind of poetic "utterance" (to use Derrida's word) that is profoundly unstable and protean in terms of the forms it can take. As a result, it is not always clearly visible as an identifiable sub-genre of poetry, in the way that forms such as the villanelle or the sestina might be, for example. Indeed, the history of poetry from classical times to the present contains countless examples of verse letters in which the more visible aspects of poetic form or genre are "mixed" and, viewed over time, they may be said to "form an open and essentially unpredictable series" like the one described here by Derrida. The verse letter, in short, knows no "law of genre"—neither at its point of origin, in the literatures of antiquity, nor in its more recent modern and postmodern manifestations. When Emily Dickinson began one of her poems by declaring "This is my letter to the World / That never wrote to me" (ll.1–2), she may on one level have been alluding to the intense but often precarious place of correspondence (with key figures such as Thomas Wentworth Higginson, for example) in the development of her work. She was also suggesting, however, that the making of lyric poetry in itself may be considered an epistolary act, one that has been performed in manifold ways in the history of poetry's development—ways that have been and continue to be both "open" and "unpredictable."

II

If, in one version of the story of modern poetry's development, the impulse towards innovation in twentieth-century poetry may be located in Ezra Pound's injunction to "make it new" in Canto LIII, then it is appropriate to note the ways in which Pound contributed towards a remaking of the verse letter in his work. *The Cantos* re-makes letters drawn from many historical sources in its intertextual weaving of materials, as in Pound's use of the letters of Thomas Jefferson in Canto LXIX. In addition to such important instances of epistolary experiment, however, the canon of Pound's shorter poems contains many examples of the poet's realization of the verse letter's formal adaptability, most notably "The River-Merchant's Wife: A Letter" and "Exile's Letter" from *Cathay* (1915). In these widely anthologized poems Pound not only reveals the verse letter's appeal across the East/West cultural divide, but he also suggests that the verse letter has a particular poignancy when dealing with issues of exile, homelessness, and loss. As an American poet who raged against what he once called the "bacillus of the land" in his blood in a letter to William Carlos Williams (*Selected Letters* 124), Pound would probably balk at the following comparison, but in realizing the verse letter's usefulness in exploring the theme of exile he was in fact contributing to and developing a tradition that can be traced back to the Colonial poet Anne Bradstreet. Bradstreet's "Letter to her Husband, Absent upon Public Employment," which Pound may have known from Charles Eliot Norton's 1897 edition of her work, is an important early American example of poetic epistolarity, and it is one of a number of poems by her in which she invokes a "postal" metaphor. Pound's poems in *Cathay* may owe their greatest formal and thematic debts to Chinese sources, but there is also a clear connection to be drawn between his work and earlier American examples, with which it may be said to engage in a kind of trans-historical epistolary exchange.

Recognizing such intertextual connections does not lessen Pound's achievement. Rather, reading his poems alongside those of Bradstreet reminds us of Pound's American inheritance while at the same time pointing to another thread of correspondence within the verse letter's complex national and international historical evolutions. At the end of his poem "Exile's Letter" the speaker calls "in the boy" and has

> him sit on his knees here
> To seal this [the letter]
> And send it a thousand miles, thinking.
>
> (ll.70–72)

The image of the letter being sent "a thousand miles" is resonant in itself, but the single word in the poem's closing clause ("thinking") signals a degree of agency, of ongoing intellectual and emotional activity, that is part of the verse letter's appeal to many of the poets who have engaged with the form. For a poet like Pound, who was often exercised by the idea that his poems should engage their audience in an active way, the verse letter is then much more than a stationary textual object. It is a thing that moves, by virtue of the fact that it is sent from the poet to a reader or readers, but the movement implied in the verse letter's posting is permanent and self-perpetuating. This is the reason why Pound's poem "Exile's Letter" ends in the present continuous tense with "thinking": it points to an ongoing process of textual engagement and relay that persists beyond the last word of the poem and, indeed, the poet. This reading of the final gesture of "Exile's Letter" may be extended to explain modernist poetry's interest in ideas of process and change, while at the same time serving to symbolize the importance of letters themselves (real and imagined) in the cultural formation of poetic modernism.

Real letters, drawn from historical and biographical sources, also play a significant and not unproblematic role in the work of Pound's close contemporary William Carlos Williams. Williams's long poem *Paterson* draws on letters from many sources—including some received from the young Allen Ginsberg—but the way Williams used letters he received from Marcia Nardi, in particular, has been the focus of some controversy. Williams knew Nardi and he was an active advocate of her work in the 1940s—he wrote an introduction for her poems in a New Directions anthology, for example, though her first book was not published until 1956—but his use of their private correspondence in *Paterson*, where he renamed her as "Cress," has raised questions for many readers about the ethics of epistolary appropriation in literature, particularly where the use of personal letters is concerned. Williams quotes long passages from Nardi's letters in *Paterson*, and in one section she ("C") writes: "My attitude towards woman's wretched position in society and my ideas about all the changes necessary there, were interesting to you, weren't they, in so far as they made for *literature?*" (emphasis in original; Williams 86). "C" (Nardi) is clearly challenging Williams's authority here (addressed as "P" in the text), but Williams ultimately ignored such challenges and quoted freely from Nardi's letters throughout *Paterson*, making their private exchanges public, turning her letters into "literature." At the end of the second Book of *Paterson*, "C" explains that "much time and much thought and much unhappiness [has] gone into those pages" (Williams 93). Williams's poem does not describe the specific events in his relationship with Nardi which might explain this, but in using her letters he alludes to a private context that some readers have suggested might have been better left out of *Paterson* altogether.

There is a distinct difference, then, between Williams's use of his personal correspondence with Nardi and Ginsberg in *Paterson* and Pound's use of the more ostensibly "public" letters of Jefferson and others in *The Cantos*, but in both cases it is clear that modernist poetic practice forced a reconsideration of the verse letter in terms of its formal, generic, thematic, and, indeed, ethical/political implications. It is possible, too, to suggest that the so-called "Middle Generation" of American poets—including Robert Lowell, John Berryman, Sylvia Plath, Randall Jarrell, Anne Sexton, and W.D. Snodgrass—found the dialectical play of private and public concerns through the use of letters in the work of Pound and Williams exemplary in their formation of a poetry and poetics that could address these contrary poles of human experience in the inter- and postwar periods. Berryman's "Letter to His Brother" is a good example of this, exploring as it does the relation between individual and communal loss—"Whatever bargain can be got / From the violent world our fathers bought" (ll.26–27). The violence of that world is given one of its most effective articulations by Karl Shapiro, a soldier poet whose work is suffused by instances of what might be called implicit and explicit epistolarity—references to or images of letters in individual poems as well as poems that take the form of verse letters. Shapiro's volume *V-Letter* (1944) signals the pervasiveness of letter-writing as well as the profundity of the epistolary moment (writing, reading, sending, or receiving a letter) in many poems, most poignantly in "Aside," which begins with these lines:

> Mail-day, and over the world in a thousand drag-nets
> The bundles of letters are dumped on the docks and beaches,
> And all that is dear to the personal conscious reaches
> Around us again like filings around iron magnets,
> And war stands aside for an hour and looks at our faces
> Of total absorption that seem to have lost their places.
>
> (ll.1–6)

The image here of "bundles of letters . . . dumped on the docks and beaches" gives urgent (twentieth-century) significance to Donne's idea that "letters mingle Soules," but the "total absorption" of the implied readers of the letters in Shapiro's poem also serves to remind us of the importance of letter-writing during World War II (and other major conflicts of the twentieth century). "When and where we arrive / Is no matter," Shapiro's poem ends, "but *how* is the question we urgently need, / How to love and to hate, how to die, how to write and read" (emphasis in original; ll.34–36). If his poem may be said to describe the war's radical reconfiguration of the experience of personal reading and writing, it also signals his desire as a poet to remake that most versatile of forms, the verse letter, as he does with particular power in his book's closing and title-poem, "V-Letter." The very title of that poem plays on an idea of loss in the allusive abbreviation of "Verse" to "V," but the poem also makes reference to "v-letters' or "v-mail"—personal letters screened and edited by censors on all sides of the conflict to prevent information from being unwittingly sent to the enemy. Shapiro's suggestion that poetry itself can be understood in terms of the "v-letter"—a kind of writing in which something is always censored, excised, or lost—advances the claim made earlier regarding the pervasiveness of epistolarity in the history of poetry, but its very real contextual significance during World War II should also be acknowledged, as well as the idea that the poem itself constitutes a kind of minor victory ("v") of the human spirit over and against the forces of war and destruction.

Despite the fact that it is a poem very much framed by the experience of war, Shapiro's "V-Letter" is also a personal poem, a love letter of a kind in which the speaker addresses the one who waits while he is away on active military service. (Shapiro's book was published while he was stationed in the Southwest Pacific.) The American poet of the generation after Williams and Pound who made the most extensive use of directly personal epistolary material in his work, however, was Robert Lowell. Lowell's late sonnets, in particular, represent an important contribution to the remaking of the verse letter in twentieth-century poetry and poetics. Lowell's early volumes contain a number of interesting poems of epistolary address—from "To Peter Taylor

on the Feast of the Epiphany" in *Lord Weary's Castle* (1946) to "To Delmore Schwartz"
in *Life Studies* (1959). The idea that the latter poem, in particular, might be considered
in epistolary terms is suggested by the place and date given in parentheses after the
title ("Cambridge 1946"), but Lowell's most interesting and indeed explicit experiments in epistolarity are in his later collections *The Dolphin, History* and *For Lizzie
and Harriet*, all published in 1973. These books are particularly interesting because
Lowell used letters he received from Elizabeth Hardwick, his second wife, to provide
the content for a number of poems, including "Foxfur," "Marriage 7: Green Sore,"
and "Marriage 8: Letter." Elizabeth Bishop questioned Lowell's method and intention
in these and other poems, pointing out that "Lizzie is not dead" and objecting in
particular to the fact that he appeared to have "*changed* her letters" in his work (emphasis in original; Travisano and Hamilton 708). She argued that "[o]ne can use one's life
as material—one does, anyway—but these letters—aren't you violating a trust?"
(708). The idea that Lowell had violated Hardwick's trust by using their private
correspondence in his poems is reminiscent of the debate regarding the ethics of
epistolary (re)production in Williams's work, and it has done a certain amount of
damage to the later poet's reputation. In particular, Lowell's explicit use of personal
materials in these poems has reinforced the view that "Confessional" poetry is essentially an art of egotistic exposure and excess. It is important to remember, however,
that Lowell's poems, like Williams's, are works of art in their own right, and while
the broader (biographical) contexts of their composition reveal sometimes disturbing
personal details they should also be seen as texts that engage in an important sense
with questions of genre and form. In their radical revision of the terms by which the
verse letter can be written, certainly, the poems of Williams and Lowell forced a major
reconsideration of the form in twentieth-century poetics.

The extent to which Lowell may be considered a poet of provocative poetic innovation is then emphasized when one considers his experiments with epistolarity, but his
work in the volumes cited is nonetheless anchored in the traditional verse form of the
sonnet. His contemporaries Robert Duncan, Allen Ginsberg, Frank O'Hara, and
Charles Olson were often more radical in their appropriations of the form. In the
preface to his volume *Letters: Poems 1953–1956*, first published in a limited edition
in 1958 and reprinted in 2003, Duncan writes: "In the Cantos [*sic*] of Ezra Pound
the voices of the guides are distorted by shifts in making. The poetry, the making,
opens gaps in the correspondence with the City of God. A poetry is possible which
will introduce peril of beauty to all the cells of history" (Duncan xii). Duncan sees
poetry *itself*—as Donne, Wordsworth, and Pound did—as a form of "correspondence,"
a kind of writing that is always, already, "epistolary." In naming his collection *Letters*
he signals the inherently "postal" aspect of his writing—his sense of the poems participating in a larger system of "correspondence" across "all the cells of history"—but
he also expands the formal frame within which the "verse letter" might be written in
poems that are remarkable for their play of punctuation, syntax, lineation, and paratactic form. Duncan refuses to use what he calls "that old line" of conventional poetic
method and forges instead a kind of poetry that seeks to undo (or, as he says, "decon-

struct") rigid form. If the difference and distance between private "letters" and public "literature" is heightened in the work of Williams and Lowell, such a distinction falls away in Duncan's belief in the idea that all poems invoke the epistolary mode by their very existence.

Throughout the thirty short sections of *Letters* Duncan appears to take the idea of the verse letter further in formal terms than any of his contemporaries, with the possible exception of Charles Olson, who makes extensive use of letters in his long work *The Maximus Poems*, written and published over two decades between 1950 and 1970. The letter has a particular function in Olson's work, serving to heighten the sense of *The Maximus Poems* as a text that speaks to and for a wide range of real and imagined communities, from New England to Oregon. Because it is a long work *The Maximus Poem* cannot be considered simply or solely as a "verse letter" but it is a text in which Olson realizes the structural and metaphorical usefulness of the letter as a way of ordering his ideas and, more importantly, of delivering them in a poem of extraordinary ambition and scope. Other poets of his generation, including Delmore Schwartz and Frank O'Hara, used the image of the letter and the epistolary mode in interesting ways throughout their work—Schwartz in "Kilroy's Carnival: A Poetic Prologue for TV," for example, and O'Hara in poems such as "To Music of Paul Bowles" and "[Dear Jap,]"—but Olson, together with Duncan, were the American poets of the post-war period who created the most engagingly innovative work in this regard. Indeed, the development of a postmodern poetics that may be said to originate in their work depended, in part, on their belief in the epistolary dimension of poetry itself, an insistence on its "projective" potential, as Olson might have put it.

III

Whether such an expansive if not open-ended understanding of poetic genre in general or the verse letter in particular is useful is open to debate. If nothing else, however, the decidedly post-modernist experiments in epistolarity that pervade the published works of poets such as Duncan and Olson suggest that the idea of poetry as a form of "postal" engagement or address has been as important to writers of the twentieth century as it was to those of earlier periods, from Donne to Wordsworth. Despite the fact that they have undergone countless transformations in practice, the activities of letter-writing and writing verse letters have enabled many poets to develop their work in fascinating ways, and these have lead to the development of new ideas about the art of poetry and its function. In the works of poets as different as Shapiro, Lowell, Duncan, and Olson, we can see that their experiments with the "verse letter" lead to the creation of works that advanced understandings of poetic form at the same time that they stimulated new ways for thinking about the role and idea of epistolarity in general in poetry as a subject of interpretative concern. Thinking about epistolarity in Olson's *Maximus Poems*, for example, leads one to an appreciation of the ways that poetry may be said to address communities of readers across space and time, while

Duncan's text *Letters* posits "Poetry" itself as the ultimate addressee of every poet's creations. In Lowell's work, also, the explicit use of epistolary material highlights the tension between private and public that is a central feature of his writing in general, while at the same time raising important questions regarding the ethics and cultural politics of literary production. In short, a consideration of the verse letter in the broad literary historical and interpretative terms sketched above reveals a great deal about twentieth-century poetic practice. However, the fundamental idea of the letter as a form of communication between the letter-writer and one or more readers remains central, and it is important to note that, in addition to being highly productive poets, all of the figures discussed so far were also prolific letter-writers. The extent to which the two activities—of writing letters and writing poems—may have overlapped in their writing is then also worth considering. As Allen Ginsberg puts it the title of one of his poems: "Fourth Floor, Dawn, Up All Night Writing Letters." For Ginsberg the art of writing poems was inseparable from the activity of letter-writing. Both activities are indeed representative of the poet's engagements with and representations of the world and what he termed the poet's "immortalizing" of it.

Ginsberg, of course, was not just interested in writing poems for their own sake, and the image of the poet "up all night writing letters" accords with the kind of intense social and political activism which was such an important part of his sense of the poet's public function. It is hard to think of a twentieth-century poet who was as engaged in public affairs as Ginsberg, but many others from a range of contexts and backgrounds used the verse letter and the idea of epistolarity to explore questions of public or political concern, from the Northern Irish poet Michael Longley's "Letters" (addressed to three other Irish poets, James Simmons, Derek Mahon, and Seamus Heaney, during the Troubles), to Chicana poet Ana Castillo's deployment of the epistolary metaphor in her long novel in verse, *Watercolor Women Opaque Men* (2005). The letter has often been used as a formal and thematic agent in works where the question of how to address certain issues and communities is problematic or unclear, as it is, for example, in the Palestinian-American poet Naomi Shihab Nye's poem "The Mother Writes to the Murderer: a Letter." Nye's consideration of one (unnamed) woman's use of a letter to explore her grief at the loss of her daughter leads to a consideration of the ethical and social function of letter-writing that echoes Karl Shapiro's *V-Letter*. It also reminds readers that letters can be as deceptive as they are candid, and that they are made things, texts that construct worlds as much as they are constructed in and by them.

In the very different examples of Longley and Castillo, verse letters and the image of the letter in verse are used in contexts where the poets concerned attempt to negotiate a kind of border-crossing through the art of poetry—across the sectarian divide between Northern Irish Catholic and Protestant communities in Longley's poem and over the Mexican–American borderlands in Castillo's longer work. Both poets realize and release the kind of political energy of the letter described in deliberately understated terms in African American poet Langston Hughes's short poem "Little Old Letter," where Hughes describes the very real power that a letter can have in changing a person's life, and especially in a context of heightened political, social, or ideological pressure such as the one he had to contend with throughout his career. Longley and Castillo realize this too, in different ways, in their poems, as does the Trinidadian poet Roi Kwabena in his poem "Letter from Sea Lots," which describes the experience of emigration in terms that evoke the complexity of postcolonial displacement and dis-possession. Not only does Kwabena's verse letter reveal the form's structural and thematic versatility, but in its foregrounding of orality it also reveals the performative aspect of all epistolary address in its invocation of an "other" to whom the poem is directed as a distinctive speech act. By emphasizing speech, indeed, Kwabena reveals the tension between what is written and what needs to be said in many verse letters, a tension that may be traced back to John Donne's sense of the form as one that "speaks" in more ways than one.

Reading the verse letters that have been written by poets as different in their backgrounds and poetics as Ginsberg, Longley, Castillo, Nye, and Kwabena, one is encouraged to conclude that the contemporary verse letter is a form that is particularly well suited to the art of poetic address across borders of community, context, and place. To these, many others present themselves as engaging examples, from American poet May Sarton's constructions of regional identity in her collection *Letters from Maine* (1984), to poems such as "Epistle from a Room in Winston-Salem, North Carolina" by Irish poet Greg Delanty and Irish American poet Thomas Lynch's "St James' Park Epistle," a pair of verse letters which, when read together, reveal two different sides of the contemporary (transatlantic) experience of emigration. W.H. Auden, of course, wrote one of the most important verse letters about the transatlantic experience in "New Year Letter" (1940), his long and complex meditation on "winter, conscience and the State," "[l]ove, language, loneliness and fear" and so much else. Auden's sense of the importance of letters in general as well as their potency in the creation of poetry is most powerfully felt in this often moving and searching poem about identity and loss, but it is also articulated elsewhere throughout his large body of work, from "The Letter" (1927) to "Epistle to a Godson" (1969) and "Posthumous Letter to Gilbert White." Auden's "New Year Letter," together with "Letter to Lord Byron" (1936), have a central place in the canon of twentieth-century epistolary poems, but the poet's sense of the pervasive importance of postal systems and metaphors in society, culture, and the life of the mind is also described in succinct detail in his short early poem "Night Mail," written as a commentary for a General Post Office film in 1935. In this poem Auden acknowledges the letter's ubiquitous power in everyday life, but his poetry also recognizes the letter as a significant agent of metaphorical, symbolic, and structural force, one that allowed him to explore a wide range of themes in his work and especially where they concerned the self's situation in different social, cultural, or temporal contexts. This is certainly the case in "New Year Letter" and "Letter to Lord Byron," poems that use the epistolary form to move between and among differ-ent cultural and historical spaces and timeframes.

Auden's "Letter to Lord Byron" and the later "Posthumous Letter to Gilbert White" also point to the verse letter's usefulness in addressing figures who have died, literary or otherwise, which in itself constitutes an interesting subset of epistolary poems written by modern and contemporary poets. Glyn Maxwell's sequence of poems "Letters to Edward Thomas" from his collection *The Breakage* (1998), is interesting in the way that it recreates the life of the earlier poet but also, in the process, constructs a narrative of Maxwell's own poetic self-construction. The consequences of such self-reflexivity are revealing of both Maxwell's influences and his sense of his own work, particularly in relation to his thinking about posterity and the afterlives of both poetry and the poet. Further examples of what might be called posthumous epistolary reflection in verse can be found in the works of Kamau Brathwaite in *The Zea Mexican Diary* (1993), Ted Hughes in *Birthday Letters* (1998), Ellen Bryant Voigt in *Kyrie* (1995), Mona Van Duyn in *Letters from a Father and Other Poems* (1982), Tess Gallagher, in *Dear Ghosts,* (2007), Donald Hall in *Without* (1998), and Pearse Hutchinson in *At Least for a While* (2008). In poems such as Hutchinson's "Letter to Alan," Brathwaite's "Letter to Zea Mexican," and Hall's "Letter in the New Year," the dynamics of intergenerational literary engagement explored in Maxwell's "Letters to Edward Thomas" give way to an affecting series of meditations on the loss of a loved one in poems that derive a great deal of rhetorical power from the fact that they are framed as letters, intimate documents from this world to the next.

These texts reveal the transcendent impulse that often informs epistolary writing, the inherent desire to project words beyond the poet's immediate world towards one that is not of his own place or time. In an important sense, however, all verse letters are poems that represent an attempt to go beyond one's local context, to reach out over borders of spatial and temporal experience with the ultimate aim of reaching an addressee who is often unnamed and may represent something like the ideal reader. Hall and Hutchinson, in their poems addressed to particular people, allow readers to witness their intimate conversations with former friends and lovers, but there are poems too in which the name or nature of the addressee is unclear. This is the case, for example, in K.A. Hays' "Letter from the End of the World," from her collection *Dear Apocalypse* (2009), in which the poet imagines the destruction of manmade conceptions of time and place represented by "the meridians," those imaginary lines of longitude and latitude by which temporal and other forms of order are maintained around the globe. The very title of Hays' collection signals her interest in epistolarity. Additionally, the first section of her book, placed after the title-poem, is called "Letters," and there are three separate poems with titles beginning "Letter from . . ." in the collection. Hays' verse letters are intriguing for a number of reasons. They are all very different in formal and structural terms, but they are also curious in the ways that they tease out the various symbolic and figurative uses to which the idea of the letter can be put by the poetic imagination. Hays' "Letters" in *Dear Apocalypse* carry the weight of a whole tradition of epistolary writing within them, but they bear their freight with astonishing dexterity and ease. They reveal the formal flexibility of the genre as well as the multiplicity of ways that epistolarity can be used to think poetically about subjects ranging from "our extinction" (in "Letter from the Afternoon") to the question of faith in "Dear Apocalypse" itself.

K.A. Hays' epistolary address to a divine presence in these poems—"Apocalypse" is a self as much as it is an event—engages in an American conversation with God through poetry that was cast in postal terms by Walt Whitman in chant 48 of "Song of Myself":

> I hear and behold God in every object, yet understand God not in the least,
> Nor do I understand who there can be more wonderful than myself.
>
> Why should I wish to see God better than this day?
> I see something of God each hour of the twenty-four, and each moment then,
> In the faces of men and women I see God, and in my own face in the glass,
> I find letters from God dropt in the street, and every one is sign'd by God's name,
> And I leave them where they are, for I know that wheresoe'er I go,
> Others will punctually come for ever and ever.
>
> (Whitman 244–45, ll.1281–88)

Whitman's poem celebrates the presence of the divine in the everyday, but it also represents the world in which the poet is projected as a kind of interpreter of letters, messages "from God dropt in the street . . . sign'd by God's name." The poet's confidence that these "letters . . . will punctually come for ever and ever" is a sign of his faith but it is also a mark of Whitman's belief in the power of poetry to persist in perpetuity. Hays is just one of a number of contemporary poets who have continued Whitman's conversation with the universe, but she and others have done so, also, by reflecting on the letter as image and form. True to the letter of Whitman's project, indeed, these poets delight in the creation of poems even when those poems seem most intensely preoccupied by difficult or gloomy subjects. As Alice Notley puts it in her poem "Dear Dark Continent" (which begins with an image of "the palpable coffin"):

> We're not the completion of myself.
>
> Not the completion of myself, but myself!
> through the whole long universe.
>
> (ll.19–21)

Notley's image—informed by Whitman's and many others before it—might then be read as a declaration of poetry's constant desire to move beyond what has been established already, an impulse towards innovation that seems to have gained momentum through the poetic movements of the twentieth century but which may, in fact, always have been a part of the art form's essential spirit. In relation to the verse letter, poets continue to experiment with new possibilities by which it might be remade, even if it is often disguised among other forms and genres, not all of which are visible or identifiable when compared with more traditional or conventional types or kinds of poetic making. There is a difference, certainly, between the verse letter in which it is clear that the poet is addressing some other (human or non-human presence) and the poem in which postal or epistolary images or terms are used for symbolic or some other kind of figurative purpose. In both cases, however, an idea of the poem as a form of address—as a kind of letter—is being invoked, whether implicitly or explicitly, and this accounts for the pervasiveness of the form throughout the history of poetic practice in and across a wide range of languages and cultures. In recent years, the advent of email and the internet has meant that the idea of epistolarity and the practice of writing verse letters—and the forms they take—have undergone ever more radical revisions and reconsiderations, from Lyn Hejinian's use of excerpts from emails in the creation of her book-length poem *The Fatalist* (2003) and Tom Chivers's *The Terrors* (2009), "a sequence of imagined emails sent from the author to inmates at London's Newgate Prison incarcerated between roughly 1700 and 1760," to the creation of a broader field that Bruce Andrew has termed "electronic poetics" which includes the work of artists such as Australian internet-based poet mezangelle or Mary-Anne Breeze. The advent of e-poetics, in fact, has created new possibilities for the material, typographical, and visual representation of epistolary poems, verse letters such as those found in Chivers's *The Terrors* which are given titles made up of "Sent," "To," and "Subject" headings.

IV

In his poem "Letter to León Felipe" the Mexican poet Octavio Paz suggests that poetry is written in absences, gaps—"the space between one word and another / a configuration of the incomplete" (97) It is interesting that Paz chose the verse-letter form in which to express this view, because the verse letter has from its earliest incarnations posited the idea of open-ended address. The formal open-endedness of epistolary writing has been succinctly described by the South African writer Breyten Breytenbach in response to the question "What happens in a letter that doesn't happen in other literary forms?" He replied:

> I imagine what it does is make it possible to focus the mind and to have a particular person in mind, even if it's an imaginary person. And I think it helps to channel thoughts one may have. It's also, nearly by definition, the suspension of other literary forms. You're liberated from having to think [about, for example,] structures of fiction.
>
> (Hartley 102)

In the preceding sections we have seen that many poets from a wide range of cultural contexts have used the idea of the letter to explore new possibilities for poetry: in writing verse letters, they discovered new modes of poetic utterance and form that have, in turn, challenged us to rethink the categories by which poetry is analyzed and understood. Breytenbach's description of the letter as "the suspension of other literary forms" relates to the verse letter's actual resistance to definition, by virtue of which the form continues to be remade in ways that exceed all of the modes, methods, and expectations by which it has been known in the past—as well as attempts at describing it.

REFERENCES AND FURTHER READING

Andrews, Bruce. "Electronic Poetics." www.ubu. com/papers/andrews_electronic.html.

Auden, W.H. *Collected Poems*, ed. Edward Mendelson. London: Faber & Faber, 1994.

Berryman, John. *Collected Poems 1937–1971*, ed. Charles Thornbury. London and Boston: Faber & Faber, 1991.

Castillo, Ana. *Watercolor Women Opaque Men: A Novel in Verse*. Willimantic, CT: Curbstone Press, 2005.

Chivers, Tom. *The Terrors*. Rugby: Nine Arches Press, 2009.

Delanty, Greg. *Collected Poems 1986–2006*. Manchester: Carcanet, 2006.

Derrida, Jacques. "The Law of Genre," trans. Avital Ronell. *Critical Inquiry* 7.1 (1980): 55–81.

Donne, John. *The Satires, Epigrams and Verse Letters*, ed. W. Milgate. Oxford: Clarendon Press, 1967.

Duncan, Robert. *Letters: Poems 1953–1956*, ed. Robert J. Bertholf. Chicago: Flood Editions, 2003.

Gallagher, Tess. *Dear Ghosts,* [sic]. Tarset, Northumberland: Bloodaxe Books, 2007.

Ginsberg, Allen. *Selected Poems, 1947–1995*. Harmondsworth: Penguin, 1997.

Hall, Donald. *Without*. Boston, MA and New York: Houghton Mifflin, 1998.

Hartley, Heather. "A Nomadic Conversation with Breyten Breytenbach." *Tin House* 11.1 (2009): 101–13.

Hays, K.A. *Dear Apocalypse*. Pittsburgh: Carnegie Mellon University Press, 2009.

Hejinian, Lyn. *The Fatalist*. Richmond, CA: Omnidawn, 2003.

Hughes, Langston. *Selected Poems*. London: Serpent's Tail. 1999.

Hutchinson, Pearse. *At Least for a While*. Oldcastle: Gallery Press, 2008.

Kwabena, Roy. "Letter from Sea Lots," in *The Oxford Book of Caribbean Verse*, ed. Stewart Brown and Mark McWatt. Oxford: Oxford University Press, 2005. 307.

Longley, Michael. *Collected Poems*. London: Jonathan Cape, 2006.

Lowell, Robert. *Collected Poems*, ed. Frank Bidart and David Gewanter. New York: Farrar, Straus and Giroux. 2003.

Lynch, Thomas. *Still Life in Milford*. London: Cape Poetry, 1998.

McGinley, Phyllis. *The Love Letters of Phyllis McGinley*. New York: Viking, 1969.

Notley, Alice. *Grave of Light: New and Selected Poems, 1970–2005*. Middletown: Wesleyan University Press, 2006.

Nye, Naomi Shihab. *Words under the Words: Selected Poems*. Portland: Eighth Mountain Press, 1995.

O'Hara, Frank. *Collected Poems*, ed. Donald Allen. Berkeley, Los Angeles and London: University of California Press, 1995.

Olson, Charles. *The Maximus Poems*, ed. George F. Butterick. Berkeley, Los Angeles, and London: University of California Press, 1983.

Paz, Octavio. *Collected Poems 1957–1987*, ed. Eliot Weinberger. London: Paladin, 1991.

Pound, Ezra. *The Cantos*. London: Faber & Faber, 1986.

Pound, Ezra. *Collected Shorter Poems*. London: Faber & Faber, 1974.

Pound, Ezra. *Selected Letters, 1907–1941*. New York: New Directions, 1971.

Preminger, Alex and T.V.F. Brogan, eds. *The New Princeton Encyclopedia of Poetry and Poetics*. Princeton: Princeton University Press, 1993.

Sarton, May. *Letters from Maine: New Poems*. New York and London: Norton and Co., 1984.

Schwartz, Delmore. *Last & Lost Poems*, ed. Robert Phillips. Rev. edn. New York: New Directions, 1989.

Shapiro, Karl. *V-Letter and Other Poems*. New York: Reynal and Hitchcock, 1944.

Travisano, Thomas and Saskia Hamilton, eds. *Words in Air: the Complete Correspondence between*

Elizabeth Bishop and Robert Lowell. London: Faber & Faber, 2008.

Van Duyn, Mona. *Selected Poems*. New York: Alfred A. Knopf, 2003.

Voigt, Ellen Bryant. *Kyrie*. New York and London: Norton and Co., 1995.

Whitman, Walt. *Complete Poetry and Prose*, ed. Justin Kaplan. New York: Library of America, 1982.

Williams, William Carlos. *Paterson*. Harmondsworth: Penguin,1983.

Wordsworth, William. *Poetical Works*. London: Edward Moxon, 1845.

36

"Containing History"
Epic Poetry and Revisions of the Genre

Alex Runchman

An Antiquated Genre?

In his 1941 essay "Epic and Novel," M.M. Bakhtin describes the epic as "a genre that has not only long since completed its development, but one that is already antiquated" (Bakhtin 3). "Whatever its origins," he suggests, "the epic has come down to us as an absolutely completed and finished generic form," one that is characterized by "a hardened and no longer flexible skeleton" and that is in sharp contrast to the fluid, open-ended nature of the novel, which is "plasticity itself" (Bakhtin 15, 3, 39). Bakhtin argues that the novel effaces the distance that characteristically separates the epic poet from the national past about which he sings, and suggests that the rise of the novel, "precisely at the point when epic distance was disintegrating," resulted in the "regeneration of all other genres" (Bakhtin 39, 7).

In the first decades of the twenty-first century, such a tendency to regard epic poetry as antiquated and perhaps exhausted seems ever more pronounced. For many, Colin Burrow notes, it has become associated with "dull officialdom [and] maleness" (Burrow 1)—and, on this point, it is striking that female practitioners of the genre remain so underrepresented. Recently, Bernard Schweizer and Jeremy M. Downes, amongst others, have championed works by women that challenge the notion of epic as "the most exclusively gender coded of all literary genres" (Schweizer 1). Schweizer argues for "a minor tradition" or "coherent sub-genre" (Schweizer 10) that becomes established in the Romantic period with such poems as Mary Tighe's *Psyche*, finds a touchstone in Elizabeth Barrett Browning's *Aurora Leigh*, and continues in such diverse twentieth-century works as H.D.'s *Helen in Egypt*, Gwendolyn Brooks's *Annie Allen*, and Sharon Doubiago's *Hard Country*. One might also add Margaret Atwood's

A Companion to Poetic Genre, First Edition. Edited by Erik Martiny.
© 2012 John Wiley & Sons, Ltd. Published 2012 by John Wiley & Sons, Ltd.

Penelopiad, her retelling of the *Odyssey* from Penelope's perspective, written in both prose and verse. The development of the female epic, Schweizer maintains, is, to an even greater extent than male epic, "marked by heightened tension between adherence to and rejection of traditional epic requirements regarding form and content" (Schweizer 4). Schweizer and Downes importantly illustrate that epic poetry need not be—and has not been—a wholly phallocentric genre, but whether this will significantly alter critical perception remains to be seen.

The word "epic" entered the English language via Latin from the Greek ἔπος meaning "word, narrative, song," but in everyday parlance it is now most likely to be used as an adjective to denote any composition, or simply event, that is grand in scale—particularly, but by no means exclusively, if it features heroic endeavor. It might be applied to anything from Peter Jackson's *Lord of the Rings* trilogy to a closely fought sports contest or even something as mundane as an interminable meeting. The *OED*'s first recorded usage of "epic" as a noun meaning "a composition comparable to an epic poem" is as late as 1840; but except in academic circles it can no longer be assumed that the word specifically refers to a poetic form.

Even within academic circles, there is a general supposition that poetry is no longer the most appropriate medium for heroic subject matter: Bakhtin is not unique in consigning the epic poem to the past. John P. McWilliams Jr. has suggested, for example, that in America the definitive epic "was far more likely to be written in prose" than verse, arguing that *Moby-Dick* has a far greater claim to this title than any of the poems written in the United States in the last two centuries (McWilliams 5). Whitman's "Song of Myself" is, for McWilliams, "not the centrepiece of American epic verse," but "the massive cause of its continuing impossibility" (McWilliams 237). The reason for this, he argues, is that the impulse behind Whitman's poem is essentially lyrical. "Song of Myself" rejects narrative progression, undermines the traditional idea of an epic hero, and is in cadenced free verse rather than the conventional blank verse. Furthermore, Whitman himself had initially asserted that the expression of the American poet "is to be indirect and not direct or descriptive or epic" (McWilliams 221; Whitman 619).

McWilliams admits that later poets influenced by what he calls Whitman's "amassing of visionary lyrics"—notably Ezra Pound in *The Cantos*, Hart Crane in *The Bridge*, William Carlos Williams in *Paterson*, John Berryman in *The Dream Songs*, Charles Olson in *The Maximus Poems*, and (unmentioned by McWilliams) Louis Zukofsky in *"A"*—created works that "bear an unmistakable if slippery connection to the epic tradition," but argues that these "will always remain long, loosely unified works, without narrative, without a culturally accepted hero, and written in a literary form valued by a miniscule fraction of the reading public" (McWilliams 242, 237). It is the lack of continuous narrative, or "epos," that strikes McWilliams as most problematic in defining these works as epics and as the principal cause of their reduced readership. Prose, like film (which now appears to be the dominant epic mode), tends to retain coherent narrative, enabling heroic works in these media to appeal to a wider public.

The influence that the novel and film have had in redefining our understanding of the epic is undeniable. However, the poet intent upon writing an epic over the last century has also had to contend with ideological and formal problems. In a 1962 *Paris Review* interview, Pound admits that to attempt an epic "in an experimental age" is rash. The difficulty, he explains, is that "the modern mind contains heteroclite elements. The past epos has succeeded when all or a great many of the answers were assumed, at least between author and audience, or a great mass of audience" (Pound, *Paris Review Interviews* 75). For the modern (and postmodern) poet, no such understanding between author and audience can be assumed. Implicit in Pound's interview is a feeling that Western civilization in the twentieth century may be characterized by its acceptance of relativity, its absorption of vast amounts of varied information, and its general skepticism. In such a community, any shared sense of an ordered universe is lost, and once-unified systems of belief break down. Western society also became increasingly wary in the last century of the kinds of national myth that epic poems, such as Virgil's *Aeneid*, have traditionally propounded. This was particularly the case after the rise of Nazism—and Pound's own association with fascism marks him very much as a writer who could not expect the majority of his readers to share his ideology. Given such a separation between poet and audience, it becomes impossible for the modern writer of epic to sound the confident tone of his poetic ancestors.

The definition of "epic" Pound gives in this interview—as simply "a poem containing history"—attests to the destabilization of the term in the twentieth century. It seems, at first, untenably broad, giving no indication as to length, structure, or even the historical moments that an epic ought to contain (Pound, *Paris Review Interviews* 75). However, any attempt at a more precise definition could only be misleading, a denial of the actual complexity and scope of the poet's consciousness. Furthermore, a poem that *contains* history and a poem that is detachedly *about* a historical subject are not the same. "Contain," as Pound uses it, bears a sense not only of inclusion but also of holding together, keeping under control. He explains that one of his aims in *The Cantos* is to find a "verbal formula" that can "combat the rise of brutality" and assert "the principle of order versus the split atom" (Pound, *Paris Review Interviews* 74). Whether such an outcome is achievable is open to debate, and for this reason any attempt at a modern epic is always likely to seem grasping, self-conscious, and incomplete. Pound asserts, nonetheless, that there remain subjects which are more epic than others, chief amongst them "the struggle for individual rights." This is a struggle that is itself reflected in his own effort to write a poem that resists the view "that Europe and civilization are going to Hell" (Pound, *Paris Review Interviews* 75).

Pound's difficulties are symptomatic of those encountered by recent writers of epic. And yet, despite the increased "novelization" of the genre, and despite an international environment unconducive to the writing of epics, it would be premature to sound the death knell for epic poetry. True, it is now difficult to talk of epic poetry in any straightforward or pure sense, but, as I shall argue, the genre has always been a composite of other genres and, contrary to Bakhtin's supposition, has always been mutable.

In Delmore Schwartz's unfinished *magnum opus* of immigration and personal development, *Genesis: Book I*, one of the ghosts who comments on the protagonist's story
remarks that it has an "epic movement": "He moves through many years with utter
ease" (Schwartz 1496–97). It is perhaps more useful to speak of poems with such "epic
movements," or with epic traits, in the late-twentieth-century than it is to attempt
to claim any of them as modern exemplars of the genre. Such movements and traits
can be discerned in a great many recent poems, from Robert Lowell's *History* and
James Merrill's *The Changing Light at Sandover* to Frank Stamford's *The Battlefield Where
the Moon Says I Love You*. Other ambitious poems, such as Derek Walcott's *Omeros*,
rework earlier epic models, whilst Frederick Turner has written two epics, *The New
World* and *Genesis*, that are set in the future. New versions, or translations, of foundational epics have also been conspicuous in recent years—amongst them, Seamus
Heaney's *Beowulf*, translations of *The Inferno* by Robert Pinsky and Ciaran Carson, and
versions of *Gilgamesh* by Stephen Mitchell and Derek Hines.

Reverence and Rebellion

Bakhtin's attribution of the changes the epic has undergone since the eighteenth
century to the influence of an increasingly widespread novelistic sensibility is compelling, but his insistence on the "absolute fusion and unfreedom of the epic subject"
exposes his blindness to the subtle transformations that have characterized the genre
since its beginnings (Bakhtin 17). The conventions of epic poetry, quite as much as
those of any other genre, have always been subject to revision. The earliest epic poets
would have recited already-familiar tales, varying them and altering their emphases
with each retelling. There would have been no fixed or official version of these orally
transmitted "primary" epics, and it is for this reason that the writing down of such
poems for the first time—thereby establishing a definitive rendering—is perhaps the
most important innovation in the history of epic poetry. Had the *Iliad* and the *Odyssey*,
the touchstones of Western epic, been scribed by a writer other than Homer, we would
have inherited a very different understanding of what constitutes epic poetry.

　　Homer's poems establish the conventions we typically associate with the epic, such
as the invocation of the Muse, the involvement of the gods, a voyage or quest, and a
visit to the underworld. Every epic written since, however—beginning with the first
"literary" epic, Virgil's *Aeneid*—has revised or challenged these conventions in some
way. As A.D. Nuttall observes, the opening words of Virgil's poem—"Arma virumque
cano . . ." ("Arms and the man I sing . . .")—are, in one respect, an act of homage to
Homer, evoking the openings of both the *Iliad* and the *Odyssey*, but they also reveal
"a rebellion at the level of grammar": by using the first-person singular, "I sing,"
rather than Homer's second-person singular, "Sing" or "Tell," and by holding back
his explicit invocation of the Muse, Virgil draws direct attention to his own role as
the maker of his poem (Nuttall 3). This shift to the first person occurs surprisingly
early in the epic's history and is a significant gesture, not least because, over many

centuries, the epic has changed from an impersonal genre that deals at a distance with the feats of gods and heroes, to one that increasingly has at its heart explorations of the self, often with the poet himself as hero.

Almost every epic poet since Virgil has written their works with a similar spirit of reverence and rebellion towards their predecessors. Dante, in casting Virgil as his guide to Hell in the *Inferno*, for example, declares the utmost admiration for the Roman poet, and yet the reader is never allowed to forget that Virgil is one of the lost souls of Limbo who died ignorant of the Christian faith, whilst Dante himself is destined for Paradise. Milton's *Paradise Lost* is even more overtly at odds with the Greek and Roman models on which he draws: for him, the classical gods are amongst Satan's fallen companions whilst Satan himself can be regarded as an anti-heroic version of Aeneas. Milton's personal ambition, as a poet, is also loftier than that of his precursor poets. Neither Homer nor Virgil saw any need or reason to justify the ways of their gods to men. Milton's stated intention to do just that attests to his own heroic aspiration—his desire to "soar / Above the Aonian mount" and to pursue "Things unattempted yet in prose or rhyme" (Milton, I.15–16). Such an image of the poet himself as hero becomes potent for Romantic and post-Romantic poets, for whom selfhood becomes a central subject.

It should be noted, too, that the epic has often tended to amalgamate other genres. Burrow, in particular, has written insightfully on "epic romance," distinguishing the works of Ariosto, Tasso, Spenser, and Milton from classical epic and arguing that they attempt to resolve the "antagonistic elements" of the two distinct genres (Burrow 5). In *The Faerie Queene*, Spenser appropriates Arthurian myth in a poem whose allegory is also richly classical. While the poem can be read as a kind of national epic, whose engagement with Elizabethan politics can be readily traced, it also aspires towards the timelessness of romance. Spenser's idiosyncratic stanza form also owes more to the lyric traditions of the canzone and the sonnet than to classical epics, and elegiac and pastoral passages are prominent too. Such conflating of genres reminds us that, although departure from the archetypal epic form may be more conspicuous in the late twentieth and early twenty-first centuries, it is anything but a new phenomenon. The epic, by its very nature, has always been a hybrid genre.

All the same, there can be little doubt that after Milton the turn away from classical epic becomes more pronounced, to the extent that it becomes increasingly difficult to categorize any given long poem straightforwardly as an epic. The later seventeenth and early eighteenth centuries are notable for the rise of mock-epic as a sub-genre in its own right, and this sensibility is perhaps best epitomized, some time later, by Byron's irreverent invocation of the Muse at the beginning of the third canto of *Don Juan*: "Hail Muse, *etc*!" (Byron, Canto III.I.1). Such flippancy is at odds with the exalted respect that the Romantics generally had for their forebears—especially Milton. The early nineteenth century was a period of "epomania" in which it was almost an expectation for serious poets to prove themselves with a long, heroic poem, fuelled, at least in part, by their preoccupation with the Revolution in France.

Relatively few of these epics have endured, but those that have, such as Wordsworth's *Prelude*, Shelley's *Prometheus Unbound*, Keats's *Hyperion*, and Blake's *Milton* are every bit as derivative as Byron's more obviously combative response to the epic genre. Of these, *The Prelude*, though unpublished in Wordsworth's lifetime, has had the most enduring influence, establishing the individual's own spiritual journey as a subject worthy of epic treatment. The wholly serious suggestion that one's inner life might deserve such elevated consideration is surprisingly close to the principles of mock-epic poetry: despite their contrasting tones, personal epic and mock-epic both arise from an impulse—possibly influenced, as Bakhtin suggests, by the rise of the novel—to present a seemingly unheroic subject heroically. It is an impulse that strengthened throughout the nineteenth century and into the twentieth and twenty-first centuries, especially in America. One might debate whether Whitman's "Song of Myself" is properly an epic or not; but it is impossible to overlook the poet's implicit claim, in presenting the self not merely as hero, but as "kosmos," that the self is not only worthy of epic treatment, but has in fact become the most epical of subjects (Whitman 497). "Song of Myself" has ultimately proved more influential on later writers of epic, on both sides of the Atlantic, than the most ambitious Victorian poems, Browning's *The Ring and the Book* and Tennyson's *Idylls of the King*, although these also suggest new directions for the epic by introducing qualities of the dramatic monologue, the novel, and (as Tennyson's title proclaims) the idyll.

Lyric and Epic, Past and Present

In announcing himself as "A Southerner soon as a Northerner," and in stating that his thoughts "are really the thoughts of all men in all ages and lands," Whitman declares himself to be a national, even an international poet (Whitman 335, 355). Many twentieth-century poets also embrace such an international vision; but there is equally a strong impulse towards the local. While this might seem to limit epic potential, a poem such as the Irish poet Patrick Kavanagh's 1938 sonnet, "Epic," challenges the notion that epic must necessarily treat elevated subjects, or that it requires an expansive form. Kavanagh imagines Homer's ghost declaring "I made the Iliad from such / A local row. Gods make their own importance" (ll.13–14). It is a validation of the epic of the everyday.

Such works as Williams's *Paterson* and Olson's *Maximus Poems*, which create myths for the locales of Paterson, New Jersey and Gloucester, Massachusetts, take this challenge further. They are no less ambitious than poems that employ a broader canvas. Williams explained that he wanted to draw a parallel between the life of a city (admittedly a large enough subject in itself) and the workings of the modern mind, and, to an extent, *Paterson* can be taken as a synecdoche for the whole of the United States. Olson, however, near the beginning of his monumental work, explicitly defines Gloucester against the nation:

> o tansy city, root city
> let them not make you
> as the nation is
>
> (Olson, letter 3; section 3; ll.3–5)

There is resistance here to the idea of a national epic, reflected in the shortness of the lines, the simplicity of the address, and the abandonment of grandiose capital letters, but this cannot detract from the immensity of *The Maximus Poems* as a whole or from the work's profound engagement with American history.

All the same, the turn towards the local is a lyric, rather than an epic, tendency, and one of the most conspicuous developments to the epic in the twentieth-century is the way in which—rather than simply absorbing lyric, or containing lyrical passages, as is often the case in *Paradise Lost*, say—it increasingly employs individual lyric poems as its constituent parts. We ought to remember that as a younger poet, Pound, the writer of perhaps the most ambitious poem of the twentieth century, had been the spokesman of Imagism, a movement which eschewed epic subjects and celebrated the fusion of thought and sense in a single image. However, as James Longenbach has stated, to continue to write in such a way in the aftermath of World War I became impossible: "a generation of studiously diminished lyric writers was confronted with an epic subject" (Longenbach 109). Not to have responded to this would have seemed to Pound a dereliction of poetic duty. But he never relinquished his commitment to the individual image, and his fascination with the Chinese ideogram, one of the most economic forms of poetic expression, remains evident throughout *The Cantos*.

M.L. Rosenthal has suggested that the modern poetic sequence might be seen as an equivalent to the classical epic. "The heroic or epic aspect of the sequence," he proposes, "lies in the protagonist's effort to pit personal, historical, and artistic memory and vision against anomie and alienation" (Rosenthal 417). Whilst American poets have generally been more probing in their examination of the dialectic between the lyric and the epic, the subjective and the all-encompassing, such an inclination is also evident in more contained British and Irish works, such as Ted Hughes's *Crow*, Geoffrey Hill's prose poem sequence *Mercian Hymns*, Paul Muldoon's *Madoc: A Mystery* (which reinvigorates Robert Southey's now largely ignored epic, *Madoc*), and Brendan Kennelly's vast *Book of Judas*. Such poems as Walcott's *Omeros* and, more loosely, Merrill's *The Changing Light at Sandover*, are divided into chapters and books. This may invite a reader to regard them as verse novels—along with Craig Raine's *History: The Home* Movie, Vikram Seth's *The Golden Gate*, and Anthony Burgess's *Byrne*, for example—rather than as epics. However, the generic distinctions are once again hazy, and Merrill and Walcott engage just as searchingly with the relationship between lyric self-containment and epic scope as they do with novelistic structures.

Robert Lowell's *History* epitomizes the trend towards sequences. Most of its unrhymed sonnet sections were originally written for Lowell's earlier volume, *Notebook*.

Though the scope of *Notebook* is no less than that of *History*, its spontaneous organization emphasizes lyric immediacy, inviting readers to find their own associations between poems. Lowell's project becomes an epic endeavor when he revises and orders these poems into a sequence that more overtly suggests the ways in which it contains—that is, includes, but also reins in—history. The ordering is loosely chronological, moving from poems contemplating man's origins through Roman civilization and early American history and culminating in poems based in Lowell's own experience, as well as elegies for contemporaries. But there is also another order of history at play in poems that conflate historical or mythical episodes with the present. "Clytemnestra," for example, can be read as a monologue spoken at the same time by Agamemnon's abandoned queen and by Lowell's own mother.

Of all poetic genres, except the elegy, the epic is most intent upon memorializing, and few poets have been as conscious as Lowell of the memorializing quality of words. He often sets this against a sense of the inadequacy of words at expressing the immediate present. However, *History*, which begins by presenting history as something living, is not a work of memorialization but one which presents history as being in continual process. Lowell writes in the final sonnet of the sequence, "[G]ods die in flesh and spirit and live in print," (Lowell, "End of a Year" l.2). This goes beyond the poetic convention of saying that what dies bodily may be remembered in verse, suggesting that words may actually animate, and reanimate, imaginatively what is past. The gods of classical epics may never have lived at all in flesh and spirit, but the imaginative life that they have been given by poets endures, and print has not fixed them in one state permanently. In *History*, though, the real hero is the poet himself, who owes his modern consciousness to the ongoing influence of the past. Roy Harvey Pearce has argued that the purpose of modern American epic "may be to create a hero rather than memorialize one" (Pearce 369). The flawed hero Lowell makes of himself in *History* supports this argument.

The conflation of historical periods distinguishes other recent poems with epic traits. The 15,283 unpunctuated lines of Stamford's *The Battlefield Where the Moon Says I Love You*, in one respect a coming-of-age poem set in Mississippi, initially appear to be structured only by free association. This poem too, however, is episodic in nature and is unified by recurring motifs, the most conspicuous of which are references to long-established epics—notably the *Inferno* and *Beowulf*. The speaker, Francis, recalls how he "liked to tell stories of wars and ships / and wolves" (ll.788–89), and in particular takes Unferth, the coward "who always liked to wag his tongue . . . and told that lie about how Beowulf couldn't swim a lick" (ll.2820–22), as epitomizing the ignoble in his own society. The poem is also rich in reference to contemporary heroes of popular culture. "I dreamed I was James Dean and Marlon Brando at the same time" (l.12,236), Francis chants; and, soon after, he dreams "Robert Burns was a merman a Beowulf with gills in Loch Ness" (l.12,281), the real and the imagined from different historical periods morphing into one in the speaker's consciousness.

As in Lowell's *History*, chronological time in Stamford's poem seems, occasionally, to collapse, a phenomenon that is also explored, in different ways by Schwartz in

Genesis: Book One and Merrill in *The Changing Light at Sandover*. The heroes of these poems both commune with the dead. Schwartz's Hershey Green—who variously identifies himself with Coriolanus, Joseph, Caesar and Orestes, and at one point declares "the child resumes history, each enacts all that has been" (Schwartz 2382)—is visited by a group of anonymous ghost commentators. Merrill, meanwhile, himself the protagonist of *Sandover*, talks with Ephraim, "[a] Greek Jew / Born AD 8 at XANTHOS" (ll.152–53) through the medium of a Ouija board. Each of these cases can be read as revisions of the classical convention of a visit to the underworld and as explorations of personal—and poetic—heritage.

The acts of translating and writing new versions of ancient epics similarly project the distant past into the present. Myths that would once have been specific to certain communities are made pertinent for contemporary societies or given more universal significance. Heaney's use of Hibernicisms, such as "bawn" and "thole," in his translation of *Beowulf* is not untrue to the original, but it invests the poem with more personal and local significance, an individual stamp. *Beowulf*, Heaney explains, seemed part of his "voice-right," partly because of the proximity he discerned between Anglo-Saxon and his own Northern Irish dialect. Using Hibernicisms, however, also enables him, as an Irish poet, "to come to terms with [a] complex history of conquest and colony, absorption and resistance, integrity and antagonism" (xxx). Heaney stresses the poem's wider resonance as well, however, suggesting that the Geat woman mourning at Beowulf's funeral "could come straight from a late twentieth century news report, from Rwanda or Kosovo" (xxi). More strident examples of "translators" appealing to modern-day sensibilities can be seen in Derrek Hines's description of Gilgamesh as "A bully. A jock. Perfecto" (Hines 7), and in Christopher Logue's *War Music*—his free version of Books 16 to 19 of The *Iliad*—at the moment when Apollo intervenes to kill Patroclus and his name—"APOLLO!"—appears in huge bold type across two pages (768). This invites the reader to view the pages more like a cinema screen or speech bubble from a comic strip, and challenges our expectation that epic poetry ought to appear in continuous verse on the page.

Frederick Turner's epics, *The New World* and *Genesis*, are, uniquely, set in the future. *Genesis* imagines the cultivation of Mars by a maverick scientist and the ensuing war that is waged with his "Ecotheist" opponents on Earth. The poem owes a debt to science fiction and films such as *Star Wars*, but it is also much more closely modeled on traditional epic than any of the other poems discussed here. The decision to set his epic in the future, which has been successful for countless films, might be seen as a way of overcoming the lack of common assumptions between author and audience. However, Turner is especially self-conscious about writing epic at a late historical moment. "The poet from Mars must make the myths from scratch, / Invent the tunes, the jokes, the references" (Turner, *Genesis* IV.v.165–66), he (or, rather, the poet of the future whose poem he claims to be transcribing) explains. His references are characteristically to Virgil, Dante, and Milton, however, backward- rather than forward-looking. The principal hero, Chance van Riebeck, for example, is accused by his enemies of "playing God," and the aim of his project is to make "Mars into a paradise" analogous to the Garden of Eden (Turner, *Genesis* I.i.310, 398). Similarly, *Genesis* itself is based upon pre-existing models. Chance's creative project and the poet's act of making are implicitly compared throughout. "The unwritten poem," Turner explains in his introduction, "is the barren planet, and the composition of the poem is its cultivation by living organisms" (Turner, *Genesis* 7). The strict form— 10,000 lines of blank verse, evenly divided into five acts, each of which contain five scenes of 400 words—represents the "historical choice-pathways" in the poem made between Mars and Earth: each decision cuts off another branch of possibility (Turner, *Genesis* 7). If *Genesis* is ingenious structurally, however, and admirable in its attempts to restore "epos" to epic poetry, it is ultimately more memorable for its anxious engagement with a past epic tradition than for its modifications of the genre.

The kinds of innovation evident in all these poems suggest that the epic is a genre that continually demands to be rewritten, a position that is vividly suggested in a metaphor towards the end of *Omeros*. Walcott describes the ocean, which knows nothing of the myths with which it has been associated, as

> An epic where every line was erased
>
> Yet freshly written in sheets of exploding surf
> In that blind violence with which one crest replaced
> Another . . .
>
>   . . . It never altered its metre
> To suit the age, a wide page without metaphors.
>
>   (Walcott, LIX.i.36–44)

This suggests that the epic is a natural phenomenon, and also that it is something constant, like the ocean, but ever-changing and without obvious beginning or ending. Individual writers may shape epic material in idiosyncratic ways, but the material is ever-present in the world around them or in their interior lives. Although the poems I have discussed are all overtly literary, they are all engaged, in different ways, with questions of rhetorical expression, reminding us of the epic's oral origins. That such refashioning of the genre is still ongoing after thousands of years reminds us that the genre remains dynamic and influential even if its traditional conventions are no longer tenable. The continued production of new translations and versions of original epics also gestures back to a time when the epic was an oral form and no single version of any given poem could be considered definitive. And, in this respect, it may be fruitful—especially in light of the fact that we are ever more receptive to the idea of reading visual media in an analogous way to that in which we would read a print text—to think of the developments in epic film not so much as competition but as further radical revisions of the genre of epic poetry.

REFERENCES AND FURTHER READING

Bakhtin, M.M., "Epic and Novel: Toward a Methodology for the Study of the Novel." In *The Dialogic Imagination*, ed. M. Holquist, trans. C. Emerson and M. Holquist. Austin: University of Texas Press, 1981. 3–40.

Burrow, Colin. *Epic Romance: Homer to Milton*. Oxford: Oxford University Press, 1993.

Byron, George Gordon, Lord. *The Major Works*, ed. Jerome McGann. Oxford: Oxford University Press, 2008.

Heaney, Seamus. *Beowulf*. London: Faber, 1999.

Hines, Derrek. *Gilgamesh*. London: Chatto & Windus, 2002.

Kavanagh, Patrick. *Selected Poems*. London: Penguin, 2000.

Logue, Christopher. *War Music*. London: Faber, 1981.

Longenbach, James. "Modern Poetry." In *The Cambridge Companion to Modernism*, ed. Michael Levenson. Cambridge: Cambridge University Press, 1999. 100–29.

Lowell, Robert. *Collected Poems*, ed. F. Bidart and D. Gewanter. London: Faber, 2003.

McWilliams, John P., Jr. *The American Epic: Transforming a Genre, 1770–1860*. Cambridge: Cambridge University Press, 1989.

Merrill, James. *The Changing Light at Sandover*. New York: Knopf, 2006.

Milton, John. *Paradise Lost*, ed. Alastair Fowler. London: Longman, 1968.

Nuttall, A.D. *Openings: Narrative Beginnings from the Epic to the Novel*. Oxford: Oxford University Press, 1992.

Olson, Charles. *The Maximus Poems*, ed. George F. Butterick. London: University of California Press, 1983.

Pearce, Roy Harvey. "Toward an American Epic." *Hudson Review* 12.3 (1959): 362–77.

Pound, Ezra. *The Cantos of Ezra Pound*. London: Faber, 1987.

Pound, Ezra. *The Paris Review Interviews, IV*. London: Picador, 2009.

Rosenthal, M.L. "Modern British and American Poetic Sequences." *Contemporary Literature* 18.3 (1977): 416–21.

Schwartz, Delmore. *Genesis: Book One*. New York: New Directions, 1943.

Schweizer, Bernard, "Introduction: Muses with Pens." In *Approaches to the Anglo and American Female Epic, 1621–1982*, ed. Bernard Schweizer. Burlington, VT: Ashgate, 2006. 1–16.

Stamford, Frank. *The Battlefield Where the Moon Says I Love You* (1977). Barrington, RI: Lost Roads, 2000.

Turner, Frederick. *Genesis: An Epic Poem*. New York: Saybrook, 1988.

Turner, Frederick. *The New World*. Princeton: Princeton University Press, 1985.

Walcott, Derek. *Omeros*. London: Faber, 1990.

Whitman, Walt. *Leaves of Grass and Other Writings*, ed. Michael Moon. London: Norton, 2002.

Williams, William Carlos. *Paterson*. Manchester: Carcanet, 1992.

37

T.S. Eliot and the Short Long Poem

Jennifer Clarvoe

T.S. Eliot asserts, in "Tradition and the Individual Talent," "no poet, no artist of any art, has his complete meaning alone. His significance, his appreciation is the appreciation of his relation to the dead poets and artists" (4). An essay from *The Chapbook*, in May 1923, seems to put Eliot's notion into playful practice, attempting to match literary monuments from the years 1800–21 with counterparts from the years 1900–21 (Munro, *Chapbook* 2–6). Conrad's *Lord Jim*, for example, is offered as a counterpart to Scott's *Waverley*. (What would we offer now, one wonders—Junot Diaz's *The Brief, Wondrous Life of Oscar Wao*?) The author cannot decide, however, where the previous year's *The Waste Land* belongs: perhaps it should be matched with Keats's *Hyperion*? In another hundred years, the author hazards, it might be compared with *Paradise Lost*. "But the comparison is more or less odious," the author continues, "because the one poem is so overwhelmingly long, and the other so disarmingly short. Who shall say, rather, that *The Waste Land* is not the *Kubla Khan* of this generation?" This offers fascinating testimony to the impact of Eliot's poem. *The Waste Land* is here awarded undeniable status, but in what genre? To what family of poems does it most properly belong? Should we trace its most important affiliations to Keats's long narrative poem, Milton's epic, or Coleridge's fragment? And what role does its length play in these affiliations? Nearly 100 years later, some of these questions are easy to resolve: *The Waste Land* is a long poem, the founding example of the modern American long poem, readily classed in a family with Pound's *Cantos*, William Carlos Williams' *Paterson*, and H.D.'s *Trilogy*, among others. And yet other questions remain vexed. Should we be aware, as Eliot's contemporaries apparently were, how "disarmingly short" the poem is? Perhaps. At the same time, the *Chapbook*'s account suggests how easily we will forget its shortness, since even Eliot's contemporaries group *The Waste Land* initially with long poems, and only later come to remind themselves that it is short.

A Companion to Poetic Genre, First Edition. Edited by Erik Martiny.
© 2012 John Wiley & Sons, Ltd. Published 2012 by John Wiley & Sons, Ltd.

This is the defining paradox of the genre: *The Waste Land* is the first long poem, and it is short.

In 2010, the phrase "long poem" presents some of the same challenges as the phrase "global warming." Both seem to refer to objective measurement—of length, of warmth—but they grapple instead with slipperier relationships between measurement and expectation. How hot is global warming? We do not register the increase in average temperature as incremental warmth, but as an intensification of extremes of heat and cold, and as an increasing unpredictability in the weather. What record did this winter's snowfall break? How many days will this heat wave continue? The only thing we can count on is that familiar, expected rhythms and patterns will be disrupted. The weather offers now, by definition, some uncomfortable departure from what it used to be in some more stable, reassuring past. Perhaps the same things may be said about the long poem. It is a poetic genre of increasing unpredictability, whose familiar, expected rhythms and patterns are disrupted. The length of the long poem (like the warmth of global warming) is length that we worry about, length that makes an issue of itself, length that finds us comparing the present against the past.

How long is a long poem? 4,000 lines? 433 lines? More than 100 lines? These measurements have, at different periods in literary history, implied something that mattered more than length alone. Keats set himself the test and trial of writing a long poem of 4,000 lines. Eliot's ground-breaking poem, "The Waste Land," comes to just 433 lines, but his friend Ezra Pound called it, "the longest poem in the English landgwidge" (Pound, *Letters* 169). Pound's own long poem, *The Cantos*, which he hoped would be "really LONG, endless, leviathanic," comes to more than 400 pages; and yet, it is not unusual for readers to refer to "The Waste Land" and *The Cantos* as long poems in the same sense. Poe claimed, famously, that a long poem was a paradox, an impossibility, and that any poem longer than 100 lines sacrificed the intensity necessary for the unity of effect required by poetry. What do we care about in considering the length of the long poem? What kinds of concerns does a long poem raise for the writer engaged in its composition, or for the reader in the middle of the process of reading? The nature, urgency, and slipperiness of these questions have changed over the last one hundred years or so. What, for example, did Pound and Eliot see, looking back at the long poems of Homer, Dante, Milton, Wordsworth, and Keats? How did their retrospective view cause them to shape their own poems differently? What do we see now, looking back at their work and its legacy, and what aspirations shape the long poem in the present moment?

The *New Princeton Encyclopedia of Poetry and Poetics* includes no listing for "long poem," as such, redirecting the reader toward entries on epic, *modern* long poem, and narrative poetry. What this signals is that it is not until the early twentieth century with the experiments of the modernists that "long poem" comes to designate not length, but genre—a genre that positions itself in relation to epic and narrative poetry, from which it seeks to distinguish itself. The modern American long poem calls attention to the problem of its length, and–above all—to the difficulty of its progress. T.S. Eliot's *The Waste Land*, Ezra Pound's *Cantos*, William Carlos Williams' *Paterson* and H.D.'s *Trilogy* are poems made out of fragments—fragments that announce themselves as fragments, without narrative or meditative glue, without regular stanzas or consistent metrical systems, without the sustaining momentum of divine inspiration or cultural approval—foregrounding by this fragmentation the problem of their own construction, which is the problem of the long poem. The resulting form is a mixture of closure and openness, compression and dispersal, certainty and uncertainty. The reader is made self-conscious about her own uncertainty in putting together the fragments of these poems as she reads.

The formal difficulty of these fragmented long poems enacts or dramatizes the tension between the centripetal pull of the interior world of the self, and the centrifugal pull of the larger exterior world, and the roles of these competing forces in shaping the poem. In effect, these long poems dramatize the tension between lyric and epic. Eliot's short long poem, *The Waste Land*, collapses the epic into the lyric, offering us a poem made of "a heap of broken images" and fragments shored against ruin. Eliot tests and checks the excesses of the nineteenth-century long poems against the rigor and intensity of the early twentieth-century lyric poem, with the important collaboration of Ezra Pound. In the century or so since then, the nature of both epic aspiration and lyric rigor has shifted significantly, not least because of the profound influence of the modern poets, on both the genre of the long poem and the lyric.

Many critics have usefully charted the transformation of the *epic* aspirations of the modern long poem, from the experiments of Eliot and Pound, through the extensions and transmogrifications of the genre in the midcentury, to the flourishing of a cornucopia of revisionist, oppositional, pluralist anti-epics in the late century. I would like to propose, however, that the urgencies driving the genre of the long poem have gradually shifted since Eliot's time, in part as aims and definitions of the *lyric* have shifted. To mark one point in this trajectory of shifting urgencies, this essay will consider John Ashbery's "Self-Portrait in a Convex Mirror" as a counter-example to Eliot's *The Waste Land*, appearing roughly half a century later, and responding to the transmutations of the lyric over that half-century. It is certainly possible to consider both of these poems as examples of the same genre (as, in quite different modes, a number of critics do), I would suggest they are to some extent opposites. If Eliot's *The Waste Land* is the shortened long poem, Ashbery's "Self-Portrait in a Convex Mirror" is the lengthened short poem. Ashbery pushes, ekphrastically, past the frame of the Parmigianino painting he considers, and past imagistic restrictions on the lyric as well. Both these poems enter into and transform the critical and creative conversations of their particular moments, offering innovation, but also crystallizing concerns of those moments.

The Short Long Poem

In 1905, A.C. Bradley's lecture, "The Long Poem in the Age of Wordsworth," raised important questions that establish a backdrop for the composition of "The Waste

Land." He offers a critical perspective on the poetry of the nineteenth century, expressing particular disappointment in the long poem in comparison to the virtues of the lyric. These are the same issues Eliot will take up in his essay, "Prose and Verse," and the concerns that *The Waste Land* attempts to address. The long poems of Wordsworth (*The Prelude, The Excursion*), Keats (*Endymion, Hyperion*), Shelley (*Alastor*), and Byron (*Childe Harolde*) are all faulted, as are the long poems of Tennyson and Browning. None of these poems, Bradley maintains, presents "a great whole" (181). Their greatness lies, instead, in certain *fragments* of the whole, and it is for the virtues of those fragments we reread them. He suggests, however, that the imperfections of the long poems and the excellence of the lyric "have a common origin," in the exploration of the poet's "inward and subjective tendencies," which are best exploited in the lyric, but weaken the long poem. He faults the age, rather than the poets (Eliot will follow him in this), but nonetheless concludes: "a single thought and mood, expressive of one aspect of things, suffices, with its melody for a lyric, but not for a long poem. That requires a substance which implicitly contains a whole 'criticism,' or interpretation of life" (197). The poems of this era, long and short alike, best explore the development of the poet's soul. What they lack, however, is the impression of "a massive, building, organizing, 'architectonic' power of imagination" (202). Finally, Bradley takes up and dismisses what he calls Poe's "delusion" that "the long poem is not merely difficult, it is impossible," and "[t]he thing called a long poem was really, as any long poem must be, a number of short ones linked together by passages of prose" (203). If this were so, Bradley argues, "it would condemn not only the long poem, but the middle-sized one, and indeed all sizes but the smallest" (203). (In fact, this almost seems to prefigure modernist editing practices like those described in Pound's narrative of the composition of his extremely short poem, "In a Station of the Metro," which begins as a long, diluted work, is later cut in half, and is finally pruned with imagist severity to its authoritative two-line version.) The correction Bradley offers to this delusion, is to recognize that "in any poem not quite short, there must be many variations and grades of poetic intensity" (204). It is this note that Eliot will pick up, in his own "Prose and Verse," emphasizing "the movement toward and from intensity, which is life itself" for a long poem (Eliot, "Prose and Verse" 5).

Eliot's long poem, *The Waste Land*, draws on the strength he saw in nineteenth-century long poems: the strength in certain fragments of the whole. Its fragmentary proceeding, paradoxically, instead of suggesting failure, suggests self-critical rigor, its awareness of the difficulties of its age. "I can connect nothing with nothing," offers a difficult truth. *The Waste Land* establishes this self-critical mode definitively, and the other modern long poems follow this pattern. What appeared in the nineteenth century in Wordsworth's *The Prelude* as a problematic but nonetheless hopeful question about poetic possibility, "Was it for this?" metamorphoses in the twentieth century into seemingly definite negative assertions—such as the *Cantos'* "Hang it all," or Williams's acknowledgment that *Paterson* must proceed by "defective means," or H.D.'s disparagement, in *Trilogy*, of the poem's "disagreeable, inconsequent syllables."

It is as if the necessary precondition for attempting the impossible is the recognition it cannot be done. These poems try to make the reader recognize mastery of the broken form as a project with more integrity—as a more difficult project—than the mastery of smooth, sustaining stanzas. Heroism in the poem comes from the struggle to resist resolving ease. The short length of *The Waste Land* is peculiar testimony to its strength. It offers a heap of broken images—but it is a heap whose fragments have nonetheless been made certain, shored against inexplicable ruin. Stanzas, sentences, rhythms, and lines have been cut down to certain fragments, certain words. The poem is about the human activity of securing and making certain, and the poem's moral is that such activity ultimately ends in fragments. Words alone are certain good. Beyond this, the poem's moral can become embedded in larger schemes, either more hopeful or more despairing; the poem encourages, brilliantly and perversely, nearly opposite readings of its fragments. We can emphasize the strength of making certain by breaking empty schemes, or we can emphasize the potentially cold comfort of such certainty.

In fact, a consideration of the work of both Eliot and Pound on the drafts of *The Waste Land* suggests just how much the construction and polishing of the long poem depended on the intensification of its fragments, interruptions, and truncations. By retaining abrupt shifts and cuts, the evidence of strenuous editorial work, it becomes a work of art whose every line announces its aim. As the long line is cut back, and made stronger, so the long poem is cut back and made stronger. "To break the pentameter," Ezra Pound claimed, "that was the first heave." The most immediate and profound sense of fragmentation in these poems comes from the ways they react to the expectations of regular meter, especially iambic pentameter. The ghost of the expected meter is a powerful presence in *The Waste Land*, something both entertained and exorcised. The poem opens with lines that waver between tetrameter phrases and pentameter lines.

> April is the cruellest month, breeding
> Lilacs out of the dead land, mixing
> Memory and desire, stirring
> Dull roots with spring rain.
>
> (ll.1–4)

This is the sound of difficult beginnings, as "dull roots" try to take hold. The tacked-on actions—breeding, mixing, stirring—are denied the force they would have if, lineated according to their syntax, they launched the second, third, and fourth lines. Instead, they wobble after each comma, and the left side of the line shrinks back to dull roots. This metrical uncertainty represents vexed attempts at action, an uncertainty the reader is forced to mime, always coming up short on the wrong beat, the wrong foot. The most powerful, rhythmic movement doesn't enter the poem until it actively questions its own progress and declaims against its weakness. Here, turned against itself, diagnosing its own limitations, the sound of the poem is strong:

> What are the roots that clutch, what branches grow
> Out of this stony rubbish? Son of man,
> You cannot say, or guess, for you know only
> A heap of broken images, where the sun beats . . .
>
>   (ll.19–22)

Unlike the wavering opening lines with their uncertain endings, these four lines offer authoritative pentameters, as in the line that closes the stanza: "I will show you fear in a handful of dust" (l.30). The poem threatens itself with dissolution: from dull roots, to broken images, to nothing but dust. What is the mode of proceeding over the poem as a whole? What is the relationship of section to section, fragment to fragment? Weak feeble progress calls forth active criticism; plaintive query is met by emptiness and silence.

Again and again, throughout *The Waste Land*, Eliot concludes sections by reduction, maiming, or truncation. The scene from the hyacinth garden, gets recounted in halting enjambments, each of which emphasizes what the speaker cannot do:

> Your arms full, and your hair wet, I could not
> Speak, and my eyes failed, I was neither
> Living nor dead, and I knew nothing,
> Looking into the heart of light, the silence,
> *Od' und leer das Meer.*
>
>   (ll.37–41)

I could not—I was neither—I knew nothing. In this passage the five-beat lines are strongly cut back to three stresses on the wide and empty sea. Or later, in Philomela's plaint,

> Twit twit twit
> Jug jug jug jug jug
> So rudely forc'd.
> Tereu.
>
>   (ll.203–06),

the line is cut back to one stress. Instead of a regular metrical pattern sustaining the whole, our expectation is being redirected toward a certain kind of fragmentation. We are made to feel the forceful truncation, which will come to suggest to the reader the "shortened" long poem.

Over the course of the poem as a whole, there is a gradual progress—away from the uncertain shrinking in the opening lines, towards a difficult certainty that expresses itself in fragments. In fact, the poem's concluding "Shantih shantih shantih" moves of from the motion of uncertain human drift to a certainty beyond human understanding. We can chart the progress of the poem as the shifting of its metrical center, so that the cutting back which is at first a sign of weakness eventually becomes a kind of strength, allowing us to shore these fragments against ruin. The truncated lines themselves embody the poem's crucial doubleness of weakness and strength, creator and editor. The interruptions make the poem feel both difficult and long.

The scene, for example, of the wide and empty sea is both a desolate corrective to the seeking love and a mirror for the silence at "the heart of light." Words fail because of the moment's emptiness—or because of its fullness. Similarly, although Philomela's song is cut short as she tries to name her violator, Tereus, the sounds themselves become stronger; the short vowels of the pitiful twit twit twit are replaced by the more forceful long vowel of "rudely," repeated in "Tereu." Examination of the drafts reveal that each of these metrical reductions arrives in revision, produced upon reread-ing. Eliot interpolates *"Od' und leer das Meer"* to conclude the section (*Drafts* 7). His variants on Philomela's plaint provide an example of his search for inevitable, deliber-ate form, before he settles on the neat reduction based on threes (*Drafts* 31, 43). This pattern shows up again in his revision of list and lines to make threes the basis of

> Jerusalem, Athens, Alexandria
> Vienna, London
> Unreal.
>
> (*Drafts* 75)

This kind of truncation, while it enacts a version of breaking forms, also produces a powerful sense of closure. The neat concluding couplet of a sonnet, for example, gets its snap of finality not just from its rhyme, but from the fact that this rhyme comes unexpectedly sooner than the pattern in the rest of the sonnet suggested. Eliot exploits techniques that, despite their seeming irregularity, out-sonnet the sonnet in exerting formal closure, in providing the sound of certainty, in aligning those three beats with authority.

In a note introducing the drafts of *The Waste Land*, Eliot is famously self-deprecating:

> Various critics have done me the honour to interpret the poem in terms of criticism of the contemporary world, have considered it indeed, as an important bit of social criti-cism. To me it was only the relief of a personal and wholly insignificant grouse against life; it is just a piece of rhythmical grumbling.
>
> (*Drafts* 1)

Self-deprecation or not, these words seem to echo the terms from Bradley's essay on the problems with the nineteenth-century long poem. Here is the substance Bradley required of the long poem, "which implicitly contains a whole 'criticism' or interpre-tation of life," the centrifugal pull of the larger world (Bradley 197). Here, too, it is set against the centripetal pull of the lyric poet's "inward and subjective tendencies" (197). The ingenious staging of the interior breakdown is designed to resonate with external chaos. The accomplishment of the poem is not to be dismissed as "rhythmical grumbling," but to be discovered precisely there. It is Eliot's distinctive mastery of a range of broken rhythms that allows his poem to embody the dynamic tension between epic aspiration and lyric precision, moving toward and from intensity that is the life of the long poem.

The Long Short Poem

John Ashbery's "Self-Portrait in a Convex Mirror" is in six unequal sections, totaling 552 lines (more than 100 lines longer than *The Waste Land*, for what it's worth). The first section is ninety-nine lines long, the middle four sections are all approximately fifty lines long, and the sixth and last section is almost as long as the rest put together again, at 241 lines. I'd like to propose that these proportions are every bit as meaningful as those of the five sections of Eliot's *The Waste Land*, in presenting us as readers with a certain kind of problem of length. One has to wonder if the first section is perversely designed to approach Poe's 100-line limit. We do not experience Ashbery's long poem as "a heap of broken images." And yet we take our cue, as readers, from the image of the englobed soul offered by that convex mirror, and the problem of such a "life englobed" (Ashbery, l.55). Does this poem, like the nineteenth-century long poems, offer us the development of the poet's soul? If so, that development is profoundly vexed, since

> the soul is a captive, treated humanely, kept
> In suspension, unable to advance much farther
> Than your look as it intercepts the picture.
>
> (ll.29–31)

Here, as in *The Waste Land*, is the long poem defined by the problem of the tension between centripetal and centrifugal forces, but the nature of the problem has changed. The progress of the poem is necessarily difficult: it is, like the soul, "unable to advance." The poem, like the soul "would like to stick one's hand / Out of the globe" (ll.56–57), and certainly the hand, like Francesco's "is big enough / to wreck the sphere" (ll.72–73) but it does not do so—it will not break into fragments. The poem's transitions are not combustible or drastic.

If the poem as a whole has a structure, it might be that of a fluid chain of soap bubbles blown tenuously through each other. As Ashbery suggests at the start of the poem's second section, "The balloon pops, the attention / Turns dully away" (ll.100–01). The first 100 lines inhabit and test the frame of the convex mirror, pressing against it, ending with a certain poise; the next section begins by popping that frame, and by turning its attention to the centripetal forces whirling us away, like a "carousel starting slowly / And going faster and faster" (ll.124–25) as our days do not cohere, but instead fly out the window. As time speeds up on us, this second section comes in at roughly half the length of the first. We get accustomed to this shorter wavelength of the middle four sections. They oscillate between centripetal and centrifugal forces. The poem offers a bubble chamber whose skin is "as tough as reptile eggs" (ll.170–71) or lapses "Like a wave breaking on a rock, giving up / its shape in a gesture which expresses that shape" (ll.199–200). Each of these gestures contributes to our sense of the poem as a variously permeable dream. Ashbery, like Eliot, directs us to unreal cities (Rome, Vienna, New York) outside the frame of the painting but informing it, so that the poem itself becomes "the movement toward and from intensity, which is life itself" ("Prose and Verse" 7). There is the breath that fills the bubble, and the wind that tears it away; both are implicated in the "breeze like the turning of a page" (l.311) that launches us into the last section of the poem.

After the middle's shorter oscillations, however, we are correspondingly unprepared for the long, long, final section. It threatens to stretch our bubble into a darkening corridor, lengthening now when we have come to wish for refuge. Then, just as we find ourselves wondering warily how long it can go on, that corridor becomes "the wrong end of the telescope" (l.530), collapsing down (along with the city around it) into "the gibbous / Mirrored eye of an insect" (ll.541–42). The structure is long enough to play with our sense of duration and dilation, but short enough to make us feel the paradox of our own contradictory wishes—that the poem let us out, let us in, keep going, come to a stop, not end so soon. We readers are made self-conscious about our relationship to this dilemma of the poem's difficult length: it is our look that inhibits the soul's progress from the globe right at the start, even as it seems to summon it. The reader of "Self-Portrait in a Convex Mirror" may be, in many ways, the "hypocrite lecteur" addressed by Eliot's poem, but Ashbery's poem does not accost us with this accusation. In fact, its first section ends with a "gesture which is neither embrace nor warning / But which holds something of both in pure / Affirmation that doesn't affirm anything" (ll.97–99). In its self-reflexive imagery, vexed discontinuous development, and fraught address to the complicit reader, "Self-Portrait in a Convex Mirror" replays central concerns of Eliot's long poem, but from a decidedly different position. It is our slippery wishes that we confront, rather than the jagged fragments of the poem.

In Eliot's poem, the reader feels pressure to find a key or keys—ones that will work precisely because they are not obvious, overarching, or schematic. The author seeks coherence beneath the rubble, and the reader seeks it too, among the fragments. In Ashbery's poem, however, we become weaned away from the wish to find such a key, as the artist, too, finds "He has omitted the thing he started out to say / in the first place" (ll.449–50). This is true in life as in art:

> Each person
> Has one big theory to explain the universe
> But it doesn't tell the whole story
> And in the end it is what is outside him
> That matters, to him and especially to us

> Who have been given no help whatever
> In decoding our own man-size quotient and must rely
> On second-hand knowledge.

(ll.499–506)

We began the poem reaching with the writer to complete the gesture Parmigianino's hand made, reaching toward us. But, at the end of the poem, "The hand holds no chalk,"

> And each part of the whole falls off
> And cannot know it knew, except
> Here and there, in cold pockets
> Of remembrance, whispers out of time.

(ll.549–52)

The centripetal bubbles and centrifugal breezes have dwindled into "cold pockets" and "whispers," which hardly seem to differ from each other. The parts will not cohere, but neither will they clash.

Postscript to the Long Poem

In a lively recent essay, "An Anatomy of the Long Poem," discussing a great range of examples (whose wildly varying lengths and natures she readily acknowledges) Rachel Zucker asserts, "long poems are imperfect" (44). But she does not mean what Bradley did when he lamented, 100 years earlier, the imperfection of long poems, in contrast to the perfection of the lyric. In fact, she celebrates this imperfection. The long poem is a terrifically fertile and flourishing genre at the present moment, taking a multiplicity of kaleidoscopic forms. It no longer defines itself against the lyric, however. In fact, the concerns of the lyric and the long poem are beginning to converge. The "unity of effect" Poe praised in the lyric of fewer than 100 lines is hardly the defining criteria of the skittery, elliptical, heterogeneous lyric of the present moment. For that matter, the "long poem" Zucker discusses at greatest length, is Randall Jarrell's "A Man Meets a Woman in the Street," which, at ninety-three lines, comes in under Poe's limit of 100 lines. Zucker admires above all, but "the 'extraneous' parts of Jarrell's poem, his digressions and diversions," not its lyric intensity. She suggests, further, that "sometimes the long poem is imperfect because striving for perfection is a questionable and problematic pursuit" (44). Zucker's claims are not programmatic; they are, if anything, happily anti-programmatic. But they definitely suggest the temper of the times, and signal a shift within the genre. Perhaps the short poem has taken to its heart the centrifugal forces of the long poem. Perhaps the phrase, long poem, will cease to be the impossibility Poe found it, and become instead a redundancy.

REFERENCES AND FURTHER READING

Ashbery, John. *Self-Portrait in a Convex Mirror.* New York: Penguin, 1975.

Baker, Peter. *Obdurate Brilliance: Exteriority and the Modern Long Poem.* Gainesville: University of Florida Press, 1991.

Bernstein, Michael. *The Tale of the Tribe: Ezra Pound and the Modern Verse Epic.* Princeton: Princeton University Press, 1980.

Bradley, A.C. "The Long Poem in the Age of Wordsworth." In A.C. Bradley, *Oxford Lectures on Poetry.* London: Macmillan, 1950. 117–205.

Dickie, Margaret. *On the Modernist Long Poem.* Iowa City: University of Iowa Press, 1986.

Eliot, T.S. "Prose and Verse." *The Chapbook* 22 (1921): 3–10.

Eliot, T.S. "Tradition and the Individual Talent." In *Selected Essays: New Edition.* New York: Harcourt, Brace and Co., 1950. 3–11.

Eliot, T.S. *The Waste Land: A facsimile and transcript of the original drafts including the annotations of Ezra Pound,* ed. Valerie Eliot. New York: Harcourt Brace Jovanovich, 1971.

Friedman, Susan Stanford. "When a 'Long' Poem Is a 'Big' Poem: Self-Authorizing Strategies in Women's Twentieth-Century 'Long Poems.'" *LIT* 2 (1990): 9–25.

Gardner, Thomas. *Discovering Ourselves in Whitman: The Contemporary American Long Poem.* Urbana and Chicago: University of Illinois Press, 1989.

Kamboureli, Smaro. *On the Edge of Genre: The Contemporary Canadian Long Poem.* Toronto: University of Toronto Press, 1991.

Keller, Lynn. "The Twentieth-Century Long Poem." In *The Columbia History of American Poetry,* ed. Jay Parini and Brett Millier. New York: Columbia University Press, 1993. 534–63.

Li, Victor P.H. "The Vanity of Length: The Long Poem as Problem in Pound's *Cantos* and Williams' *Paterson.*" *Genre* 19.1 (1986): 3–20.

McHale, Brian. *The Obligation toward the Difficult Whole: Postmodernist Long Poems.* Tuscaloosa: University of Alabama Press, 2004.

Miller James, E., Jr. *The American Quest for a Supreme Fiction: Whitman's Legacy in the Personal Epic.* Chicago: University of Chicago Press, 1979.

Munro, H.H. "Editor's Notes." *The Chapbook* 37 (1923): 2–6.

Pearce, Roy Harvey. "The Long View: An American Epic." In Roy Harvey Pearce, *The Continuity of American Poetry.* Princeton: Princeton University Press, 1960. 59–136.

Pound, Ezra. *Selected Letters of Ezra Pound, 1907–1941.* New York: New Directions, 1971.

Riddell, Joseph N., ed. *The Long Poem in the Twentieth Century. Genre* 11 (1978): 459–687.

Rosenthal, M.L. and Sally M. Gall, *The Modern Poetic Sequence: The Genius of Modern Poetry.* New York: Oxford University Press, 1983.

Williams, Nerys. "The Monstrosity of the Long Poem." *Poetry Wales* 45.2 (2009). http://poems.com/special_features/prose/essay_williams-n.php.

Zucker, Rachel. "An Anatomy of the Long Poem." *American Poet* 37 (2009): 41–44.

38

Making War Poetry Contemporary

Rainer Emig

War poetry is among the most ancient literary genres. The epic is in essence a war poem, and its extant relics take us back to the origins of civilization—with texts such as the story of Gilgamesh dating from around 2,400 BC. Homer's *Iliad* is one of the founding texts of Western literature and has managed to bridge the gap between Classical Antiquity, the Middle Ages (when it was busily adapted) and our modern or postmodern age. In this sense, war poetry is always traditional. Yet it has also adapted itself not only to developments in warfare, but also to changing literary tastes. Good examples are Dryden's neoclassical rewritings of Virgil and Chaucer.

Pinpointing the emergence of contemporary war poetry therefore remains tricky, and the present chapter does not claim to do it complete justice. However, it makes sense to locate the emergence of contemporary war poems at a time when the modernization of warfare coincided with a crucial development in literature, yet one that affected poetry only belatedly: the rise of Realism. Improvements in strategy, the streamlining of logistics with steam trains and ships as more reliable means of transport, but most importantly the rise of faster communication with the aid of the telegraph make the Crimean War the first modern war. The telegraph and journalism entered an alliance in it, and it was journalism that triggered a celebrated Victorian war poem that also employed realist techniques: Alfred Lord Tennyson's "The Charge of the Light Brigade" (1854).

Tennyson's poem owes one of its most potent images, the "thin red line" to a phrase in a report by William Howard Russell for *The Times*. Yet it does more than use a topical battle to demonstrate to the Victorian public the deficiencies of their military leaders. The poem also employs journalistic conventions, those of a Realism that had entered prose fiction from the eighteenth century onwards, yet had largely remained outside poetry, especially war poetry. There, heightened rhetoric and the uncritical

A Companion to Poetic Genre, First Edition. Edited by Erik Martiny.
© 2012 John Wiley & Sons, Ltd. Published 2012 by John Wiley & Sons, Ltd.

celebration of individual heroism remained the norm, as can be glimpsed in the famous lines of Felicia Hemans' "Casabianca" (1826): "The boy stood on the burning deck" (l.1) and

> Yet beautiful and bright he stood,
> As born to rule the storm;
> A creature of heroic blood,
> A proud, though child-like form.
>
>   (ll.5–8)

Hemans' poem, lest one forget, is about a boy allowing himself to be blown up on an abandoned British boat in the Battle of the Nile in 1798.

In stark contrast, Tennyson's poem knows only collective effort, and though heroic, it is nonetheless tempered by the incompetence of the leadership that condemns the British cavalry to a suicide attack against Russian forces during the Battle of Balaclava on October 25, 1854. Moreover, the language of its opening verses already displays the drastic Realism of a shouted command and only contains one symbolic term that instantly evokes disaster:

> Half a league, half a league,
> Half a league onward,
> All in the valley of Death
> Rode the six hundred.
>
>   (ll.1–4)

The poem retains inversion and capitalizes on repetition, yet one that echoes rather the mechanics of attack than those of traditional poetry:

> Cannon to right of them,
> Cannon to left of them,
> Cannon in front of them
> Volley'd and thunder'd;
> Storm'd at with shot and shell,
> Boldly they rode and well,
> Into the jaws of Death,
> Into the mouth of Hell
> Rode the six hundred.
>
>   (ll.18–26)

Contemporary martial vocabulary is evident in "Volley'd." Equally untraditional is the anonymity of the collective "six hundred." Though ancient war epics sometimes stressed numbers, they tended to highlight individual courage as well, as did Hemans' "Casabianca." Equally anonymous remain those responsible for the desperate attack. The repeated line "All the world wonder'd" (ll.31 and 51) that sets up a distant rhyme with the earlier verse "Some one had blunder'd" (l.12) contains a subtle yet powerful critique of leadership. Once again Tennyson's poem displays its debt to journalism. Although it concludes in a seemingly traditional way that still chimes with epic conventions ("Honour the charge they made! / Honour the Light Brigade, / Noble six hundred!" ll.52–54), the poem is as much a description of the bravery of ordinary soldiers as an inquiry into the reasons for such futile self-sacrifice.

A rift has opened up in war poetry that permits the inclusion of anti-heroic elements. A related rift concerns the poem's form: it manages to combine traditional and anti-traditional elements in a mixture that recognizes the war poem as an established genre, yet opens up possibilities for the future. The combination of old-style camaraderie and its attendant jargon and modern cynical attitudes paved the way for seminal war poems, such as the ones collected in Rudyard Kipling's *Barrack Room Ballads* (1892/1896), to which the English language owes expressions such as "Tommy" for British soldier.

Contemporary war poetry was moreover deeply influenced by a mode of thinking that emerged in the later years of the nineteenth century and blossomed in the early twentieth: psychoanalysis. Tennyson's six hundred share an intention, but lack individual psychology. The same is true for Hemans' boy hero. The arrival of a modern view of psychic activity and dispositions in war poetry paradoxically coincided with the removal of individuality from the battlefield in the mechanized First World War. The gap thus created produces significantly contradictory war poems, such as heroic pro-war ones by the likes of Rupert Brooke and the satirical anti-war tracts of Siegfried Sassoon. Yet it is writers like Isaac Rosenberg and, even more pronouncedly, Wilfred Owen, who incorporate individual psychic anxieties into war poetry. The outstanding example is Owen's "Strange Meeting," which forms another stepping stone in the direction of contemporary war poetry. The poem marries everyday images and terms with highly charged motifs and rhetoric. Already its title prepares for the strategic imprecision that governs the text. What exactly is the nature of the encounter, and what kind of strangeness is experienced? The poem's opening continues this theme:

> It seemed that out of battle I escaped
> Down some profound dull tunnel, long since scooped
> Through granites which titanic wars had groined.
>
> (ll.1–3)

The "it seemed" introduces a dream vision not unlike those of Medieval allegories. As it turns out, the lyrical I reports from beyond death. Terms such as "out of battle" or "escape" are part of the recent realist heritage of war poetry, but even commonsense terms such as "tunnel" is accompanied by contradictory adjectives: "profound" (as in physically or conceptually "deep") and "dull" (which could stand for sound qualities or lack of distractions). The "titanic wars" that form the only obvious symbolically charged term make war a quasi-mythological feat, yet the strange verb "groined" instantly links this with bodily intimacy and even sexuality, and by doing so attaches the poem to psychoanalytic paradigms.

The lyrical I understands the nature of its strange location only in the moment of another recognition: when one of the sleepers of this tunnel wakes up and smiles at it. Discovery equals self-discovery, and what is discovered is at least twofold. War's destructive nature is no surprise to speaker or reader, yet what is startling is the willing acceptance of its destructiveness. War is not an accident of culture and civilization, but one of their possible outcomes: "Courage was mine, and I had mystery, / Wisdom was mine, and I had mastery" (ll.30–31). The convenient tale of individuals stumbling blindly into a war that they neither want nor control is rejected by the poem, an exculpation that still featured behind even the tragic stories contained in "Casabianca" and "The Charge of the Light Brigade."

This cultural bracketing of war forms the macrocosmic equivalent of the individual mirroring of speaker and enemy, the stranger of the strange encounter who ends up calling the lyrical I "friend": "I am the enemy you killed, my friend. / I knew you in this dark" (ll.40–41). The oxymoronic formula makes sense when one recognizes (in the same shocking way that the poem proposes for the cultural "nature" of war) the indivisible identity of "the soldier"—who is always the same, no matter on which side he fights. It is not merely his subjection to war that robs him of a self, but also his attachment to an impersonal unconscious (the dark of the tunnel, dream, memory, or vision). The poem's shock is not merely the intimacy that unites speaker and enemy at the poem's close ("Let us sleep now . . ."; 44), but the resulting lack of identity of the speaker who now truly becomes a "universal soldier," yet without thereby gaining any fixed meaning or value.

Owen's poem is radical in its imagery, yet still fairly conventional in its form. The First World War is frequently credited with having triggered the Modernist movement in literature, yet very few poems resulting from this war really bear the marks of Modernist styles. A notable exception that balances on the borderline of poetry in the same way as T.S. Eliot's *The Waste Land* is David Jones's *In Parenthesis* (1937). Jones freely mixes genres: lyrical fragments, dramatic direct speech, and epic passages. He uses intertextuality to link the First World War with much earlier ones, such as the historical defeat of 300 Welsh Warriors at Catreath, which forms the basis of the epic *Y Gododdin*, written around the sixth century—extracts from which precede each of the seven sections of Jones's text. Finally, *In Parenthesis* merges the meaningless slaughter of trench warfare with Christian notions of sacrifice—to achieve a typically Modernist mixture that sometimes resembles Eliot's later poetry, especially *Four Quartets*.

But when one takes a closer look at *In Parenthesis*, the differences to *Four Quartets* could not be greater. These couch their interest in war in allegories and metaphysical speculations. *In Parenthesis* instead acknowledges its endeavor to make sense of war—even at the price of its own form. War is described as a void, an absence of sense into which human existence tumbles. In it history as a linear narrative becomes suspended and the notion of a unified self obliterated. This void, however, creates the very space in which the aesthetics of Modernism find their realm. There they can produce their own reworking of the Romantic sublime in the stress on the uniqueness of the moment that eludes representation—only to immediately attempt a representation of this loss and absence.

Making the representation of war itself a theme is also a good shorthand description for the most controversial war poem of the 1930s, W.H. Auden's "Spain 1937." Originally written as a pamphlet to finance medical aid during the Spanish Civil War, the poem nonetheless refuses to engage in a straightforward propagandistic taking of sides. It does not even remain in Spain, but instead philosophizes about world history, knowledge, religion, and power. In its panoptic view of the origins of war, it includes all of these and, even more insistently, the individual psychological failures of ordinary people. Yet while Owen's psychology is existential, Auden's is mundane and often casual. Much less casual is his view of power, which is more pronounced and historically determined than in the previous examples of war poetry. War is both the specific effect of ideology, anchored in what Marx calls the base structure of politics and economy, and the result of individual weakness, choices, and decisions. Ethics therefore enter the equation in much more pressing form than in the general accusations and laments of earlier war poems:

> And the life, if it answers at all, replies from the heart
> And the eyes and the lungs, from the shops and squares of the city:
> "O no, I am not the Mover,
> Not to-day, not to you. To you I'm the
>
> "Yes-man, the bar-companion, the easily-duped:
> I am whatever you do; I am your vow to be
> Good, your humorous story;
> I am your business voice; I am your marriage.
>
> "What's your proposal? To build the Just City? I will.
> I agree. Or is it the suicide pact, the romantic
> Death? Very well, I accept, for
> I am your choice, your decision: yes, I am Spain."
>
> (ll.45–56)

This radical linking of war with its historical and ideological origins and individual failure as well as its depiction in clinical and largely "unpoetic" language also characterizes another famous war poem in Auden's oeuvre, "September 1, 1939," which commemorates the start of the Second World War in lines such as

> Faces along the bar
> Cling to their average day:
> The lights must never go out,
> The music must always play,

> All the conventions conspire
> To make this fort assume
> The furniture of home.
>
>   (ll.45–51)

One of the most drastic changes that warfare underwent in the twentieth century was the abolishment of the distinction between war zones and peaceful areas. Aerial bombardment did away with it and created, now in a literal sense, the 'home front." Edith Sitwell's "Still Falls the Rain," subtitled "The Raids, 1940. Night and Dawn," frames in poetry the experience of the London Blitz on non-combatants. Its language echoes religious poetry, but also contains down-to-earth references to the present situation:

> Still falls the Rain—
> Dark as the world of man, black as our loss—
> Blind as the nineteen hundred and forty nails
> Upon the Cross.
>
>   (ll.1–4)

Learned allusions to the Bible and antiquity shade over into concrete locations, such as the Potter's Field, a pauper cemetery. Yet despite the religious framing of the poem that resembles Eliot's contemporaneous efforts in *Four Quartets*, one can never be sure whether the poem promises consolation or even redemption in lines such as the concluding one " 'Still do I love, still shed my innocent light, my Blood, for thee' " (l.33). Marked as direct speech and prefaced by "the voice of One who like the heart of man / Was once a child who among beasts has lain" (ll.31–32), it figures as Christ's voice. Yet only a few lines above the poem had employed religious verse in a clearly anachronistic way: "O Ile leape up to my God: who pulles me doune" (l.25). The quotation from Christopher Marlowe's *Doctor Faustus* is voiced by a character who refuses to be saved. Easy consolations, even of the religious kind, are apparently no longer appropriate in modern war poetry. Richard Eberhard's "The Fury of Aerial Bombardment" (1941) makes this even more explicit in its questioning of God's and men's historical responsibility.

Easy sympathy and clichéd compassion are risks that contemporary war poems have had to face ever since they ceased to be unanimously patriotic or nationalistic, in other words, ever since identities and positions in them became blurred or problematic. More self-reflexive war poetry makes this part of its structures, as does Auden's "The Shield of Achilles" (1953), which links the Homeric heroic motif of its title with images that bring to mind prisoner-of-war camps, the Holocaust, and perhaps also Hiroshima and Nagasaki. Yet of course war poetry continues to be written, both by survivors and (often belated) onlookers, which simply represents a direct emotional (and thereby often naive) response to war's traumas.

As naive as some of these poetic responses was also the terrible misnaming of the time after 1945 as the "postwar" era, when in fact no other era in human history saw such a proliferation and simultaneity of armed conflicts. The Second World War did not so much make way for as become the Cold War, out of which the Korean War and the Vietnam War emerged. Vietnam has proved a decisive cultural trauma for the United States, and it is no coincidence that war poetry responded to its challenges.

Robert Bly counters this trauma by framing it in nature images that derive from his attachment to a tradition instigated by Henry David Thoreau. In "Driving through Minnesota during the Hanoi Bombings" (1967) terrifying events such as the random killing of a tortured boy become

> crystals,
> Particles
> The grass cannot dissolve.
>
> (ll.13–15)

Bly's mythopoetic and archetypal vision, however, also takes him into problematic territory, for example when he implicitly compares the Vietnamese to ants in "Johnson's Cabinet Watched by Ants" (1967).

Denise Levertov wrote a number of poems about the inability to make a meaningful poetic comment on the atrocities committed in Vietnam from a secure and privileged position in the United States. In them, lines such as "all my tears . . . are used up" from "In Thai Binh (Peace) Province" (1975) (ll.4–5) often resort to an easy subjectivism that laments poetic inability, itself a long-standing cliché in poetry. Yet she also managed to write more successful Vietnam poems, such as "The Pilots" (1975), by reversing perspectives: it presents American prisoners of war and delves into their attitudes, convictions, and backgrounds from a simulated outsider perspective, a Vietnamese one or that of a court of human rights. Lines such as

> Yes, they knew
> the names of the bombs they dropped
> but didn't say whether they understood what these bombs
> are designed to do
> to human flesh.
>
> (ll.3–7)

reduce the already sparse language of modern war poetry even further to a quality that indeed resembles court notes. The horror that is imminent in the conjunction of bland terms such as "bombs," "dropped," "do," and "flesh" is not so much felt by the lyrical I, but created in the reader. The reader also feels the ethical appeal hidden and unveiled simultaneously in the subtle use of the verb "designed."

Allen Ginsberg's poetry is a far cry from making the war a personal issue. "War Profit Litany" (1967; published 1972) that he tellingly dedicates to Ezra Pound, a would-be theorist of usury and notorious defender of the Second World War and Mussolini's fascism, starts with the lines "These are the names of the companies that have made / money from this war" (ll.1–2). It continues with top managers, ambassadors, lobbyists, generals, and ends, as in Auden's poems, with ordinary employees who have also profited from the Vietnam War. Needless to say, names are never given. Yet through its repetitive phrasing and paratactic structure the poem resembles a religious litany: "nineteenhundredsixtyeight Annodomini fourthousand / eighty Hebraic" (ll.3–4). Rather than a lament, however, the poem is an elaborate accusation—or rather self-accusation—of America getting rich on war through one of its sons.

Lawrence Ferlinghetti opted for a prose poem when he wrote "Where Is Vietnam?" in 1964. Any poetic form, including free verse, is abandoned as too conventional. Instead, a sort of Joycean stream of consciousness rejects even the ordering intrusion of commas and full stops. "Meanwhile back at the ranch the then President also known as Colonel Cornpone got out a blank Army draft and began to fill in the spaces with men" (201) opens the poem that includes not merely ironic set-pieces (such as the "Meanwhile, back at the ranch" convention of low-budget radio, cinema, and television of the 1960s), but also phrases that resemble political and advertising slogans, such as "Vietnam was not a place but a state of mind" or "The world really does rotate Westward don't it?" (202).

Structure itself becomes a problem for contemporary war poetry when even the most radical forms have been used up and entered convention and canonical tradition. A similar conundrum affects protest: of course a war poem from the middle of the First World War onwards is generally an anti-war poem. Yet when does protesting against yet another war become a mere fashionable stance, or worse, *de rigueur*? These are the issues that contemporary war poems have to address if they do not want to be consigned to the critical garbage heap of "yet another war poem." It is interesting to notice that, as a consequence of these impasses, much recent war poetry opts for surprising "sideways" or even seeming "backward" moves when it comes to its own tradition and that of poetry in general.

That the Modernist radicalizing of form is generally not continued might not surprise considering the fact that further fragmentation and erosion of form would only lead to unreadable texts and the danger of art for art's sake that would immediately disqualify itself in the context of war. What might be more surprising, in an age that has seen literary and cultural theories enter the mainstream of cultural debates, is that few texts nowadays follow the complex political and ethical inquiries that poems by the likes of Auden and Ginsberg represent. Many recent war poems are short, and many are ostensibly simple, if not simplistic, in form. Yet behind the return to what often appears to be cheap sloganeering often lurk very conscious deployments of older literary conventions and reflexive engagements with an old chestnut that has accompanied war poetry from its epic beginnings: propaganda.

Traditional pro-war poems as much as ancient epics were always propagandistic. Even the earliest examples of modern war poems cannot help but uphold heroic patriotic notions. Uncritical attachment to such general ideologies became shaken and ultimately shattered through the experience of dehumanized modern warfare at least from the First World War onwards. Yet this does not mean that contemporary anti-war poetry is not ideological. As we have seen, its immediate precursors (by Owen, Sitwell or Auden) worked through individualistic and psychological, religious, historicist, and Humanist paradigms. These created a tradition of their own, out of which, for instance, American Vietnam poems emerge as variations, even when they seemingly employ what is now called "post-humanist" positions, as in the mythopoetic nature references in Bly's poems. Psychologized individual anxiety and/or criticism of "the system" have now replaced the traditional celebration of heroism and camaraderie. It is these new "traditions" in war poetry that most recent war poems write against. This is particularly evident in British war poems about the recent or still current conflicts in Bosnia, Iraq, and Afghanistan.

The old alliance between war poetry and journalism was reactivated recently when *The Guardian* commissioned Tony Harrison to go to war-torn Bosnia and submit poems from there. One can regard this as a critical intervention by a leftist newspaper to counter the still current practice of the British government to commission war artists. Yet Harrison himself claims that the power of poetry emerges particularly from catastrophic events such as war. He finds in poetry

> a reaffirmation of the power of the word, eroded by other media and by some of the speechless events of our worst century. Sometimes, despite the fact that the range of poetry has been diminished by the apparently effortless way that the mass media seem to depict reality, I believe that, maybe, poetry, the word at its most eloquent, is one medium which could concentrate our attention on our worst experiences without leaving us with the feeling, as other media can, that life in this century has had its affirmative spirit burnt out.

> ("Author Statement")

Already in 1991 Harrison had, again in *The Guardian*, responded to the media images of charred Iraqi soldiers in the aftermath of the Second Gulf War with the poem "A Cold Coming":

> I saw the charred Iraqi lean towards me from bomb-blasted screen,
> his windscreen wiper like a pen ready to write down thoughts for men,
>
> his windscreen wiper like a quill he's reaching for to make his will.
> I saw the charred Iraqi lean like someone made of Plasticine.

> (ll. 1–4)

The deliberately artless, though in fact elaborate rhythm and the mundane vocabulary are used to create a seemingly objective everyday image. Its irony lies in the fact that the outrageous image has become routine viewing ever since television started to broadcast war into every home during the Vietnam War. This was further perfected in the real-time coverage of the Second Gulf War. Its effect, many media scholars argue, is ironically a loss of reality of what is presented, in the same way that the mutilated corpse of an Iraqi soldier becomes equated with a toy.

The poem combines obscenity (its title refers to rumors that Allied soldiers had their sperm frozen before they entered a war zone where they expected biological and chemical weapons), Classical references and newspaper headlines such as the *Sun*'s infamous "GOTCHA" that celebrated the sinking of the Argentine ship Belgrano during the Falklands War in 1982. But it also contains references to poetry and poets. These are by no means shown as privileged moralists or detached observers, but as part of the modern media machine that digests war in the same way as it does any other news. In fact, poetry in Harrison is a job, as is demonstrated by the cynical line "That's your job, poet, to pretend I want my foe to be my friend" (l.77). It mocks the Humanist detachment of much anti-war poetry that pretends to feel as much for the enemy as for one's own side, a tendency visible in some of Levertov's poems. But Harrison's poetry also reproduces the macho posturing so prevalent in war in many of its own features.

This is not be expected in the poems that the current British Poet Laureate Carol Ann Duffy commissioned in response to the ongoing conflict in Afghanistan and the now official inquiry into Britain's involvement in the third Iraq War. Her poem "Big Ask" makes cruel fun of the procedures of such an inquiry by presenting it as the mixture of a catechism and a TV quiz show with mythical issues thrown in and politicians' evasive answers:

> What was it Sisyphus pushed up the hill?
> *I wouldn't call it a rock.*
> Will you solemnly swear on the Bible?
> *I couldn't swear on a book.*

> (ll.1–4)

What becomes evident in the poems collected by Duffy from male and female British poets of her generation is that war poetry has now become post-war poetry in the sense of already dealing with the cultural and media fallout of conflicts. Thus Amanda Dalton's poem "Untidiness" depicts the National Museum of Iraq in Baghdad after the successful invasion by American troops. Yet when its opening lines tell us that "Some time after the looting, the locked gates, / the US tank stood idle in a gallery" (ll.1–2), it by no means indicates that war is now safely stored away as a cultural memory. Culture has been damaged, and the threat of further destruction continues to loom large.

The poetry commissioned by Duffy has also become meta-war poetry in the sense of reflecting about the possibilities and impasses faced by contemporary war writing. Reponses to the challenge take on wildly different forms. These can be impressionistically personal as in Gillian Clarke's "Listen," that is, nonetheless, in no way existential or psychological, when the poem asks its readers to listen

> to the chant that tranced me thirty years ago
> in Samarkand: the call to prayer at dawn;

> to that voice again, years and miles from then,
> in the blood-red mountains of Afghanistan.
>
> (ll.1–4)

In stark contrast to such seemingly apolitical stances, some of this poetry deliberately approaches propaganda. Paul Muldoon's "Afghanistan," for instance, is content to use simple word play on "dark" as in "obscure" to criticize the British government's Afghanistan policy. Daljit Nagra's "Have I Got Old News for You" pokes cruel fun at both the "special relationship" that Britain claims to entertain with the United States and at the equally special relationship of the British public with a mediatized reality. Already the poem's title parodies the British TV show "Have I Got News for You" that uses the previous week's headlines for a celebrity quiz.

There is also much awareness of the time-honored (and therefore perhaps not so honorable) rituals surrounding war, from the reference to "our brave boys" (l.3) in Carole Satyamurti's "Battle Lines" to the established symbol of war commemoration in Jane Weir's "Poppies." But there are also insistent images that hark back to the existential challenge posed in Owen's "Strange Meeting" while adding to it the shocking impersonality that is characteristic of modern warfare as much as of genocide. A haunting example of this merger of traditional war poetry atmospherics with the antihuman challenge of contemporary warfare is Robert Minhinnick's poem "After the Stealth Bomber" that commemorates the civilians killed by a so-called "smart bomb" in a shelter in the Amiriya suburb of Baghdad:

> all a fog of flesh.
> one body with four hundred souls
> is exposed in a photographic flash.
> They pick the wedding rings and wisdom teeth
> from crematorium ash.
>
> (ll.10–14)

The poem talks about the atrocities created by modern war's supposedly enlightened technology, but it also exposes the challenges and media competition (especially with ubiquitous images) that contemporary war poetry has to face. It demonstrates how by making the used-up images of the mass media and the long-established clichés of war poetry their material, contemporary war poems can inject them with renewed immediacy and critical potential.

References and Further Reading

Auden, Wystan Hugh. *The English Auden: Poems, Essays and Dramatic Writings 1927–1939*, ed. Edward Mendelson. London and Boston, MA: Faber & Faber, 1977.

Bly, Robert. *Selected Poems*. New York: Harper & Row, 1986.

Duffy, Carol Ann. "Exit Wounds." 25 July 2009. *The Guardian*. www.guardian.co.uk/books/2009/jul/25/war-poetry-carol-ann-duffy.

Ferlinghetti, Lawrence. "Where Is Vietnam?" *New Directions* 19 (1966): 201–02.

Ginsberg, Allen. *The Fall of America: Poems of these States 1965–1971*. San Francisco: City Lights, 1972.

Harrison, Tony. "Author Statement." *British Council Contemporary Writers*. www.contemporarywriters.com/authors/?p=auth188.

Harrison, Tony, *The Gaze of the Gorgon*. Newcastle upon Tyne: Bloodaxe Books, 1992.

Hemans, Felicia Dorothea. *The Poetical Works of Felicia Dorothea Hemans*. London: Oxford University Press, 1914.

Levertov, Denise. *The Freeing of the Dust*. New York: New Directions, 1975.

Owen, Wilfred. *The Collected Poems of Wilfred Owen*, ed. Cecil Day Lewis. London: Chatto & Windus, 1963.

Sitwell, Edith. *Selected Poems*. Harmondsworth: Penguin, 1952.

Tennyson, Alfred, Lord. *Poems*, ed. Hallam Lord Tennyson. 2 vols. Vol. 2. London: Macmillan, 1908.

39

Bestiary USA

The Modern American Bestiary Poem

Jo Gill

The origins of the bestiary (in its simplest and broadest terms defined as the representation of non-human and sometimes fantastical animals for the purposes of instruction and/or amazement) seem as old as language itself. John Berger in his 1977 essay "Why Look at Animals?" traces the ancient lineage of this tradition of representing—and even literally inscribing—animals: "The first subject matter for painting was animal. Probably the first paint was animal blood. Prior to that, it is not unreasonable to suppose that the first metaphor was animal" (7). From the earliest time, then, to imagine and realize ourselves as humans, we have imagined and realized ourselves in relation to (which may also mean as different from) animals. The nature and limitations of this potential relationship underpin the bestiary tradition as it has developed from the ancient world through its flowering in the medieval period to its emergence in the modern American context that is my main focus here.

Modern inflections of the bestiary tradition feature in a number of different cultures. In England, for example, Ted Hughes's *The Hawk in the Rain* (1957) and *Crow* (1970) have made extensive use of incidents and motifs from the animal world. His Australian contemporary Les Murray similarly invokes whales, elephants, dogs, insects, pigs, sea lions, and a plethora of other animals in collections such as *Translations from the Natural World* (1993). It is in the American context, though, that we can most clearly trace the emergence and achievement of modern forms of this ancient mode, and for this reason I focus on modern American bestiary poems in the discussion that follows.

According to T.H. White in the foreword to his 1954 work, *The Book of Beasts being a Translation from a Latin Bestiary of the Twelfth Century*, the bestiary's "sources go back to the most distant past, to the Fathers of the Church, to Rome, to Greece, to Egypt,

A Companion to Poetic Genre, First Edition. Edited by Erik Martiny.
© 2012 John Wiley & Sons, Ltd. Published 2012 by John Wiley & Sons, Ltd.

to mythology, ultimately to oral tradition" (231). The bestiaries of the medieval period represented, in Debra Hassig's words, "the culmination and apogee of allegorical functions for animals, assembling stories and pictures of beasts and birds for purposes of moral instruction and courtly entertainment" (xi). Among its earliest known precursors are Aristotle's *Historia Animalium* (fourth century BC), an account, said to have been commissioned by Alexander the Great, of the sum of contemporary understanding of the animal world (Berger 10; Clark 15–16), and Pliny the Elder's *The Natural History* (first century AD), a study in thirty-seven volumes of "just about all of the classical zoological 'knowledge'" (Schaefer xiii). More important even than these to the emergence of what we might now recognize as a bestiary, was the *Physiologus*. This was probably produced first in Greek between the fifth and second centuries BC and was widely translated, copied, and supplemented such that over the succeeding centuries its original inventory of some forty-nine beasts grew to over 140 (White 231, 234; Schaefer xiii). As Arnold Clayton Henderson concludes, an important feature of the bestiary tradition from the outset has been this propensity for change: "innovation," he suggests, has long been a "sought-after good" (40).

During the Renaissance, the "relatively brief" and predominantly allegorical bestiaries of the Middle Ages were supplemented by more expansive "animal histories" whose aim was to "collect all the available learning on each animal" (Edwards 72, 73). By the early 1600s, the emphasis had begun to shift from the old "emblematic tradition" (Edwards 5) whereby the animal was understood to represent some other— usually human and moral value—to the "study of real animals" (Schaeffer xiv). This move was stimulated, in part, by emerging opportunities for exploration and collecting (Edwards 99; Clark 21).

By the nineteenth century with the work of Charles Darwin and his peers, this process seemed complete. Human understanding—and thus dominance—of the animal world had left little apparent use for a tradition reaching back to the medieval period and beyond. Yet as is evident in the work of the modern American poets discussed below, the bestiary retains—and from some perspectives has consolidated—its place as an important form. It functions now, of course, in an entirely different context and for different purposes than in its medieval heyday. Nevertheless, in the work of Countee Cullen, Marianne Moore, Kenneth Rexroth, Gary Snyder, Anne Sexton, and many others, we find unexpected "testimony to the flexibility and power of the genre" (Hassig xii).

Moral Lessons

One of the most important features of the medieval bestiary was its moral purpose. In Anne Clark's terms, the bestiary of this period was "a moral and religious treatise in which the supposed characteristics of animals are used to illustrate points of doctrinal and moral significance" (26). Clearly a post-Darwinian, post-Freudian America thinks in rather different ways. Nevertheless, the bestiaries of the modern American poets considered here do retain elements of this didactic intent. Indeed, for the purposes of this essay, we might define the modern American bestiary poem as not just a poem about animals, but as a poem featuring animals that also invites a moral, ethical, or philosophical reading. Arguably such poetry epitomizes a long-standing American tendency—one whose influences derive from Puritan typology and Transcendentalist ideals of enlightenment and improvement—to turn "to nature in order to pose epistemological and esthetic questions" (Rotella ix). It also draws on the legacy of Native American cultures and a poetry which inherits a particular relationship with the earth and its creatures.

Countee Cullen's joyful, provocative, genre-crossing bestiary, *The Lost Zoo* (1940), like the best examples of the medieval tradition, combines "moral instruction" with "entertainment" (Hassig xi). Its lessons are both personal (about the folly of pride, as represented by the figure of "The Snake-That-Walked-Upon-His-Tail") and political (about the oppressive silencing of a race). The book tells the story of those "Very Unfortunate Few We Never Shall See in Any Zoo" (45)—the eight or more fantastical animals who, for reasons which the collection goes on to explain, failed to make it into Noah's Ark. Like earlier bestiaries, but rather unlike most other twentieth-century examples, *The Lost Zoo* uses illustration as a way of nuancing or amplifying the poems' meanings—to different effect as illustrators have changed over successive editions (see Gillian Adams). Also like earlier bestiaries, the collection includes animals both familiar (the L.E. Phant and the bear) and imaginary (the "Ha-ha-ha" and the "Sleepamitemore"). Randy Malamud suggests a comparison with the creatures in Conrad Aiken's 1977 book *Who's Zoo* and concludes that "Cullen's animals are all imaginary . . . as fancifully extravagant as Aiken's, and as unfettered by any human constraint" (*Reading* 318). Imaginary they may be, but as we will see in a moment, their fanciful features are precisely conceived in order to expose their very "human constraint." Cullen inherits from his antecedents the knowledge that, in Berger's gnomic words, "animals offered explanations" (8).

Like its medieval antecedents, *The Lost Zoo* is profoundly allegorical. It features a dual narrative voice which yokes Cullen (or the human speaker) with his cat, Christopher. As Gillian Adams has shown, much of the fascination of the book, and its allegorical bite, come from its exposure of the processes of silencing and marginalization which have hitherto denied oppressed animals (the cat, Christopher) or, allegorically, African-American citizens, a voice in their own representation. The human speaker's confession of his shock on being asked by Christopher to acknowledge his value by crediting him as the book's co-author is deeply telling: "'I must confess that I was astonished. Such a thing had never entered my head. A cat, as part author of a book? Whoever in the world had heard of such a thing?'" So, too, Christopher's response exposes the hypocrisy of the author's (for which read white America's) habitual denial of African-American agency: "'Now don't go telling me that you never heard of such a thing,' he said, shaking a paw at me. 'That's what you people always say when you don't want to do the fair thing by us animals'" (20–21).

Kenneth Rexroth's 1944 sequence, "The Phoenix and the Tortoise (1940–1944)" (*Collected Longer*) similarly takes an animal fable and the relationship between a real and an imagined creature as the starting point for an exposé of the political turmoil of the age. The World War II context is signaled in the dates of the subtitle and in the emphatic pathetic fallacy of the opening stanza wherein "All night vast rollers exploded / Offshore" (ll.7–8). Here, atypically of the bestiary tradition, animals suffer as a direct consequence of human action:

> Broken starfish, a dead octopus,
> And everywhere, swarming like ants,
> Innumerable hermit crabs,
> Hungry and efficient as maggots.

(ll.12–15)

No longer mere abstractions, animals are physically implicated in the human failings they might hitherto only have emblematized.

Rexroth's later "A Bestiary" (*Collected Shorter*), although less explicitly focusing on political themes, nevertheless references these important contexts. Throughout, the short, end-stopped lines give a cautious and admonitory tone. Some of the animals' characteristics are to be expected ("The eagle is very proud" [l.1]; "The Fox is very clever" [l.1]). Others less so. And it is this mixing of the familiar and the unexpected that gives the sequence its unsettling edge. "A Bestiary" works hard to construct and then erode the reader's sense of security. "Cow," for instance, comically opens: "The contented cow gives milk" (l.1), but then turns and addresses the reader in the second person—and thus in the position of the cow—and commands: "When they ask, 'Do you give milk?' / As they surely will, say 'No'" (ll.2–3). "Seal" sets up an initially endearing picture of the seal in its native habitat but rapidly and shockingly turns into an indictment of what happens when "He goes on dry land and men / Kill him with clubs" (ll.4–5). "Trout" encodes a warning about deception: "Confronted with fraud, keep your / Mouth shut and don't volunteer" (ll.3–4). The poem "I" offers a chilling repudiation of any larger spiritual value to life while another, "Uncle Sam," exposes the mythologization and idealization of the nation. The appearance of entries for "I" and "Uncle Sam" in the bestiary is a sign of the interchangeability of human and animal traits which in turn undermines conventional orthodoxies about human superiority. In these poems, the speaker's authority and the implied dominance of humans over animals is profoundly troubled. An exploration of the porosity of such categories is, as we will see in a moment, one of the distinctive concerns of the modern American bestiary poem.

Other contemporary poets encode moral and ethical messages in their bestiaries. Gary Snyder's "What Happened Here Before," like Cullen's *The Lost Zoo*, revisits and reinterprets the Creation story. In Snyder's account, there is no Noah and, by implication, no God. From the outset, the narrative is detailed, specific and emphatically material in its description of the vast and ancient processes by which the natural world came into being. Instead of imaginary creatures, the poem presents us with the marvelously real, precisely rendered in number and in kind. From its opening line ("300,000,000") the poem counts down through the ages ("80,000,000"; "3,000,000"; "40,000"; "125" [ll.9, 20, 32, 38]) to a "now" (74) of fear and uncertainty. Emphatic present participles ("loading, compressing, heating, crumpling, / crushing, recrystallising, infiltrating" [ll.3–4]), alliterative and onomatopoeic description ("in streambeds / slate and schist rock-riffles catch it" [ll.16–17]) and attentive rendering of the rich variety of the animal world ("deer, coyote, bluejay, gray squirrel / ground squirrel, fox, blacktail hair" [ll.28–29]) make this a compelling vision. Its disruption, then, with stanza 5's abrupt "Then came the white man" (l.39) is all the more unsettling. The organic and natural are corrupted by the human and social. Hard-won glimpses of "sunlight" and "forest" (ll.68, 76) in the closing stanzas of the poem are crowded out by the taxes, treaties and "worked-out mining claim" (50) of a new and potentially devastating order. The threat is registered even, or particularly, by the animals. The human figures at the end of "What Happened Here Before" (the speaker's sons, speaking metonymically for a wider humanity) are reduced to uncertainty: "Who are we?" they ask, "Who are they?" (ll.78, 83). Only the bluejay sees and knows enough to screech a final warning.

Snyder is not alone in his concern about human impact on the American environment. Poet Wendell Berry laments that: "The pristine America that the first white man saw is a lost continent, sunk like Atlantis in the sea. The thought of what was here once and is gone forever will not leave me as long as I live. It is as though I walk knee-deep in its absence" (qtd. in Elder 59). The "didactic function" of the (medieval) bestiary (Syme 163) becomes in Snyder and a number of other contemporary poets, an environmental and ethical imperative. Look at the world in this way, these poems say, and see what you have done. Look at the world in this way, and learn to live better. Native American poet Joy Harjo's work, including the poems "Invisible Fish" and "Song for the Deer and Myself to Return On" (*How We Became Human*), similarly seeks to reconcile the animal and the human, the past, the present and the future. Narratives from such traditions have proved an important influence on the resurgence of animal and eco-poetry in the late twentieth century. As John Elder puts it: "Snyder evokes a wholeness of life greater than our American culture has achieved since the colonial origins of the nation . . . Native American models also serve as an avenue to enhanced sympathy and identification with animals" (43). This is not, though, an unproblematic relationship. As Catherine Rainwater points out, "a tangle of unexamined cultural assumptions about nature and indigenous people underlies much of the discourse of early, and even present-day America" (261).

In addition to Native American sources, the growing interest in Chinese and Japanese writing and in various forms of Buddhist philosophy across the twentieth century from Ezra Pound's era through the midcentury popularity of Japanese poet Bashō to the Beat poets' embracing of Eastern cultures, opened up for American poetry an alternative set of figures and perspectives. One might argue that in their midcentury heyday at least such influences offered a new inflection on the spiritual foundations of the bestiary. Where the medieval bestiary offers a Christian message based on the biblical interpretation of animal symbols, some modern American bestiaries offer a message based on Eastern religions, albeit reformulated for Western ears.

Human–Animal Relationships

In the examples examined thus far, the basic tenets of the bestiary tradition wherein certain animals are credited with, and stand in for, certain human values and capacities, are subtly reworked such that the animal (the bluejay in Snyder's poem, for example) is not simply the object of the (superior) human's will, but instead takes the moral and ethical lead. In the medieval tradition, animals (both real and imaginary) are figments of the human imagination; they exist only to fulfill the human's moral intentions. In the twentieth-century bestiaries considered here, animals assert or are given—the distinction is moot—their own existence and agency.

One of the strategies which modern bestiarists have used which would not have been contemplated by their antecedents is to encourage a close identification with animals. From the medieval period to the late twentieth century, "the relationship between people and non-human animals [has been] codified in social culture as hierarchical and fundamentally impermeable" (Malamud, *Poetic* 3). More recently: "The ecological movement has . . . brought forth a vision of a fragile interdependence between human culture and non-human nature, in which the role of humans cannot be taken for granted but has to be negotiated" (Gymnich and Costa 69). Mary Oliver's poetry invites a unification of people and animals. Her poem "Wild Geese," from the 2004 collection of the same name, urges "You only have to let the soft animal of your body / love what it loves" (ll.4–5); "Spring" self-reflexively makes connections between self, animal, and world; "The Dipper" laments the failure of human language and seeks some other mode of engagement:

> there being no words to transcribe, I had to
> bend forward, as it were,
> into his frame of mind.
>
> (ll.9–11)

"Such Singing in the Wild Branches" gives way to a sublime fantasy of communication and mutual understanding. As Malamud argues, this erasure of the boundaries is, in part, a symptom of a wider postmodern rethinking of hitherto unquestionable categories that have "traditionally separated 'us' from 'them': absolute boundaries between people and animals are giving way to blurry ones" (*Reading Zoos* 36).

The importance of birdsong in Oliver's bestiary (for example, in the poem "Such Singing in the Wild Branches") should not be overlooked. Song, of course, has long been used as a metaphor for poetry and specifically for lyric verse. For Oliver the threat to the environment is metaphorically represented by the potential silencing of the birds which, by extension, poses a threat to the poet's song. Simultaneously though, and reciprocally, the threat to the birds' song (as also in the screeching bluejay in Gary Snyder's "What Happened Here Before") inspires the voice of the poet whose own singing thereby becomes an important weapon in the birds' defense.

The 1962 publication of Rachel Carson's wake-up call about environmental damage, *Silent Spring*, is an important context here. As her title indicates, it is the absence of bird song which Carson takes as a signifier of the environmental catastrophe threatening the nation: "Over increasingly large areas of the United States, spring now comes unheralded by the return of the birds, and the early mornings are strangely silent where once they were filled with the beauty of bird song" (100). Elder has pointed to a "great tradition of birdsong in American literature from Whitman and Thoreau to Levertov." Mary Oliver, he argues, "offers the experience as well as the idea of birdsong in her heavily cadenced catalog, filled with the sensuality of lines like 'Carolina wren, chickadee, nuthatch, english' in which consonants collide and break the line into a pulsing syncopation" (222). Oliver's description, like Snyder's list in "What Happened Here Before" (quoted earlier) bears comparison with a passage from Carson's *Silent Spring* which catalogues warblers killed by DTT spraying: "the black-and-white, the yellow, the magnolia, and the Cape May; the oven-bird whose call throbs in the May-time woods; the Blackburnian, whose wings are touched with flame" (107). In every case, the list of birds is used to didactic effect.

Like her contemporary Mary Oliver, Sharon Olds explores the newly vulnerable threshold between the animal and the human. Her "Bestiary," though, is less concerned with allegorizing environmental concerns than with critiquing orthodox boundaries of sexuality and gender. In "Bestiary," which reports a child's enthusiastic fantasies of cross-species reproduction, the latent commonality of animals and humans is registered in the opening line: "Nostrils flared, ears pricked." The delayed allusion to a subject here (line two's "our son") leaves the referent of the first line pleasingly unclear—is it animal or human? On one level, it is the son whose nostrils are "flared" and whose ears are "pricked" in an evocation of childish excitement which also, pertinently, conveys his animal-like instincts. On another, it is the animals themselves (which the mother and son proceed to discuss) whose senses are alerted. Later in the poem as the son contemplates the strangeness of animals, their very strangeness becomes a part of him and his own consciousness:

> fur and
> skin and hooves and teeth and tails
> whirling in his brain.

(ll.4–6)

Mother and son are explicitly likened to animals, "rolling on the floor / laughing like hyenas" (ll.8–9). The excitement of this overstepping of the assumed barriers between animals and humans motivates the poem. There is a charge or thrill (hence "flushed, panting / Hot" in ll.15 and 16) in rethinking the orthodox divide, in recognizing the possibilities of diverse sexual practices and arrangements ("lynxes / eagles, pythons, mosquitoes, girls" [ll.16–17]). The conventional and socially determined explanation for sexuality ("Too late, / I remember love" [ll.9–10]) seems tired and inadequate in light of the "glittering" (l.18) possibilities imagined by the son.

May Swenson's slightly earlier poem "Beast" (*Nature*) daringly imagines a bestial subjectivity comprising "my brown self" (1). The absence of punctuation throughout the poem replicates the transgression of the established restrictions and parameters that the poem describes. As Carol Adams and Josephine Donovan suggest "theorising about animals is inevitable for feminism. Historically, the ideological justification for women's alleged inferiority has been made by appropriating them to animals: from Aristotle on, women's bodies have been seen to intrude upon their rationality" (qtd. in McKay 208). In Margaret Atwood's work, animals have been used in order to defamiliarize and thereby expose an aggressive masculinism ("The Animals in That Country") or to mourn lost opportunity, restriction, and denial ("Dreams of the Animals") (*Selected*). As Kathleen Vogt puts it, in Atwood's work "references to the animal world are obvious metaphors for what humans do to one another" (169).

John Updike's "Bestiary" in his 1964 collection *Telephone Poles* examines the relationship—a still-pertinent one even in this secular age—between spirit (or soul) and body, the abstract and the material, human and animal. The poem opens with an epigraph from Sallustius which imagines an uncanny scenario where the "rational souls" of humans are relegated to chasing or shadowing the lives of mere "brutes"; "Unable to enter, they float / Behind" (ll.6–7). The image recalls the shadow of the "man-moth" trailing behind him in Bishop's poem of that title. The poem concludes with a couplet which is as chilling as it is comic: "For each squirrel feels a rational squirrel / pressing on its ears" (ll.11–12). The epistemological question for Updike, as for many of his contemporaries, concerns the connection between humans and animals. Until the nineteenth century, as Berger suggests, "anthropomorphism was integral to the relationship between man and animal and was an expression of their proximity" (11). In the Modernist period, as Andrew M. Lakritz has argued, here citing Margot Norris, animals have been removed from their "normative cultural context—lions 'mean' courage, elephants 'mean' memory, and so on"—and "anthropomorphic projections" have been replaced by other forms of scrutiny and interpretation (131).

In Marianne Moore's poetry we find particular attention to the detail of animal existence. "The Jerboa," for instance, or "The Frigate Pelican" or "Elephants" reveal a careful—even relentless—examination of what, precisely, the animal is rather than, as in earlier examples of the genre, what it stands for. The characteristic Moore approach of careful delineation reads like a fascinated (even dogged) attempt to realize the unrealizable—to establish some meaningful point of understanding or connection between human observer and animal object. She tries to establish identity rather than concede alterity—even against the odds and even while her detailed accounts of the astonishing characteristics of her animal subjects takes them ever further away from the human realm. Inevitably, perhaps, the impossibility of rendering the full complexity of animal life throws the focus back on human attempts so to do. The animals risk slipping out of sight such that we are left only with a record of the chase. The emphasis moves from the animals themselves to human attempts to understand them.

Moore's "The Buffalo" opens by considering and then stepping beyond symbolic or emblematic readings of the animal ("Black in blazonry means / prudence" [ll.1–2]). Thereafter the poem's approach is circuitous, cautious. It uses the conditional tense ("might"), qualifications ("yet") and repeated questions, often about meaning ("what would that express?" [ll.2, 22, 8]). Barely able to establish a point of connection, it can only negate the similarities it attempts to establish (it does "not look like"; it is "unlike the elephant" [ll.13, 26]). In some of Elizabeth Bishop's poems, too, the determined use, and questioning, of similes foregrounds the challenges of establishing an identification across apparently disparate species. Bishop's "The Fish," for example, uses emphatic and thereby unstable similes in order to show that the fish cannot easily be assimilated (unstable in that the repeated insistence that the fish is "like ancient wallpaper" or "like full-blown roses" or "like feathers" indicates that the fish is, in fact, none of these things [ll.11, 14, 28]). Bishop's prose-poem sequence "Rainy Season; Sub-Topics" takes this separation a stage further. These animals are not only alienated from people, but from each other. Spoken in the voices of the apparently ugly, marginalized "Giant Toad," "Strayed Crab," and "Giant Snail," the sequence blends hostility, pride, and fear in its evocation of the animals' defensive and allegorical position. As the giant snail puts it: "withdrawal is always best."

In Bishop's and Moore's work, the preoccupation is often with the nature and limits of human imagination. What and how do we see? Can our vision match the astonishing reality? In "The Plumet Basilisk" Moore exploits the observer's sense of wonder and incredulity in order to open out and examine the relationships between different species (the basilisk, incidentally, in the medieval tradition has "an obvious and well-established symbolic reference to Satan") (Edwards 91). Moore's animals are no mere abstractions. Rather, they are precisely located: "In Costa Rica" and "In Guatavita Lake" (I.4, 11). Moore plays with the species barrier, giving us reptiles that are likened to birds and fish and insects and bats and mythological creatures (dragons). As a stanza in the second "In Costa Rica" section concedes:

> the basilisk portrays
> mythology's wish
> to be interchangeably man and fish—
>
> (IV.34–36)

Similarly, in "The Frigate Pelican" Moore blends the descriptively accurate with the fanciful. This is the bird, the poem says, but this is also and more importantly how we read the bird. The poem describes the Frigate Pelican as it swoops, dives, feints, and sweeps other birds' prey from their grasp. The poem's own form and focus mimic that display. The present participles from the first line onwards convey motion and immediacy while the expanding and receding long and short lines arranged in eight and nine-line stanzas and the mostly regular syllabic lines represent both the pelican's movements ("cruising or lying," "fishing," and "rising" [ll.1, 8, 15]) and the poem's own processes and effects.

Moore's poetry and correspondence reveal what Alison Rieke calls a "kind of reverse anthropomorphism" (155). Instead of projecting human characteristics onto animals, she absorbs animal characteristics into her own human subjectivity. This becomes, in a poem like "He 'Digesteth Harde Yron'" a profoundly ethical issue and one which forces us to face up to our own responsibilities to non-human creatures (here ostriches). The title of the poem distances the reader and returns us to a pre-modern world wherein we might read these poems credulously, as messages from an unknown realm about barely conceivable animals. The poem foregrounds some important paradoxes and contradictions. It opens with the extinction of ("the aepyornis / or roc") but thereby asserts the existence of its own object—the "camel-sparrow" which "was and *is*" (ll.4, 6) (my emphasis). It describes the male bird as "maternal" and "mother[ly]" and juxtaposes the sentient bird with foolish men (who are "actor-like in ostrich-skins") (9, 10, 18). Even more contradictory and non-sensical, though, is the sober description in the final three-stanza section of the poem, separated from the earlier part by an explicit and extended ellipsis, of the real folly—which is also the historical fact—of ostriches being exploited by humans as food, glassware or transportation. Redeemingly, though, the camel-sparrow ("sparrow-camel" in the final line) resists and persists. Faced with such violent avarice, the "remaining rebel" lives on (57). The poem is about the ostrich and about our sordid attempts to master it. But it is also, finally, about our inability—literally and figuratively—so to do.

Moore's extended bestiary simultaneously registers the strangeness and the familiarity of animals. By the use of unexpected juxtapositions, metaphorical associations and suggestive form, her poetry invokes awe but also establishes moments of recognition. Post-Darwinian leaps in scientific knowledge notwithstanding, it is the retention of the space for wonder which was so much part of the medieval bestiary tradition, that is vital to the poem's success. One might argue of the achievement of Moore's work (and, for that matter, of prose bestiaries such as Jorge Luis Borges's 1967 *The Book of Imaginary Beings*) that it speaks to a desire for imaginative possibility in an otherwise reductive scientific world. By invoking the echoes of an ancient tradition, these bestiaries invite us to test our otherwise-jaded belief, to relinquish some of the power which comes with our knowledge and to admit the incredible.

The Anti-Bestiary

Not all American poets, though, have found the mode quite so positive or the world of beasts quite so rich with possibilities. Anne Sexton's superb, if often overlooked sequence *Bestiary USA* (published posthumously in 1970) is far more troubling than many of the other examples discussed thus far. These eighteen poems were originally entitled "Anne's Bestiary" and written in some haste between the end of May and the middle of June 1972. On the final day of writing (June 18), Sexton inscribes her manuscript ("6 poems in one day of pain and sickness") (*45 Mercy* manuscript).

In *Bestiary USA*, Sexton devises a complex and idiosyncratic set of symbolic values. Her first-person speaker identifies herself with the lowest of creatures (the dog, the bat, the rat, the snake, the cockroach, and the earthworm) as though to test to the extreme the possibilities of any kind of spiritual redemption. As Gymnich and Costa explain, identification with or transformation into animals has typically been presented in literary texts as a form of "punishment" and as a sign of "helplessness" and "utter degradation" (71, 70). For Sexton, as the epigraph to *Bestiary USA* makes clear, the animal world provides a reassuring model against which to measure her own bestiality: "I look at the strangeness in them and the naturalness they cannot help, in order to find some virtue in the beast in me" (497).

The first poem of the sequence, "Bat," opens with astonishment, which is also horror, as the speaker contemplates the bat's "awful skin." It proceeds to test, exemplify, and qualify the possibilities of human/animal identification. The bat's skin is "like my skin," we are told, "here between my fingers" (3). The extended simile tries to make the bat known to us, to assimilate it into a recognizably human world. Yet the connection proves difficult to sustain. The speaker herself seems unsure of the kinship she ostensibly seeks and the poem is riddled with questions, negatives, and pleas for reassurance ("Not well"; "not to be seen"; "surely . . . / surely" [ll.7, 9, 5–6]). Perhaps what she seeks is not, in fact, to be animal but rather, no longer to be human. Certainly the speaker rejects ideals of femininity and domesticity which are represented in this poem by the grotesque image of self as despised bat, hanging in the cemetery "like a misshapen udder" (l.20). Elizabeth Bishop's magnificent poem "The Man-Moth" features a similarly grotesque and marginalized human/animal, lurking out of sight and offering an oblique commentary on the everyday world of the humans. Like Sexton's bat, the man-moth's perspective is attenuated; his experience is displaced or deferred (he "does not see the moon" [l.6], for example, but only the light it casts) yet he somehow carries the burden of humanity's suffering.

Repeatedly throughout *Bestiary USA*, Sexton uses animals as a way of figuring her own abjection and of indicting the violence of the contemporary world. In "Hog" the speaker identifies with the hog's role as producer in an obsessively consumerist society. Similarly, "Sheep" excoriates the exploitation of animals but turns the condemnation on the animals themselves who are vilified for their complicity. "Porcupine," a thirty-seven-line poem of mostly one- to four-word lines is a blade-like excoriation of a troubled nation. The poems opens with the colloquial name "Spine hog" but then offers a sequence of images ("steel wings," "steel bullets," "four-inch / screws") to describe its vicious armor (ll.3, 7, 9–10). It proceeds to situate this threat in the context of modern America by referencing the "White House," "Martin / Luther King" and "a Kennedy" (ll.24, 26–27, 28) and arguing that the threat has moved beyond these and is posed now to the earth itself. In this way the subject, her wider society, and the natural environment are united in their pain and mutually assured destruction. Selim Sarwar sees a similarly apocalyptic nihilism in the "marching bestial horror" of Robert Lowell's "Skunk Hour." For Sarwar, like for Wendell Berry quoted earlier, such degradation is a mark of the disappointed promise of American civilization.

The rhetoric throughout *Bestiary USA* is of sickness, violence, and death. The final poem, "Gull," tries to soar above this sordid world and builds an elaborate chain of synaesthetic metaphors in an attempt to do so: "crying out like friends who sing from the tavern / of fighting hands" (ll.7–8). But even this poem ends with images of death—both material ("dead fruit") and, most damagingly we must assume for the poet, figurative: "all that flies today / is crooked and vain and has been cut from a book" (ll.18–20).

Sexton's *Bestiary USA* is, then, a failed or an anti-bestiary. If there is a bond between humans and animals, the evidence from this sequence is that it is built on mutual exploitation, reciprocal violence, and profound despair. The only lesson that animals can teach us, it seems, is that it is too late (hence the corpse-like bat and the hog which is more bacon than pig). These poems expose not the spiritual promise of creation but its vulnerability to corruption. Nevertheless, even here in Sexton's grotesque modern American bestiary we might argue that traces of the tradition remain. Sexton, like many of the contemporaries discussed above, and like her medieval antecedents, uses animals in her poetry in order to examine and illuminate the condition of her culture as she finds it. Her identification with the beasts may be unsettling but it is precisely this transgression which inspires awe and provides illumination. In this respect at least, Sexton's *Bestiary USA* is a worthy inheritor and example of this important genre.

References and Further Reading

Adams, Gillian. "Missing the Boat: Countee Cullen's *The Lost Zoo*." *The Lion and the Unicorn* 2.1 (1997): 40–58.

Aristotle. *Historia Animalium*. http://etext.virginia.edu/toc/modeng/public/AriHian.html.

Atwood, Margaret. *Selected Poems*. Toronto: Oxford University Press, 1976.

Berger, John. "Why Look at Animals?" in John Berger, *About Looking*. London: Bloomsbury, 2009. 3–28.

Bishop, Elizabeth. *The Complete Poems: 1927–1979*. New York: Farrar, Straus and Giroux, 1980.

Borges, Jorge Luis. *The Book of Imaginary Beings*, trans. Norman Thomas di Giovanni. London: Vintage, 2002.

Carson, Rachel. *Silent Spring*. Harmondsworth: Penguin, 2000.

Clark, Anne. *Beasts and Bawdy*. London: Dent, 1975.

Cullen, Countee. *The Lost Zoo by Christopher Cat and Countee Cullen*. Chicago and New York: Follett Publishing, 1969.

Edwards, Karen. *Milton and the Natural World*. Cambridge: Cambridge University Press, 1999.

Elder, John. *Imagining the Earth: Poetry and the Vision of Nature*. 2nd edn. Athens, GA: University of Georgia Press, 1996.

Gymnich, Marion and Alexandre Segão Costa. "Of Humans, Pigs, Fish, and Apes: The Literary Motif of Human–Animal Metamorphosis and Its Multiple Functions in Contemporary Fiction." *L'Esprit Créateur* 46.2 (2006): 68–88.

Harjo, Joy. *How We Became Human: New and Selected Poems 1975–2001*. New York: Norton, 2002.

Hassig, Debra, ed. *The Mark of the Beast: The Medieval Bestiary in Art, Life, and Literature.* New York and London: Garland, 1999.

Henderson, Arnold Clayton. "Medieval Beasts and Modern Cages: The Making of Meaning in Fables and Bestiaries." *PMLA* 97.1 (1982): 40–49.

Hughes, Ted. *Crow.* London: Faber & Faber, 1970.

Hughes, Ted. *The Hawk in the Rain.* London: Faber & Faber, 1957.

Lakritz, Andrew M. *Modernism and the Other in Stevens, Frost and Moore.* Gainesville: University Press of Florida, 1996.

Malamud, Randy. *Poetic Animals and Animal Souls.* Basingstoke: Palgrave, 2003.

Malamud, Randy. *Reading Zoos: Representations of Animals and Captivity.* Basingstoke: Macmillan, 1998.

McKay, Robert. "'Identifying with the Animals': Language, Subjectivity and the Animal Politics of Margaret Atwood's *Surfacing*," in *Figuring Animals: Essays on Animal Images in Art, Literature, Philosophy and Popular Culture*, ed. Mary Sanders Pollock and Catherine Rainwater. New York: Palgrave Macmillan, 2005. 207–27.

Moore, Marianne. *Complete Poems.* London: Faber & Faber, 1984.

Murray, Les. *Translations from the Natural World.* Manchester: Carcanet, 1993.

Olds, Sharon. *Strike Sparks: Selected Poems 1980–2002.* New York: Knopf, 2004.

Oliver, Mary. *Wild Geese: Selected Poems.* Tarset: Bloodaxe, 2004.

Pliny. *The Natural History.* http://old.perseus.tufts.edu/cgibin/ptext?lookup=Plin.+Nat.+toc.

Pollock, Mary Sanders and Catherine Rainwater, eds. *Figuring Animals: Essays on Animal Images in Art, Literature, Philosophy and Popular Culture.* New York: Palgrave Macmillan, 2005.

Rainwater, Catherine. "Who May Speak for the Animals? Deep Ecology in Linda Hogan's *Power* and A.A. Carr's *Eye Killers*," in *Figuring Animals: Essays on Animal Images in Art, Literature, Philosophy and Popular Culture*, ed. Mary Sanders Pollock and Catherine Rainwater. New York: Palgrave Macmillan, 2005. 261–80.

Rexroth, Kenneth. *The Collected Longer Poems of Kenneth Rexroth.* New York: New Directions, 1968.

Rexroth, Kenneth. *The Collected Shorter Poems of Kenneth Rexroth.* New York: New Directions, 1966.

Rieke, Alison. "'Plunder' or 'Accessibility to Experience': Consumer Culture and Marianne Moore's Self-Fashioning." *Journal of Modern Literature* 27.1/2 (2003): 149–70.

Rotella, Guy. *Reading and Writing Nature: The Poetry of Robert Frost, Wallace Stevens, Marianne Moore, and Elizabeth Bishop.* Boston, MA: Northeastern University Press, 1991.

Sarwar, Selim. "Robert Lowell: Scripting the Midcentury Eschatology." *Journal of Modern Literature* 25.2 (2001–02): 111–30.

Schaefer, Jack. *An American Bestiary.* Boston, MA: Houghton Mifflin, 1975.

Sexton, Anne. *The Complete Poems.* Boston, MA: Houghton Mifflin, 1981.

Sexton, Anne. *45 Mercy Street.* Manuscript. Harry Ransom Humanities Research Center, University of Texas at Austin.

Snyder, Gary. *Turtle Island.* New York: New Directions, 1974.

Swenson, May. *Nature: Poems Old and New.* Boston, MA: Houghton Mifflin, 1994.

Syme, Alison. "Taboo and the Holy in Bodley 764," in *The Mark of the Beast: The Medieval Bestiary in Art, Life, and Literature*, ed. Debra Hassig. New York and London: Garland, 1999. 163–79.

Updike, John. *Telephone Poles and Other Poems.* London: Andre Deutsch, 1964.

Vogt, Kathleen. "Real and Imaginary Animals in the Poetry of Margaret Atwood," in *Margaret Atwood: Visions and Forms*, ed. Kathryn VanSpanckeren and Jan Garden Castro. Carbondale and Edwardsville: Southern Illinois University Press, 1988. 163–82.

White, T.H. *The Book of Beasts Being a Translation from a Latin Bestiary of the Twelfth Century.* London: Jonathan Cape, 1954.

40

"From Arcadia to Bunyah"

Mutation and Diversity in the Pastoral Mode

Karina Williamson

The term "pastoral" denotes both a *genre* (a group of texts observing common conventions of form, style, and subject-matter) and a *mode* (the expression of a certain ethos or set of attitudes). Poems of many other genres, such as odes and ballads, can be modally pastoral but *idylls* (or *idyls*), *eclogues*, and *bucolic(s)*, are specifically pastoral subgenres. The roots of pastoral lie in classical poetry, with the invention of "bucolic" (poems about herdsmen) by Theocritus in his *Idylls*, and the development of Theocritean interests and practices by Virgil in his *Bucolica* or *Eclogues*, from which pastoral derives its generic identity (Alpers 154). Pastoral was absorbed into European vernacular literature in the Renaissance, reaching its finest flowering in England during the sixteenth and seventeenth centuries, in Scotland in the eighteenth century. It flourished as a mode in drama and prose romance as well as poetry, and gained a place in Renaissance critical theory alongside other literary kinds such as epic, tragedy, and satire.

Pastoral Poetry from the Sixteenth to Nineteenth Century

Conventional pastorals are short poems of rural life (descriptive, narrative, amatory), often in dialogue form and supposedly uttered by simple rustics. They present idealized images of the countryside and country life modeled on Virgil's Arcadia. Agricultural labor (the province of *georgic* poetry) is not represented in classical pastoral, which rests on the fiction that a shepherd's life allows more leisure and is "attended with more tranquillity than any other rural employment" (Pope 1:297). The fictionality of the pastoral world was underlined in English poetry by the use of

A Companion to Poetic Genre, First Edition. Edited by Erik Martiny.
© 2012 John Wiley & Sons, Ltd. Published 2012 by John Wiley & Sons, Ltd.

classical names for personae, but in Scotland Allan Ramsay localized the genre by using Scottish personal names. Piping, singing, and rural crafts are shown as the principal recreations of shepherds, making the genre a ready channel for discussion of the poetic craft itself. Pastoral elegy for the death of a poet, based on Theocritus' first *Idyll* (the lament of the shepherd Thyrsis for Daphnis, a legendary herdsman-poet) developed into a lofty tradition, with its own repertory of thematic and structural conventions including an appeal to the Muses or other supernatural powers, a catalogue of flowers, the rhetorical strategy known as "pathetic fallacy" (whereby nature is endowed with the capacity to express human sympathies), and a movement from despair to hope and transcendence. The classic English examples are Spenser's *Astrophel*, Milton's *Lycidas*, Shelley's *Adonais* and Arnold's *Thyrsis*.

Central to the pastoral ethos was the Epicurean ideal of *otium*: a state of peaceful leisure, withdrawal from public business, and a simple manner of living, such as that described by the Duke in exile in Shakespeare's *As You Like It*. The pastoral site was an imagined *locus amoenus* ("delightful place," Hopkins's "sweet especial rural scene"), evoking classical and Christian myths of origin: Arcadia or Eden, the Golden Age or prelapsarian state of happiness and innocence. The countryside was conceived as humankind's native (spiritual, psychological) "home," but ideas of pastness and loss were embedded in the pastoral mode, giving rise to themes of return or retreat, and hence to the critical contention that nostalgia is the "basic emotion" of pastoral (Lerner 41). Pastoral has never been entirely backward-looking, however. Contrast between the peaceful, harmonious world of myth and the perceived reality of contemporary society and manners made it an effective medium for satire, while the dream of a lost felicity could be projected into the future in the form of utopian fantasies or redemptive visions.

Since pastoral poetry was written in fact not by simple rustics but by sophisticated urban poets, intrinsic to the genre is a gap between semblance and actuality, "between the complex existence of poet and reader and the designedly naïve dream of rural simplicity" (Chaudhuri 1). Pastoral poetry was thus *ab origo* "an ironic form, based on a perceivable distance between the alleged and the implied" (Ettin 12). It is thus distinguished from nature poetry in general by its figurative character: it encodes social, political, ethical, or aesthetic values in a pattern of opposition between country and city, nature and civilization. From this pattern arises the dialectical tendency of the genre, leading typically to tension or paradox rather than synthesis. The contradiction between the equally valid but irreconcilable claims of nature and civilization is encapsulated in a simile by Andrew Marvell in "A Dialogue between the Soul and Body." Each speaker accuses the other of enslaving and tormenting them, until "Body" at last acknowledges their necessary but painful interdependence. The poet concludes: "So architects do square and hew / Green trees that in the forest grew." Pastoral declined in the early eighteenth century. Neoclassical theory and practice debased it as a medium for serious poetry by emphasizing its artificiality, playfulness, and decorative qualities. A swing from pastoral to georgic as the dominant mode of rural poetry in the same period signaled a shift in ethos, with the concept of *otium* as the highest good giving way to the ideal of productive labor. The swing cannot be explained in literary-ethical terms alone, however. Following in the wake of Raymond Williams' influential study *The Country and the City* (1973), literary historians have ascribed the changes in rural poetry during the eighteenth century to economic developments in the world outside the text, and to the struggle by poets to reconfigure their conceptions of social and political order accordingly. Both pastoral *and* georgic in the eighteenth century, Richard Feingold argues, "record an effort of political understanding." Under the strain, the two genres ceased to be categorically watertight, if indeed they ever were: "we find each coloring the other, quite freely combined within single poems as if to announce an ideal of optimal civilization, a blend of *otium* and *ponos* [labor] itself figuring forth an ideal pattern of life in a good social order" (17).

At the end of the eighteenth century, conventional pastoral was routed under the double impact of Crabbe's anti-pastoral, *The Village* (1783), and Wordsworth's condemnation of artificial representations of rural life, in the Preface to the second edition of *Lyrical Ballads* (1800). Instead of rendering pastoral unusable as a genre, however, Wordsworth revivified it in a changed form. In *The Ruined Cottage*, in "Michael: A Pastoral Poem," in parts of *The Prelude*, and in numerous lyrics, he inaugurated a new line of pastoral realism, using colloquial language and detailed, matter-of-fact description and offering transvalued ideals of rural life, based on the actual conditions of Cumbrian shepherds' lives. Where the older pastoral model of social harmony had been based on the manorial ideal (a benevolent squirearchy supporting and supported by a sturdy peasantry), Wordsworth valorized the figure of the self-reliant countryman, subservient to no human master though at the mercy of natural disasters and political and economic circumstance.

Occasional uses or adaptations for serious purposes of traditional pastoral forms (the eclogue, idyll, and pastoral elegy) in the nineteenth and early twentieth century by Shelley, Keats, Tennyson, Whittier, Arnold, Yeats, and others (such as William Barnes, with eclogues in Dorset dialect), demonstrated that the older genre had not been entirely killed off by neoclassical trivialization. Nevertheless, it was Wordsworth's pastoral realism and his revival of Virgilian eclogue that paved the way for the recovery of pastoral in the twentieth century (Alpers 261).

Modern Pastoral

Abandonment of the conventions by which pastoral was generically defined left the concept prey to theoretical and critical controversy in the twentieth century, starting with William Empson's brilliant but idiosyncratic study, *Some Versions of Pastoral*. His famous formula, "the pastoral process of putting the complex into the simple" (23), is generally accepted as a necessary but insufficient condition for the definition of pastoral literature; few critics today use it to identify as pastoral *any* text which fits that description. On the other hand, the loose assumption that pastoral is simply another name for "nature poetry" too often muddies the waters of critical discussion. Modern pastoral poetry is not necessarily concerned with the natural world, while not all nature poetry is pastoral, modally or generically. A more recent debate concerns pastoral ideology: "pastoral" has been used by some English critics as a derogatory term for the kind of pastoralism, associated especially with the Georgian poets, which promoted the fantasy of rural England as a changeless refuge of beauty, tranquility, and social harmony from the evils of the contemporary world. Pastoral, on such a view, means nostalgic escapism, failure to recognize the effects of socio-economic and environmental change, and a simplistic view of the physical and economic relations between town and country (Gifford chapter 1).

Pejorative uses of the label in critical argument have not in practice deterred modern poets from finding non-escapist uses for pastoral forms, often though not necessarily under generic titles: usually "Bucolics" or "Pastoral" for lyrics, "Eclogue" mainly for dialogues in rhymed or unrhymed pentameters. At the same time, the abundance of anti-pastoral and counter-pastoral forms is back-handed testimony to the continuing vitality of pastoral itself. As John Kinsella points out, "variations of a form are always an outcome of it" (*Contrary Rhetoric* 131). The wit of Sylvia Plath's "Bucolics" (*Collected Poems*, 1956), for example, a mock-pastoral amatory lyric with a bitter ending, depends for its shock effect on recognition of pastoral *jouissance* as a modal norm.

The acknowledged father of modern pastoral is Robert Frost, "a pastoralist of Theocritean and Wordsworthian range and variety" (Alpers 307), whose poetry both maintains and modifies earlier pastoral tradition and has exerted an influence on later twentieth-century writing throughout the English-speaking world. One of his earliest poems, "Pan with Us" (in *A Boy's Will*, 1913), proclaimed his abandonment of pastoral fantasy, as alien to a New World sensibility in the modern age:

> He tossed his pipes, too hard to teach
> A new-world song, far out of reach,
> . . .
> They were pipes of pagan mirth,
> And the world had found new words of worth.
>
> (ll.16–17, 26–27)

The poem ends with a question: "Play? Play?—What should he play?" The answer is implicit in "Mowing," which embraces a new pastoral ethos, rejecting *otium* ("no dream of the gift of idle hours") in favor of "fact" and "labour": "The fact is the sweetest dream that labour knows" (l.13). In his second collection, *North of Boston*, Frost reverted to tradition by re-establishing the eclogue as the basic pastoral form, but relocating Arcadia in the New England countryside. The majority of the poems in *North of Boston* are dialogues, not labeled "eclogues" but referred to as such by contemporary readers and by Frost himself. Reviewing the book in 1914, Frost's friend Edward Thomas described him as following Wordsworth in his use of colloquial language while differing in his closer empathy with country people: "[Frost] sympathizes where Wordsworth contemplates. The result is a unique type of eclogue, homely, racy, and touched by a spirit that might, under other circumstances, have made pure lyric on the one hand or drama on the other" (Thomas 24).

Frost's eclogues and pastoral lyrics show many of the generic traits of traditional pastoral: ideas of home and homelessness; the linkage of paradisal imagery with ideas of loss (in "Never Again Would Birds' Song Be the Same"), and awareness of the paradoxical core of the pastoral imaginary (in "The Need of Being Versed in Country Things"). His eclogues exploit to the full the potential for irony latent in the artifice of a dialogue between rustic speakers; especially when one of them is the author, self-represented as a homely New England farmer, down-to-earth but ostensibly more thoughtful and worldly wise than his interlocutor. Refining on the technique of ironic reversal in Wordsworth's dialogues ("We Are Seven," for instance), whereby the naïve speaker ultimately appears wiser than the poet, Frost leaves the outcome of his exchanges ambiguous ("Mending Wall" is a famous example). Lastly, even in the replacement of *otium* by georgic values of labor, cultivation (in "Putting in the Seed"), and good workmanship (in "The Wood Pile," "The Ax-Helve"), Frost preserves the basic function of the genre as "contrast, implicit or expressed, between pastoral life and some more complex type of civilization" (Greg 4).

Frost's texts depart most obviously from tradition in their exploration of the dark obverse of pastoral myth. Tragic eclogues such as "Home Burial," "The Death of the Hired Man," and "Out, Out—," may arguably be too troubled in their realism to "count as pastoral": they do not "sustain the mode of their genre" (Alpers 309). Nevertheless, the pastoral code was enlarged rather than violated by Frost's intimations of a darker aspect of the rural idyll in the notes of mystery, fear, or foreboding that may disturb the surface, even in such tranquil lyrics as "Stopping by Woods on a Snowy Evening." Except in its most escapist versions, later pastoral poetry has seldom attempted to recover the serene quality of idyll possible within earlier tradition. Seamus Heaney indeed argues that pastoral has stayed alive precisely through "its ability to meet the challenges of new and sometimes tragic historical circumstances" (Heaney, "Eclogues *In Extremis*" 1).

In Frost's own time, Edward Thomas showed that a precarious balance between tragic realism and pastoral idealism was still achievable. Although sometimes grouped with the Georgians, Thomas never contributed to the *Georgian Poetry* series and "Lob" is the only poem in which he subscribes to the myth of a changeless rural England. Indeed his eclogue, "As the Team's Head-Brass," written in 1915 (the same year as Thomas Hardy's famous lyric "In Time of 'The Breaking of Nations,'" with its images of rural immutability) "symbolises war's intrusion into rural England, and into English (and European) pastoral" (Longley 300). It circles round from idyllic prelude (a plowman driving his team of horses, lovers disappearing into a wood, the narrator seated on a fallen tree at the edge of a field) into casual dialogue between the narrator and plowman about the war, deaths of men from the farm, and the "different world" confronting the speakers, before returning to the opening scene:

> The lovers came out of the wood again:
> The horses started and for the last time
> I watched the clods crumble and topple over
> After the ploughshare and the stumbling team.

(ll.33–36)

The phrase "for the last time" carries heavy weight here: against the backdrop of war and death it has an elegiac resonance which challenges without wholly negating the hint of regeneration suggested by the lovers.

For the Georgians, as for Thomas, pastoral was predominantly a response to the immediate or remembered horror of World War I; a peculiarly English reaction according to Paul Fussell:

> Recourse to the pastoral is an English mode of both fully gauging the calamities of the Great War and imaginatively protecting oneself against them. Pastoral reference, whether to literature or to actual rural localities and objects, is a way of invoking a code to hint by antithesis at the indescribable . . . The Golden Age posited by Classical and Renaissance literary pastoral now finds its counterparts in ideas of "home" and "the summer of 1914."

(*Great War* 235)

While acknowledging that pastoral imaginings, so motivated, could collapse into sentimental escapism, Fussell shows how pastoral *topoi* nevertheless gave subtlety and edge to some of the finest lyrics of the war poets, such as Isaac Rosenberg's "Break of Day in the Trenches" and Ivor Gurney's "To His Love" (250–54).

Pastoral reference for Edmund Blunden was far more than a comfort in time of war, although it could be precisely that too (as in "11th R.S.R."). It was the staple of his verse before, during, and after his front-line service in France: *Pastorals*, a collection of lyrics he wrote between leaving school and going out to France, was published in 1916. Blunden soon shed the immature romanticism of these early efforts, but not the conception that pre-war English country life enshrined an order of values at the opposite pole to the savagery of war. Pastoral reference and contrast appear with almost monotonous regularity in his war poetry, but when re-invigorated by sardonic language and wit, as in "Rural Economy," and "La Quinque Rue," they can lend startling force to his texts.

The images of rural England on which the pastoralism of Blunden's generation was based became increasingly unrealistic from the 1930s onwards. John Heath-Stubbs, addressed Blunden on his sixtieth birthday as "the last and truly-tempered voice / Of all our lovely, dead, and pastoral England" ("To Edmund Blunden," ll.4–5). As Randall Stevenson shows, the most obvious cause of the fading of pastoral from English poetry in the later twentieth century was social and economic: the despoliation of the countryside. "Nature and its idylls . . . were banished . . . by traffic, pollution, and urban sprawl" (243–50). Heath-Stubbs, rare among modern English poets in his use of traditional genres, turns pastoral into a weapon of environmental protest in "The Green Man's Last Will and Testament: An Eclogue" (1982). The testator, a "green daemon of England's wood," speaking from "a ragged spinney (scheduled / For prompt development as a bijou housing estate)," passionately declaims against the destruction of wildlife and the landscape (ll.1–3) by all three agencies named by Stevenson. Earlier, however, his "Shepherd's Bush Eclogue" (1954) gave a new twist to the eighteenth-century subgenre of "town eclogue": setting primal innocence against the sense of "exile," loss, and mortality in a city environment and finding something "truly pastoral" in the Spring skyscape, "azure and virginal / Fields of pure air that over London lie" (ll.3–4).

Earlier still, Heath-Stubbs's attempt in *Wounded Thammuz* (1942) to address the contemporary condition through "a tripartite sequential pastoral elegy on the themes of seasonal and historical recurrence and resurrection" (25), mingling classical conventions and idioms with a tired modernist rhetoric, was an ambitious failure. The failure was probably inevitable: by 1942 the traditional conventions of pastoral elegy had become culturally too time-bound to be viable. The dereliction of the old tradition is wittily exposed in a recent poem by Conor O'Callaghan, "The Modern Pastoral Elegy: A Tick-Where-Appropriate Template." Beginning with a parody of the rhetoric of obituaries for dead poets, it ends with derisive echoes of Arnold pastoral elegies:

> Something something something *world*,
> Something something something *grope*.
> Something something something *unfurled*,
> Something something something *hope*.
>
> (ll.51–54)

Having abandoned the conventions which made it a distinctive form in its heyday, pastoral elegy has become a subgenre of elegy.

The scarcity of pastoral poetry in England and Scotland since the 1920s has been obscured by the loose application by critics of the term "pastoral" to other more thriving forms of nature poetry. For example, Norman Nicholson's poetry of landscape and country life in his native Cumbria is classed as pastoral by Terry Gifford; yet it is categorically non-pastoral judged by the principle that it is the representative character of pastoral, its investment with meaning or value beyond the particular, that distinguishes it from nature poetry in general. One of Nicholson's strengths is his steadfast resistance to abstraction: the Cumbrian countryside and the people of Millom are observed in all their particularity with a fine exactitude in his poetry.

In fact the most notable pastoralist in English poetry in the second half of the twentieth century is Philip Larkin, not a "nature poet" at all in the usual sense, although he too wrote about the vanishing countryside. As Stevenson points out, the impact of environmental change on pastoral conceptions of England can be traced in the progression in Larkin's poetry from "Here" (1961), to "Going, Going" (1972). The first is ironic pastoral, in that it inverts the traditional rural-urban polarity by finding "a terminate and fishy-smelling / Pastoral of ships up streets" (ll.19–20) in the unlovely, bustling city (clearly Hull), but frames it within the tranquil beauty, solitude, and "unfenced existence" of the country (l.31). Ten years later, "Going, Going" foretells the disappearance of rural England itself: "England gone / The shadows, the meadows, the lanes," destroyed by "greeds / And garbage," "bricked in," until "all that remains / For us will be concrete and tyres" (ll.47–48). The pastoral impulse nevertheless finds expression throughout Larkin's poetry, from the early lyric "At Grass" onwards, in images of paradisal innocence in the lives of ordinary people ("The Whitsun Weddings") and of transcendence over decay and death ("The Trees"). Larkin's most distinctive contribution to pastoral is in the glimpses of a regenerative power in social rituals. In "Show Saturday," as the people leave the showground to return to their mundane "local lives," and the "dismantled Show / . . . dies back into the area of work," the poet pleads:

> Let it stay hidden there like strength,
> . . . something they share
> That breaks ancestrally each year into
> Regenerate union. Let it always be there.

> (ll.59–64)

Similarly, in "To the Sea," the middle-aged speaker, observing holiday-makers on the beach, is reassured to find that the remembered pattern of seaside holidays still occurs, "As half an annual pleasure, half a rite / . . . Still going on, all of it, still going on!" (ll.10, 18). Nostalgia, images of innocent rituals, and the yearning for permanence combine to make this one of the great pastoral lyrics of the twentieth century.

Postcolonial Pastoral: Ireland, the Caribbean, and Australia

The pastoral mode, both positive and negative versions, has played a significant role in Irish poetry in the post-Revival period. Patrick Kavanagh in *The Great Hunger* (1942) and John Montague in *The Rough Field* (1972), use pastoral and anti-pastoral modalities with powerful force to channel their perceptions of conditions in postcolonial Ireland. Kavanagh's anti-pastoral text fiercely combats the pastoral rhetoric of Anglo-Irish revivalist writers and politicians, which, by creating an idyllic vision of rural Ireland, obscured the bitter realities of poverty and deprivation in the Republic of Kavanagh's time (Kiberd 477–78). Montague's complex work, a long sequence of lyrical poems written at the time of the Troubles and centered on his family's rural home in County Tyrone, is at once realistic and profoundly pastoral in its vision of contemporary Ireland in historical context. The pastoral myth of loss is itself historicized in "Sound of a Wound," when "the pain of a lost . . . pastoral rhythm" is set in the long perspective of Irish colonization, beginning with the seventeenth-century Plantation and its legacy of "bitterness" and "race hatred": "I assert / a civilisation died here" (ll.44–45). The "Epilogue" balances realism against pastoral grief at "the changing rural pattern." Although "Only a sentimentalist" would want to return to the "degradation" of farming life in his father's generation, yet "something" in him mourns for "Our finally lost dream of man at home / in a rural setting" (ll.82–83).

Among pastoral genres, the eclogue has proved especially serviceable as an "enabling device," in David Duff's phrase (Duff 2), for Irish poets from Louis MacNeice to Michael Longley, Seamus Heaney, and Peter McDonald. Frost's influence on poets of Heaney's generation doubtless contributed to its resurgence, but the translation of Virgil's *Eclogues* in 1966 by the Anglo-Irish poet Cecil Day-Lewis may have been another contributory factor. MacNeice however seems to have rediscovered the genre independently, employing it as a medium for social and political debate in five poems written in 1933–34, all with "Eclogue" in their original titles (33–54). The first, "An Eclogue for Christmas," is a dialogue concerned with the sickness of contemporary society between spokesmen for the country and the city respectively. But instead of representing the country as a refuge from the evils of the city, the poem pillories urban and rural life with even-handed ferocity: viewing the poem in retrospect, MacNeice saw it as a diatribe against the Decline of the West. "Eclogue from Iceland," though no less bleak in its world-view, is more conventionally pastoral in its "comparison of a sophisticated society with a simpler past" (Marsack 30). The dialectic is resolved, however, in ethical rather than social terms, with the conclusion that "Hatred of hatred, assertion of human values" is the "only duty" and the "only chance" for moral survival (47). MacNeice's eclogues, like some of Frost's, do not fully "sustain the mode of their genre," but for a different reason: they lack a positive pastoral *locus* to set against sophisticated society. The apparent exception is "Valediction" (subtitled "an eclogue" when first published), with its nostalgia for rural Ireland,

> the chequered and the quiet hills
> . . .
> your hens running in and out of the white house,
> Your absent-minded goats along the road.
>
>   (ll.99–104)

But its sour conclusion, with "Your drums and your dolled-up Virgins and your ignorant dead" (l.106), casts an anti-pastoral shadow retrospectively over the whole text. MacNeice's ambivalence here is in contrast to the forays into pastoral by his English contemporary and friend, W.H. Auden. In Auden's texts, mode and genre are firmly separated. "In Praise of Limestone" is pastoral in mode but not in form, while both his long poem, *Age of Anxiety: A Baroque Eclogue* (1948), and his "Bucolics" (1955: 15–32), a set of short lyrics on a common theme, are anti-pastoral. The titular subjects ("Woods," "Mountains," "Lakes," and so on) provide pegs on which to hang an argument pitting civilization against primitivism, in which traditional pastoralism is exposed as false to history and socially and ethically irresponsible (Hyde 343–44).

Seamus Heaney showed his commitment to the georgic-pastoral mode in his first collection, *Death of a Naturalist* (1966). The opening poem, "Digging," celebrates the spade-work of his forebears as a form of heroic action ("My grandfather cut more turf in a day / Than any other man on Toner's bog"), then turns "digging" into an emblem of the poet's craft:

> But I've no spade to follow men like them.
> Between my finger and my thumb
> The squat pen rests.
> I'll dig with it.
>
> (ll.28–31)

The volume is steeped in recollections of Heaney's childhood on a farm in Mossbawn, County Derry. It describes rural activities ("Churning," "The Forge," "Thatcher") with the exactitude of language which Heaney admired in Frost, and offers images of pastoral fertility and plenitude. Yet even at this early stage, his rural poetry offers no "uncontaminated idyll" (O'Donoghue 108). An ominous note is struck with the opening lines of "Digging" itself: "Between my finger and my thumb / The squat pen rests; snug as a gun" (ll.1–2). "At a Potato Digging," later, looks back at the horrors of the great famine in nineteenth-century Ireland (ll.19, 23–24). Less sensationally, in "Blackberry-Picking," the innocent connotations of the title are undercut by disturbingly voluptuous language, and pastoral fertility gives way to decay as the stored fruit ferments, "rat-grey fungus, glutting on our cache," until "all the lovely canfuls smelt of rot. / Each year I hoped they'd keep, knew they would not" (20). Country trades and the people who practice them, however, are abiding positives in Heaney's pastoral repertoire: thirty years after *Death of a Naturalist* he paid tribute in *The Spirit Level*, with totally unsentimental family piety, to the "journeyman tailor who was my antecedent" ("At Banagher," l.2). Heaney's cottage in Glanmore, County Wicklow, succeeded Mossbawn as his remembered *"locus amoenus"* ("The Cot," l.6). "Glanmore Eclogue" is one of three eclogues which are central to his recent collection, *Electric Light*. Unusually for Heaney, this is a light-hearted pastoral, though touches of caustic realism ("Outsiders own / The country nowadays / . . . Small farmers are priced out of the market," *Electric Light* 35–36) recall Virgil's ninth eclogue, Heaney's translation of which appears in the same volume. As Bernard O'Donoghue points out, Virgil's "broadly post-colonial themes of land confiscation . . . have a resonance in the Irish context" (112).

Peter McDonald is one of the most recent poets from Northern Ireland to employ pastoral forms. His *Pastorals* (2004) include four poems which indicate openly or by intertextual allusion their generic identity: "Eclogue" (imitating Virgil, *Eclogue I*),

"The Cup" (translating part of Theocritus, *Idyll I*), and two lyrics, "Pastoral" (a love poem) and "Damon the Mower," which sardonically reworks Marvell's pastoral lyric of that title. The volume as a whole invites a sustained reappraisal of pastoral as a way of relating present to past: through personal experience, as in "The Road to Rome," in which the poet confesses himself to be "deep in thrall / to the peculiar pastoral" that is "part history and part escape" (ll.175–77); through bereavement (in several elegiac poems), or through collective fantasy, as in the sequence titled "The Victory Weekend." It centers on celebrations of the fiftieth anniversary of the end of World War II: popular public rites which allow the brutality and sorrow of war, refracted through the false nostalgia of commemoration, to be safely tidied away, "for this was pastoral" (*Pastorals* 26).

Modern pastoral poetry is mainly a male preserve. Eavan Boland, another Irish poet, offers an eloquent rationale for this coupling of gender and genre in "The New Pastoral." The speaker (a woman) traces the genesis of pastoral back to the conquest of nature through technology by the "first man," which has left her "in the dark" as "last inhabitant . . . in a pastoral chaos" (ll.4–6). Attempting to reconcile mechanized nature ("the switch and tick of / new herds," ll.8–9) with her housewife's perception of its denaturing methods ("this lamb's knuckle, butchered from its last crooked suckling"), she finally recognizes pastoral as a myth concealing a causal chain: "these chance sights" are all "amnesias of a rite / I danced once on a frieze" (ll.24–25).

For writers in more distant parts of the former British Empire, the pastoral mode is tainted by association with colonial pastoralism. From the earliest years of European expansionism, writers projected paradisal images of the undeveloped world of the Americas as a pastoral haven in contrast to the Old World. The Caribbean islands, in particular, were celebrated for their lush natural beauty and fertility, the innocence or noble savagery of their inhabitants, and, not least, their potential for economic exploitation. The absorption of the Caribbean into the pastoral imaginary is typified by a passage in James Grainger's long poem, *The Sugar-Cane* (1764), based on the author's experience of plantation life on St. Kitts. The poem is georgic in form, but Grainger resorts to pastoral as the only adequate mode for eulogy:

> Such, green St. Christopher, thy happy soil!—
> Not Grecian Tempé, where Arcadian Pan,
> Knit with the Graces, tun'd his sylvan pipe, . . .
> Can vie, blest-Isle, with thee.—Tho' no soft sound
> Of pastoral stop thine echoes e'er awak'd.
>
> (Book I, ll.60–68)

Pastoral and paradisal imagery became standard currency for descriptions of the Caribbean in romantic fiction, travel writing, and tourist literature down to the modern era. Pastoral penetrated even into early twentieth-century attempts to adopt a distinctive West Indian poetic voice, in for example the verse of the Irish-Jamaican writer Thomas MacDermot ("Tom Redcam"), a leading figure in the promotion of a genuinely "Jamaican" literature.

For non-European Caribbean writers, however, the pastoral tradition is inherently alien. Classical and Christian pastoral myth is a myth of western civilization, predicated on the assumption of historical and cultural continuity from a primeval human state up to the present: not the state of *all* humankind, however, but implicitly that of the peoples of Europe. The traditional pastoral space, Arcadia or Eden, was in effect an ethnic homeland, excluding Caribbean people of African or Asian descent, who were separated from *their* ancestral homelands by a disrupted history of transportation, slavery or indentured service, and exile. "Les Antilles sont le lieu d'une histoire faite de ruptures et dont le commencement est un arrachement brutal, la Traite" (Glissant 223): "the Antilles are the site of a history made up of ruptures, beginning with a savage uprooting, the slave trade." When pastoral appears in post-colonial Caribbean poetry, then, it is typically in negative mode: anti-pastoral or satirical. David Dabydeen's "Guyana Pastoral" in *Slave Song* (1984) is an anti-pastoral elegy in Creole: a lament for the rape and murder of a young girl, told in "hard, brutal rhythms," as the poet explains, to "signify the violent aspect of Guyanese existence" (49).

Derek Walcott's anti-pastoralism takes the form of "writing back" to colonial pastoral. A line from Marvell's "Bermudas" is used as the title of his early collection, *In a Green Night* (1962), the title-poem itself implying that the vision of Bermuda in Marvell's poem as an earthly paradise was a pastoral delusion. "As John to Patmos," in the same volume, flirts with pastoralism, only to undermine it by irony. "This island is heaven," it declares, "—away from the dustblown blood of cities; / See the curve of bay, . . . pretty is / The wing'd sound of trees" The stanza ends: "For beauty has surrounded / Its black children, and freed them of homeless ditties" (ll.9–11). The lines draw on traditional urban-rural contrast ("dustblown" city versus rural "beauty") to suggest a Caribbean *locus amoenus*, but the banal rhyme-words alone (*cities* / *pretty is* / *ditties*), mock any pastoral interpretation. An intertextual reading, moreover, turns the contrast upside-down: according to the New Testament, what St. John saw on the island of Patmos was a vision of the "holy city." The island-city contrast is used, satirically again, in "Prelude," where the reality of Caribbean life is shown as "lost" to the eyes of tourists who "have known cities and think us here happy" (l.9).

Walcott's most delicate, complex exercise in postcolonial pastoral comes in a long political poem, "The Star-Apple Kingdom" (1979), in which pastoral fantasy itself is conceived as instrumental in Jamaican colonial history. Beginning "There were still shards of ancient pastoral / in those shires of the island," the first paragraph portrays a typical Jamaican plantation through the double lens of colonial insider and postcolonial observer, evoking the way in which owners strove to reproduce in their plantations the order, beauty and "epochal happiness" of an English country estate. The second paragraph shatters

> that dream
> of slow rivers and lily-like parasols, in snaps
> of fine old colonial families

(ll.33–35)

by showing the ugly reality of slavery which it hid: "the groom, the cattle boy, the housemaid, the gardeners" who sustained it, and the "rancour of hatred" it bred (l.38). The text however is (anti-colonial) pastoral, rather than (postcolonial) anti-pastoral, for pastoral fantasy as such is not demolished. Walcott's rhetoric gives it even a peculiar beauty of its own. As Peter Balakian perceives, by sheer force of language the text contrives "to hold in tension the pastoral munificence of the colonial world and its morally rotten underpinnings" (353). Thirty years later, in "Pastoral" (*White Egrets*, 2010), Walcott finds a similar contradiction in rural Pennsylvania.

Australia has a different heritage of colonial pastoral. Rural poetry written by descendants of settlers, living on land appropriated from its Aboriginal inhabitants, constructed a hybrid European-Australian Arcadia, in which the indigenous culture was either romantically idealized or simply erased. Ethel Anderson's "Bucolic Eclogues" (from *Squatter's Luck*, 1954), for example, sprang from her "desire to bring the pleasantries of Virgil and Theocritus to this new land" (Preface). Anderson, a fifth-generation Australian, whose eclogues owe as much to Virgil's *Georgics* as to his bucolics, celebrates the heroic struggle of Australian farmers to wrest a living out of an unyielding environment, without so much as mentioning the previous occupants of the "new land."

Reaction against this tradition generated a variety of negative versions of pastoral in twentieth-century Australian poetry, variously termed "anti-pastoral," "neo-pastoral," "radical pastoral," and so on. There is nothing negative, however, about Les Murray's fine early poem, "Noonday Axeman" (from *The Ilex Tree*, 1965), which is a modern eclogue in everything but name, complete with poet-as-rustic-speaker (the axman of the title), and constructed round the opposition of country to city. His later poem-cycle, *The Idyll-Wheel: Cycle of a Year at Bunyah, New South Wales* (1989) is reminiscent in its structure of John Clare's *Shepherd's Calendar*. It again is "anti-pastoral" only in its realism and its refusal to romanticize the rural past, as when his farming ancestors' land is referred to as the "ruins of an idyll" (300, l.19). *The Idyll-Wheel* is in the same mode as Frost's and Heaney's rural poetry in its blending of georgic and pastoral: the "landscape" of his farm at Bunyah is described as "a haughty pastoral / bent fitfully to farming's fourteen-hour days" ("Leaf Spring," ll.15–16).

John Kinsella, Australia's most dedicated pastoralist, calls his poems "counter-pastorals." His conception of Australian pastoral and his practice as a poet are forged on the one hand out of an intimate knowledge of pastoral genres and the literary history of pastoral poetry, and on the other out of acute consciousness of the dispossession of Australia's original inhabitants, and of the forces threatening or destroying the environment. Of the latter he writes, in "Is there an Australian Pastoral?"

> The destruction of environments does not reduce the discourse of pastoral, but increases the need for it. This is a case not simply of nostalgia for what has been lost, but of the need to create an exchange, a discourse between differing voices and points of view within the landscape picture.
>
> (*Contrary Rhetoric* 131–32).

The eclogue provides Kinsella with a tailor-made form for such a discourse. Formal conventions in "First Eclogue" and "Second Eclogue" (from *The Hunt*, 1998) act as a frame for dialogues between workers in the Australian wheatlands, and a foil to their down-to-earth topics (and in "Second Eclogue" to the racy colloquialism of their speech). "The Rabbiters: A Pastoral," however, is bitingly anti-pastoral: its field of pastoral reference—Theocritus and Frost: "the Theocritan ute [utility vehicle] has been versed / in country things"—provides the ground for remorseless "rituals" of animal slaughter (*The Hunt and Other Poems* 83). Kinsella nevertheless insists that even negative or subversive uses of pastoral, "steeped in death and destruction as they might be, are actually affirming as much as they are condemning" (*Contrary Rhetoric* 132).

Conclusion

The emergence of pastoral, anti-pastoral, and counter-pastoral in Ireland, Australia, and the Caribbean, at a time when pastoral had long ceased to be a favored, let alone a dominant poetic genre in the English-speaking literary world at large, seems to bear out the contention that genre is "culture-specific" and "historically determined" (Perloff 7). There is as yet no proven method for mapping genres on to cultures, synchronically or diachronically, but recent developments in genre theory, Duff argues, make it "now possible to conceive of a type of literary history that has an accurate perception of the genre spectrum that obtains at any given period," and which would yield understanding of "the conditions of possibility for the existence of particular genres, and the reasons for their flourishing or decline" (18). Pastoral, enmeshed as it is not only in competing literary theories but also in eco-critical debate about the interrelation of humans and the natural world, stands peculiarly in need of such a history.

The adoption of both positive and negative forms of pastoral in postcolonial literatures illustrates, further, the generative, epistemological functions of genre, a subject which has become prominent in recent theoretical discussion. The power of genres to "generate and shape knowledge of the world" is the central thesis of John Frow's *Genre* (2). Where debate formerly revolved round the conflict between "a neoclassical understanding of genre as prescriptive taxonomy and as a constraint on textual energy," and the "Romantic revolt" by Jacques Derrida and others against it, Frow advocates a reconception of genres as "performative structures that shape the world in the very process of putting it into speech" ("'Reproducibles, Rubrics'" 1633). Critical perception and poetic practice has run ahead of theory on this issue. Heaney, arguing for "the staying power of pastoral" in 2002, cited texts by several contemporary authors to show how "the literariness of the pastoral mode allows the poet to shed new or clearer light on truth and reality" ("Eclogues *In Extremis*" 1). The vigor and inventiveness with which poets in the modern age have reclaimed, adapted, or subverted pastoral, for this and other purposes, testifies to the power of genres to generate textual energy rather than constrain it.

REFERENCES AND FURTHER READING

Alpers, Paul. *What Is Pastoral?* Chicago: University of Chicago Press, 1996

Anderson, Ethel. *Squatter's Luck with Other Bucolic Eclogues*. Melbourne: Melbourne University Press, 1954.

Auden, W.H. *The Shield of Achilles*. London: Faber & Faber, 1955.

Balakian, Peter. "The Poetry of Derek Walcott," in *Critical Perspectives on Derek Walcott*, ed. Robert D. Hamner. Washington, DC: Three Continents Press, 1993.

Blunden, Edmund. *Poems of Many Years*. London: Collins, 1957.

Boland, Eavan. *Collected Poems*. Manchester: Carcanet. 1995.

Chaudhuri, Sukanta. *Renaissance Pastoral and Its English Developments*. Oxford: Clarendon Press, 1989.

Dabydeen, David. *Slave Song*. Mundelstrup: Dangaroo Press, 1984.

Duff, David (ed.). *Modern Genre Theory*. Harlow: Longman, 2000.

Empson, William. *Some Versions of Pastoral*. London: Chatto & Windus. 1935.

Ettin, Andrew V. *Literature and the Pastoral*. New Haven: Yale University Press, 1984.

Feingold, Richard. *Nature and Society: Later Eighteenth-Century Uses of the Pastoral and Georgic*. Hassocks: Harvester Press, 1978.

Frost, Robert. *Robert Frost: Collected Poems, Prose, and Plays*, ed. Richard Poirier and Mark Richardson. New York: Library of America, 1995.

Frow, John. *Genre*. London: Routledge, 2006.

Frow, John. "'Reproducibles, Rubrics, and Everything You Need': Genre Theory Today," *PMLA* 122.5 (2007), 1626–34.

Fussell, Paul. *The Great War and Modern Memory*. Oxford: Oxford University Press, 1975.

Gilmore, John. *The Poetics of Empire: A Study of James Grainger's "The Sugar-Cane."* London: Athlone Press, 2000.

Gifford, Terry. *Green Voices: Understanding Contemporary Nature Poetry*. Manchester: Manchester University Press, 1995.

Glissant, Edouard. *Le Discours antillais*. Paris: Gallimard, 1997.

Greg, Walter W. *Pastoral Poetry and Pastoral Drama*. London: A.H. Bullen, 1906.

Heaney, Seamus. "Eclogues *In Extremis*: On the Staying Power of Pastoral" [a paper delivered in Dublin, 2002], *Proceedings of the Royal Irish Academy* 103C:1 (2003): 1–12.

Heaney, Seamus. *Electric Light*. London: Faber & Faber, 2001.

Heaney, Seamus. *Death of a Naturalist*. London: Faber & Faber, 1966.

Heaney, Seamus. *Opened Ground: Poems 1966–1996*. London: Faber & Faber, 1998.

Heath-Stubbs, John. *Collected Poems, 1942–1987*. Manchester: Carcanet, 1988.

Hyde, Virginia M. "The Pastoral Formula of W.H. Auden and Piero di Cosimo," *Contemporary Literature* 14 (1973): 332–46.

Kiberd, Declan. *Inventing Ireland: The Literature of the Modern Nation*. London: Jonathan Cape, 1995.

Kinsella, John. *Contrary Rhetoric: Lectures on Landscape and Language*, ed. Glen Phillips and Andrew Taylor. Fremantle: Fremantle Press, 2008.

Kinsella, John. *The Hunt and Other Poems*. Newcastle upon Tyne: Bloodaxe, 1998.

Larkin, Philip. *Collected Poems*, ed. Anthony Thwaite. London: Marvell Press; Faber & Faber, 2003.

Lerner, Laurence. *The Uses of Nostalgia: Studies in Pastoral Poetry*. London: Chatto and Windus, 1972.

Longley, Edna (ed.). *Edward Thomas: The Annotated Collected Poems*. Tarset: Bloodaxe, 2008.

MacNeice, Louis. *The Collected Poems of Louis MacNeice*, ed. E.R. Dodds. London: Faber & Faber, 1966.

Marsack, Robyn. *The Cave of Making: The Poetry of Louis MacNeice*. Oxford: Clarendon Press, 1982.

McDonald, Peter. *Mistaken Identities: Poetry and Northern Ireland*. Oxford: Clarendon Press, 1997.

McDonald, Peter. *Pastorals*. Manchester: Carcanet, 2004.

Montague, John. *The Rough Field* (1972), 3rd edn. Dublin: Dolmen Press, 1979.

Murray, Les. *Collected Poems*. Melbourne: Black Inc., 2006.

O'Callaghan, Conor. "The Modern Pastoral Elegy: A Tick-Where-Appropriate Template," in *Poetry* (July 2005): 297.

O'Donoghue, Bernard. "Heaney's Classics and the Bucolic," in *The Cambridge Companion to Seamus Heaney*, ed. O'Donoghue. Cambridge: Cambridge University Press, 2009. 106–21.

Perloff, Marjorie (ed.). *Postmodern Genres*. London: University of Oklahoma Press, 1995.

Pope, Alexander. "A Discourse of Pastoral Poetry" (*Works*, 1717): *The Prose Works of Alexander Pope*, ed. Norman Ault, 2 vols. Oxford: Basil Blackwell, 1968. 297–302.

Stevenson, Randall. *The Last of England?* Oxford English Literary History 12: 1960–2000. Oxford: Oxford University Press, 2004.

Thomas, Edward. *Elected Friends: Robert Frost and Edward Thomas to one Another*, ed. Matthew Spencer. New York: Handsel, 2003.

Walcott, Derek. *Collected Poems 1948–1984*. New York: Noonday Press, Farrar, Straus & Giroux, 1986.

41

Another Green World

Contemporary Garden Poetry

Mark Scroggins

The garden is one of the primary topoi of the Western imagination. Gardens in classical literature, like the famous Garden of Alcinous in *Odyssey* VII, gesture towards a lost "Golden Age," while the controlling Judaeo-Christian narrative begins in a garden, the Eden in which the Lord placed the first human beings. In "Of Gardens" (1625), Francis Bacon argues that all human gardening is an attempt to emulate or recover that primal paradise: "GOD *Almightie* first planted a *Garden*. And indeed, it is the Purest of Humane pleasures . . . And a Man shall ever see, that when Ages grow to Civility and Elegancie, Men come to *Build Stately*, sooner than to *Garden Finely*: As if *Gardening* were the Greater Perfection" (qtd. in Hunt and Willis 51).

Gardening is an art of *milieu*, of place-making, a complex negotiation between the human imagination and the shape of the land, the motion of water, the growing patterns of vegetation. If the primary meaning of "nature" is the environment untouched by human hands, and if human technology, by planting fields and building roads and structures, reshapes that into what Cicero calls *alteram naturam*, or a "second" nature, then the garden can be read, in the phrase of the Renaissance humanist Jacobo Bonfadio, as a "third nature," a self-conscious intervention marrying natural materials and human artifice in a *milieu* that flaunts its very liminality between the found and the made (Hunt, *Greater Perfections* 33–34).

The garden, a complex emblem of humans' relationship to their worldly environment, has exerted an irresistible fascination for poets, though garden poetry has received rather less critical attention than one might expect, given its pervasiveness and perdurability. The tradition of garden poetry dates back at least as far as Homer and the Hebrew Bible; it overlaps with the contiguous traditions of pastoral and georgic poetry, as well as with the poetry of architecture. And while contemporary

A Companion to Poetic Genre, First Edition. Edited by Erik Martiny.
© 2012 John Wiley & Sons, Ltd. Published 2012 by John Wiley & Sons, Ltd.

English-language garden poetry, in an increasingly urbanized and ecologically threatened world, has taken radically different forms from those of its heyday in the eighteenth century, it continues a vital and intellectually challenging tradition.

English garden poetry, a tradition which predates Chaucer, is at its most energetic during the seventeenth and eighteenth centuries, when powerful poets found themselves in the company of rich landowners for whom elaborate gardens were a necessary element of their property. In "Upon Appleton House," for instance, Andrew Marvell celebrates the estate of his employer General Fairfax as an ordered and reclaimed microcosm of a disorderly outside world:

> 'Tis not, what it once was, the world,
> But a rude heap together hurled,
> All negligently overthrown,
> Gulfs, deserts, precipices, stone.
> Your lesser world contains the same,
> But in more decent order tame;
> You, heaven's centre, Nature's lap,
> And paradise's only map.

(ll.761–69)

Marvell's was an age of formal gardens, of boxwoods, shrubs, and flowers laid out in flat, geometrical parterres. It is unsurprising, then, that the principal tension underlying his famous garden poems is that between the formal, the artificial, and the wild, or natural. In "The Mower against Gardens," the mower excoriates fallen, "Luxurious" man for having imposed an artificial order upon the vegetative world:

> He first enclosed within the gardens square
> A dead and standing pool of air,
> And a more luscious earth for them did knead,
> which stupefied them while it fed.

(ll.5–8)

To the mower, whose vocation is the simple maintenance of pastoral meadows, the formal garden is an insult to the innocence of pristine nature:

> 'Tis all enforced, the fountain and the grot,
> While the sweet fields do lie forgot:
> Where willing nature does to all dispense
> A wild and fragrant innocence.

(ll.31–34)

"Fauns and fairies" might grace the garden in the form of statues, but their real presences can still be found only in the ungardened meadows: "howsoe'er the figures do excel, / The gods themselves with us do dwell" (ll.39–40).

In the century after Marvell, the tension between formal garden and pastoral nature dramatized in the "Mower" poems takes on a new complexion, as gardening in geometrical shapes—a style associated with the Dutch and French traditions—was displaced by a new "English" style of landscape gardening, among whose pioneering theorists was Alexander Pope. The English garden would no longer impose an order upon a passive nature, but would rather seek to draw out the beauties already inherent in the landscape, to work in conjunction with the *genius loci*. As Pope enjoins the garden designer in the "Epistle to Burlington,"

> Consult the Genius of the Place in all;
> That tells the Waters or to rise, or fall,
> Or helps th' ambitious Hill the heav'n to scale,
> Or scoops in circling theatres the Vale,
> Calls in the Country, catches opening glades,
> Joins willing woods, and varies shades from shades,
> Now breaks or now directs, th' intending Lines;
> Paints as you plant, and, as you work, designs.
>
> (ll. 57–64)

The new English garden is known as the *picturesque* garden, and implicit in that term (Pope's coinage) is a shift from gardening as a branch of architecture to gardening that takes painting as its paradigmatic art. As Pope remarked to Joseph Spence, "All gardening is landscape painting" (Spence 104).

The eighteenth-century heyday of the English landscape garden, under such renowned garden designers as William Kent, Lancelot "Capability" Brown, and Humphrey Repton, is something of a golden age for the poet-gardener. Besides laboring intensively on his own garden at Twickenham, Pope advised his landowning friends on matters of garden design and recorded his principles of gardening in a number of poems. The poet William Shenstone sought in his landscape at The Leasowes to design a garden that, like Pope's, drew upon a rich humus of literary and historical associations. And numerous verses praised, described, and explicated the picturesque landscapes that were becoming the rage on English country estates—some of them, notably Lord Cobham's Stowe in Buckinghamshire, aiming to create a complex experience of landscape and poetical allusion: Stowe includes, along with any number of classical inscriptions, a monument to Congreve, a Fane of Pastoral Poetry, and a Temple of British Worthies (including Shakespeare, Milton, and Pope).

Once this Augustan moment of conjunction between the arts of poetry and garden design has passed, however, it is not to return. Romanticism brought with it a fascination with the sublime scenes of *untamed* nature—Snowdon or Mont Blanc, rather than the gardens of Stowe or Castle Howard. And the dissolution of the patronage economy in literature meant that poets for the most part no longer moved in intimate company with garden-building landowners, nor felt impelled to honor the achievements of the nobility and gentry's landscape designers.

Poets continue to write garden poems through the Victorian era and into the twentieth century, but one no longer apprehends—as one does with Marvell and Pope—that the poet's art moves hand in hand with the garden designer's. The two aesthetic pursuits have parted company, and there is only intermittently the sense that poem-making and garden-making are two parallel and potentially intertwined arts. If poets of the nineteenth and twentieth century are gardeners, they are for the most part cultivators of small urban or suburban gardens, like other members of the middle class. John Dixon Hunt is right, however, to find "a special richness and variety in twentieth-century garden poetry" (*Oxford Book* 23). Several outstanding contemporary poets have recognized the primal kinship of the poem and the garden, and have explored that kinship both metaphorically and in terms of the very formal structure of their poems, to dazzling effect.

Marvell's best-known garden poem, of course, is "The Garden," which invokes the garden as a psychic retreat where the mind can "[withdraw] into its happiness," "Annihilating all that's made / To a green thought in a green shade" (ll.47–48). The poem ends with a depiction of a vegetable sun-dial:

> How well the skilful gardener drew
> Of flowers and herbs this dial new,
> where from above the milder sun
> Does through a fragrant zodiac run;
> And, as it works, the industrious bee
> Computes its time as well as we.
> How could such sweet and wholesome hours
> Be reckoned but with herbs and flowers!
>
> (ll.65–72)

This passage, in which time is "computed" only with "herbs and flowers," might serve as an epigraph to the American poet Louis Zukofsky's last collection, *80 Flowers* (1978), a book which takes as metaphorical model the Medieval and Renaissance botanical garden, and which explores an aspect of the garden which perhaps most fascinates and eludes its celebrants: the garden's existence over the fourth dimension of time.

By the time he finished his long poem *"A"* in 1974, at the age of seventy, Zukofsky had laid the groundwork for a sequence of eighty-one short poems, each of them dealing with a particular flower or plant, to be completed by his eightieth birthday. The eighty plants of *80 Flowers* would include "Only those flowers I have actually seen and whatever botany I can learn in 10 years," as Zukofsky noted in a draft overview of the book (qtd. in Leggott 12). The poems, then, would be based upon the plants already growing in and around his home in Long Island, and plants acquired and cultivated over the course of the book's composition.

Eighty separate species is a range of growing things far larger than the ordinary suburban garden; and Zukofsky's working method, which involved intensive research into botanical and literary lore surrounding each plant, would draw many more flowers into his poems than their four score ostensible subjects. Indeed, *80 Flowers* represents less a detailed walk-through of an individual garden than a compact recreation of the Renaissance botanic garden, which aimed at a *universal* representation of all plants known to humanity. As John Prest describes it, "The Garden was an encyclopedia" (6), a single location at which the whole botanic aspect of the Book of Nature could be read in all of its variety. In *80 Flowers*, Zukofsky aspires to a similar comprehensiveness; and further, through his methods of extreme citationality and condensation, Zukofsky aims ultimately to wind in *every* aspect of human culture, much as his 1963 *Bottom: on Shakespeare* had sought to cover all of Western letters.

In his late work Zukofsky had forged a particularly dense and obdurate lyrical poetic. On the structure of a word-count line he would dispose linguistic material which—in a radical extension of the modernist practice of such poems as *The Waste Land* or *The Cantos*—is almost entirely derived from preexisting sources, words quoted, translated, or transliterated from earlier texts. *80 Flowers'* opening unnumbered and untitled "epigraph" exemplifies this late poetic:

> Heart us invisibly thyme time
> round rose bud fire downland
> bird tread quagmire dry gill-over-the-ground
> stem-square leaves-cordate earth race horsethyme
> breath neighbors a mace nays
> sorrow of harness pulses pent
> *thus* fruit pod split four
> one-fourth *ripens* unwithering gaping.

> *(Complete Short Poetry* 325)

This form, eight five-word lines, is a constant throughout *80 Flowers*. The epigraph revolves around four specific plants: a thyme bush near the Zukofskys' house; a rose bush; "gill-over-the-ground," an old name for ground ivy (*Nepeta hederacea*); and the common catnip, or *Nepeta cataria*. Zukofsky devises his poem by running down every imaginable historical, literary, etymological association of his plant names, and then sifting a careful selection of what he has found into his forty-word formal framework.

The epigraph's opening "Heart us" is Zukofsky's rough transliteration of the Greek *artos*, or bread—made from flour, a homophone for "flower." "[R]ose bud fire" condenses a quotation from Isaac D'Israeli's essay "Introduction of Tea, Coffee, and Chocolate." "[U]nwithering" translates "amaranth," which Zukofsky plucks from a passage in Herman Melville's *Pierre*, where it is contrasted with the humble catnip. "[F]ruit pod split four" is taken directly from *Taylor's Encyclopedia of Gardening*, as is "stem-square leaves-cordate," both descriptions of catnip. "[H]orsethyme" is a name for *Thymus vulgaris*, the common "thyme" of the first line. Indeed, practically every word of the poem can, with enough patience and ingenuity, be "sourced" in Zukofsky's preparatory reading for *80 Flowers*.

This epigraph, revolving around the thyme/time pun, evoking the speed of a "race," and alluding to horses—which in Zukofsky's late work symbolize the poet, working in the "sorrow of harness"—is concerned with the passage of *time*, the forward temporal movement that "ripens" both poems and plants. Zukofsky knew that he was working against time on this project, and had resolved as well to make the passage of time an integral element of the collection. As Hunt notes, the garden "not only exists in but also takes its special character from *four* dimensions" (*Greater Perfections* 15): as fundamental to the garden as its site, arrangement, and plant materials is its existence across time, the fact that the garden will present a different face over each of the four seasons, that its plants are continually growing, maturing, in decline. In the case of the botanic garden that is *80 Flowers*, Zukofsky builds the passage of time into the very sequence of his flowers. While the collection ends with an alphabetical series—"Vines," "Weeds," " 'X,' " "Yaupon," and "Zinnia"—unsurprising for a poet given to numerology and word-games, often the sequence of the flowers treated depends on the order of the plants' blooming season, and even the particular date on which a given flower bloomed in the Zukofskys' household.

Even more striking perhaps is the degree to which *80 Flowers* serves its poet as a vegetable calendar, a "dial" which "reckons" time "with herbs and flowers." As his compositional notes make clear, Zukofsky seeded his flower poems with references to their dates of composition, marking especially specific talismanic dates. "Mountain Laurel," written late in January, alludes to the death of Zukofsky's mother on January 29, 1927. Other flowers remember the deaths of the poet's father ("Forsythia") and sister ("Petunia"). Poems written in mid-February ("Honesty," "Tulip") are intended as valentines—a holiday of great significance to the sentimental poet; Rosh Hashanah is celebrated in "Dahlia" and "Artemesia." Other poems remember the birthdays of Zukofsky's wife and son and such cultural figures as Bach and Shakespeare. The poems do not openly trumpet these anniversaries; rather, they are encoded in the language and references of each flower, and ultimately function as one of the primary compositional impulses of the collection.

While the prickly, unpunctuated word-blocks of the poems initially present an appearance of obdurate density to the reader, an exploration of Zukofsky's citational poetics and time-based compositional process reveals that *80 Flowers* is not merely a striking linguistic reinvention of the botanic garden, but a compelling meditation on the passage of time as measured by the cycles of the green world: a late modernist floral sun-dial.

"To the extent that gardens depend on natural materials, they are at best ever-changing," Hunt writes, "but at worst they are destined for dilapidation and ruin from their very inception." (*Greater Perfections* 15). Perhaps the most momentous temporal change that the great private gardens of the renaissance and baroque periods have undergone is a *social* refunctioning, from the pleasure-grounds of royalty and nobility to public parks. In her 2008 collection *Ours*, American poet Cole Swensen imagines the French queen consort Marie de Medici (1575–1642) awakening in 2007 to see Paris's Luxembourg Gardens transformed into a space of bourgeois public relaxation:

> Walking out on the first day of summer, 2007, Marie
> sees hundreds of people playing on the lawns and in the paths
> which have been completely redrawn, and the green metal chairs,
> their particular sound as they're dragged across gravel. And the green metal chairs
> full of people quietly reading paperbacks and newspapers, who look up,
> startled to see her.
>   She stood a full minute, shocked, and then started screaming.
> The rue d'Assas has cut off the entire northwest sector, and half the trees are gone.
> The other half have unconscionably grown.
>
>   (53)

Swensen's book revolves around the life, career, and gardens of André Le Nôtre (1613–1700), chief garden designer to the "Sun King" Louis XIV. In its very title, the book underlines how the gardens Le Nôtre designed as displays of absolutist power have become the property of the people—*ours*, the literal translation of Le Nôtre's surname.

The poems of *Ours* are conscious that they regard Le Nôtre from three centuries' distance. "Every thing he ever planted is now dead," Swensen writes (5). The garden, like any other human making, exists in time; but while the text of a poem or the shape of a sculpture might remain more or less constant even as the context of its interpretation changes, a garden necessarily shifts over time: its plants grow, mature, die, and are replaced; over the basic form of its underpinning landscape (which itself can be altered over time), the shapes of the garden's *allées*, parterres, and groves will inevitably change, radically or subtly. It is difficult, then, to recapture a gardener's original intentions when the garden itself is a moving target; and to do so is to recapture an entirely different world-frame: "Any garden," Swensen writes, "is a description / of its era's metaphysics" (13).

The "metaphysics" of Le Nôtre's royal gardens is a metaphysics of absolutism, "the subordination of architecture and nature to a total hallucinatory statement of power" (Adams 123). It is also a metaphysics of Cartesian rationalism, of geometrical order, and of the conviction that the natural world can yield its secrets and conform itself to the human mind: "It was an age that felt that nature could be corrected" (Swensen 73). Yet even as Swensen touches upon these themes in such poems as "The Divinity of the Sun King" and "The Garden as a Map of Louis XIV," she remains acutely aware of the garden's polysemy. The garden *is* no one thing, but an array of different frames by which one views the world, frames that Swensen poses and explores in poem after poem: "The Garden as Architecture Itself," "The Garden as Word Game," "The Garden as Extension," "A Garden as a Letter," "A Garden as Between," "A Garden as a Unit of Measure." If the garden is "a way of making nature account for the mind," "the world counted / and found analogue in nature," it is also true that "Gardens lie beyond the eye" (20, 31, 24).

"Gardens lie beyond the eye," sometimes literally: it was impossible for a single gaze to take in the whole of Versailles's 8,000-hectare landscape. But they lie beyond the eye as well because of their experiential and semantic richness, the degree to which they spur the ambulative, observing, and speculative mind into vistas beyond the garden's immediate concrete presence. The gardens of Swensen's *Ours* are both the landscapes designed by André Le Nôtre *as they exist now* and those landscapes as imaginary palimpsest over their appearance in Le Nôtre's day; and furthermore, the conceptual landscapes and gardens to which the principles of Le Nôtre's garden art give rise in the poet's own imagination.

"It might appear," John Prest writes, that the renaissance botanic garden marks "the beginnings of modern science, the collection of data, and the patient, detailed observation of causes and effects" (6). But while the botanic garden does indeed point in the direction of Baconian empiricism, its original intention was far different: to recreate Eden, that first garden where the Lord planted "every tree that is pleasant to the sight, and good for food" and in which he placed Adam "to dress it and keep it" (Genesis 2.9, 15). The American poet Ronald Johnson places the Adamic imperative near the end of the first section of his long poem *ARK*, in a segment titled "*The Garden*":

> "To do as Adam did"
> through the twilight's fluoride glare Mercury in perihilion
> (rotating exactly three times
> while circling the sun twice)
> to Pluto foot tilt up the slide at either plane
> and build a Garden of the brain.
>
> (*ARK*, BEAM 30, *The Garden*)

Adam's task was twofold: he was to name the animals the Lord had made to inhabit his newly created world—and Johnson's poem is much involved with celebrating, caressing, and reconfiguring the words humans use to describe the world around them—and he was to *garden*, to maintain ("dress and keep") the growing things with which the Lord had filled the Garden.

ARK is a ninety-nine-section poem much in the tradition of such works as Pound's *Cantos*, William Carlos Williams's *Paterson*, Zukofsky's "*A*," and Charles Olson's *The Maximus Poems*. But while Pound and company wrote poems that set contemporaneity within a rich, even encyclopedic, historical context, Johnson seeks instead to write a long poem outside of history: "If my confreres wanted to write a work with all history in its maw," Johnson comments, he conceives *ARK* as "structure rather than diatribe, artifact rather than argument, a veritable shell of the chambered nautilus, sliced and polished, bound for Ararat unknown" (*ARK*, "A Note").

ARK is a poem of visionary physics, a celebration of human perception and natural process, of how the eye and everything it perceives "may be said to be sun in other form" (BEAM 4). Johnson conceives of the poem's tripartite structure of "Beams,"

"Spires," and "Arches" as forming "Literally an architecture" (*ARK*, "A Note"), and is delighted with the neatness and sense of finality with which the notion of architecture invests his poem: "when you make it an architecture, then you're settled at being finished" (O'Leary 565). But *ARK* can be read as readily as a *garden*—an idiosyncratic, late-modernist variation upon some hybrid of the renaissance formal garden and the English picturesque landscape—as an architectural structure.

In his architectural models, Johnson inclines toward such naïve visionary structures as the Facteur Cheval's "Palais Idéal," built out of randomly collected stones, or Simon Rodia's Watts Towers; it is therefore only natural, argues Eric Selinger, to find an analogue to *ARK* in the visionary environments, "gardens of revelation" (John Beardsley's phrase) constructed by isolated eccentrics across the United States. *ARK* has much in common with these gardens, seeded with naïve images of Biblical characters and patriotic heroes, statues of angels, demons, and deities, American flags and bits of popular culture. The poem is suffused with an enthusiastic Whitmanian democracy, celebrating the nation's bicentennial in one Beam, formally miming the Statue of Liberty in a "Spire of Liberty," and indulging in a run of Currier and Ives-like fireworks in other Spires; its various sections draw on Henry James, Henry David Thoreau, the Bible, patriotic songs, and Protestant hymnals. While Johnson always acknowledges the modernist pedigree of his poetics of quotation and collage, he is as willing to call his poetry a species of amateur bricolage akin to the work of Beardsley's eccentric gardeners.

One is tempted to identify these "gardens of revelation" as a home-grown, populist version of the statue- and inscription-strewn gardens of the early eighteenth century. In place of the neoclassicism of the Augustan garden—nymph-inhabited grottoes, Latin inscriptions, columned temples—these works refer to the vernacular icons of American history and above all else to the Bible. Johnson, in fashioning *ARK* as a garden of ecstatic, visionary celebration of natural process, as opposed to an American-keyed scriptural revelation, ropes in as well any number of references to classical and neo-classical garden *topoi*: there are grottoes here, and herms (ithyphallic statues of the god Hermes); there seems to be a labyrinth at every turn; and one of the governing myths of the poem as a whole is the story of Orpheus and Eurydice.

If architecture is the explicit, "public" formal model for *ARK*, its governing metaphor is clearly the garden, in an eclectic array of its various forms. And while the poem's relative scarcity of reference to particular *flora* make it rather unlike a botanic garden, the poem certainly makes gestures towards being a *zoological* garden. One of the implications of its very title, in addition to a mathematical arc, the Ark of the Covent, and the rainbow (*arc-en-ciel*), is Noah's Ark: allusions to the Ark and the Flood punctuate the book, and ARK 83, *Arches XVIII, The Ramp* consists of a lineated list of collective names of animals ("a pedylyng of ducks, a skein of / geese, muster of / peacocks")—a catalogue of the fauna to be preserved from a deluge.

The "gardening" in which the poet of *ARK* is engaged is an activity of composition and revelation, of revealing the hidden harmonies within the visible world. The literal gardener works with soil, plants, water, and architectural detail; Johnson works with the bright juxtaposition of words, arranging his quotations, allusions, and descriptions into harmonic patterns:

> Love itself is a kind of *mirage* nestling it all
> together. Around a center
> no one can see the end of, at the Well of The Bottomless,
> I have placed parallels of bright guardians
> "along with the trill
> of the Nightingale,
> and the call of the European quail"
> as in The Pastoral.
> (Signed) THE GARDENER
>
> (BEAM 30, *The Garden*)

Johnson recovers Eden in *ARK*, not least in the poem's garden-like vision of the human being's place in the natural world. Johnson's work is strikingly free from social angst, from the pervasive pessimism and tragedy of much twentieth-century writing. Rather than enduring a state of abjection, alienation, or Heideggerian *Geworfenheit*, for Johnson the human being is fundamentally at home in the world, is both a caretaker and himself a mode of the natural processes that make the world a garden-home.

In the last years of his life Johnson worked as a gardener on a historic estate in his home state of Kansas, and it is unsurprising that it was there he wrote his last work, a sequence of poems entitled *The Shrubberies*. They are his most thorough-going garden-based poetry, and they make explicit the gardening metaphor at the heart of all of his mature writing:

> quincunx of succulents
> subtle colors and forms
> succinct in dust
>
> appropriate the pot
> assigned, set each
> for spill into Other
>
> always my core dream
> winding a garden
> secret in every sense
>
> (67)

The shift from formal to "landscape" gardening was not the only evolution undergone by garden practice over the eighteenth century. As Hunt explains, there was as well a movement from "emblematic" to "expressive" gardens: from gardens that, through their meaning-bearing inscriptions, sculptures, and buildings, solicited an active, even "allegorical" interpretation from those who visited them; to gardens which aimed at making an impression upon visitors in a less overtly semantic manner (*Gardens* 75–102). In contrast to a garden such as Pope's Twickenham, the picturesque garden of the late eighteenth century "no longer requires the learned attention to detailed meaning; it makes no claim upon our intellect" it is "a landscape that seems to answer our moods, that allows a unique and individual response by each visitor to its unobtrusive character" (87). The affinity between such a designed landscape and the ensuing Romantic attitude towards untamed nature should be evident.

The earlier Augustan garden, however, was emphatically "emblematic." As Ronald Paulson notes, by the middle of the eighteenth century the English landscape garden, dotted with statuary, temples, and inscriptions, had become "as allusive a structure as the poem" (qtd. in Brownell 246). That allusiveness disappeared in the latter part of the century, and largely vanished from garden design for at least a hundred years afterwards. It has been revived with a vengeance, however, in the gardens of the Scottish poet-artist Ian Hamilton Finlay. His crowning achievement, the garden known as Little Sparta in Lanarkshire, Scotland, is not merely a contemporary landscape design, but a fascinating and complex *poem* in its own right.

Finlay began his career as a conventional print poet, but by the mid-1960s, he had become one of the most prominent practitioners of "concrete poetry." In a 1963 letter to Pierre Garnier, Finlay described this turn as in part a reaction against "the now-fashionable poetry of anguish and doubt": the concrete poem "is a model, of order, even if set in a space which is full of doubt" (qtd. in Scobie 188). That principle—setting a "model of order" within a given space—would become the basis of his aesthetic practice over the next four decades. In 1966 Finlay moved to "Stonypath," an abandoned croft in the hills south of Edinburgh, and in the years following he would begin to reshape its buildings and landscapes into an astonishingly rich and complex garden site.

The two hectares of Little Sparta contain a wide variety of landscapes and garden features: there are glades, formal gardens, a kitchen garden (the "Kailyard," a vernacular Scots allusion), allées, a Wild Garden, ponds, and a stretch of "English"-style landscape. The garden, simply in terms of its exquisite architecture, careful landscaping, and alternately dense and sparse plantings, is a striking aesthetic experience. What is even more striking, however, is the density of *inscription* in the garden: at every turn, one comes upon a sign, a plaque, a bit of statuary with writing upon it; there are inscribed plinths, benches, bird-baths; there are inscriptions on the stiles, the bridges, the bricks of the paths, the very stepping stones over the pond. These inscriptions are not the anodyne platitudes of contemporary garden stones but evoke the semantic density of some of Pope's inscriptions at Twickenham. On the statues of two river gods which flanked his garden's Thames landing-place, Pope intended the inscriptions "Hic placido fluit amne Meles" [Here softly flows the Meles] and "Magnis ubi flexibus errat Mincius" [Where the Mincius wanders with great windings], quotations—from Politian's *Ambra* and Virgil's *Georgics* respectively—that refer us to the poets associated with those rivers, Homer and Virgil, and remind the reader of Virgil's goal "of enlarging and enriching the national culture by causing to be poured into it the great works of classical antiquity": a goal shared, seventeen centuries later, by Pope himself (Mack 37–40).

Finlay's inscriptions are equally as allusive, if usually more compact. The initials "AD" are inscribed on a tablet in a space of turf and hanging from a tree by a leather thong, transforming those two scenes into "quotations" of two of Albrecht Dürer's paintings; the name "CLAUDI," carved on a pink concrete bridge, makes the scene a landscape by Claude Lorrain (Sheeler 107–08, 28–29). On a Greek stele at the foot of a copse of maples and hornbeams one finds the inscription "BRING BACK THE BIRCH"; the immediate reference is of course to the (absent) birch tree, but the inescapable allusion to corporal punishment underscores the element of harshness, even violence, present throughout the otherwise peaceful Arcadia of Finlay's garden. As he remarks in one of his "Unconnected Sentences on Gardening," "Certain gardens are described as retreats when they are really attacks" (qtd. in Hunt, *Nature* 22). Little Sparta, that is, is not merely an idyllic retreat among the windswept hills of southern Scotland, but in Stephen Bann's words "the emplacement of a political and cultural offensive which the poet directs against the wider world" (103).

As its very name indicates ("Little *Sparta*," in contrast to Edinburgh, the "Athens of the North"), Finlay conceives of his garden as a statement of strict neo-classical morality, a signifying space of ethical and aesthetic purity against the muddied political and artistic world at large. In this his totemic figures are the French Revolutionaries, who also clothed their aspirations for cultural revitalization in the garments of classical republicanism. (Camille Desmoulins referred to the Patriot-populated villages of France as "little Spartas" [Schama 499].) Throughout Little Sparta there are remembrances of Revolutionary figures, in particular Robespierre and Saint-Just, whose words "THE PRESENT ORDER IS THE DISORDER OF THE FUTURE" are inscribed on a "flock" of massive stones across a moor.

Little Sparta's Garden Temple is dedicated "To APOLLO / HIS MUSIC / HIS MISSILES / HIS MUSES"; this Apollo, as a bust inscribed "APOLLON TERRORISTE" indicates, is a figure of both art and violence. Terror is the flip side of virtue, as indicated on a medal Finlay had struck in 1984, on one face a guillotine with the inscription "Terror," on the other a visual "rhyme," a pair of Corinthian columns with the inscription "Virtue"; Robespierre spoke of "virtue without which terror is harmful and terror without which virtue is impotent" (Abrioux 259; Schama 828). But it would be mistaken to overstress the violence of Finlay's revolutionary vision, which is always leavened, especially in the softening atmosphere of the garden, with gentle wit and a good degree of whimsy. If, in a set of aphorisms for a 1987 exhibition, he writes "Classicism aims at Beauty, neo-classicism at Virtue," he also writes "Neo-classicism is classicism which has virtuously lost weight" (Finlay, *Inter Artes* n.p.).

In Little Sparta we seem to have come full circle back to Pope's Twickenham or Shenstone's The Leasowes: a garden designed by a poet, making ample use of *words*, the poet's most fundamental medium. Maynard Mack writes of Twickenham that "To be a great satirist, a man must have, literally and figuratively, a place to stand, an angle of vision . . . the garden and the grotto supplied this" (232). Little Sparta is indeed Finlay's "place to stand" in his often whimsical "war" against contemporary mores, but it is more importantly a signifying space, a "model of order": as poem of words, plants, landscapes, and architecture Little Sparta is itself Finlay's complex commentary on the Western cultural heritage in the latter half of the twentieth century.

REFERENCES AND FURTHER READING

Abrioux, Yves. *Ian Hamilton Finlay: A Visual Primer*. 2nd edn. Cambridge, MA: MIT Press, 1992.

Adams, William Howard. *Gardens through History: Nature Perfected*. New York: Abbeville Press, 1991.

Bann, Stephen. "Nature Over Again after Poussin: Some Discovered Landscapes." In *Wood Notes Wild: Essays on the Poetry and Art of Ian Hamilton Finlay*, ed. Alec Finlay. Edinburgh: Polygon, 1995. 98–106.

Beardsley, John. *Gardens of Revelation: Environments by Visionary Artists*. New York: Abbeville, 1995.

Bettridge, Joel and Eric Murphy Selinger, eds. *Ronald Johnson: Life and Works*. Orono, ME: National Poetry Foundation, 2008.

Brownell, *Alexander Pope and the Arts of Georgian England*. Oxford: Clarendon Press, 1978.

Finlay, Alec, ed. *Wood Notes Wild: Essays on the Poetry and Art of Ian Hamilton Finlay*. Edinburgh: Polygon, 1995.

Finlay, Ian Hamilton. *Inter Artes et Naturam*. Paris: ARC, 1987.

Hunt, John Dixon. *Gardens and the Picturesque: Studies in the History of Landscape Architecture*. Cambridge, MA: MIT Press, 1992.

Hunt, John Dixon. *Greater Perfections: The Practice of Garden Theory*. London: Thames & Hudson, 2000.

Hunt, John Dixon. *Nature Over Again: The Garden Art of Ian Hamilton Finlay*. London: Reaktion, 2008.

Hunt, John Dixon, ed. *The Oxford Book of Garden Verse*. Oxford: Oxford University Press, 1993.

Hunt, John Dixon and Peter Willis, eds. *The Genius of the Place: The English Landscape Garden 1620–1820* (1975). Cambridge, MA: MIT Press, 1988.

Johnson, Ronald. *ARK*. Albuquerque: Living Batch Press, 1996.

Johnson, Ronald. *The Shrubberies*, ed. Peter O'Leary. Chicago: Flood Editions, 2001.

Leggott, Michele J. *Reading Zukofsky's 80 Flowers*. Baltimore: Johns Hopkins University Press, 1989.

Mack, Maynard. *The Garden and the City: Retirement and Politics in the Later Poetry of Pope, 1731–1743*. Toronto: University of Toronto Press, 1969.

Marvell, Andrew. *The Collected Poems*, ed. Elizabeth Story Donno. Harmondsworth: Penguin, 1972.

O'Leary, Peter. "An Interview with Ronald Johnson (1995)." In *Ronald Johnson: Life and Works*, ed. Joel Bettridge and Eric Murphy Selinger. Orono, ME: National Poetry Foundation, 2008. 561–85.

Pope, Alexander. *Poetry and Prose of Alexander Pope*, ed. Aubrey Williams. Boston, MA: Houghton Mifflin, 1969.

Prest, John. *The Garden of Eden: The Botanic Garden and the Re-Creation of Paradise*. New Haven: Yale University Press, 1981.

Schama, Simon. *Citizens: A Chronicle of the French Revolution*. New York: Knopf, 1989.

Scobie, Stephen. "Models of Order." In *Wood Notes Wild: Essays on the Poetry and Art of Ian Hamilton Finlay*, ed. Alec Finlay. Edinburgh: Polygon, 1995. 177–204.

Selinger, Eric Murphy. "*ARK* as a Garden of Revelation." In *Ronald Johnson: Life and Works*, ed. Joel Bettridge and Eric Murphy Selinger.

Orono, ME: National Poetry Foundation, 2008. 323–42.

Sheeler, Jessie. *Little Sparta: The Garden of Ian Hamilton Finlay*. Photographs by Andrew Lawson. London: Frances Lincoln, 2003.

Spence, Joseph. *Anecdotes, Observations and Characters of Books and Men*, ed. Samuel Weller Singer. Carbondale: Southern Illinois University Press, 1978.

Swensen, Cole. *Ours*. Berkeley: University of California Press, 2008.

Zukofsky, Louis. *Complete Short Poetry*. Baltimore: Johns Hopkins University Press, 1991.

42

Scenic, or Topographical, Poetry

Stephen Burt

When American critics mention a "scenic mode" in contemporary poetry, they are probably using the term as an insult. Writing in 1982, Charles Altieri identified a kind of poem whose "highly crafted moments of scenic empathy" show how a place fits a poet's mood, usually staying close to prose sense and plain diction, and concluding in numinous awe (452). Such often anthologized works as James Wright's "Lying in a Hammock on William Duffy's Farm in Pine Island, Minnesota," William Stafford's "Ceremony," and Robert Hass's "Meditation at Lagunitas" for example, satisfy "a mimetic criterion of naturalness, an ethical standard of humility, a visionary dream of self-transcendence, and a praise of foregrounded craft" (456). Yet (Altieri continued) their "authentic feeling" emerges at the expense of "analytic intellect" (458).

Such poems did seem to dominate the 1970s, and not only in the United States: ambitious writers reacted against them. Yet what we might also call a scenic mode persists, in English, on several continents, among poets who have little else in common. These poems describe a real place where the poet has been, and they stake their aesthetic success on their ability to connect their own memorable formal features, salient phrases, and arguments to place, prospect, site, scene. This mode connects poets at work today to poems 250 and 350 years old; at its best it is also contemporary in its self-consciousness, its self-skepticism, or its ecological awareness, and its attraction to fact, even to reportage, responds to contemporary doubts about the figurative work poems can do.

The best single name for this mode is "topographical poetry," though scenic poem, prospect poem, or local poem would do almost as well. Robert Aubin in 1936 defined topographical verse as "poetry [which] aims at describing *specifically named actual localities*" (italics his): such poems flourished throughout the eighteenth century, as his

A Companion to Poetic Genre, First Edition. Edited by Erik Martiny.

exhaustive study shows (vii). John Barrell calls the topographical poem a "deliberate attempt to give a sense of the individuality of the place being described" (35): attempts do not necessarily imply success, and Barrell argues that in eighteenth-century England such attempts usually failed—the poems sounded too much alike (and too clearly indebted to Claude Lorrain). By contrast, Barrell continues, John Clare's best poems say "*this* is how it is *here* . . . the knowledge that Clare has in Helpston he has only there" (131). It is a *ne plus ultra*, an epistemologically freighted extreme, of the effect sought in all topographical poems, whose prehistory runs from late antiquity (Ausonius's *Mosella*) to the English Renaissance country house poem (Ben Jonson's "To Penshurst"), the descriptive, often satirical poem about London (Jonson's "On the Famous Voyage"), and that anomalous effort to describe all of England in verse, Michael Drayton's *Poly-Olbion*. But the ideal-typical English topographical poem, invoked and imitated for a century, turned out to be John Denham's "Cooper's Hill" (1642, rev. 1655), with its view of the Thames and far-off Windsor Castle. That view testifies to a right order in nature as in the monarchical state:

> With such an easy, and unforc'd ascent,
> Windsor her gentle bosom doth present;
> Where no stupendious cliff, no threat'ning heights
> Access deny, no horrid steep affrights,
> But such a rise, as doth at once invite
> A pleasure, and a reverence from the sight.
>
> (ll.42–47)

Digressive and given to inset narratives, Denham does not confine himself to description. Yet he does describe: and Denham's extended analogy between landscape and something outside landscape (in this case, government) provides both structure and texture for the whole poem, giving point to the smooth versification in Denham's famous apostrophe to the Thames:

> O could I flow like thee, and make thy stream
> My great example, as it is my theme!
> Though deep, yet clear, though gentle, yet not dull,
> Strong without rage, without o'er-flowing full.
>
> (ll.189–92)

The moderate river stays within its course, the hill within its gentle slope, as English society ought to stay within its inherited bounds.

Cooper's Hill adopted a physical (as well as a political) point of view: the speaker stood at a specified place, surveying and describing what he saw. So did John Dyer in "Grongar Hill" (1726), which also fastened maxims to descriptions:

> See on the mountain's southern side,
> Where the prospect opens wide,

> Where the evening gilds the tide;
> How close and small the hedges lie!
> What streaks of meadows cross the eye!
> A step, methinks, may pass the stream,
> So little distant dangers seem:
> So we mistake the Future's face,
> Ey'd thro' Hope's deluding glass:
> As yon summits soft and fair,
> Clad in colours of the air,
> Which to those who journey near,
> Barren, brown, and rough appear.
>
>   (ll.114–26)

Pursuing the layered perspective and the peaceful variety that would soon be codified as "picturesque," "Grongar Hill" reflects Dyer's training as a painter—"no other prospect poem," says John Dixon Hunt, "managed . . . painterly manoeuvres . . . with so much skill" (Hunt 226–27). Denham's work, and seventy years later Dyer's, corresponds (as all their critics note) to the growing and changing prestige of landscape painting, which encouraged yet more topographical poems. "Only one who has waded extensively in it," sighs Aubin, "can possibly realize what a constantly widening pool of descriptive-topographical poetry flooded the press" from Dyer to Wordsworth: hills, mountains, rivers, castles, estates, seashores, cliffs, farms, cities and towns, in couplets, in blank verse (after James Thomson's *The Seasons*), and, from the 1780s on, in sonnets, such as those by Charlotte Smith and W.L. Bowles (50).

The streams of eighteenth-century prospect and landscape poems fed the wilder, broader course of Romantic lyric. Effects we may now call Romantic are sometimes far older: Mary Sidney (1561–1621 wrote, in a sonnet about "a little spring hard by Kiddington house," "I saw & felt, was moved with the sight / Kindly me thought the place did sympathize" (ll.9–10). The spring, whose "trickling crystalls fall" straight out of solid rock, matches her sudden grief. Yet such effects of imagined sympathy, of moods and memories found in and through named places, became central to an entire kind of poetry only with the rise of what M.H. Abrams named the greater Romantic lyric, a cluster of influential poems including Samuel Taylor Coleridge's "Frost at Midnight" and William Wordsworth's "Lines Composed a Few Miles Above Tintern Abbey." In the greater Romantic lyric as defined by Abrams "the speaker begins with a description of the landscape, [and] an aspect or change of aspect in the landscape evokes a varied but integral process of memory, thought, anticipation and feeling . . . closely intervolved with the outer scene . . . Often the poem rounds upon itself and ends where it began" (201). Romantic poets, Abrams argued, create the greater Romantic lyric by interiorizing, cross-hatching with meditation, descriptive modes traced back to Denham: "The local poem has been lyricized" (Abrams 209, 213). Intermediate between the pure descriptive poem of location and the greater Romantic lyric are the midcentury poems of prospect and sentiment such as Thomas

Gray's "Ode on a Distant Prospect of Eton College," and the poems of sensibility, of extreme moods amid landscape, such as Smith's.

The pattern of the greater Romantic lyric fits not only the work by Wordsworth and Coleridge that Abrams went on to analyze, but many of the most famous poems of the last 200 years—Matthew Arnold's "Dover Beach," Walt Whitman's "Crossing Brooklyn Ferry," Robert Lowell's "For the Union Dead":

> The old South Boston Aquarium stands
> in a Sahara of snow now. Its broken windows are boarded.
> The bronze weathervane cod has lost half its scales.
> The airy tanks are dry.
>
> Once my nose crawled like a snail on the glass.
>
> (ll.1–5)

Many other modern poems about places become more comprehensible if we see them as permutations, expansions, or alterations of the greater Romantic lyric: Philip Larkin's "The Whitsun Weddings" is a greater Romantic lyric whose beginning and ending place is the compartment of a train, and Basil Bunting's *Briggflatts*—named for the place, subtitled "An Autobiography"—is a greater Romantic lyric expanded almost beyond recognition. Other famous modern poems follow other established kinds of topographical verse: Yeats's "Coole Park and Ballylee, 1931," for example, a country house poem. We might see Altieri's "scenic mode" as the far less ambitious descendant of the poetry Abrams described. But we should not neglect the rest of the topographical family tree.

Abrams called the greater Romantic lyric a genre; it would be better to call its descendants, and modern topographical poetry generally, a mode. "Modal terms never imply a complete external form," explains Alastair Fowler; a mode's "existence presupposes an earlier kind of which it is an extension" (107, 167). The history of topographical poetry shows just the pattern that Fowler identifies: what starts as a genre, a label for a complete work that implied expectations about length and form (at first, a few hundred lines, in couplets), became by the twentieth century a mode, compatible with almost any form and length, from the modernist collage-epic (William Carlos Williams's *Paterson,* the Gloucester of Charles Olson's *Maximus* poems) and the book-length, internally heterogeneous study (Arun Kolatkar's *Jejuri*) to the sonnet sequence (Heaney's "Glanmore Sonnets"), the miniature (Williams's "Nantucket"), or fragments of lyrical prose (Jen Hadfield's *Nigh-no-Place*).

A mode, like a genre, requires some line of descent: poets adopt it more or less self-consciously, having read, or misread, prior examples. Many contemporary poets who write topographically have never read "Grongar Hill." They have, however, read the Romantic inheritors ("Tintern Abbey," "Dover Beach," "Crossing Brooklyn Ferry") and the midcentury followers ("The End of March," "For the Union Dead," "The Whitsun Weddings," "A Step Away from Them," *Briggflatts*) who have carried the mode along. Not simply a name for a subject, topographical poetry remains (once we look for it) legible as a mode because it comes with a set of formal signals: the name of the place, often in the title, sometimes with a preposition—"At," "Above"; deictics ("here," "there," "now"); present tense (we stand, walk, ride along with the poet, right now); and a structure involving movement or perspective, following the eye or the body as it moves across or through the site.

Present-day topographical poets, like their eighteenth-century predecessors, may view apparently wild, unaltered "nature," or a built environment, or some combination of both. They may emphasize the presence of the past, the way that history interacts with the sense to produce what we think we can see. Contemporary topographical poems may also emphasize the paradox in trying to make a physical site, and the experience of that site, apparent to readers in a necessarily disembodied medium that uses words alone. For all their disagreements contemporary topographical poems are as one in organizing themselves around perception and cognition cued by a uniquely identified place. Often they seek to replicate what Tony Hiss in *The Experience of Place* calls "simultaneous perception," the "evenhanded, instantaneous and outward-looking flow of attention" to ground and air, sight, sound and scent, by which "we are connected to the people and things around us—as part of a family, a crowd, a community, a species, the biosphere" (21–22).

Probably no living British poet has explored the topographical poem more thoroughly than Roy Fisher, so much of whose output (including the long poem *CITY*) characterizes either Birmingham or the terrain nearby. Fisher also pursues the apparent impersonality that separates many recent topographical poems from their Romantic heritage. His poem "For Realism" takes place "at the corner of Farm and Wheeler Streets":

> For "realism":
> the sight of Lucas's
> lamp factory on a summer night;
> a shift coming off about nine,
> pale light, dispersing,
> runnels of people chased
> by pavements drying off.
>
>   (ll.1–6)

The poem follows sightlines; the line follows the eye. Fisher waits till the end of the poem to signal, with the deictic, his presence as an observer: the experience of the place becomes what Fisher in the early poem "Wonders of Obligation" called "common property," not just the background to one writer's life (l.56). Fisher puts "realism" in quote marks, as if to remind us that even the most purely descriptive poem implies a recording consciousness, a "point of view" both geographic and psychological, with judgments of value and moods: "what silver filth these drains have run" (l.47). "At Brough-on-Noe," from his recent book *Standard Midland*, also shows its eighteenth-century roots:

> What's good
> is the way there seem to be
> more waters than there are, poured
> out of the rows of hills
> in the valley bottom. There seem
> to be more side lanes and alleys
> than there ever were.
>
> (ll.1–70)

The sentences run from water into townscape, apparently unimproved nature into an obviously built environment, imitating with their own flow of comparatives and adjectival phrases the watercourse as it runs down the multiple hills. It is a mimetic goal familiar from Denham, whose polished lines copy a smooth waterway.

Robert Minhinnick's "The Porthcawl Preludes," about the seaside town in Wales, also makes a superb example of the modern topographical poem, and it shows how the topographical poem is not a genre properly so-called but a mode, since it accommodates Minhinnick's invented form, in which each stanza has a separate point of view and a separate, personified speaker. Here is "Lighthouse":

> I fly a kite around my head
> A restless, broken thing.
> Is no one there who'd let me rest
> And take the silver string?
>
> (ll.32–35)

The "restless, broken" spirit makes a contrast with the nursery-rhyme form, and the contrast suggests the disordered disappointment that is the keynote of Minhinnick's Porthcawl. In "Neap" the figures who should be most at home on the beach seem most compromised, sad to be there:

> Surfer, cursing the calm,
> Oystercatcher beeping like a smoke-alarm,
>   Anglers weighting their lines:
> Now and forever the sea's concubines.
>
> (ll.12–15)

Any one of the forty-two stanzas could present itself as a poem about any one of innumerable beaches; together, all forty-two describe the human geography, and the damaged economy, the endangered ecology specific to Porthcawl, where "this sea's not what it was" (l.115).

Other poets invent other forms, and other special effects, in order to put into words the sensory experience of a particular place. The title poem in Donald Revell's *My Mojave*, with its narrow (but expanding) cone of syllables, imitates the narrow shade in the desert at noon:

```
Sha-
Dow,
As of
A meteor
At mid-
Day; it goes
From there.
```
                                                              (ll.1–7)

This place of bright light, long sightlines, and stark contrasts leaves the observer open (as a more built-up or crowded place would not) to the sublime, to the divine:

```
At midday
My soul wants only to go
The black road which is the white road,
```
                                                            (ll.81–82)

a road towards God. In their opposition to instrumental reason, their direct mimesis of sight and sound, Revell's desert poems may seem to fit Altieri's condemnation of the scenic lyric as anti-intellectual. In fact, though, the poems end up dense with implicit argument about Revell's panentheistic, Thoreau-inflected Christianity. They show how he can live as an ecology-minded lover of open space, under what another desert poem names as "The Government of Heaven," taking his bearing not from any political entity (any human government) but from sky and dry land, from what he can see (20).

Some topographical poets try to escape human history; others cannot get enough of it. Eiléan ni Chuilleanáin's sequence "Cork" describes her city by making insistent connections between its water-dominated sites and its maritime past. Take the right view of the city today, ni Chuilleanáin implies, and you will be able to see back in time, for example, to the days when its port received Catholic refugees:

```
the river, flat and luminous
At its fullest, images the defences:
Ribbed quays and stacked rooves
Plain warehouse walls as high as churches
Insolent flights of steps,

Encamped within, the hurried exiles
Sheltered against the tide
A life in waiting,
Waking, reach out for a door and find a banister,
Reach for a light and find their hands in water,
Their rooms all swamped by dreams.
```
                                                            (ll.6–16)

To see Cork rightly, for ni Chuilleanáin, just is to see the history that its river and "defences" imply; the lines too, as they change length and break on the phrase, might be said to move back and forth, hypnogogically, like a tide.

Topographical poetry has always paid attention to cultural capitals: consider John Gay's London, Whitman's and then Frank O'Hara's Manhattan, the London of Michael Hofmann or of Iain Sinclair (in poems and prose). Yet topographical poetry has held a special appeal to poets who start out, or remain, in places not prestigiously central: "second cities" such as Birmingham or Cork, bedraggled or proud suburbs such as those in Lavinia Greenlaw's Essex, and remote rural sites such as Clare's Helpston, Gary Snyder's Cascade Mountains, or the lakeland of southern Wisconsin, home to Lorine Niedecker, whose longest poem is entitled "Paean to Place." By writing topographical poetry, these writers were and are not only announcing their difference from the writers of the metropolis: they are doing something for which there can be no metropolitan competition, something that writers in London, New York, San Francisco cannot do.

Critics who praise modern poems about wild places, finding them environmentalist opposition to exploitative Western ideas, can overlook the way that these poems also draw on conventions centuries old: the way they belong to their mode. Gary Snyder writes of named sites often, insisting that "our place is part of what we are" (*Practice* 27). His verse line, unadorned and informal, derives from East Asian classics and from Beat goals of apparently improvised speech, not from obvious English or European models. Yet his poems can follow precisely the structure of the eighteenth-century prospect poems: we view, from a height, a wild scene, layer by layer, with moral or maxim then stated or clearly implied. Early poems drawn from his work as a fire lookout work this way ("Above Pate Valley," for example), and so do many poems from the 1970s, such as "By Frazier Creek Falls": "Standing up on lifted, folded rock, / looking out and down," the poet sees "clear sky / strong wind in the / stiff glittering needle clusters / of the pine," then concludes "We could live on this Earth / without clothes or tools!" (1–2, 6–8, 18–19)

Topographical poetry may also incorporate other poetic kinds: ekphrasis, ars poetica, self-portrait, prayer. Jorie Graham's "San Sepolcro," well known in America, is a poem of vocation, of motherhood and pregnancy; an ars poetica, showing what poems, or lyric poems, in general try to do; and an ekphrasis, presenting Piero della Francesca's Annunciation, which hangs in a church in the eponymous town. Yet it begins as a prospect poem:

> In this blue light
> I can take you there,
> snow having made me
> a world of bone
> seen through to. This
> is my house,
>
> my section of Etruscan
> wall, my neighbor's

                    lemontrees, and just below
                      the lower church,
                    the airplane factory.

                                                                (ll.1–11)

Graham decides (like a painter) on the time of day (dawn), the quality of the light, and the journey the eye will make over the scene, from the sky with its mingled blue and white (suggestive of Piero's brilliant tones) down and across the town. Movement through this landscape with its characteristically Tuscan features turns into movement towards childbirth, towards the opening of Mary's dress and the creation of a new body (Piero's Madonna is, famously, visibly pregnant). To go from "outside the walls" of the town, inside the church, to visit the depicted Virgin, is for Graham to become present in a new body, within which we might find the soul: the work of discovering a new place resembles the work of poetry, which resembles the human work of gestation and the angelic work of Annunciation (bringing the good news to Mary). These are the kinds of work Graham's poem, by way of its sense of place, says that it can do.

Other topographical poems end up skeptical as to whether they can "take you there": whether the sense of a place can be intuited, the intuition shared. Rae Armantrout's "Double" appears to describe the poet's return (after more than a decade away) to a street in San Diego, where she grew up. "So these are the hills of home," the poem begins: their "Hazy tiers" are "nearly subliminal," so that "To see them is to see / double," not to be sure what we see (ll.1–2, 5). The poet moves through her hills along with us, indicating her presence by deictics ("these") and concentrating on the aspects (hills, "tiers" of tract housing, "junipers") that set the place apart. Yet there may be no essence of San Diego *to* see, and the poem may describe, not a genuine return, but a dream: "Rising from my sleep, the road is more / and less the road"; "to *look* / reveals no more" (italics hers) (ll.7–8). Other poets are cannier, or less decisive, as to how well we can know their place. John Tranter's "The Beach" combines apparent fluency, even spontaneity, and obvious artifice, being both a prose poem and a sestina: each paragraph ends with one of six repeating words. It is, too, both a topographical poem, set "in the inner western suburbs of Sydney" and at the famous Bondi Beach, and a poem about the way that memory, habit, expectation, and exhaustion can prevent us from seeing, or even imagining, any site to our own satisfaction. "So our feelings write themselves onto the view, turning geography into landscape," Tranter says, "and when you finally arrive at Bondi Beach you trudge along the famous golden sand spike with rusty needles soaked with hepatitis . . . wondering what the 'style' of the place really represents" (324–25).

"Landscape," "scene," "nature," "prospect," "environment": each term encodes a history of debate, and each one feeds back into (and has been in turn influenced by) the intertwined histories of painting and poetry, garden design and city planning. For Bonnie Costello "the structure of landscape" (by which she means a mode of seeing "nature," whether in paintings or in poems) "retains an opposition between mastering spectator and expansive scene that masks our involvement in what we view . . . But modern poets have exposed this structure in order to reconfigure it" (8). Costello responds to a line of critics, among them Barrell and W. J. T. Mitchell, for whom "landscape," in writing as in the visual arts, both signifies, and extends, a culpable attempt to govern both the rural poor and the natural world. Giving an impression of good order (and placing their sounds in good order, too), prospect poems can (as Tim Fulford recently put it) "turn . . . the viewing of landscape into a confirmation of the landed classes' right to power" (112). Yet their sights, these days, may also serve left-wing claims. Adrienne Rich's "The Spirit of Place" begins as a prospect poem: looking "Over the hills in Shutesbury, Leverett" (towns in Vermont) Rich examines the local flora and the history of New England ("mountain laurel in bloom / constructed like needlework"; Emily Dickinson; the end of the Underground Railroad) in order to find, in the spirit of this region, encouragement for the political Left (1, 32–33).

Armantrout and Tranter (for example) write as if they suspect (along with Mitchell) that the making of place into "landscape," of site into representation, amounts to a kind of colonization, an imposition, an occlusion of the real. Other poets of place treat visual art less warily: it is *through* visual art that these poets (like their eighteenth century precursors) present the spirit of their place. "Escaped Trees of Lynchburg," by Forrest Gander, describes both a site (in the terrain where Gander grew up) and a photograph by Denny Moers:

> Trees, the central figures
> of their own originality,　　come bare down the slope
> to bathe.　　Sudden raptus in the land,
> arborescing.　　The poplar
> and its reflection　　are disturbing, like twins.
>
> 　　　　　　　　　　　　　　　(ll.3–6)

It is a double, and fruitful, "reflection" indeed.

August Kleinzahler has topographical poems in every one of his books, set in Montreal, Auckland, San Francisco, Austin, Berlin, as well as his native northern New Jersey. He owes as much to visual art (to models of seeing) as any eighteenth-century landscape poet, but the kinds of visual art vary wildly: newspaper photography, film noir, classical East Asian brushwork, the Ashcan School. "Storm over Hackensack" becomes explicit about its multiple analogues: though the clouds may look "like an angry bruise about to burst / on City Hall," nonetheless

> for a moment the light
> downtown
> 　belongs someplace else,
> not here
> or any town close.
> Look at the shoppers, how palpable
> and bright

> against gathering dark
> like storied figures in stereoscope.
>
> (ll.4–12)

Stereoscopes were early 3-D pictures, in which two eyes saw two different views: it is as if Kleinzahler wanted to demonstrate that any artistic tradition—not only high culture landscape, not only art photography—may inform our vision of a place, give models for a prospect poem. Both stereoscope and Hackensack, moreover, may seem outmoded, or obsolete.

Kleinzahler's other topographical poems can owe less to visual art, less to vision, and more to the other bodily senses. "Sleeping It Off in Rapid City" begins by following sound: we *hear* what happens in Kleinzahler's Rapid City, what he hears from his hotel room—trains in the night, for example. But Rapid City also holds monuments and tourist attractions: "empty missile silos," and Mount Rushmore, and a sculpture of "Crazy Horse too, 30 stories high":

> The bronze is cold in the High Plains night
> The eyes they gaze out of are holes
> Here at the exact dead center of America
> Or close enough, just north of here, off Highway 79
> The buffalo roam in these hills.
>
> (ll.100–04)

In a United States built on Indian removal and nuclear deterrence (thus the pun "dead center") the poet says that he has found a real "sacred place," found "surcease here from all my cares" (120, 124). We may not trust his claim; he may not trust himself, and the poem will not rest with his feelings. It is too busy with people, with information, with the sounds (not only sights) of the High Plains night, as if the poet wanted to (but could not) get around the Romantic heritage, back to a less personal descriptive mode.

Is Rapid City a place, or a set of places? You can stay in a hotel in Rapid City, and you can stand on a balcony there, but you cannot stand "on" or "at" Rapid City: it is not a single vantage point. The same can be said for Cork, and for the Mojave. Revell, ni Chuilleanáin, and the other poets quoted above describe both an immediate area bounded by what the poet hears or sees, and a larger area ("Cork," say) with historical, cultural or ecological coherence. We might call these small and large areas (following the philosopher Edward P. Casey, though the terms are not his) *region* and *site*: topographical poems can focus on one or the other, as they can seek harmony, or discord, between the two. Fisher's Birmingham is in this sense a region; the corner of Farm and Wheeler Streets is a site. All topographical poems, from Dyer to Fisher, have both region and site, though other poems (Heaney's "Bogland," for example) evoke a region without specifying a site.

It may be oversimplification, though, to speak of region in the singular. Any point on a map—as Lawrence Buell has explained—belongs to overlapping regions, to "concentric zones," each with connotations that poets can evoke or avoid (65). Snyder's descriptive verse attempts to replace our sense of political region (California, Oregon) with another sense based on geology and biota ("Shasta Bioregion") (*Practice* 39). Ciaran Carson's *Belfast Confetti* works very hard to make clear that the city, not the larger entities called Ireland or Ulster, makes up the relevant region; not coincidentally, Carson also works to show that the truth of his place is never the truth of the eye, but rather the truth of history—the best "map of the city" shows "the bridge that was never built" (1). Carson's "Turn Again," though it does suggest the confusions of old city streets, is—like Armantrout's "Double"—a kind of anti-topography: it asserts that the truth of Belfast cannot be seen.

Even the visible present scene, the truth of a site, can present itself as unknowable, in an undeniably topographical poem. The Newfoundland poet Mary Dalton has emphasized her location throughout her career: *Merrybegot* (2005), relies on Newfoundland dialect words. *Red Ledger* attends instead to the geography of her island, to the variety within its places. In "Casse-Cœur," "Secrets litter the beach," but also "burden the beach" (1, 10). It is a beach first characterized by detritus, rejecta, and corpses, "a shattered sea urchin / dropped from the hungry gull's beak" (ll.2–3). But it is also a place of unbreachable integrity, a place whose litter of detritus renders it, not abject, but invitingly secretive. Trying to find what the place truly means, and to like it, visiting *"appreciators"* (italics hers)

> inscribe surfaces, reach for
> the handiest myth, find parables
> among the beach rocks, their colours,
> thinking to read the littoral
> meanings, gather them up for
> their knick-knack, their book, shelf in town.
>
> (ll.22–27)

The pebbles, once dry on a shelf, will of course lose their colors; taken away from the tidal zone, they will lose their "littoral" meanings, too. Dalton confronts a paradox that most earlier topographical poets (Clare notwithstanding) avoid—if the place has unique meanings embodied in it, if you have to go there to encounter them, how can a poet take those meanings away from the place by embedding them into her poem?

It might be better to say, not a paradox, but a set of paradoxes, or impossible tasks: to reduce the multi-sensory, site-specific experience of place into a string of words; to make an essentially place-bound experience portable; to make the spirit of a place apparent both to a resident (who will compare it to other places quite nearby) and to a visitor (who will have no such comparisons handy); to establish, for resident and for visitor, a difference between region (what typifies Newfoundland, or typifies the Avalon Peninsula) and site (what represents the unique experience of standing, walking, looking here and now). A kind of poetry that began by tying the figuration of poetic language to literal fact (to facts on the ground, as it were) thus ends up, by our own era, emphasizing the limits and the contradictions in claims that a poem can make the world present to us, can place us (as topographical poetry promises) in the poet's shoes. For Leonard Scigaj, as for other ecology-minded critics, poetry that seeks a sense of place (for Scigaj it is always a "natural" place) must thereby acknowledge "originary perception initiated by stimuli from events in the natural world . . . The preverbal experience is primary" (29). The harder a modern topographical poem (and not only a poem about "nature") works to capture the experience of a place, the more it may alert us to the aspects of such experience that both precede, and evade, language, the aspects for which you just have to be there.

Analyzing, and advocating, modern poems about place, critics have tried to set them apart from their precursors. Roger Gilbert distinguishes poems organized around walks from "topographical or descriptive poetry" (ix). "The walk poem differs from both the standard local poem and the greater Romantic lyric" in that "it takes as its subject not a landscape . . . but an experience," becoming "transcriptive rather than descriptive" (8). But the experience of seeing a certain place from a certain vantage point is Dyer's subject too. Angus Fletcher, proposing a new American genre called the "environment-poem," has argued that such poems oppose bounded, traditional definitions of place and space, observer and observed: "It almost looks as if this type were not a genre at all, because it evinces a careless want of traditional form" (123). Being "shapeless" or boundless, such a poem seems to instantiate ecological principles of interconnection: but long and heterogeneous poems devoted to journeys through places (such as C.D. Wright's *Deepstep Come Shining* or Alice Oswald's *Dart*) may be "environment-poems" in Fletcher's sense and topographical poems as well.

As much as they continue modes and projects specific to poetry, contemporary topographical poets also take up goals that began outside the craft of verse. They may, as Buell put it, "press the case of systematically abused places," overlooked rural sites or hard-up towns (78). They may instead praise—and try to share with us—the experience of sites well known for beauty, whether far away or at home. They may defend the individuality of wild places against destructive homogenization (as in most of the poems Scigaj considers), and they may be investigating the phenomenology of place, how and whether the particulars of simultaneous perception can carry over into words. They may belong to older subgenres (the graveyard poem, the river poem) or to such newer subgenres as the lyric of superposition, where the immigrant or traveler "sees" two places at once (Arthur Nortje's "Cosmos in London"); the visit to a battlefield or historic site (Laura Kasischke's "At Gettysburg," Tom Pickard's "A History Lesson from My Son on Hadrian's Wall"); or the documentary sequence about a place, interspersing physical views with transcribed interviews (Mark Nowak's *Revenants*).

All these poets, all these kinds of poem (and more), are engaged in what the geographer Yi-Fu Tuan calls "making place," establishing their own and their readers' potential felt relations to some location, relations that may include nonhuman biota, geology, atmosphere, buildings, and human history ("Language" 684). These poets hence (in the terms Tuan also prefers) establish a bounded, intuitive sense of "place" as against "more abstract . . . undifferentiated space" (*Space* 6). In Western thought since the Enlightenment, Casey complains, "place has been subordinated to other terms taken as putative absolutes: most notably, Space and Time" (x). Casey writes that "the encroachment of an indifferent sameness-of-place on a global scale—to the point where at times you cannot be sure what city you are in . . . makes the human subject long for a diversity of places, that is, difference-of-place," hence for an art that makes apprehensible that diversity: for poems (to update Wordsworth) not on the naming, but on the differentiation, the simple existence, of places (Casey xiii).

But why *poems*? The most famous books of place-making in English are not poems: Thoreau's *Walden* and Jane Jacobs' *The Death and Life of Great American Cities* come to mind. Critics concerned with ecology and poetry have struggled to explain what sort of place-making function poems are best suited to serve: some of the most convincing such critics find in poetry a resistance to the denotative, expository functions in language, acknowledging what in nonhuman nature we cannot control or even fully represent. Scott Bryson, for example, finds in W.S. Merwin's "process of place-making . . . a space-conscious awareness of the limitations of human insight, language and even poetry itself" (105). And yet to emphasize the inarticulacy of the nonhuman, the resistance to language, in contemporary poems of place is to leave out most of what I have been emphasizing: the particulars of *that* place and not this one, the particular ways of seeing, hearing, walking, remembering that constitute the poem, and that are as likely to occur in a built-up environment as in one that looks wild.

Only some contemporary topographical poets (Minhinnick, Snyder) certainly write as environmentalists too. All these poets, however, are drawn to fact: all have chosen a mode in which poetry not only can but must take on some of the functions of expository nonfiction prose, of local reportage or of travel writing, which (as Ian Jack once quipped) relies on our sense that the writer "did not make it up" (Hulme and Youngs 10). The contemporary topographical poet, like the travel writer, participates in an apparently "minor" kind, one not dependent on a stance of authority, nor on private afflatus. Rather, travel writing, like topographical poetry, depends upon observable, verifiable fact: it is as if the poet said to us, "Whatever poems now cannot do—prophecy, dream-vision, beautiful escape, politically efficacious social critique—they can at least do this: they can say something true about something real." No wonder topographical modes appeal to poets—Kleinzahler, Fisher, Greenlaw, Armantrout—who have remained especially skeptical about the grander claims for poetry that their coevals advance. The topographical poem, moreover, can say what it says, show what it shows, through the devices (suggestion, linguistic density, sonic mimesis) that are the strengths of poetry as such. Revell could not imitate his shadows at noon without the use of his line breaks, nor Fisher emulate his streets and streams without the heightened attention to syntax produced by the frame of a poem. If you care for place-making—these achievements imply—then you might care for the techniques of poems.

Susan Stewart writes that "poetry's role . . . has to do with a transfer of sense impressions" from the writer to the reader, accomplished in part through "deictic terms": here, now, there, this (152). Such terms almost require us to imagine somebody, some body, located with respect to the things described, with a sense of "here versus there, front versus back, near versus far, and so forth," as Casey has put it; these senses, in turn "begin in the bodily experience of place" (237). Poetry as such, for Stewart, "creates an *eidos* [image] of the human figure, a presence in space [that] creates . . . other versions of the 'here' and 'now'" (197). And here is a role for poetry in general that topographical poems, in particular, seem well suited to play. Topographical poetry is at once factual and phenomenological, showing what it is like to be this figure in this place, now and here: how it looks (or sounds, or smells) to her. And here the special suitability of poems for place-making, the way that good poems can create a sense of place, depends upon the distance that the modern topo-graphical poet can achieve from the greater Romantic lyric. Only if the "I" in a poem could seemingly or fictively be you, or me, or anyone, all the way through, can the poem put the place (not the poet) first.

Topographical poetry as a mode, then, defends poetry as a set of techniques for representing at once an external world and an observing consciousness; it lends itself to defenses of poetry that are not claims about poets' exalted roles, but rather claims about what poems make present to us (besides the poet herself). And it may be no coincidence that one poet whose reputation has risen dramatically over the past few decades (as poetry has become "minor" in Anglophone cultures at large) has been a poet unusually committed to topographical writing. She is the author of *North and South*, of *Questions of Travel*, and *Geography III*, and I have been avoiding her until now not just because I want to show a wider, and still current, international, mode, but because her work makes a good place to conclude.

Elizabeth Bishop did not only write poems about named places, poems in which region and site, things discovered immediately by the senses and things remembered or known, conjoin collide; she wrote well in every one of the subgenres into which Aubin and others sort eighteenth-century topographical poems—the country house poem ("Song for the Rainy Season"), the journey down a river ("Santarém"), the journey overland ("The Moose"), the city view ("Varick Street"; "Under the Window: Ouro Preto"), the beach and ocean ("At the Fishhouses," "Cape Breton"), the poem about a landscape that is also a poem about a landscape painting ("Poem"); the pros-pect as such, with foreground and background, weather and sloping hill ("The Armadillo"). All but the last name the place they present, and "The Armadillo," moving from sky down a "mountain height" to land, portraying a dangerous custom of Rio de Janeiro, describes its place as surely as it describes its sad events (4). If some of these poems fit Altieri's narrow "scenic mode," with its neo-Romantic gestures towards transcendence, others ("Poem," for example, with its arguments about memory) surely do not; and all of them follow at once the trace of a history and the course of the eye across a site. Our readings of Bishop might be enriched—along with our readings of so many still active poets—if we see her, too, as a poet who took advantage of the variety within the mode of the topographical poem.

REFERENCES AND FURTHER READING

Abrams, M.H. "Structure and Style in the Greater Romantic Lyric" (1965). Repr. *Romanticism and Consciousness*, ed. Harold Bloom. New York: Norton, 1970. 201–29.

Altieri, Charles. "Sensibility, Rhetoric and Will: Some Tensions in Contemporary Poetry." *Contemporary Literature* 23:4 (1982): 451–79.

Armantrout, Rae. *Precedence*. Providence, RI: Burning Deck, 1985.

Aubin, Robert. *Topographical Poetry in Eighteenth-Century England*. New York: Modern Language Association, 1936.

Barrell, John. *The Idea of Landscape and the Sense of Place 1730–1840*. Cambridge: Cambridge University Press, 1972.

Bryson, J. Scott. "Place and Space in W.S. Merwin." In *Ecopoetry*, ed. J. Scott Bryson. Salt Lake City: University of Utah Press, 2002. 101–16.

Buell, Lawrence. *Writing for an Endangered World*. Cambridge, MA: Harvard University Press, 2001.

Carson, Ciaran. *Belfast Confetti*. Oldcastle, Meath: Gallery, 1989.

Casey, Edward. *The Fate of Place*. Berkeley: University of California Press, 1998.

Costello, Bonnie. *Shifting Ground: Reinventing Landscape in Modern American Poetry*. Cambridge, MA: Harvard University Press, 2003.

Dalton, Mary. *Red Ledger*. Montreal: Signal, 2006.

Denham, John. *Cooper's Hill*, ed. John D. Baird. http://rpo.library.utoronto.ca/poem/3399.html.

Dyer, John. "Grongar Hill," ed. Jack Lynch. http://ethnicity.rutgers.edu/ jlynch/Texts/grongar.html.

Fisher, Roy. *The Long and the Short of It: Poems 1955–2005*. Tarset: Bloodaxe, 2005.

Fisher, Roy. *Standard Midland*. Tarset: Bloodaxe, 2010.

Fletcher, Angus. *A New Theory for American Poetry*. Cambridge, MA: Harvard University Press, 2004.

Fulford, Tim. " 'Nature' poetry." In *The Cambridge Companion to Eighteenth-Century Poetry*, ed. John Sitter. Cambridge: Cambridge University Press, 2001. 109–32.

Gander, Forrest. *Science and Steepleflower*. New York: New Directions, 1998.

Gilbert, Roger. *Walks in the World*. Princeton: Princeton University Press, 1991.

Graham, Jorie. *Erosion*. Princeton: Princeton University Press, 1983.

Hiss, Tony. *The Experience of Place*. New York: Random House, 1991.

Hulme, Peter and Tim Youngs, eds. *The Cambridge Companion to Travel Writing*. Cambridge: Cambridge University Press, 2003.

Hunt, John Dixon. *The Figure in the Landscape*. Baltimore: Johns Hopkins University Press, 1976.

Kleinzahler, August. *Sleeping It Off in Rapid City*. New York: Farrar, Straus and Giroux, 2008.

Lowell, Robert. *Selected Poems: Expanded Edition*. New York: Farrar, Straus and Giroux, 2006.

Minhinnick, Robert. *After the Hurricane*. Manchester: Carcanet, 2002.

Ni Chuilleanain, Eileen. *Selected Poems*. Winston-Salem: Wake Forest University, 2009.

Revell, Donald. *My Mojave*. Farmington: Alice James, 2003.

Rich, Adrienne. *The Fact of a Doorframe: Selected Poems 1950–2001*. New York: Norton, 2002.

Schlueter, June and Paul Schlueter. "Halfe maim'd? Five Unknown Poems by Mary Sidney Herbert, Countess of Pembroke." *TLS*, July 23, 2010. 14–15.

Scigaj, Leonard. *Sustainable Poetry*. Lexington: University Press of Kentucky, 1999.

Snyder, Gary. *The Practice of the Wild*. New York: North Point, 1990.

Snyder, Gary. *Turtle Island*. New York: New Directions, 1974.

Stewart, Susan. *Poetry and the Fate of the Senses*. Chicago: University of Chicago Press, 2002.

Tranter, John. *Urban Myths: 210 Poems*. Cambridge: Salt, 2006.

Tuan, Yi-Fu. "Language and Place." *Annals of the Association of American Geographers* 81:4 (1991): 684–96.

Tuan, Yi-Fu. *Space and Place*. Minneapolis: University of Minnesota Press, 1977.

43
Ekphrastic Poetry
In and Out of the Museum

Jonathan Ellis

Human beings have always been attracted to describing things that are beautiful. As Elaine Scarry points out, the presence of beauty

> seems to incite, even to require, the act of replication . . . Beauty brings copies of itself into being. It makes us draw it, take photographs of it, or describe it to other people. Sometimes it gives rise to exact replication and other times to resemblances and still other times to things whose connection to the original site of inspiration is unrecognizable.
>
> (3)

For Scarry, beauty is rather like friendly bacteria multiplying and mutating across various art forms and media. A beautiful face in the street becomes a portrait in a museum becomes a poem in a book becomes the essay you have just begun reading. Every photograph taken is a record of this process; every postcard delivered a way of saying not simply "Wish you were here," but also "Wish you could see this!"

Ekphrasis is an awkward-sounding word for this everyday activity: the habit, one might say the necessity, of describing things in words. More precisely, ekphrasis is a literary term that refers to the art of speaking about visual objects, the transformation of things seen into poetry or prose read or spoken. John Hollander helpfully distinguishes between two forms of ekphrasis: "actual" ekphrasis in which a real artwork is being addressed or described and "notional" ekphrasis in which the visual object is a fictional painting or sculpture brought to life through language (3–91). The most famous ekphrastic description is probably Walter Pater's lyrical response to Leonardo da Vinci's *Mona Lisa*. "Set it for a moment beside one of those white Greek goddesses or beautiful women of antiquity, and how they would be troubled by this beauty, into

A Companion to Poetic Genre, First Edition. Edited by Erik Martiny.
© 2012 John Wiley & Sons, Ltd. Published 2012 by John Wiley & Sons, Ltd.

which the soul with all its maladies had passed!" (129–30). For Pater, da Vinci's painting was not just the most beautiful object he had ever seen; it somehow contained and was the summation of all previous human encounters with beauty.

> All the thoughts and experience of the world have etched and moulded there, in that which they have of power to refine and make expressive the outward form, the animalism of Greece, the lust of Rome, the mysticism of the middle age with its spiritual ambition and imaginative loves, the return of the Pagan world, the sins of the Borgias.
>
> (130)

Da Vinci's painting, it is worth remembering, was itself a copy, a portrait not just of a real person (or an amalgamation of various real people) but of an ancient ideal of beauty. In this sense, Pater's prose response was a copy of a copy, at least two removes from the original source of beauty. In seeing the painting through Pater's eyes (or rather reading it via Pater's words) one is simultaneously in the presence of three distinct objects of beauty: the "real" Mona Lisa, da Vinci's painting of her, and Pater's prose response to it. Flesh becomes word via canvas. Yet does Pater actually *see* the *Mona Lisa* here? As Angela Leighton points out, "the passage is more about time than it is about a picture in an art gallery . . . The way that Pater reads the Mona Lisa almost unframes it altogether, marking no division between the art object and the swimmingly impressionistic memories which it inspires" (87–88). Art critics have increasingly lamented the extent to which Pater's words obscure our capacity to see da Vinci's painting anew. His words rival and perhaps even usurp their original object of attention. What was once simply a description of the *Mona Lisa* quickly became *the* description of the *Mona Lisa*.

Ekphrastic writing often has a parasitic relationship to the visual work it commemorates. It can attach itself to the prior work of art without adding anything individual or new. In order to have its own afterlife, however, ekphrastic literature has to be more than just a copy. The term "ekphrasis" comes from the Greek words *ek* (out) and *phrassein* (to tell, to speak). As a technical term connected to the study and practice of rhetoric, its origins go back to the first century AD when it was used to denote "any elaborate digressive description embedded within rhetorical discourse" (Smith 10). A love of ekphrasis in terms of digression is still popular in the contemporary period as evidenced by the career of Frank O'Hara whose day job at the Museum of Modern Art brought him into close contact with twentieth-century artists such as Joan Miró and Jackson Pollock but in whose poetry we learn as much about the poet's lunch-time desires and feelings as his work-time thoughts about painters and paintings. O'Hara even titled one of his poems about paintings, "Digression on *Number 1, 1948*," fully aware of the extent to which poems often get in the way of seeing things well. Although the poem in question recollects "a fine day for seeing" (l.5), the poet cannot see beyond his own minor ailments and irritations. "I am ill today but I am not / too ill" (ll.1–2), the poem begins. "I am tired today but I am not / too tired" (ll.11–12), he says elsewhere. For O'Hara, as for many other twentieth-century writers, poems are like paintings only in a very roundabout way. Visual art is part of his world, not the world of his art.

Digression is just one element of ekphrastic writing, however. In the third and fourth centuries AD ekphrasis began to be used as a term for the description of visual art rather than just a rhetorical mode of speaking. The earliest known example of ekphrasis in the western world is the lengthy description of Achilles' shield in Homer's *Iliad*. As James Heffernan points out: "Since Homer's epics are generally dated to the eighth century B.C., about the time that writing originates in Greece, it is hardly an exaggeration to say that ekphrasis is as old as writing itself in the western world" (9). Heffernan defines ekphrasis as "the verbal representation of visual representation" (3). This definition is, he admits, "simple in form but complex in its implications" (3). Heffernan focuses attention on ekphrasis as "speaking out" or "telling in full" (6): "Ekphrasis speaks not only *about* works of art but also *to* and *for* them. In so doing, it stages—within the theater of language itself—a revolution of the image against the word" (7). Heffernan's definition of ekphrasis in terms of a contest between words and images has a long history. Plutarch set the terms for the debate almost 2,000 years ago when describing painting as mute poetry, poetry as speaking picture. As Stephen Cheeke observes, definitions of this kind created

> the seeds of a whole tradition of thinking about the meaning of what each art *lacks* in relation to the other . . . Painting is poetry that perhaps would wish to speak but cannot, and therefore wishes poetry to speak for it. (Is this so?) And poetry is painting that would wish to see, and therefore requires painting to illustrate it.
>
> (20–21)

Other binary oppositions develop out of this seeing/speaking division of roles, not least the seductively simple if ultimately reductive idea that a painting exists in space whereas a poem exists in time. Not all painting is still life, one might protest, but all paintings do freeze time in certain irrevocable ways. The sea might appear to heave in J.M.W. Turner's *The Slave Ship*, for example, but the waves never really shift. The slaves, too, are always in the process of drowning, never to be saved. Poems, though we often encounter them through the space of a page, permit characters to travel through time. They tell stories, if not always with a beginning, middle, and end, then at least with a before and after. The very fact that a poem needs to be read, whether aloud or in one's head, also creates a sense of time. Events unfold line by line and cannot be seen whole, as in a painting.

And yet such rigid separations surely speak to our need for order rather than a real understanding of the differences between paintings and poems. As anyone who has actually looked at a Turner painting for some time can testify, the scene might be frozen but the story that it tells is anything but. We continue its temporarily frozen narrative outside the frame of the painting. The same process occurs in the opposite direction when reading poetry. Expectations of narrative movement are often frustrated and we are suddenly caught in a moment that upsets or reverses chronological time, "Surprised by joy" as Wordsworth memorably puts it in an eponymous elegy for his three-year-old daughter. Pattern poetry and concrete poetry are two further poetic genres in which the shape of a poem on a page, its visual appearance, is almost as important as what the poem actually says. One only has to glance at George Herbert's "Easter Wings" to guess it has something to do with religious flight. John Hollander's "Swan and Shadow" can similarly be at least partially understood without reading a single line. While there are ekphrastic writers who speak on behalf of the visual object as if speaking were what visual objects always desired, most respect the silence of painting and sculpture not as something lost or missing but about which poetry can make a new work of art.

The most famous ekphrastic poem in the English canon, John Keats's "Ode on a Grecian Urn," leaves us in little doubt about the speaker's belief that the Grecian urn exists if not fully outside of history then at least in a "slow time" (2) where lovers can be lovers forever: "For ever warm and still to be enjoy'd / For ever panting, and for ever young" (ll.26–27). The poem concludes by appearing to let the urn speak though it does not have the final word:

> Thou, silent form, dost tease us out of thought
> As dost eternity: Cold Pastoral!
> When old age shall this generation waste,
> Thou shalt remain, in midst of other woe
> Than ours, a friend to man, to whom thou say'st,
> 'Beauty is truth, truth beauty,'—that is all
> Ye know on earth, and all ye need to know.
>
> (ll.44–50)

These lines have been much debated, imitated, and indeed parodied. Is Keats envious of the urn's "Cold" detachment from human existence where mere mortal hearts die and can only dream of immortality? Or is he mocking the lover depicted on the urn's surface who may be "Bold" but "never, never canst thou kiss, / Though winning near the goal" (ll.17–18). By the poem's conclusion, I doubt whether we are any the wiser. The urn's aphoristic words of wisdom, "Beauty is truth, truth beauty," appear like most aphorisms to be impossible to pin down conclusively. Visual art works often appear to "say" things to poets but what they "say" is not easy to paraphrase or indeed write a poem about. They are a prompt to thought rather than a ready-made statement. Keats's poem remains memorable not because of its relationship to the Grecian urn that inspired it, if indeed a particular urn ever existed, but because of its articulation of the dilemma every ekphrastic poet faces when writing on another object. Is it ethical to impose one's own ideas *on* an object that cannot object to somebody else's interpretation? Is a poet's way of knowing something and speaking about that knowledge necessarily the same or indeed similar to the knowledge etched on and in material objects?

Contemporary poets often return to Keats's questions. The American poet Mark Doty has written an entire book on the significance of everyday objects. Like Keats, Doty is attracted to the silence of visual objects and their unique relationship to time:

> Painting creates silence. You could examine the objects themselves, the actors in a Dutch still life—this knobbed beaker, this pewter salver, this knife—and, lovely as all antique utilitarian objects are, they are not, would not be, poised on the edge these same things inhabit when they are represented. These things exist—if indeed they are still around at all—in time. It is the act of painting them that makes them perennially poised, an emergent truth about to be articulated, a word waiting to be spoken. Single word that has been forming all these years in the light on the knife's pearl handle, in the drops of moisture on nearly translucent grapes: At the end of time, will that word be said?
>
> (ll.18–19)

Doty's love of objects that are "perennially poised" is a modern version of Keats's equally poised lovers. In a sense, Doty's book, just like Keats's poem, breaks the silence that the visual object creates. It attempts to find an "emergent truth" about life that the painting is only ever "about" to articulate, leaving behind a trail of words where previously but a single word lay "waiting to be spoken." At the same time of course, Doty draws attention to his own garrulousness in the presence of painting and perhaps even to the pointlessness of his task. His truths do not complete the painting's story. Indeed, it is as if the painting is still "forming" before his eyes, in the "light on the knife's pearl handle" and "the drops of moisture on nearly translucent grapes." The painting, in other words, is not still at all, or completely silent either.

Ekphrastic writing, unlike other poetic genres (the epic, the long poem, or the villanelle, for example), has never really gone out of fashion. James Heffernan's seminal book on the subject, *Museum of Words: The Poetics of Ekphrasis from Homer to Ashbery*, mentions nearly every English-speaking poet of note from Shakespeare to the present day. Or rather Heffernan mentions most English-speaking male poets (Chaucer, Spencer, Shakespeare, Wordsworth, Keats, Shelley, Byron, Browning, and Auden). Female poets do not get much of a look-in. To his credit, Heffernan admits as much in his opening remarks when he writes of ekphrastic literature as offering a challenge to "the controlling authority of the male gaze and the power of the male word" (7). He never quite addresses why women poets do not also object to being objectified in visual art. The obvious answer is that they did and still do, in the contemporary period more than perhaps ever before.

The Scottish poet Carol Ann Duffy has written some of the most brilliant ekphrastic poems of her generation. Before becoming Poet Laureate on the strength of her feminist rewritings of history in collections such as *The World's Wife* and *Feminine Gospels*, Duffy was best known for her dramatic monologues, many of which engage directly with a male artistic tradition. The title poem from her 1985 collection, *Standing Female Nude*, has been interpreted by Deryn Rees-Jones as in direct dialogue with the Cubist paintings of Georges Braque (the name, "Georges," is mentioned in line 16). Yet, as Angelica Michelis and Antony Rowland observe, it is in fact impossible to identify which Braque painting, if any, Duffy may have had in mind when writing the poem:

> The model's complaint would suggest that the painting is from his Cubist phase, but 'Standing' features in only a few of Braque's titles—none of them from this stage of his career—such as *Standing Woman with Basket* (1929) and the *Standing Women* sculpture (1920). Duffy may not be referring, of course, to a distinct art work; if she is, the post-Cubist *Canephora* series based on sketches of 'standing' nudes in the 1920s become prime suspects.
>
> (14)

For all their clever detective work, Michelis and Rowland cannot identify the painting in question. In fact, they leave open the possibility that it might be a sculpture or just a sketch. Such bafflement is understandable. At times it is difficult to tell who is even speaking: the artist, the model, or perhaps even the painting?

> Six hours like this for a few francs.
> Belly nipple arse in the window light,
> he drains the colour from me. Further to the right,
> Madame. And do try to be still.
> I shall be represented analytically and hung
> in great museums. The bourgeoisie will coo
> at such an image of a river-whore. They call it Art.
>
> (ll.1–7)

The stanza's heart—"Further to the right, / Madame. And do try to be still"—sounds like the sort of thing a supercilious painter might say. The surrounding lines are more ambiguous, however. Would a "Standing Female Nude" who spends her time-off making her living as she can, "with wine and dance around the bars" (l.26), necessarily speak in the voice of an art critic or Marxist historian? "I shall be represented analytically and hung / in great museums," this voice announces immediately after being told to "be still." Rather than the model speaking back to the artist as she seems to be doing in the first lines of the poem ("Six hours like this for a few francs"), might this be the imagined voice of the painting, speaking back not in the present moment to the painter but in a future time to the bourgeois reader/viewer?

The point is not that one can tell either way, but that the poem makes both possibilities equally plausible. It brings the formerly "still" woman and the permanently "still" painting back to life. In the best tradition of ekphrastic writing, whether written by a man or a woman, Duffy gets her own back on a visual world that has often confined women to the role of silent object. Yet her greatest achievement here is probably linguistic rather than political. After reading the poem, we do not know who has been speaking out: Georges Braque himself, Braque's anonymous model, or one of more than a hundred possible works of art that may or may not have been the work of Braque at all? Could Duffy actually have written a poem about Georges Seurat, for example? Might the ambiguous he/she of the poem's narrative voice that the poet never divides by quotation marks actually be a reflection of the male names and masks (George Eliot and George Sand among them) behind which many women artists felt compelled to hide throughout the eighteenth and nineteenth centuries?

Duffy is not the only contemporary poet to have fun with visual art. Few contemporary poets leave out the ekphrastic poem from their repertoire. Poems about photographs have been particularly popular as demonstrated by Stephen Cheeke's decision to devote a whole chapter of his recent book on ekphrasis to the subject. In Cheeke's opinion,

> writing about photography frequently displays an even greater ambivalence, a sharper disquiet about the rival medium, than texts about paintings . . . the apparent excision of an organising artistic consciousness in photography, the impersonality or authorlessness of the medium, exerts a fascination for poets something like the draw of the "cold pastoral" of Keats's urn.
>
> (146–47)

Cheeke's argument focuses on poems by Philip Larkin, Ted Hughes, and John Ashbery, each of whom objects to the photographic medium's rather smug knowledge of reality. "But o photography! as no art is" (l.16), Larkin complains in "Lines on a Young Lady's Photograph Album":

> Faithful and disappointing! that records
> Dull days as dull, and hold-it smiles as frauds,
> And will not censor blemishes
> Like washing-lines.
>
> (ll.17–20)

Not all poets are so disappointed by photography. Paul Muldoon, a poet who was born in Northern Ireland but has spent the last two decades living and working in North America, is, as his literal travels across the Atlantic might suggest, well practiced in imagining himself in somebody else's shoes. In *Plan B*, a 2009 book-length collaboration between Muldoon and the Scottish photographer Norman McBeath, only one McBeath photograph is directly invoked by Muldoon's poetry. Muldoon admits to being

> very conscious of the difficulties of poems and photographs responding to each other in kind, of one given "in return" for the other . . . It was with all this in mind that I sat down one evening with the photographs and copies of the poems contained in *Plan B* and, like the kind of party host we've all been encouraged to believe ourselves to be, allowed them to get into conversation with each other . . . It would not be too much of a stretch, then, to say that this combination of poems and photographs was curated neither by Norman McBeath nor me but by the poems and photographs themselves.
>
> (Muldoon and McBeath 7)

Muldoon presents himself not as the author, or even the co-author of the book, but as a "kind of party host" to two interesting guests, both known to him separately, neither having met one another before. He does not attempt to speak for or to the photograph as often occurs in much ekphrastic writing. On the contrary, he seems reluctant to go near the photographs at all. Images and words thus exist alongside each other not as rivals for attention but as different art forms rubbing shoulders rather as new friends might do, or indeed old enemies. The book, in this sense, is more an artistic happening than a planned collaboration, very much a Plan B as the title indicates. As Peter Barry points out in a perceptive article on "Contemporary Poetry and Ekphrasis": "Writing a poem about (say) a photograph seems to involve tacitly accepting that poetry can only deal with *representations* of reality, never with reality itself" (157). *Plan B*'s dust-jacket boldly credits Muldoon for having created "a distinctly new genre—photoetry." Yet perhaps the poet's casual treatment of visual images, his self-conscious digressions, are not as original as he thinks. After all, as Barry suggests, surely most poets are guilty of taking photographs for granted at some point. Muldoon simply makes this process visible.

The elements that cause Muldoon to hesitate before writing ekphrastic poetry, specifically the problem of exchange—what does one get in return for the other?—can be felt half a century earlier in the statements of various Movement writers like Kingsley Amis and Philip Larkin who both derided what they saw as Modernist enthrallment to art galleries and museums in preference to real people and places. In a statement first published in 1955 Amis famously included ekphrasis in a long list of things he hated about contemporary poetry: "Nobody wants any more poems about philosophers or paintings or novelists or art galleries or mythology or foreign cities or other poems" (17–18). Edna Longley, in an essay on Irish poets Derek Mahon and Paul Durcan, restated Amis's point thirty years later. "Addiction to the practice (e.g. Wallace Stevens) can be a form of imaginative auto-eroticism" (227), she declared in a piece first published in 1991. "Poetry's consciousness of painting inevitably highlights and measures its *aesthetic* self-consciousness, tilts the see-saw away from history" (227). Longley explicitly connects the age of ekphrasis to a feeling of living at the end of history (a sense particularly present in the early 1990s after the fall of the Berlin Wall and the collapse of Communism in Eastern Europe). When poets run out of things to say about the world, she implies, they inevitably turn to saying things about themselves. Poems about paintings, in other words, are too often simply poems about poetry. Longley interestingly exempts Irish poets from this imaginative cul-de-sac. In any comparison, "Ireland comes off well" (227), she suggests.

National point-scoring aside, what are the reasons behind this continued interest in ekphrasis, not just in Ireland, but in every English-speaking poetic tradition? Arguably the popularity of ekphrastic writing goes back at least as far as the early nineteenth-century when the museum became the place where most people, including poets, encountered visual art. For Heffernan, "the first truly distinguished specimens of self-sufficient ekphrastic poetry emerge in the romantic period, when . . . the establishment of the museum began to make individual works available for detailed scrutiny" (138). In the twentieth century, the museum itself became the subject for ekphrastic writing. Two of the most iconic ekphrastic poems of the last century, W.H. Auden's "Musée des Beaux Arts" and John Ashbery's "Self-Portrait in a Convex Mirror," are as much about the context in which visual art is seen as visual art itself. Both poems focus on that which lies outside the frame just as much as that which lies inside of it. In Heffernan's opinion, this is "what distinguishes the ekphrastic poetry of this [twentieth] century from its predecessors. Twentieth-century ekphrasis springs from the museum, the shrine where all poets worship in a secular age" (138). For Susan Rosenbaum, this idea of the "museum as muse" is central to our thinking about twentieth-century art and twentieth-century poetry (64–68). Indeed, she argues that many poets and visual artists were "involved in a shared project of institutional reflection and critique, a project that involves self-consciously invoking the institutions that influence artistic production and reception" (67). Rosenbaum gives Elizabeth Bishop, Marcel Duchamp, and Joseph Cornell as examples, focusing in particular on their creation of a series of "miniature museums" that seek "to undo the acquisitive values of the official museum from within" (87).

Bishop is one of the most original twentieth-century ekphrastic poets, not least because of her refusal to follow many of the established conventions and tropes of much ekphrastic poetry. *North & South*, her first collection of poetry, has several memorable ekphrastic passages. In the book's very first poem, "The Map," Bishop engages with the vexed history of words against images. The poem is an example of both actual and notional ekphrasis in that it clearly refers to a real map but not one we can ever identify. On the one hand, the map described in the poem is a visual representation of something real. It stands in for cities and countries that we can obviously locate (Newfoundland, Labrador, and Norway). At the same time, as Gertrude Stein might have put it, a map is a map is a map. It represents the world not as it is, but as the individual mapmaker decides. "Are they assigned, or can the countries pick their colors? / —What suits the character or the native waters best" (ll.24–25). Maps, like other visual representations of the world, may look "flat and still" (l.9), but in every detail included or excluded they bear witness to human touch, human excitement and human bias. Bishop adds to our understanding of visual culture by revealing the extent to which visual artists add to and subtract from what is already there. She shows the person behind the visual representations we sometimes take for real.

One of Bishop's main artistic heroes was not a painter or poet but the English naturalist, Charles Darwin. She took his books with her to Brazil in the 1950s and in a famous 1964 letter to Anne Stevenson described his way of looking at the world as a model for any artist, visual or verbal:

Reading Darwin, one admires the beautiful solid case being built up out of his endless heroic *observations*, almost unconscious or automatic—and then comes a sudden relaxation, a forgetful phrase, and one *feels* the strangeness of his undertaking, sees the lonely young man, his eyes fixed on facts and minute details, sinking or sliding giddily off

into the unknown. What one seems to want in art, in experiencing it, is the same thing
that is necessary for its creation, a self-forgetful, perfectly useless concentration.

(Bishop, *Poems, Prose, and Letters* 861; emphasis in the original)

Darwin's "heroic *observations*," particularly the movement from "facts and minute
details" to something "unknown," is the dream of all artists. In Bishop's mind, it is
the dream of readers and viewers too. After all, "endless" looking only takes Darwin
so far. His "observations" have to become something "solid" one can actually read. If
in "The Map" we find the mapmaker, in reading Darwin we find "the lonely young
man."

Bishop, unlike Keats, does not see art as akin to a funeral urn, the traces of its
maker long since gone. Her art objects are never cold or still, but always warm to the
touch, as if they have literally just been painted or set in stone the second before
the poet arrived on the scene. In "Large Bad Picture," for example, Bishop delights
in the painting's failures as much as its successes. She pays particular attention to the
visible signs not just of a painter painting but also of a great-uncle remembering.

> Remembering the Strait of Belle Isle or
> some northerly harbour of Labrador,
> before he became a schoolteacher
> a great-uncle painted a big picture.
>
> (ll.1–4)

In placing "Remembering" first in the poem, Bishop accepts the fact she may be
losing sight of the "big picture." Unlike Keats or Pater, she is not seeking Beauty or
Truth in the canvas before her. Her aim in looking and then writing about visual art
is more modest, more skeptical. As she says at the end of the poem of the ships
depicted in the painting: "It would be hard to say what brought them there, / commerce or contemplation" (ll.31–32). The works of art she celebrates in her poetry do
not tend to be found in an art gallery or museum. She finds art not just in everyday
life but in everyday objects too. One cannot usually compare her poetic descriptions
with an image in a book to see how they measure up. They are family relics, heirlooms,
mementoes lost and mislaid.

Bishop's museum, in other words, is not in any city or country but in her own
attic, real or invented. She commemorates the paintings, photographs, and sculptures
that she can lay her hands on, in both the literal sense of such objects being close at
hand and the religious sense of confirming value in someone or something through
touch. In "The Monument," another early poem from *North & South*, the act of observing something closely, whether "solid" or "hollow" (l.72), is almost as important as
the object in view. It is as if she is encouraging us to read the poem with a pencil in
hand:

> Now can you see the monument? It is of wood
> built somewhat like a box. No. Built
> like several boxes in descending sizes
> one above the other.
> Each is turned half-way round so that
> its corners point toward the sides
> of the one below and the angles alternate.
> Then on the topmost cube is set
> a sort of fleur-de-lys of weathered wood,
> long petals of board, pierced with odd holes,
> four-sided, stiff, ecclesiastical.

(ll.1–11)

As an experiment, I've often asked friends to make a sketch based on this description. Nobody ever draws the same thing, or even anything remotely similar. There's always a fair amount of rubbing out and revising too. The point is not that Bishop's description is imprecise or that poetic language itself is imprecise (though many theorists might argue this), but that the act of writing about the objects we see is nearly always completely subjective. None of us really see what the other sees, regardless of whether one is a painter, poet, or reader. Something always gets in the way of shared perception, whether it be a color-association, a memory, a narrative on the wall, or simply a very tall person blocking one's view. Bishop's ekphrastic poems make us look harder and think about how we look more seriously. More so even perhaps than Muldoon, she lets us curate poems and visual art for ourselves.

Individual poets like Bishop, Duffy, Larkin, and Muldoon obviously respond to visual culture in their own ways. What, if anything, links their various ekphrastic practices? Perhaps no more than a fascination with visual art not just as a subject for poetry but as *the* subject that makes them question their own aesthetic choices. It has become a commonplace among cultural historians to speak of a "pictorial" or "visual turn" in contemporary culture. W.J.T. Mitchell coined the term in his still influential book, *Picture Theory* (1994), though he later attempted to put the record straight in *What Do Pictures Want?* (2005). "The pictorial or visual turn . . . is not unique to our time," Mitchell argues in the later work.

> It is a repeated narrative figure that takes on a very specific form today, but which seems to be available in its schematic form in an innumerable variety of circumstances . . . The invention of photography, of oil painting, of artificial perspective, of sculptural casting, of the Internet, of writing, of mimesis itself are conspicuous occasions when a new way of making visual images seemed to mark a historical turning point for better or worse. The mistake is to construct a grand binary model of history centered on just one of these turning points, and to declare a single 'great divide' between the 'age of literacy' (for instance) and the 'age of visuality.' These kinds of narratives are beguiling, handy for the purposes of presentist polemics, and useless for the purposes of genuine historical

criticism. . . . Let us try out, as a counteraxiom, the notion that all media are mixed media, and see where that leads us.

(348–50)

Mitchell's "counteraxiom, the notion that all media are mixed media," is the theoretical equivalent of Bishop's shape-shifting map that is both "flat and still" (l.9) and etched upon with human "emotion" and "feeling" (ll.17 and 19). Rather than speak of paintings and poems as if they were different species, constantly fighting for survival, one needs to come up with a different language to represent representation. A painting exists in the mind just as much as it exists on a canvas. It certainly exists in a poem just as much as it exists on the walls of a museum. Poems similarly float free of their verbal forms. In fact, perhaps most poems begin life as visual objects, words and phrases still waiting to be framed by lines and stanzas. The best ekphrastic poetry of this and earlier ages has not only always been conscious of these mixed messages. It has actively gone out of its way to disseminate them.

References and Further Reading

Amis, Kingsley. In *Poets of the 1950s*, ed. D.J. Enright. Tokyo: Kenkyusha, 1955.

Barry, Peter. "Contemporary Poetry and Ekphrasis." *Cambridge Quarterly* 31.2. 2002: 155–65.

Bishop, Elizabeth. *Complete Poems*. London: Chatto & Windus, 1983.

Bishop, Elizabeth. *Poems, Prose, and Letters*. Eds. Robert Giroux and Lloyd Schwartz. New York: Library of America, 2008.

Cheeke, Stephen. *Writing for Art: The Aesthetics of Ekphrasis*. Manchester and New York: Manchester University Press, 2008.

Doty, Mark. *Still Life with Oysters and Lemons*. Boston, MA: Beacon Press, 2001.

Duffy, Carol Ann. *Standing Female Nude*. London: Anvil, 1985.

Heffernan, James. *Museum of Words: The Poetry of Ekphrasis from Homer to Ashbery*. Chicago and London: University of Chicago Press, 1993.

Hollander, John. *The Gazer's Spirit: Poems Speaking to Silent Works of Art*. Chicago and London: University of Chicago Press, 1995.

Keats, John. *Selected Poems*. Ed. Nicholas Roe. London: Everyman, 1995.

Larkin, Philip. *Collected Poems*. Ed. Anthony Thwaite. London: Faber & Faber, 1988.

Leighton, Angela. *On Form: Poetry, Aestheticism, and the Legacy of a Word*. Oxford: Oxford University Press, 2007.

Longley, Edna. "No More Poems about Paintings?" In *The Living Stream: Literature & Revisionism in Ireland* (pp.). Newcastle: Bloodaxe Books, 1994. 227–251.

Meek, Richard. "Ekphrasis in *The Rape of Lucrece* and *The Winter's Tale*." *Studies in English Literature* 46.2. 2006: 389–414.

Michelis, Angelica and Antony Rowland. "Introduction." In *The Poetry of Carol Ann Duffy: "Choosing Tough Words,"* ed. Michelis and Rowland. Manchester: Manchester University Press, 2003. 1–32.

Mitchell, W.J.T. *Picture Theory: Essays on Verbal and Visual Representation*. Chicago and London: University of Chicago Press, 1994.

Mitchell, W.J.T. *What Do Pictures Want? The Lives and Loves of Images*. Chicago and London: University of Chicago Press, 2005.

Muldoon, Paul and Norman McBeath. *Plan B*. London: Enitharmon, 2009.

O'Hara, Frank. *The Collected Poems of Frank O'Hara*. Ed. Donald Allen. Berkeley: University of California Press, 1995.

Pater, Walter. *The Renaissance: Studies in Art and Poetry*. London and New York: Macmillan, 1888 ["Notes on Leonardo da Vinci" first appeared in *The Fortnightly Review* in 1869].

Rosenbaum, Susan. "Elizabeth Bishop and the Miniature Museum." *Journal of Modern Literature* 28.2. 2005: 61–99.

Scarry, Elaine. *On Beauty and Being Just*. Princeton and Oxford: Princeton University Press, 1999.

Smith, Mack. *Literary Realism and the Ekphrastic Tradition*. University Park: Pennsylvania State University Press, 1995.

Spiegelman, Willard. *How Poets See the World: The Art of Description in Contemporary Poetry*. Oxford: Oxford University Press, 2005.

Webb, Ruth. "*Ekphrasis* Ancient and Modern: The Invention of a Genre." *Word & Image* 15.1. 1999: 7–18.

Index

A Companion to Poetic Genre, First Edition. Edited by Erik Martiny.
© 2012 John Wiley & Sons, Ltd. Published 2012 by John Wiley & Sons, Ltd.